[JOINT COMMI

GENERAL EXPLANATION OF TAX LEGISLATION ENACTED IN THE 108TH CONGRESS

PREPARED BY THE STAFF

OF THE

JOINT COMMITTEE ON TAXATION

MAY 2005

U.S. GOVERNMENT PRINTING OFFICE

21–118 WASHINGTON : 2005 JCS–5–05

For sale by the Superintendent of Documents, U.S. Government Printing Office
Internet: bookstore.gpo.gov Phone: toll free (866) 512-1800; DC area (202) 512-1800
Fax: (202) 512-2250 Mail: Stop SSOP, Washington, DC 20402-0001

ISBN 0-16-072517-8

JOINT COMMITTEE ON TAXATION

109TH CONGRESS, 1ST SESSION

HOUSE

WILLIAM M. THOMAS, California, *Chairman*
E. CLAY SHAW, JR., Florida
NANCY L. JOHNSON, Connecticut
CHARLES B. RANGEL, New York
FORTNEY PETE STARK, California

SENATE

CHARLES E. GRASSLEY, Iowa, *Vice Chairman*
ORRIN G. HATCH, Utah
TRENT LOTT, Mississippi
MAX BAUCUS, Montana
JOHN D. ROCKEFELLER IV, West Virginia

GEORGE K. YIN, *Chief of Staff*
BERNARD A. SCHMITT, *Deputy Chief of Staff*
THOMAS A. BARTHOLD, *Deputy Chief of Staff*

CONTENTS

INTRODUCTION

This document,[1] prepared by the staff of the Joint Committee on Taxation in consultation with the staffs of the House Committee on Ways and Means and the Senate Committee on Finance, provides an explanation of tax legislation enacted in the 108th Congress. The explanation follows the chronological order of the tax legislation as signed into law.

For each provision, the document includes a description of present and prior law, explanation of the provision, and effective date. Present and prior law describes the law in effect immediately prior to enactment. Prior law indicates the portion of the law that was changed by the provision. For most provisions, the reasons for change are also included. In some instances, provisions included in legislation enacted in the 108th Congress were not reported out of committee before enactment. As a result, the legislative history of such provisions does not include the reasons for change normally included in a committee report. In the case of such provisions, no reasons for change are included with the explanation of the provision in this document.

Part One of this document is an explanation of the provisions of the Jobs and Growth Tax Relief Reconciliation Act of 2003 (Pub. L. No. 108–27), relating to the acceleration of certain previously enacted tax reductions, growth incentives for businesses, reduction in taxes on dividends and capital gains, and corporate estimated tax payments.

Part Two is an explanation of the provision of Surface Transportation Extension Act of 2003 (Pub. L. No. 108–88) relating to the extension of the Highway Trust Fund and Aquatic Resources Trust Fund expenditure authority.

Part Three is an explanation of provisions relating to disclosure of return information relating to student loans, extension of IRS user fees, and extension of custom user fees of an Act to extend the Temporary Assistance for Needy Families block grant program and certain tax and trade programs and for other purposes (Pub. L. No. 108–89).

Part Four is an explanation of the provisions of the Military Family Tax Relief Act of 2003 (Pub. L. No. 108–121), relating to improving tax equity for military personnel and extension of custom user fees.

Part Five is an explanation of the provisions of the Medicare Prescription Drug, Improvement, and Modernization Act (Pub. L. No. 108–173) relating to disclosure of return information for purposes under the Medicare discount card program, disclosure of return information relating to income-related reduction in Part B Premium

[1] This document may be cited as follows: Joint Committee on Taxation, General Explanation of Tax Legislation Enacted in the 108th Congress (JCS–5–05), May 2005.

subsidy, health savings accounts, exclusion from gross income of certain Federal subsidies for prescription drug plans, and an exception to information reporting for certain health arrangements.

Part Six is an explanation of the provisions of the Vision 100-Century of Aviation Reauthorization Act (Pub. L. No. 108–176) relating to the extension of expenditure authority.

Part Seven is an explanation of the provision of the Servicemembers Civil Relief Act (Pub. L. No. 108–189) relating to tax collection of servicemembers.

Part Eight is an explanation of the provision of the Surface Transportation Extension Act of 2004 (Pub. L. No. 108–202) relating to extension of the Highway Trust Fund and Aquatic Resources Trust Fund expenditure authority.

Part Nine is an explanation of the revenue provisions of the Social Security Protection Act of 2004 (Pub. L. No. 108–203) relating to the treatment of individual work plans under the Ticket to Work program, FICA and SECA tax exemptions individuals subject to the laws of a tantalization agreement partner, and other technical amendments.

Part Ten is an explanation of the provisions of the Pension Funding Equity Act of 2004 (Pub. L. No. 108–218), relating to temporary replacement of the 30-year Treasury rate and election of alternative deficit reduction contribution, multiemployer plan funding notices, deferral of the charge for a portion of net experience loss of multiemployer plans, and other provisions.

Part Eleven is an explanation of the provision of the Surface Transportation Extension Act of 2004, Part II (Pub. L. No. 108–224) relating to the extension of the Highway Trust Fund and Aquatic Resources Trust Fund expenditure authority.

Part Twelve is an explanation of the provision of the Surface Transportation Extension Act of 2004, Part III (Pub. L. No. 108–263) relating to the extension of the Highway Trust Fund and Aquatic Resources Trust Fund expenditure authority.

Part Thirteen is an explanation of the provision of the Surface Transportation Extension Act of 2004, Part IV (Pub. L. No. 108–280) relating to the extension of the Highway Trust Fund and Aquatic Resources Trust Fund expenditure authority.

Part Fourteen is an explanation of the provision of the Surface Transportation Extension Act of 2004, Part V (Pub. L. No. 108–310) relating to the extension of the Highway Trust Fund and Aquatic Resources Trust Fund expenditure authority.

Part Fifteen is an explanation of the provisions of the Working Families Tax Relief Act of 2004 (Pub. L. No. 108–311), relating to extension of certain expiring provisions, uniform definition of child and tax technical corrections.

Part Sixteen is an explanation of the provision to clarify the tax treatment of bonds and other obligations issued by the Government of American Samoa (Pub. L. No. 108–326).

Part Seventeen is an explanation of the provisions of the America Jobs Creation Act of 2004 (Pub. L. No. 108–357), relating to the repeal of exclusion for extraterritorial income, business tax incentives, tax relief for agriculture and small manufacturers, tax reform and simplification for United States businesses, deduction of State and local sales taxes, miscellaneous and revenue provisions.

Part Eighteen is an explanation of the revenue provisions of the Ronald W. Reagan National Defense Authorization Act for Fiscal Year 2005 (Pub. L. No. 108–375) relating to the exclusion from gross income of travel benefits under Operation Hero Miles.

Part Nineteen is an explanation of the revenue provisions of the Consolidated Appropriations Act, 2005 (Pub. L. No. 108–447) relating to the application of ERISA anticutback rules to certain multiemployer plan amendments.

Part Twenty is an explanation of the provisions of the Act to treat certain arrangements maintained by the YMCA Retirement Fund as church plans for the purposes of certain provisions of the Internal Revenue Code of 1986, and for other purposes (Pub. L. No. 109–476).

Part Twenty-One is an explanation of the provision of the Act to modify the taxation of arrow components (Pub. L. No. 108–493).

The Appendix provides the estimated budget effects of tax legislation enacted in the 108th Congress.

The first footnote in each part gives the legislative history of each of the Acts of the 108th Congress discussed.

PART ONE: JOBS AND GROWTH TAX RELIEF RECONCILIATION ACT OF 2003 (PUBLIC LAW 108–27) [2]

I. ACCELERATION OF CERTAIN PREVIOUSLY ENACTED TAX REDUCTIONS

A. Accelerate the Increase in the Child Tax Credit (sec. 101 of the Act and sec. 24 of the Code)

Present and Prior Law

In general

For 2003, an individual may claim a $600 tax credit for each qualifying child under the age of 17. In general, a qualifying child is an individual for whom the taxpayer can claim a dependency exemption and who is the taxpayer's son or daughter (or descendent of either), stepson or stepdaughter (or descendent of either), or eligible foster child.

Under prior law, the child tax credit was scheduled to increase to $1,000, phased-in over several years.

Table 1, below, shows the scheduled increases of the child tax credit as provided under the Economic Growth and Tax Relief Reconciliation Act of 2001 ("EGTRRA").

Table 1.—Scheduled Increase of the Child Tax Credit

Taxable year	Credit amount per child
2003–2004	$600
2005–2008	$700
2009	$800
2010 [1]	$1,000

[1] The credit reverts to $500 in taxable years beginning after December 31, 2010, under the sunset provision of EGTRRA.

The child tax credit is phased-out for individuals with income over certain thresholds. Specifically, the otherwise allowable child tax credit is reduced by $50 for each $1,000 (or fraction thereof) of modified adjusted gross income over $75,000 for single individuals or heads of households, $110,000 for married individuals filing joint returns, and $55,000 for married individuals filing separate re-

[2] H.R. 2. The House Committee on Ways and Means reported the bill on May 8, 2003 (H.R. Rep. No. 108–94). The House passed the bill on May 9, 2003. The Senate Committee on Finance reported S. 1054 on May 13, 2003 (S. Prt. No. 108–26). The Senate passed H. R. 2, as amended by the provisions of S. 1054, on May 15, 2003. The conference report was filed on May 22, 2003 (H.R. Rep. No. 108–126), and was passed by the House on May 23, 2003, and the Senate on May 23, 2003. The President signed the bill on May 28, 2003.

turns.[3] The length of the phase-out range depends on the number of qualifying children. For example, the phase-out range for a single individual with one qualifying child is between $75,000 and $87,000 of modified adjusted gross income. The phase-out range for a single individual with two qualifying children is between $75,000 and $99,000.

The amount of the tax credit and the phase-out ranges are not adjusted annually for inflation.

Refundability

For 2003, the child credit is refundable to the extent of 10 percent of the taxpayer's earned income in excess of $10,500.[4] The percentage is increased to 15 percent for taxable years 2005 and thereafter. Families with three or more children are allowed a refundable credit for the amount by which the taxpayer's social security taxes exceed the taxpayer's earned income credit, if that amount is greater than the refundable credit based on the taxpayer's earned income in excess of $10,500 (for 2003). The refundable portion of the child credit does not constitute income and is not treated as resources for purposes of determining eligibility or the amount or nature of benefits or assistance under any Federal program or any State or local program financed with Federal funds. For taxable years beginning after December 31, 2010, the sunset provision of EGTRRA applies to the rules allowing refundable child credits.

Alternative minimum tax liability

The child credit is allowed against the individual's regular income tax and alternative minimum tax. For taxable years beginning after December 31, 2010, the sunset provision of EGTRRA applies to the rules allowing the child credit against the alternative minimum tax.

Reasons for Change

The Jobs and Growth Tax Relief Reconciliation Act of 2003 ("the Act") accelerated the increase in the child tax credit in order to provide additional tax relief to families to help offset the significant costs of raising a child. Further, the Act provided immediate tax relief to American taxpayers in the form of the advance payment of the increased amount of the child credit. The Congress believed that such immediate tax relief might encourage short-term growth in the economy by providing individuals with additional cash to spend.

Explanation of Provision

Under the Act, the amount of the child credit is increased to $1,000 for 2003 and 2004.[5] After 2004, the child credit will revert

[3] Modified adjusted gross income is the taxpayer's total gross income plus certain amounts excluded from gross income (i.e., excluded income of: U.S. citizens or residents living abroad (sec. 911), residents of Guam, American Samoa, and the Northern Mariana Islands (sec. 931), and residents of Puerto Rico (sec. 933)). Unless otherwise indicated, all section references are to the Internal Revenue Code.

[4] The $10,500 amount is indexed for inflation.

[5] The increase in refundability to 15 percent of the taxpayer's earned income, scheduled for calendar years 2005 and thereafter, is not accelerated under the provision.

to the levels provided under present and prior law, as described above. For 2003, the increased amount of the child credit will be paid in advance beginning in July, 2003, on the basis of information on each taxpayer's 2002 return filed in 2003. The IRS is not expected to issue advance payment checks to an individual who did not claim the child credit for 2002. Such payments will be made in a manner similar to the advance payment checks issued by the Treasury in 2001 to reflect the creation of the 10-percent regular income tax rate bracket.[6]

Effective Date

The provision is effective for taxable years beginning after December 31, 2002, and before January 1, 2005.

B. Accelerate Marriage Penalty Relief (secs. 102 and 103 of the Act and secs. 1 and 63 of the Code)

1. Standard deduction marriage penalty relief

Present and Prior Law

Marriage penalty

A married couple generally is treated as one tax unit that must pay tax on the couple's total taxable income. Although married couples may elect to file separate returns, the rate schedules and other provisions are structured so that filing separate returns usually results in a higher tax than filing a joint return. Other rate schedules apply to single persons and to single heads of households.

A "marriage penalty" exists when the combined tax liability of a married couple filing a joint return is greater than the sum of the tax liabilities of each individual computed as if they were not married. A "marriage bonus" exists when the combined tax liability of a married couple filing a joint return is less than the sum of the tax liabilities of each individual computed as if they were not married.

Basic standard deduction

Taxpayers who do not itemize deductions may choose the basic standard deduction (and additional standard deductions, if applicable),[7] which is subtracted from adjusted gross income ("AGI") in arriving at taxable income. The size of the basic standard deduction varies according to filing status and is adjusted annually for inflation.[8] Under prior law for 2003, the basic standard deduction for married couples filing a joint return was 167 percent of the basic standard deduction for single filers. (Stated alternatively, under prior law for 2003, the basic standard deduction amount for single filers was 60 percent of the basic standard deduction amount for married couples filing joint returns). Thus, two unmarried individ-

---

[6] The size of the child credit for taxable years beginning after December 31, 2004, was modified by the Working Families Tax Relief Act of 2004, described in Part Fifteen of this document.

[7] Additional standard deductions are allowed with respect to any individual who is elderly (age 65 or over) or blind.

[8] For 2003 the basic standard deduction amounts are: (1) $4,750 for unmarried individuals; (2) $7,950 for married individuals filing a joint return; (3) $7,000 for heads of households; and (4) $3,975 for married individuals filing separately.

uals have standard deductions whose sum exceeds the standard deduction for a married couple filing a joint return.

EGTRRA increased the basic standard deduction for a married couple filing a joint return to twice the basic standard deduction for an unmarried individual filing a single return.[9] The increase in the standard deduction for married taxpayers filing a joint return is scheduled to be phased-in over five years beginning in 2005 and will be fully phased-in for 2009 and thereafter. Table 2, below, shows the standard deduction for married couples filing a joint return as a percentage of the standard deduction for single individuals.

Table 2.—Size of the Basic Standard Deduction for Married Couples Filing Joint Returns

Taxable year	Standard deduction for married couples filing joint returns as percentage of standard deduction for unmarried individual returns
2003–2004	167
2005	174
2006	184
2007	187
2008	190
2009 and 2010 [1]	200

[1] The basic standard deduction increases are repealed for taxable years beginning after December 31, 2010, under the sunset provision of EGTRRA.

Reasons for Change

The Congress remained concerned about the inequity that arises when two working single individuals marry and experience a tax increase solely by reason of their marriage. Any attempt to address the marriage tax penalty involves the balancing of several competing principles, including equal tax treatment of married couples with equal incomes, the determination of equitable relative tax burdens of single individuals and married couples with equal incomes, and the goal of simplicity in compliance and administration. The Congress believed that the acceleration of the increase in the standard deduction for married couples filing a joint return was a responsible reduction of the marriage tax penalty.

Explanation of Provision

The Act increases the basic standard deduction amount for joint returns to twice the basic standard deduction amount for single returns effective for 2003 and 2004. For taxable years beginning after

[9] The basic standard deduction for a married taxpayer filing separately will continue to equal one-half of the basic standard deduction for a married couple filing jointly; thus, the basic standard deduction for unmarried individuals filing a single return and for married couples filing separately will be the same after the phase-in period.

2004, the applicable percentages will revert to those allowed under present and prior law, as described above in Table 2.[10]

Effective Date

The provision is effective for taxable years beginning after December 31, 2002, and before January 1, 2005.

2. Accelerate the expansion of the 15-percent rate bracket for married couples filing joint returns

Present and Prior Law

In general

Under the Federal individual income tax system, an individual who is a citizen or resident of the United States generally is subject to tax on worldwide taxable income. Taxable income is total gross income less certain exclusions, exemptions, and deductions. An individual may claim either a standard deduction or itemized deductions.

An individual's income tax liability is determined by computing his or her regular income tax liability and, if applicable, alternative minimum tax liability.

Regular income tax liability

Regular income tax liability is determined by applying the regular income tax rate schedules (or tax tables) to the individual's taxable income and then is reduced by any applicable tax credits. The regular income tax rate schedules are divided into several ranges of income, known as income brackets, and the marginal tax rate increases as the individual's income increases. The income bracket amounts are adjusted annually for inflation. Separate rate schedules apply based on filing status: Single individuals (other than heads of households and surviving spouses), heads of households, married individuals filing joint returns (including surviving spouses), married individuals filing separate returns, and estates and trusts. Lower rates may apply to capital gains.

In general, the bracket breakpoints for single individuals are approximately 60 percent of the rate bracket breakpoints for married couples filing joint returns.[11] The rate bracket breakpoints for married individuals filing separate returns are exactly one-half of the rate brackets for married individuals filing joint returns. A separate, compressed rate schedule applies to estates and trusts.

15-percent regular income tax rate bracket

EGTRRA increased the size of the 15-percent regular income tax rate bracket for a married couple filing a joint return to twice the size of the corresponding rate bracket for a single individual filing a single return. The increase is phased-in over four years, beginning in 2005. Therefore, this provision is fully effective (i.e., the size of the 15-percent regular income tax rate bracket for a married

[10] The size of the basic standard deduction for taxable years beginning after December 31, 2004, was modified by the Working Families Tax Relief Act of 2004, described in Part Fifteen of this document.

[11] Under present law, the rate bracket breakpoint for the 38.6 percent marginal tax rate is the same for single individuals and married couples filing joint returns.

couple filing a joint return is twice the size of the 15-percent regular income tax rate bracket for an unmarried individual filing a single return) for taxable years beginning after December 31, 2007. Table 3, below, shows the size of the 15-percent bracket.

Table 3.—Size of the 15-Percent Rate Bracket for Married Couples Filing Joint Returns

Taxable year	End point of 15-percent rate bracket for married couples filing joint returns as percentage rate bracket for unmarried individuals
2003–2004	167
2005	180
2006	187
2007	193
2008 and 2010[1]	200

[1] The increases in the 15-percent rate bracket for married couples filing a joint return are repealed for taxable years beginning after December 31, 2010, under the sunset of EGTRRA.

Reasons for Change

The Congress believed that accelerating the expansion of the 15-percent rate bracket for married couples filing joint returns, in conjunction with the expansion of the standard deduction amount for joint filers, would alleviate the effects of the marriage tax penalty. These provisions significantly reduced the most widely applicable marriage penalties.

Explanation of Provision

The Act increases of the size of the 15-percent regular income tax rate bracket for joint returns to twice the width of the 15-percent regular income tax rate bracket for single returns for taxable years beginning in 2003 and 2004. For taxable years beginning after 2004, the applicable percentages will revert to those allowed under present and prior law, as described above.[12]

Effective Date

The provision is effective for taxable years beginning after December 31, 2002, and before January 1, 2005.

[12] The size of the 15-percent regular rate bracket for joint returns for taxable years beginning after December 31, 2004, was modified by the Working Families Tax Relief Act of 2004, described in Part Fifteen of this document.

C. Accelerate Reductions in Individual Income Tax Rates (secs. 104, 105, and 106 of the Act and secs. 1 and 55 of the Code)

Present and Prior Law

In general

Under the Federal individual income tax system, an individual who is a citizen or a resident of the United States generally is subject to tax on worldwide taxable income. Taxable income is total gross income less certain exclusions, exemptions, and deductions. An individual may claim either a standard deduction or itemized deductions.

An individual's income tax liability is determined by computing his or her regular income tax liability and, if applicable, alternative minimum tax liability.

Regular income tax liability

Regular income tax liability is determined by applying the regular income tax rate schedules (or tax tables) to the individual's taxable income. This tax liability is then reduced by any applicable tax credits. The regular income tax rate schedules are divided into several ranges of income, known as income brackets, and the marginal tax rate increases as the individual's income increases. The income bracket amounts are adjusted annually for inflation. Separate rate schedules apply based on filing status: single individuals (other than heads of households and surviving spouses), heads of households, married individuals filing joint returns (including surviving spouses), married individuals filing separate returns, and estates and trusts. Lower rates may apply to capital gains.

For 2003, the regular income tax rate schedules for individuals are shown in Table 4, below. The rate bracket breakpoints for married individuals filing separate returns are exactly one-half of the rate brackets for married individuals filing joint returns. A separate, compressed rate schedule applies to estates and trusts.

Table 4.—Individual Regular Income Tax Rates for 2003

If taxable income is over:	But not over:	Then regular income tax equals:
Single Individuals		
$0	$6,000	10% of taxable income
$6,000	$28,400	$600, plus 15% of the amount over $6,000
$28,400	$68,800	$3,960.00, plus 27% of the amount over $28,400
$68,800	$143,500	$14,868.00, plus 30% of the amount over $68,800
$143,500	$311,950	$37,278.00, plus 35% of the amount over $143,500

Table 4.—Individual Regular Income Tax Rates for 2003—Continued

If taxable income is over:	But not over:	Then regular income tax equals:
Over $311,950 ...	....	$96,235.50, plus 38.6% of the amount over $311,950
Head of Households		
$0	$10,000	10% of taxable income
$10,000	$38,050	$1,000, plus 15% of the amount over $10,000
$38,050	$98,250	$5,207.50, plus 27% of the amount over $38,050
$98,250	$159,100 ...	$21,461.50, plus 30% of the amount over $98,250
$159,100	$311,950 ...	$39,716.50, plus 35% of the amount over $159,100
Over $311,950 ...	....	93,214, plus 38.6% of the amount over $311,950
Married Individuals Filing Joint Returns		
$0	$12,000	10% of taxable income
$12,000	$47,450	$1,200, plus 15% of the amount over $12,000
$47,450	$114,650 ...	$6,517.50, plus 27% of the amount over $47,450
$114,650	$174,700 ...	$24,661.50, plus 30% of the amount over $114,650
$174,700	$311,950 ...	$42,676.50, plus 35% of the amount over $174,700
Over $311,950 ...	....	$90,714, plus 38.6% of the amount over $311,950

Ten-percent regular income tax rate

Under prior law, the 10-percent rate applied to the first $6,000 of taxable income for single individuals, $10,000 of taxable income for heads of households, and $12,000 for married couples filing joint returns. Effective beginning in 2008, the $6,000 amount will increase to $7,000 and the $12,000 amount will increase to $14,000.

The taxable income levels for the 10-percent rate bracket will be adjusted annually for inflation for taxable years beginning after December 31, 2008. The bracket for single individuals and married individuals filing separately is one-half for joint returns (after adjustment of that bracket for inflation).

The 10-percent rate bracket will expire for taxable years beginning after December 31, 2010, under the sunset provision of the Economic Growth and Tax Relief Reconciliation Act of 2001 ("EGTRRA").

Reduction of other regular income tax rates

Prior to EGTRRA, the regular income tax rates were 15 percent, 28 percent, 31 percent, 36 percent, and 39.6 percent.[13] EGTRRA added the 10-percent regular income tax rate, described above, and retained the 15-percent regular income tax rate. Also, the 15-percent regular income tax bracket was modified to begin at the end of the 10-percent regular income tax bracket. EGTRRA also made other changes to the 15-percent regular income tax bracket.[14]

Also, under EGTRRA, the 28 percent, 31 percent, 36 percent, and 39.6 percent rates are phased down over six years to 25 percent, 28 percent, 33 percent, and 35 percent, effective after June 30, 2001. The taxable income levels for the rates above the 15-percent rate in all taxable years are the same as the taxable income levels that apply under the prior-law rates.

Table 5, below, shows the schedule of regular income tax rate reductions.

Table 5.—Scheduled Regular Income Tax Rate Reductions

Taxable year	28% rate reduced to:	31% rate reduced to:	36% rate reduced to:	39.6% rate reduced to:
2001–2003 [1]	27	30	35	38.6
2004–2005	26	29	34	37.6
2006–2010 [2]	25	28	33	35.0

[1] Effective July 1, 2001.

[2] The reduction in the regular income tax rates are repealed for taxable years beginning after December 31, 2010, under the sunset provision of EGTRRA.

Alternative minimum tax exemption amounts

The alternative minimum tax is the amount by which the tentative minimum tax exceeds the regular income tax. An individual's tentative minimum tax is the sum of (1) 26 percent of so much of the taxable excess as does not exceed $175,000 ($87,500 in the case of a married individual filing a separate return) and (2) 28 percent of the remaining taxable excess. The taxable excess is so much of the alternative minimum taxable income ("AMTI") as exceeds the exemption amount. The maximum tax rates on net capital gain and dividends used in computing the regular tax are used in computing the tentative minimum tax. AMTI is the individual's taxable income adjusted to take account of specified preferences and adjustments.

Under prior law, the exemption amounts were: (1) $49,000 ($45,000 in taxable years beginning after 2004) in the case of married individuals filing a joint return and surviving spouses; (2) $35,750 ($33,750 in taxable years beginning after 2004) in the case of other unmarried individuals; (3) $24,500 ($22,500 in taxable years beginning after 2004) in the case of married individuals filing

[13] The regular income tax rates will revert to these percentages for taxable years beginning after December 31, 2010, under the sunset of EGTRRA.

[14] See the discussion of the provision regarding marriage penalty relief in the 15–percent regular income tax bracket, above.

a separate return; and (4) $22,500 in the case of an estate or trust. The exemption amounts are phased out by an amount equal to 25 percent of the amount by which the individual's AMTI exceeds (1) $150,000 in the case of married individuals filing a joint return and surviving spouses, (2) $112,500 in the case of other unmarried individuals, and (3) $75,000 in the case of married individuals filing separate returns or an estate or a trust. These amounts are not indexed for inflation.

Reasons for Change

The Congress believed that high marginal individual income tax rates reduce incentives for taxpayers to work, to save, and to invest and, thereby, have a negative effect on the long-term health of the economy. The higher that marginal tax rates are, the greater is the disincentive for individuals to increase their work effort. Lower marginal tax rates provide greater incentives to taxpayers to be entrepreneurial risk takers; the Congress believed that the higher marginal tax rates of prior-law discourage success. The Congress believed that this tax cut will lead to increased investment by these businesses, promoting long-term growth and stability in the economy and rewarding the businessmen and women who provide a foundation for our country's success.

In addition, lower marginal tax rates help remove the barriers that lower-income families face as they try to enter the middle class. The lower the marginal tax rates for lower-income families, the greater is the incentive to work. The expanded 10-percent rate bracket provides an incentive for these taxpayers to increase their work effort.

Finally, there were signs that the economy was not growing as fast as desirable. The Congress believed that immediate tax relief could encourage growth in the economy by providing individuals with additional tax relief. The Congress recognized that it was important to act quickly so that taxpayers become aware of the commitment of the President and the Congress to enact this tax cut and to adjust income tax withholding tables.

Explanation of Provision

Ten-percent regular income tax rate

The Act accelerates the increase in the taxable income levels for the 10-percent rate bracket previously scheduled for 2008 to be effective in 2003 and 2004. Specifically, for 2003 and 2004, the Act increases the taxable income level for the 10-percent regular income tax rate brackets for unmarried individuals from $6,000 to $7,000 and for married individuals filing jointly from $12,000 to $14,000. The taxable income levels for the 10-percent regular income tax rate bracket will be adjusted annually for inflation for taxable years beginning after December 31, 2003.

For taxable years beginning after December 31, 2004, the taxable income levels for the 10-percent rate bracket will revert to the levels allowed under prior law. Therefore, for 2005, 2006, and 2007, the levels will revert to $6,000 for unmarried individuals and $12,000 for married individuals filing jointly. In 2008, the taxable income levels for the 10-percent regular income tax rate brackets will be $7,000 for unmarried individuals and $14,000 for married individuals filing jointly. The taxable income levels for the 10-percent rate bracket will be adjusted annually for inflation for taxable years beginning after December 31, 2008.[15]

Reduction of other regular income tax rates

The Act accelerates the reductions in the regular income tax rates in excess of the 15-percent regular income tax rate that were scheduled for 2004 and 2006. Therefore, for 2003–2010, the regular income tax rates in excess of 15 percent under the bill are 25 percent, 28 percent, 33 percent, and 35 percent.

Alternative minimum tax exemption amounts

The Act increases the AMT exemption amount for married taxpayers filing a joint return and surviving spouses to $58,000, and for unmarried taxpayers to $40,250, for taxable years beginning in 2003 and 2004.

Effective Date

The provision generally is effective for taxable years beginning after December 31, 2002. The Congress recognized that withholding at statutorily mandated rates (such as pursuant to backup withholding under section 3406) had already occurred. The Congress intended that taxpayers who have been overwithheld as a consequence of this obtain a refund of this overwithholding through the normal process of filing an income tax return, and not through the payor. In addition, the Congress anticipated that the Treasury would provide a brief, reasonable period of transition for payors to implement these changes in these statutorily mandated withholding rates.

[15] The size of the 10-percent rate bracket for taxable years beginning after December 31, 2004, was modified by the Working Families Tax Relief Act of 2004, described in Part Fifteen of this document.

II. GROWTH INCENTIVES FOR BUSINESS

A. Increase and Extension of Bonus Depreciation (sec. 201 of the Act and sec. 168 of the Code)

Present and Prior Law

In general

A taxpayer is allowed to recover, through annual depreciation deductions, the cost of certain property used in a trade or business or for the production of income. The amount of the depreciation deduction allowed with respect to tangible property for a taxable year is determined under the modified accelerated cost recovery system ("MACRS"). Under MACRS, different types of property generally are assigned applicable recovery periods and depreciation methods. The recovery periods applicable to most tangible personal property (generally tangible property other than residential rental property and nonresidential real property) range from 3 to 25 years. The depreciation methods generally applicable to tangible personal property are the 200-percent and 150-percent declining balance methods, switching to the straight-line method for the taxable year in which the depreciation deduction would be maximized.

Section 280F limits the annual depreciation deductions with respect to passenger automobiles to specified dollar amounts, indexed for inflation.

Section 167(f)(1) provides that capitalized computer software costs, other than computer software to which section 197 applies, are recovered ratably over 36 months.

In lieu of depreciation, a taxpayer with a sufficiently small amount of annual investment generally may elect to deduct up to $25,000 of the cost of qualifying property placed in service for the taxable year (sec. 179). In general, qualifying property is defined as depreciable tangible personal property that is purchased for use in the active conduct of a trade or business.

Additional first year depreciation deduction

The Job Creation and Worker Assistance Act of 2002[16] ("JCWAA") allows an additional first-year depreciation deduction equal to 30 percent of the adjusted basis of qualified property.[17] The amount of the additional first-year depreciation deduction is not affected by a short taxable year. The additional first-year depreciation deduction is allowed for both regular tax and alternative minimum tax purposes for the taxable year in which the property

[16] Pub. L. No. 107–147, sec. 101 (2002).

[17] The additional first-year depreciation deduction is subject to the general rules regarding whether an item is deductible under section 162 or subject to capitalization under section 263 or section 263A.

is placed in service.[18] The basis of the property and the depreciation allowances in the year of purchase and later years are appropriately adjusted to reflect the additional first-year depreciation deduction. In addition, there are no adjustments to the allowable amount of depreciation for purposes of computing a taxpayer's alternative minimum taxable income with respect to property to which the provision applies. A taxpayer is allowed to elect out of the additional first-year depreciation for any class of property for any taxable year.

In order for property to qualify for the additional first-year depreciation deduction it must meet all of the following requirements. First, the property must be (1) property to which MACRS applies with an applicable recovery period of 20 years or less, (2) water utility property (as defined in section 168(e)(5)), (3) computer software other than computer software covered by section 197, or (4) qualified leasehold improvement property (as defined in section 168(k)(3)).[19] Second, the original use[20] of the property must commence with the taxpayer on or after September 11, 2001.[21] Third, the taxpayer must purchase the property within the applicable time period. Finally, the property must be placed in service before January 1, 2005. An extension of the placed in service date of one year (i.e., to January 1, 2006) is provided for certain property with a recovery period of ten years or longer and certain transportation property.[22] Transportation property is defined as tangible personal property used in the trade or business of transporting persons or property.

The applicable time period for acquired property is (1) after September 10, 2001, and before September 11, 2004, but only if no binding written contract for the acquisition is in effect before September 11, 2001, or (2) pursuant to a binding written contract which was entered into after September 10, 2001, and before September 11, 2004.[23] With respect to property that is manufactured, constructed, or produced by the taxpayer for use by the taxpayer, the taxpayer must begin the manufacture, construction, or production of the property after September 10, 2001, and before Sep-

---

[18] However, the additional first-year depreciation deduction is not allowed for purposes of computing earnings and profits.

[19] A special rule precludes the additional first-year depreciation deduction for any property that is required to be depreciated under the alternative depreciation system of MACRS.

[20] The term "original use" means the first use to which the property is put, whether or not such use corresponds to the use of such property by the taxpayer.

If in the normal course of its business a taxpayer sells fractional interests in property to unrelated third parties, then the original use of such property begins with the first user of each fractional interest (i.e., each fractional owner is considered the original user of its proportionate share of the property).

[21] A special rule applies in the case of certain leased property. In the case of any property that is originally placed in service by a person and that is sold to the taxpayer and leased back to such person by the taxpayer within three months after the date that the property was placed in service, the property would be treated as originally placed in service by the taxpayer not earlier than the date that the property is used under the leaseback.

If property is originally placed in service by a lessor (including by operation of section 168(k)(2)(D)(i)), such property is sold within three months after the date that the property was placed in service, and the user of such property does not change, then the property is treated as originally placed in service by the taxpayer not earlier than the date of such sale.

[22] In order for property to qualify for the extended placed in service date, the property is required to have a production period exceeding two years or an estimated production period exceeding one year and a cost exceeding $1 million.

[23] Property does not fail to qualify for the additional first-year depreciation merely because a binding written contract to acquire a component of the property is in effect prior to September 11, 2001.

tember 11, 2004. Property that is manufactured, constructed, or produced for the taxpayer by another person under a contract that is entered into prior to the manufacture, construction, or production of the property is considered to be manufactured, constructed, or produced by the taxpayer. For property eligible for the extended placed in service date, a special rule limits the amount of costs eligible for the additional first year depreciation. With respect to such property, only the portion of the basis that is properly attributable to the costs incurred before September 11, 2004 ("progress expenditures") is eligible for the additional first-year depreciation.[24]

Property does not qualify for the additional first-year depreciation deduction when the user of such property (or a related party) would not have been eligible for the additional first-year depreciation deduction if the user (or a related party) were treated as the owner. For example, if a taxpayer sells to a related party property that was under construction prior to September 11, 2001, the property does not qualify for the additional first-year depreciation deduction. Similarly, if a taxpayer sells to a related party property that was subject to a binding written contract prior to September 11, 2001, the property does not qualify for the additional first-year depreciation deduction. As a further example, if a taxpayer (the lessee) sells property in a sale-leaseback arrangement, and the property otherwise would not have qualified for the additional first-year depreciation deduction if it were owned by the taxpayer-lessee, then the lessor is not entitled to the additional first-year depreciation deduction.

The limitation on the amount of depreciation deductions allowed with respect to certain passenger automobiles (sec. 280F) is increased in the first year by $4,600 for automobiles that qualify (and do not elect out of the increased first year deduction). The $4,600 increase is not indexed for inflation.

Reasons for Change

The Congress believed that increasing and extending the additional first-year depreciation would accelerate purchases of equipment, promote capital investment, modernization, and growth, and would help to spur an economic recovery.

Explanation of Provision

The Act provides an additional first-year depreciation deduction equal to 50 percent of the adjusted basis of qualified property.[25] Qualified property is defined in the same manner as for purposes of the 30-percent additional first-year depreciation deduction provided by the JCWAA except that the applicable time period for acquisition (or self construction) of the property is modified. In addition, property must be placed in service before January 1, 2005 to

---

[24] For purposes of determining the amount of eligible progress expenditures, it is intended that rules similar to sec. 46(d)(3) as in effect prior to the Tax Reform Act of 1986 shall apply.

[25] A taxpayer is permitted to elect out of the 50-percent additional first-year depreciation deduction for any class of property for any taxable year.

qualify.[26] Property for which the 50-percent additional first year depreciation deduction is claimed is not eligible for the 30-percent additional first year depreciation deduction.

Under the Act, in order to qualify the property must be acquired after May 5, 2003, and before January 1, 2005, and no binding written contract for the acquisition is in effect before May 6, 2003.[27] With respect to property that is manufactured, constructed, or produced by the taxpayer for use by the taxpayer, the taxpayer must begin the manufacture, construction, or production of the property after May 5, 2003. For property eligible for the extended placed in service date (i.e., certain property with a recovery period of 10 years or longer and certain transportation property), a special rule limits the amount of costs eligible for the additional first year depreciation. With respect to such property, only progress expenditures properly attributable to the costs incurred before January 1, 2005, shall be eligible for the additional first year depreciation.[28]

The Congress wishes to clarify that the adjusted basis of qualified property acquired by a taxpayer in a like kind exchange or an involuntary conversion is eligible for the additional first year depreciation deduction.

The Act also increases the limitation on the amount of depreciation deductions allowed with respect to certain passenger automobiles (sec. 280F) in the first year by $7,650 (in lieu of the $4,600 provided under the JCWAA) for automobiles that qualify (and do not elect out of the increased first year deduction). The $7,650 increase is not indexed for inflation.

The Act also extends the placed in service date requirement for certain property with a recovery period of 10 years or longer and certain transportation property to property placed in service prior to January 1, 2006 (instead of January 1, 2005).[29] In addition, progress expenditures eligible for the 30-percent additional first year depreciation is extended to include costs incurred prior to January 1, 2005 (instead of September 11, 2004).

Effective Date

The provision applies to taxable years ending after May 5, 2003.

[26] An extension of the placed in service date of one year (i.e., January 1, 2006) is provided for certain property with a recovery period of 10 years or longer and certain transportation property as defined for purposes of the JCWAA.

[27] Property does not fail to qualify for the additional first-year depreciation merely because a binding written contract to acquire a component of the property is in effect prior to May 6, 2003. However, no 50-percent additional first-year depreciation is permitted on any such component. No inference is intended as to the proper treatment of components placed in service under the 30 percent additional first-year depreciation provided by the JCWAA.

[28] For purposes of determining the amount of eligible progress expenditures, it is intended that rules similar to sec. 46(d)(3) as in effect prior to the Tax Reform Act of 1986 are to apply.

[29] Property that is otherwise eligible for the extended placed-in-service rules, and that is acquired and placed in service during 2005 pursuant to a written binding contract which was entered into after May 5, 2003, and before January 1, 2005, is eligible for the 50-percent additional first-year depreciation deduction. A technical correction may be necessary so that the statute reflects this intent.

B. Increased Expensing for Small Business (sec. 202 of the Act and sec. 179 of the Code)

Present and Prior Law

In lieu of depreciation, a taxpayer with a sufficiently small amount of annual investment may elect to deduct up to $25,000 (for taxable years beginning in 2003 and thereafter) of the cost of qualifying property placed in service for the taxable year (sec. 179).[30] In general, qualifying property is defined as depreciable tangible personal property that is purchased for use in the active conduct of a trade or business. The $25,000 amount is reduced (but not below zero) by the amount by which the cost of qualifying property placed in service during the taxable year exceeds $200,000. An election to expense these items generally is made on the taxpayer's original return for the taxable year to which the election relates, and may be revoked only with the consent of the Commissioner.[31] In general, taxpayers may not elect to expense off-the-shelf computer software.[32]

The amount eligible to be expensed for a taxable year may not exceed the taxable income for a taxable year that is derived from the active conduct of a trade or business (determined without regard to this provision). Any amount that is not allowed as a deduction because of the taxable income limitation may be carried forward to succeeding taxable years (subject to similar limitations). No general business credit under section 38 is allowed with respect to any amount for which a deduction is allowed under section 179.

Reasons for Change

The Congress believed that section 179 expensing provides two important benefits for small businesses. First, it lowers the cost of capital for tangible property used in a trade or business. With a lower cost of capital, the Congress believed small business will invest in more equipment and employ more workers. Second, it eliminates depreciation recordkeeping requirements with respect to expensed property. In order to increase the value of these benefits and to increase the number of taxpayers eligible, the Act increases the amount allowed to be expensed under section 179 and increases the amount of the phase-out threshold, as well as indexing these amounts.

The Congress also believed that purchased computer software should be included in the section 179 expensing provision so that it is not disadvantaged relative to developed software. In addition, the Congress believed that the process of making and revoking section 179 elections should be made simpler and more efficient for

---

[30] Additional section 179 incentives are provided with respect to a qualified property used by a business in the New York Liberty Zone (sec. 1400L(f)), an empowerment zone (sec. 1397A), or a renewal community (sec. 1400J).

[31] Section 179(c)(2). A taxpayer may make the election on the original return (whether or not the return is timely), or on an amended return filed by the due date (including extensions) for filing the return for the tax year the property was placed in service. If the taxpayer timely filed an original return without making the election, the taxpayer may still make the election by filing an amended return within six months of the due date of the return (excluding extensions). Treas. Reg. sec. 1.179-5.

[32] Section 179(d)(1) requires that property be tangible to be eligible for expensing; in general, computer software is intangible property.

taxpayers by eliminating the requirement of the consent of the Commissioner.

Explanation of Provision [33]

The Act provides that the maximum dollar amount that may be deducted under section 179 is increased to $100,000 for property placed in service in taxable years beginning in 2003, 2004, and 2005. In addition, the $200,000 amount is increased to $400,000 for property placed in service in taxable years beginning in 2003, 2004, and 2005. The dollar limitations are indexed annually for inflation for taxable years beginning after 2003 and before 2006. The provision also includes off-the-shelf computer software placed in service in a taxable year beginning in 2003, 2004, or 2005, as qualifying property. With respect to a taxable year beginning after 2002 and before 2006, the provision permits taxpayers to make or revoke expensing elections on amended returns without the consent of the Commissioner.

Effective Date

The provision is effective for taxable years beginning after December 31, 2002.

[33] The provision was subsequently extended in section 201 of the American Jobs Creation Act of 2004, Pub. L. No. 108–357, described in Part Seventeen.

III. REDUCTION IN TAXES ON DIVIDENDS AND CAPITAL GAINS

A. Reduction in Capital Gains Rates for Individuals; Repeal of Five-Year Holding Period Requirement (sec. 301 of the Act and sec. 1(h) of the Code)

Present and Prior Law

In general, gain or loss reflected in the value of an asset is not recognized for income tax purposes until a taxpayer disposes of the asset. On the sale or exchange of a capital asset, any gain generally is included in income. Any net capital gain of an individual is taxed at maximum rates lower than the rates applicable to ordinary income. Net capital gain is the excess of the net long-term capital gain for the taxable year over the net short-term capital loss for the year. Gain or loss is treated as long-term if the asset is held for more than one year.

Capital losses generally are deductible in full against capital gains. In addition, individual taxpayers may deduct capital losses against up to $3,000 of ordinary income in each year. Any remaining unused capital losses may be carried forward indefinitely to another taxable year.

A capital asset generally means any property except: (1) inventory, stock in trade, or property held primarily for sale to customers in the ordinary course of the taxpayer's trade or business; (2) depreciable or real property used in the taxpayer's trade or business; (3) specified literary or artistic property; (4) business accounts or notes receivable; (5) certain U.S. publications; (6) certain commodity derivative financial instruments; (7) hedging transactions; and (8) business supplies. In addition, the net gain from the disposition of certain property used in the taxpayer's trade or business is treated as long-term capital gain. Gain from the disposition of depreciable personal property is not treated as capital gain to the extent of all previous depreciation allowances. Gain from the disposition of depreciable real property is generally not treated as capital gain to the extent of the depreciation allowances in excess of the allowances that would have been available under the straight-line method of depreciation.

Under prior law, the maximum rate of tax on the adjusted net capital gain of an individual was 20 percent. In addition, any adjusted net capital gain which otherwise would have been taxed at a 15-percent rate was taxed at a 10-percent rate. These rates applied for purposes of both the regular tax and the alternative minimum tax.

The "adjusted net capital gain" of an individual is the net capital gain reduced (but not below zero) by the sum of the 28-percent rate gain and the unrecaptured section 1250 gain. The net capital gain is reduced by the amount of gain that the individual treats as investment income for purposes of determining the investment interest limitation under section 163(d).

The term "28-percent rate gain" means the amount of net gain attributable to long-term capital gains and losses from the sale or exchange of collectibles (as defined in section 408(m) without regard to paragraph (3) thereof), an amount of gain equal to the amount of gain excluded from gross income under section 1202 (relating to certain small business stock),[34] the net short-term capital loss for the taxable year, and any long-term capital loss carryover to the taxable year.

"Unrecaptured section 1250 gain" means any long-term capital gain from the sale or exchange of section 1250 property (i.e., depreciable real estate) held more than one year to the extent of the gain that would have been treated as ordinary income if section 1250 applied to all depreciation, reduced by the net loss (if any) attributable to the items taken into account in computing 28-percent rate gain. The amount of unrecaptured section 1250 gain (before the reduction for the net loss) attributable to the disposition of property to which section 1231 applies shall not exceed the net section 1231 gain for the year.

The unrecaptured section 1250 gain is taxed at a maximum rate of 25 percent, and the 28-percent rate gain is taxed at a maximum rate of 28 percent. Any amount of unrecaptured section 1250 gain or 28-percent rate gain otherwise taxed at a 10- or 15-percent rate is taxed at that rate.

Under prior law, any gain from the sale or exchange of property held more than five years that would otherwise have been taxed at the 10-percent rate was taxed at an 8-percent rate. Any gain from the sale or exchange of property held more than five years and the holding period for which began after December 31, 2000, which would otherwise have been taxed at a 20-percent rate was taxed at an 18-percent rate.

Reasons for Change

The Congress believed that, by reducing the effective tax rates on capital gains, American households will respond by increasing savings. The Congress believed it is important to encourage risk-taking and believed that a reduction in the taxation of capital gains will have that effect. The Congress also believed that a reduction in the taxation of capital gains will improve the efficiency of the markets, because the taxation of capital gains upon realization encourages investors who have accrued past gains to keep their monies "locked in" to such investments even when better investment opportunities present themselves. A reduction in the taxation of capital gains should reduce this "lock in" effect.

The Congress believed it is important that tax policy be conducive to economic growth. Economic growth cannot occur without savings, investment, and the willingness of individuals to take risks. The greater the pool of savings, the greater will be the monies available for business investment. It is through such invest-

[34] This results in a maximum effective regular tax rate on qualified gain from small business stock of 14 percent.

ment that the United States' economy can increase output and productivity. It is through increases in productivity that workers earn higher real wages. Hence, a greater saving rate is necessary for all Americans to benefit from a higher standard of living.

Explanation of Provision

The Act reduces the 10- and 20-percent rates on the adjusted net capital gain of an individual to five (zero for taxable years beginning after 2007) and 15 percent, respectively. These lower rates apply to both the regular tax and the alternative minimum tax. The lower rates apply to assets held more than one year.

Effective Date

The provision applies to taxable years ending on or after May 6, 2003, and beginning before January 1, 2009.

For taxable years that include May 6, 2003, the lower rates apply to amounts properly taken into account for the portion of the year on or after that date. This generally has the effect of applying the lower rates to capital assets sold or exchanged (and installment payments received) on or after May 6, 2003. In the case of gain and loss taken into account by a pass-through entity, the date taken into account by the entity is the appropriate date for applying this rule.

B. Dividend Income of Individuals Taxed at Capital Gain Rates (sec. 302 of the Act and sec. 1(h) of the Code)

Present and Prior Law

Under prior law, dividends received by an individual[35] were included in gross income and taxed as ordinary income at rates up to 38.6 percent.[36]

Under prior law, the rate of tax on the net capital gain of an individual generally was 20 percent (10 percent[37] with respect to income which would otherwise be taxed at the 10- or 15-percent rate).[38] Net capital gain means net gain from the sale or exchange of capital assets held for more than one year in excess of net loss from the sale or exchange of capital assets held not more than one year.

Reasons for Change

Under prior law, the United States had a "classical" system of taxing corporate income. Under this system, corporations and their shareholders are treated as separate persons. A tax was imposed on the corporation on its taxable income, and after-tax earnings distributed to individual shareholders as dividends are included in the individual's income and taxed at the individual's tax rate. This system created the so-called "double taxation of dividends."

---

[35] The rates applicable to individuals also apply to trusts and estates.

[36] Section 105 of the Act reduced the maximum rate to 35 percent.

[37] An eight-percent rate applied to property held more than five years.

[38] Section 301 of the Act reduced the capital gain rates to five (zero for taxable years beginning after 2007) and 15 percent, respectively.

The Congress noted that economically, the issue was not that dividends were taxed twice, but rather the magnitude of the total tax burden on income from different investments. The Congress believed the prior system, by placing different tax burdens on different investments, resulted in economic distortions. The Congress observed that prior law distorted corporate financial decisions. The Congress observed that because interest payments on the debt are deductible, prior law encouraged corporations to finance using debt rather than equity and created incentives for financial engineering to achieve interest deductions from financial instruments with substantial equity characteristics. The Congress believed that the increase in corporate leverage, while beneficial to each corporation from a tax perspective, may have placed the economy at risk of more bankruptcies during an economic downturn. In addition, the Congress found that prior law encouraged corporations to retain earnings rather than to distribute them as taxable dividends. If dividends are discouraged, shareholders may prefer that corporate management retain and reinvest earnings rather than pay out dividends, even if the shareholder might have an alternative use for the funds that could offer a higher rate of return than that earned on the retained earnings. This was another source of inefficiency as the opportunity to earn higher pre-tax returns was by-passed in favor of lower pre-tax returns.

The Congress believed it is important that tax policy be conducive to economic growth. Economic growth is impeded by tax-induced distortions in the capital markets. Mitigating these distortions will improve the efficiency of the capital markets. In addition, reducing the aggregate tax burden on investments made by corporations will lower the cost of capital needed to finance new investments and lead to increases in aggregate national investment by the private sector. It is through such investment that the United States' economy can increase output and productivity. It is through increases in productivity that workers earn higher real wages and all Americans benefit from a higher standard of living.

Explanation of Provision[39]

Under the Act, dividends received by a non-corporate shareholder from domestic corporations and qualified foreign corporations are taxed at the same rates that apply to net capital gain. This treatment applies for purposes of both the regular tax and the alternative minimum tax. Thus, under the Act, dividends received by an individual, estate, or trust are taxed at rates of five (zero for taxable years beginning after 2007) and 15 percent.[40]

If a shareholder does not hold a share of stock for more than 60 days during the 121-day period beginning 60 days before the ex-dividend date (as measured under section 246(c)),[41] dividends received on the stock are not eligible for the reduced rates. Also, the reduced rates are not available for dividends to the extent that the

[39] The provision is described as amended by the technical corrections enacted by section 402 of the Working Families Relief Act of 2004. See H.R. Rep. No. 108–696, the Conference Report to accompany H.R. 1308, pp. 87–88 (Sept. 23, 2004).

[40] Payments in lieu of dividends are not eligible for the lower rates. See section 6045(d) relating to statements required to be furnished by brokers regarding these payments.

[41] In the case of preferred stock, the period is 90 days within a 181-day period beginning 90 days before the ex-dividend date.

taxpayer is obligated to make related payments with respect to positions in substantially similar or related property.

Qualified dividend income includes otherwise qualified dividends received from a qualified foreign corporation. The term "qualified foreign corporation" includes a foreign corporation that is eligible for the benefits of a comprehensive income tax treaty with the United States which the Treasury Department determines to be satisfactory and which includes an exchange of information program.[42] In addition, a foreign corporation is treated as a qualified foreign corporation with respect to any dividend paid by the corporation with respect to stock that is readily tradable on an established securities market in the United States.[43]

Dividends received from a foreign corporation that was a foreign investment company (as defined in section 1246(b)), a passive foreign investment company (as defined in section 1297), or a foreign personal holding company (as defined in section 552) in either the taxable year of the distribution or the preceding taxable year are not qualified dividends.[44]

Special rules apply in determining a taxpayer's foreign tax credit limitation under section 904 in the case of qualified dividend income. For these purposes, rules similar to the rules of section 904(b)(2)(B) concerning adjustments to the foreign tax credit limitation to reflect any capital gain rate differential will apply to any qualified dividend income. Additionally, it is anticipated that regulations promulgated under this provision will coordinate the operation of the rules applicable to qualified dividend income and capital gain.

If an individual, estate, or trust receives an extraordinary dividend (within the meaning of section 1059(c)) eligible for the reduced rates with respect to any share of stock, any loss on the sale of the stock is treated as a long-term capital loss to the extent of the dividend.

A dividend is treated as investment income for purposes of determining the amount of deductible investment interest only if the taxpayer elects to treat the dividend as not eligible for the reduced rates.

The deduction for estate taxes under section 691(c) paid on any qualified dividend that is income in respect of a decedent reduces the amount eligible for the lower tax rates.

The amount of dividends qualifying for reduced rates that may be paid by a regulated investment company ("RIC") for any taxable year in which the qualified dividend income received by the company is less than 95 percent of its gross income (as specially computed) may not exceed the sum of (i) the qualified dividend income of the RIC for the taxable year and (ii) the amount of earnings and profits accumulated in a non-RIC taxable year that were distributed by the RIC during the taxable year.

---

[42] IRS Notice 2003–69 (I.R.B. 2003–42, Oct. 20, 2003) provides a list of treaties satisfying this requirement.

[43] IRS Notice 2003–71 (I.R.B. 2003–43, Oct. 27, 2003), IRS Notice 2003–79 (I.R.B. 2003–50, December 15, 2003), and IRS Notice 2004–71 (I.R.B. 2004–45, November 8, 2004) provide guidance on when stock of a foreign corporation is considered readily tradable on an established securities market in the United States for this purpose.

[44] IRS Notice 2004–70 (I.R.B. 2004–44, Nov. 1, 2004) provides guidance on dividend treatment for amounts received by shareholders from foreign corporations subject to anti-deferral regimes.

The amount of dividends qualifying for reduced rates that may be paid by a real estate investment trust ("REIT") for any taxable year may not exceed the sum of (i) the qualified dividend income of the REIT for the taxable year, (ii) an amount equal to the excess of the income subject to the taxes imposed by section 857(b)(1) and the regulations prescribed under section 337(d) for the preceding taxable year over the amount of these taxes for the preceding taxable year, and (iii) the amount of earnings and profits accumulated in a non-REIT taxable year that were distributed by the REIT during the taxable year.

The reduced rates do not apply to dividends received from an organization that was exempt from tax under section 501 or was a tax-exempt farmers' cooperative in either the taxable year of the distribution or the preceding taxable year; dividends received from a mutual savings bank that received a deduction under section 591; or deductible dividends paid on employer securities.

In the case of brokers and dealers who engage in securities lending transactions, short sales, or other similar transactions on behalf of their customers in the normal course of their trade or business, the Congress intended that the IRS would exercise its authority under section 6724(a) to waive penalties where dealers and brokers attempt in good faith to comply with the information reporting requirements under sections 6042 and 6045, but were unable to reasonably comply because of the period necessary to conform their information reporting systems to the retroactive rate reductions on qualified dividends provided by the Act. In addition, the Congress expected that individual taxpayers who received payments in lieu of dividends from these transactions could treat the payments as dividend income to the extent that the payments were reported to them as dividend income on their Forms 1099–DIV received for calendar year 2003, unless they knew or had reason to know that the payments were in fact payments in lieu of dividends rather than actual dividends.[45]

The tax rate for the accumulated earnings tax (sec. 531) and the personal holding company tax (sec. 541) is reduced to 15 percent.

Amounts treated as ordinary income on the disposition of certain preferred stock (sec. 306) are treated as dividends for purposes of applying the reduced rates.

The collapsible corporation rules (sec. 341) are repealed.

Effective Date

The provision is effective for taxable years beginning after December 31, 2002. In the case of a RIC, REIT, S corporation, partnership, estate, trust, or common trust fund, the provision applies to taxable years ending after December 31, 2002, with respect to dividends received after that date.

The provision does not apply to taxable years beginning after December 31, 2008.

---

[45] IRS Notice 2003–67 (I.R.B. 2003–40, Oct. 6, 2003) provides guidance to brokers and individuals regarding information reporting for payments in lieu of dividends. IRS Notice 2003–79 (I.R.B 2003–50, December 15, 2003) and IRS Notice 2004–71 (I.R.B. 2004–45, November 8, 2004) provide guidance to brokers and individuals regarding information reporting for foreign dividends.

IV. CORPORATE ESTIMATED TAX PAYMENTS FOR 2003

A. Time for Payment of Corporate Estimated Taxes (sec. 501 of the Act)

Present and Prior Law

In general, corporations are required to make quarterly estimated tax payments of their income tax liability (sec. 6655). For a corporation whose taxable year is a calendar year, these estimated tax payments must be made by April 15, June 15, September 15, and December 15.

Reasons for Change

The Congress believed it was appropriate to modify the corporate estimated tax requirements.

Explanation of Provision

With respect to corporate estimated tax payments otherwise due on September 15, 2003, 25 percent is not required to be paid until October 1, 2003.

Effective Date

The provision is effective on the date of enactment (May 26, 2003)

PART TWO: SURFACE TRANSPORTATION EXTENSION ACT OF 2003 (PUBLIC LAW 108–88)[46]

A. Extension of Highway Trust Fund and Aquatic Resources Trust Fund Expenditure Authority (sec. 12 of the Act)

Present and Prior Law

Under prior law, the Internal Revenue Code (sec. 9503) authorized expenditures (subject to appropriations) to be made from the Highway Trust Fund through September 30, 2003, for purposes provided in specified authorizing legislation as in effect on the date of enactment of the most recent authorizing Act (the Transportation Equity Act for the 21st Century).

Under prior law, expenditures also were authorized from the Aquatic Resources Trust Fund through September 30, 2003.

Highway Trust Fund spending is limited by anti-deficit provisions internal to the Highway Trust Fund, the so-called "Harry Byrd rule." The rule requires the Treasury Department to determine, on a quarterly basis, the amount (if any) by which unfunded highway authorizations exceed projected net Highway Trust Fund tax receipts for the 24-month period beginning at the close of each fiscal year (sec. 9503(d)). Similar rules apply to unfunded Mass Transit Account authorizations. If unfunded authorizations exceed projected 24-month receipts, apportionments to the States for specified programs funded by the relevant Trust Fund Account are to be reduced proportionately. Because of the Harry Byrd rule, taxes dedicated to the Highway Trust Fund typically are scheduled to expire at least two years after current authorizing Acts.

Explanation of Provision[47]

The Act extends the authority to make expenditures (subject to appropriations) from the Highway Trust Fund through February 29, 2004. The Act also updates the Highway Trust Fund cross references to authorizing legislation to include expenditure purposes in this Act and prior authorizing legislation as in effect on the date of enactment.

Instead of extending the taxes dedicated to the Highway Trust Fund, the Act creates a temporary rule (through February 29, 2004) for purposes of the anti-deficit provisions of the Highway Trust Fund. For purposes of determining 24 months of projected

[46] H.R. 3087. The House passed the bill on the suspension calendar on September 24, 2003. The Senate passed the bill by unanimous consent on September 26, 2003. The President signed the bill on September 30, 2003.

[47] The expiration dates described herein were subsequently extended by the Surface Transportation Extension Act of 2004; the Surface Transportation Extension Act of 2004, Part II; the Surface Transportation Extension Act of 2004, Part III; the Surface Transportation Extension Act of 2004, Part IV; and the Surface Transportation Extension Act of 2004, Part V, described in Part Eight, Part Eleven, Part Twelve, Part Thirteen, and Part Fourteen, respectively.

revenues for the anti-deficit provisions, the Secretary of the Treasury is instructed to treat each expiring provision relating to appropriations and transfers to the Highway Trust Fund to have been extended through the end of the 24-month period and to assume that the rate of tax during such 24-month period remains the same as the rate in effect on the date of enactment of the Act.

The Act extends the authority to make expenditures (subject to appropriations) from the Aquatics Resources Trust Fund through February 29, 2004. The Act also updates the Aquatics Resources Trust Fund cross references to authorizing legislation to include expenditure purposes as in effect on the date of enactment of this Act.

Effective Date

The provision is effective on the date of enactment (September 30, 2003).

PART THREE: TO EXTEND THE TEMPORARY ASSISTANCE FOR NEEDY FAMILIES BLOCK GRANT PROGRAM, AND CERTAIN TAX AND TRADE PROGRAMS, AND FOR OTHER PURPOSES (PUBLIC LAW 108–89)[48]

A. Disclosure of Return Information Relating to Student Loans (sec. 201 of the Act and sec. 6103(l) of the Code)

Present and Prior Law

Present and prior law prohibit the disclosure of returns and return information, except to the extent specifically authorized by the Code.[49] An exception is provided for disclosure to the Department of Education (but not to contractors thereof) of a taxpayer's filing status, adjusted gross income and identity information (i.e., name, mailing address, taxpayer identifying number) to establish an appropriate repayment amount for an applicable student loan.[50] Under prior law, the Department of Education disclosure authority was scheduled to expire after September 30, 2003.

Explanation of Provision

The Act extends the disclosure authority relating to the disclosure of return information to carry out income-contingent repayment of student loans. The disclosure authority does not apply to any request made after December 31, 2004.[51]

Effective Date

The provision is effective with respect to requests for disclosures made after September 30, 2003.

B. Extension of IRS User Fees (sec. 202 of the Act and new sec. 7528 of the Code)

Present and Prior Law

The IRS provides written responses to questions of individuals, corporations, and organizations relating to their tax status or the effects of particular transactions for tax purposes. The IRS generally charges a fee[52] for requests for a letter ruling, determination

[48] H.R. 3146. The House passed the bill on the suspension calendar on September 24, 2003. The Senate passed the bill with an amendment by unanimous consent on September 30, 2003. The House passed the bill as amended by the Senate by unanimous consent on September 30, 2003. The President signed the bill on October 1, 2003.

[49] Sec. 6103.

[50] Sec. 6103(l)(13).

[51] The provision predated the enactment of H.R. 1308, Pub. L. No. 108–311 (the "Working Families Tax Relief Act of 2004"), which further extended the disclosure authority through December 31, 2005.

[52] These user fees were originally enacted in section 10511 of the Revenue Act of 1987 (Pub. L. No. 100–203, December 22, 1987) but were not originally placed in the Code.

letter, opinion letter, or other similar ruling or determination. Under prior law,[53] the statutory authorization for these user fees was extended through September 30, 2003.

Explanation of Provision

The Act extends the statutory authorization for IRS user fees through December 31, 2004.[54] The Act also moves the statutory authorization for these fees into the Code[55] and repeals the off-Code statutory authorization for these fees.

Effective Date

The provision is effective for requests made after the date of enactment (October 1, 2003).

C. Extension of Customs User Fees (sec. 301 of the Act)

Present and Prior Law

Section 13031 of the Consolidated Omnibus Budget Reconciliation Act of 1985 (COBRA)[56] authorized the Secretary of the Treasury to collect certain service fees. Section 412 of the Homeland Security Act of 2002[57] authorized the Secretary of the Treasury to delegate such authority to the Secretary of Homeland Security. Provided for under 19 U.S.C. 58c, these fees include: processing fees for air and sea passengers, commercial trucks, rail cars, private aircraft and vessels, commercial vessels, dutiable mail packages, barges and bulk carriers, merchandise, and Customs broker permits. COBRA was amended on several occasions but most recently by Pub. L. No. 103–182, which extended authorization for collection of these fees through September 30, 2003.

Explanation of Provision

The Act extends the authorization for the collection of customs user fees though March 31, 2004.[58]

Effective Date

The provision is effective on the date of enactment (October 1, 2003).

---

[53] Pub. L. No. 104–117, an Act to provide that members of the Armed Forces performing services for the peacekeeping efforts in Bosnia and Herzegovina, Croatia, and Macedonia shall be entitled to tax benefits in the same manner as if such services were performed in a combat zone, and for other purposes (March 20, 1996).

[54] Section 891 of the American Jobs Creation Act of 2004 (Pub. L. No. 108–357, October 22, 2004) further extended the statutory authorization for these user fees through September 30, 2014.

[55] Sec. 7528. The Act also moved into the Code the user fee provision relating to pension plans that was enacted in section 620 of the Economic Growth and Tax Relief Reconciliation Act of 2001 (Pub. L. No. 107–16, June 7, 2001).

[56] Pub. L. No. 99–272.

[57] Pub. L. No. 107–296.

[58] The expiration date was subsequently extended by the Military Family Tax Relief Act of 2003, and the American Jobs Creation Act of 2004, described in Part Four and Part Seventeen, respectively. Present law provides authorization for the collection of these fees through September 30, 2014 (sec. 201; 117 Stat. 1335).

PART FOUR: MILITARY FAMILY TAX RELIEF ACT OF 2003 (PUBLIC LAW 108–121)[59]

I. IMPROVING TAX EQUITY FOR MILITARY PERSONNEL

A. Exclusion of Gain on Sale of a Principal Residence by a Member of the Uniformed Services or the Foreign Service (sec. 101 of the Act and sec. 121 of the Code)

Present and Prior Law

Under present and prior law, an individual taxpayer may exclude up to $250,000 ($500,000 if married filing a joint return) of gain realized on the sale or exchange of a principal residence. To be eligible for the exclusion, the taxpayer must have owned and used the residence as a principal residence for at least two of the five years ending on the sale or exchange. A taxpayer who fails to meet these requirements by reason of a change of place of employment, health, or, to the extent provided under regulations, unforeseen circumstances is able to exclude an amount equal to the fraction of the $250,000 ($500,000 if married filing a joint return) that is equal to the fraction of the two years that the ownership and use requirements are met. Under prior law, there were no special rules relating to members of the uniformed services or the Foreign Service of the United States.

Reasons for Change[60]

The Congress believed that members of the uniformed services and the Foreign Service of the United States who would otherwise qualify for the exclusion of the gain on the sale of a principal residence should not be deprived the exclusion because of service to their country. The Congress believed that it is unfair that members of the uniformed services and the Foreign Service of the United States are unable to avail themselves of the exclusion due to relocations required by service to their country.

Explanation of Provision

Under the Act, an individual may elect to suspend for a maximum of 10 years the five-year test period for ownership and use during certain absences due to service in the uniformed services or the Foreign Service of the United States. The uniformed services

[59] H.R. 3365. The House passed the bill on the suspension calendar on October 29, 2003. The Senate passed the bill with an amendment by unanimous consent on November 3, 2003. The House passed the bill as amended by the Senate on the suspension calendar on November 5, 2003. The President signed the bill on November 11, 2003.

[60] See S. 351, the "Armed Forces Tax Fairness Act of 2003," which was reported by the Senate Committee on Finance on February 11, 2003 (S. Rep. No. 108–3) and H.R. 878, the "Armed Forces Tax Fairness Act of 2003," which was reported by the House Committee on Ways and Means on March 5, 2003 (H.R. Rep. No. 108–23).

include: (1) the Armed Forces (the Army, Navy, Air Force, Marine Corps, and Coast Guard); (2) the commissioned corps of the National Oceanic and Atmospheric Administration; and (3) the commissioned corps of the Public Health Service. If the election is made, the five-year period ending on the date of the sale or exchange of a principal residence does not include any period up to five years during which the taxpayer or the taxpayer's spouse is on qualified official extended duty as a member of the uniformed services or in the Foreign Service of the United States. For these purposes, qualified official extended duty is any period of extended duty while serving at a place of duty at least 150 miles away from the taxpayer's principal residence or under orders compelling residence in Government furnished quarters. Extended duty is defined as any period of duty pursuant to a call or order to such duty for a period in excess of 180 days or for an indefinite period. The election may be made with respect to only one property for a suspension period.

Effective Date

The provision is effective for sales or exchanges after May 6, 1997.

B. Exclusion from Gross Income of Certain Death Gratuity Payments (sec. 102 of the Act and sec. 134 of the Code)

Present and Prior Law

Present and prior law provides that qualified military benefits are not included in gross income. Generally, a qualified military benefit is any allowance or in-kind benefit (other than personal use of a vehicle) which: (1) is received by any member or former member of the uniformed services of the United States or any dependent of such member by reason of such member's status or service as a member of such uniformed services; and (2) was excludable from gross income on September 9, 1986, under any provision of law, regulation, or administrative practice which was in effect on such date. Generally, other than certain cost of living adjustments, no modification or adjustment of any qualified military benefit after September 9, 1986, is taken into account for purposes of this exclusion from gross income. Qualified military benefits include certain death gratuities. The amount of the military death gratuity benefit has been increased since September 9, 1986, to $6,000 pursuant to Chapter 75 of Title 10 of the United States Code. Under prior law, the amount of the exclusion from gross income was not increased to take into account this change.

Reasons for Change [61]

The Congress believed that the amount of the exclusion for these death gratuities should be conformed to the levels of such death gratuities. Further, the Congress believed that the amount of the

[61] See S. 351, the "Armed Forces Tax Fairness Act of 2003," which was reported by the Senate Committee on Finance on February 11, 2003 (S. Rep. No. 108–3) and H.R. 878, the "Armed Forces Tax Fairness Act of 2003," which was reported by the House Committee on Ways and Means on March 5, 2003 (H.R. Rep. No. 108–23).

exclusion should be automatically adjusted for future changes in these death gratuities.

Explanation of Provision

The Act extends the exclusion from gross income for military benefits to any adjustment to the amount of the death gratuity payable under Chapter 75 of Title 10 of the United States Code that is pursuant to a provision of law enacted after September 9, 1986, with respect to the death of certain members of the Armed services on active duty, inactive duty training, or engaged in authorized travel.[62]

Effective Date

The provision is effective with respect to deaths occurring after September 10, 2001.

C. Exclusion for Amounts Received Under Department of Defense Homeowners Assistance Program (sec. 103 of the Act and sec. 132 of the Code)

Present and Prior Law

Homeowners Assistance Program payment

The Department of Defense Homeowners Assistance Program ("HAP") provides payments to certain employees and members of the Armed Forces to offset the adverse effects on housing values that result from a military base realignment or closure.[63]

In general, under HAP, eligible individuals receive either: (1) a cash payment as compensation for losses that may be or have been sustained in a private sale, in an amount not to exceed the difference between (a) 95 percent of the fair market value of their property prior to public announcement of intention to close all or part of the military base or installation and (b) the fair market value of such property at the time of the sale; or (2) as the purchase price for their property, an amount not to exceed 90 percent of the prior fair market value as determined by the Secretary of Defense, or the amount of the outstanding mortgages.

Tax treatment

Unless specifically excluded, gross income for Federal income tax purposes includes all income from whatever source derived. Amounts received under HAP are received in connection with the performance of services. Under prior law, these amounts were includible in gross income as compensation for services to the extent such payments exceed the fair market value of the property relinquished in exchange for such payments. Additionally under prior law, such payments were wages for Federal Insurance Contributions Act ("FICA") tax purposes (including Medicare).

---

[62] The Act also increases the death gratuity benefit from $6,000 to $12,000.

[63] The payments are authorized under the provisions of 42 U.S.C. sec. 3374.

Reasons for Change[64]

The Congress believed that an exclusion from gross income and FICA taxes was necessary to provide full compensation for the losses in home values incurred as a result of military base realignment or closure. The Congress further believed that this would help to facilitate necessary military base realignment or closure.

Explanation of Provision

The Act generally exempts from gross income amounts received under the HAP (as in effect on the date of enactment of this Act). Amounts received under the program also are not considered wages for FICA tax purposes (including Medicare). The excludable amount is limited to the reduction in the fair market value of property.

Effective Date

The provision is effective for payments made after the date of enactment (November 11, 2003).

D. Expansion of Combat Zone Filing Rules to Contingency Operations (sec. 104 of the Act and sec. 7508 of the Code)

Present and Prior Law

General time limits for filing tax returns

Individuals generally must file their Federal income tax returns by April 15 of the year following the close of a taxable year. The Secretary may grant reasonable extensions of time for filing such returns. Treasury regulations provide an additional automatic two-month extension (until June 15 for calendar-year individuals) for United States citizens and residents in military or naval service on duty on April 15 of the following year (the otherwise applicable due date of the return) outside the United States. No action is necessary to apply for this extension, but taxpayers must indicate on their returns (when filed) that they are claiming this extension. Unlike most extensions of time to file, this extension applies to both filing returns and paying the tax due.

Treasury regulations also provide, upon application on the proper form, an automatic four-month extension (until August 15 for calendar-year individuals) for any individual timely filing that form and paying the amount of tax estimated to be due.

In general, individuals must make quarterly estimated tax payments by April 15, June 15, September 15, and January 15 of the following taxable year. Wage withholding is considered to be a payment of estimated taxes.

Suspension of time periods

In general, the period of time for performing various acts under the Code, such as filing tax returns, paying taxes, or filing a claim

[64] See S. 351, the "Armed Forces Tax Fairness Act of 2003," which was reported by the Senate Committee on Finance on February 11, 2003 (S. Rep. No. 108–3) and H.R. 878, the "Armed Forces Tax Fairness Act of 2003," which was reported by the House Committee on Ways and Means on March 5, 2003 (H.R. Rep. No. 108–23).

for credit or refund of tax, is suspended for any individual serving in the Armed Forces of the United States in an area designated as a “combat zone” during the period of combatant activities. An individual who becomes a prisoner of war is considered to continue in active service and is therefore also eligible for these suspension of time provisions. The suspension of time also applies to an individual serving in support of such Armed Forces in the combat zone, such as Red Cross personnel, accredited correspondents, and civilian personnel acting under the direction of the Armed Forces in support of those Forces. The designation of a combat zone must be made by the President in an Executive Order. The President must also designate the period of combatant activities in the combat zone (the starting date and the termination date of combat).

The suspension of time encompasses the period of service in the combat zone during the period of combatant activities in the zone, as well as (1) any time of continuous qualified hospitalization resulting from injury received in the combat zone[65] or (2) time in missing in action status, plus the next 180 days.

The suspension of time applies to the following acts:

1. Filing any return of income, estate, or gift tax (except employment and withholding taxes);
2. Payment of any income, estate, or gift tax (except employment and withholding taxes);
3. Filing a petition with the Tax Court for redetermination of a deficiency, or for review of a decision rendered by the Tax Court;
4. Allowance of a credit or refund of any tax;
5. Filing a claim for credit or refund of any tax;
6. Bringing suit upon any such claim for credit or refund;
7. Assessment of any tax;
8. Giving or making any notice or demand for the payment of any tax, or with respect to any liability to the United States in respect of any tax;
9. Collection of the amount of any liability in respect of any tax;
10. Bringing suit by the United States in respect of any liability in respect of any tax; and
11. Any other act required or permitted under the internal revenue laws specified by the Secretary of the Treasury.

Individuals may, if they choose, perform any of these acts during the period of suspension. Spouses of qualifying individuals are entitled to the same suspension of time, except that the spouse is ineligible for this suspension for any taxable year beginning more than two years after the date of termination of combatant activities in the combat zone.

[65] Two special rules apply to continuous hospitalization inside the United States. First, the suspension of time provisions based on continuous hospitalization inside the United States are applicable only to the hospitalized individual; they are not applicable to the spouse of such individual. Second, in no event do the suspension of time provisions based on continuous hospitalization inside the United States extend beyond five years from the date the individual returns to the United States. These two special rules do not apply to continuous hospitalization outside the United States.

Reasons for Change[66]

The Congress believed that military personnel deployed outside the United States away from their permanent duty station while participating in a contingency operation should be entitled to utilize the same suspension of time provisions as those deployed in a combat zone.

Explanation of Provision

The Act applies the special suspension of time period rules to persons deployed outside the United States away from the individual's permanent duty station while participating in an operation designated by the Secretary of Defense as a contingency operation or that becomes a contingency operation. A contingency operation is defined[67] as a military operation that is designated by the Secretary of Defense as an operation in which members of the Armed Forces are or may become involved in military actions, operations, or hostilities against an enemy of the United States or against an opposing military force, or results in the call or order to (or retention of) active duty of members of the uniformed services during a war or a national emergency declared by the President or Congress.

Effective Date

The provision applies to any period for performing an act that has not expired before the date of enactment (November 11, 2003).

E. Modification of Membership Requirement for Exemption from Tax for Certain Veterans' Organizations (sec. 105 of the Act and sec. 501(c)(19) of the Code)

Present and Prior Law

Under present and prior law, a veterans' organization as described in section 501(c)(19) of the Code generally is exempt from taxation. The Code defines such an organization as a post or organization of past or present members of the Armed Forces of the United States: (1) that is organized in the United States or any of its possessions; (2) no part of the net earnings of which inures to the benefit of any private shareholder or individual; and (3) that meets certain membership requirements. The membership requirements are that (1) at least 75 percent of the organization's members are past or present members of the Armed Forces of the United States, and, under prior law, that (2) substantially all of the remaining members are cadets or are spouses, widows, or widowers of past or present members of the Armed Forces of the United States or of cadets. Under present and prior law, no more than 2.5 percent of an organization's total members may consist of individuals who are not veterans, cadets, or spouses, widows, or widowers of such individuals.

---

[66] See S. 351, the "Armed Forces Tax Fairness Act of 2003," which was reported by the Senate Committee on Finance on February 11, 2003 (S. Rep. No. 108–3) and H.R. 878, the "Armed Forces Tax Fairness Act of 2003," which was reported by the House Committee on Ways and Means on March 5, 2003 (H.R. Rep. No. 108–23).

[67] The definition is by cross-reference to 10 U.S.C. sec. 101.

Contributions to an organization described in section 501(c)(19) may be deductible for Federal income or gift tax purposes if the organization is a post or organization of war veterans.

Reasons for Change[68]

As the membership of veterans' organizations changes due to aging and the deaths of members, veterans' organizations that currently qualify for tax exemption under section 501(c)(19) may cease to qualify for exempt status under that section, even though the membership, apart from changes due to deaths, remains the same. The Congress believed that a limited expansion of the membership of veterans' organizations will enable certain of such organizations to retain exempt status, which might otherwise be in jeopardy, and will not unduly expand the membership base beyond persons with a close connection to members of the Armed Forces or cadets.

Explanation of Provision

The Act permits ancestors or lineal descendants of past or present members of the Armed Forces of the United States or of cadets to qualify as members for purposes of the "substantially all" test. The Act does not change the requirement that 75 percent of the organization's members must be past or present members of the Armed Forces of the United States or the 2.5 percent rule.

Effective Date

The provision is effective for taxable years beginning after the date of enactment (November 11, 2003).

F. Clarification of Treatment of Certain Dependent Care Assistance Programs Provided to Members of the Uniformed Services of the United States (sec. 106 of the Act and sec. 134 of the Code)

Present and Prior Law

Present and prior law provides that qualified military benefits are not included in gross income. Generally, a qualified military benefit is any allowance or in-kind benefit (other than personal use of a vehicle) which: (1) is received by any member or former member of the uniformed services of the United States or any dependent of such member by reason of such member's status or service as a member of such uniformed services; and (2) was excludable from gross income on September 9, 1986, under any provision of law, regulation, or administrative practice which was in effect on such date. Generally, other than certain cost of living adjustments, no modification or adjustment of any qualified military benefit after September 9, 1986, is taken into account for purposes of this exclusion from gross income. Under prior law, questions arose as to the scope of the exclusion with respect to the dependent care credit.

---

[68] See S. 351, the "Armed Forces Tax Fairness Act of 2003," which was reported by the Senate Committee on Finance on February 11, 2003 (S. Rep. No. 108–3) and H.R. 878, the "Armed Forces Tax Fairness Act of 2003," which was reported by the House Committee on Ways and Means on March 5, 2003 (H.R. Rep. No. 108–23).

Reasons for Change[69]

The Congress believed that it is important to remove any uncertainty regarding the tax treatment of dependent care assistance provided to members of the uniformed services.

Explanation of Provision

The Act clarifies that dependent care assistance provided under a dependent care assistance program (as in effect on the date of enactment of this Act) for a member of the uniformed services by reason of such member's status or service as a member of the uniformed services is excludable from gross income as a qualified military benefit subject to the present-law rules. The uniformed services include: (1) the Armed Forces (the Army, Navy, Air Force, Marine Corps, and Coast Guard); (2) the commissioned corps of the National Oceanic and Atmospheric Administration; and (3) the commissioned corps of the Public Health Service. Amounts received under the program also are not considered wages for Federal Insurance Contributions Act tax purposes (including Medicare).

Effective Date

The provision is effective for taxable years beginning after December 31, 2002. No inference is intended as to the tax treatment of such amounts for prior taxable years.

G. Treatment of Service Academy Appointments as Scholarships for Purposes of Qualified Tuition Programs and Coverdell Education Savings Accounts (sec. 107 of the Act and secs. 529 and 530 of the Code)

Present and Prior Law

The Code provides tax-exempt status to qualified tuition programs, meaning programs established and maintained by a State or agency or instrumentality thereof or by one or more eligible educational institutions under which a person (1) may purchase tuition credits or certificates on behalf of a designated beneficiary which entitle the beneficiary to the waiver or payment of qualified higher education expenses of the beneficiary, or (2) in the case of a program established by and maintained by a State or agency or instrumentality thereof, may make contributions to an account which is established for the purpose of meeting the qualified higher education expenses of the designated beneficiary of the account. Contributions to qualified tuition programs may be made only in cash. Qualified tuition programs must have adequate safeguards to prevent contributions on behalf of a designated beneficiary in excess of amounts necessary to provide for the qualified higher education expenses of the beneficiary.

The Code provides tax-exempt status to Coverdell education savings accounts ("ESAs"), meaning certain trusts or custodial ac-

[69] See S. 351, the "Armed Forces Tax Fairness Act of 2003," which was reported by the Senate Committee on Finance on February 11, 2003 (S. Rep. No. 108–3) and H.R. 878, the "Armed Forces Tax Fairness Act of 2003," which was reported by the House Committee on Ways and Means on March 5, 2003 (H.R. Rep. No. 108–23).

counts which are created or organized in the United States exclusively for the purpose of paying the qualified education expenses of a designated beneficiary. Contributions to ESAs may be made only in cash. Annual contributions to ESAs may not exceed $2,000 per beneficiary (except in cases involving certain tax-free rollovers) and may not be made after the designated beneficiary reaches age 18.

Earnings on contributions to an ESA or a qualified tuition program generally are subject to tax when withdrawn. However, distributions from an ESA or qualified tuition program are excludable from the gross income of the distributee to the extent that the total distribution does not exceed the qualified education expenses incurred by the beneficiary during the year the distribution is made.

If the qualified education expenses of the beneficiary for the year are less than the total amount of the distribution from an ESA or qualified tuition program, then the qualified education expenses are deemed to be paid from a pro-rata share of both the principal and earnings components of the distribution. In such a case, only a portion of the earnings is excludable (i.e., the portion of the earnings based on the ratio that the qualified education expenses bear to the total amount of the distribution) and the remaining portion of the earnings is includible in the beneficiary's gross income.

The earnings portion of a distribution from an ESA or a qualified tuition program that is includible in income is generally subject to an additional 10-percent tax. The 10-percent additional tax does not apply if a distribution is made on account of the death or disability of the designated beneficiary, or on account of a scholarship received by the designated beneficiary (to the extent it does not exceed the amount of the scholarship).

Service obligations are required of recipients of appointments to the United States Military Academy, the United States Naval Academy, the United States Air Force Academy, the United States Coast Guard Academy, or the United States Merchant Marine Academy. Because of these service obligations, appointments to the Academies are not considered scholarships for purposes of the waiver of the additional 10 percent tax on withdrawals from ESAs and qualified tuition programs that are not used for qualified education purposes.

Reasons for Change [70]

The Congress believed that it was appropriate to treat appointments to a United States Service Academy in a manner similar to the treatment of qualified scholarships. Accordingly, Congress believed that it was appropriate to waive the additional 10-percent tax on withdrawals from ESAs and qualified tuition programs that are not used for qualified education purposes because the designated beneficiary received an appointment to a United States Service Academy.

The Congress believed that imposing an additional tax on earnings from educational savings accounts and qualified tuition plans is inappropriate in the case of individuals who choose to serve their

[70] See S. 351, the "Armed Forces Tax Fairness Act of 2003," which was reported by the Senate Committee on Finance on February 11, 2003 (S. Rep. No. 108–3) and H.R. 878, the "Armed Forces Tax Fairness Act of 2003," which was reported by the House Committee on Ways and Means on March 5, 2003 (H.R. Rep. No. 108–23).

country as a member of the military and who, as a part of that service, obtain their education at one of the Service Academies.

Explanation of Provision

Under the Act, the additional 10-percent tax does not apply to withdrawals from Coverdell education savings accounts and qualified tuition programs made on account of the attendance of the beneficiary at the United States Military Academy, the United States Naval Academy, the United States Air Force Academy, the United States Coast Guard Academy, or the United States Merchant Marine Academy.

The amount of funds that can be withdrawn without the additional tax is limited to the costs of advanced education as defined in 10 U.S.C. section 2005(e)(3) (as in effect on the date of the enactment of the Act) at such Academies.

Effective Date

The provision applies to taxable years beginning after December 31, 2002.

H. Suspension of Tax-Exempt Status of Terrorist Organizations (sec. 108 of the Act and sec. 501 of the Code)

Present and Prior Law

Under present and prior law, the Internal Revenue Service generally issues a letter revoking recognition of an organization's tax-exempt status only after (1) conducting an examination of the organization, (2) issuing a letter to the organization proposing revocation, and (3) allowing the organization to exhaust the administrative appeal rights that follow the issuance of the proposed revocation letter. In the case of an organization described in section 501(c)(3), the revocation letter immediately is subject to judicial review under the declaratory judgment procedures of section 7428. To sustain a revocation of tax-exempt status under section 7428, the IRS must demonstrate that the organization is no longer entitled to exemption. Under prior law, there was no procedure for the IRS to suspend the tax-exempt status of an organization.

To combat terrorism, the Federal government has designated a number of organizations as terrorist organizations or supporters of terrorism under the Immigration and Nationality Act, the International Emergency Economic Powers Act, and the United Nations Participation Act of 1945.

Reasons for Change [71]

The Congress believed that an organization that has been designated or otherwise identified by the Federal government as a terrorist organization pursuant to certain authority should not be exempt from Federal income tax and that contributions to such organizations should not be deductible for Federal income tax purposes.

[71] See S. 351, the "Armed Forces Tax Fairness Act of 2003," which was reported by the Senate Committee on Finance on February 11, 2003 (S. Rep. No. 108–3) and H.R. 878, the "Armed Forces Tax Fairness Act of 2003," which was reported by the House Committee on Ways and Means on March 5, 2003 (H.R. Rep. No. 108–23).

The Congress believed that the Federal government's designation or identification of an organization as a terrorist organization is ground for suspension of tax-exempt status, and that in such cases a separate investigation of the organization by the Internal Revenue Service is not necessary. Further, because a terrorist organization may challenge the Federal government's designation or identification of the organization under the law authorizing the designation or identification, recourse to the declaratory judgment procedures of the Internal Revenue Code to challenge the suspension of tax-exemption is not appropriate.

Explanation of Provision

The Act suspends the tax-exempt status of an organization that is exempt from tax under section 501(a) for any period during which the organization is designated or identified by U.S. Federal authorities as a terrorist organization or supporter of terrorism. The Act also makes such an organization ineligible to apply for tax-exemption under section 501(a). The period of suspension runs from the date the organization is first designated or identified (or from the date of enactment of the bill, whichever is later) to the date when all designations or identifications with respect to the organization have been rescinded pursuant to the law or Executive Order under which the designation or identification was made.

The Act describes a terrorist organization as an organization that has been designated or otherwise individually identified (1) as a terrorist organization or foreign terrorist organization under the authority of section 212(a)(3)(B)(vi)(II) or section 219 of the Immigration and Nationality Act; (2) in or pursuant to an Executive Order that is related to terrorism and issued under the authority of the International Emergency Economic Powers Act or section 5 of the United Nations Participation Act for the purpose of imposing on such organization an economic or other sanction; or (3) in or pursuant to an Executive Order that refers to the provision and is issued under the authority of any Federal law if the organization is designated or otherwise individually identified in or pursuant to such Executive Order as supporting or engaging in terrorist activity (as defined in section 212(a)(3)(B) of the Immigration and Nationality Act) or supporting terrorism (as defined in section 140(d)(2) of the Foreign Relations Authorization Act, Fiscal Years 1988 and 1989). During the period of suspension, no deduction for any contribution to a terrorist organization is allowed under the Code, including under sections 170, 545(b)(2), 556(b)(2), 642(c), 2055, 2106(a)(2), or 2522.

No organization or other person may challenge, under section 7428 or any other provision of law, in any administrative or judicial proceeding relating to the Federal tax liability of such organization or other person, the suspension of tax-exemption, the ineligibility to apply for tax-exemption, a designation or identification described above, the timing of the period of suspension, or a denial of deduction described above. The suspended organization may maintain other suits or administrative actions against the agency or agencies that designated or identified the organization, for the purpose of challenging such designation or identification (but not the suspension of tax-exempt status under this provision).

If the tax-exemption of an organization is suspended and each designation and identification that has been made with respect to the organization is determined to be erroneous pursuant to the law or Executive Order making the designation or identification, and such erroneous designation results in an overpayment of income tax for any taxable year with respect to such organization, a credit or refund (with interest) with respect to such overpayment shall be made. If the operation of any law or rule of law (including res judicata) prevents the credit or refund at any time, the credit or refund may nevertheless be allowed or made if the claim for such credit or refund is filed before the close of the one-year period beginning on the date that the last remaining designation or identification with respect to the organization is determined to be erroneous.

The Act directs the IRS to update the listings of tax-exempt organizations to take account of organizations that have had their exemption suspended and to publish notice to taxpayers of the suspension of an organization's tax-exemption and the fact that contributions to such organization are not deductible during the period of suspension.

Effective Date

The provision is effective for designations made before, on, or after the date of enactment (November 11, 2003).

I. Above-the-Line Deduction for Overnight Travel Expenses of National Guard and Reserve Members (sec. 109 of the Act and sec. 162 of the Code)

Present and Prior Law

Under prior law, National Guard and Reserve members could claim itemized deductions for their nonreimbursable expenses for transportation, meals, and lodging when they must travel away from home (and stay overnight) to attend National Guard and Reserve meetings. These overnight travel expenses were combined with other miscellaneous itemized deductions on Schedule A of the individual's income tax return and were deductible only to the extent that the aggregate of these deductions exceeds two percent of the taxpayer's adjusted gross income. Under present and prior law, no deduction is generally permitted for commuting expenses to and from drill meetings.

Reasons for Change [72]

The Congress believed that all National Guard and Reserve members incurring unreimbursed overnight expenses to attend National Guard and Reserve meetings should be able to deduct these expenses from their income, not just those who itemize their deductions. Accordingly, the Congress provided an above-the-line deduction for these expenses.

[72] See S. 351, the "Armed Forces Tax Fairness Act of 2003," which was reported by the Senate Committee on Finance on February 11, 2003 (S. Rep. No. 108–3) and H.R. 878, the "Armed Forces Tax Fairness Act of 2003," which was reported by the House Committee on Ways and Means on March 5, 2003 (H.R. Rep. No. 108–23).

Explanation of Provision

The Act provides an above-the-line deduction for the overnight transportation, meals, and lodging expenses of National Guard and Reserve members who must travel away from home more than 100 miles (and stay overnight) to attend National Guard and Reserve meetings. Accordingly, these individuals incurring these expenses can deduct them from gross income regardless of whether they itemize their deductions. The amount of the expenses that may be deducted may not exceed $1,500 per taxable year and is only available for any period during which the individual is more than 100 miles from home in connection with such services.

Effective Date

The provision is effective with respect to amounts paid or incurred in taxable years beginning after December 31, 2002.

J. Extension of Certain Tax Relief Provisions to Astronauts (sec. 110 of the Act and secs. 101, 692, and 2201 of the Code)

Present and Prior Law

In general

The Victims of Terrorism Tax Relief Act of 2001 (the "Victims Act") provided certain income and estate tax relief to individuals who die from wounds or injury incurred as a result of the terrorist attacks against the United States on September 11, 2001, and April 19, 1995 (the bombing of the Alfred P. Murrah Federal Building in Oklahoma City), or as a result of illness incurred due to an attack involving anthrax that occurred on or after September 11, 2001, and before January 1, 2002.

Income tax relief

The Victims Act extended relief similar to the present-law treatment of military or civilian employees of the United States who die as a result of terrorist or military activity outside the United States to individuals who die as a result of wounds or injury which were incurred as a result of the terrorist attacks that occurred on September 11, 2001, or April 19, 1995, and individuals who die as a result of illness incurred due to an attack involving anthrax that occurs on or after September 11, 2001, and before January 1, 2002. Under the Victims Act, such individuals generally are exempt from income tax for the year of death and for prior taxable years beginning with the taxable year prior to the taxable year in which the wounds or injury occurred.[73] The exemption applies to these individuals whether killed in an attack (e.g., in the case of the September 11, 2001, attack in one of the four airplanes or on the ground) or in rescue or recovery operations.

Present and prior law provides tax relief of at least $10,000 to each eligible individual regardless of the income tax liability of the individual for the eligible tax years. If an eligible individual's income tax for years eligible for the exclusion under the provision is less than $10,000, the individual is treated as having made a tax

[73] Present law does not provide relief from self-employment tax liability.

payment for such individual's last taxable year in an amount equal to the excess of $10,000 over the amount of tax not imposed under the provision.

Subject to rules prescribed by the Secretary, the exemption from tax does not apply to the tax attributable to (1) deferred compensation which would have been payable after death if the individual had died other than as a specified terrorist victim, or (2) amounts payable in the taxable year which would not have been payable in such taxable year but for an action taken after September 11, 2001. Thus, for example, the exemption does not apply to amounts payable from a qualified plan or individual retirement arrangement to the beneficiary or estate of the individual. Similarly, amounts payable only as death or survivor's benefits pursuant to deferred compensation preexisting arrangements that would have been paid if the death had occurred for another reason are not covered by the exemption. In addition, if the individual's employer makes adjustments to a plan or arrangement to accelerate the vesting of restricted property or the payment of nonqualified deferred compensation after the date of the particular attack, the exemption does not apply to income received as a result of that action.[74] Also, if the individual's beneficiary cashed in savings bonds of the decedent, the exemption does not apply. On the other hand, the exemption does apply, for example, to a final paycheck of the individual or dividends on stock held by the individual when paid to another person or the individual's estate after the date of death but before the end of the taxable year of the decedent (determined without regard to the death). The exemption also applies to payments of an individual's accrued vacation and accrued sick leave.

The tax relief does not apply to any individual identified by the Attorney General to have been a participant or conspirator in any terrorist attack to which the provision applies, or a representative of such individual.

Exclusion of death benefits

The Victims Act generally provides an exclusion from gross income for amounts received if such amounts are paid by an employer (whether in a single sum or otherwise[75]) by reason of the death of an employee who dies as a result of wounds or injury which were incurred as a result of the terrorist attacks that occurred on September 11, 2001, or April 19, 1995, or as a result of illness incurred due to an attack involving anthrax that occurred on or after September 11, 2001, and before January 1, 2002. Subject to rules prescribed by the Secretary, the exclusion does not apply to amounts that would have been payable if the individual had died for a reason other than the attack. The exclusion does apply, however, to death benefits provided under a qualified plan that satisfy the incidental benefit rule.

For purposes of the exclusion, self-employed individuals are treated as employees. Thus, for example, payments by a partnership to the surviving spouse of a partner who died as a result of

[74] Such amounts may, however, be excludable from gross income under the death benefit exclusion provided in section 102 of the Victims Act.

[75] Thus, for example, payments made over a period of years could qualify for the exclusion.

the September 11, 2001, attacks may be excludable under the provision.

The tax relief does not apply to any individual identified by the Attorney General to have been a participant or conspirator in any terrorist attack to which the provision applies, or a representative of such individual.

Estate tax relief

Present and prior law provides a reduction in Federal estate tax for taxable estates of U.S. citizens or residents who are active members of the U.S. Armed Forces and who are killed in action while serving in a combat zone (sec. 2201). This provision also applies to active service members who die as a result of wounds, disease, or injury suffered while serving in a combat zone by reason of a hazard to which the service member was subjected as an incident of such service.

In general, the effect of section 2201 is to replace the Federal estate tax that would otherwise be imposed with a Federal estate tax equal to 125 percent of the maximum State death tax credit determined under section 2011(b). Credits against the tax, including the unified credit of section 2010 and the State death tax credit of section 2011, then apply to reduce (or eliminate) the amount of the estate tax payable.

Generally, the reduction in Federal estate taxes under section 2201 is equal in amount to the "additional estate tax." The additional estate tax is the difference between the Federal estate tax imposed by section 2001 and 125 percent of the maximum State death tax credit determined under section 2011(b) as in effect prior to its repeal by EGTRRA.

The Victims Act generally treats individuals who die from wounds or injury incurred as a result of the terrorist attacks that occurred on September 11, 2001, or April 19, 1995, or as a result of illness incurred due to an attack involving anthrax that occurred on or after September 11, 2001, and before January 1, 2002, in the same manner as if they were active members of the U.S. Armed Forces killed in action while serving in a combat zone or dying as a result of wounds or injury suffered while serving in a combat zone for purposes of section 2201. Consequently, the estates of these individuals are eligible for the reduction in Federal estate tax provided by section 2201. The tax relief does not apply to any individual identified by the Attorney General to have been a participant or conspirator in any terrorist attack to which the provision applies, or a representative of such individual.

The Victims Act also changed the general operation of section 2201, as it applies to both the estates of service members who qualify for special estate tax treatment under present and prior law and to the estates of individuals who qualify for the special treatment only under the Act. Under the Victims Act, the Federal estate tax is determined in the same manner for all estates that are eligible for Federal estate tax reduction under section 2201. In addition, the executor of an estate that is eligible for special estate tax treatment under section 2201 may elect not to have section 2201 apply to the estate. Thus, in the event that an estate may receive more favorable treatment without the application of section 2201 in the year of death than it would under section 2201, the executor may elect not to apply the provisions of section 2201, and the estate tax owed (if any) would be determined pursuant to the generally applicable rules.

Under the Victims Act, section 2201 no longer reduces Federal estate tax by the amount of the additional estate tax. Instead, the Victims Act provides that the Federal estate tax liability of eligible estates is determined under section 2001 (or section 2101, in the case of decedents who were neither residents nor citizens of the United States), using a rate schedule that is equal to 125 percent of the pre-EGTRRA maximum State death tax credit amount. This rate schedule is used to compute the tax under section 2001(b) or section 2101(b) (i.e., both the tentative tax under section 2001(b)(1) and section 2101(b), and the hypothetical gift tax under section 2001(b)(2) are computed using this rate schedule). As a result of this provision, the estate tax is unified with the gift tax for purposes of section 2201 so that a single graduated (but reduced) rate schedule applies to transfers made by the individual at death, based upon the cumulative taxable transfers made both during lifetime and at death.

In addition, while the Victims Act provides an alternative reduced rate table for purposes of determining the tax under section 2001(b) or section 2101(b), the amount of the unified credit nevertheless is determined as if section 2201 did not apply, based upon the unified credit as in effect on the date of death. For example, in the case of victims of the September 11, 2001, terrorist attack, the applicable unified credit amount under section 2010(c) would be determined by reference to the actual section 2001(c) rate table.

Reasons for Change [76]

The Congress wished to honor the bravery of individuals who lost their lives in the space shuttle Columbia disaster. Further, the Congress believed it appropriate to provide these tax relief measures to those individuals and their families.

Explanation of Provision

The Act extends the exclusion from income tax, the exclusion for death benefits, and the estate tax relief available under the Victims of Terrorism Tax Relief Act of 2001 to astronauts who lose their lives on a space mission (including the individuals who lost their lives in the space shuttle Columbia disaster).

Effective Date

The provision is generally effective for qualified individuals whose lives are lost on a space mission after December 31, 2002.

[76] See S. 351, the "Armed Forces Tax Fairness Act of 2003," which was reported by the Senate Committee on Finance on February 11, 2003 (S. Rep. No. 108–3) and H.R. 878, the "Armed Forces Tax Fairness Act of 2003," which was reported by the House Committee on Ways and Means on March 5, 2003 (H.R. Rep. No. 108–23).

II. REVENUE PROVISION

A. Extension of Customs User Fees (sec. 201 of the Act)

Present and Prior Law

Section 13031 of the Consolidated Omnibus Budget Reconciliation Act of 1985 (COBRA) (Pub. L. No. 99–272), authorized the Secretary of the Treasury to collect certain service fees. Section 412 of the Homeland Security Act of 2002 (Pub. L. No. 107–296) authorized the Secretary of the Treasury to delegate such authority to the Secretary of Homeland Security. Provided for under 19 U.S.C. sec. 58c, these fees include: processing fees for air and sea passengers, commercial trucks, rail cars, private aircraft and vessels, commercial vessels, dutiable mail packages, barges and bulk carriers, merchandise, and customs broker permits. COBRA was amended on several occasions but most recently by Pub. L. No. 108–89, which extended authorization for the collection of these fees through March 31, 2004.[77]

Explanation of Provision

The Act extends the authorization for the collection of customs user fees though March 1, 2005.[78]

Effective Date

The provision is effective on the date of enactment (November 11, 2003).

[77] Sec. 201; 117 Stat. 1335.

[78] The expiration date was subsequently extended by the American Jobs Creation Act of 2004, described in Part Seventeen. Present law provides authorization for the collection of these fees through September 30, 2014 (sec. 201; 117 Stat. 1935).

PART FIVE: MEDICARE PRESCRIPTION DRUG, IMPROVEMENT, AND MODERNIZATION ACT OF 2003 (PUBLIC LAW 108–173) [79]

A. Disclosure of Return Information for Purposes of Providing Transitional Assistance Under Medicare Discount Card Program (sec. 105(e) of the Act and sec. 6103(l)(19) of the Code)

Present and Prior Law

The Internal Revenue Code prohibits disclosure of returns and return information, except to the extent specifically authorized by the Code (sec. 6103(a)). Unauthorized disclosure is a felony punishable by a fine not exceeding $5,000 or imprisonment of not more than five years, or both, together with the costs of prosecution (sec. 7213). Unauthorized inspection of such information is a misdemeanor, punishable by a fine not exceeding $1,000 or imprisonment of not more than one year, or both, together with the costs of prosecution (sec. 7213A). An action for civil damages also may be brought for unauthorized disclosure (sec. 7431). No return or return information may be furnished by the Internal Revenue Service ("IRS") to another agency unless the other agency establishes procedures satisfactory to the IRS for safeguarding the information it receives (sec. 6103(p)).

Explanation of Provision

The Act establishes a new optional Medicare prescription drug benefit program, effective January 1, 2006. Until the new permanent program is effective, the Secretary of Health and Human Services is required to establish a program to endorse prescription drug discount programs in order to provide access to prescription drug discounts for discount card-eligible individuals and to provide for transitional assistance for eligible individuals enrolled in such endorsed programs.

An individual who wishes to be treated as a "transitional assistance eligible individual" has the option of self-certifying under penalty of perjury as to the amount of the individual's income, family size, and prescription drug coverage (if any). The Secretary of Health and Human Services is authorized to verify eligibility for individuals seeking to enroll in an endorsed program and for individuals who provide self-certification as to the foregoing items. In its verification process, the Department of Health and Human

[79] H.R. 1. The House passed the bill, with the text of H.R. 2596 (a bill relating to Health Savings Accounts) appended thereto, on June 27, 2003. The Senate Committee on Finance reported S. 1 on June 13, 2003. The Senate passed H.R. 1, as amended by the provisions of S. 1, on July 7, 2003. The conference report was filed on November 21, 2003 (H.R. Rep. No. 108–391). The conference bill passed the House on November 22, 2003, and the Senate on November 25, 2003. The President signed the bill on December 8, 2003.

Services may obtain and use return information from the IRS. Specifically, the provision authorizes the IRS to disclose to employees and contractors of the Department of Health and Human Services whether adjusted gross income, as modified in accordance with definitions that will be specified by the Secretary of Health and Human Services, exceeds amounts that are 100 and 135 percent of the official poverty line.[80] The IRS also is authorized to disclose the applicable year (as defined below) and whether the return was a joint return. If no return has been filed for such year, the IRS is authorized to disclose the fact that no return has been filed for such taxpayer. "Applicable year" means the most recent taxable year for which information is available in the IRS data information systems generally for all taxpayers, or if there is no return filed for such taxpayer for such year, the prior taxable year. Return information disclosed may only be used for the purposes of determining eligibility for and administering the transitional assistance program as established under the provision. Employees and contractors of the Department of Health and Human Services are subject to the penalties for unauthorized disclosure and inspection, as well as the applicable safeguard requirements.

Effective Date

The provision is effective for disclosures made after the date of enactment (December 8, 2003).

B. Disclosure of Return Information Relating to Income-Related Reduction in Part B Premium Subsidy (sec. 811(c) of the Act and sec. 6103(l)(20) of the Code)

Present and Prior Law

The Internal Revenue Code prohibits disclosure of returns and return information, except to the extent specifically authorized by the Code (sec. 6103(a)). Unauthorized disclosure is a felony punishable by a fine not exceeding $5,000 or imprisonment of not more than five years, or both, together with the costs of prosecution (sec. 7213). Unauthorized inspection of such information is a misdemeanor, punishable by a fine not exceeding $1,000 or imprisonment of not more than one year, or both, together with the costs of prosecution (sec. 7213A). An action for civil damages also may be brought for unauthorized disclosure (sec. 7431). No return or return information may be furnished by the Internal Revenue Service ("IRS") to another agency unless the other agency establishes procedures satisfactory to the IRS for safeguarding the information it receives (sec. 6103(p)).

Explanation of Provision

To facilitate the income-related reduction in Part B premium subsidy, the Act authorizes the disclosure of certain return information to employees and contractors of the Social Security Administration. Upon written request from the Commissioner of Social

[80] For this purpose, the official poverty line is defined in section 673(3) of the Community Services Block Grant Act, 42 U.S.C. sec. 9902(2).

Security, the IRS may disclose certain items of return information with respect to a taxpayer whose premium may be subject to a subsidy adjustment.[81] With respect to such taxpayers, the IRS may disclose (1) taxpayer identity information; (2) filing status; (3) adjusted gross income; (4) the amounts excluded from such taxpayer's gross income under sections 135 and 911 of the Code (relating to income from United States Savings bonds used to pay higher education tuition and fees, and foreign earned income); (5) tax-exempt interest received or accrued during the taxable year to the extent such information is available; (6) amounts excluded from such taxpayer's gross income by sections 931 and 933 of the Code (relating to income from sources within Guam, American Samoa, the Northern Mariana Islands, or Puerto Rico); (7) for nonfilers only, such other information relating to the liability of the taxpayer as the Secretary may prescribe by regulation, as might indicate that the amount of the premium of the taxpayer may be subject to adjustment (including estimated tax payments and income information derived from Form W–2, Form 1099, and similar information returns); and (8) the taxable year with respect to which the preceding information relates. Return information disclosed under this authority may be used by employees and contractors of the Social Security Administration only for purposes of, and to the extent necessary in, establishing the appropriate amount of any Part B premium adjustment. Employees and contractors of the Social Security Administration are subject to the penalties for unauthorized disclosure and inspection, as well as the applicable safeguard requirements.

Effective Date

The provision is effective for premium adjustments under section 1839(i) of the Social Security Act for months beginning with January 2007.

C. Health Savings Accounts (sec. 1201 of the Act and new sec. 223 of the Code)

Present and Prior Law

Overview

A number of provisions dealing with the Federal tax treatment of health expenses and health insurance coverage exist under present and prior law.

Employer-provided health coverage

In general, employer contributions to an accident or health plan are excludable from an employee's gross income (and wages for employment tax purposes).[82] This exclusion generally applies to coverage provided to employees (including former employees) and their spouses, dependents, and survivors. Benefits paid under employer-provided accident or health plans are also generally excludable from income to the extent they are reimbursements for medical

---

[81] Adjustments are determined pursuant to section 1839(i) of the Social Security Act (as added by the provision).

[82] Secs. 106, 3121(a)(2), and 3306(b)(2).

care.[83] If certain requirements are satisfied, employer-provided accident or health coverage offered under a cafeteria plan is also excludable from an employee's gross income and wages.[84]

Two general employer-provided arrangements can be used to pay for or reimburse medical expenses of employees on a tax-favored basis: flexible spending arrangements ("FSAs") and health reimbursement arrangements ("HRAs"). While these arrangements provide similar tax benefits (i.e., the amounts paid under the arrangements for medical care are excludable from gross income and wages for employment tax purposes), they are subject to different rules. A main distinguishing feature between the two arrangements is that while FSAs are generally part of a cafeteria plan and contributions to FSAs are made on a salary reduction basis, HRAs cannot be part of a cafeteria plan and contributions cannot be made on a salary-reduction basis.[85]

Amounts paid or accrued by an employer within a taxable year for a sickness, accident, hospitalization, medical expense, or similar health plan for its employees are generally deductible as ordinary and necessary business expenses.[86]

Self-employed individuals

The exclusion for employer-provided health coverage does not apply to self-employed individuals. However, self-employed individuals (i.e., sole proprietors or partners in a partnership)[87] are entitled to deduct 100 percent of the amount paid for health insurance for themselves and their spouse and dependents.[88]

Itemized deduction for medical expenses

Individuals who itemize deductions may deduct amounts paid during the taxable year (to the extent not reimbursed by insurance or otherwise) for medical care of the taxpayer, the taxpayer's spouse, and dependents, to the extent that the total of such expenses exceeds 7.5 percent of the taxpayer's adjusted gross income.[89]

Archer medical savings accounts

In general

In general, an Archer medical savings account ("MSA") is a tax-exempt trust or custodial account created exclusively for the benefit of the account holder that is subject to rules similar to those applicable to individual retirement arrangements.[90]

---

[83] Sec.105. In the case of a self-insured medical reimbursement arrangement, the exclusion applies to highly compensated employees only if certain nondiscrimination rules are satisfied. Sec. 105(h). Medical care is defined as under section 213(d) and generally includes amounts paid for qualified long-term care insurance and services.

[84] Secs. 125, 3121(a)(5)(G), and 3306(b)(5)(G). Long-term care insurance and services may not be provided through a cafeteria plan.

[85] Notice 2002–45, 2002–28 I.R.B. 93 (July 15, 2002); Rev. Rul. 2002–41, 2002–28 I.R.B. 75 (July 15, 2002).

[86] Sec. 162.

[87] Self-employed individuals include more than two-percent shareholders of S corporations who are treated as partners for purposes of fringe benefits rules pursuant to section 1372.

[88] Sec. 162(l).

[89] Sec. 213. The adjusted gross income percentage is 10 percent for purposes of the alternative minimum tax. Sec. 56(b)(1)(B).

[90] Sec. 220.

Within limits, contributions to an Archer MSA are deductible in determining adjusted gross income if made by an eligible individual and are excludable from gross income and wages for employment tax purposes if made by the employer of an eligible individual. Earnings on amounts in an Archer MSA are not includible in gross income in the year earned (i.e., inside buildup is not taxable). Distributions from an Archer MSA for qualified medical expenses are not includible in gross income. Distributions not used for qualified medical expenses are includible in gross income and subject to an additional 15-percent tax unless the distribution is made after death, disability, or the individual attains the age of Medicare eligibility (i.e., age 65).

Qualified medical expenses are generally defined as under section 213(d), except that qualified medical expenses do not include expenses for health insurance other than long-term care insurance, premiums for health coverage during any period of continuation coverage required by Federal law, and premiums for health care coverage while an individual is receiving unemployment compensation under Federal or State law. For purposes of determining the itemized deduction for medical expenses, distributions from an Archer MSA for qualified medical expenses are not treated as expenses paid for medical care under section 213.

Eligible individuals

Archer MSAs are available only to employees of a small employer who are covered under an employer-sponsored high deductible health plan and to self-employed individuals covered under a high deductible health plan.[91] An employer is a small employer if it employed, on average, no more than 50 employees on business days during either of the two preceding calendar years. An individual is not eligible for an Archer MSA if he or she is covered under any other health plan that is not a high deductible health plan (other than a plan providing certain limited types of coverage). Individuals entitled to benefits under Medicare are not eligible individuals. Eligible individuals do not include individuals who may be claimed as a dependent on another person's tax return.

Treatment of contributions

Individual contributions to an Archer MSA are deductible (within limits) in determining adjusted gross income (i.e., "above-the-line"). In addition, employer contributions are excludable from gross income and wages for employment tax purposes (within the same limits). Contributions to an Archer MSA may not be made through a cafeteria plan. In the case of an employee, contributions can be made to an Archer MSA either by the individual or by the individual's employer, but not by both.

The maximum annual contribution that can be made to an Archer MSA for a year is 65 percent of the annual deductible under the high deductible health plan in the case of self-only coverage and 75 percent of the annual deductible in the case of family coverage.

---

[91] Self-employed individuals include more than two-percent shareholders of S corporations who are treated as partners for purposes of fringe benefit rules pursuant to section 1372.

If an employer provides a high deductible health plan coupled with Archer MSAs for employees and makes employer contributions to the Archer MSAs, the employer must make available a comparable contribution on behalf of all employees with comparable coverage during the same period. Contributions are considered comparable if they are either of the same amount or the same percentage of the deductible under the high deductible health plan. If employer contributions do not satisfy the comparability rule during a period, then the employer is subject to an excise tax equal to 35 percent of the aggregate amount contributed by the employer to Archer MSAs of the employer for that period.

Definition of high deductible health plan

For 2003, a high deductible health plan is a health plan with an annual deductible of at least $1,700 and no more than $2,500 in the case of self-only coverage and at least $3,350 and no more than $5,050 in the case of family coverage. In addition, the maximum out-of-pocket expenses with respect to allowed costs must be no more than $3,350 in the case of self-only coverage and no more than $6,150 in the case of family coverage (for 2003).[92] Out-of-pocket expenses include deductibles, co-payments, and other amounts (other than premiums) that the individual must pay for covered benefits under the plan. A plan does not fail to qualify as a high deductible health plan merely because it does not have a deductible for preventive care as required under State law. A plan does not qualify as a high deductible health plan if substantially all of the coverage under the plan is certain permitted insurance or is coverage (whether provided through insurance or otherwise) for accidents, disability, dental care, vision care, or long-term care.

Treatment of death of account holder

Upon death, any balance remaining in the decedent's Archer MSA is includible in his or her gross estate. If the account holder's surviving spouse is the named beneficiary of the Archer MSA, then, after the death of the account holder, the Archer MSA becomes the Archer MSA of the surviving spouse and the amount of the Archer MSA balance may be deducted in computing the decedent's taxable estate, pursuant to the estate tax marital deduction.[93] If, upon the account holder's death, the Archer MSA passes to a named beneficiary other than the decedent's surviving spouse, the Archer MSA ceases to be an Archer MSA as of the date of the decedent's death, and the beneficiary is required to include the fair market value of the Archer MSA assets as of the date of death in gross income for the taxable year that includes the date of death. The amount includible in gross income is reduced by the amount in the Archer MSA used, within one year after death, to pay qualified medical expenses incurred prior to the death. If there is no named beneficiary for the decedent's Archer MSA, the Archer MSA ceases to be an Archer MSA as of the date of death, and the fair market value of the

[92] The deductible and out-of-pocket expenses dollar amounts are indexed for inflation in $50 increments.
[93] Sec. 2056.

assets in the Archer MSA as of such date is includible in the decedent's gross income for the year of the death.

Limit on number of MSAs; termination of MSA availability

The number of taxpayers benefiting annually from an Archer MSA contribution is limited to a threshold level (generally 750,000 taxpayers). The number of Archer MSAs established has not exceeded the threshold level.

After 2003, no new contributions could be made to Archer MSAs except by or on behalf of individuals who previously had Archer MSA contributions and employees who are employed by a participating employer.[94]

Explanation of Provision

In general

The Act adds provisions for health savings accounts (HSAs), effective for taxable years beginning after December 31, 2003. In general, HSAs provide tax-favored treatment for current medical expenses as well as the ability to save on a tax-favored basis for future medical expenses. In general, HSAs are tax-exempt trusts or custodial accounts created exclusively to pay for the qualified medical expenses of the account holder and his or her spouse and dependents that are subject to rules similar to those applicable to individual retirement arrangements.[95]

Within limits, contributions to an HSA made by or on behalf of an eligible individual are deductible by the individual. Contributions to an HSA are excludable from income and employment taxes if made by the employer. Earnings on amounts in HSAs are not taxable. Distributions from an HSA for qualified medical expenses are not includible in gross income. Distributions from an HSA that are not used for qualified medical expenses are includible in gross income and are subject to an additional tax of 10 percent, unless the distribution is made after death, disability, or the individual attains the age of Medicare eligibility (i.e., age 65).

Eligible individuals

Eligible individuals for HSAs are individuals who are covered by a high deductible health plan and no other health plan that is not a high deductible health plan and which provides coverage for any benefit which is covered under the high deductible health plan. Individuals entitled to benefits under Medicare are not eligible to make contributions to an HSA. Eligible individuals do not include individuals who may be claimed as a dependent on another person's tax return.

An individual with other coverage in addition to a high deductible health plan is still eligible for an HSA if such other coverage is certain permitted insurance or permitted coverage. Permitted insurance is: (1) insurance if substantially all of the coverage provided under such insurance relates to (a) liabilities incurred under

[94] Under Pub. L. No. 108–311, new contributions to Archer MSAs can be made through 2005.

[95] The present-law requirement applicable to insurance companies that certain policy acquisition expenses must be capitalized and amortized (sec. 848) does not apply in the case of any contract that is an HSA.

worker's compensation law, (b) tort liabilities, (c) liabilities relating to ownership or use of property (e.g., auto insurance), or (d) such other similar liabilities as the Secretary may prescribe by regulations; (2) insurance for a specified disease or illness; and (3) insurance that provides a fixed payment for hospitalization. Permitted coverage is coverage (whether provided through insurance or otherwise) for accidents, disability, dental care, vision care, or long-term care.

A high deductible health plan is a health plan that has a deductible that is at least $1,000 for self-only coverage or $2,000 for family coverage and that has an out-of-pocket expense limit that is no more than $5,000 in the case of self-only coverage and $10,000 in the case of family coverage.[96] As under present and prior law, out-of-pocket expenses include deductibles, co-payments, and other amounts (other than premiums) that the individual must pay for covered benefits under the plan. A plan is not a high deductible health plan if substantially all of the coverage is for permitted coverage or coverage that may be provided by permitted insurance, as described above.

A plan does not fail to be a high deductible health plan by reason of failing to have a deductible for preventive care. Except as otherwise provided by the Secretary, preventive care is defined as under section 1871 of the Social Security Act. It is intended that the Secretary of the Treasury will amend the definition of preventive care if the definition used under the Social Security Act is inconsistent with the purposes of the provision.

Tax treatment of and limits on contributions

Contributions to an HSA by or on behalf of an eligible individual are deductible (within limits) in determining adjusted gross income (i.e., "above-the-line") of the individual. Thus, for example, contributions made by an eligible individual's family members are deductible by the eligible individual to the extent the contributions would be deductible if made by the individual.[97] In addition, employer contributions to HSAs (including salary reduction contributions made through a cafeteria plan) are excludable from gross income and wages for employment tax purposes.[98] In the case of an employee, contributions to an HSA may be made by both the individual and the individual's employer. All contributions are aggregated for purposes of the maximum annual contribution limit. Contributions to Archer MSAs reduce the annual contribution limit for HSAs.

---

[96] The $1,000 and $5,000 limits are indexed for inflation. The family coverage limits will always be twice the self-only coverage limits (as indexed for inflation). In the case of the plan using a network of providers, the plan does not fail to be a high deductible health plan (if it would otherwise meet the requirements of a high deductible health plan) solely because the out-of-pocket expense limit for services provided outside of the network exceeds the $5,000 and $10,000 out-of-pocket expense limits. In addition, such plan's deductible for out-of-network services is not taken into account in determining the annual contribution limit (i.e., the deductible for services with the network is used for such purpose).

[97] Under present law, contributions made on behalf of another individual are generally treated as gifts. The present-law gift tax rules apply to contributions made on behalf of another individual.

[98] Employer contributions to an HSA are excludable from wages for employment tax purposes if, at the time of payment, it is reasonable to believe that the employee will be able to exclude such payment from income.

The maximum aggregate annual contribution that can be made to an HSA is the lesser of (1) 100 percent of the annual deductible under the high deductible health plan, or (2) the maximum deductible permitted under an Archer MSA high deductible health plan under present and prior law, as adjusted for inflation.[99] For 2004, the amount of the maximum deductible under an Archer MSA high deductible health plan is $2,600 in the case of self-only coverage and $5,150 in the case of family coverage. The annual contribution limits are increased for individuals who have attained age 55 by the end of the taxable year. In the case of policyholders and covered spouses who are age 55 or older, the HSA annual contribution limit is greater than the otherwise applicable limit by $500 in 2004, $600 in 2005, $700 in 2006, $800 in 2007, $900 in 2008, and $1,000 in 2009 and thereafter.[100] Contributions, including catch-up contributions, cannot be made once an individual is eligible for Medicare.

An excise tax applies to contributions in excess of the maximum contribution amount for the HSA. The excise tax is generally equal to six percent of the cumulative amount of excess contributions that are not distributed from the HSA.

Amounts can be rolled over into an HSA from another HSA or from an Archer MSA.

If an employer makes contributions to employees' HSAs, the employer must make available comparable contributions on behalf of all employees with comparable coverage during the same period. Contributions are considered comparable if they are either of the same amount or the same percentage of the deductible under the plan. The comparability rule is applied separately to part-time employees (i.e., employees who are customarily employed for fewer than 30 hours per week).

If employer contributions do not satisfy the comparability rule during a period, then the employer is subject to an excise tax equal to 35 percent of the aggregate amount contributed by the employer to HSAs for that period. The excise tax is designed as a proxy for the denial of the deduction for employer contributions. In the case of a failure to comply with the comparability rule which is due to reasonable cause and not to willful neglect, the Secretary may waive part or all of the tax imposed to the extent that the payment of the tax would be excessive relative to the failure involved. For purposes of the comparability rule, employers under common control are aggregated.

Taxation of distributions

Distributions from an HSA for qualified medical expenses of the individual and his or her spouse or dependents generally are excludable from gross income. In general, amounts in an HSA can be used for qualified medical expenses even if the individual is not currently eligible for contributions to the HSA.

---

[99] The annual contribution limit is the sum of the limits determined separately for each month, based on the individual's status and health plan coverage as of the first day of the month.

[100] As in determining the general annual contribution limit, the increase in the annual contribution limit for individuals who have attained age 55 is also determined on a monthly basis.

Qualified medical expenses generally are defined as under section 213(d) and include expenses for diagnosis, cure, mitigation, treatment, or prevention of disease, including prescription drugs, transportation primarily for and essential to such care, and qualified long-term care expenses of the account holder and his or her spouse or dependents. Qualified medical expenses do not include expenses for insurance other than for (1) long-term care insurance, (2) premiums for health coverage during any period of continuation coverage required by Federal law, (3) premiums for health care coverage while an individual is receiving unemployment compensation under Federal or State law, or (4) in the case of an account beneficiary who has attained the age of Medicare eligibility, health insurance premiums for Medicare, other than premiums for Medigap policies. Such qualified health insurance premiums include, for example, Medicare Part A and Part B premiums, Medicare HMO premiums, and the employee share of premiums for employer-sponsored health insurance including employer-sponsored retiree health insurance.

For purposes of determining the itemized deduction for medical expenses, distributions from an HSA for qualified medical expenses are not treated as expenses paid for medical care under section 213.

Distributions from an HSA that are not for qualified medical expenses are includible in gross income. Distributions includible in gross income are also subject to an additional 10-percent tax unless made after death, disability, or the individual attains the age of Medicare eligibility (i.e., age 65).

Tax treatment of HSAs after death

Upon death, any balance remaining in the decedent's HSA is includible in his or her gross estate.

If the HSA holder's surviving spouse is the named beneficiary of the HSA, then, after the death of the HSA holder, the HSA becomes the HSA of the surviving spouse and the amount of the HSA balance may be deducted in computing the decedent's taxable estate, pursuant to the estate tax marital deduction.[101] The surviving spouse is not required to include any amount in gross income as a result of the death; the general rules applicable to the HSA apply to the surviving spouse's HSA (e.g., the surviving spouse is subject to income tax only on distributions from the HSA for nonqualified expenses). The surviving spouse can exclude from gross income amounts withdrawn from the HSA for expenses incurred by the decedent prior to death, to the extent they otherwise are qualified medical expenses.

If, upon death, the HSA passes to a named beneficiary other than the decedent's surviving spouse, the HSA ceases to be an HSA as of the date of the decedent's death, and the beneficiary is required to include the fair market value of HSA assets as of the date of death in gross income for the taxable year that includes the date of death. The amount includible in income is reduced by the amount in the HSA used, within one year after death, to pay qualified medical expenses incurred by the decedent prior to the death.

[101] Sec. 2056.

As is the case with other HSA distributions, whether the expenses are qualified medical expenses is determined as of the time the expenses were incurred. In computing taxable income, the beneficiary may claim a deduction for that portion of the Federal estate tax on the decedent's estate that was attributable to the amount of the HSA balance.[102]

If there is no named beneficiary of the decedent's HSA, the HSA ceases to be an HSA as of the date of death, and the fair market value of the assets in the HSA as of such date is includible in the decedent's gross income for the year of the death. This rule applies in all cases in which there is no named beneficiary, even if the surviving spouse ultimately obtains the right to the HSA assets (e.g., if the surviving spouse is the sole beneficiary of the decedent's estate).

Reporting requirements

Employer contributions are required to be reported on the employee's Form W–2. Trustees of HSAs may be required to report to the Secretary of the Treasury amounts with respect to contributions, distributions, the return of excess contributions, and other matters as determined appropriate by the Secretary. In addition, the Secretary may require providers of high deductible health plans to make reports to the Secretary and to account beneficiaries as the Secretary determines appropriate.

Effective Date

The provision is effective for taxable years beginning after December 31, 2003.

D. Exclusion from Gross Income of Certain Federal Subsidies for Prescription Drug Plans (sec. 1202 of the Act and new sec. 139A of the Code)

Present and Prior Law

Gross income includes all income from whatever source derived unless a specific exclusion applies.[103]

Explanation of Provision

The Act provides that gross income does not include any special subsidy payment received under section 1860D–22 of the Social Security Act. The exclusion applies for purposes of both the regular tax and the alternative minimum tax (including the adjustment for adjusted current earnings).

The exclusion is not taken into account in determining whether a deduction is allowable with respect to costs taken into account in determining the subsidy payment. Accordingly, a taxpayer could claim a deduction for prescription drug expenses incurred even though the taxpayer also received an excludible subsidy related to the same expenses.

---

[102] The deduction is calculated in accordance with the present-law rules relating to income in respect of a decedent set forth in section 691(c).

[103] Sec. 61.

Effective Date

The provision is effective for taxable years ending after the date of enactment (December 8, 2003).

E. Exception to Information Reporting Requirements for Certain Health Arrangements (sec. 1203 of the Act and sec. 6041 of the Code)

Present and Prior Law

Any person in a trade or business who, in the course of that trade or business, makes specified payments to another person totaling $600 or more in a year, must provide an information report to the IRS (as well as a copy to the recipient) on the payments.[104] Reporting is required to be done on Form 1099. In general, these information reports remind taxpayers of amounts of income that should be reflected on their tax returns and assist the IRS in verifying that taxpayers have correctly reported these amounts.

Treasury regulations specify that fees for professional services, including the services of physicians, must be reported.[105] Treasury regulations also provide a general exception from these information reporting requirements for payments made to corporations, except that this exception is inapplicable if the corporation is "engaged in providing medical and health care services."[106]

In 2003, the IRS issued a revenue ruling describing when employer-provided expense reimbursements made through debit or credit cards or other electronic media are excludible from gross income.[107] The ruling stated that "payments made to medical service providers through the use of debit, credit, and stored value cards are reportable by the employer on Form 1099–MISC under section 6041."[108]

Reasons for Change[109]

The Congress wished to encourage electronic reimbursement of medical expenses through the use of debit or store-valued cards. The Congress believed that the regulatory reporting requirement discouraged the use of such cards and that such burden should be removed.

Explanation of Provision

The Act provides an exception from the generally applicable information reporting provisions for payments for medical care made under either: (1) a flexible spending arrangement,[110] or (2) a health reimbursement arrangement that is treated as employer-provided coverage.

---

[104] Sec. 6041.

[105] Treas. Reg. sec. 1.6041–1(d)(2).

[106] Treas. Reg. sec. 1.6041–3(p)(1). These regulations also provide an exception from these information reporting requirements if the payment is made to a hospital that is tax-exempt or that is owned and operated by a governmental entity.

[107] Rev. Rul. 2003–43, 2003–21 I.R.B. 935 (May 27, 2003).

[108] Id.

[109] See H.R. 2351, the "Health Savings Account Availability Act," which was reported by the House Committee on Ways and Means on June 25, 2003 (H.R. Rep. No. 108–177).

[110] This term is defined in sec. 106(c)(2).

Effective Date

The provision applies to payments made after December 31, 2002.

PART SIX: VISION 100–CENTURY OF AVIATION REAUTHORIZATION ACT (PUBLIC LAW 108–176)[111]

A. Extension of Expenditure Authority (secs. 901 and 902 of the Act)

Present and Prior Law

The Airport and Airway Trust Fund (the "Trust Fund") was created in 1970 to finance a major portion of the Federal expenditures on national aviation programs. Prior to that time, these expenditures had been financed with General Fund monies. The statutory provisions relating to the Trust Fund were placed in the Code in 1982.[112]

Under prior law, the Internal Revenue Code authorized expenditures to be made from the Trust Fund through September 30, 2003, for purposes provided in specified authorizing legislation as in effect on the date of enactment of the most recent authorizing Act (the Wendell H. Ford Aviation Investment and Reform Act for the 21st Century).

To support the Trust Fund, the Code imposes taxes on both commercial and noncommercial aviation. Commercial aviation is the carriage of persons or property by air for compensation (air transportation "for hire"). All other air transportation is defined as noncommercial aviation.[113]

The taxes imposed to finance the aviation trust fund are:

1. ticket taxes imposed on commercial passenger transportation;
2. a waybill tax imposed on freight transportation; and
3. fuel taxes imposed on gasoline and jet fuel used in commercial aviation and non-commercial aviation.

Most domestic air passenger transportation is subject to a two-part ticket tax. First, the Code imposes a tax at the rate of 7.5 percent of the amount paid for taxable transportation. Second, the Code imposes a flight segment tax of $3 for each domestic segment of taxable transportation. Beginning with calendar year 2003, the domestic flight segment portion of the ticket tax is adjusted for inflation annually.

---

[111] H.R. 2115. The House Committee on Transportation reported the bill on June 6, 2003 (H.R. Rep. No. 108–143). The House passed the bill on June 11, 2003. The Senate Committee on Commerce, Science, and Transportation reported S. 824 on May 2, 2003 (S. Rep. No. 108–41). The Senate passed H.R. 2115, as amended by the provisions of S. 824, on June 12, 2003. The conference report was filed on October 29, 2003 (H.R. Rep. No. 108–334). The conference report passed the House on October 30, 2003 and the Senate on November 21, 2003. The President signed the bill on December 12, 2003.

[112] Sec. 9502.

[113] Sec. 4041(c)(2). Because these definitions are based on whether an amount is paid for the transportation, it is possible for the same aircraft to be used at times in commercial aviation and at times in non-commercial aviation. This determination is made on a flight-by-flight basis. For example, a corporate-owned aircraft transporting employees of the corporation is engaged in non-commercial aviation (and subject only to fuels excise tax) while the same aircraft when transporting non-employees is engaged in commercial aviation (and subject to a mix of ticket and fuels taxes).

Explanation of Provisions

Trust Fund expenditure authority

The Act extends the authority to make expenditures (subject to appropriations) from the Trust Fund through September 30, 2007. The Act also updates the Trust Fund cross references to authorizing legislation to include expenditure purposes in this Act and prior authorizing legislation as in effect on the date of enactment of the Act.

Domestic flight segment tax

The Act makes a technical correction to the domestic flight segment portion of the airline ticket tax. Beginning with calendar year 2003, the domestic flight segment portion of the airline ticket tax is adjusted for inflation annually. The technical correction clarifies that, in the case of amounts paid for transportation before the beginning of the year in which the transportation is to occur, the rate of tax is the rate in effect for the calendar year in which the amount is paid.

Effective Dates

The provision extending expenditure authority is effective on the date of enactment (December 12, 2003).

The provision relating to the domestic flight segment tax for flight segments beginning after December 31, 2002, is effective as if included in the provisions of the Taxpayer Relief Act of 1997 to which it relates.

PART SEVEN: SERVICEMEMBERS CIVIL RELIEF ACT (PUBLIC LAW 108–189)[114]

A. Servicemembers Civil Relief (sec. 510 of the Act)

Explanation of Provision

Section 510 of the Servicemembers Civil Relief Act reenacts section 573 of the Soldiers' and Sailors' Civil Relief Act of 1940, with only minor technical changes. First, section 510 requires notice to the IRS or the tax authority of a State or a political subdivision thereof to be effective. Second, the six month maximum effective period under the 1940 Act has been changed to a 180–day period.

[114] H.R. 100. The House Committee on Veterans' Affairs reported the bill on April 30, 2003 (H.R. Rep. No. 108–81). The House passed the bill on the suspension calendar on May 7, 2003. The Senate Committee on Veterans' Affairs reported S. 1136 on November 11, 2003 (S. Rep. No. 108–197). The Senate passed H.R. 100, as amended by the provisions of S. 1136, by unanimous consent on November 21, 2003. The House passed the bill, as amended by the Senate, by unanimous consent on December 12, 2003. The President signed the bill on December 19, 2003.

PART EIGHT: SURFACE TRANSPORTATION EXTENSION ACT OF 2004 (PUBLIC LAW 108–202) [115]

A. Extension of Highway Trust Fund and Aquatic Resources Trust Fund Expenditure Authority (sec. 12 of the Act)

Prior Law

Under prior law, the Internal Revenue Code (sec. 9503) authorized expenditures (subject to appropriations) to be made from the Highway Trust Fund through February 29, 2004, for purposes provided in specified authorizing legislation as in effect on the date of enactment of the most recent authorizing Act (the Surface Transportation Extension Act of 2003).

Under prior law, expenditures also were authorized from the Aquatic Resources Trust Fund through February 29, 2004.

Highway Trust Fund spending is limited by anti-deficit provisions internal to the Highway Trust Fund, the so-called "Harry Byrd rule". The rule requires the Treasury Department to determine, on a quarterly basis, the amount (if any) by which unfunded highway authorizations exceed projected net Highway Trust Fund tax receipts for the 24-month period beginning at the close of each fiscal year (sec. 9503(d)). Similar rules apply to unfunded Mass Transit Account authorizations. If unfunded authorizations exceed projected 24-month receipts, apportionments to the States for specified programs funded by the relevant Trust Fund Account are to be reduced proportionately.. Because of the Harry Byrd rule, taxes dedicated to the Highway Trust Fund typically are scheduled to expire at least two years after current authorizing Acts.

The Surface Transportation Extension Act of 2003, created a temporary rule (through February 29, 2004) for purposes of the anti-deficit provisions of the Highway Trust Fund. For purposes of determining 24 months of projected revenues for the anti-deficit provisions, the Secretary of the Treasury is instructed to treat each expiring provision relating to appropriations and transfers to the Highway Trust Fund to have been extended through the end of the 24-month period and to assume that the rate of tax during such 24-month period remains the same as the rate in effect on the date of enactment of that Act.

[115] H.R. 3850. The House passed the bill by unanimous consent on February 26, 2004. The Senate passed the bill by unanimous consent on February 27, 2004. The President signed the bill on February 29, 2004.

Explanation of Provision[116]

The Act extends the authority to make expenditures (subject to appropriations) from the Highway Trust Fund through April 30, 2004. The Act also updates the Highway Trust Fund cross references to authorizing legislation to include expenditure purposes in this Act and prior authorizing legislation as in effect on the date of enactment.

For purposes of the anti-deficit provisions of the Highway Trust Fund, the Act extends the temporary rule (through April 30, 2004) created by the Surface Transportation Extension Act of 2003.

The Act extends the authority to make expenditures (subject to appropriations) from the Aquatics Resources Trust Fund through April 30, 2004. The Act also updates the Aquatics Resources Trust Fund cross references to authorizing legislation to include expenditure purposes as in effect on the date of enactment of this Act.

Effective Date

The provision is effective on the date of enactment (February 29, 2004).

[116] The expiration dates described herein were subsequently extended by the Surface Transportation Extension Act of 2004, Part II; the Surface Transportation Extension Act of 2004, Part III; the Surface Transportation Extension Act of 2004, Part IV; and the Surface Transportation Extension Act of 2004, Part V, described in Part Eleven, Part Twelve, Part Thirteen, and Part Fourteen, respectively.

PART NINE: THE SOCIAL SECURITY PROTECTION ACT OF 2004 (PUBLIC LAW 108–203) [117]

A. Technical Amendment Clarifying Treatment for Certain Purposes of Individual Work Plans under the Ticket to Work and Self-Sufficiency Program (sec. 405 of the Act, sec. 1148(g)(1) of the Social Security Act, and sec. 51 of the Code)

Present and Prior Law

The work opportunity tax credit is a temporary credit available on an elective basis for employers hiring individuals from one or more of eight targeted groups.[118] The credit generally equals 40 percent (25 percent for employment of 400 hours or less) of qualified first-year wages. Generally, qualified first-year wages are qualified wages (not in excess of $6,000) attributable to service rendered by a member of a targeted group during the one-year period beginning with the day the individual began work for the employer. Therefore, the maximum credit per employee is generally $2,400 (40 percent of the first $6,000 of qualified first-year wages).

For purposes of the credit, the eight targeted groups are: (1) certain families eligible to receive benefits under the Temporary Assistance for Needy Families Program; (2) high-risk youth; (3) qualified ex-felons; (4) vocational rehabilitation referrals; (5) qualified summer youth employees; (6) qualified veterans; (7) families receiving food stamps; and (8) persons receiving certain Supplemental Security Income (SSI) benefits.

For purposes of the credit, the term "vocational rehabilitation referral" means any individual who is certified by the local designated agency as: (1) having a physical or mental disability that, for the individual, constitutes or results in a substantial handicap to employment; and (2) having been referred to the employer upon completion of (or while receiving) rehabilitative services pursuant to either an individualized written plan for employment under a State plan for vocational rehabilitation services approved under the Rehabilitation Act of 1973, or a program of vocational rehabilitation for veterans carried out under applicable Federal law.

The Ticket to Work and Work Incentives Improvement Act of 1999 established the "Ticket to Work" program under the Social

---

[117] H.R. 743. The House Committee on Ways and Means reported the bill on March 24, 2003 (H.R. Rep. No. 108–46). The House passed the bill on April 2, 2003. The Senate Committee on Finance reported the bill on October 29, 2003 (S. Rep. No. 108–176). The Senate passed the bill, as amended, on December 9, 2003. The bill, as amended, passed the House on February 11, 2004. The President signed the bill on March 2, 2004.

[118] Section 303 of the Working Class Families Tax Relief Act of 2004, also described in Part Fifteen of this document, provides for the extension of the work opportunity tax credit for two years, i.e., for wages paid to qualified individuals who begin work for an employer after December 31, 2003, and before January 1, 2006.

Security Act.[119] Under this program, a disabled individual may be employed pursuant to an individual work plan developed by an approved employment network, which may include private organizations, rather than pursuant to an individualized written plan for employment under a State plan approved under the Rehabilitation Act of 1973.

Reasons for Change

The Congress noted that the Ticket to Work program was designed to increase choice available to beneficiaries when they select providers of employment services. The Congress believed that employers hiring individuals with disabilities should be able to qualify for the work opportunity tax credit, regardless of whether the employment referral is made by a public or private service provider. The Congress believed the eligibility criteria for the work opportunity tax credit should be updated to conform to the expansion of employment services and the increase in number and range of vocational rehabilitation providers as a result of the enactment of the Ticket to Work Act.

Explanation of Provision

Under the Act, an individual work plan established pursuant to the Ticket to Work program under the Social Security Act is treated, for purposes of the work opportunity tax credit, as an individualized written plan for employment under a State plan approved under the Rehabilitation Act of 1973.

Effective Date

The provision is effective as if included in the Ticket to Work and Work Incentives Improvement Act of 1999.

B. Clarification Respecting the FICA and SECA Tax Exemptions for an Individual Whose Earnings Are Subject to the Laws of a Totalization Agreement Partner (sec. 415 of the Act and secs. 1401(c), 3101(c), and 3111(c) of the Code)

Present and Prior Law

Under the Federal Insurance Contributions Act ("FICA"), which is part of the Code, a tax is imposed on the wages paid by an employer to an employee.[120] FICA tax consists of two parts: (1) old age, survivor and disability insurance ("OASDI"), which correlates to the Social Security program that provides monthly benefits after retirement, disability, or death; and (2) Medicare hospital insurance ("HI"). The OASDI tax rate is 6.2 percent on both the employee and employer (for a total rate of 12.4 percent). The OASDI tax rate applies to compensation up to the OASDI wage base ($87,900 for 2004). The HI tax rate is 1.45 percent on both the employee and the employer (for a total rate of 2.9 percent). Unlike the OASDI tax, the HI tax is not limited to a specific amount of compensation.

[119] Pub. L. No. 106–170.
[120] Code secs. 3101–3128.

FICA tax generally applies only to employees, not to individuals engaged in a trade or business. Instead, such individuals are subject to tax under the Self-Employment Compensation Act ("SECA") on their self-employment income.[121] Like FICA tax, SECA tax consists of two parts, OASDI and HI.

Under the Social Security Act, an individual receives credit for his or her wages and self-employment income, which is used to determine eligibility for monthly Social Security benefits and Medicare coverage.

The United States may enter into agreements (referred to as "totalization" agreements) with foreign countries (referred to as "totalization agreement partners") to coordinate coverage and contributions (or taxes) under the Social Security program with similar programs of other countries.[122] These agreements generally eliminate dual social security coverage and taxes for the same work and earnings. Wages and self-employment income are exempt from FICA and SECA to the extent that, under a totalization agreement with a foreign country, the wages or self-employment income is subject to taxes or contributions for similar purposes under the Social Security system of the foreign country.

Reasons for Change

The Congress noted that, under U.S. totalization agreements, a person's work is generally subject to the Social Security laws of the country in which the work is performed. The Congress further noted that, in most cases, the worker (whether subject to the laws of the United States or the other country) is compulsorily covered and required to pay contributions in accordance with the laws of that country; in some instances, however, work that would be compulsorily covered in the United States is excluded from compulsory coverage in the other country (such as Germany). The Congress was concerned that, in such cases, the IRS had questioned the exemption from U.S. Social Security tax for workers who elect not to make contributions to the foreign country's retirement system. The Congress believed that any question should be removed regarding the exemption, in a manner consistent with the general philosophy behind the coverage rules of totalization agreements.

Explanation of Provision

Under the Act, wages and self-employment income are exempt from FICA and SECA to the extent that, under a totalization agreement with a foreign country, the wages or self-employment income is subject exclusively to the laws applicable to the Social Security system of the foreign country. As a result, an individual's earnings are exempt from FICA and SECA in cases in which the earnings are subject to a foreign country's Social Security system in accordance with a totalization agreement, but the foreign country's law does not require compulsory contributions on those earnings. The Act establishes that such earnings are exempt from FICA and SECA regardless of whether the individual elects to make contributions to the foreign country's Social Security system.

---

[121] Code secs. 1401–1403.
[122] Sec. 233 of the Social Security Act.

Effective Date

The provision is effective on the date of enactment (March 2, 2004).

C. Technical Amendments

1. Technical correction relating to retirement benefits of ministers (sec. 422 of the Act and sec. 211(a)(7) of the Social Security Act)

Present and Prior Law

Under the Self-Employment Compensation Act ("SECA"), which is part of the Code, an individual engaged in a trade or business is subject to tax on his or her self-employment income, which is based on net earnings from self-employment.[123] SECA tax consists of two parts: (1) old age, survivor and disability insurance ("OASDI"), which correlates to the Social Security program that provides monthly benefits after retirement, disability, or death; and (2) Medicare hospital insurance ("HI"). The Code contains definitions of "self-employment income" and "net earnings from self-employment" that apply for SECA purposes.

Under the Social Security Act, an individual receives credit for his or her self-employment income, which is used to determine insured status, that is, eligibility for monthly Social Security benefits and Medicare coverage, as well as the amount of monthly benefits. The Social Security Act contains definitions of "self-employment income" and "net earnings from self-employment" that parallel the Code definitions. Generally, if a statutory change is made to these definitions, it is made both in the Code and in the Social Security Act.

The Small Business Job Protection Act of 1996[124] amended the Code to provide that, in the case of a minister or member of a religious order, net earnings from self-employment does not include the rental value of a parsonage or parsonage allowance provided after the individual retires or any other retirement benefit received from a church plan after the individual retires. This amendment was effective for years beginning before, on, or after December 31, 1994.

Reasons for Change

The Congress noted that the Small Business Job Protection Act of 1996 provided that certain retirement benefits received by ministers and members of religious orders are not subject to SECA taxes. However, a conforming change was not made to the Social Security Act to exclude these benefits from being counted for the purpose of acquiring insured status and calculating Social Security benefit amounts. The Congress was concerned that this income was therefore not treated in a uniform manner. The Congress believed that the Social Security Act should be conformed to the Code with respect to such income.

---

[123] Secs. 1401–1403.
[124] Pub. L. No. 104–188.

Explanation of Provision

The Act makes a conforming change to the definition of net earnings from self-employment under the Social Security Act to exclude the rental value of a parsonage or a parsonage allowance provided after a minister or member of a religious order retires or any other retirement benefit received from a church plan after the individual retires. Thus, these benefits are not included in earnings for purposes of determining insured status or the amount of monthly Social Security benefits.

Effective Date

The provision is effective for years beginning before, on, or after December 31, 1994.

2. Technical correction relating to domestic employment (sec. 423 of the Act, sec. 3121(a)(7)(B) and (g)(5) of the Code, and secs. 209(a)(6)(B) and 210(f)(5) of the Social Security Act)

Present and Prior Law

Under the Federal Insurance Contributions Act ("FICA"), which is part of the Code, a tax is imposed on the wages paid by an employer to an employee.[125] FICA tax consists of two parts: (1) old age, survivor and disability insurance ("OASDI"), which correlates to the social security program that provides monthly benefits after retirement, disability, or death; and (2) Medicare hospital insurance ("HI"). For this purpose, "wages" is defined as all remuneration for employment, with certain specified exceptions.

This definition of wages provides an exception for cash remuneration paid by an employer to an employee for agricultural labor unless the total cash remuneration paid to the employee in the calendar year is $150 or more. For this purpose, under prior law, agricultural labor included service performed on a farm operated for profit if the service was domestic service in the private home of the employer. In addition, for years beginning after December 31, 1994, wages does not include cash remuneration paid to an employee in the private home of the employer if the total cash remuneration paid to the employee in the calendar year is less than a specified amount ($1,400 for 2004).

Under the Social Security Act, an individual receives credit for his or her wages, which is used to determine insured status, that is, eligibility for monthly Social Security benefits and Medicare coverage, as well as the amount of monthly benefits. The Social Security Act contains a definition of wages that parallels the Code definitions, including exceptions for cash remuneration paid for agricultural labor or domestic service.

Reasons for Change

The Congress recognized that, prior to 1994, domestic service on a farm was treated as agricultural labor and was subject to the wage threshold for agricultural labor. The Congress noted that, ac-

---

[125] Secs. 3101–3128.

cording to the Social Security Administration, in 1994, when Congress amended the law with respect to domestic employment, the intent was that domestic employment on a farm would be subject to the wage threshold for domestic employees instead of the threshold for agricultural labor. However, the Congress believed that the prior-law language was unclear, making it appear as if domestic employees on farms were subject to both thresholds.

Explanation of Provision

Under the Act, domestic service on a farm operated for profit is treated as domestic service in a private home, rather than as agricultural labor. As a result, the same wage threshold applies to cash remuneration for domestic service on a farm as applies to domestic service in a private home. That is, cash remuneration paid to an employee for domestic service on a farm operated for profit is not wages if the total cash remuneration paid to the employee in the calendar year is less than a specified amount ($1,400 for 2004).

Effective Date

The provision is effective on the date of enactment (March 2, 2004).

3. Technical correction of outdated references (sec. 424 of the Act, sec. 3102(a) of the Code, and sec. 211(a)(15) of the Social Security Act)

Present and Prior Law

Various provisions of the Code and the Social Security Act contain cross-references to other statutory provisions.

Reasons for Change

The Congress noted that, over the years, provisions in the Social Security Act, the Code and other related laws have been deleted, redesignated or amended; however, necessary conforming changes have not always been made. The Congress further noted that, consequently, prior law contained some outdated references.

Explanation of Provision

Under the Act, language referring to a previously repealed 20-day work test for agricultural labor is deleted from the Code, and a cross-reference in the Social Security Act to a Code provision is corrected.

Effective Date

The provision is effective on the date of enactment (March 2, 2004).

4. Technical correction respecting self-employment income in community property States (sec. 425 of the Act, sec. 1402(a)(5) of the Code, and sec. 211(a)(5) of the Social Security Act)

Present and Prior Law

The Code and the Social Security Act define "net earnings from self-employment" in order to determine self-employment income, which is subject to tax under the Code and is credited as earnings under the Social Security Act. Under prior law, the Code and the Social Security Act provided that, in determining net earnings from self-employment, if any income derived from a trade or business (other than a partnership) is community income under applicable community property laws, all of the income and deductions attributable to the trade or business are treated as the income and deductions of the husband unless the wife exercises substantially all of the management and control of the trade or business, in which case all of the income and deductions are treated as income and deductions of the wife.

This rule was held to be unconstitutional, and, as a result, the same rule for attributing the income and deductions of a trade or business to a spouse applied to taxpayers in community property States and in non-community States.[126] Under this rule, income and deductions of a trade or business (other than a partnership) are attributed to the spouse carrying on the trade or business.

Reasons for Change

The Congress noted that then-present law was found to be unconstitutional in several court cases in 1980 and that, since then, income from a trade or business that is not a partnership in a community property State has been treated the same as income from a trade or business that is not a partnership in a non-community property State, that is, it is taxed and credited to the spouse who is found to be carrying on the business. The Congress believed that a change should be made to conform the provisions in the Social Security Act and the Internal Revenue Code to current practice in both community property and non-community property States.

Explanation of Provision

Under the Act, in determining net earnings from self-employment, if any income derived from a trade or business (other than a partnership) is community income under applicable community property laws, the income and deductions attributable to the trade or business are treated as the income and deductions of the spouse carrying on the trade or business or, if the trade or business is jointly operated, treated as the income and deductions of each spouse on the basis of their respective distributive shares of the income and deductions. The Act thus conforms the statutory definition of net earnings from self-employment with administrative practice.

---

[126] See Rev. Rul. 82–39, 1982–1 C.B. 119.

Effective Date

The provision is effective on the date of enactment (March 2, 2004).

PART TEN: PENSION FUNDING EQUITY ACT OF 2004 (PUBLIC LAW 108–218) [127]

I. PENSION FUNDING

A. Temporary Replacement of 30-Year Treasury Rate and Election of Alternative Deficit Reduction Contribution (secs. 101 and 102 of the Act and secs. 404, 412 and 415 of the Code)

Present and Prior Law

In general

The interest rate on 30-year Treasury securities is generally used for several purposes related to defined benefit pension plans, specifically: (1) in determining current liability for purposes of the funding and deduction rules; (2) in determining unfunded vested benefits for purposes of Pension Benefit Guaranty Corporation ("PBGC") variable rate premiums; and (3) in determining the minimum required value of lump-sum distributions from a defined benefit pension plan and maximum lump-sum values for purposes of the limits on benefits payable under a defined benefit pension plan.

Funding rules

In general

The Internal Revenue Code (the "Code") and the Employee Retirement Income Security Act of 1974 ("ERISA") impose minimum funding requirements with respect to defined benefit pension plans.[128] Under the funding rules, the amount of contributions required for a plan year is generally the plan's normal cost for the year (i.e., the cost of benefits allocated to the year under the plan's funding method) plus that year's portion of other liabilities that are amortized over a period of years, such as benefits resulting from a grant of past service credit.

Additional contributions for underfunded plans

Under special funding rules (referred to as the "deficit reduction contribution" rules),[129] an additional contribution to a plan is generally required if the plan's funded current liability percentage is

---

[127] H.R. 3108. The House passed the bill on October 8, 2003. The Senate passed the bill on January 28, 2004. The conference report was filed on April 1, 2004 (H.R. Rep. No. 108–457). The conference report passed the House on April 2, 2004, and the Senate on April 8, 2004. The President signed the bill on April 10, 2004.

[128] Code sec. 412; ERISA sec. 302. The Code also imposes limits on deductible contributions, as discussed below.

[129] The deficit reduction contribution rules apply to single-employer plans, other than single-employer plans with no more than 100 participants on any day in the preceding plan year. Single-employer plans with more than 100 but not more than 150 participants are generally subject to lower contribution requirements under these rules.

less than 90 percent.[130] A plan's "funded current liability percentage" is the actuarial value of plan assets[131] as a percentage of the plan's current liability. In general, a plan's current liability means all liabilities to employees and their beneficiaries under the plan.

The amount of the additional contribution required under the deficit reduction contribution rules is the sum of two amounts: (1) the excess, if any, of (a) the deficit reduction contribution (as described below), over (b) the contribution required under the normal funding rules; and (2) the amount (if any) required with respect to unpredictable contingent event benefits.[132] The amount of the additional contribution cannot exceed the amount needed to increase the plan's funded current liability percentage to 100 percent.

The deficit reduction contribution is the sum of (1) the "unfunded old liability amount," (2) the "unfunded new liability amount," and (3) the expected increase in current liability due to benefits accruing during the plan year.[133] The "unfunded old liability amount" is the amount needed to amortize certain unfunded liabilities under 1987 and 1994 transition rules. The "unfunded new liability amount" is the applicable percentage of the plan's unfunded new liability. Unfunded new liability generally means the unfunded current liability of the plan (i.e., the amount by which the plan's current liability exceeds the actuarial value of plan assets), but determined without regard to certain liabilities (such as the plan's unfunded old liability and unpredictable contingent event benefits). The applicable percentage is generally 30 percent, but is reduced if the plan's funded current liability percentage is greater than 60 percent.

Required interest rate and mortality table

Specific interest rate and mortality assumptions must be used in determining a plan's current liability for purposes of the special funding rule. The interest rate used to determine a plan's current liability is generally required to be within a permissible range of the weighted average[134] of the interest rates on 30-year Treasury securities for the four-year period ending on the last day before the plan year begins. The permissible range is generally from 90 percent to 105 percent.[135] The interest rate used under the plan was

[130] Under an alternative test, a plan is not subject to the deficit reduction contribution rules for a plan year if (1) the plan's funded current liability percentage for the plan year is at least 80 percent, and (2) the plan's funded current liability percentage was at least 90 percent for each of the two immediately preceding plan years or each of the second and third immediately preceding plan years.

[131] The actuarial value of plan assets is the value determined under an actuarial valuation method that takes into account fair market value and meets certain other requirements. The use of an actuarial valuation method allows appreciation or depreciation in the market value of plan assets to be recognized gradually over several plan years. Sec. 412(c)(2); Treas. Reg. sec. 1.412(c)(2)–1.

[132] A plan may provide for unpredictable contingent event benefits, which are benefits that depend on contingencies that are not reliably and reasonably predictable, such as facility shutdowns or reductions in workforce. An additional contribution is generally not required with respect to unpredictable contingent event benefits unless the event giving rise to the benefits has occurred.

[133] If the Secretary of the Treasury prescribes a new mortality table to be used in determining current liability, as described below, the deficit reduction contribution may include an additional amount.

[134] The weighting used for this purpose is 40 percent, 30 percent, 20 percent and 10 percent, starting with the most recent year in the four-year period. Notice 88–73, 1988–2 C.B. 383.

[135] If the Secretary of the Treasury determines that the lowest permissible interest rate in this range is unreasonably high, the Secretary may prescribe a lower rate, but not less than 80 percent of the weighted average of the 30-year Treasury rate.

required to be consistent with the assumptions which reflect the purchase rates which would be used by insurance companies to satisfy the liabilities under the plan.[136]

The Job Creation and Worker Assistance Act of 2002 [137] temporarily amended the permissible range of the statutory interest rate used in calculating a plan's current liability for purposes of applying the additional contribution requirements, so that the permissible range was from 90 percent to 120 percent for plan years beginning after December 31, 2001, and before January 1, 2004.

Prior law did not provide a special interest rate rule for plan years beginning after December 31, 2003, and before January 1, 2006.

The IRS generally publishes the interest rate on 30-year Treasury securities on a monthly basis. The Department of the Treasury does not currently issue 30-year Treasury securities. As of March 2002, the IRS published the average yield on the 30-year Treasury bond maturing in February 2031 as a substitute.

The Secretary of the Treasury is required to prescribe mortality tables and to periodically review (at least every five years) and update such tables to reflect the actuarial experience of pension plans and projected trends in such experience.[138] The Secretary of the Treasury has required the use of the 1983 Group Annuity Mortality Table.[139]

Full funding limitation

No contributions are required under the minimum funding rules in excess of the full funding limitation. The full funding limitation is the excess, if any, of (1) the accrued liability under the plan (including normal cost), over (2) the lesser of (a) the market value of plan assets or (b) the actuarial value of plan assets.[140] However, the full funding limitation may not be less than the excess, if any, of 90 percent of the plan's current liability (including the current liability normal cost) over the actuarial value of plan assets. In general, current liability is all liabilities to plan participants and beneficiaries accrued to date, whereas the accrued liability under the full funding limitation may be based on projected future benefits, including future salary increases.

---

[136] Code sec. 412(b)(5)(B)(iii)(II); ERISA sec. 302(b)(5)(B)(iii)(II). Under Notice 90–11, 1990–1 C.B. 319, the interest rates in the permissible range are deemed to be consistent with the assumptions reflecting the purchase rates that would be used by insurance companies to satisfy the liabilities under the plan.

[137] Pub. L. No. 107–147.

[138] Code sec. 412(l)(7)(C)(ii); ERISA sec. 302(d)(7)(C)(ii).

[139] Rev. Rul. 95–28, 1995–1 C.B. 74. The IRS and the Treasury Department have announced that they are undertaking a review of the applicable mortality table and have requested comments on related issues, such as how mortality trends should be reflected. Notice 2003–62, 2003–38 I.R.B. 576; Announcement 2000–7, 2000–1 C.B. 586.

[140] For plan years beginning before 2004, the full funding limitation was generally defined as the excess, if any, of (1) the lesser of (a) the accrued liability under the plan (including normal cost) or (b) a percentage (170 percent for 2003) of the plan's current liability (including the current liability normal cost), over (2) the lesser of (a) the market value of plan assets or (b) the actuarial value of plan assets, but in no case less than the excess, if any, of 90 percent of the plan's current liability over the actuarial value of plan assets. Under the Economic Growth and Tax Relief Reconciliation Act of 2001 ("EGTRRA"), the full funding limitation based on 170 percent of current liability is repealed for plan years beginning in 2004 and thereafter. The provisions of EGTRRA generally do not apply for years beginning after December 31, 2010.

Timing of plan contributions

In general, plan contributions required to satisfy the funding rules must be made within 8½ months after the end of the plan year. If the contribution is made by such due date, the contribution is treated as if it were made on the last day of the plan year.

In the case of a plan with a funded current liability percentage of less than 100 percent for the preceding plan year, estimated contributions for the current plan year must be made in quarterly installments during the current plan year.[141] The amount of each required installment is 25 percent of the lesser of (1) 90 percent of the amount required to be contributed for the current plan year or (2) 100 percent of the amount required to be contributed for the preceding plan year.[142]

Funding waivers

Within limits, the IRS is permitted to waive all or a portion of the contributions required under the minimum funding standard for a plan year.[143] A waiver may be granted if the employer (or employers) responsible for the contribution could not make the required contribution without temporary substantial business hardship and if requiring the contribution would be adverse to the interests of plan participants in the aggregate. Generally, no more than three waivers may be granted within any period of 15 consecutive plan years.

If a funding waiver is in effect for a plan, subject to certain exceptions, no plan amendment may be adopted that increases the liabilities of the plan by reason of any increase in benefits, any change in the accrual of benefits, or any change in the rate at which benefits vest under the plan. In addition, the IRS is authorized to require security to be granted as a condition of granting a funding waiver if the sum of the plan's accumulated funding deficiency and the balance of any outstanding waived funding deficiencies exceeds $1 million.

Excise tax

An employer is generally subject to an excise tax if it fails to make minimum required contributions and fails to obtain a waiver from the IRS.[144] The excise tax is generally 10 percent of the amount of the funding deficiency. In addition, a tax of 100 percent may be imposed if the funding deficiency is not corrected within a certain period.

---

[141] Code sec. 412(m); ERISA sec. 302(e).

[142] In connection with the expanded interest rate range available for 2002 and 2003, special rules applied in determining current liability for the preceding plan year for purposes of applying the quarterly contributions requirements to plan years beginning in 2002 (when the expanded range first applied) and 2004 (when the expanded range no longer applied). In each of those years ("present year"), current liability for the preceding year was to be redetermined, using the permissible range applicable to the present year. This redetermined current liability was to be used for purposes of the plan's funded current liability percentage for the preceding year, which could affect the need to make quarterly contributions, and for purposes of determining the amount of any quarterly contributions in the present year, which is based in part on the preceding year.

[143] Code sec. 412(d); ERISA sec. 303.

[144] Code sec. 4971.

Deductions for contributions

Employer contributions to qualified retirement plans are deductible, subject to certain limits. In the case of a defined benefit pension plan, the employer generally may deduct the greater of: (1) the amount necessary to satisfy the minimum funding requirement of the plan for the year; or (2) the amount of the plan's normal cost for the year plus the amount necessary to amortize certain unfunded liabilities over ten years, but limited to the full funding limitation for the year.[145] However, the maximum amount of deductible contributions is generally not less than the plan's unfunded current liability.[146]

PBGC premiums

Because benefits under a defined benefit pension plan may be funded over a period of years, plan assets may not be sufficient to provide the benefits owed under the plan to employees and their beneficiaries if the plan terminates before all benefits are paid. The PBGC generally insures the benefits owed under defined benefit pension plans (up to certain limits) in the event a plan is terminated with insufficient assets. Employers pay premiums to the PBGC for this insurance coverage.

PBGC premiums include a flat-rate premium and, in the case of an underfunded plan, a variable rate premium based on the amount of unfunded vested benefits.[147] In determining the amount of unfunded vested benefits, the interest rate used is generally 85 percent of the annual yield on 30-year Treasury securities for the month preceding the month in which the plan year begins.

Under the Job Creation and Worker Assistance Act of 2002, for plan years beginning after December 31, 2001, and before January 1, 2004, the interest rate used in determining the amount of unfunded vested benefits for PBGC variable rate premium purposes was increased to 100 percent of the annual yield on 30-year Treasury securities for the month preceding the month in which the plan year begins.

Prior law did not provide a special interest rate rule for plan years beginning after December 31, 2003, and before January 1, 2006.

Lump-sum distributions

Accrued benefits under a defined benefit pension plan generally must be paid in the form of an annuity for the life of the participant unless the participant consents to a distribution in another form. Defined benefit pension plans generally provide that a participant may choose among other forms of benefit offered under the plan, such as a lump-sum distribution. These optional forms of benefit generally must be actuarially equivalent to the life annuity benefit payable to the participant.

---

[145] Code sec. 404(a)(1).

[146] Code sec. 404(a)(1)(D). In the case of a plan that terminates during the year, the maximum deductible amount is generally not less than the amount needed to make the plan assets sufficient to fund benefit liabilities as defined for purposes of the PBGC termination insurance program (sometimes referred to as "termination liability").

[147] ERISA sec. 4006.

A defined benefit pension plan must specify the actuarial assumptions that will be used in determining optional forms of benefit under the plan in a manner that precludes employer discretion in the assumptions to be used. For example, a plan may specify that a variable interest rate will be used in determining actuarial equivalent forms of benefit, but may not give the employer discretion to choose the interest rate.

Statutory assumptions must be used in determining the minimum value of certain optional forms of benefit, such as a lump sum.[148] That is, the lump sum payable under the plan may not be less than the amount of the lump sum that is actuarially equivalent to the life annuity payable to the participant, determined using the statutory assumptions. The statutory assumptions consist of an applicable mortality table (as published by the IRS) and an applicable interest rate.

The applicable interest rate is the annual interest rate on 30-year Treasury securities, determined as of the time that is permitted under regulations. The regulations provide various options for determining the interest rate to be used under the plan, such as the period for which the interest rate will remain constant ("stability period") and the use of averaging.

Limits on benefits

Annual benefits payable under a defined benefit pension plan generally may not exceed the lesser of: (1) 100 percent of average compensation; or (2) $165,000 (for 2004).[149] The dollar limit generally applies to a benefit payable in the form of a straight life annuity beginning no earlier than age 62. The limit is reduced if benefits are paid before age 62. In addition, if the benefit is not in the form of a straight life annuity, the benefit generally is adjusted to an equivalent straight life annuity. In making these reductions and adjustments, the interest rate used generally must be not less than the greater of: (1) five percent; or (2) the interest rate specified in the plan. However, for purposes of adjusting a benefit in a form that is subject to the minimum value rules (including the use of the interest rate on 30-year Treasury securities), such as a lump-sum benefit, the interest rate used generally must be not less than the greater of: (1) the interest rate on 30-year Treasury securities; or (2) the interest rate specified in the plan. Prior law did not provide a special interest rate rule for plan years beginning in 2004 and 2005.

Explanation of Provision

Interest rate for determining current liability and PBGC premiums

Under the Act, the interest rate used for plan years beginning after December 31, 2003, and before January 1, 2006, in determining current liability for funding and deduction purposes and in determining PBGC variable rate premiums is generally the rate of

[148] Code sec. 417(e)(3); ERISA sec. 205(g)(3).
[149] Code sec. 415(b).

interest on amounts invested conservatively in long-term investment-grade corporate bonds.[150]

For purposes of determining a plan's current liability for plan years beginning after December 31, 2003, and before January 1, 2006, the interest rate used must be within a permissible range of the weighted average of the rates of interest on amounts invested conservatively in long-term investment-grade corporate bonds during the four-year period ending on the last day before the plan year begins. The permissible range for these years is from 90 percent to 100 percent. The interest rate is to be determined by the Secretary of the Treasury on the basis of two or more indices that are selected periodically by the Secretary and are in the top three quality levels available.

The interest rate on long-term corporate bonds is to be calculated pursuant to a method, prescribed by the Secretary of the Treasury, which relies on publicly available indices of high-quality bonds (i.e., the top three quality levels). The Secretary may use bonds with average maturities of 20 years or more in determining the rate. The Secretary of Treasury may prescribe that two thirds of the rate may be based on two or more indices that are in the top three quality levels, and one third of such rate may be based on two or more indices that are in the third quality level. The Secretary has discretion to determine which publicly available indices to use.

The Secretary is directed to make the permissible range of the interest rate, as well as the indices and methodology used to determine the average rate, publicly available. The methodology used by the Secretary to arrive at a single rate is to be publicly available (including for a subscription fee or other charge). The Secretary is to publish the rate on a monthly basis, along with an updated four-year weighted average of the rate and an updated permissible range. The Secretary is to consider and monitor the current marketplace indices to produce the specified rate to ensure that the indices continue to be appropriate for this purpose. Through regulations, the Secretary is to make, as appropriate, prospective changes in the indices used to determine the rate.

For purposes of determining the four-year weighted average of interest rates under the temporary provision, the weighting applicable before the Act continues to apply (i.e., 40 percent, 30 percent, 20 percent and 10 percent, starting with the most recent year in the four-year period). In addition, consistent with current IRS guidance, the interest rates in the permissible range under the temporary provision are deemed to be consistent with the assumptions reflecting the purchase rates that would be used by insurance companies to satisfy the liabilities under the plan. Thus, any interest rate in the permissible range may be used in determining current liability while the temporary provision is in effect.

The temporary interest rate generally applies in determining current liability for purposes of determining the maximum amount of deductible contributions to a defined benefit pension plan (regardless of whether the plan is subject to the deficit reduction contribution requirements). However, an employer may elect to disregard

[150] The Act also repeals the prior-law rule under which, for purposes of applying the quarterly contributions requirements to plan years beginning in 2004, current liability for the preceding year is redetermined.

the temporary interest rate change for purposes of determining the maximum amount of deductible contributions (regardless of whether the plan is subject to the deficit reduction contribution requirements). In such a case, the interest rate used in determining current liability for that purpose must be within the permissible range (90 to 105 percent) of the weighted average of the interest rates on 30-year Treasury securities for the preceding four-year period. This is intended solely as a temporary provision to ensure that, pending long-term reform of the funding and deduction rules, the deduction limit is neither increased nor decreased so that employers are not penalized for fully funding their plans. Because the 30-year Treasury rate is an obsolete rate, its use must be revisited promptly in the context of long-term funding and deduction reform. However, the use of the 30-year Treasury rate for the purposes of determining maximum deduction limits should not be considered precedent for the determination of other pension plan calculations. Furthermore, the use of different interest rates for certain pension plan calculations in the context of this temporary bill should not be considered precedent for the use of different discount rates to measure pension plan liabilities.

Under the Act, in determining the amount of unfunded vested benefits for PBGC variable rate premium purposes for plan years beginning after December 31, 2003, and before January 1, 2006, the interest rate used is 85 percent of the annual rate of interest determined by the Secretary of the Treasury on amounts invested conservatively in long-term investment-grade corporate bonds for the month preceding the month in which the plan year begins (subject to the same requirements applicable to the determination of the interest rate used in determining current liability).

Interest rate used to apply benefit limits to lump sums

Under the Act, in the case of plan years beginning in 2004 or 2005, in adjusting a form of benefit that is subject to the minimum value rules, such as a lump-sum benefit, for purposes of applying the limits on benefits payable under a defined benefit pension plan, the interest rate used must be not less than the greater of: (1) 5.5 percent; or (2) the interest rate specified in the plan.

Plan amendments

The Act permits certain plan amendments made pursuant to the interest rate provision of the bill to be retroactively effective. If certain requirements are met, the plan will be treated as being operated in accordance with its terms, and the amendment will not violate the anticutback rules (except as provided by the Secretary of the Treasury).[151] In order for this treatment to apply, the plan amendment must be made on or before the last day of the first plan year beginning on or after January 1, 2006. In addition, the amendment must apply retroactively as of the date on which the interest rate provision became effective with respect to the plan and the plan must be operated in compliance with the interest rate provision until the amendment is made.

[151] Code sec. 411(d)(6); ERISA sec. 204(g).

A plan amendment will not be considered to be pursuant to the interest rate provision of the bill if it has an effective date before the effective date of the interest rate provision. Similarly, relief from the anticutback rules does not apply for periods prior to the effective date of the interest rate provision or the plan amendment.

Alternative deficit reduction contribution for certain plans

In general

The Act allows certain employers ("applicable employers") to elect a reduced amount of additional required contribution under the deficit reduction contribution rules (an "alternative deficit reduction contribution") with respect to certain plans for applicable plan years. An applicable plan year is a plan year beginning after December 27, 2003, and before December 28, 2005, for which the employer elects a reduced contribution. If an employer so elects, the amount of the additional deficit reduction contribution for an applicable plan year is the greater of: (1) 20 percent of the amount of the additional contribution that would otherwise be required; or (2) the additional contribution that would be required if the deficit reduction contribution for the plan year were determined as the expected increase in current liability due to benefits accruing during the plan year.

An election of an alternative deficit reduction contribution may be made only with respect to a plan that was not subject to the deficit reduction contribution rules for the plan year beginning in 2000.[152] An election may not be made with respect to more than two plan years. An election is to be made at such time and in such manner as the Secretary of the Treasury prescribes. An election does not invalidate any obligation pursuant to a collective bargaining agreement in effect on the date of the election to provide benefits, to change the accrual of benefits, or to change the rate at which benefits vest under the plan.

An applicable employer is an employer that is: (1) a commercial passenger airline; (2) primarily engaged in the production or manufacture of a steel mill product, or the processing of iron ore pellets; or (3) an organization described in section 501(c)(5) that established the plan for which an alternative deficit reduction contribution is elected on June 30, 1955.

Restrictions on amendments

Certain plan amendments may not be adopted during an applicable plan year (i.e., a plan year for which an alternative deficit reduction contribution is elected). This restriction applies to an amendment that increases the liabilities of the plan by reason of any increase in benefits, any change in the accrual of benefits, or any change in the rate at which benefits vest under the plan. The restriction applies unless: (1) the plan's enrolled actuary certifies (in such form and manner as prescribed by the Secretary of the Treasury) that the amendment provides for an increase in annual

[152] Whether a plan was subject to the deficit reduction contribution rules for the plan year beginning in 2000 is determined without regard to the rule that allows the temporary interest rate based on amounts invested conservatively in long-term investment-grade corporate bonds to be used for lookback rule purposes, as discussed below.

contributions that will exceed the increase in annual charges to the funding standard account attributable to such amendment; or (2) the amendment is required by a collective bargaining agreement that is in effect on the date of enactment of the provision.

If a plan is amended during an applicable plan year in violation of the provision, an election of an alternative deficit reduction contribution does not apply to any applicable plan year ending on after the date on which the amendment is adopted.

Notice requirement

The Act amends ERISA to provide that, if an employer elects an alternative deficit reduction contribution for any applicable plan year, the employer must provide written notice of the election to participants and beneficiaries and to the PBGC within 30 days of filing the election. The notice to participants and beneficiaries must include: (1) the due date of the alternative deficit reduction contribution; (2) the amount by which the required contribution to the plan was reduced as a result of the election; (3) a description of the benefits under the plan that are eligible for guarantee by the PBGC; and (4) an explanation of the limitations on the PBGC guarantee and the circumstances in which the limitations apply, including the maximum guaranteed monthly benefits that the PBGC would pay if the plan terminated while underfunded. The notice to the PBGC must include: (1) the due date of the alternative deficit reduction contribution; (2) the amount by which the required contribution to the plan was reduced as a result of the election; (3) the number of years it will take to restore the plan to full funding if the employer makes only the required contributions; and (4) information as to how the amount by which the plan is underfunded compares with the capitalization of the employer.

An employer that fails to provide the required notice to a participant, beneficiary, or the PBGC may (in the discretion of a court) be liable to the participant, beneficiary, or PBGC in the amount of up to $100 a day from the date of the failure, and the court may in its discretion order such other relief as it deems proper.

Effective date

Interest rate for determining current liability and PBGC premiums

The provision relating to the interest rate used to determine current liability and PBGC premiums is generally effective for plan years beginning after December 31, 2003. For purposes of applying certain rules ("lookback rules") to plan years beginning after December 31, 2003, the amendments made by the provision may be applied as if they had been in effect for all years beginning before the effective date. For purposes of the provision, "lookback rules" means: (1) the rule under which a plan is not subject to the additional funding requirements for a plan year if the plan's funded current liability percentage was at least 90 percent for each of the two immediately preceding plan years or each of the second and third immediately preceding plan years; and (2) the rule under which quarterly contributions are required for a plan year if the plan's funded current liability percentage was less than 100 percent for the preceding plan year. The amendments made by the provision may be applied for purposes of the lookback rules, regardless of the funded current liability percentage reported for the plan on the plan's annual reports (i.e., Form 5500) for preceding years.

Interest rate used to apply benefit limits to lump sums

The provision relating to the interest rate used to apply the benefit limits to certain forms of benefit is generally effective for plan years beginning after December 31, 2003. Under a special rule, in the case of a distribution made to a participant or beneficiary after December 31, 2003, and before January 1, 2005, in a form of benefit that is subject to the minimum value rules, such as a lump-sum benefit, and that is subject to adjustment in applying the limit on benefits payable under a defined benefit pension plan, the amount payable may not, solely by reason of the provision, be less than the amount that would have been payable if the amount payable had been determined using the applicable interest rate in effect as of the last day of the last plan year beginning before January 1, 2004.

Alternative deficit reduction contribution for certain plans

The provision relating to alternative deficit reduction contributions is effective on the date of enactment (April 10, 2004).

B. Multiemployer Plan Funding Notices (sec. 103 of the Act and secs. 101 and 502 of ERISA)

Present and Prior Law

Defined benefit plans are generally required to meet certain minimum funding rules. These rules are designed to help ensure that such plans are adequately funded. Both single-employer plans and multiemployer plans are subject to minimum funding requirements; however, the requirements for each type of plan differ in various ways.

Similarly, the Pension Benefit Guaranty Corporation ("PBGC") insures certain benefits under both single-employer and multiemployer defined benefit plans, but the rules relating to the guarantee vary for each type of plan. In the case of multiemployer plans, the PBGC guarantees against plan insolvency. Under its multiemployer program, PBGC provides financial assistance through loans to plans that are insolvent (that is, plans that are unable to pay basic PBGC-guaranteed benefits when due).

Employers maintaining single-employer defined benefit plans are required to provide certain notices to plan participants relating to the funding status of the plan. For example, ERISA requires an employer of a single-employer defined benefit plan to notify plan participants if the employer fails to make required contributions (unless a request for a funding waiver is pending).[153] In addition, in the case of an underfunded plan for which variable rate PBGC premiums are required, the plan administrator generally must notify plan participants of the plan's funding status and the limits on

[153] ERISA sec. 101(d).

the PBGC benefit guarantee if the plan terminates while underfunded.[154]

Reasons for Change[155]

The Congress believed that participants in multiemployer plans should be furnished with information about the plan's funded status and the limitations on the guarantee of benefits by the PBGC, including the circumstances in which the guarantee would come into effect. The Congress also believed that such participants should be provided with information about the value of the plan's assets and the amount of benefit payments as well as the rules governing insolvent multiemployer plans. Requiring administrators of multiemployer plans to provide participants with annual notices regarding plan funding will help keep participants in multiemployer plans adequately informed about their retirement benefits.

Explanation of Provision

In general

The Act requires the administrator of a defined benefit plan which is a multiemployer plan to provide an annual funding notice to: (1) each participant and beneficiary; (2) each labor organization representing such participants or beneficiaries; (3) each employer that has an obligation to contribute under the plan; and (4) the PBGC.

Such a notice must include: (1) identifying information, including the name of the plan, the address and phone number of the plan administrator and the plan's principal administrative officer, each plan sponsor's employer identification number, and the plan identification number; (2) a statement as to whether the plan's funded current liability percentage for the plan year to which the notice relates is at least 100 percent (and if not, a statement of the percentage); (3) a statement of the value of the plan's assets, the amount of benefit payments, and the ratio of the assets to the payments for the plan year to which the report relates; (4) a summary of the rules governing insolvent multiemployer plans, including the limitations on benefit payments and any potential benefit reductions and suspensions (and the potential effects of such limitations, reductions, and suspensions on the plan); (5) a general description of the benefits under the plan which are eligible to be guaranteed by the PBGC and the limitations of the guarantee and circumstances in which such limitations apply; and (6) any additional information which the plan administrator elects to include to the extent it is not inconsistent with regulations prescribed by the Secretary of Labor.

The annual funding notice must be provided no later than two months after the deadline (including extensions) for filing the plan's annual report for the plan year to which the notice relates. The funding notice must be provided in a form and manner pre-

---

[154] ERISA sec. 4011. Multiemployer plans are not required to pay variable rate premiums.

[155] These reasons for change were included for a substantially similar provision in S. 2424, the "National Employee Savings and Trust Equity Guarantee Act," which was reported by the Senate Committee on Finance on May 14, 2004 (S. Rep. No. 108–266), subsequent to the enactment of Pub. L. No. 108–218.

scribed in regulations by the Secretary of Labor. Additionally, it must be written so as to be understood by the average plan participant and may be provided in written, electronic, or some other appropriate form to the extent that it is reasonably accessible to persons to whom the notice is required to be provided.

The Secretary of Labor is directed to issue regulations (including a model notice) necessary to implement the provision no later than one year after the date of enactment.

Sanction for failure to provide notice

In the case of a failure to provide the annual multiemployer plan funding notice, the Secretary of Labor may assess a civil penalty against a plan administrator of up to $100 per day for each failure to provide a notice. For this purpose, each violation with respect to a single participant or beneficiary is treated as a separate violation.

Effective Date

The provision is effective for plan years beginning after December 31, 2004.

C. Election for Deferral of Charge for Portion of Net Experience Loss of Multiemployer Plans (sec. 104 of the Act, sec. 302(b)(7) of ERISA, and sec. 412(b)(7) of the Code)

Present and Prior Law

General funding requirements

The Code and ERISA impose minimum funding requirements with respect to defined benefit plans.[156] Under the minimum funding rules, the amount of contributions required for a plan year is generally the plan's normal cost for the year (i.e., the cost of benefits allocated to the year under the plan's funding method) plus that year's portion of other liabilities that are amortized over a period of years, such as benefits resulting from a grant of past service credit.[157] A plan's normal cost and other liabilities must be determined under an actuarial cost method permissible under the Code and ERISA.

Funding standard account

As an administrative aid in the application of the funding requirements, a defined benefit plan is required to maintain a special account called a "funding standard account" to which specified charges and credits (including credits for contributions to the plan), plus interest, are made for each plan year. If, as of the close of a plan year, the account reflects credits equal to or in excess of charges, the plan is generally treated as meeting the minimum funding standard for the year. Thus, as a general rule, the minimum contribution for a plan year is determined as the amount by

[156] Code sec. 412; ERISA sec. 302.

[157] Under special funding rules (referred to as the "deficit reduction contribution" rules), an additional contribution may be required to a single-employer plan if the plan's funded current liability percentage is less than 90 percent. The deficit reduction contribution rules do not apply to multiemployer plans.

which the charges to the account would exceed credits to the account if no contribution were made to the plan. If, as of the close of the plan year, charges to the funding standard account exceed credits to the account, then the excess is referred to as an "accumulated funding deficiency." [158]

Experience gains and losses

In determining plan funding under an actuarial cost method, a plan's actuary generally makes certain assumptions regarding the future experience of a plan. These assumptions typically involve rates of interest, mortality, disability, salary increases, and other factors affecting the value of assets and liabilities, such as increases or decreases in asset values. The actuarial assumptions are required to be reasonable and may be subject to other restrictions. If, on the basis of these assumptions, the contributions made to the plan result in actual unfunded liabilities that are less than those anticipated by the actuary, then the excess is an experience gain. If the actual unfunded liabilities are greater than those anticipated, then the difference is an experience loss.

If a plan has a net experience gain, the funding standard account is credited with the amount needed to amortize the net experience gain over a certain period. If a plan has a net experience loss, the funding standard account is charged with the amount needed to amortize the net experience loss over a certain period. In the case of a multiemployer plan, the amortization period for net experience gains and losses is 15 years.

Funding waivers

Within limits, the IRS is permitted to waive all or a portion of the contributions required under the minimum funding standard for a plan year.[159] A waiver may be granted if the employer (or employers) responsible for the contribution could not make the required contribution without temporary substantial business hardship and if requiring the contribution would be adverse to the interests of plan participants in the aggregate. In the case of a multiemployer plan, no more than five waivers may be granted within any period of 15 consecutive plan years.

If a funding waiver is in effect for a plan, subject to certain exceptions, no plan amendment may be adopted that increases the liabilities of the plan by reason of any increase in benefits, any change in the accrual of benefits, or any change in the rate at which benefits vest under the plan.

Excise tax

An employer is generally subject to an excise tax if it fails to make minimum required contributions and fails to obtain a waiver from the IRS.[160] The excise tax is 10 percent of the amount of the funding deficiency (five percent in the case of a multiemployer

---

[158] In addition to the funding standard account, a reconciliation account is sometimes used to balance certain items for purposes of reporting actuarial information about the plan on the plan's annual report (Schedule B of Form 5500).

[159] Sec. 412(d).

[160] Sec. 4971.

plan). In addition, a tax of 100 percent may be imposed if the funding deficiency is not corrected within a certain period.

Explanation of Provision

The Act allows the plan sponsor of an eligible multiemployer plan to elect to defer certain charges to the funding standard account that would otherwise be made to the plan's funding standard account for a plan year beginning after June 30, 2003, and before July 1, 2005. The charges may be deferred to any plan year selected by the plan sponsor from either of the two plan years immediately succeeding the plan year for which the charge would otherwise be made. An election may be made with respect to up to 80 percent of the charge to the funding standard account attributable to the amortization of a net experience loss for the first plan year beginning after December 31, 2001. An election is to be made at such time and in such manner as the Secretary of the Treasury prescribes. For the plan year to which a charge is deferred under the plan sponsor's election, the funding standard account is required to be charged with interest at the short-term Federal rate on the deferred charge for the period of the deferral.

An eligible multiemployer plan is a multiemployer plan: (1) that, for the first plan year beginning after December 31, 2001, had an actual net investment loss of at least 10 percent of the average fair market value of plan assets during the plan year; and (2) with respect to which the plan's enrolled actuary certifies that (not taking into account the deferral of charges under the provision and based on the actuarial assumptions used for the last plan year before date of enactment of the provision), the plan is projected to have an accumulated funding deficiency for any plan year beginning after June 30, 2003, and before July 1, 2006. In addition, a plan is not treated as an eligible multiemployer plan if: (1) for any taxable year beginning during the ten-year period preceding the first plan year for which an election is made under the provision, any employer required to contribute to the plan failed to timely pay an excise tax imposed on the plan for failure to make required contributions; (2) for any plan year beginning after June 30, 1993, and before the first plan year for which an election is made under the provision, the average contribution required to be made to the plan by all employers does not exceed 10 cents per hour, or no employer is required to make contributions to the plan; or (3) with respect to any plan year beginning after June 30, 1993, and before the first plan year for which an election is made under the provision, a funding waiver or extension of an amortization period was granted to the plan.

Certain plan amendments may not be adopted during the period for which a charge is deferred. This restriction applies to an amendment that increases the liabilities of the plan by reason of any increase in benefits, any change in the accrual of benefits, or any change in the rate at which benefits vest under the plan. The restriction applies unless: (1) the plan's enrolled actuary certifies (in such form and manner as prescribed by the Secretary of the Treasury) that the amendment provides for an increase in annual contributions that will exceed the increase in annual charges to the funding standard account attributable to such amendment; or (2) the amendment is required by a collective bargaining agreement that is in effect on the date of enactment of the provision. If a plan is amended in violation of the provision, an election under the provision does not apply to any plan year ending on or after the date on which the amendment is adopted.

If a plan sponsor elects to defer charges attributable to a net experience loss, the plan administrator must provide written notice of the election within 30 days to participants and beneficiaries, to each labor organization representing participants and beneficiaries, to each employer that has an obligation to contribute under the plan, and to the PBGC. The notice must include: (1) the amount of the charges to be deferred under the election and the period of the deferral; and (2) the maximum guaranteed monthly benefits that the PBGC would pay if the plan terminated while underfunded. If a plan administrator fails to comply with the notice requirement, the Secretary of Labor may assess a civil penalty of not more than $1,000 a day for each violation.

Effective Date

The provision is effective on the date of enactment (April 10, 2004).

II. OTHER PROVISIONS

A. Two-Year Extension of Transition Rule to Pension Funding Requirements for Interstate Bus Company (sec. 201 of the Act, and sec. 769(c) of the Retirement Protection Act of 1994 (as added by sec. 1508 of the Taxpayer Relief Act of 1997))

Present and Prior Law

Defined benefit pension plans are required to meet certain minimum funding rules. In some cases, additional contributions are required if a single-employer defined benefit pension plan is underfunded. Additional contributions generally are not required in the case of a plan with a funded current liability percentage of at least 90 percent. A plan's funded current liability percentage is the value of plan assets as a percentage of current liability. In general, a plan's current liability means all liabilities to employees and their beneficiaries under the plan. In the case of a plan with a funded current liability percentage of less than 100 percent for the preceding plan year, estimated contributions for the current plan year must be made in quarterly installments during the current plan year.

The PBGC insures benefits under most single-employer defined benefit pension plans in the event the plan is terminated with insufficient assets to pay for plan benefits. The PBGC is funded in part by a flat-rate premium per plan participant, and a variable rate premium based on the amount of unfunded vested benefits under the plan. A specified interest rate and a specified mortality table apply in determining unfunded vested benefits for this purpose.

A special rule modifies the minimum funding requirements in the case of certain plans. The special rule applies in the case of plans that (1) were not required to pay a variable rate PBGC premium for the plan year beginning in 1996, (2) do not, in plan years beginning after 1995 and before 2009, merge with another plan (other than a plan sponsored by an employer that was a member of the controlled group of the employer in 1996), and (3) are sponsored by a company that is engaged primarily in interurban or interstate passenger bus service.

The special rule generally treats a plan to which it applies as having a funded current liability percentage of at least 90 percent for plan years beginning after 1996 and before 2005 if for such plan year the funded current liability percentage is at least 85 percent. If the funded current liability of the plan is less than 85 percent for any plan year beginning after 1996 and before 2005, the relief from the minimum funding requirements generally applies only if certain specified contributions are made.

For plan years beginning after 2004 and before 2010, the funded current liability percentage generally will be deemed to be at least 90 percent if the actual funded current liability percentage is at least at certain specified levels. The relief from the minimum funding requirements generally applies for a plan year beginning in 2005, 2006, 2007, or 2008 only if contributions to the plan for the plan year equal at least the expected increase in current liability due to benefits accruing during the plan year.

Under prior law, the special rule did not include a provision applicable specifically for plan years beginning in 2004 and 2005.

Reasons for Change [161]

The Congress believed that the special funding rules for plans maintained by certain interstate bus companies were enacted because the generally applicable funding rules required greater contributions for such plans than were warranted give the special characteristics of such plans. In particular, these plans are closed to new participants and have demonstrated mortality significantly greater than that predicted under mortality tables that the plans would otherwise be required to use for minimum funding purposes. The Congress believed that it was appropriate to provide an extension of the special minimum funding rules for these plans for two years.

Explanation of Provision

The Act temporarily modifies the special funding rules for plans sponsored by a company engaged primarily in interurban or interstate passenger bus service by providing that, for plan years beginning in 2004 and 2005, the funded current liability percentage of the plan will be treated as at least 90 percent for purposes of determining the amount of required contributions (100 percent for purposes of determining whether quarterly contributions are required). As a result, for these years, additional contributions and quarterly contributions are not required with respect to the plan. In addition, for these years, the mortality table used under the plan is used in determining the amount of unfunded vested benefits under the plan for purposes of calculating PBGC variable rate premiums.

Effective Date

The provision effective for plan years beginning after December 31, 2003.

B. Procedures Applicable to Disputes Involving Pension Plan Withdrawal Liability (sec. 202 of the Act and sec. 4221 of ERISA)

Present and Prior Law

Under ERISA, when an employer withdraws from a multiemployer plan, the employer is generally liable for its share of un-

[161] These reasons for change were included for an identical provision in S. 2424, the "National Employee Savings and Trust Equity Guarantee Act," which was reported by the Senate Committee on Finance on May 14, 2004 (S. Rep. No. 108–266), subsequent to the enactment of Pub. L. No. 108–218.

funded vested benefits, determined as of the date of withdrawal (generally referred to as the "withdrawal liability"). Whether and when a withdrawal has occurred and the amount of the withdrawal liability is determined by the plan sponsor. The plan sponsor's assessment of withdrawal liability is presumed correct unless the employer shows by a preponderance of the evidence that the plan sponsor's determination of withdrawal liability was unreasonable or clearly erroneous. A similar standard applies in the event the amount of the plan's unfunded vested benefits is challenged.

The first payment of withdrawal liability determined by the plan sponsor is generally due no later than 60 days after demand, even if the employer contests the determination of liability. Disputes between an employer and plan sponsor concerning withdrawal liability are resolved through arbitration, which can be initiated by either party. Even if the employer contests the determination, payments of withdrawal liability must be made by the employer until the arbitrator issues a final decision with respect to the determination submitted for arbitration.

For purposes of withdrawal liability, all trades or businesses under common control are treated as a single employer. In addition, the plan sponsor may disregard a transaction in order to assess withdrawal liability if the sponsor determines that the principal purpose of the transaction was to avoid or evade withdrawal liability. For example, if a subsidiary of a parent company is sold and the subsidiary then withdraws from a multiemployer plan, the plan sponsor may assess withdrawal liability as if the subsidiary were still part of the parent company's controlled group if the sponsor determines that a principal purpose of the sale of the subsidiary was to evade or avoid withdrawal liability.

Explanation of Provision

Under the Act, a special rule may apply if a transaction is disregarded by a plan sponsor in determining that a withdrawal has occurred or that an employer is liable for withdrawal liability. If the transaction that is disregarded by the plan sponsor occurred before January 1, 1999, and at least five years before the date of the withdrawal, then (1) the determination by the plan sponsor that a principal purpose of the transaction was to evade or avoid withdrawal liability is not be presumed to be correct, (2) the plan sponsor, rather than the employer, has the burden to establish, by a preponderance of the evidence, the elements of the claim that a principal purpose of the transaction was to evade or avoid withdrawal liability, and (3) if an employer contests the plan sponsor's determination through an arbitration proceeding, or through a claim brought in a court of competent jurisdiction, the employer is not obligated to make any withdrawal liability payments until a final decision in the arbitration proceeding, or in court, upholds the plan sponsor's determination. The Act does not modify the burden of establishing other elements of a claim for withdrawal liability other than whether the purpose of the transaction was to evade or avoid withdrawal liability.

Effective Date

The provision applies to an employer that receives a notification of withdrawal liability and demand for payment under ERISA section 4219(b)(1) after October 31, 2003.

C. Sense of Congress Regarding Defined Benefit Pension System Reform (sec. 203 of the Act)

Prior Law

No provision.

Explanation of Provision

Under the Act, it is the sense of the Congress that the Congress must ensure the financial health of the defined benefit pension system by working to promptly implement: (1) a permanent replacement for the discount rate used for defined benefit pension plan calculations; and (2) comprehensive funding reforms for all defined benefit pension plans aimed at achieving accurate and sound pension plan funding to enhance retirement security for workers who rely on defined benefit pension plan benefits, to reduce the volatility of contributions, to provide plan sponsors with predictability for plan contributions, and to ensure adequate disclosures for plan participants in the case of underfunded plans.

Effective Date

The provision is effective on the date of enactment (April 10, 2004).

D. Extension of Provision Permitting Qualified Transfers of Excess Pension Assets to Retiree Health Accounts (sec. 204 of the Act, sec. 420 of the Code, and secs. 101, 403, and 408 of ERISA)

Present and Prior Law

Defined benefit plan assets generally may not revert to an employer prior to termination of the plan and satisfaction of all plan liabilities. In addition, a reversion may occur only if the plan so provides. A reversion prior to plan termination may constitute a prohibited transaction and may result in plan disqualification. Any assets that revert to the employer upon plan termination are includible in the gross income of the employer and subject to an excise tax. The excise tax rate is 20 percent if the employer maintains a replacement plan or makes certain benefit increases in connection with the termination; if not, the excise tax rate is 50 percent. Upon plan termination, the accrued benefits of all plan participants are required to be 100-percent vested.

A pension plan may provide medical benefits to retired employees through a separate account that is part of such plan. A qualified transfer of excess assets of a defined benefit plan to such a separate account within the plan may be made in order to fund retiree health benefits.[162] A qualified transfer does not result in plan disqualification, is not a prohibited transaction, and is not treated as a reversion. Thus, transferred assets are not includible in the gross income of the employer and are not subject to the excise tax on reversions. No more than one qualified transfer may be made in any taxable year. A qualified transfer can be made only from a single-employer plan.

Excess assets generally means the excess, if any, of the value of the plan's assets[163] over the greater of (1) the accrued liability under the plan (including normal cost) or (2) 125 percent of the plan's current liability.[164] In addition, excess assets transferred in a qualified transfer may not exceed the amount reasonably estimated to be the amount that the employer will pay out of such account during the taxable year of the transfer for qualified current retiree health liabilities. No deduction is allowed to the employer for (1) a qualified transfer or (2) the payment of qualified current retiree health liabilities out of transferred funds (and any income thereon).

Transferred assets (and any income thereon) must be used to pay qualified current retiree health liabilities for the taxable year of the transfer. Transferred amounts generally must benefit pension plan participants, other than key employees, who are entitled upon retirement to receive retiree medical benefits through the separate account. Retiree health benefits of key employees may not be paid out of transferred assets.

Amounts not used to pay qualified current retiree health liabilities for the taxable year of the transfer are to be returned to the general assets of the plan. These amounts are not includible in the gross income of the employer, but are treated as an employer reversion and are subject to a 20-percent excise tax.

In order for the transfer to be qualified, accrued retirement benefits under the pension plan generally must be 100-percent vested as if the plan terminated immediately before the transfer (or in the case of a participant who separated in the one-year period ending on the date of the transfer, immediately before the separation).

In order for a transfer to be qualified, the employer generally must maintain retiree health benefits at the same level for the taxable year of the transfer and the following four years.

In addition, the ERISA provides that, at least 60 days before the date of a qualified transfer, the employer must notify the Secretary of Labor, the Secretary of the Treasury, employee representatives, and the plan administrator of the transfer, and the plan administrator must notify each plan participant and beneficiary of the transfer.[165]

---

[162] Sec. 420.

[163] The value of plan assets for this purpose is the lesser of fair market value or actuarial value.

[164] In the case of plan years beginning before January 1, 2004, excess assets generally means the excess, if any, of the value of the plan's assets over the greater of (1) the lesser of (a) the accrued liability under the plan (including normal cost) or (b) 170 percent of the plan's current liability (for 2003), or (2) 125 percent of the plan's current liability. The current liability full funding limit was repealed for years beginning after 2003. Under the general sunset provision of EGTRRA, the limit is reinstated for years after 2010.

[165] ERISA sec. 101(e). ERISA also provides that a qualified transfer is not a prohibited transaction under ERISA or a prohibited reversion.

Under prior law, no qualified transfer could be made after December 31, 2005.

Reasons for Change [166]

The Congress believed it was appropriate to extend the ability of employers to transfer assets set aside for pension benefits to a section 401(h) account for retiree health benefits as long as the security of employees' pension benefits is not thereby threatened.

Explanation of Provision

The Act allows qualified transfers of excess defined benefit plan assets through December 31, 2013.

Effective Date

The provision is effective on the date of enactment (April 10, 2004).

E. Repeal of Reduction of Deductions for Mutual Life Insurance Companies (sec. 205 of the Act and sec. 809 of the Code)

Present and Prior Law

In general, a corporation may not deduct amounts distributed to shareholders with respect to the corporation's stock. The Deficit Reduction Act of 1984 added a provision to the rules governing insurance companies that was intended to remedy the failure of prior law to distinguish between amounts returned by mutual life insurance companies to policyholders as customers, and amounts distributed to them as owners of the mutual company.

Under the provision, section 809, a mutual life insurance company is required to reduce its deduction for policyholder dividends by the company's differential earnings amount. If the company's differential earnings amount exceeds the amount of its deductible policyholder dividends, the company is required to reduce its deduction for changes in its reserves by the excess of its differential earnings amount over the amount of its deductible policyholder dividends. The differential earnings amount is the product of the differential earnings rate and the average equity base of a mutual life insurance company.

The differential earnings rate is based on the difference between the average earnings rate of the 50 largest stock life insurance companies and the earnings rate of all mutual life insurance companies. The mutual earnings rate applied under the provision is the rate for the second calendar year preceding the calendar year in which the taxable year begins. The differential earnings rate cannot be a negative number.

---

[166] The reasons for change were included for an identical provision in S. 2424, the "National Employee Savings and Trust Equity Guarantee Act," which was reported by the Senate Committee on Finance on May 14, 2004 (S. Rep. No. 108–266), subsequent to the enactment of Pub. L. No. 108–218. See also, H.R. 2896, the "American Jobs Creation Act of 2003," which was reported by the House Committee on Ways and Means on November 21, 2003 (H.R. Rep. No. 108–393).

A company's equity base equals the sum of: (1) its surplus and capital increased by 50 percent of the amount of any provision for policyholder dividends payable in the following taxable year; (2) the amount of its nonadmitted financial assets; (3) the excess of its statutory reserves over its tax reserves; and (4) the amount of any mandatory security valuation reserves, deficiency reserves, and voluntary reserves. A company's average equity base is the average of the company's equity base at the end of the taxable year and its equity base at the end of the preceding taxable year.

A recomputation or "true-up" in the succeeding year is required if the differential earnings amount for the taxable year either exceeds, or is less than, the recomputed differential earnings amount. The recomputed differential earnings amount is calculated taking into account the average mutual earnings rate for the calendar year (rather than the second preceding calendar year, as above). The amount of the true-up for any taxable year is added to, or deducted from, the mutual company's income for the succeeding taxable year.

For taxable years beginning in 2001, 2002, or 2003, the differential earnings amount is treated as zero for purposes of computing both the differential earnings amount and the recomputed differential earnings amount (true-up).

Explanation of Provision

The Act repeals the rule requiring reduction in certain deductions of a mutual life insurance company (section 809).

Effective Date

The provision is effective for taxable years beginning after December 31, 2004. Thus, for taxable years beginning in 2003, the differential earnings amount is treated as zero; for taxable years beginning in 2004, this rule does not apply and section 809 is in effect (including the true-up applicable with respect to taxable years beginning in 2004).

F. Modify Qualification Rules for Tax-Exempt Property and Casualty Insurance Companies (sec. 206 of the Act and secs. 501 and 831 of the Code)

Present and Prior Law

A property and casualty insurance company generally is subject to tax on its taxable income (sec. 831(a)). The taxable income of a property and casualty insurance company is determined as the sum of its underwriting income and investment income (as well as gains and other income items), reduced by allowable deductions (sec. 832).

A property and casualty insurance company is eligible to be exempt from Federal income tax if its net written premiums or direct written premiums (whichever is greater) for the taxable year do not exceed $350,000 (sec. 501(c)(15)).

A property and casualty insurance company may elect to be taxed only on taxable investment income if its net written premiums or direct written premiums (whichever is greater) for the taxable year exceed $350,000, but do not exceed $1.2 million (sec. 831(b)).

For purposes of determining the amount of a company's net written premiums or direct written premiums under these rules, premiums received by all members of a controlled group of corporations of which the company is a part are taken into account. For this purpose, a more-than-50-percent threshhold applies under the vote and value requirements with respect to stock ownership for determining a controlled group, and rules treating a life insurance company as part of a separate controlled group or as an excluded member of a group do not apply (secs. 501(c)(15), 831(b)(2)(B) and 1563).

Reasons for Change[167]

The Congress became aware of abuses in the area of tax-exempt insurance companies. Considerable media attention has focused on the inappropriate use of tax-exempt insurance companies to shelter investment income.[168] It is believed that the use of these organizations as vehicles for sheltering income was never contemplated by Congress. The proliferation of these organizations as a means to avoid tax on income, sometimes on large investment portfolios, is inconsistent with the original narrow scope of the provision, which has been in the tax law for decades. The Congress believed it is necessary to limit the availability of tax-exempt status under the provision so that it cannot be abused as a tax shelter. To that end, the Act applies a gross receipts test and requires that premiums received for the taxable year be greater than 50 percent of gross receipts.

The Act correspondingly expands the availability of the present-law election of a property and casualty insurer to be taxed only on taxable investment income to companies with premiums below $350,000. This provision of present law provides a relatively simple tax calculation for small property and casualty insurers, and because the election results in the taxation of investment income, the Congress does not believe that it is abused to avoid tax on investment income. Thus, the bill provides that a company whose net written premiums (or if greater, direct written premiums) do not exceed $1.2 million (without regard to the $350,000 threshhold of present law) is eligible for the simplification benefit of this election.

Explanation of Provision

The Act modifies the requirements for a property and casualty insurance company to be eligible for tax-exempt status, and to elect to be taxed only on taxable investment income.

Under the Act, a property and casualty insurance company is eligible to be exempt from Federal income tax if (a) its gross receipts for the taxable year do not exceed $600,000, and (b) the premiums

[167] The reasons for change were included for a substantially similar provision in S. 2424, the "National Employee Savings and Trust Equity Guarantee Act," which was reported by the Senate Committee on Finance on May 14, 2004 (S. Rep. No. 108–266), subsequent to the enactment of Pub. L. No. 108–218.

[168] See David Cay Johnston, *Insurance Loophole Helps Rich,* N.Y. Times, April 1, 2003; David Cay Johnston, *Tiny Insurers Face Scrutiny as Tax Shields,* N.Y. Times, April 4, 2003, at C1; Janet Novack, *Are You a Chump?,* Forbes, March 5, 2001.

received for the taxable year are greater than 50 percent of its gross receipts. For purposes of determining these amounts, amounts received by all members of a controlled group of corporations of which the company is a part are taken into account. The Act expands the present-law controlled group rule so that it also takes into account foreign and tax-exempt corporations.

A company that does not meet the definition of an insurance company is not eligible to be exempt from Federal income tax under the Act. For this purpose, the term "insurance company" means any company, more than half of the business of which during the taxable year is the issuing of insurance or annuity contracts or the reinsuring of risks underwritten by insurance companies (sec. 816(a) and new sec. 831(c)). A company whose investment activities outweigh its insurance activities is not considered to be an insurance company for this purpose.[169] It is intended that IRS enforcement activities address the misuse of present-law section 501(c)(15).

The Act also provides that a property and casualty insurance company may elect to be taxed only on taxable investment income if its net written premiums or direct written premiums (whichever is greater) do not exceed $1.2 million (without regard to whether such premiums exceed $350,000) (sec. 831(b)). For purposes of determining the amount of a company's net written premiums or direct written premiums under this rule, premiums received by all members of a controlled group of corporations (as defined in section 831(b)) of which the company is a part are taken into account.

It is intended that regulations or other Treasury guidance provide for anti-abuse rules so as to prevent improper use of the provision, including, for example, by attempts to characterize as premiums any income that is other than premium income.

Under the Act, an additional special rule provides that a mutual property and casualty insurance company is eligible to be exempt from Federal income tax under the provision if (a) its gross receipts for the taxable year do not exceed $150,000, and (b) the premiums received for the taxable year are greater than 35 percent of its gross receipts, provided certain requirements are met. The requirements are that no employee of the company or member of the employee's family is an employee of another company that is exempt from tax under section 501(c)(15) (or that would be exempt but for this rule). The limitation to mutual companies and the limitation on employees are intended to address the conferees' concern about the inappropriate use of tax-exempt insurance companies to shelter investment income, including in the case of companies with gross receipts under $150,000. For example, it is intended that the provision not permit the use of small companies with common owners or employees to shelter investment income for the benefit of such owners or employees.

Effective Date

The provision generally is effective for taxable years beginning after December 31, 2003.

---

[169] See, e.g., *Inter-American Life Insurance Co.* v. Comm'r, 56 T.C. 497, *aff'd per curiam,* 469 F.2d 697 (9th Cir. 1972).

Under the provision, a special transition rule applies with respect to certain companies. This transition rule applies in the case of a company that, (1) for its taxable year that includes April 1, 2004, meets the requirements of present-law section 501(c)(15)(A) (as in effect for the taxable year beginning before January 1, 2004), and (2) on April 1, 2004, is in a receivership, liquidation or similar proceeding under the supervision of a State court. Under the transition rule, in the case of such a company, the general rule of the provision applies to taxable years beginning after the earlier of (1) the date the proceeding ends, or (2) December 31, 2007.

For such a company, the limitations on the carryover of net operating losses to or from years in which the company was not subject to tax (including section 831(b)(3)) continue to apply. A company that is not otherwise eligible for tax-exempt status under present-law section 501(c)(15) (e.g., a company that is or becomes a life insurance company, or a company with net (or, if greater, direct) written premiums exceeding $350,000 for the taxable year) is not eligible for the transition rule.

G. Definition of Insurance Company for Property and Insurance Company Tax Rules (sec. 206 of the Act and sec. 831 of the Code)

Present and Prior Law

Specific rules are provided for taxation of the life insurance company taxable income of a life insurance company (sec. 801), and for taxation of the taxable income of an insurance company other than a life insurance company (sec. 831) (generally referred to as a property and casualty insurance company). For Federal income tax purposes, a life insurance company means an insurance company that is engaged in the business of issuing life insurance and annuity contracts, or noncancellable health and accident insurance contracts, and that meets a 50-percent test with respect to its reserves (sec. 816(a)). This statutory provision applicable to life insurance companies explicitly defines the term "insurance company" to mean any company, more than half of the business of which during the taxable year is the issuing of insurance or annuity contracts or the reinsuring of risks underwritten by insurance companies (sec. 816(a)).

The life insurance company statutory definition of an insurance company does not explicitly apply to property and casualty insurance companies, although a long-standing Treasury regulation[170] that is applied to property and casualty companies provides a somewhat similar definition of an "insurance company" based on the company's "primary and predominant business activity."[171]

---

[170] The Treasury regulation provides that "the term 'insurance company' means a company whose primary and predominant business activity during the taxable year is the issuing of insurance or annuity contracts or the reinsuring of risks underwritten by insurance companies. Thus, though its name, charter powers, and subjection to State insurance laws are significant in determining the business which a company is authorized and intends to carry on, it is the character of the business actually done in the taxable year which determines whether a company is taxable as an insurance company under the Internal Revenue Code." Treas. Reg. sec. 1.801–3(a)(1).

[171] Court cases involving a determination of whether a company is an insurance company for Federal tax purposes have examined all of the business and other activities of the company. In considering whether a company is an insurance company for such purposes, courts have consid-

When enacting the statutory definition of a life insurance company in 1984, Congress stated, "[b]y requiring [that] more than half rather than the 'primary and predominant business activity' be insurance activity, the bill adopts a stricter and more precise standard for a company to be taxed as a life insurance company than does the general regulatory definition of an insurance company applicable for both life and nonlife insurance companies . . . Whether more than half of the business activity is related to the issuing of insurance or annuity contracts will depend on the facts and circumstances and factors to be considered will include the relative distribution of the number of employees assigned to, the amount of space allocated to, and the net income derived from, the various business activities."[172]

Reasons for Change[173]

The Congress believed that the law will be made clearer and more exact and tax administration will be improved by conforming the definition of an insurance company for purposes of the property and casualty insurance tax rules to the existing statutory definition of an insurance company under the life insurance company tax rules. Further, the Congress expected that IRS enforcement activities to prevent abuse of the provision relating to tax-exempt insurance companies will be simplified and improved by this provision of the Act.

Explanation of Provision

The Act provides that, for purposes of determining whether a company is a property and casualty insurance company, the term "insurance company" is defined to mean any company, more than half of the business of which during the taxable year is the issuing of insurance or annuity contracts or the reinsuring of risks underwritten by insurance companies. Thus, the Act conforms the definition of an insurance company for purposes of the rules taxing property and casualty insurance companies to the rules taxing life insurance companies, so that the definition is uniform. The Act

---

ered, among other factors, the amount and source of income received by the company from its different activities. See *Bowers v. Lawyers Mortgage Co., 285 U.S. 182 (1932); United States v. Home Title Insurance Co., 285 U.S. 191 (1932).* See also *Inter-American Life Insurance Co. v. Comm'r, 56 T.C. 497, aff'd per curiam,* 469 F.2d 697 (9th Cir. 1972), in which the court concluded that the company was not an insurance company: "The . . . financial data clearly indicates that petitioner's primary and predominant source of income was from its investments and not from issuing insurance contracts or reinsuring risks underwritten by insurance companies. During each of the years in issue, petitioner's investment income far exceeded its premiums and the amounts of earned premiums were de minimis during those years. It is equally as clear that petitioner's primary and predominant efforts were not expended in issuing insurance contracts or in reinsurance. Of the relatively few policies directly written by petitioner, nearly all were issued to [family members]. Also, Investment Life, in which [family members] each owned a substantial stock interest, was the source of nearly all of the policies reinsured by petitioner. These facts, coupled with the fact that petitioner did not maintain an active sales staff soliciting or selling insurance policies . . ., indicate a lack of concentrated effort on petitioner's behalf toward its chartered purpose of engaging in the insurance business. . . . For the above reasons, we hold that during the years in issue, petitioner was not 'an insurance company . . . engaged in the business of issuing life insurance' and hence, that petitioner was not a life insurance company within the meaning of section 801." 56 T.C. 497, 507–508.

[172] H.R. Rep. No. 98–432, part 2, at 1402–1403 (1984); S. Prt. No. 98–169, vol. I, at 525–526 (1984); see also H.R. Rep. No. 98–861 at 1043–1044 (1985) (Conference Report).

[173] The reasons for change were included for an identical provision in S. 2424, the "National Employee Savings and Trust Equity Guarantee Act," which was reported by the Senate Committee on Finance on May 14, 2004 (S. Rep. No. 108–266), subsequent to the enactment of Pub. L. No. 108–218.

adopts a stricter and more precise standard than the "primary and predominant business activity" test contained in Treasury Regulations. A company whose investment activities outweigh its insurance activities is not considered to be an insurance company under the Act.[174] It is not intended that a company whose sole activity is the run-off of risks under the company's insurance contracts be treated as a company other than an insurance company, even if the company has little or no premium income.

Effective Date

The provision applies to taxable years beginning after December 31, 2003.

[174] See *Inter-American Life Insurance Co. v. Comm'r,* supra.

PART ELEVEN: SURFACE TRANSPORTATION EXTENSION ACT OF 2004, PART II (PUBLIC LAW 108–224) [175]

A. Extension of Highway Trust Fund and Aquatic Resources Trust Fund Expenditure Authority (sec. 10 of the Act)

Prior Law

Under prior law, the Internal Revenue Code (sec. 9503) authorized expenditures (subject to appropriations) to be made from the Highway Trust Fund through April 30, 2004, for purposes provided in specified authorizing legislation as in effect on the date of enactment of the most recent authorizing Act (the Surface Transportation Extension Act of 2004).

Under prior law, expenditures also were authorized from the Aquatic Resources Trust Fund through April 30, 2004.

Highway Trust Fund spending is limited by anti-deficit provisions internal to the Highway Trust Fund, the so-called "Harry Byrd rule". The rule requires the Treasury Department to determine, on a quarterly basis, the amount (if any) by which unfunded highway authorizations exceed projected net Highway Trust Fund tax receipts for the 24-month period beginning at the close of each fiscal year (sec. 9503(d)). Similar rules apply to unfunded Mass Transit Account authorizations. If unfunded authorizations exceed projected 24-month receipts, apportionments to the States for specified programs funded by the relevant Trust Fund Account are to be reduced proportionately. Because of the Harry Byrd rule, taxes dedicated to the Highway Trust Fund typically are scheduled to expire at least two years after current authorizing Acts.

The Surface Transportation Extension Act of 2003, created a temporary rule (through February 29, 2004) for purposes of the anti-deficit provisions of the Highway Trust Fund. For purposes of determining 24 months of projected revenues for the anti-deficit provisions, the Secretary of the Treasury is instructed to treat each expiring provision relating to appropriations and transfers to the Highway Trust Fund to have been extended through the end of the 24-month period and to assume that the rate of tax during such 24-month period remains the same as the rate in effect on the date of enactment of that Act. The Surface Transportation Extension Act of 2004 extended this rule through April 30, 2004.

---

[175] H.R. 4219. The House passed the bill on the suspension calendar on April 28, 2004. The Senate passed the bill by unanimous consent on April 29, 2004. The President signed the bill on April 30, 2004.

Explanation of Provision[176]

The Act extends the authority to make expenditures (subject to appropriations) from the Highway Trust Fund through June 30, 2004. The Act also updates the Highway Trust Fund cross references to authorizing legislation to include expenditure purposes in this Act and prior authorizing legislation as in effect on the date of enactment. For purposes of the anti-deficit provisions of the Highway Trust Fund, the Act extends the temporary rule through June 30, 2004.

The Act extends the authority to make expenditures (subject to appropriations) from the Aquatics Resources Trust Fund through June 30, 2004. The Act also updates the Aquatics Resources Trust Fund cross references to authorizing legislation to include expenditure purposes as in effect on the date of enactment of this Act.

Effective Date

The provision is effective on the date of enactment (April 30, 2004).

[176] The expiration dates described herein were subsequently extended by the Surface Transportation Extension Act of 2004, Part III; the Surface Transportation Extension Act of 2004, Part IV; and the Surface Transportation Extension Act of 2004, Part V, described in Part Twelve, Part Thirteen, and Part Fourteen, respectively.

PART TWELVE: SURFACE TRANSPORTATION EXTENSION ACT OF 2004, PART III (PUBLIC LAW 108–263) [177]

A. Extension of Highway Trust Fund and Aquatic Resources Trust Fund Expenditure Authority (sec. 10 of the Act)

Prior Law

Under prior law, the Internal Revenue Code (sec. 9503) authorized expenditures (subject to appropriations) to be made from the Highway Trust Fund through June 30, 2004, for purposes provided in specified authorizing legislation as in effect on the date of enactment of the most recent authorizing Act (the Surface Transportation Extension Act of 2004, Part II).

Under prior law, expenditures also were authorized from the Aquatic Resources Trust Fund through June 30, 2004.

Highway Trust Fund spending is limited by anti-deficit provisions internal to the Highway Trust Fund, the so-called "Harry Byrd rule". The rule requires the Treasury Department to determine, on a quarterly basis, the amount (if any) by which unfunded highway authorizations exceed projected net Highway Trust Fund tax receipts for the 24-month period beginning at the close of each fiscal year (sec. 9503(d)). Similar rules apply to unfunded Mass Transit Account authorizations. If unfunded authorizations exceed projected 24-month receipts, apportionments to the States for specified programs funded by the relevant Trust Fund Account are to be reduced proportionately. Because of the Harry Byrd rule, taxes dedicated to the Highway Trust Fund typically are scheduled to expire at least two years after current authorizing Acts.

The Surface Transportation Extension Act of 2003, created a temporary rule (through February 29, 2004) for purposes of the anti-deficit provisions of the Highway Trust Fund. For purposes of determining 24 months of projected revenues for the anti-deficit provisions, the Secretary of the Treasury is instructed to treat each expiring provision relating to appropriations and transfers to the Highway Trust Fund to have been extended through the end of the 24-month period and to assume that the rate of tax during such 24-month period remains the same as the rate in effect on the date of enactment of that Act. The Surface Transportation Extension Act of 2004 extended this rule through April 30, 2004. The Surface Transportation Extension Act of 2004, Part II, extended this rule through June 30, 2004.

[177] H.R. 4635. The House passed the bill on the suspension calendar on June 23, 2004. The Senate passed the bill by unanimous consent on June 23, 2004. The President signed the bill on June 30, 2004.

Explanation of Provision [178]

The Act extends the authority to make expenditures (subject to appropriations) from the Highway Trust Fund through July 31, 2004. The Act also updates the Highway Trust Fund cross references to authorizing legislation to include expenditure purposes in this Act and prior authorizing legislation as in effect on the date of enactment.

For purposes of the anti-deficit provisions of the Highway Trust Fund, the Act extends the temporary rule through July 31, 2004.

The Act extends the authority to make expenditures (subject to appropriations) from the Aquatics Resources Trust Fund through July 31, 2004. The Act also updates the Aquatics Resources Trust Fund cross references to authorizing legislation to include expenditure purposes as in effect on the date of enactment of this Act.

Effective Date

The provision is effective on the date of enactment (June 30, 2004).

[178] The expiration dates described herein were subsequently extended by the Surface Transportation Extension Act of 2004, Part IV; and the Surface Transportation Extension Act of 2004, Part V, described in Part Thirteen, and Part Fourteen, respectively.

PART THIRTEEN: SURFACE TRANSPORTATION EXTENSION ACT OF 2004, PART IV (PUBLIC LAW 108–280) [179]

A. Extension of Highway Trust Fund and Aquatic Resources Trust Fund Expenditure Authority (sec. 10 of the Act)

Prior Law

Under prior law, the Internal Revenue Code (sec. 9503) authorized expenditures (subject to appropriations) to be made from the Highway Trust Fund through July 31, 2004, for purposes provided in specified authorizing legislation as in effect on the date of enactment of the most recent authorizing Act (the Surface Transportation Extension Act of 2004, Part III).

Under prior law, expenditures also were authorized from the Aquatic Resources Trust Fund through July 31, 2004.

Highway Trust Fund spending is limited by anti-deficit provisions internal to the Highway Trust Fund, the so-called "Harry Byrd rule". The rule requires the Treasury Department to determine, on a quarterly basis, the amount (if any) by which unfunded highway authorizations exceed projected net Highway Trust Fund tax receipts for the 24-month period beginning at the close of each fiscal year (sec. 9503(d)). Similar rules apply to unfunded Mass Transit Account authorizations. If unfunded authorizations exceed projected 24-month receipts, apportionments to the States for specified programs funded by the relevant Trust Fund Account are to be reduced proportionately. Because of the Harry Byrd rule, taxes dedicated to the Highway Trust Fund typically are scheduled to expire at least two years after current authorizing Acts.

The Surface Transportation Extension Act of 2003, created a temporary rule (through February 29, 2004) for purposes of the anti-deficit provisions of the Highway Trust Fund. For purposes of determining 24 months of projected revenues for the anti-deficit provisions, the Secretary of the Treasury is instructed to treat each expiring provision relating to appropriations and transfers to the Highway Trust Fund to have been extended through the end of the 24-month period and to assume that the rate of tax during such 24-month period remains the same as the rate in effect on the date of enactment of that Act. The Surface Transportation Extension Act of 2004 extended this rule through April 30, 2004. The Surface Transportation Extension Act of 2004, Part II, extended this rule through June 30, 2004. The Surface Transportation Extension Act of 2004, Part III, extended this rule through July 31, 2004.

[179] H.R. 4916. The House passed the bill by unanimous consent on July 22, 2004. The Senate passed the bill without amendment by unanimous consent on July 22, 2004. The President signed the bill on July 30, 2004.

Explanation of Provision [180]

The Act extends the authority to make expenditures (subject to appropriations) from the Highway Trust Fund through September 30, 2004. Core highway programs are authorized through September 24, 2004. The term "core highway program" means any program (other than any program carried out by the National Highway Traffic Safety Administration and any program carried out by the Federal Motor Carrier Administration) funded by the Highway Trust fund (other than the Mass Transit Account). The Act also updates the Highway Trust Fund cross references to authorizing legislation to include expenditure purposes in this Act and prior authorizing legislation as in effect on the date of enactment.

For purposes of the anti-deficit provisions of the Highway Trust Fund, the Act extends the temporary rule through September 30, 2004.

The Act extends the authority to make expenditures (subject to appropriations) from the Aquatics Resources Trust Fund through September 30, 2004. The Act also updates the Aquatics Resources Trust Fund cross references to authorizing legislation to include expenditure purposes as in effect on the date of enactment of this Act.

Effective Date

The provision is effective on the date of enactment (July 30, 2004).

[180] The expiration dates described herein were subsequently extended by the Surface Transportation Extension Act of 2004, Part V, described in Part Fourteen.

PART FOURTEEN: SURFACE TRANSPORTATION EXTENSION ACT OF 2004, PART V (PUBLIC LAW 108–310)[181]

A. Extension of Highway Trust Fund and Aquatic Resources Trust Fund Expenditure Authority (sec. 13 of the Act)

Present and Prior Law

Expenditure authority

Under prior law, the Internal Revenue Code (sec. 9503) authorized expenditures (subject to appropriations) to be made from the Highway Trust Fund generally through September 30, 2004, for purposes provided in specified authorizing legislation as in effect on the date of enactment of the most recent authorizing Act (the Surface Transportation Extension Act of 2004, Part IV).[182]

Under prior law, expenditures also were authorized from the Aquatic Resources Trust Fund through September 30, 2004.

Highway Trust Fund spending is limited by anti-deficit provisions internal to the Highway Trust Fund, the so-called "Harry Byrd rule". The rule requires the Treasury Department to determine, on a quarterly basis, the amount (if any) by which unfunded highway authorizations exceed projected net Highway Trust Fund tax receipts for the 24-month period beginning at the close of each fiscal year (sec. 9503(d)). Similar rules apply to unfunded Mass Transit Account authorizations. If unfunded authorizations exceed projected 24-month receipts, apportionments to the States for specified programs funded by the relevant Trust Fund Account are to be reduced proportionately. Because of the Harry Byrd rule, taxes dedicated to the Highway Trust Fund typically are scheduled to expire at least two years after current authorizing Acts.

The Surface Transportation Extension Act of 2003, created a temporary rule (through February 29, 2004) for purposes of the anti-deficit provisions of the Highway Trust Fund. For purposes of determining 24 months of projected revenues for the anti-deficit provisions, the Secretary of the Treasury is instructed to treat each expiring provision relating to appropriations and transfers to the Highway Trust Fund to have been extended through the end of the 24-month period and to assume that the rate of tax during such 24-month period remains the same as the rate in effect on the date of enactment of that Act. The Surface Transportation Extension Act of 2004 extended this rule through April 30, 2004. The Surface Transportation Extension Act of 2004, Part II, extended this rule

---

[181] H.R. 5183. The House passed the bill on September 30, 2004. The Senate passed the bill without amendment by unanimous consent on September 30, 2004. The President signed the bill on September 30, 2004.

[182] Core highway programs were authorized through September 24, 2004. The term "core highway program" means any program (other than any program carried out by the National Highway Traffic Safety Administration and any program carried out by the Federal Motor Carrier Administration) funded by the Highway Trust fund (other than the Mass Transit Account).

through June 30, 2004. The Surface Transportation Extension Act of 2004, Part III, extended this rule through July 31, 2004. The Surface Transportation Extension Act of 2004, Part IV, extended this rule through September 30, 2004.

Alcohol fuel taxes

In general, 18.3 cents per gallon of the gasoline excise tax is deposited in the Highway Trust Fund and 0.1 cent per gallon is deposited in the Leaking Underground Storage Tank Trust Fund (the "LUST" rate). Under prior law, in the case of gasohol with respect to which a reduced excise tax is paid,[183] 2.5 cents per gallon of the reduced tax was retained in the General Fund. The balance of the reduced rate (less the LUST rate) was deposited in the Highway Trust Fund. Also under prior law, of the reduced tax rate on gasoline to be blended into an alcohol fuel, 2.8 cents per gallon of the reduced tax was retained in the General Fund. The balance of the reduced rate (less the LUST rate) was deposited in the Highway Trust Fund.

Explanation of Provision

Expenditure authority

The Act extends the authority to make expenditures (subject to appropriations) from the Highway Trust Fund through May 31, 2005. The Act also updates the Highway Trust Fund cross references to authorizing legislation to include expenditure purposes in this Act and prior authorizing legislation as in effect on the date of enactment.

For purposes of the anti-deficit provisions of the Highway Trust Fund, the Act extends the temporary rule through May 31, 2005.

The Act extends the authority to make expenditures (subject to appropriations) from the Aquatics Resources Trust Fund through May 31, 2005. The Act also updates the Aquatics Resources Trust Fund cross references to authorizing legislation to include expenditure purposes as in effect on the date of enactment of this Act.

All alcohol fuel taxes transferred to Highway Trust Fund for FY 2004

For the period beginning October 1, 2003, through September 30, 2004, the Act authorizes the transfer to the Highway Trust Fund of the 2.5 and 2.8 cents per gallon of tax imposed on alcohol fuels that had been retained by the General Fund.

Effective Date

The provisions relating to expenditure authority are effective on the date of enactment (September 30, 2004). The provision relating to the transfer of alcohol fuel taxes to the Highway Trust Fund is effective for taxes imposed after September 30, 2003.

---

[183] For example, under prior law, a 10 percent ethanol/gasoline blend was taxed at 13.2 cents per gallon. Gasoline for use in producing gasohol consisting of 10 percent ethanol was taxed at 14.666 cents per gallon.

PART FIFTEEN: WORKING FAMILIES TAX RELIEF ACT OF 2004 (PUBLIC LAW 108–311)[184]

I. EXTENSION OF CERTAIN EXPIRING PROVISIONS

A. Extension of the Child Tax Credit, Acceleration of Refundability of the Child Tax Credit and Treatment of Combat Pay as Earned Income for Purposes of the Child Tax Credit and Earned Income Credit (secs. 101–104 of the Act and sec. 24 and 32 of the Code)

Present and Prior Law

In general

For 2004, an individual may claim a $1,000 tax credit for each qualifying child under the age of 17. In general, a qualifying child is an individual for whom the taxpayer can claim a dependency exemption and who is the taxpayer's son or daughter (or descendent of either), stepson or stepdaughter (or descendent of either), or eligible foster child.

The child tax credit is scheduled to revert to $700 in 2005, and then, over several years, increase to $1,000.

Table 6, below, shows the scheduled amount of the child tax credit.

Table 6.—Scheduled Amount of the Child Tax Credit

Taxable year	Credit amount per child
2003–2004	$1,000
2005–2008	700
2009	800
2010[1]	1,000

[1] The credit reverts to $500 in taxable years beginning after December 31, 2010, under the sunset provision of EGTRRA (the "Economic Growth and Tax Relief Reconciliation Act of 2001," Pub. L. No. 107–16).

The child tax credit is phased out for individuals with income over certain thresholds. Specifically, the otherwise allowable child tax credit is reduced by $50 for each $1,000 (or fraction thereof) of modified adjusted gross income over $75,000 for single individuals

[184] H.R. 1308. The House passed the bill on the suspension calendar on March 19, 2003. The Senate passed the bill, as amended, on June 5, 2003. The House passed the bill with a further amendment on June 12, 2003. The conference report was filed on September 23, 2004 (H.R. Rep. No. 108–696). The conference report passed the House on September 23, 2004, and passed the Senate on September 23, 2004. The President signed the bill on October 4, 2004.

or heads of households, $110,000 for married individuals filing joint returns, and $55,000 for married individuals filing separate returns.[185] The length of the phase-out range depends on the number of qualifying children. For example, the phase-out range for a single individual with one qualifying child is between $75,000 and $95,000 of modified adjusted gross income. The phase-out range for a single individual with two qualifying children is between $75,000 and $115,000.

The amount of the tax credit and the phase-out ranges are not adjusted annually for inflation.

Refundability

For 2004, the child credit is refundable to the extent of 10 percent of the taxpayer's taxable earned income (which is taken into account in determining taxable income) in excess of $10,750.[186] The percentage is increased to 15 percent for taxable years 2005 and thereafter. Families with three or more children are allowed a refundable credit for the amount by which the taxpayer's social security taxes exceed the taxpayer's earned income credit, if that amount is greater than the refundable credit based on the taxpayer's taxable earned income in excess of $10,750 (for 2004). The refundable portion of the child credit does not constitute income and is not treated as resources for purposes of determining eligibility or the amount or nature of benefits or assistance under any Federal program or any State or local program financed with Federal funds. For taxable years beginning after December 31, 2010, the sunset provision of EGTRRA applies to the 15-percent rule for allowing refundable child credits.

Alternative minimum tax liability

The child credit is allowed against the individual's regular income tax and alternative minimum tax. For taxable years beginning after December 31, 2010, the sunset provision of EGTRRA applies to the rules allowing the child credit against the alternative minimum tax.

Explanation of Provision

In general

The Act increases the child credit to $1,000 for taxable years 2005–2009. Therefore, the maximum child tax credit is $1,000 per child for taxable years 2005–2010. All modifications to the child credit under the Act are subject to the sunset provision of EGTRRA.[187]

---

[185] Modified adjusted gross income is the taxpayer's total gross income plus certain amounts excluded from gross income (i.e., excluded income of U.S. citizens or residents living abroad (sec. 911); residents of Guam, American Samoa, and the Northern Mariana Islands (sec 931); and residents of Puerto Rico (sec. 933)).

[186] The $10,750 amount is indexed for inflation.

[187] The credit reverts to $500 in taxable years beginning after December 31, 2010, under the sunset provision of EGTRRA.

Refundability

The Act accelerates to 2004 the increase in refundability of the child credit to 15 percent of the taxpayer's earned income in excess of $10,750 (with indexing).

Combat pay treated as earned income

The Act provides that combat pay that is otherwise excluded from gross income under section 112 is treated as earned income which is taken into account in computing taxable income for purposes of calculating the refundable portion of the child credit.

The Act provides that any taxpayer may elect to treat combat pay that is otherwise excluded from gross income under section 112 as earned income for purposes of the earned income credit. This election is available with respect to any taxable year ending after the date of enactment and before January 1, 2006.

Effective Dates

The provision generally applies to taxable years beginning after December 31, 2004. The provision relating to the acceleration of the refundability of the child credit applies to taxable years beginning after December 31, 2003. The provision relating to the treatment of combat pay as earned income for purposes of the child credit is effective for taxable years beginning after December 31, 2003. The earned income credit election is effective for taxable years ending after the date of enactment (October 4, 2004) and before January 1, 2006.

B. Extend Marriage Penalty Relief (sec. 101 of the Act and secs. 1 and 63 of the Code)

1. Standard deduction marriage penalty relief (sec. 63 of the Code)

Present and Prior Law

Marriage penalty

A married couple generally is treated as one tax unit that must pay tax on the couple's total taxable income. Although married couples may elect to file separate returns, the rate schedules and other provisions are structured so that filing separate returns usually results in a higher tax than filing a joint return. Other rate schedules apply to single persons and to single heads of households.

A "marriage penalty" exists when the combined tax liability of a married couple filing a joint return is greater than the sum of the tax liabilities of each individual computed as if they were not married. A "marriage bonus" exists when the combined tax liability of a married couple filing a joint return is less than the sum of the tax liabilities of each individual computed as if they were not married.

Basic standard deduction

Taxpayers who do not itemize deductions may choose the basic standard deduction (and additional standard deductions, if applicable),[188] which is subtracted from adjusted gross income ("AGI") in arriving at taxable income. The size of the basic standard deduction varies according to filing status and is adjusted annually for inflation.[189] In general, two unmarried individuals have standard deductions whose sum exceeds the standard deduction for a married couple filing a joint return. EGTRRA increased the basic standard deduction for a married couple filing a joint return, providing for a phase-in of the increase until the basic standard deduction for a married couple filing a joint return equaled twice the basic standard deduction for an unmarried individual filing a single return by 2009.[190] The Jobs and Growth Tax Relief Reconciliation Act of 2003 ("JGTRRA") accelerated the phase-in, providing that the basic standard deduction for a married couple filing a joint return equaled twice the basic standard deduction for an unmarried individual filing a single return for 2003 and 2004, reverting to the phase-in schedule provided by EGTRAA for 2005–2009.

Table 7, below, shows the standard deduction for married couples filing a joint return as a percentage of the standard deduction for single individuals.

Table 7.—Amount of the Basic Standard Deduction for Married Couples Filing Joint Returns

Taxable year	Standard deduction for married couples filing joint returns as percentage of standard deduction for unmarried individual returns
2003–2004	200
2005	174
2006	184
2007	187
2008	190
2009 and 2010 [1]	200

[1] The basic standard deduction increases are repealed for taxable years beginning after December 31, 2010, under the sunset provision of EGTRRA.

Explanation of Provision

The Act increases the basic standard deduction amount for joint returns to twice the basic standard deduction amount for single returns effective for 2005–2008. Therefore, the basic standard deduction for joint returns is twice the basic standard deduction for single returns for taxable years 2005–2010. All modifications to the

[188] Additional standard deductions are allowed with respect to any individual who is elderly (age 65 or over) or blind.

[189] For 2004 the basic standard deduction amounts are: (1) $4,850 for unmarried individuals; (2) $9,700 for married individuals filing a joint return; (3) $7,150 for heads of households; and (4) $4,850 for married individuals filing separately.

[190] The basic standard deduction for a married taxpayer filing separately will continue to equal one-half of the basic standard deduction for a married couple filing jointly; thus, the basic standard deduction for unmarried individuals filing a single return and for married couples filing separately will be the same after the phase-in period.

basic standard deduction under the Act are subject to the sunset provision of EGTRRA.

Effective Date

The provision is effective for taxable years beginning after December 31, 2004.

2. Increase the size of the 15-percent rate bracket for married couples filing joint returns (sec. 1 of the Code)

Present and Prior Law

In general

Under the Federal individual income tax system, an individual who is a citizen or resident of the United States generally is subject to tax on worldwide taxable income. Taxable income is total gross income less certain exclusions, exemptions, and deductions. An individual may claim either a standard deduction or itemized deductions.

An individual's income tax liability is determined by computing his or her regular income tax liability and, if applicable, alternative minimum tax liability.

Regular income tax liability

Regular income tax liability is determined by applying the regular income tax rate schedules (or tax tables) to the individual's taxable income and then is reduced by any applicable tax credits. The regular income tax rate schedules are divided into several ranges of income, known as income brackets, and the marginal tax rate increases as the individual's income increases. The income bracket amounts are adjusted annually for inflation. Separate rate schedules apply based on filing status: single individuals (other than heads of households and surviving spouses), heads of households, married individuals filing joint returns (including surviving spouses), married individuals filing separate returns, and estates and trusts. Lower rates may apply to capital gains.

In general, the bracket breakpoints for single individuals are approximately 60 percent of the rate bracket breakpoints for married couples filing joint returns.[191] The rate bracket breakpoints for married individuals filing separate returns are exactly one-half of the rate brackets for married individuals filing joint returns. A separate, compressed rate schedule applies to estates and trusts.

15-percent regular income tax rate bracket

EGTRRA increased the size of the 15-percent regular income tax rate bracket for a married couple filing a joint return to twice the size of the corresponding rate bracket for a single individual filing a single return, phasing in the increase over four years, beginning in 2005. JGTRRA accelerated these increases, making the size of the 15-percent regular income tax rate bracket for a married couple filing a joint return equal to twice the size of the corresponding rate bracket for a single individual filing a single return for taxable

[191] Under present law, the rate bracket breakpoint for the 35-percent marginal tax rate is the same for single individuals and married couples filing joint returns.

years beginning in 2003 and 2004. For taxable years beginning after 2004, the applicable percentages will revert to those provided by EGTRRA. Table 8, below, shows the size of the 15-percent bracket.

Table 8.—Size of the 15-Percent Rate Bracket for Married Couples Filing Joint Returns

Taxable year	End point of 15-percent rate bracket for married couples filing joint returns as percentage of end point of 15-percent rate bracket for unmarried individual
2003–2004	200
2005	180
2006	187
2007	193
2008 and 2010 [1]	200

[1] The increases in the 15-percent rate bracket for married couples filing a joint return are repealed for taxable years beginning after December 31, 2010, under the sunset provision of EGTRRA.

Explanation of Provision

The Act increases the size of the 15-percent rate bracket for joint returns to twice the size of the corresponding rate bracket for single returns effective for 2005–2007. Therefore, the size of the 15-percent rate bracket for joint returns is twice the size of the corresponding rate bracket for single returns for taxable years 2005–2010. The modification to the 15-percent rate bracket under the Act is subject to the sunset provision of EGTRRA.

Effective Date

The provision is effective for taxable years beginning after December 31, 2004.

C. Extend Size of 10-Percent Rate Bracket for Individuals (sec. 103 of the Act and sec. 1 of the Code)

Present and Prior Law

In general

Under the Federal individual income tax system, an individual who is a citizen or a resident of the United States generally is subject to tax on worldwide taxable income. Taxable income is total gross income less certain exclusions, exemptions, and deductions. An individual may claim either a standard deduction or itemized deductions.

An individual's income tax liability is determined by computing his or her regular income tax liability and, if applicable, alternative minimum tax liability.

Regular income tax liability

Regular income tax liability is determined by applying the regular income tax rate schedules (or tax tables) to the individual's taxable income. This tax liability is then reduced by any applicable tax credits. The regular income tax rate schedules are divided into several ranges of income, known as income brackets, and the marginal tax rate increases as the individual's income increases. The income bracket amounts are adjusted annually for inflation. Separate rate schedules apply based on filing status: single individuals (other than heads of households and surviving spouses), heads of households, married individuals filing joint returns (including surviving spouses), married individuals filing separate returns, and estates and trusts. Lower rates may apply to capital gains.

Ten-percent regular income tax rate

EGTRRA created a new 10-percent rate that applied to the first $6,000 of taxable income for single individuals, $10,000 of taxable income for heads of households, and $12,000 for married couples filing joint returns, and provided a scheduled increase effective beginning in 2008 under which the $6,000 amount would increase to $7,000 and the $12,000 amount would increase to $14,000, with such amounts adjusted annually for inflation for taxable years beginning after December 31, 2008. JGTRRA accelerated the scheduled increases to 2003 and 2004 (with indexing). For 2004, the size of the 10-percent bracket for single individuals is $7,150 ($14,300 for married individuals filing a joint return). For 2005–2010, the size of the 10-percent bracket reverts to the levels provided under EGTRRA. Thus the amounts drop to $6,000 for single individuals, $10,000 for heads of households and $12,000 for married individuals filing a joint return) for 2005–2007. In 2008, the amounts will increase to $7,000 ($14,000 for married individuals filing a joint return). These amounts ($7,000 for single individuals, $10,000 for heads of households and $14,000 for married individuals) are adjusted annually for inflation for taxable years beginning after December 31, 2008. The 10-percent rate bracket will expire for taxable years beginning after December 31, 2010, under the sunset provision of EGTRRA.

Explanation of Provision

The Act extends the size of the 10-percent rate bracket through 2010. Specifically, the size of the 10-percent rate bracket for 2005 through 2010 is set at the 2003 level ($7,000 for single individuals, $10,000 for heads of households and $14,000 for married individuals) with annual indexing from 2003. The modifications to the 10-percent rate bracket under the Act are subject to the sunset provision of EGTRRA.

Effective Date

The provision is effective for taxable years beginning after December 31, 2004.

D. Extend Alternative Minimum Tax Exemption for Individuals (sec. 104 of the Act and sec. 55 of the Code)

Present and Prior Law

The alternative minimum tax is the amount by which the tentative minimum tax exceeds the regular income tax. An individual's tentative minimum tax is the sum of (1) 26 percent of so much of the taxable excess as does not exceed $175,000 ($87,500 in the case of a married individual filing a separate return) and (2) 28 percent of the remaining taxable excess. The taxable excess is so much of the alternative minimum taxable income ("AMTI") as exceeds the exemption amount. The maximum tax rates on net capital gain and dividends used in computing the regular tax are used in computing the tentative minimum tax. AMTI is the individual's taxable income adjusted to take account of specified preferences and adjustments.

Under prior law, the exemption amounts were: (1) $45,000 ($58,000 for taxable years beginning before 2005) in the case of married individuals filing a joint return and surviving spouses; (2) $33,750 ($40,250 for taxable years beginning before 2005) in the case of other unmarried individuals; (3) $22,500 ($29,000 for taxable years beginning before 2005) in the case of married individuals filing a separate return; and (4) $22,500 in the case of an estate or trust. The exemption amounts are phased out by an amount equal to 25 percent of the amount by which the individual's AMTI exceeds (1) $150,000 in the case of married individuals filing a joint return and surviving spouses, (2) $112,500 in the case of other unmarried individuals, and (3) $75,000 in the case of married individuals filing separate returns, an estate, or a trust. These amounts are not indexed for inflation.

Explanation of Provision

The Act extends the increased AMT exemption amounts to taxable years beginning in 2005.

Effective Date

The provision applies to taxable years beginning after December 31, 2004.

II. UNIFORM DEFINITION OF CHILD

A. Establish Uniform Definition of a Qualifying Child (secs. 201–208 of the Act and secs. 2, 21, 24, 32, 151, and 152 of the Code)

Present and Prior Law

In general

Present and prior law contains five commonly used provisions that provide benefits to taxpayers with children: (1) the dependency exemption; (2) the child credit; (3) the earned income credit; (4) the dependent care credit; and (5) head of household filing status. Under prior law, each provision had separate criteria for determining whether the taxpayer qualified for the applicable tax benefit with respect to a particular child. The separate criteria included factors such as the relationship (if any) the child must bear to the taxpayer, the age of the child, and whether the child must live with the taxpayer. Thus, with respect to the same individual, a taxpayer was required to determine eligibility for each benefit separately, and an individual who qualified a taxpayer for one provision did not automatically qualify the taxpayer for another provision.

Dependency exemption [192]

In general

Under present and prior law, taxpayers are entitled to a personal exemption deduction for the taxpayer, his or her spouse, and each dependent. The deduction for personal exemptions is phased out for taxpayers with incomes above certain thresholds.[193]

Under prior law, in general, a taxpayer was entitled to a dependency exemption for an individual if the individual: (1) satisfied a relationship test or was a member of the taxpayer's household for the entire taxable year; (2) satisfied a support test; (3) satisfied a gross income test or was a child of the taxpayer under a certain age; (4) was a citizen or resident of the U.S. or resident of Canada or Mexico;[194] and (5) did not file a joint return with his or her

[192] Secs. 151 and 152. Under the prior-law statutory structure, section 151 provided for the deduction for personal exemptions with respect to "dependents." The term "dependent" was defined in section 152. Most of the requirements regarding dependents were contained in section 152; section 151 contained additional requirements that had to be satisfied in order to obtain a dependency exemption with respect to a dependent (as so defined). In particular, section 151 contained the gross income test, the rules relating to married dependents filing a joint return, and the requirement for a taxpayer identification number. The other rules discussed here also were contained in section 151.

[193] Sec. 151(d)(3).

[194] Under present and prior law, a legally adopted child who does not satisfy the residency or citizenship requirement may nevertheless qualify as a dependent (provided other applicable

Continued

spouse for the year.[195] In addition, under present and prior law, the taxpayer identification number of the individual must be included on the taxpayer's return.

Relationship or member of household test

Relationship test.—Under prior law, the relationship test was satisfied if an individual was the taxpayer's (1) son or daughter or a descendant of either (e.g., grandchild or great-grandchild); (2) stepson or stepdaughter; (3) brother or sister (including half brother, half sister, stepbrother, or stepsister); (4) parent, grandparent, or other direct ancestor (but not foster parent); (5) stepfather or stepmother; (6) brother or sister of the taxpayer's father or mother; (7) son or daughter of the taxpayer's brother or sister; or (8) the taxpayer's father-in-law, mother-in-law, son-in-law, daughter-in-law, brother-in-law, or sister-in-law.

Under prior law, an adopted child (or a child who was a member of the taxpayer's household and who had been placed with the taxpayer for adoption) was treated as a child of the taxpayer. Under prior law, a foster child was treated as a child of the taxpayer if the foster child was a member of the taxpayer's household for the entire taxable year.

Member of household test.—Under prior law, if the relationship test was not satisfied, then the individual may have been considered the dependent of the taxpayer if the individual was a member of the taxpayer's household for the entire year. Thus, a taxpayer may have been eligible to claim a dependency exemption with respect to an unrelated child who lived with the taxpayer for the entire year.

Under present and prior law, for the member of household test to be satisfied, the taxpayer must both maintain the household and occupy the household with the individual.[196] A taxpayer or other individual does not fail to be considered a member of a household because of "temporary" absences due to special circumstances, including absences due to illness, education, business, vacation, and military service.[197] Similarly, an individual does not fail to be considered a member of the taxpayer's household due to a custody agreement under which the individual is absent for less than six months.[198] Indefinite absences that last for more than the taxable year may be considered "temporary." For example, the IRS has ruled that an elderly woman who was indefinitely confined to a nursing home was temporarily absent from a taxpayer's household. Under the facts of the ruling, the woman had been an occupant of the household before being confined to a nursing home, the confinement had extended for several years, and it was possible that the woman would die before becoming well enough to return to the taxpayer's household. There was no intent on the part of the taxpayer or the woman to change her principal place of abode.[199]

---

requirements are met) if (1) the child's principal place of abode is the taxpayer's home and (2) the taxpayer is a citizen or national of the United States. Sec. 152(b)(3).

[195] This restriction did not apply if the return was filed solely to obtain a refund and no tax liability would exist for either spouse if they filed separate returns. Rev. Rul. 54–567, 1954–2 C.B. 108.

[196] Treas. Reg. sec. 1.152–1(b).

[197] Id.

[198] Id.

[199] Rev. Rul. 66–28, 1966–1 C.B. 31.

Support test

In general.—Under present and prior law, the support test is satisfied if the taxpayer provides over one half of the support of the individual for the taxable year. To determine whether a taxpayer has provided more than one half of an individual's support, the amount the taxpayer contributed to the individual's support is compared with the entire amount of support the individual received from all sources, including the individual's own funds.[200] Governmental payments and subsidies (e.g., Temporary Assistance to Needy Families, food stamps, and housing) generally are treated as support provided by a third party. Expenses that are not directly related to any one member of a household, such as the cost of food for the household, must be divided among the members of the household. If any person furnishes support in kind (e.g., in the form of housing), then the fair market value of that support must be determined.

Multiple support agreements.—In some cases, no one taxpayer provides more than one half of the support of an individual. Instead, two or more taxpayers, each of whom would be able to claim a dependency exemption but for the support test, together provide more than one half of the individual's support. If this occurs, under prior law (and in cases under present law where support remains relevant) the taxpayers may agree to designate that one of the taxpayers who individually provides more than 10 percent of the individual's support can claim a dependency exemption for the child. Each of the others must sign a written statement agreeing not to claim the exemption for that year. The statements must be filed with the income tax return of the taxpayer who claims the exemption.

Special rules for divorced or legally separated parents.—Under present and prior law, special rules apply in the case of a child of divorced or legally separated parents (or parents who live apart at all times during the last six months of the year) who provide over one half the child's support during the calendar year.[201] If such a child is in the custody of one or both of the parents for more than one half of the year, then the parent having custody for the greater portion of the year is deemed to satisfy the support test; however, the custodial parent may release the dependency exemption to the noncustodial parent by filing a written declaration with the IRS.[202] Special support rules also apply in the case of certain pre-1985 agreements between divorced or legally separated parents.

Gross income test

In general, under prior law (and in certain cases under present law), an individual may not be claimed as a dependent of a taxpayer if the individual has gross income that is at least equal to

[200] Under present and prior law, in the case of a son, daughter, stepson, or stepdaughter of the taxpayer who is a full-time student, scholarships are not taken into account for the support test. Sec. 152(d) (prior to amendment by the Act).

[201] For purposes of this rule, a "child" means a son, daughter, stepson, or stepdaughter (including an adopted child or foster child, or child placed with the taxpayer for adoption). Sec. 152(e)(1)(A) (prior to amendment by the Act).

[202] Sec. 152(e)(4) (prior to amendment by the Act).

the personal exemption amount for the taxable year.[203] Under prior law, if the individual was the child of the taxpayer and under age 19 (or under age 24, if a full-time student), the gross income test did not apply.[204] For purposes of this prior-law rule, a "child" means a son, daughter, stepson, or stepdaughter (including an adopted child of the taxpayer, a foster child who resides with the taxpayer for the entire year, or a child placed with the taxpayer for adoption by an authorized adoption agency).

Earned income credit[205]

In general

In general, the earned income credit is a refundable credit for low-income workers. The amount of the credit depends on the earned income of the taxpayer and whether the taxpayer has one, more than one, or no "qualifying children." Under present and prior law, in order to be a qualifying child for the earned income credit, an individual must satisfy a relationship test, a residency test, and an age test. In addition, the name, age, and taxpayer identification number of the qualifying child must be included on the return.

Relationship test

Under prior law, an individual satisfied the relationship test under the earned income credit if the individual was the taxpayer's: (1) son, daughter, stepson, or stepdaughter, or a descendant of any such individual;[206] (2) brother, sister, stepbrother, or stepsister, or a descendant of any such individual, who the taxpayer cared for as the taxpayer's own child; or (3) eligible foster child. An eligible foster child was an individual (1) who was placed with the taxpayer by an authorized placement agency, and (2) who the taxpayer cared for as her or his own child. Under present and prior law, a married child of the taxpayer is not treated as meeting the relationship test unless the taxpayer is entitled to a dependency exemption with respect to the married child or would be entitled to the exemption if the taxpayer had not waived the exemption to the noncustodial parent.[207]

Residency test

Under present and prior law, the residency test is satisfied if the individual has the same principal place of abode as the taxpayer for more than one half of the taxable year. The residence must be in the United States.[208] Temporary absences due to special circumstances, including absences due to illness, education, business,

---

[203] Certain income from sheltered workshops is not taken into account in determining the gross income of permanently and totally disabled individuals. Sec. 151(c)(5) (prior to amendment by the Act).

[204] Sec. 151(c). The IRS has issued guidance stating that for purposes of the dependency exemption, an individual attains a specified age on the anniversary of the date that the child was born (e.g., a child born on January 1, 1987, attains the age of 17 on January 1, 2004). Rev. Rul. 2003–72, 2003–33 I.R.B. 346.

[205] Sec. 32.

[206] A child who is legally adopted or placed with the taxpayer for adoption by an authorized adoption agency is treated as the taxpayer's own child. Sec. 32(c)(3)(B)(iv).

[207] Sec. 32(c)(3)(B).

[208] The principal place of abode of a member of the Armed Services is treated as in the United States during any period during which the individual is stationed outside the United States on active duty. Sec. 32(c)(4).

vacation, and military service are not treated as absences for purposes of determining whether the residency test is satisfied.[209] Under the earned income credit, there is no requirement that the taxpayer maintain the household in which the taxpayer and the qualifying individual reside.

Age test

Under present and prior law, in general, the age test is satisfied if the individual has not attained age 19 as of the close of the calendar year.[210] In the case of a full-time student, the age test is satisfied if the individual has not attained age 24 as of the close of the calendar year. In the case of an individual who is permanently and totally disabled, no age limit applies.

Child credit[211]

Taxpayers with incomes below certain amounts are eligible for a child credit for each qualifying child of the taxpayer. The amount of the child credit is up to $1,000, in the case of taxable years beginning before 2011, and then declines to $500 in taxable year 2011.[212] Under prior law, for purposes of this credit, a qualifying child was an individual: (1) with respect to whom the taxpayer was entitled to a dependency exemption for the year; (2) who satisfied the same relationship test applicable to the earned income credit; and (3) who had not attained age 17 as of the close of the calendar year.[213] In addition, under present and prior law, the child must be a citizen or resident of the United States.[214] A portion of the child credit is refundable under certain circumstances.[215]

Dependent care credit[216]

Under prior law, the dependent care credit could be claimed by a taxpayer who maintained a household that included one or more qualifying individuals and who had employment-related expenses. Under prior law, a qualifying individual included (1) a dependent of the taxpayer under age 13 for whom the taxpayer was entitled to a dependency exemption,[217] (2) a dependent of the taxpayer who

---

[209] IRS Publication 596, Earned Income Credit (EIC), at 14. H.R. Rep. No. 101–964 (October 27, 1990), at 1037.

[210] The IRS has issued guidance stating that for purposes of the earned income credit, an individual attains a specified age on the anniversary of the date that the child was born (e.g., a child born on January 1, 1987, attains the age of 17 on January 1, 2004). Rev. Rul. 2003–72, 2003–33 I.R.B. 346.

[211] Sec. 24.

[212] EGTRRA, Pub. L. No. 107–16, sec. 901(a) (2001). Prior to enactment of the Act, the maximum credit was $700 for taxable years 2005–2008, and $800 for taxable years beginning in 2009.

[213] The IRS has issued guidance stating that for purposes of the child credit, an individual attains a specified age on the anniversary of the date that the child was born (e.g., a child born on January 1, 1987, attains the age of 17 on January 1, 2004). Rev. Rul. 2003–72, 2003–33 I.R.B. 346.

[214] Under present and prior law, the child credit does not apply with respect to a child who is a resident of Canada or Mexico and is not a U.S. citizen, even if a dependency exemption is available with respect to the child. Sec. 24(c)(2). The child credit is, however, available with respect to a child dependent who is not a resident or citizen of the United States if: (1) the child has been legally adopted by the taxpayer; (2) the child's principal place of abode is the taxpayer's home; and (3) the taxpayer is a U.S. citizen or national. See sec. 24(c)(2) and sec. 152(b)(3).

[215] Sec. 24(d).

[216] Sec. 21.

[217] The IRS has issued guidance stating that for purposes of the dependent care credit, an individual attains a specified age on the anniversary of the date that the child was born (e.g.,

Continued

was physically or mentally incapable of caring for himself or herself,[218] or (3) the spouse of the taxpayer, if the spouse was physically or mentally incapable of caring for himself or herself. In addition, under present and prior law, a taxpayer identification number for the qualifying individual must be included on the return.

Under prior law, a taxpayer was considered to maintain a household for a period if over one half the cost of maintaining the household for the period was furnished by the taxpayer (or, if married, the taxpayer and his or her spouse). Costs of maintaining the household included expenses such as rent, mortgage interest (but not principal), real estate taxes, insurance on the home, repairs (but not home improvements), utilities, and food eaten in the home.

Under present and prior law, a special rule applies in the case of a child who is under age 13 or is physically or mentally incapable of caring for himself or herself if the custodial parent has waived his or her dependency exemption to the noncustodial parent.[219] For the dependent care credit, such a child is treated as a qualifying individual with respect to the custodial parent, not the parent entitled to claim the dependency exemption.

Head of household filing status [220]

Under prior law, a taxpayer could claim head of household filing status if the taxpayer was unmarried (and not a surviving spouse) and paid more than one half of the cost of maintaining as his or her home a household which was the principal place of abode for more than one half of the year of (1) an unmarried son, daughter, stepson or stepdaughter of the taxpayer or an unmarried descendant of the taxpayer's son or daughter, (2) an individual described in (1) who is married, if the taxpayer may claim a dependency exemption with respect to the individual (or could claim the exemption if the taxpayer had not waived the exemption to the noncustodial parent), or (3) a relative with respect to whom the taxpayer may claim a dependency exemption.[221] Under present and prior law, if certain other requirements are satisfied, head of household filing status also may be claimed if the taxpayer is entitled to a dependency exemption with respect to one of the taxpayer's parents.

Reasons for Change [222]

Prior law contained five commonly used provisions that provided benefits to taxpayers with children: (1) the dependency exemption; (2) the child credit; (3) the earned income credit; (4) the dependent care credit; and (5) head of household filing status. Each provision had separate criteria for determining whether the taxpayer quali-

---

a child born on January 1, 1987, attains the age of 17 on January 1, 2004). Rev. Rul. 2003–72, 2003–33 I.R.B. 346.

[218] Although such an individual must have been a dependent of the taxpayer as defined in section 152, it was not required that the taxpayer be entitled to a dependency exemption with respect to the individual under section 151. Thus, such an individual may have been a qualifying individual for purposes of the dependent care credit, even though the taxpayer was not entitled to a dependency exemption because the individual did not meet the gross income test.

[219] Sec. 21(e)(5).

[220] Sec. 2(b).

[221] Sec. 2(b)(1)(A)(ii), as qualified by sec. 2(b)(3)(B). An individual for whom the taxpayer is entitled to claim a dependency exemption by reason of a multiple support agreement does not qualify the taxpayer for head of household filing status.

[222] See S. 882, the "Tax Administration Good Government Act," which was reported by the Senate Committee on Finance on May 4, 2004 (S. Rep. No. 108–257).

fied for the applicable tax benefit with respect to a particular child. The separate criteria included factors such as the relationship (if any) the child must bear to the taxpayer, the age of the child, and whether the child must live with the taxpayer. Thus, a taxpayer was required to apply different definitions to the same individual when determining eligibility for these provisions, and an individual who qualified a taxpayer for one provision did not automatically qualify the taxpayer for another provision. The use of different tests to determine whether a taxpayer may claim one or more of these tax benefits with respect to a child caused complexity for taxpayers and the IRS. The different tests relating to qualifying children were a source of errors for taxpayers both because the rules for each provision were different and because of the complexity of particular rules. The variety of rules caused taxpayers inadvertently to claim tax benefits for which they did not qualify, as well as to fail to claim tax benefits for which they did qualify. Adopting a uniform definition of qualifying child for five commonly used provisions (the dependency exemption, the child credit, the earned income credit, the dependent care credit, and head of household filing status) achieves simplification by making it easier for taxpayers to determine whether they qualify for the various tax benefits relating to children, reduces inadvertent taxpayer errors arising from confusion due to differing rules, and makes the applicable provisions easier for the IRS to administer.

Explanation of Provision

In general

In general

The Act establishes a uniform definition of qualifying child for purposes of the dependency exemption, the child credit, the earned income credit, the dependent care credit, and head of household filing status. A taxpayer generally may claim an individual who does not meet the uniform definition of qualifying child (with respect to any taxpayer) as a dependent if the present-law dependency requirements are satisfied. The Act generally does not modify other parameters of each tax benefit (e.g., the earned income requirements of the earned income credit) or the rules for determining whether individuals other than children of the taxpayer qualify for each tax benefit.

Under the uniform definition, in general, a child is a qualifying child of a taxpayer if the child satisfies each of three tests: (1) the child has the same principal place of abode as the taxpayer for more than one half the taxable year; (2) the child has a specified relationship to the taxpayer; and (3) the child has not yet attained a specified age. A tie-breaking rule applies if more than one taxpayer claims a child as a qualifying child.

Under the Act, the present-law support and gross income tests for determining whether an individual is a dependent generally do not apply to a child who meets the requirements of the uniform definition of qualifying child.

Residency test

Under the uniform definition's residency test, a child must have the same principal place of abode as the taxpayer for more than one half of the taxable year. It is intended that, as is the case under present law, temporary absences due to special circumstances, including absences due to illness, education, business, vacation, or military service, are not treated as absences.

Relationship test

In order to be a qualifying child under the Act, the child must be the taxpayer's son, daughter, stepson, stepdaughter, brother, sister, stepbrother, stepsister, or a descendant of any such individual. The Act modifies the definition of adopted child, for purposes of determining whether an adopted child is treated as a child by blood, to mean an individual who is legally adopted by the taxpayer, or an individual who is lawfully placed with the taxpayer for legal adoption by the taxpayer. A foster child who is placed with the taxpayer by an authorized placement agency or by judgment, decree, or other order of any court of competent jurisdiction is treated as the taxpayer's child.[223]

Age test

Under the Act, the age test varies depending upon the tax benefit involved. In general, a child must be under age 19 (or under age 24 in the case of a full-time student) in order to be a qualifying child.[224] In general, no age limit applies with respect to individuals who are totally and permanently disabled within the meaning of section 22(e)(3) at any time during the calendar year. The Act retains the present-law requirements that a child must be under age 13 (if he or she is not disabled) for purposes of the dependent care credit, and under age 17 (whether or not disabled) for purposes of the child credit.

Children who support themselves

Under the Act, a child who provides over one half of his or her own support generally is not considered a qualifying child of another taxpayer. The Act retains the present-law rule, however, that a child who provides over one half of his or her own support may constitute a qualifying child of another taxpayer for purposes of the earned income credit.

Tie-breaking rules

If a child would be a qualifying child with respect to more than one individual (e.g., a child lives with his or her mother and grandmother in the same residence) and more than one person claims a benefit with respect to that child, then the following "tie-breaking" rules apply. First, if only one of the individuals claiming the child as a qualifying child is the child's parent, the child is deemed the qualifying child of the parent. Second, if both parents claim the child and the parents do not file a joint return, then the child is

[223] The Act eliminates the present-law rule requiring that if a child is the taxpayer's sibling or stepsibling or a descendant of any such individual, the taxpayer must care for the child as if the child were his or her own child.

[224] The Act retains the present-law definition of full-time student set forth in section 151(c)(4).

deemed a qualifying child first with respect to the parent with whom the child resides for the longest period of time, and second with respect to the parent with the highest adjusted gross income. Third, if the child's parents do not claim the child, then the child is deemed a qualifying child with respect to the claimant with the highest adjusted gross income.

Interaction with present-law rules

Taxpayers generally may claim an individual who does not meet the uniform definition of qualifying child with respect to any taxpayer as a dependent if the present-law dependency requirements (including the gross income and support tests) are satisfied.[225] Thus, for example, as under present law, a taxpayer may claim a parent as a dependent if the taxpayer provides more than one half of the support of the parent and the parent's gross income is less than the exemption amount. As another example, under the Act a grandparent may claim a dependency exemption with respect to a grandson who does not reside with any taxpayer for over one half the year, if the grandparent provides more than one half of the support of the grandson and the grandson's gross income is less than the exemption amount.

Citizenship and residency

Children who are U.S. citizens living abroad or non-U.S. citizens living in Canada or Mexico may qualify as a qualifying child, as is the case under the present-law dependency tests. A legally adopted child who does not satisfy the residency or citizenship requirement may nevertheless qualify as a qualifying child (provided other applicable requirements are met) if (1) the child's principal place of abode is the taxpayer's home and (2) the taxpayer is a citizen or national of the United States.

Children of divorced or legally separated parents

The Act retains the present-law rule that allows a custodial parent to release the claim to a dependency exemption (and, therefore, the child credit) to a noncustodial parent.[226] Thus, under the Act, custodial waivers that are in place and effective on the date of enactment will continue to be effective after the date of enactment if they continue to satisfy the waiver rule. In addition, the Act retains the custodial waiver rule for purposes of the dependency exemption (and, therefore, the child credit) for decrees of divorce or separate maintenance or written separation agreements that become effective after the date of enactment. Under the Act, as under present law, the custodial waiver rules do not affect eligibility with respect to children of divorced or legally separated parents for purposes of the earned income credit, the dependent care credit, and head of household filing status.

While retaining the substantive effect of the present-law waiver provisions, the Act modifies the mechanical structure of the rules. Under present law, a waiver may be made with respect to the dependency exemption. The waiver then automatically carries over to

[225] Individuals who satisfy the present-law dependency tests and who are not qualifying children are referred to as "qualifying relatives" under the Act.

[226] A technical correction may be necessary so that the statute reflects this intent.

the child credit, because in order to claim the child credit, the taxpayer must be allowed the dependency exemption with respect to the child. Thus, if the dependency exemption is waived, the child credit applies to the taxpayer who is allowed the dependency exemption under the waiver.

The Act obtains the same result, but through a slightly modified statutory structure. Under the Act, if a waiver is made, the waiver applies for purposes of determining whether a child meets the definition of a qualifying child or a qualifying relative under section 152(c) or 152(d) as amended by the provision. While the definition of qualifying child is generally uniform, for purposes of the earned income credit, head of household status, and the dependent care credit, the definition of qualifying child is made without regard to the waiver provision.[227] Thus, as under present law, a waiver that applies for the dependency exemption will also apply for the child credit, and the waiver will not apply for purposes of the other provisions.

Other provisions

The Act retains the applicable present-law requirements that a taxpayer identification number for a child be provided on the taxpayer's return. For purposes of the earned income credit, a qualifying child is required to have a social security number that is valid for employment in the United States (that is, the child must be a U.S. citizen, permanent resident, or have a certain type of temporary visa).

Effect on particular tax benefits

Dependency exemption

For purposes of the dependency exemption, the Act defines a dependent as a qualifying child or a qualifying relative. The qualifying child test eliminates the support test (other than in the case of a child who provides more than one half of his or her own support), and replaces it with the residency requirement described above. Further, the present-law gross income test does not apply to a qualifying child. The rules relating to multiple support agreements do not apply with respect to qualifying children because the support test does not apply to them. Special tie-breaking rules (described above) apply if more than one taxpayer claims a qualifying child under the Act. These tie-breaking rules do not apply if a child constitutes a qualifying child with respect to multiple taxpayers, but only one eligible taxpayer actually claims the qualifying child.

The Act generally permits taxpayers to continue to apply the present-law dependency exemption rules to claim a dependency exemption for a qualifying relative who does not satisfy the qualifying child definition. In such cases, the present-law gross income and support tests, including the special rules for multiple support agreements, the special rules relating to income of handicapped dependents, and the special support test in case of students, continue to apply for purposes of the dependency exemption.

As is the case under present law, a child who provides over half of his or her own support is not considered a dependent of another

---

[227] See secs. 2(b)(1)(A)(i) and 32(c)(3)(A) as amended by the Act, and sec. 21(e)(5).

taxpayer under the Act. Further, an individual shall not be treated as a dependent of any taxpayer if such individual has filed a joint return with the individual's spouse for the taxable year.

Earned income credit

In general, the Act adopts a definition of qualifying child that is similar to the present-law definition under the earned income credit. The present-law requirement that a foster child and certain other children be cared for as the taxpayer's own child is eliminated. The present-law tie-breaker rule applicable to the earned income credit is used for purposes of the uniform definition of qualifying child. The Act retains the present-law requirement that the taxpayer's principal place of abode must be in the United States.

Child credit

The present-law child credit generally uses the same relationships to define an eligible child as the uniform definition. The present-law requirement that a foster child and certain other children be cared for as the taxpayer's own child is eliminated. The age limitation under the Act retains the present-law requirement that the child must be under age 17, regardless of whether the child is disabled.

Dependent care credit

The present-law requirement that a taxpayer maintain a household in order to claim the dependent care credit is eliminated. Thus, if other applicable requirements are satisfied, a taxpayer may claim the dependent care credit with respect to a child who lives with the taxpayer for more than one half the year, even if the taxpayer does not provide more than one half of the cost of maintaining the household.

The rules for determining eligibility for the credit with respect to an individual who is physically or mentally incapable of caring for himself or herself are amended to include a requirement that the taxpayer and the dependent have the same principal place of abode for more than one half the taxable year.

Head of household filing status

Under the Act, a taxpayer is eligible for head of household filing status only with respect to a qualifying child or an individual for whom the taxpayer is entitled to a dependency exemption. Under the Act, a taxpayer may claim head of household filing status if the taxpayer is unmarried (and not a surviving spouse) and pays more than one half of the cost of maintaining as his or her home a household which is the principal place of abode for more than one half the year of (1) a qualifying child, or (2) an individual for whom the taxpayer may claim a dependency exemption. As under present law, a taxpayer may claim head of household status with respect to a parent for whom the taxpayer may claim a dependency exemption and who does not live with the taxpayer, if certain requirements are satisfied.

Technical and conforming amendments

The Act makes a number of technical and conforming amendments regarding the change in the definition of dependent for other purposes of the Code. The conforming amendments provide that an individual may qualify as a dependent for certain purposes (e.g., sec. 105, sec. 125, and sec. 213) without regard to whether the individual has gross income that exceeds an otherwise applicable gross income limitation or is married and files a joint return. In addition, an individual who is treated as a dependent under the conforming amendment provisions generally is not subject to the general rule that a dependent of a taxpayer shall be treated as having no dependents for the taxable year of such individual beginning in such calendar year.[228]

Effective Date

The provision is effective for taxable years beginning after December 31, 2004.

[228] A technical correction may be necessary so that the statute reflects this intent with respect to certain other provisions of the Code, such as with respect to health savings accounts (sec. 223(d)(2)(A)), and the dependent care credit and dependent care assistance programs (sec. 21(b)(1)(B)).

III. EXTENSIONS OF CERTAIN EXPIRING PROVISIONS

A. Extension of the Research Credit (sec. 301 of the Act and sec. 41 of the Code)

Present and Prior Law

Section 41 provided a research tax credited equal to 20 percent of the amount by which a taxpayer's qualified research expenses for a taxable year exceeded its base amount for that year. Taxpayers were permitted to elect an alternative incremental research credit regime in which the taxpayer was assigned a three-tiered fixed-base percentage and the credit rate likewise was reduced. Under the alternative credit regime, a credit rate of 2.65 percent applied to the extent that a taxpayer's current-year research expenses exceed a base amount computed by using a fixed-base percentage of one percent but do not exceed a base amount computed by using a fixed-base percentage of 1.5 percent. A credit rate of 3.2 percent applied to the extent that a taxpayer's current-year research expenses exceeded a base amount computed by using a fixed-base percentage of 1.5 percent but did not exceed a base amount computed by using a fixed-base percentage of two percent. A credit rate of 3.75 percent applied to the extent that a taxpayer's current-year research expenses exceeded a base amount computed by using a fixed-base percentage of two percent.

A 20-percent research tax credit also applied to the excess of (1) 100 percent of corporate cash expenses (including grants or contributions) paid for basic research conducted by universities (and certain nonprofit scientific research organizations) over (2) the sum of (a) the greater of two minimum basic research floors plus (b) an amount reflecting any decrease in nonresearch giving to universities by the corporation as compared to such giving during a fixed-base period, as adjusted for inflation.

The research tax credit expired and generally does not apply to amounts paid or incurred after June 30, 2004.

Reasons for Change[229]

The Congress acknowledged that research is important to the economy. Research is the basis of new products, new services, new industries, and new jobs for the domestic economy. Therefore the Congress believed it was appropriate to extend the prior-law research credit.

[229] See H.R. 4520, the "American Jobs Creation Act of 2004", which was reported by the House Committee on Ways and Means on June 16, 2004 (H.R. Rep. No. 108–548).

Explanation of Provision

The Act extends the prior-law research credit to qualified amounts paid or incurred before January 1, 2006.

Effective Date

The provision is effective for amounts paid or incurred after June 30, 2004.

B. Extension of Parity in the Application of Certain Limits to Mental Health Benefits (sec. 302 of the Act, sec. 9812 of the Code, sec. 712 of ERISA, and section 2705 of the PHSA)

Present and Prior Law

The Mental Health Parity Act of 1996 amended the Employee Retirement Income Security Act of 1974 ("ERISA") and the Public Health Service Act ("PHSA") to provide that group health plans that provide both medical and surgical benefits and mental health benefits cannot impose aggregate lifetime or annual dollar limits on mental health benefits that are not imposed on substantially all medical and surgical benefits. The provisions of the Mental Health Parity Act were initially effective with respect to plan years beginning on or after January 1, 1998, for a temporary period. Since enactment, the mental health parity requirements in ERISA and the PHSA have been extended on more than one occasion and currently are scheduled to expire with respect to benefits for services furnished on or after December 31, 2004.

The Taxpayer Relief Act of 1997 added to the Code the requirements imposed under the Mental Health Parity Act, and imposed an excise tax on group health plans that fail to meet the requirements. The excise tax is equal to $100 per day during the period of noncompliance and is generally imposed on the employer sponsoring the plan if the plan fails to meet the requirements. The maximum tax that can be imposed during a taxable year cannot exceed the lesser of 10 percent of the employer's group health plan expenses for the prior year or $500,000. No tax is imposed if the Secretary determines that the employer did not know, and exercising reasonable diligence would not have known, that the failure existed.

The Code provisions were initially effective with respect to plan years beginning on or after January 1, 1998, for a temporary period.[230] The Code provisions have been extended on a number of occasions, and, under prior law, expired with respect to benefits for services furnished after December 31, 2003.

Reasons for Change[231]

The Congress recognized that the Code provisions relating to mental health parity are important to carrying out the purposes of the Mental Health Parity Act. Thus, the Congress believed that ex-

---

[230] The excise tax does not apply to benefits for services furnished on or after September 30, 2001, and before January 10, 2002.

[231] See H.R. 4520, the American Jobs Creation Act of 2004, which was reported by the House Committee on Ways and Means on June 16, 2004 (H.R. Rep. No. 108–548).

tending the Code provisions relating to mental health parity was warranted.

Explanation of Provision

The Act extends the ERISA and PHSA provisions relating to mental health parity to benefits for services furnished before January 1, 2006. The Act also extends the Code provisions relating to mental health parity to benefits for services furnished on or after the date of enactment and before January 1, 2006. Thus, the excise tax on failures to meet the requirements imposed by the Code provisions does not apply after December 31, 2003, and before the date of enactment.

Effective Date

The provision is effective on the date of enactment (October 4, 2004).

C. Extension of the Work Opportunity Tax Credit (sec. 303 of the Act and sec. 51 of the Code)

Present and Prior Law

Work opportunity tax credit

Targeted groups eligible for the credit

The work opportunity tax credit is available on an elective basis for employers hiring individuals from one or more of eight targeted groups. The eight targeted groups are: (1) certain families eligible to receive benefits under the Temporary Assistance for Needy Families Program; (2) high-risk youth; (3) qualified ex-felons; (4) vocational rehabilitation referrals; (5) qualified summer youth employees; (6) qualified veterans; (7) families receiving food stamps; and (8) persons receiving certain Supplemental Security Income (SSI) benefits.

A qualified ex-felon is an individual certified as: (1) haven been convicted of a felony under State or Federal law; (2) being a member of an economically disadvantaged family; and (3) having a hiring date within one year of release from prison or conviction.

Qualified wages

Generally, qualified wages are defined as cash wages paid by the employer to a member of a targeted group. The employer's deduction for wages is reduced by the amount of the credit.

Calculation of the credit

The credit equals 40 percent (25 percent for employment of 400 hours or less) of qualified first-year wages. Generally, qualified first-year wages are qualified wages (not in excess of $6,000) attributable to service rendered by a member of a targeted group during the one-year period beginning with the day the individual began work for the employer. Therefore, the maximum credit per employee is $2,400 (40 percent of the first $6,000 of qualified first-year wages). With respect to qualified summer youth employees, the maximum credit is $1,200 (40 percent of the first $3,000 of qualified first-year wages).

Minimum employment period

No credit is allowed for qualified wages paid to employees who work less than 120 hours in the first year of employment.

Coordination of the work opportunity tax credit and the welfare-to-work tax credit

An employer cannot claim the work opportunity tax credit with respect to wages of any employee on which the employer claims the welfare-to-work tax credit.

Other rules

The work opportunity tax credit is not allowed for wages paid to a relative or dependent of the taxpayer. Similarly wages paid to replacement workers during a strike or lockout are not eligible for the work opportunity tax credit. Wages paid to any employee during any period for which the employer received on-the-job training program payments with respect to that employee are not eligible for the work opportunity tax credit. The work opportunity tax credit generally is not allowed for wages paid to individuals who had previously been employed by the employer. In addition, many other technical rules apply.

Expiration date

Under prior law, the credit is effective for wages paid or incurred to a qualified individual who begins work for an employer before January 1, 2004.

Reasons for Change[232]

The Congress believed that a temporary extension of this credit will allow the Congress and the Treasury and Labor Departments to continue to examine the effectiveness of the credit in expanding employment opportunities among the eight targeted groups.

Explanation of Provision

The Act extends the work opportunity tax credit for two years (through December 31, 2005).

Effective Date

The extension of the work opportunity tax credit is effective for wages paid or incurred for individuals beginning work after December 31, 2003.

---

[232] See H.R. 4520, the "American Jobs Creation Act of 2004", which was reported by the House Committee on Ways and Means on June 16, 2004 (H.R. Rep. No. 108–548).

D. Extension of the Welfare-to-Work Tax Credit (sec. 303 of the Act and sec. 51A of the Code)

Present and Prior Law

Welfare-to-work tax credit

Targeted group eligible for the credit

The welfare-to-work tax credit is available on an elective basis to employers of qualified long-term family assistance recipients. Qualified long-term family assistance recipients are: (1) members of a family that has received family assistance for at least 18 consecutive months ending on the hiring date; (2) members of a family that has received such family assistance for a total of at least 18 months (whether or not consecutive) after August 5, 1997 (the date of enactment of the welfare-to-work tax credit) if they are hired within 2 years after the date that the 18-month total is reached; and (3) members of a family who are no longer eligible for family assistance because of either Federal or State time limits, if they are hired within 2 years after the Federal or State time limits made the family ineligible for family assistance.

Qualified wages

Qualified wages for purposes of the welfare-to-work tax credit are defined more broadly than for purposes of the work opportunity tax credit. Unlike the definition of wages for the work opportunity tax credit which includes simply cash wages, the definition of wages for the welfare-to-work tax credit includes cash wages paid to an employee plus amounts paid by the employer for: (1) educational assistance excludable under a section 127 program (or that would be excludable but for the expiration of sec. 127); (2) health plan coverage for the employee, but not more than the applicable premium defined under section 4980B(f)(4); and (3) dependent care assistance excludable under section 129. The employer's deduction for wages is reduced by the amount of the credit.

Calculation of the credit

The welfare-to-work tax credit is available on an elective basis to employers of qualified long-term family assistance recipients during the first two years of employment. The maximum credit is 35 percent of the first $10,000 of qualified first-year wages and 50 percent of the first $10,000 of qualified second-year wages. Qualified first-year wages are defined as qualified wages (not in excess of $10,000) attributable to service rendered by a member of the targeted group during the one-year period beginning with the day the individual began work for the employer. Qualified second-year wages are defined as qualified wages (not in excess of $10,000) attributable to service rendered by a member of the targeted group during the one-year period beginning immediately after the first year of that individual's employment for the employer. The maximum credit is $8,500 per qualified employee.

Minimum employment period

No credit is allowed for qualified wages paid to a member of the targeted group who does not work at least 400 hours or 180 days in the first year of employment.

Coordination of the work opportunity tax credit and the welfare-to-work tax credit

An employer cannot claim the work opportunity tax credit with respect to wages of any employee on which the employer claims the welfare-to-work tax credit.

Other rules

The welfare-to-work tax credit incorporates directly or by reference many of these other rules contained on the work opportunity tax credit.

Expiration date

Under prior law, the welfare to work credit is effective for wages paid or incurred to a qualified individual who begins work for an employer before January 1, 2004.

Reasons for Change[233]

The Congress believed that the welfare-to-work credit should be temporarily extended to provide the Congress and Treasury and Labor Departments a better opportunity to continue to assess the operation and effectiveness of the credit in meeting its goals. These goals are: (1) to provide an incentive to hire long-term welfare recipients; (2) to promote the transition from welfare to work by increasing access to employment for these individuals; and (3) to encourage employers to provide these individuals with training, health coverage, dependent care and ultimately better job attachment.

Explanation of Provision

The Act extends the welfare-to-work tax credit for two years (through December 31, 2005).

Effective Date

The extension of the welfare-to-work tax credit is effective for wages paid or incurred for individuals beginning work after December 31, 2003.

E. Qualified Zone Academy Bonds (sec. 304 of the Act and sec. 1397E of the Code)

Present and Prior Law

Generally, "qualified zone academy bonds" are bonds issued by a State or local government, provided that at least 95 percent of the proceeds are used for one or more qualified purposes with respect to a "qualified zone academy" and private entities have promised

---

[233] See H.R. 4520, the "American Jobs Creation Act of 2004", which was reported by the House Committee on Ways and Means on June 16, 2004 (H.R. Rep. No. 108–548).

to contribute to the qualified zone academy certain equipment, technical assistance or training, employee services, or other property or services with a value equal to at least 10 percent of the bond proceeds. Qualified purposes with respect to any qualified zone academy are (1) rehabilitating or repairing the public school facility in which the academy is established, (2) providing equipment for use at such academy, (3) developing course materials for education at such academy, and (4) training teachers and other school personnel. A total of $400 million of qualified zone academy bonds was authorized to be issued annually in calendar years 1998 through December 31, 2003.

Reasons for Change[234]

The Congress believed that extension of authority to issue qualified zone academy bonds was appropriate in light of the educational needs that exist today.

Explanation of Provision

The Act extends the authority to issue qualified zone academy bonds through 2005.

Effective Date

The provision is effective for obligations issued after December 31, 2003.

F. Extension of Cover Over of Excise Tax on Distilled Spirits to Puerto Rico and Virgin Islands (sec. 305 of the Act and sec. 7652 of the Code)

Present and Prior Law

A $13.50 per proof gallon (a proof gallon is a liquid gallon consisting of 50 percent alcohol) excise tax is imposed on distilled spirits produced in or imported into the United States.

The Code provides for cover over (payment) to Puerto Rico and the Virgin Islands of the excise tax imposed on rum imported into the United States, without regard to the country of origin. The amount of the cover over is generally limited under section 7652(f) to $10.50 per proof gallon. However, the limitation is increased to $13.25 per proof gallon during the period July 1, 1999 through December 31, 2003.

Thus, tax amounts attributable to rum produced in Puerto Rico are covered over to Puerto Rico. Tax amounts attributable to rum produced in the Virgin Islands are covered over to the Virgin Islands. Tax amounts attributable to rum produced in neither Puerto Rico nor the Virgin Islands are divided and covered over to the two possessions under a formula. All of the amounts covered over are subject to the limitation.

---

[234] See H.R. 4520, the "American Jobs Creation Act of 2004," which was reported by the House Committee on Ways and Means on June 16, 2004 (H.R. Rep. No. 108–548).

Reasons For Change[235]

The Congress believed that the needs of Puerto Rico and the Virgin Islands justified the extension of the cover over amount of $13.25 per proof gallon through December 31, 2005.

Explanation of Provision

The Act temporarily suspends the $10.50 per proof gallon limitation on the amount of excise taxes on rum covered over to Puerto Rico and the Virgin Islands. Under the Act, the cover over amount of $13.25 per proof gallon is extended for rum brought into the United States after December 31, 2003 and before January 1, 2006. After December 31, 2005, the cover over amount reverts to $10.50 per proof gallon.

Effective Date

The provision is effective for articles brought into the United States after December 31, 2003.

G. Charitable Contributions of Computer Technology and Equipment Used for Educational Purposes (sec. 306 of the Act and sec. 170 of the Code)

Present and Prior Law

A deduction by a corporation for charitable contributions of computer technology and equipment generally is limited to the corporation's basis in the property. However, certain corporations may claim a deduction in excess of basis for a qualified computer contribution. Under prior law, such enhanced deduction expired for contributions made during any taxable year beginning after December 31, 2003.

Reasons for Change[236]

The Congress believed that educational organizations and public libraries continue to have a need for computer equipment and that it was appropriate to extend the enhanced deduction for contributions of such equipment to such institutions.

Explanation of Provision

The Act extends the enhanced deduction for qualified computer contributions to contributions made during any taxable year beginning before January 1, 2006.

Effective Date

The provision is effective for taxable years beginning after December 31, 2003.

---

[235] See H.R. 4520, the "American Jobs Creation Act of 2004," which was reported by the House Committee on Ways and Means on June 16, 2004 (H.R. Rep. No. 108–548).

[236] See H.R. 4520, the "American Jobs Creation Act of 2004," which was reported by the House Committee on Ways and Means on June 16, 2004 (H.R. Rep. No. 108–548).

H. Certain Expenses of Elementary and Secondary School Teachers (sec. 307 of the Act and sec. 62 of the Code)

Present and Prior Law

In general, ordinary and necessary business expenses are deductible (sec. 162). However, in general, unreimbursed employee business expenses are deductible only as an itemized deduction and only to the extent that the individual's total miscellaneous deductions (including employee business expenses) exceed two percent of adjusted gross income. An individual's otherwise allowable itemized deductions may be further limited by the overall limitation on itemized deductions, which reduces itemized deductions for taxpayers with adjusted gross income in excess of a threshold amount. In addition, miscellaneous itemized deductions are not allowable under the alternative minimum tax.

Certain expenses of eligible educators are allowed an above-the-line deduction. Specifically, for taxable years beginning in 2002 and 2003, an above-the-line deduction is allowed for up to $250 annually of expenses paid or incurred by an eligible educator for books, supplies (other than nonathletic supplies for courses of instruction in health or physical education), computer equipment (including related software and services) and other equipment, and supplementary materials used by the eligible educator in the classroom. To be eligible for this deduction, the expenses must be otherwise deductible under 162 as a trade or business expense. A deduction is allowed only to the extent the amount of expenses exceeds the amount excludable from income under section 135 (relating to education savings bonds), 529(c)(1) (relating to qualified tuition programs), and section 530(d)(2) (relating to Coverdell education savings accounts).

An eligible educator is a kindergarten through grade 12 teacher, instructor, counselor, principal, or aide in a school for at least 900 hours during a school year. A school means any school which provides elementary education or secondary education, as determined under State law.

Under prior law, the above-the-line deduction for eligible educators was not allowed for taxable years beginning after December 31, 2003.

Reasons for Change

The Congress recognized that elementary and secondary educations often incur substantial unreimbursed expenses in the course of their teacher duties, and believed that an extension of the deduction for such expenses was warranted to continue to provide tax relief to educators who incur such expenses on behalf of their students.[237]

Explanation of Provision

The Act extends the above-the-line deduction for two years, i.e., for taxable years beginning in 2004 and 2005.

[237] See H.R. 4520, the "American Jobs Creation Act of 2004," which was reported by the House Committee on Ways and Means on June 16, 2004 (H.R. Rep. No. 108–548).

Effective Date

The provision is effective for taxable years beginning in 2004 and 2005.

I. Expensing of Environmental Remediation Costs (sec. 308 of the Act and sec. 198 of the Code)

Present and Law

Taxpayers can elect to treat certain environmental remediation expenditures that would otherwise be chargeable to capital account as deductible in the year paid or incurred (sec. 198). The deduction applies for both regular and alternative minimum tax purposes. The expenditure must be incurred in connection with the abatement or control of hazardous substances at a qualified contaminated site.

A "qualified contaminated site" generally is any property that (1) is held for use in a trade or business, for the production of income, or as inventory and (2) is at a site on which there has been a release (or threat of release) or disposal of certain hazardous substances as certified by the appropriate State environmental agency (so called "brownfields"). However, sites that are identified on the national priorities list under the Comprehensive Environmental Response, Compensation, and Liability Act of 1980 cannot qualify as targeted areas.

Under prior law, eligible expenditures were those paid or incurred before January 1, 2004.

Reasons for Change[238]

The Congress observed that by lowering the net capital cost of a development project the expensing of brownfields remediation costs promotes the goal of environmental remediation and promotes new investment and employment opportunities. In addition, the Congress believed that the increased investment in the qualifying areas has spillover effects that are beneficial to the neighboring communities. Therefore, the Congress believed it was appropriate to extend the present-law provision permitting the expensing of environmental remediation costs.

Explanation of Provision

The Act extends the prior law expensing provision for two years (through December 31, 2005).

Effective Date

Effective for expenses paid or incurred after December 31, 2003.

[238] See H.R. 4520, the "American Jobs Creation Act of 2004," which was reported by the House Committee on Ways and Means on June 16, 2004 (H.R. Rep. No. 108–548).

J. New York Liberty Zone Provisions (sec. 309 of the Act and sec. 1400L of the Code)

Present and Prior Law

An aggregate of $8 billion in tax-exempt private activity bonds is authorized for the purpose of financing the construction and repair of infrastructure in New York City ("Liberty Zone bonds"). The bonds must be issued before January 1, 2005.

Certain bonds used to fund facilities located in New York City are permitted one additional advance refunding before January 1, 2005 ("advance refunding bonds"). In addition to satisfying other requirements, the bond refunded must be (1) a State or local bond that is a general obligation of New York City, (2) a State or local bond issued by the New York Municipal Water Finance Authority or Metropolitan Transportation Authority of the City of New York, or (3) a qualified 501(c)(3) bond which is a qualified hospital bond issued by or on behalf of the State of New York or the City of New York. The maximum amount of advance refunding bonds is $9 billion.

Reasons for Change[239]

The Congress was committed to aiding the City of New York's economic recovery from the terrorist attacks of September 11, 2001. Therefore, the Congress believed that an extension of the authority to issue New York Liberty Bonds was appropriate.

Explanation of Provisions

The Act extends authority to issue Liberty Zone bonds through December 31, 2009. The Act also extends the additional advance refunding authority through December 31, 2005. In addition, the Act provides that bonds of the Municipal Assistance Corporation are eligible for advance refunding.

The purpose in extending the New York Liberty Bond program through December 31, 2009, is to facilitate the full designation of New York Liberty Bond authority. Congress could consider a further extension of the New York Liberty Bond program beyond 2009 if circumstances justify such an extension.

Effective Date

The Liberty Zone bonds and general additional advance refunding provisions are effective on the date of enactment (October 4, 2004). The provision relating to the advance refunding of bonds of the Municipal Assistance Corporation is effective as if included in the amendments made by section 301 of the Job Creation and Worker Assistance Act of 2002.

---

[239] See H.R. 4520, the "American Jobs Creation Act of 2004," which was reported by the House Committee on Ways and Means on June 16, 2004 (H.R. Rep. No. 108–548).

K. Tax Incentives for Investment in the District of Columbia (sec. 310 of the Act and secs. 1400, 1400A, 1400B, 1400C, and 1400F of the Code)

Present and Prior Law

Certain economically depressed census tracts within the District of Columbia were designated as the District of Columbia Enterprise Zone (the "D.C. Zone") within which businesses and individual residents are eligible for special tax incentives. Under prior law, the designation expired on December 31, 2003.

First-time homebuyers of a principal residence in the District of Columbia were eligible for a nonrefundable tax credit of up to $5,000 of the amount of the purchase price. Under prior law, the credit expired for property purchased after December 31, 2003.

Reasons for Change[240]

Congress believed that the incentives should temporarily be extended to provide the Congress and the Treasury Department a better opportunity to continue to assess the overall operation and effectiveness of the tax incentives to revitalize the D.C. Zone and to promote homeownership therein.

Explanation of Provision

The Act extends the D.C. Zone designation and related tax incentives for two years (through December 31, 2005). The provision extends the first-time homebuyer credit for two years (through December 31, 2005).

Effective Date

The extension of the D.C. Zone designation and related tax incentives is generally effective on January 1, 2004, except that the provision relating to tax-exempt financing incentives applies to obligations issued after the date of enactment (October 4, 2004).

L. Combined Employment Tax Reporting (sec. 311 of the Act and sec. 6103(d)(5) of the Code)

Present and Prior Law

Traditionally, Federal tax forms are filed with the Federal government and State tax forms are filed with individual States. This necessitates duplication of items common to both returns.

The Taxpayer Relief Act of 1997 permitted implementation of a limited demonstration project to assess the feasibility and desirability of expanding combined Federal and State reporting. First, it was limited to the sharing of information between the State of Montana and the IRS. Second, it was limited to employment tax reporting. Third, it was limited to disclosure of the name, address, TIN, and signature of the taxpayer, which is information common to both the Montana and Federal portions of the combined form.

[240] See H.R. 4520, the "American Jobs Creation Act of 2004," which was reported by the House Committee on Ways and Means on June 16, 2004 (H.R. Rep. No. 108–548).

Fourth, it was limited to a period of five years (expiring August 5, 2002).

Reasons for Change[241]

The Congress believed that authorizing and expanding this project for a year will provide the Congress with information to assess the usefulness of the program and whether further expansions are warranted.

Explanation of Provision

The Act provides authority through December 31, 2005, for any State to participate in a combined Federal and State employment tax reporting program, provided that the program has been approved by the Secretary. The Secretary may disclose the name, address, TIN and signature of the taxpayer to any agency, body, or commission of a State for purposes of carrying out the approved program with such agency, body, or commission.

Effective Date

The provision is effective on the date of enactment (October 4, 2004).

M. Nonrefundable Personal Credits Allowed Against the Alternative Minimum Tax (sec. 312 of the Act and sec. 26 of the Code)

Present and Prior Law

Present and prior law provides for certain nonrefundable personal tax credits (i.e., the dependent care credit, the credit for the elderly and disabled, the adoption credit, the child tax credit,[242] the credit for interest on certain home mortgages, the HOPE Scholarship and Lifetime Learning credits, the credit for savers, and the D.C. first-time homebuyer credit).

For taxable years beginning in 2003, all the nonrefundable personal credits were allowed to the extent of the full amount of the individual's regular tax and alternative minimum tax.

For taxable years beginning after 2003, the credits (other than the adoption credit, child credit and credit for savers) were allowed only to the extent that the individual's regular income tax liability exceeds the individual's tentative minimum tax, determined without regard to the minimum tax foreign tax credit. The adoption credit, child credit, and IRA credit are allowed to the full extent of the individual's regular tax and alternative minimum tax.

Reasons for Change[243]

The Congress believed that the nonrefundable personal credits should be useable without limitation by reason of the alternative

---

[241] See H.R. 4520, the "American Jobs Creation Act of 2004," which was reported by the House Committee on Ways and Means on June 16, 2004 (H.R. Rep. No. 108–548).

[242] A portion of the child credit may be refundable.

[243] See H.R. 4520, the "American Jobs Creation Act of 2004," which was reported by the House Committee on Ways and Means on June 16, 2004 (H.R. Rep. No. 108–548).

minimum tax. This provision will result in significant simplification.

Explanation of Provision

The Act extends the provision allowing the nonrefundable personal credits to the full extent of the regular tax and the alternative minimum tax for taxable years beginning in 2004 and 2005.

Effective Date

The provision applies to taxable years beginning after December 31, 2003.

N. Extension of Credit for Electricity Produced from Certain Renewable Resources (sec. 313 of the Act and sec. 45 of the Code)

Present and Prior Law

An income tax credit is allowed for the production of electricity from either qualified wind energy, qualified "closed-loop" biomass, or qualified poultry waste facilities. The amount of the credit is 1.8 cents per kilowatt hour for 2004. The credit amount is indexed for inflation.

The credit applies to electricity produced by a wind energy facility placed in service after December 31, 1993, and before January 1, 2004, to electricity produced by a closed-loop biomass facility placed in service after December 31, 1992, and before January 1, 2004, and to a poultry waste facility placed in service after December 31, 1999, and before January 1, 2004. The credit is allowable for production during the 10-year period after a facility is originally placed in service.

Reasons for Change[244]

The Congress recognized that the section 45 production credit has fostered additional electricity generation capacity in the form of non-polluting wind power. The Congress believed it was important to continue this tax credit by extending the placed in service date for such facilities to bring more wind energy to the U. S. electric grid. The Congress further believed that, to encourage entrepreneurial exploration of alternative sources for electricity generation, it was appropriate to extend the present-law provision relating to facilities that use closed-loop biomass as an energy source, to give those potential fuel sources an opportunity in the market place.

[244] While there were no committee reports for H.R. 1308, H.R. 4520 which was reported by the House Committee on Ways and Means on June 16, 2004 (H.R. Rep. No. 108–54) and passed the House of Representatives on June 17, 2004, contained a nearly identical provision. H.R. 4520 as passed by the House did not extend that part of present law relating to poultry waste facilities.

Explanation of Provision

The Act extends the placed in service date for wind energy facilities, "closed-loop" biomass facilities, and poultry waste facilities to include facilities placed in service prior to January 1, 2006.[245]

Effective Date

Effective for facilities placed in service after December 31, 2003.

O. Suspension of 100-Percent-of-Net-Income Limitation on Percentage Depletion for Oil and Gas from Marginal Wells (sec. 314 of the Act and sec. 613A of the Code)

Present and Prior Law

Percentage depletion method for oil and gas properties applies to independent producers and royalty owners. Generally, under the percentage depletion method, 15 percent of the taxpayer's gross income from an oil- or gas-producing property is allowed as a deduction in each taxable year. The amount deducted generally may not exceed 100 percent of the net income from the property in any year (the "net-income limitation"). Under prior law, the 100–percent net-income limitation for marginal wells was suspended for taxable years beginning after December 31, 1997, and before January 1, 2004.

Reasons for Change[246]

Domestic production from marginal wells is an appropriate part of establishing national energy security and reducing dependence on foreign oil. The Congress believed the suspension of the 100-percent net-income limitation for marginal wells should be extended to encourage continued operation of such wells.

Explanation of Provision

The Act extends the suspension of the net-income limitation for marginal wells for taxable years beginning before January 1, 2006.

Effective Date

The provision is effective for taxable years beginning after December 31, 2003.

P. Indian Employment Tax Credit (sec. 315 of the Act and sec. 45A of the Code)

Present and Prior Law

In general, a credit against income tax liability is allowed to employers for the first $20,000 of qualified wages and qualified employee health insurance costs paid or incurred by the employer with respect to certain employees (sec. 45A). The credit is equal to

[245] Sec. 45 was subsequently modified to include additional qualifying facilities by the American Jobs Creation Act of 2004, described in Part Seventeen.

[246] See H.R. 4520, the "American Jobs Creation Act of 2004," which was reported by the House Committee on Ways and Means on June 16, 2004 (H.R. Rep. No. 108–548).

20 percent of the excess of eligible employee qualified wages and health insurance costs during the current year over the amount of such wages and costs incurred by the employer during 1993. The credit is an incremental credit, such that an employer's current-year qualified wages and qualified employee health insurance costs (up to $20,000 per employee) are eligible for the credit only to the extent that the sum of such costs exceeds the sum of comparable costs paid during 1993. No deduction is allowed for the portion of the wages equal to the amount of the credit.

Under prior law, the wage credit was available for wages paid or incurred on or after January 1, 1994, in taxable years that begin before January 1, 2005.

Reasons for Change [247]

The Congress believed that extending the wage credit tax incentive will expand employment opportunities for members of Indian tribes.

Explanation of Provision

The Act extends the Indian employment credit incentive for one year (to taxable years beginning before January 1, 2006).

Effective Date

The provision is effective on the date of enactment (October 4, 2004).

Q. Accelerated Depreciation for Business Property on Indian Reservations (sec. 316 of the Act and sec. 168(j) of the Code)

Present and Prior Law

With respect to certain property used in connection with the conduct of a trade or business within an Indian reservation, depreciation deductions under section 168(j) will be determined using the following recovery periods:

3-year property	2 years
5-year property	3 years
7-year property	4 years
10-year property	6 years
15-year property	9 years
20-year property	12 years
Nonresidential real property	22 years

"Qualified Indian reservation property" eligible for accelerated depreciation includes property which is (1) used by the taxpayer predominantly in the active conduct of a trade or business within an Indian reservation, (2) not used or located outside the reservation on a regular basis, (3) not acquired (directly or indirectly) by the taxpayer from a person who is related to the taxpayer (within the meaning of section 465(b)(3)(C)), and (4) described in the recovery-period table above. In addition, property is not "qualified Indian reservation property" if it is placed in service for purposes of

[247] See H.R. 4520, the "American Jobs Creation Act of 2004," which was reported by the House Committee on Ways and Means on June 16, 2004 (H.R. Rep. No. 108–548).

conducting gaming activities. Certain "qualified infrastructure property" may be eligible for the accelerated depreciation even if located outside an Indian reservation, provided that the purpose of such property is to connect with qualified infrastructure property located within the reservation (e.g., roads, power lines, water systems, railroad spurs, and communications facilities).

The depreciation deduction allowed for regular tax purposes is also allowed for purposes of the alternative minimum tax. Under prior law, the accelerated depreciation for Indian reservations was available with respect to property placed in service on or after January 1, 1994, and before January 1, 2005.

Reasons for Change[248]

The Congress believed that extending the depreciation incentive will encourage economic development within Indian reservations and expand employment opportunities on such reservations.

Explanation of Provision

The Act extends eligibility for the special depreciation periods to property placed in service before January 1, 2006.

Effective Date

The provision is effective on the date of enactment (October 4, 2004).

R. Disclosure of Return Information Relating to Student Loans (sec. 317 of the Act and sec. 6103(l)(13) of the Code)

Present and Prior Law

Present and prior law prohibit the disclosure of returns and return information, except to the extent specifically authorized by the Code.[249] An exception to the general rule prohibiting disclosure is provided for disclosure to the Department of Education (but not to contractors thereof) of a taxpayer's filing status, adjusted gross income and identity information (i.e. name, mailing address, taxpayer identifying number) to establish an appropriate repayment amount for an applicable student loan. Under prior law, the Department of Education disclosure authority was scheduled to expire after December 31, 2004.[250]

Reasons for Change[251]

The Congress believed that the Department of Education should be provided with access to tax return information to assist it in carrying out the income-contingent repayment program. Thus, the Congress believed that it is appropriate to provide a further extension of this disclosure authority.

---

[248] See H.R. 4520, the "American Jobs Creation Act of 2004," which was reported by the House Committee on Ways and Means on June 16, 2004 (H.R. Rep. No. 108–548).

[249] Sec. 6103.

[250] Pub. L. No. 108–89 (2003).

[251] See H.R. 4520, the "American Jobs Creation Act of 2004," which was reported by the House Committee on Ways and Means on June 16, 2004 (H.R. Rep. No. 108–548).

Explanation of Provision

The Act extends the disclosure authority relating to the disclosure of return information to carry out income-contingent repayment of student loans for an additional year. The disclosure authority does not apply to any request made after December 31, 2005.

Effective Date

The provision is effective on the date of enactment (October 4, 2004).

S. Credit for Qualified Electric Vehicles (sec. 318 of the Act and sec. 30 of the Code)

Present and Prior Law

A 10-percent tax credit is provided for the cost of a qualified electric vehicle, up to a maximum credit of $4,000. A qualified electric vehicle generally is a motor vehicle that is powered primarily by an electric motor drawing current from rechargeable batteries, fuel cells, or other portable sources of electrical current. The full amount of the credit is available for purchases prior to 2004. Under prior law, the credit phases down in the years 2004 through 2006, and is unavailable for purchases after December 31, 2006. Under the phase down, the credit for 2004 is 75 percent of the otherwise allowable credit.

Reasons for Change[252]

The Congress believed it was necessary to continue to provide the full benefit of the tax subsidy to the purchase of these innovative vehicles to enable such vehicles to demonstrate their road-worthiness to the consumer. However, in the future, the Congress expects such vehicles to compete in the market without subsidy.

Explanation of Provision

The Act repeals the phase down of the allowable tax credit for electric vehicles in 2004 and 2005. Thus, a taxpayer who purchases a qualifying vehicle may claim 100 percent of the otherwise allowable credit for vehicles purchased in 2004 and 2005. For vehicles purchased in 2006 the credit remains at 25 percent of the otherwise allowable amount as under present law.

Effective Date

The provision is effective for vehicles placed in service after December 31, 2003.

---

[252] See H.R. 4520, the "American Jobs Creation Act of 2004," which was reported by the House Committee on Ways and Means on June 16, 2004 (H.R. Rep. No. 108–548).

T. Deduction for Qualified Clean-Fuel Vehicle Property (sec. 319 of the Act and sec. 179A of the Code)

Present and Prior Law

Certain costs of qualified clean-fuel vehicle may be expensed and deducted when such property is placed in service. Qualified clean-fuel vehicle property includes motor vehicles that use certain clean-burning fuels (natural gas, liquefied natural gas, liquefied petroleum gas, hydrogen, electricity and any other fuel at least 85 percent of which is methanol, ethanol, any other alcohol or ether). The Secretary has determined that certain hybrid (gas-electric) vehicles are qualified clean-fuel vehicles.

The maximum amount of the deduction is $50,000 for a truck or van with a gross vehicle weight over 26,000 pounds or a bus with a seating capacity of at least 20 adults; $5,000 in the case of a truck or van with a gross vehicle weight between 10,000 and 26,000 pounds; and $2,000 in the case of any other motor vehicle. Under prior law, the deduction phases down in the years 2004 through 2006, and is unavailable for purchases after December 31, 2006. Under the phase down, the deduction permitted for 2004 is 75 percent of the otherwise allowable amount.

Reasons for Change[253]

The Congress believed it was necessary to continue to provide the full benefit of the tax subsidy to the purchase of these innovative vehicles to enable such vehicles to demonstrate their road-worthiness to the consumer. However, in the future, the Congress expects such vehicles to compete in the market without subsidy.

Explanation of Provision

The Act repeals the phase down of the allowable deduction for clean-fuel vehicles in 2004 and 2005. Thus, a taxpayer who purchases a qualifying vehicle may claim 100 percent of the otherwise allowable deduction for vehicles purchased in 2004 and 2005. For vehicles purchased in 2006 the deduction remains at 25 percent of the otherwise allowable amount as under present law.

Effective Date

The provision is effective for vehicles placed in service after December 31, 2003.

U. Disclosures Relating to Terrorist Activities (sec. 320 of the Act and sec. 6103(i)(3) and (i)(7) of the Code)

Present and Prior Law

Present and prior law prohibit the disclosure of returns and return information except to the extent specifically authorized by the Code. In connection with terrorist activities, the Code permits the IRS to disclose return information, other than taxpayer return in-

[253] See H.R. 4520, the "American Jobs Creation Act of 2004," which was reported by the House Committee on Ways and Means on June 16, 2004 (H.R. Rep. No. 108–548).

formation,[254] to officers and employees of any Federal law enforcement agency upon a written request.[255] The Code requires the request to be made by the head of the Federal law enforcement agency (or his delegate) involved in the response to or investigation of terrorist incidents, threats, or activities, and set forth the specific reason or reasons why such disclosure may be relevant to a terrorist incident, threat, or activity. Disclosure of the information is permitted to officers and employees of the Federal law enforcement agency who are personally and directly involved in the response to or investigation of terrorist incidents, threats, or activities. The information is to be used by such officers and employees solely for such response or investigation.

The Code permits the head of the Federal law enforcement agency to redisclose the information received under such authority to officers and employees of any State or local law enforcement agency personally and directly engaged in the response to or investigation of the terrorist incident, threat, or activity.[256] The State or local law enforcement agency is required to be part of an investigative or response team with the Federal law enforcement agency for these disclosures to be made.

Return information includes a taxpayer's identity.[257] If a taxpayer's identity is taken from a return or other information filed with or furnished to the IRS by or on behalf of the taxpayer, it is taxpayer return information. Under prior law, since taxpayer return information was not covered by the disclosure authorization for Federal law enforcement agencies, taxpayer identity information submitted by or on behalf of the taxpayer could not be disclosed pursuant to that authority and thus could not be associated with other information being provided to such agencies.

The Code also allows the IRS to disclose return information (other than taxpayer return information) upon the written request of an officer or employee of the Department of Justice or Treasury who is appointed by the President with the advice and consent of the Senate, or who is the Director of the U.S. Secret Service, if such individual is responsible for the collection and analysis of intelligence and counterintelligence concerning any terrorist incident, threat, or activity.[258] A taxpayer's identity for this purpose is not considered taxpayer return information. Such written request is required to set forth the specific reason or reasons why such disclosure may be relevant to a terrorist incident, threat, or activity. Disclosures under this authority are permitted to be made to those officers and employees of the Department of Justice, Department of the Treasury, and Federal intelligence agencies who are personally and directly engaged in the collection or analysis of intelligence and counterintelligence information or investigation concerning any terrorist incident, threat, or activity. Such disclosures are permitted solely for the use of such officers and employees in such investigation, collection, or analysis.

---

[254] Sec. 6103(b)(3).
[255] Sec. 6103(i)(7)(A).
[256] Sec. 6103(i)(7)(A)(ii).
[257] Sec. 6103(b)(2)(A).
[258] Sec. 6103(i)(7)(B).

The IRS, on its own initiative, is permitted to disclose in writing return information (other than taxpayer return information) that may be related to a terrorist incident, threat, or activity to the extent necessary to apprise the head of the appropriate investigating Federal law enforcement agency.[259] A taxpayer's identity for this purpose is not considered taxpayer return information. The head of the agency is permitted to redisclose such information to officers and employees of such agency to the extent necessary to investigate or respond to the terrorist incident, threat, or activity.

Except for the limited exceptions noted above relating to a taxpayer's identity, if taxpayer return information is to be disclosed, the disclosure is required to be made pursuant to the ex parte order of a Federal district court judge or magistrate.

Under prior law, no disclosures could be made under any of the above provisions after December 31, 2003.

Reasons for Change[260]

The Congress believed that a renewal of this disclosure authority will provide additional time to evaluate the effectiveness of the provision and whether any modifications need to be implemented to enhance the provision.

Explanation of Provision

The Act extends the disclosure authority relating to terrorist activities. Under the Act, no disclosures can be made after December 31, 2005.

The Act also makes a technical change to clarify that a taxpayer's identity is not treated as taxpayer return information for purposes of disclosures to law enforcement agencies regarding terrorist activities.

Effective Dates

The provision extending authority is effective for disclosures made on or after the date of enactment (October 4, 2004). The technical change is effective as if included in section 201 of the Victims of Terrorism Tax Relief Act of 2001.

V. Extension of Joint Review of Strategic Plans and Budget for the Internal Revenue Service (sec. 321 of the Act and secs. 8021 and 8022 of the Code)

Prior Law

The Code required the Joint Committee on Taxation to conduct a joint review[261] of the strategic plans and budget of the IRS from 1999 through 2003.[262] The Code also required the Joint Committee

---

[259] Sec. 6103(i)(3)(C).

[260] See H.R. 4520, the "American Jobs Creation Act of 2004," which was reported by the House Committee on Ways and Means on June 16, 2004 (H.R. Rep. No. 108–548).

[261] The joint review was required to include two members of the majority and one member of the minority of the Senate Committees on Finance, Appropriations, and Governmental Affairs, and of the House Committees on Ways and Means, Appropriations, and Government Reform and Oversight.

[262] Sec. 8021(f).

to provide an annual report[263] from 1999 through 2003 with respect to:

- Strategic and business plans for the IRS;
- Progress of the IRS in meeting its objectives;
- The budget for the IRS and whether it supports its objectives;
- Progress of the IRS in improving taxpayer service and compliance;
- Progress of the IRS on technology modernization; and
- The annual filing season.

Reasons for Change[264]

The Congress believed that a joint review of the IRS should be held for one additional year and that the report provided by the Joint Committee on Taxation should be tailored to the specific issues addressed in the joint review.

Explanation of Provision

The Act requires that the Joint Committee conduct a joint review before June 1, 2005. The Act also requires that the Joint Committee provide an annual report with respect to such joint review, and specifies that the content of the annual report is the matters addressed in the joint review.[265]

Effective Date

The provision is effective on the date of enactment (October 4, 2004).

W. Extension of Archer Medical Savings Accounts ("MSAs") (sec. 322 of the Act and sec. 220 of the Code)

Present and Prior Law

In general

Within limits, contributions to an Archer MSA are deductible in determining adjusted gross income if made by an eligible individual and are excludable from gross income and wages for employment tax purposes if made by the employer of an eligible individual. Earnings on amounts in an Archer MSA are not currently taxable. Distributions from an Archer MSA for medical expenses are not includible in gross income. Distributions not used for medical expenses are includible in gross income. In addition, distributions not used for medical expenses are subject to an additional 15-percent tax unless the distribution is made after age 65, death, or disability.

Eligible individuals

Archer MSAs are available to employees covered under an employer-sponsored high deductible plan of a small employer and self-

[263] Sec. 8022(3)(C).

[264] See H.R. 4520, the "American Jobs Creation Act of 2004," which was reported by the House Committee on Ways and Means on June 16, 2004 (H.R. Rep. No. 108–548).

[265] Accordingly, the provision deletes the specific list of matters required to be covered in the annual report.

employed individuals covered under a high deductible health plan.[266] An employer is a small employer if it employed, on average, no more than 50 employees on business days during either the preceding or the second preceding year. An individual is not eligible for an Archer MSA if he or she is covered under any other health plan in addition to the high deductible plan.

Tax treatment of and limits on contributions

Individual contributions to an Archer MSA are deductible (within limits) in determining adjusted gross income (i.e., "above-the-line"). In addition, employer contributions are excludable from gross income and wages for employment tax purposes (within the same limits). Contributions to an Archer MSA may not be made through a cafeteria plan. In the case of an employee, contributions can be made to an Archer MSA either by the individual or by the individual's employer.

The maximum annual contribution that can be made to an Archer MSA for a year is 65 percent of the deductible under the high deductible plan in the case of individual coverage and 75 percent of the deductible in the case of family coverage.

Definition of high deductible plan

For 2004, a high deductible plan is a health plan with an annual deductible of at least $1,700 and no more than $2,600 in the case of individual coverage and at least $3,450 and no more than $5,150 in the case of family coverage. In addition, the maximum out-of-pocket expenses with respect to allowed costs (including the deductible) must be no more than $3,450 in the case of individual coverage and no more than $6,300 in the case of family coverage (for 2004).[267] A plan does not fail to qualify as a high deductible plan merely because it does not have a deductible for preventive care as required by State law. A plan does not qualify as a high deductible health plan if substantially all of the coverage under the plan is for permitted coverage (as described above). In the case of a self-insured plan, the plan must in fact be insurance (e.g., there must be appropriate risk shifting) and not merely a reimbursement arrangement.

Cap on taxpayers utilizing Archer MSAs and expiration of pilot program

The number of taxpayers benefiting annually from an Archer MSA contribution is limited to a threshold level (generally 750,000 taxpayers). The number of Archer MSAs established has not exceeded the threshold level.

Under prior law, after 2003, no new contributions could be made to Archer MSAs except by or on behalf of individuals who previously had Archer MSA contributions and employees who are employed by a participating employer.

Trustees of Archer MSAs are generally required to make reports to the Treasury by August 1 regarding Archer MSAs established by July 1 of that year. If any year is a cut-off year, the Secretary is

[266] Self-employed individuals include more than two-percent shareholders of S corporations who are treated as partners for purposes of fringe benefit rules pursuant to section 1372.

[267] These amounts are indexed for inflation, rounded to the nearest $50.

required to make and publish such determination by October 1 of such year.

Reasons for Change[268]

The Congress believed that individuals should be encouraged to save for future medical care expenses and that individuals should be allowed to save for such expenses on a tax-favored basis. The Congress believed that consumers who spend their own savings on health care will make cost-conscious decisions, thus reducing the rising cost of health care. The Congress believed that Archer MSAs have been an important tool in allowing certain individuals to save for future medical expenses on a tax-favored basis.

The Congress was aware that recently enacted health savings accounts offer more advantageous tax treatment than Archer MSAs and that amounts can be rolled over into a health savings account from an Archer MSA on a tax-free basis. Still, the Congress believed that individuals should be allowed the choice to continue the use of Archer MSAs. Thus, the Congress believed that it was appropriate to extend Archer MSAs.

Explanation of Provision

The Act extends Archer MSAs through December 31, 2005. The Act also provides that the reports required by MSA trustees for 2004 are treated as timely if made within 90 days after the date of enactment. In addition, the determination of whether 2004 is a cut-off year and the publication of such determination is to be made within 120 days of the date of enactment. If 2004 is a cut-off year, the cut-off date will be the last day of such 120-day period.

Effective Date

The provision is generally effective on January 1, 2004. The provisions relating to reports and the determination by the Secretary are effective on the date of enactment (October 4, 2004).

[268] See H.R. 4520, the "American Jobs Creation Act of 2004", which was reported by the House Committee on Ways and Means on June 16, 2004 (H.R. Rep. No. 108–548).

IV. TAX TECHNICAL CORRECTIONS
(secs. 401–408 of the Act)

Present and Prior Law

Certain recently enacted tax legislation needs technical, conforming, and clerical amendments in order properly to carry out the intention of the Congress.[269]

Explanation of Provisions

The Act includes technical corrections to recently enacted tax legislation. Except as otherwise provided, the amendments made by the technical corrections contained in the Act take effect as if included in the original legislation to which each amendment relates. The following is a description of the provisions contained in the technical corrections title:

Amendments Related to the Medicare Prescription Drug, Improvement, and Modernization Act of 2003

Additional tax relating to health savings accounts.—Code section 26(b) provides that "regular tax liability" does not include certain "additional taxes" and similar amounts. Under prior law, regular tax liability did not include the additional tax on Archer MSA distributions not used for qualified medical expenses (sec. 220(f)(4)). The provision adds to the list of such amounts the additional tax on distributions not used for qualified medical expenses (sec. 223(f)(4)) under the rules relating to health savings accounts.

Health coverage tax credit.—Code section 35(g)(3) provides that any amount distributed from an Archer MSA will not be taken into account for purposes of determining the amount of health coverage tax credit ("HCTC") an individual is eligible to receive. Under the provision, section 35(g)(3) is amended to provide that amounts distributed from health savings accounts are not to be taken into account for purposes of determining the amount of HCTC an individual is entitled to receive.

Amendments Related to the Jobs and Growth Tax Relief Reconciliation Act of 2003

Dividends taxed at capital gain rates.—Section 302 of the Jobs and Growth Tax Relief Reconciliation Act of 2003 ("JGTRRA") generally provides that qualified dividend income of taxpayers other than corporations is taxed at the same tax rates as the net capital gain. The provision makes the following amendments to the provisions adopted by that section:[270]

---

[269] Tax technical corrections legislation, the "Tax Technical Corrections Act of 2003," was introduced in the House of Representatives (H.R. 3654) on December 8, 2003, and in the Senate (S. 1984) on December 9, 2003.

The provision clarifies that the determination of net capital gain, for purposes of determining the amount taxed at the 25-percent rate (section 1(h)(1)(D)(i)), is made without regard to qualified dividend income.

The deduction for estate taxes paid on gain that is income in respect of a decedent reduces the amount of gain otherwise taken into account in computing the amount eligible for the lower tax rates on net capital gain (sec. 691(c)(4)). Since it is not entirely clear whether this provision also applies to qualified dividends eligible for the lower tax rates on net capital gain, the provision clarifies that the provision does so apply.

The provision clarifies that the extraordinary dividend rule applies to trusts and estates as well as individuals.

The provision rewrites portions of the provisions relating to the treatment of dividends received from a regulated investment company ("RIC") or a real estate investment trust ("REIT") to set forth the rules directly rather than be reference to rules applicable to dividends received by corporate shareholders.

The provision provides that all distributions by a RIC or REIT of the earnings and profits from C corporation years can be treated as qualifying dividends eligible for the lower rate.

The provision extends the 60-day period for notifying shareholders of the amount of the qualified dividend income distributed by a RIC or REIT for taxable years ending on or before November 30, 2003, to the date the 1099–DIV for 2003 is required.

The provision provides that, in the case of partnerships, S corporations, common trust funds, trusts, and estates, section 302 of JGTRRA applies to taxable years ending after December 31, 2002, except that dividends received by the entity prior to January 1, 2003, are not treated as qualified dividend income. JGTRRA provided a similar rule in the case of RICs and REITs.

Satisfaction of certain holding period requirements if stock is acquired on the day before ex-dividend date.—Under several similar holding period requirements relating to the tax consequences of receiving dividends, a taxpayer who acquires stock the day before the ex-dividend date cannot satisfy these holding period requirements with respect to the dividend. The provision modifies the stock holding period requirements to permit taxpayers to satisfy the requirements when they acquire stock on the day before the ex-dividend date of the stock. Specifically, the provision modifies the holding period requirement for the dividends-received deduction under section 246(c) (as modified by section 1015 of the Taxpayer Relief Act of 1997) by changing from 90 days to 91 days (and from 180 days to 181 days in the case of certain dividends on preferred stock) the period within which a taxpayer may satisfy the requirement. In addition, the provision modifies the holding period requirement for foreign tax credits with respect to dividends under section 901(k) (enacted in section 1053 of the Taxpayer Relief Act of 1997) by changing from 30 days to 31 days (and from 90 days to 91 days in the case of certain dividends on preferred stock) the period within which a taxpayer may satisfy the requirement. The provision modi-

[270] IR–2004–22 (February 19, 2004) announced that the IRS agreed to make the technical correction provisions relating to dividends contained in the Technical Corrections Act of 2003, as introduced, available to taxpayers in advance of their passage.

fies the holding period requirement for dividends to be taxed at the tax rates applicable to net capital gain under section 1(h)(11) (enacted in section 302 of JGTRRA) by changing from 120 days to 121 days (and from 180 days to 181 days in the case of certain dividends on preferred stock) the period within which a taxpayer may satisfy the requirement.

Amendments Related to the Job Creation and Worker Assistance Act of 2002

Bonus depreciation.—Section 101 of the Job Creation and Worker Assistance Act of 2002 ("JCWA") provides generally for 30-percent additional first-year depreciation for qualifying property. Qualifying property is defined to include certain property subject to the capitalization rules of section 263A by reason of having an estimated production period exceeding 2 years or an estimated production period exceeding 1 year and a cost exceeding $1 million (secs. 168(k)(2)(B)(i)(III) and 263A(f)(1)(B)(ii) or (iii)). An unintended interpretation of this rule could preclude property from qualifying for bonus depreciation if it meets this description but is subject to the capitalization rules of section 263A by reason of section 263A(f)(1)(B)(i) (having a long useful life). The provision clarifies that qualifying property includes such property that is subject to the capitalization rules of section 263A and is described in the provisions requiring an estimated production period exceeding 2 years or an estimated production period exceeding 1 year and a cost exceeding $1 million.

Section 101 of JCWA provides a binding contract rule in determining property that qualifies for it. The requirements that must be satisfied in order for property to qualify include that (1) the original use of the property must commence with the taxpayer on or after September 11, 2001, (2) the taxpayer must acquire the property after September 10, 2001, and before September 11, 2004, and (3) no binding written contract for the acquisition of the property is in effect before September 11, 2001 (or, in the case of self-constructed property, manufacture, construction, or production of the property does not begin before September 11, 2001). In addition, JCWA provides a special rule in the case of certain leased property. In the case of any property that is originally placed in service by a person and that is sold to the taxpayer and leased back to such person by the taxpayer within three months after the date that the property was placed in service, the property is treated as originally placed in service by the taxpayer not earlier than the date that the property is used under the leaseback. JCWA did not specifically address the syndication of a lease by the lessor.

The provision clarifies that property qualifying for additional first-year depreciation does not include any property if the user or a related party to the user or owner of such property had a written binding contract in effect for the acquisition of the property at any time on or before September 10, 2001 (or, in the case of self-constructed property, the manufacture, construction, or production of the property began on or before September 10, 2001). For example, if a taxpayer sells to a related party property that was under construction on or prior to September 10, 2001, the property does not qualify for the additional first-year depreciation deduction. Similarly, if a taxpayer sells to a related party property that was subject to a binding written contract on or prior to September 10, 2001, the property does not qualify for the additional first-year depreciation deduction. As a further example, if a taxpayer sells property and leases the property back in a sale-leaseback arrangement, and the lessee had a binding written contract in effect for the acquisition of such property on or prior to September 10, 2001, then the lessor is not entitled to the additional first-year depreciation deduction.

In addition, the provision provides that if property is originally placed in service by a lessor (including by operation of section Code 168(k)(2)(D)(i)), such property is sold within three months after the date that the property was placed in service, and the user of such property does not change, then the property is treated as originally placed in service by the taxpayer not earlier than the date of such sale.

Five-year carryback of net operating losses ("NOLs").—Section 102 of JCWA temporarily extends the NOL carryback period to five years (from two years, or three years in certain cases) for NOLs arising in taxable years ending in 2001 and 2002. The JCWA was enacted in March 2002, after some taxpayers had filed returns for 2001.

The provision (1) clarifies that only the NOLs arising in taxable years ending in 2001 and 2002 qualify for the 5-year period, and (2) provides that any election to forego any carrybacks of NOLs arising in 2001 or 2002 can be revoked prior to November 1, 2002. The provision also allows taxpayers until November 1, 2002, to use the tentative carryback adjustment procedures of section 6411 for NOLs arising in 2001 and 2002 (without regard to the 12-month limitation in section 6411). In addition, the provision clarifies that an election to disregard the 5-year carryback for certain NOLs is treated as timely made if made before November 1, 2002 (notwithstanding that section 172(j) requires the election to be made by the due date (including extensions) for filing the taxpayer's return for the year of the loss).[271]

The provision also makes several clerical changes to the NOL provisions relating to the alternative minimum tax.

New York Liberty Zone bonus depreciation.—Section 301 of JCWA provides tax benefits for the area of New York City damaged in terrorist attacks on September 11, 2001 (an area defined in the provision and named the New York Liberty Zone). Under these rules, an additional first-year depreciation deduction is allowed equal to 30 percent of the adjusted basis of qualified New York Liberty Zone ("Liberty Zone") property. A taxpayer is allowed to elect out of the additional first-year depreciation for any class of property for any taxable year. In addition, the Act provides a special rule in the case of certain leased property. In the case of any property that is originally placed in service by a person and that is sold to the taxpayer and leased back to such person by the taxpayer within three months after the date that the property was placed in service, the property would be treated as originally placed

---

[271] The corrections are consistent with the guidance issued by the IRS (Rev. Proc. 2002–40, 2002–1 C.B. 1096).

in service by the taxpayer not earlier than the date that the property is used under the leaseback. JCWA did not specifically address the syndication of a lease by the lessor.

The provision clarifies that property qualifying for additional first-year depreciation does not include any property if the user or a related party to the user or owner of such property had a written binding contract in effect for the acquisition of the property at any time before September 11, 2001 (or in the case of self constructed property the manufacture, construction, or production of the property began before September 11, 2001). In addition, the provision provides that if property is originally placed in service by a lessor (including by operation of section 168(k)(2)(D)(i)), such property is sold within three months after the date that the property was placed in service, and the user of such property does not change, then the property is treated as originally placed in service by the taxpayer not earlier than the date of such sale.

New York Liberty Zone expensing.—Section 301 of JCWA increases the amount a taxpayer may expense under section 179 to the lesser of $35,000 or the cost of Liberty Zone property placed in service for the year. In addition, section 301(a) of the Act states that if property qualifies for both the general additional first-year depreciation and Liberty Zone additional first-year depreciation, it is deemed to be eligible for the general additional first-year depreciation and is not considered Liberty Zone property (i.e., only one 30-percent additional first-year depreciation deduction is allowed). Because only Liberty Zone property is eligible for the increased section 179 expensing amount, this rule has the unintended consequence of denying the increased section 179 expensing to Liberty Zone property. The provision corrects this unintended result (such that qualifying Liberty Zone property qualifies for both the 30-percent additional first-year depreciation and the additional section 179 expensing).

Provide election out of Liberty Zone five-year depreciation for leasehold improvements.—Code section 1400L(c), as added by section 301 of JCWA, provides for a 5-year recovery period for depreciation of qualified New York Liberty Zone leasehold improvement property that is placed in service after September 10, 2001, and before January 1, 2007 (and meets certain other requirements). Unlike the rules relating to bonus depreciation and to Liberty Zone bonus depreciation property (see Code sections 168(k)(2)(C)(iii) and 1400L(b)(2)(C)(iv)), which permit a taxpayer to elect out, this 5-year depreciation rule is not elective. The provision adds a rule permitting taxpayers to elect out of the 5-year recovery period.

Interest rate for defined benefit plan funding requirements.—Section 405(c) of JCWA increases the interest rate used in determining the amount of unfunded vested benefits for PBGC variable rate premium purposes for plan years beginning in 2002 or 2003 from 85 percent to 100 percent of the interest rate on 30-year Treasury securities for the month preceding the month in which the applicable plan year begins. The provision makes conforming changes so that this rule applies for purposes of notices and reporting required under Title IV of ERISA with respect to underfunded plans.

Exclusion for employer-provided adoption assistance.—The provision corrects an incorrect reference in a technical correction to a provision relating to the exclusion for employer-provided adoption assistance.

Amendments Related to the Economic Growth and Tax Relief Reconciliation Act of 2001

Coverdell education savings accounts.—The provision corrects the application of a conforming change to the rule coordinating Coverdell education savings accounts with Hope and Lifetime Learning credits and qualified tuition programs. The conforming change was made in connection with the expansion of Coverdell education savings accounts to elementary and secondary education expenses in section 401 of the Economic Growth and Tax Relief Reconciliation Act of 2001 ("EGTRRA").

Base period for cost-of-living adjustments to Indian employment credit rule.—The Indian employment credit is not available with respect to an employee whose wages exceed $30,000 (sec. 45A). For years after 1994, this $30,000 amount is adjusted for cost-of-living increases at the same time, and in the same manner, as cost-of-living adjustments to the dollar limits on qualified retirement plan benefits and contributions under section 415. Section 611 of EGTRAA increases the dollar limits under section 415 and adds a new base period for making cost-of-living adjustments. The provision clarifies that the pre-existing base period applies for purposes of the Indian employment credit.

Rounding rule for retirement plan benefit and contribution limits.—Section 611 of EGTRRA increases the dollar limits on qualified retirement plan benefits and contributions under Code section 415, and adds a new rounding rule for cost-of-living adjustments to the dollar limit on annual additions to defined contribution plans. This new rounding rule is in addition to a pre-existing rounding rule that applies to benefits payable under defined benefit plans. The provision clarifies that the pre-existing rounding rule applies for purposes of other Code provisions that refer to Code section 415 and do not contain a specific rounding rule.

Excise tax on nondeductible contributions.—Under section 614 of EGTRRA, the limits on deductions for employer contributions to qualified retirement plans do not apply to elective deferrals, and elective deferrals are not taken into account in applying the deduction limits to other contributions. The provision makes a conforming change to the Code provision that applies an excise tax to nondeductible contributions.

SIMPLE plan contributions for domestic or similar workers.—Section 637 of EGTRRA provides an exception to the application of the excise tax on nondeductible retirement plan contributions in the case of contributions to a SIMPLE IRA or SIMPLE section 401(k) plan that are nondeductible solely because they are not made in connection with a trade or business of the employer (e.g., contributions on behalf of a domestic worker). Section 637 of EGTRRA did not specifically modify the present-law requirement that compensation for purposes of determining contributions to a SIMPLE plan must be wages subject to income tax withholding, even though wages paid to domestic workers are not subject to income tax withholding. The provision revises the definition of compensation for purposes of determining contributions to a SIMPLE plan to include wages paid to domestic workers, even though such amounts are not subject to income tax withholding.

Rollovers among various types of retirement plans.—Section 641 of EGTRRA expanded the rollover rules to allow rollovers among various types of tax-favored retirement plans. The provision makes a conforming change to the cross-reference to the rollovers rules in the Code provision relating to qualified retirement annuities.

Amendment Related to the Community Renewal Tax Relief Act of 2000

Tax treatment of options and securities futures contracts.—The provision clarifies that the Secretary of the Treasury has the authority to prescribe regulations regarding the status of an option or a contract the value of which is determined directly or indirectly by reference to an index which becomes (or ceases to be) a narrow-based security index (as defined in section 1256(g)(6)). This authority includes, but is not limited to, regulations that provide for preserving the status of such an option or contract as appropriate.

Amendments Related to the Taxpayer Relief Act of 1997

Qualified tuition programs.—Section 211 of the Taxpayer Relief Act of 1997 modified section 529(c)(5), relating to gift tax rules for qualified tuition programs, but did not include in the statutory language the requirement that, upon a change in the designated beneficiary of the program, the new beneficiary must be a member of the family of the old beneficiary for gift taxes not to apply. The legislative history for the provision stated that the new beneficiary had to be of the same generation as the old beneficiary and a member of the family of the old beneficiary for gift taxes not to apply. The provision clarifies that the gift taxes apply unless the new beneficiary is of the same (or higher) generation than the old beneficiary and is a member of the family of the old beneficiary.

Coverdell education savings accounts.—The provision corrects Code section 530(d)(4)(B)(iii), relating to Coverdell education savings accounts, by substituting for the undefined term "account holder" the defined term "designated beneficiary."

Constructive sale exception.—Section 1001(a) of the Taxpayer Relief Act of 1997 provides an exception from constructive sale treatment for any transaction that is closed before the end of the thirtieth day after the close of the taxable year in which the transaction was entered into, provided certain requirements are met after closing the transaction (section 1259(c)(3)). In the case of positions that are reestablished following a closed transaction but prior to satisfying the requirements for the exception from constructive sale treatment, the exception applies in a similar manner if the reestablished position itself is closed and similar requirements are met after closing the reestablished position. The provision clarifies that the exception applies in the same manner to all closed transactions, including reestablished positions that are closed.

Basis adjustments for QZAB held by S corporation.—Under present law, a shareholder of an S corporation that is an eligible financial institution may claim a credit with respect to a qualified zone academy bond ("QZAB") held by the S corporation. The amount of the credit is included in gross income of the shareholder.

An unintended interpretation of these rules would be that the shareholder's basis in the stock of the S corporation is increased by the amount of the income inclusion, notwithstanding that the benefit of the credit flows directly to the shareholder rather than to the corporation, and the corporation has no additional assets to support the basis increase. The provision clarifies that the basis of stock in an S corporation is not affected by the QZAB credit.

Capital gains and AMT.—The provision provides that the maximum amount of adjusted net capital gain eligible for the five-percent rate under the alternative minimum tax is the excess of the maximum amount of taxable income that may be taxed at a rate of less than 25 percent under the regular tax (for example, $56,800 for a joint return in 2003) over the taxable income reduced by the adjusted net capital gain.

The provision may be illustrated by the following example:

For example, assume that a married couple with no dependents in 2003 has $32,100 of salary, $82,000 of long-term capital gain from the sale of stock, $73,000 of itemized deductions consisting entirely of state and local taxes and allowable miscellaneous itemized deductions. For purposes of the regular tax, the taxable income is $35,000 ($32,100 plus $82,000 minus $73,000 minus $6,100 deduction for personal exemptions). For purposes of the alternative minimum tax, the taxable excess is $56,100 ($32,100 plus $82,000 less the $58,000 exemption amount).

The amount taxed under the regular tax at five percent is $35,000 (the lesser of (i) taxable income ($35,000), (ii) adjusted net capital gain ($82,000), or (iii) the excess of the maximum amount taxed at the 10- and 15-percent rates ($56,800 in 2003) over the ordinary taxable income (zero)). Thus, the regular tax is $1,750.

Under prior law, $35,000 was taxed at five percent in computing the alternative minimum tax (the lesser of (i) amount of the adjusted net capital gain which is taxed at the five percent under the regular tax ($35,000), or (ii) the taxable excess ($56,100)). The remaining $21,100 of taxable excess was taxed at 15 percent, for a total tentative minimum tax of $4,915.

Under the provision, in computing the alternative minimum tax, $56,100 is taxed at five percent (the lesser of (i) the taxable excess ($56,100), (ii) the adjusted net capital gain ($82,000), or (iii) the excess of the maximum amount taxed at the 10- and 15-percent rates under the regular tax ($56,800) over the ordinary taxable income (zero)). The tentative minimum tax is $2,805.

Amendment Related to the Small Business Job Protection Act of 1996

S corporation post-termination transition period.—Shareholders of an S corporation whose status as an S corporation terminates are allowed a period of time after the termination (the post-termination transition period ("PTTP")) to utilize certain of the benefits of S corporation status. The shareholders may claim losses and deductions previously suspended due to lack of stock or debt basis up to the amount of the stock basis as of the last day of the PTTP (sec. 1366(d)). Also, shareholders may receive cash distributions from the corporation during the PTTP that are treated as returns of capital to the extent of any balance in the S corporation's accumulated adjustments account ("AAA") (sec. 1371(e)).

The PTTP generally begins on the day after the last day of the corporation's last tax year as an S corporation and ends on the later of the day which is one year after such last day or the due date for filing the return for such last year as an S corporation (including extensions). Section 1307 of the Small Business Job Protection Act of 1996 added a new 120-day PTTP following an audit of the corporation that adjusts an S corporation item of income, loss, or deduction arising during the most recent period while the corporation was an S corporation. This provision was enacted to allow the tax-free distribution of any additional income determined in the audit.

As a result of the 1996 legislation, an S corporation shareholder might take the position that an audit adjustment allows the shareholder to utilize suspended losses and deductions in excess of the amount of the audit deficiency. For example, assume that, at the end of the one-year PTTP following the termination of a corporation's S corporation status, a shareholder has $1 million of suspended losses in the corporation. Later, the shareholder purchases additional stock in the corporation for $1 million. The corporation's audit determines a $25,000 increase in the S corporation's income. Although the $25,000 increase in income would allow $25,000 of suspended losses to be allowed, the shareholder might take the position that the entire $1,000,000 of suspended losses could be utilized during the 120-day PTTP following the end of the audit. Similarly, an S corporation that had failed to distribute the entire amount in its AAA during the one-year PTTP following the loss of S corporation status might argue that it could distribute that amount, in addition to the amount determined in the audit, during the 120-day period following the audit.

The provision provides that the 120-day PTTP added by the 1996 Act does not apply for purposes of allowing suspended losses to be deducted (since the increased income determined in the audit can be offset with the losses), and allows tax-free distributions of money by the corporation during the 120-day period only to the extent of any increase in the AAA by reason of adjustments from the audit.

Defined contribution plans.—The Small Business Job Protection Act of 1996 amended section 401(a)(26) (generally requiring that a qualified retirement plan benefit the lesser of 50 employees or 40 percent of the employer's workforce) so that it no longer applies to defined contribution plans. Section 401(a)(26)(C) (which treats employees as benefiting in certain circumstances) was not repealed even though it relates only to defined contribution plans. The provision repeals section 401(a)(26)(C).

Clerical amendments

The provision makes a number of clerical and typographical amendments.

PART SIXTEEN: TO CLARIFY THE TAX TREATMENT OF BONDS AND OTHER OBLIGATIONS ISSUED BY THE GOVERNMENT OF AMERICAN SAMOA (PUBLIC LAW 108–326) [272]

A. Clarification of Tax Treatment of Bonds and Other Obligations Issued by the Government of American Samoa (secs. 1 and 2 of the Act)

Present and Prior Law

The interest on obligations issued by American Samoa is generally exempt from Federal income tax.[273] This is consistent with the treatment of interest on obligations issued by other possessions of the United States. Prior law did not, however, provide an exemption from State, local, and territorial taxes for the interest paid on all obligations issued by American Samoa.[274] Rather, prior law only provided an exemption from State, local, and territorial taxes for certain industrial development bonds issued by American Samoa.[275] In contrast, Congress has provided statutory exemptions from State, local, and territorial taxes for all obligations issued by Guam,[276] the Virgin Islands,[277] Puerto Rico,[278] and the Northern Mariana Islands,[279] in addition to the exemption from Federal income tax.

Explanation of Provision

The Act provides that the interest on any obligation issued by the Government of American Samoa is exempt from State, local,

---

[272] H.R. 982. The House Committee on Judiciary reported the bill on May 15, 2003, (H.R. Rep. No. 108–102, Part I) and the House Committee on Resources reported the bill on October 7, 2003, (H.R. Rep. No. 108–102 Part II). The House passed the bill on the suspension calendar on November 4, 2003. The Senate Committee on Finance reported the bill, without amendment, on July 20, 2004. The Senate passed the bill by unanimous consent on September 29, 2004. The President signed the bill on October 16, 2004.

[273] 26 U.S.C. sec. 103(c).

[274] 48 U.S.C. sec. 1670.

[275] 48 U.S.C. sec. 1670(b). The power of Congress to make rules and regulations respecting "the Territory or other Property belonging to the United States" is generally derived from Article IV, section 3, clause 2 of the Constitution.

[276] "All bonds issued by the government of Guam or by its authority shall be exempt . . . from taxation by the Government of the United States or by the government of Guam, or by any State or Territory or any political subdivision thereof, or by the District of Columbia." 48 U.S.C. sec. 1423a.

[277] Bonds issued by the government of the Virgin Islands are "exempt from taxation . . . by any State, Territory, or possession or by any political subdivision of any State, Territory, or possession, or by the District of Columbia." 48 U.S.C. sec. 1403.

[278] "All bonds issued by the Government of Puerto Rico, or by its authority, shall be exempt from taxation by the Government of the United States, or by the Government of Puerto Rico or of any political or municipal subdivision thereof, or by any State, Territory, or possession, or by any county, municipality, or other municipal subdivision of any State, Territory, or possession of the United States, or by the District of Columbia." 48 U.S.C. sec. 745.

[279] Bonds issued by the Northern Mariana Islands are "exempt, as to principal and interest, from taxation by the United States, or by any State, territory or possession of the United States, or any political subdivision of any of them." 48 U.S.C. sec. 1801.

and territorial taxes. This exemption does not apply to gift, estate, inheritance, legacy, succession, or other wealth transfer taxes.

Effective Date

The provision is effective for obligations issued after the date of enactment (October 16, 2004).

PART SEVENTEEN: AMERICAN JOBS CREATION ACT OF 2004 (PUBLIC LAW 108–357)[280]

I. PROVISIONS RELATING TO REPEAL OF EXCLUSION FOR EXTRATERRITORIAL INCOME

A. Repeal of Extraterritorial Income Regime (sec. 101 of the Act and secs. 114 and 941 through 943 of the Code)

Present and Prior Law

Like many other countries, the United States has long provided export-related benefits under its tax law. In the United States, for most of the last two decades, these benefits were provided under the foreign sales corporation ("FSC") regime. In 2000, the European Union succeeded in having the FSC regime declared a prohibited export subsidy by the World Trade Organization ("WTO"). In response to this WTO finding, the United States repealed the FSC rules and enacted a new regime, under the FSC Repeal and Extraterritorial Income Exclusion Act of 2000.[281] The European Union immediately challenged the extraterritorial income ("ETI") regime in the WTO, and in January of 2002 the WTO Appellate Body held that the ETI regime also constituted a prohibited export subsidy under the relevant trade agreements.

Under the ETI regime, an exclusion from gross income applies with respect to "extraterritorial income," which is a taxpayer's gross income attributable to "foreign trading gross receipts." This income is eligible for the exclusion to the extent that it is "qualifying foreign trade income." Qualifying foreign trade income is the amount of gross income that, if excluded, would result in a reduction of taxable income by the greatest of: (1) 1.2 percent of the foreign trading gross receipts derived by the taxpayer from the transaction; (2) 15 percent of the "foreign trade income" derived by the taxpayer from the transaction;[282] or (3) 30 percent of the "foreign sale and leasing income" derived by the taxpayer from the transaction.[283]

---

[280] H.R. 4520. The House Committee on Ways and Means reported the bill on June 16, 2004 (H.R. Rep. No. 108–548). The House passed the bill on June 17, 2004. The Senate Committee on Finance reported S. 1637 on November 7, 2003 (S. Rep. No. 108–192). The Senate passed H.R. 4520, as amended by the provisions of S. 1637, on July 15, 2004. The conference report was filed on October 7, 2004 (H.R. Rep No. 108–755), and was passed by the House on October 7, 2004, and the Senate on October 11, 2004. The President signed the bill on October 22, 2004.

[281] Transition rules delayed the repeal of the FSC rules and the effective date of ETI for transactions before January 1, 2002. An election was provided, however, under which taxpayers could adopt ETI at an earlier date for transactions after September 30, 2000. This election allowed the ETI rules to apply to transactions after September 30, 2000, including transactions occurring pursuant to pre-existing binding contracts.

[282] "Foreign trade income" is the taxable income of the taxpayer (determined without regard to the exclusion of qualifying foreign trade income) attributable to foreign trading gross receipts.

[283] "Foreign sale and leasing income" is the amount of the taxpayer's foreign trade income (with respect to a transaction) that is properly allocable to activities that constitute foreign economic processes. Foreign sale and leasing income also includes foreign trade income derived by

Foreign trading gross receipts are gross receipts derived from certain activities in connection with "qualifying foreign trade property" with respect to which certain economic processes take place outside of the United States. Specifically, the gross receipts must be: (1) from the sale, exchange, or other disposition of qualifying foreign trade property; (2) from the lease or rental of qualifying foreign trade property for use by the lessee outside the United States; (3) for services which are related and subsidiary to the sale, exchange, disposition, lease, or rental of qualifying foreign trade property (as described above); (4) for engineering or architectural services for construction projects located outside the United States; or (5) for the performance of certain managerial services for unrelated persons. A taxpayer may elect to treat gross receipts from a transaction as not foreign trading gross receipts. As a result of such an election, a taxpayer may use any related foreign tax credits in lieu of the exclusion.

Qualifying foreign trade property generally is property manufactured, produced, grown, or extracted within or outside the United States that is held primarily for sale, lease, or rental in the ordinary course of a trade or business for direct use, consumption, or disposition outside the United States. No more than 50 percent of the fair market value of such property can be attributable to the sum of: (1) the fair market value of articles manufactured outside the United States; and (2) the direct costs of labor performed outside the United States. With respect to property that is manufactured outside the United States, certain rules are provided to ensure consistent U.S. tax treatment with respect to manufacturers.

Reasons for Change

While recognizing that there are problems with the WTO dispute settlement system that need to be addressed, the Congress believed it is important that the United States, and all members of the WTO, make every effort to come into compliance with their WTO obligations. The Appellate Body found that the ETI regime constitutes a prohibited export-contingent subsidy contrary to U.S. obligations under the WTO. The Congress believed that the ETI regime should be repealed, and that it was necessary and appropriate to provide transition relief comparable to that which has been included in measures taken by WTO members to bring their laws into compliance with WTO decisions and obligations.

In developing a transition for this provision, the Congress was guided by the latitude demonstrated by the United States toward the European Union in the context of the so-called "Bananas" dispute. With respect to both the Bananas and FSC/ETI disputes, the efforts to comply with the applicable WTO decisions entail the sizable disruption of commercial relations and expectations that developed over the course of decades.

In the Bananas case, the United States joined other complainants in challenging the European Union's banana import regime under the WTO. The United States and the European Union eventually reached an Understanding to resolve the WTO dispute over

the taxpayer in connection with the lease or rental of qualifying foreign trade property for use by the lessee outside the United States.

the European Union's import regime for bananas. By virtue of that Understanding, the European Union imposed a transitional banana import regime that will not end until seven years after the initial deadline established by the WTO for the European Union to come into compliance. The European Union subsequently obtained from the Doha Ministerial Conference of the WTO a waiver from paragraphs 1 and 2 of Article XIII of the GATT 1994 with respect to its transitional banana import regime. That waiver was necessary for the transitional banana import regime to remain consistent with the WTO obligations of the European Union. The United States did not object to that waiver. The United States also did not object to a second waiver granted to the European Union by the Doha Ministerial Conference, under which paragraph 1 of Article I of the GATT 1994 was waived with respect to the European Union's preferential tariff treatment for products originating in the African, Caribbean and Pacific Group of States. This latter waiver extends until December 31, 2007. As a result of the foregoing waivers consented to by the United States, the European Union will not be required to grant non-discriminatory market access for bananas until a full nine years after the compliance deadline established by the WTO. The Congress noted that the transition provided for in the provision expires well before the nine-year anniversary of the compliance deadline established by the WTO with respect to the FSC regime. Just as the European Union approached the issue of compliance in the Bananas dispute, the Congress believed that it is necessary and appropriate to provide a reasonable transition period during which the affected businesses may adjust to the new environment following repeal of the ETI regime.

A second transitional element provided for in the provision is the grandfathering of existing contracts entered into under the FSC and ETI tax regimes. These contracts are comprised primarily of long-term leasing arrangements. These arrangements typically entail a U.S. lessor purchasing the manufactured good from the manufacturer and subsequently entering into a long-term lease with a foreign lessee. Under these circumstances, the FSC/ETI tax benefit accrues to the lessor rather than the manufacturer of the leased good. The lessor must report the FSC/ETI tax benefit immediately for purposes of financial statement accounting under generally accepted accounting principles.

Leasing is a service and is recognized as such within the WTO. The provision of non-discriminatory subsidies to service suppliers is not prohibited under the WTO General Agreement on Trade in Services ("GATS"). Thus, an extension of FSC/ETI benefits for suppliers of leasing services under existing long-term contracts does not appear to be inconsistent with the WTO obligations of the United States under GATS. Moreover, the extension of FSC/ETI benefits for existing long-term leasing contracts will have no effect on future exports. Accordingly, a principal rationale for the European Union's challenge to the FSC/ETI regimes is not implicated because future trade patterns will not be distorted by virtue of the grandfather clause. On the other hand, the absence of a grandfather clause for existing long-term contracts would effectively dictate winners and losers based upon preexisting contractual relationships, and would inflict additional harm by forcing lessors to restate their financial statements. Neither of those outcomes was equitable in the view of the Congress, nor did the architects of the WTO dispute settlement system contemplate such punitive results. Accordingly, the Congress believed it was necessary and appropriate to continue to provide FSC and ETI tax benefits to existing long-term contracts that currently benefit from the FSC/ETI tax regimes.

The Congress also believed that it was important to use the opportunity afforded by the repeal of the ETI regime to reform the U.S. tax system in a manner that makes U.S. businesses and workers more productive and competitive. To this end, the Congress believed that it was important to provide tax cuts to U.S. domestic manufacturers and to update the U.S. international tax rules, which are over 40 years old and which the Congress concluded made U.S. companies uncompetitive in the United States and abroad. The Congress believed that the replacement tax regime provided for in the Act was consistent with U.S. obligations under the WTO and brought the United States into compliance with the Appellate Body decision.

Explanation of Provision

The Act repeals the ETI exclusion. For transactions prior to 2005, taxpayers retain 100 percent of their ETI benefits. For transactions after 2004, the Act provides taxpayers with 80 percent of their otherwise-applicable ETI benefits for transactions during 2005 and 60 percent of their otherwise-applicable ETI benefits for transactions during 2006. However, the Act provides that the ETI exclusion provisions remain in effect for transactions in the ordinary course of a trade or business if such transactions are pursuant to a binding contract[284] between the taxpayer and an unrelated person and such contract is in effect on September 17, 2003, and at all times thereafter.

In addition, foreign corporations that elected to be treated for all Federal tax purposes as domestic corporations in order to facilitate the claiming of ETI benefits are allowed to revoke such elections within one year of the date of enactment of the Act without recognition of gain or loss, subject to anti-abuse rules.

Effective Date

The provision is effective for transactions after December 31, 2004.

[284] This rule also applies to a purchase option, renewal option, or replacement option that is included in such contract. For this purpose, a replacement option will be considered enforceable against a lessor notwithstanding the fact that a lessor retained approval of the replacement lessee.

B. Deduction Relating to Income Attributable to United States Production Activities (sec. 102 of the Act and new sec. 199 of the Code)

Present and Prior Law

Under prior law, there was no provision in the Code that generally permitted taxpayers to claim a deduction equal to a percentage of taxable income attributable to domestic production activities.

Reasons for Change

The Congress believed that creating new jobs is an essential element of economic recovery and expansion, and that tax policies designed to foster economic strength also will contribute to the continuation of the recent increases in employment levels. To accomplish this objective, the Congress believed that it should enact tax laws that enhance the ability of domestic businesses, and domestic manufacturing firms in particular, to compete in the global marketplace. The Congress further believed that it should enact tax laws that enable small businesses to maintain their position as the primary source of new jobs in this country.

The Congress understood that simply repealing the ETI regime, while bringing our tax laws into compliance with our obligations under the WTO, would diminish the prospects for recovery from the recent economic downturn by the manufacturing sector. Consequently, the Congress believed that it was appropriate and necessary to replace the ETI regime with new provisions that reduce the tax burden on domestic manufacturers, including small businesses engaged in manufacturing. The Congress was of the view that a reduced tax burden on domestic manufacturers will improve the cash flow of domestic manufacturers and make investments in domestic manufacturing facilities more attractive. Such investment will assist in the creation and preservation of U.S. manufacturing jobs.

Explanation of Provision

In general

The Act provides a deduction equal to a specified percent of the lesser of the taxpayer's (1) qualified production activities income or (2) taxable income (determined without regard to this deduction) for the taxable year.[285] For taxable years beginning after 2009, the percent is nine percent; for taxable years beginning in 2005 and 2006, the percent is three percent; and for taxable years beginning 2007, 2008, and 2009, the percent is six percent. However, the deduction for a taxable year is limited to 50 percent of the wages paid by the taxpayer during the calendar year that ends in such taxable year.[286] In the case of corporate taxpayers that are members of cer-

[285] In the case of an individual, the limit is applied using adjusted gross income rather than taxable income.

[286] For purposes of the Act, "wages" include the sum of the aggregate amounts of wages and elective deferrals that the taxpayer is required to include on statements with respect to the employment of employees of the taxpayer during the taxpayer's taxable year. Elective deferrals include elective deferrals as defined in section 402(g)(3), amounts deferred under section 457, and, for taxable years beginning after December 31, 2005, designated Roth contributions (as defined in section 402A). The Act does not specifically require such statements (i.e., Forms W–2) actu-

tain affiliated groups[287], the deduction is determined by treating all members of such groups as a single taxpayer and the deduction is allocated among such members in proportion to each member's respective amount (if any) of qualified production activities income.

Qualified production activities income

In general, "qualified production activities income" is equal to domestic production gross receipts, reduced by the sum of: (1) the costs of goods sold that are allocable to such receipts;[288] (2) other deductions, expenses, or losses that are directly allocable to such receipts; and (3) a proper share of other deductions, expenses, and losses that are not directly allocable to such receipts or another class of income.[289]

Domestic production gross receipts

"Domestic production gross receipts" generally are gross receipts of a taxpayer that are derived from: (1) any sale, exchange or other disposition, or any lease, rental or license, of qualifying production property that was manufactured, produced, grown or extracted by the taxpayer in whole or in significant part within the United States;[290] (2) any sale, exchange or other disposition, or any lease, rental or license, of qualified film produced by the taxpayer; (3) any sale, exchange or other disposition electricity, natural gas, or potable water produced by the taxpayer in the United States; (4) con-

---

ally to be filed, and does not specify whether the employees must be the common law employees of the taxpayer. However, it is intended that a taxpayer may take into account only wages that are paid to the common law employees of the taxpayer and that are reported on a Form W–2 filed with the Social Security Administration no later than 60 days after the extended due date for the Form W-2. Thus, the taxpayer may not take into account wages that were not actually reported. A technical correction may be necessary so that the statute reflects this intent, and to address situations in which the employer uses an agent to report its wages.

[287] Members of an expanded affiliated group for purposes of the provision generally include those corporations which would be members of an affiliated group if such membership were determined based on an ownership threshold of "more than 50%" rather than "at least 80%." A technical correction may be necessary to reflect this intent.

[288] For purposes of determining such costs, any item or service that is imported into the United States without an arm's length transfer price shall be treated as acquired by purchase, and its cost shall be treated as not less than its value when it entered the United States. A similar rule shall apply in determining the adjusted basis of leased or rented property where the lease or rental gives rise to domestic production gross receipts. With regard to property previously exported by the taxpayer for further manufacture, the increase in cost or adjusted basis shall not exceed the difference between the value of the property when exported and the value of the property when re-imported into the United States after further manufacture. Except as provided by the Secretary, the value of property for this purpose shall be its customs value (as defined in section 1059A(b)(1)).

[289] The Secretary shall prescribe rules for the proper allocation of items of income, deduction, expense, and loss for purposes of determining qualified production activities income. Where appropriate, such rules shall be similar to and consistent with relevant present-law rules (e.g., sec. 263A, in determining the cost of goods sold, and sec. 861, in determining the source of such items). Other deductions, expenses or losses that are directly allocable to such receipts include, for example, selling and marketing expenses. A proper share of other deductions, expenses, and losses that are not directly allocable to such receipts or another class of income include, for example, general and administrative expenses allocable to selling and marketing expenses. It is intended that, in computing qualified production activities income, the domestic production activities deduction itself is not an allocable deduction. In addition, no inference is intended with regard to the interpretive relationship between the cost allocation rules provided in this provision and cost allocation rules provided in provisions elsewhere in the Act (e.g., incentives to reinvest foreign earnings in the United States). Technical corrections may be necessary so that the statute reflects this intent.

[290] Domestic production gross receipts include gross receipts of a taxpayer derived from any sale, exchange or other disposition of agricultural products with respect to which the taxpayer performs storage, handling or other processing activities (other than transportation activities) within the United States, provided such products are consumed in connection with, or incorporated into, the manufacturing, production, growth or extraction of qualifying production property (whether or not by the taxpayer).

struction activities performed in the United States;[291] or (5) engineering or architectural services performed in the United States for construction projects located in the United States.[292] However, domestic production gross receipts do not include any gross receipts of the taxpayer derived from property that is leased, licensed or rented by the taxpayer for use by any related person.[293]

Sale of food or beverages prepared at a retail establishment

The Act provides that domestic production gross receipts do not include any gross receipts of the taxpayer that are derived from the sale of food or beverages prepared by the taxpayer at a retail establishment. It is intended that food processing, which generally is a qualified production activity under the Act, does not include food preparation activities carried out at a retail establishment. Thus, under the Act, while the gross receipts of a meat packing establishment are qualified domestic production gross receipts, the activities of a master chef who creates a venison sausage for his or her restaurant menu cannot be construed as a qualified production activity.

However, it is recognized that some taxpayers may own facilities at which the predominant activity is domestic production as defined in the Act and other facilities at which they engage in the retail sale of the taxpayer's produced goods and also sell food and beverages that are prepared by the taxpayer at the retail establishment. It is intended that the Act draw a distinction between activities that constitute domestic production under the Act and other activities. Therefore, it is not intended that the retail activities of the taxpayer, which themselves do not constitute domestic production under the Act, also disqualify other activities of the taxpayer that do constitute domestic production under the Act. As is the case under the Act generally, with respect to gross receipts that are attributable to both domestic production activities and other activities performed by the taxpayer, gross receipts that are attributable to both the domestic production of food or beverages by the taxpayer and the sale of food or beverages prepared by the taxpayer at a retail establishment are to be allocated or apportioned between the domestic production activities and retail activities, including circumstances in which the food or beverages domestically pro-

[291] For this purpose, construction activities include activities that are directly related to the erection or substantial renovation of residential and commercial buildings and infrastructure. Substantial renovation would include structural improvements, but not mere cosmetic changes, such as painting that is not performed in connection with activities that otherwise constitute substantial renovation.

[292] With regard to the definition of "domestic production gross receipts" as it relates to construction performed in the United States and engineering or architectural services performed in the United States for construction projects in the United States, it is intended that the term refer only to gross receipts derived from the construction of real property by a taxpayer engaged in the active conduct of a construction trade or business, or from engineering or architectural services performed with respect to real property by a taxpayer engaged in the active conduct of an engineering or architectural services trade or business. Technical corrections may be necessary so that the statute reflects this intent.

[293] It is intended that principles similar to those under the present-law extraterritorial income regime apply for this purpose. See Temp. Treas. Reg. sec. 1.927(a)–1T(f)(2)(i). For example, this exclusion generally does not apply to property leased by the taxpayer to a related person if the property is held for sublease, or is subleased, by the related person to an unrelated person for the ultimate use of such unrelated person. Similarly, the license of computer software to a related person for reproduction and sale, exchange, lease, rental or sublicense to an unrelated person for the ultimate use of such unrelated person is not treated as excluded property by reason of the license to the related person.

duced by the taxpayer also are involved subsequently in the preparation of food or beverages by the taxpayer at a retail establishment.

For example, assume that the taxpayer buys coffee beans and roasts those beans at a facility, the primary activity of which is the roasting and packaging of roasted coffee. The taxpayer sells the roasted coffee beans (either whole or ground) through a variety of unrelated third-party vendors and also sells roasted coffee beans at the taxpayer's own retail establishments. In addition, at the taxpayer's retail establishments, the taxpayer prepares brewed coffee and other foods. Consistent with the general operation of the Act, it is intended that to the extent the gross receipts of the taxpayer's retail establishment represent receipts from the sale of its roasted coffee beans to customers, the receipts are qualified domestic production gross receipts, but to the extent that the gross receipts of the taxpayer's retail establishment represent receipts from the sale of brewed coffee or food prepared at the retail establishment, the receipts are not qualified domestic production gross receipts. To the extent that the taxpayer uses its own roasted coffee beans in the brewing of coffee at the taxpayer's retail establishment, the taxpayer may allocate part of the receipts from the sale of the brewed coffee as qualified domestic production gross receipts to the extent of the value of the roasted coffee beans used to brew the coffee. It is anticipated that the Secretary will provide guidance drawing on the principles of section 482 by which such a taxpayer can allocate gross receipts between qualified domestic production gross receipts and other, nonqualified, gross receipts. In the preceding example, the taxpayer's sales of roasted coffee beans to unrelated third parties would provide a value for the beans used in brewing a cup of coffee for retail sale.

It is intended that the disqualification of gross receipts derived from the sale of food and beverage prepared by the taxpayer at a retail establishment not be construed narrowly to apply only to establishments at which customers dine on premises. The receipts of a facility that prepares food and beverage solely for take out service would not be qualified production gross receipts. Likewise, it is intended that the disqualification of gross receipts derived from the sale of food and beverages prepared by the taxpayer need not be limited to retail establishments primarily engaged in the dining trade. For example, if a taxpayer operates a supermarket and as part of the supermarket the taxpayer operates an in-store bakery, the same allocation described above would apply to determine the extent to which the taxpayer's gross receipts represent qualified domestic production gross receipts.

Electricity, natural gas, or potable water transmission or distribution

Although domestic production gross receipts include the gross receipts from the production in the United States of electricity, gas, and potable water, the Act excludes gross receipts from the transmission or distribution of electricity, gas, and potable water. Thus, in the case of a taxpayer who owns a facility for the production of electricity (either as part of a regulated utility or an independent power facility), the taxpayer's gross receipts from the production of electricity at that facility are qualified domestic production gross receipts. However, to the extent that the taxpayer is an integrated producer that generates electricity and delivers electricity to end users, any gross receipts properly attributable to the transmission of electricity from the generating facility to a point of local distribution and any gross receipts properly attributable to the distribution of electricity to final customers are not qualified domestic production gross receipts.

For example, taxpayer A owns a wind turbine that generates electricity and taxpayer B owns a high-voltage transmission line that passes near taxpayer A's wind turbine and ends near the system of local distribution lines of taxpayer C. Taxpayer A sells the electricity produced at the wind turbine to taxpayer C and contracts with taxpayer B to transmit the electricity produced at the wind turbine to taxpayer C who sells the electricity to his or her customers using taxpayer C's distribution network. The gross receipts received by taxpayer A for the sale of electricity produced at the wind turbine constitute qualifying domestic production gross receipts. The gross receipts of taxpayer B from transporting taxpayer A's electricity to taxpayer C are not qualifying domestic production gross receipts. Likewise, the gross receipts of taxpayer C from distributing the electricity are not qualifying domestic production gross receipts. Also, if taxpayer A made direct sales of electricity to customers in taxpayer C's service area and taxpayer C received remuneration for the distribution of electricity, the gross receipts of taxpayer C are not qualifying domestic production gross receipts. If taxpayers A, B, and C are all related taxpayers, then taxpayers A, B, and C must allocate gross receipts to production activities, transmission activities, and distribution activities in a manner consistent with the preceding example.

The same principles apply in the case of the natural gas and water supply industries. In the case of natural gas, production activities generally are all activities involved in extracting natural gas from the ground and processing the gas into pipeline quality gas. Such activities would produce qualifying domestic production gross receipts. However, gross receipts of a taxpayer attributable to transmission of pipeline quality gas from a natural gas field (or from a natural gas processing plant) to a local distribution company's citygate (or to another customer) are not qualified domestic production gross receipts. Likewise, gas purchased by a local gas distribution company and distributed from the citygate to the local customers does not give rise to domestic production gross receipts.

In the case of the production of potable water, activities involved in the production of potable water include the acquisition, collection, and storage of raw water (untreated water). It also includes the transportation of raw water to a water treatment facility and treatment of raw water at such a facility. However, any gross receipts from the storage of potable water after the water treatment facility or delivery of potable water to customers does not give rise to qualifying domestic production gross receipts. It is intended that a taxpayer that both produces potable water and distributes potable water will properly allocate gross receipts across qualifying and non-qualifying activities.

Qualifying production property

"Qualifying production property" generally includes any tangible personal property, computer software, or sound recordings. "Qualified film" includes any motion picture film or videotape[294] (including live or delayed television programming, but not including certain sexually explicit productions) if 50 percent or more of the total compensation relating to the production of such film (including compensation in the form of residuals and participations[295]) constitutes compensation for services performed in the United States by actors, production personnel, directors, and producers.[296]

Other rules

Qualified production activities income of partnerships and S corporations

With respect to the domestic production activities of a partnership or S corporation, the deduction under the Act is determined at the partner or shareholder level. In performing the calculation, each partner or shareholder generally will take into account such person's allocable share of the components of the calculation (including domestic production gross receipts; the cost of goods sold allocable to such receipts; and other expenses, losses, or deductions allocable to such receipts) from the partnership or S corporation as well as any items relating to the partner or shareholder's own qualified production activities, if any.[297]

In applying the wage limitation, each partner or shareholder is treated as having been allocated wages from the partnership or S corporation in an amount that is equal to the lesser of: (1) such person's allocable share of wages, as determined under regulations prescribed by the Secretary; or (2) twice the appropriate deductible percentage of such person's qualified production activities income attributable to items allocated from the partnership or S corporation. This limitation is intended to prevent a partner or shareholder from claiming a deduction with respect to its own activities in excess of that which would be allowed if such person were not a member of the partnership or S corporation.

Qualified production activities of trusts and estates

In the case of a trust or estate, the components of the calculation are to be apportioned between (and among) the beneficiaries and the fiduciary under regulations prescribed by the Secretary.[298]

Qualified production activities income of agricultural and horticultural cooperatives

With regard to member-owned agricultural and horticultural cooperatives formed under Subchapter T of the Code, the Act pro-

[294] The Congress intends that the nature of the material on which properties described in section 168(f)(3) are embodied and the methods and means of distribution of such properties shall not affect their qualification under this provision.

[295] To the extent that a taxpayer has included an estimate of participations and/or residuals in its income forecast calculation under section 167(g), the taxpayer must use the same estimate of participations and/or residuals for purposes of determining total compensation.

[296] It is intended that the Secretary will provide appropriate rules governing the determination of total compensation for services performed in the United States.

[297] A technical correction may be necessary so that the statute reflects this intent.

[298] A technical correction may be necessary so that the statute reflects this intent.

vides the same treatment of qualified production activities income derived from agricultural or horticultural products that are manufactured, produced, grown, or extracted by cooperatives,[299] or that are marketed through cooperatives, as it provides for qualified production activities income of other taxpayers (i.e., the cooperative may claim a deduction from qualified production activities income).

Alternatively, the Act provides that the amount of any patronage dividends or per-unit retain allocations paid to a member of an agricultural or horticultural cooperative (to which Part I of Subchapter T applies), which is allocable to the portion of qualified production activities income of the cooperative that is deductible under the provision, is deductible from the gross income of the member. In order to qualify, such amount must be designated by the organization as allocable to the deductible portion of qualified production activities income in a written notice mailed to its patrons not later than the payment period described in section 1382(d). The cooperative cannot reduce its income under section 1382 (e.g., cannot claim a dividends-paid deduction) for such amounts.

Alternative minimum tax

The deduction provided by the Act is allowed for purposes of computing alternative minimum taxable income (including adjusted current earnings). The deduction in computing alternative minimum taxable income is determined by reference to the lesser of the qualified production activities income (as determined for the regular tax) or the alternative minimum taxable income (in the case of an individual, adjusted gross income as determined for the regular tax) without regard to this deduction.[300]

Timber cutting

Under the Act, an election made for a taxable year ending on or before the date of enactment, to treat the cutting of timber as a sale or exchange, may be revoked by the taxpayer without the consent of the IRS for any taxable year ending after that date. The prior election (and revocation) is disregarded for purposes of making a subsequent election.

Exploration of fundamental tax reform

The Congress acknowledges that it has not reduced the statutory corporate income tax rate since 1986. According to the Organisation of Economic Cooperation and Development ("OECD"), the combined corporate income tax rate, as defined by the OECD, in most instances is lower than the U.S. corporate income tax rate.[301] Higher corporate tax rates factor into the United States' ability to attract and retain economically vibrant industries, which create good jobs and contribute to overall economic growth.

This legislation was crafted to repeal an export tax benefit that was deemed inconsistent with obligations of the United States under the Agreement on Subsidies and Countervailing Measures

---

[299] For this purpose, agricultural or horticultural products also include fertilizer, diesel fuel and other supplies used in agricultural or horticultural production that are manufactured, produced, grown, or extracted by the cooperative.

[300] A technical correction may be necessary so that the statute reflects this intent.

[301] Organisation of Economic Cooperation and Development, Table 1.5, Tax Data Base Statistics, Tax Policy and Administration, Summary Tables (2003).

and other international trade agreements. This legislation replaces the benefit with tax relief specifically designed to be economically equivalent to a 3-percentage point reduction in U.S.-based manufacturing.

The Congress recognizes that manufacturers are a segment of the economy that has faced significant challenges during the nation's recent economic slowdown. The Congress recognizes that trading partners of the United States retain subsidies for domestic manufacturers and exports through their indirect tax systems. The Congress is concerned about the adverse competitive impact of these subsidies on U.S. manufacturers.

These concerns should be considered in the context of the benefits of a unified top tax rate for all corporate taxpayers, including manufacturers, in terms of efficiency and fairness. The Congress also expects that the tax-writing committees will explore a unified top corporate tax rate in the context of fundamental tax reform.

Effective Date

The provision is effective for taxable years beginning after December 31, 2004.

II. BUSINESS TAX INCENTIVES

A. Two-Year Extension of Increased Expensing for Small Business (sec. 201 of the Act and sec. 179 of the Code)

Present and Prior Law

In lieu of depreciation, a taxpayer with a sufficiently small amount of annual investment may elect to deduct such costs. The Jobs and Growth Tax Relief Reconciliation Act of 2003 ("JGTRRA")[302] increased the amount a taxpayer may deduct, for taxable years beginning in 2003 through 2005, to $100,000 of the cost of qualifying property placed in service for the taxable year.[303] In general, qualifying property is defined as depreciable tangible personal property (and certain computer software) that is purchased for use in the active conduct of a trade or business. The $100,000 amount is reduced (but not below zero) by the amount by which the cost of qualifying property placed in service during the taxable year exceeds $400,000. The $100,000 and $400,000 amounts are indexed for inflation.

Prior to the enactment of JGTRRA (and for taxable years beginning in 2006 and thereafter) a taxpayer with a sufficiently small amount of annual investment could elect to deduct up to $25,000 of the cost of qualifying property placed in service for the taxable year. The $25,000 amount was reduced (but not below zero) by the amount by which the cost of qualifying property placed in service during the taxable year exceeds $200,000. In general, qualifying property is defined as depreciable tangible personal property that is purchased for use in the active conduct of a trade or business.

The amount eligible to be expensed for a taxable year may not exceed the taxable income for a taxable year that is derived from the active conduct of a trade or business (determined without regard to this provision). Any amount that is not allowed as a deduction because of the taxable income limitation may be carried forward to succeeding taxable years (subject to similar limitations). No general business credit under section 38 is allowed with respect to any amount for which a deduction is allowed under section 179.

An expensing election is made under rules prescribed by the Secretary.[304] Applicable Treasury regulations provide that an expensing election generally is made on the taxpayer's original return for the taxable year to which the election relates.[305]

[302] Pub. L. No. 108–27, sec. 202 (2003).

[303] Additional section 179 incentives are provided with respect to a qualified property used by a business in the New York Liberty Zone (sec. 1400L(f)), an empowerment zone (sec. 1397A), or a renewal community (sec. 1400J).

[304] Sec. 179(c)(1).

[305] Under Treas. Reg. sec. 1.179–5, applicable to property placed in service in taxable years ending after January 25, 1993 (but not including property placed in service in taxable years beginning after 2002 and before 2006), a taxpayer may make the election on the original return (whether or not the return is timely), or on an amended return filed by the due date (including

Prior to the enactment of JGTRRA (and for taxable years beginning in 2006 and thereafter), an expensing election may be revoked only with consent of the Commissioner.[306] JGTRRA permits taxpayers to revoke expensing elections on amended returns without the consent of the Commissioner with respect to a taxable year beginning after 2002 and before 2006.[307]

Reasons for Change

The Congress believed that section 179 expensing provides two important benefits for small businesses. First, it lowers the cost of capital for property used in a trade or business. With a lower cost of capital, the Congress believed small businesses will invest in more equipment and employ more workers. Second, it eliminates depreciation recordkeeping requirements with respect to expensed property. In JGTRRA, Congress acted to increase the value of these benefits and to increase the number of taxpayers eligible for taxable years through 2005. The Congress believed that these changes to section 179 expensing will continue to provide important benefits if extended, and the Act therefore extends these changes for an additional two years.

Explanation of Provision

The Act extends the increased amount that a taxpayer may deduct, and other changes that were made by JGTRRA, for an additional two years. Thus, the Act provides that the maximum dollar amount that may be deducted under section 179 is $100,000 for property placed in service in taxable years beginning before 2008 ($25,000 for taxable years beginning in 2008 and thereafter). In addition, the $400,000 amount applies for property placed in service in taxable years beginning before 2008 ($200,000 for taxable years beginning in 2008 and thereafter). The Act extends, through 2007 (from 2005), the indexing for inflation of both the maximum dollar amount that may be deducted and the $400,000 amount. The Act also includes off-the-shelf computer software placed in service in taxable years beginning before 2008 as qualifying property. The Act permits taxpayers to revoke expensing elections on amended returns without the consent of the Commissioner with respect to a taxable year beginning before 2008. The Congress expects that the Secretary will prescribe regulations to permit a taxpayer to make an expensing election on an amended return without the consent of the Commissioner.

Effective Date

The provision is effective on the date of enactment (October 22, 2004).

---

extensions) for filing the return for the tax year the property was placed in service. If the taxpayer timely filed an original return without making the election, the taxpayer may still make the election by filing an amended return within six months of the due date of the return (excluding extensions).

[306] Sec. 179(c)(2).

[307] Id. Under Prop. and Temp. Treas. Reg. sec. 179–5T, applicable to property placed in service in taxable years beginning after 2002 and before 2006, a taxpayer is permitted to make or revoke an election under section 179 without the consent of the Commissioner on an amended Federal tax return for that taxable year. This amended return must be filed within the time prescribed by law for filing an amended return for the taxable year. T.D. 9146, August 3, 2004.

B. Depreciation

1. Recovery period for depreciation of certain leasehold improvements (sec. 211 of the Act and sec. 168 of the Code)

Present and Prior Law

In general

A taxpayer generally must capitalize the cost of property used in a trade or business and recover such cost over time through annual deductions for depreciation or amortization. Tangible property generally is depreciated under the modified accelerated cost recovery system ("MACRS"), which determines depreciation by applying specific recovery periods, placed-in-service conventions, and depreciation methods to the cost of various types of depreciable property (sec. 168). The cost of nonresidential real property is recovered using the straight-line method of depreciation and a recovery period of 39 years. Nonresidential real property is subject to the mid-month placed-in-service convention. Under the mid-month convention, the depreciation allowance for the first year property is placed in service is based on the number of months the property was in service, and property placed in service at any time during a month is treated as having been placed in service in the middle of the month.

Depreciation of leasehold improvements

Depreciation allowances for improvements made on leased property are determined under MACRS, even if the MACRS recovery period assigned to the property is longer than the term of the lease.[308] This rule applies regardless of whether the lessor or the lessee places the leasehold improvements in service.[309] If a leasehold improvement constitutes an addition or improvement to nonresidential real property already placed in service, the improvement is depreciated using the straight-line method over a 39-year recovery period, beginning in the month the addition or improvement was placed in service.[310]

Qualified leasehold improvement property

The additional first-year depreciation deduction generally equals either 30 percent or 50 percent of the adjusted basis of qualified property placed in service before January 1, 2005. Qualified prop-

[308] Sec. 168(i)(8). The Tax Reform Act of 1986 modified the Accelerated Cost Recovery System ("ACRS") to institute MACRS. Prior to the adoption of ACRS by the Economic Recovery Tax Act of 1981, taxpayers were allowed to depreciate the various components of a building as separate assets with separate useful lives. The use of component depreciation was repealed upon the adoption of ACRS. The Tax Reform Act of 1986 also denied the use of component depreciation under MACRS.

[309] Former sections 168(f)(6) and 178 provided that, in certain circumstances, a lessee could recover the cost of leasehold improvements made over the remaining term of the lease. The Tax Reform Act of 1986 repealed these provisions.

[310] Secs. 168(b)(3), (c), (d)(2), and (i)(6). If the improvement is characterized as tangible personal property, ACRS or MACRS depreciation is calculated using the shorter recovery periods, accelerated methods, and conventions applicable to such property. The determination of whether improvements are characterized as tangible personal property or as nonresidential real property often depends on whether or not the improvements constitute a "structural component" of a building (as defined by Treas. Reg. sec. 1.48–1(e)(1)). See, e.g., Metro National Corp v. Commissioner, 52 TCM (CCH) 1440 (1987); King Radio Corp Inc. v. U.S., 486 F.2d 1091 (10th Cir. 1973); Mallinckrodt, Inc. v. Commissioner, 778 F.2d 402 (8th Cir. 1985) (with respect to various leasehold improvements).

erty includes qualified leasehold improvement property. For this purpose, qualified leasehold improvement property is any improvement to an interior portion of a building that is nonresidential real property, provided certain requirements are met. The improvement must be made under or pursuant to a lease either by the lessee (or sublessee), or by the lessor, of that portion of the building to be occupied exclusively by the lessee (or sublessee). The improvement must be placed in service more than three years after the date the building was first placed in service. Qualified leasehold improvement property does not include any improvement for which the expenditure is attributable to the enlargement of the building, any elevator or escalator, any structural component benefiting a common area, or the internal structural framework of the building.

Treatment of dispositions of leasehold improvements

A lessor of leased property that disposes of a leasehold improvement that was made by the lessor for the lessee of the property may take the adjusted basis of the improvement into account for purposes of determining gain or loss if the improvement is irrevocably disposed of or abandoned by the lessor at the termination of the lease. This rule conforms the treatment of lessors and lessees with respect to leasehold improvements disposed of at the end of a term of lease.

Reasons for Change

The Congress believed that taxpayers should not be required to recover the costs of certain leasehold improvements beyond the useful life of the investment. The 39-year recovery period for leasehold improvements extends well beyond the useful life of such investments. Although lease terms differ, the Congress believed that lease terms for commercial real estate typically are shorter than the present-law 39-year recovery period. In the interests of simplicity and administrability, a uniform period for recovery of leasehold improvements is desirable. The Act therefore shortened the recovery period for leasehold improvements to a more realistic 15 years.

Explanation of Provision

The Act provides a statutory 15-year recovery period for qualified leasehold improvement property placed in service before January 1, 2006.[311] The Act requires that qualified leasehold improvement property be recovered using the straight-line method.

Qualified leasehold improvement property is defined as under present and prior law for purposes of the additional first-year depreciation deduction,[312] with the following modification. If a lessor makes an improvement that qualifies as qualified leasehold improvement property, such improvement does not qualify as qualified leasehold improvement property to any subsequent owner of such improvement. An exception to the rule applies in the case of

[311] Qualified leasehold improvement property continues to be eligible for the additional first-year depreciation deduction under sec. 168(k).

[312] Sec. 168(k).

death and certain transfers of property that qualify for non-recognition treatment.

Effective Date

The provision is effective for property placed in service after the date of enactment (October 22, 2004).

2. Recovery period for depreciation of certain restaurant improvements (sec. 211 of the Act and sec. 168 of the Code)

Present and Prior Law

A taxpayer generally must capitalize the cost of property used in a trade or business and recover such cost over time through annual deductions for depreciation or amortization. Tangible property generally is depreciated under the modified accelerated cost recovery system ("MACRS"), which determines depreciation by applying specific recovery periods, placed-in-service conventions, and depreciation methods to the cost of various types of depreciable property (sec. 168). The cost of nonresidential real property is recovered using the straight-line method of depreciation and a recovery period of 39 years. Nonresidential real property is subject to the mid-month placed-in-service convention. Under the mid-month convention, the depreciation allowance for the first year property is placed in service is based on the number of months the property was in service, and property placed in service at any time during a month is treated as having been placed in service in the middle of the month.

Reasons for Change

The Congress believed that unlike other commercial buildings, restaurant buildings generally are more specialized structures. Restaurants also experience considerably more traffic, and remain open longer than most retail properties. This daily assault causes rapid deterioration of restaurant properties and forces restaurateurs to constantly repair and upgrade their facilities. As such, restaurant facilities have a much shorter life span than other commercial establishments. The Act reduced the 39-year recovery period for improvements made to restaurant buildings and more accurately reflected the true economic life of the properties by reducing the recovery period to 15 years.

Explanation of Provision

The Act provides a statutory 15-year recovery period for qualified restaurant property placed in service before January 1, 2006.[313] For purposes of the provision, qualified restaurant property means any improvement to a building if such improvement is placed in service more than three years after the date such building was first placed in service and more than 50 percent of the building's square footage is devoted to the preparation of, and seating for, on-prem-

[313] Qualified restaurant property becomes eligible for the additional first-year depreciation deduction under sec. 168(k) by virtue of the assigned 15-year recovery period.

ises consumption of prepared meals. The Act requires that qualified restaurant property be recovered using the straight-line method.

Effective Date

The provision is effective for property placed in service after the date of enactment (October 22, 2004).

C. Community Revitalization

1. Modification of targeted areas and low-income communities designated for new markets tax credit (sec. 221 of the Act and sec. 45D of the Code)

Present and Prior Law

Section 45D provides a new markets tax credit for qualified equity investments made to acquire stock in a corporation, or a capital interest in a partnership, that is a qualified community development entity ("CDE").[314] The amount of the credit allowable to the investor (either the original purchaser or a subsequent holder) is (1) a five-percent credit for the year in which the equity interest is purchased from the CDE and for each of the following two years, and (2) a six-percent credit for each of the following four years. The credit is determined by applying the applicable percentage (five or six percent) to the amount paid to the CDE for the investment at its original issue, and is available for a taxable year to the taxpayer who holds the qualified equity investment on the date of the initial investment or on the respective anniversary date that occurs during the taxable year. The credit is recaptured if at any time during the seven-year period that begins on the date of the original issue of the investment the entity ceases to be a qualified CDE, the proceeds of the investment cease to be used as required, or the equity investment is redeemed.

A qualified CDE is any domestic corporation or partnership: (1) whose primary mission is serving or providing investment capital for low-income communities or low-income persons; (2) that maintains accountability to residents of low-income communities by their representation on any governing board of or any advisory board to the CDE; and (3) that is certified by the Secretary as being a qualified CDE. A qualified equity investment means stock (other than nonqualified preferred stock) in a corporation or a capital interest in a partnership that is acquired directly from a CDE for cash, and includes an investment of a subsequent purchaser if such investment was a qualified equity investment in the hands of the prior holder. Substantially all of the investment proceeds must be used by the CDE to make qualified low-income community investments. For this purpose, qualified low-income community investments include: (1) capital or equity investments in, or loans to, qualified active low-income community businesses; (2) certain financial counseling and other services to businesses and residents in low-income communities; (3) the purchase from another CDE of any loan made by such entity that is a qualified low-income com-

[314] Section 45D was added by section 121(a) of the Community Renewal Tax Relief Act of 2000, Pub. L. No. 106–554 (December 21, 2000).

munity investment; or (4) an equity investment in, or loan to, another CDE.

Under prior law, a "low-income community" was defined as a population census tract with either (1) a poverty rate of at least 20 percent or (2) median family income which does not exceed 80 percent of the greater of metropolitan area median family income or statewide median family income (for a non-metropolitan census tract, does not exceed 80 percent of statewide median family income). Under prior law, the Secretary could designate any area within any census tract as a low-income community provided that (1) the boundary is continuous, (2) the area (if it were a census tract) would otherwise satisfy the poverty rate or median income requirements, and (3) an inadequate access to investment capital exists in the area.

A qualified active low-income community business is defined as a business that satisfies, with respect to a taxable year, the following requirements: (1) at least 50 percent of the total gross income of the business is derived from the active conduct of trade or business activities in any low-income community; (2) a substantial portion of the tangible property of such business is used in a low-income community; (3) a substantial portion of the services performed for such business by its employees is performed in a low-income community; and (4) less than five percent of the average of the aggregate unadjusted bases of the property of such business is attributable to certain financial property or to certain collectibles.

The maximum annual amount of qualified equity investments is capped at $2.0 billion per year for calendar years 2004 and 2005, and at $3.5 billion per year for calendar years 2006 and 2007.

Explanation of Provision

The Act modifies the Secretary's authority to designate certain areas as low-income communities to provide that the Secretary shall prescribe regulations to designate "targeted populations" as low-income communities for purposes of the new markets tax credit. For this purpose, a "targeted population" is defined by reference to section 103(20) of the Riegle Community Development and Regulatory Improvement Act of 1994 (12 U.S.C. 4702(20)) to mean individuals, or an identifiable group of individuals, including an Indian tribe, who (A) are low-income persons; or (B) otherwise lack adequate access to loans or equity investments. Under the Act, "low-income" means (1) for a targeted population within a metropolitan area, less than 80 percent of the area median family income; and (2) for a targeted population within a non-metropolitan area, less than the greater of 80 percent of the area median family income or 80 percent of the statewide non-metropolitan area median family income.[315] Under the Act, a targeted population is not required to be within any census tract. In addition, a population census tract with a population of less than 2,000 is treated under the Act as a low-income community for purposes of the credit if such tract is within an empowerment zone, the designation of which is in effect

[315] 12. U.S.C. 4702(17) (defines "low-income" for purposes of 12. U.S.C. 4702(20)).

under section 1391, and is contiguous to one or more low-income communities.

Effective Date

The targeted population provision is effective for designations made after the date of enactment (October 22, 2004). The low-population provision is effective for investments made after the date of enactment (October 22, 2004).

2. Expansion of designated renewal community area based on 2000 census data (sec. 222 of the Act and sec. 1400E of the Code)

Present and Prior Law

Section 1400E provides for the designation of certain communities as renewal communities.[316] An area designated as a renewal community is eligible for the following tax incentives: (1) a zero-percent rate for capital gain from the sale of qualifying assets; (2) a 15–percent wage credit to employers for the first $10,000 of qualified wages; (3) a "commercial revitalization deduction" that allows taxpayers (to the extent allocated by the appropriate State agency) to deduct either (a) 50 percent of qualifying expenditures for the taxable year in which a qualified building is placed in service, or (b) all of the qualifying expenditures ratably over a 10-year period beginning with the month in which such building is placed in service; (4) an additional $35,000 of section 179 expensing for qualified property; and (5) an expansion of the work opportunity tax credit with respect to individuals who live in a renewal community.

Under prior law, to be designated as a renewal community, a nominated area was required to meet the following criteria: (1) each census tract must have a poverty rate of at least 20 percent; (2) in the case of an urban area, at least 70 percent of the households have incomes below 80 percent of the median income of households within the local government jurisdiction; (3) the unemployment rate is at least 1.5 times the national unemployment rate; and (4) the area is one of pervasive poverty, unemployment, and general distress. There are no geographic size limitations placed on renewal communities. Instead, the boundary of a renewal community must be continuous. In addition, under prior law, the renewal community must have had a minimum population of 4,000 if the community is located within a metropolitan statistical area (at least 1,000 in all other cases), and a maximum population of not more than 200,000. Under present and prior law, the population limitations do not apply to any renewal community that is entirely within an Indian reservation.

The designations of renewal communities were required to have been made by December 31, 2001, using 1990 census data to determine relevant populations and poverty rates.

---

[316] Section 1400E was added by section 101(a) of the Community Renewal Tax Relief Act of 2000, Pub. L. No. 106–554 (December 21, 2000).

Explanation of Provision

The Act authorizes the Secretary of Housing and Urban Development, at the request of all of the governments that nominated a renewal community, to add a contiguous census tract to a renewal community in the following circumstances. First, the renewal community, including any tract to be added, would have met the renewal community eligibility requirements at the time of the community's original nomination, and any tract to be added has a poverty rate using 2000 census data that exceeds the poverty rate of such tract using 1990 census data. Second, a tract may be added to a renewal community even if the addition of such tract to such community would have caused the community to fail one or more eligibility requirements when originally nominated using 1990 census data, provided that: (1) the renewal community after the inclusion of such tract does not have a population that exceeds 200,000 using either 1990 or 2000 census data; (2) such tract has a poverty rate of at least 20 percent using 2000 census data; and (3) such tract has a poverty rate using 2000 census data that exceeds the poverty rate of such tract using 1990 census data. Census tracts that did not have a poverty rate determined by the Bureau of the Census using 1990 data may be added to an existing renewal community without satisfying requirement (3) above. Third, a tract may be added to an existing renewal community if such tract: (1) has no population using 2000 census data or no poverty rate for such tract is determined by the Bureau of the Census using 2000 census data; (2) such tract is one of general distress; and (3) the renewal community, including such tract, is within the jurisdiction of one or more local governments and has a continuous boundary.

Effective Date

The provision is effective as if included in the amendments made by section 101 of the Community Renewal Tax Relief Act of 2000.

3. Modification of income requirement for census tracts within high migration rural counties for new markets tax credit (sec. 223 of the Act and sec. 45D of the Code)

Present and Prior Law

Section 45D provides a new markets tax credit for qualified equity investments made to acquire stock in a corporation, or a capital interest in a partnership, that is a qualified community development entity ("CDE").[317] The amount of the credit allowable to the investor (either the original purchaser or a subsequent holder) is (1) a five-percent credit for the year in which the equity interest is purchased from the CDE and for each of the following two years, and (2) a six-percent credit for each of the following four years. The credit is determined by applying the applicable percentage (five or six percent) to the amount paid to the CDE for the investment at its original issue, and is available for the taxable year to the taxpayer who holds the qualified equity investment on the date of the

[317] Section 45D was added by section 121(a) of the Community Renewal Tax Relief Act of 2000, Pub. L. No. 106–554 (December 21, 2000).

initial investment or on the respective anniversary date that occurs during the taxable year. The credit is recaptured if at any time during the seven-year period that begins on the date of the original issue of the investment the entity ceases to be a qualified CDE, the proceeds of the investment cease to be used as required, or the equity investment is redeemed.

A qualified CDE is any domestic corporation or partnership: (1) whose primary mission is serving or providing investment capital for low-income communities or low-income persons; (2) that maintains accountability to residents of low-income communities by their representation on any governing board of or any advisory board to the CDE; and (3) that is certified by the Secretary as being a qualified CDE. A qualified equity investment means stock (other than nonqualified preferred stock) in a corporation or a capital interest in a partnership that is acquired directly from a CDE for cash, and includes an investment of a subsequent purchaser if such investment was a qualified equity investment in the hands of the prior holder. Substantially all of the investment proceeds must be used by the CDE to make qualified low-income community investments. For this purpose, qualified low-income community investments include: (1) capital or equity investments in, or loans to, qualified active low-income community businesses; (2) certain financial counseling and other services to businesses and residents in low-income communities; (3) the purchase from another CDE of any loan made by such entity that is a qualified low-income community investment; or (4) an equity investment in, or loan to, another CDE.

Under prior law, a "low-income community" was defined as a population census tract with either (1) a poverty rate of at least 20 percent or (2) median family income which does not exceed 80 percent of the greater of metropolitan area median family income or statewide median family income (for a non-metropolitan census tract, does not exceed 80 percent of statewide median family income). Under prior law, the Secretary could designate any area within any census tract as a low-income community provided that (1) the boundary is continuous, (2) the area (if it were a census tract) would otherwise satisfy the poverty rate or median income requirements, and (3) an inadequate access to investment capital exists in the area.

A qualified active low-income community business is defined as a business that satisfies, with respect to a taxable year, the following requirements: (1) at least 50 percent of the total gross income of the business is derived from the active conduct of trade or business activities in any low-income community; (2) a substantial portion of the tangible property of such business is used in a low-income community; (3) a substantial portion of the services performed for such business by its employees is performed in a low-income community; and (4) less than five percent of the average of the aggregate unadjusted bases of the property of such business is attributable to certain financial property or to certain collectibles.

The maximum annual amount of qualified equity investments is capped at $2.0 billion per year for calendar years 2004 and 2005, and at $3.5 billion per year for calendar years 2006 and 2007.

Explanation of Provision

The Act modifies the low-income test for high migration rural counties. Under the Act, in the case of a population census tract located within a high migration rural county, low-income is defined by reference to 85 percent (rather than 80 percent) of statewide median family income. For this purpose, a high migration rural county is any county that, during the 20-year period ending with the year in which the most recent census was conducted, has a net out-migration of inhabitants from the county of at least 10 percent of the population of the county at the beginning of such period.

Effective Date

The provision is effective as if included in the amendment made by section 121(a) of the Community Renewal Tax Relief Act of 2000.

D. S Corporation Reform and Simplification (secs. 231–240 of the Act and secs. 1361–1379 and 4975 of the Code)

Overview

In general, an S corporation is not subject to corporate-level income tax on its items of income and loss. Instead, an S corporation passes through its items of income and loss to its shareholders. The shareholders take into account separately their shares of these items on their individual income tax returns. To prevent double taxation of these items when the stock is later disposed of, each shareholder's basis in the stock of the S corporation is increased by the amount included in income (including tax-exempt income) and is decreased by the amount of any losses (including nondeductible losses) taken into account. A shareholder's loss may be deducted only to the extent of his or her basis in the stock or debt of the S corporation. To the extent a loss is not allowed due to this limitation, the loss generally is carried forward with respect to the shareholder.

Reasons for Change

The Act contains a number of general provisions relating to S corporations. The Congress adopted these provisions that modernize the S corporation rules and eliminate undue restrictions on S corporations in order to expand the application of the S corporation provisions so that more corporations and their shareholders will be able to enjoy the benefits of subchapter S status.

The Congress was aware of obstacles that have prevented banks from electing subchapter S status.[318] The Act contains provisions that apply specifically to banks in order to remove these obstacles and make S corporation status more readily available to banks.

The Act also revises the prohibited transaction rules applicable to employee stock ownership plans ("ESOPs") maintained by S corporations in order to expand the ability to use distributions made with respect to S corporation stock held by an ESOP to repay a

[318] See, for example, General Accounting Office GAO/GGD–00–159, *Banking Taxation: Implications of Proposed Revisions Governing S-Corporations on Community Banks* (June 23, 2000).

loan used to purchase the stock, subject to the same conditions that apply to C corporation dividends used to repay such a loan.

1. Members of family treated as one shareholder

Present and Prior Law

A small business corporation may elect to be an S corporation with the consent of all its shareholders, and may terminate its election with the consent of shareholders holding more than 50 percent of the stock. Under prior law, a "small business corporation" was defined as a domestic corporation which is not an ineligible corporation and which has (1) no more than 75 shareholders, all of whom are individuals (and certain trusts, estates, charities, and qualified retirement plans)[319] who are citizens or residents of the United States, and (2) only one class of stock. For purposes of the numerical-shareholder limitation, a husband and wife are treated as one shareholder. An "ineligible corporation" means a corporation that is a financial institution using the reserve method of accounting for bad debts, an insurance company, a corporation electing the benefits of the Puerto Rico and possessions tax credit, or a Domestic International Sales Corporation ("DISC") or former DISC.

Explanation of Provision

The Act provides an election to allow all members of a family (and their estates)[320] to be treated as one shareholder in determining the number of shareholders in the corporation (for purposes of section 1361(b)(1)(A)).

A family is defined as the common ancestor and all lineal descendants of the common ancestor, as well as the spouses, or former spouses, of these individuals. An individual shall not be a common ancestor if, as of the later of the time of the election or the effective date of this provision, the individual is more than six generations removed from the youngest generation of shareholders who would (but for this rule) be members of the family. For purposes of this rule, a spouse or former spouse is treated as being in the same generation as the member of the family to whom the individual is (or was) married.[321]

Except as provided by Treasury regulations, the election for a family may be made by any member of the family, and the election remains in effect until terminated.

Effective Date

The provision applies to taxable years beginning after December 31, 2004.

---

[319] If a qualified retirement plan (other than an employee stock ownership plan) or a charity holds stock in an S corporation, the interest held is treated as an interest in an unrelated trade or business, and the plan or charity's share of the S corporation's items of income, loss, or deduction, and gain or loss on the disposition of the S corporation stock, are taken into account in computing unrelated business taxable income.

[320] A technical correction may be necessary so that the statute reflects this intent.

[321] Members of a family may be treated as one shareholder for the purpose of determining the number of shareholders, whether a family member holds stock directly or is treated as a shareholder under section 1361(c)(2)(B) by reason being a beneficiary of certain types of trusts.

2. Increase in maximum number of shareholders to 100

Present and Prior Law

A small business corporation may elect to be an S corporation with the consent of all its shareholders, and may terminate its election with the consent of shareholders holding more than 50 percent of the stock. Under prior law, a "small business corporation" was defined as a domestic corporation which is not an ineligible corporation and which has (1) no more than 75 shareholders, all of whom are individuals (and certain trusts, estates, charities, and qualified retirement plans)[322] who are citizens or residents of the United States, and (2) only one class of stock. For purposes of the numerical-shareholder limitation, a husband and wife are treated as one shareholder. An "ineligible corporation" means a corporation that is a financial institution using the reserve method of accounting for bad debts, an insurance company, a corporation electing the benefits of the Puerto Rico and possessions tax credit, or a Domestic International Sales Corporation ("DISC") or former DISC.

Explanation of Provision

The Act increases the maximum number of shareholders from 75 to 100.

Effective Date

The provision applies to taxable years beginning after December 31, 2004.

3. Expansion of bank S corporation eligible shareholders to include IRAs

Present and Prior Law

An individual retirement account ("IRA") is a trust or account established for the exclusive benefit of an individual and his or her beneficiaries. There are two general types of IRAs: traditional IRAs, to which both deductible and nondeductible contributions may be made, and Roth IRAs, contributions to which are not deductible. Amounts held in a traditional IRA are includible in income when withdrawn (except to the extent the withdrawal is a return of nondeductible contributions). Amounts held in a Roth IRA that are withdrawn as a qualified distribution are not includible in income; distributions from a Roth IRA that are not qualified distributions are includible in income to the extent attributable to earnings. A qualified distribution is a distribution that: (1) is made after the five-taxable year period beginning with the first taxable year for which the individual made a contribution to a Roth IRA, and (2) is made after attainment of age 59½, on account of death or disability, or is made for first-time homebuyer expenses of up to $10,000.

---

[322] If a qualified retirement plan (other than an employee stock ownership plan) or a charity holds stock in an S corporation, the interest held is treated as an interest in an unrelated trade or business, and the plan or charity's share of the S corporation's items of income, loss, or deduction, and gain or loss on the disposition of the S corporation stock, are taken into account in computing unrelated business taxable income.

Under prior law, an IRA could not be a shareholder of an S corporation.

Certain transactions are prohibited between an IRA and the individual for whose benefit the IRA is established, including a sale of property by the IRA to the individual. If a prohibited transaction occurs between an IRA and the IRA beneficiary, the account ceases to be an IRA, and an amount equal to the fair market value of the assets held in the IRA is deemed distributed to the beneficiary.

Explanation of Provision

The Act allows an IRA (including a Roth IRA) to be a shareholder of a bank that is an S corporation, but only to the extent of bank stock held by the IRA on the date of enactment of the provision (October 22, 2004). Under the Act, the present-law rules treating S corporation stock held by a qualified retirement plan (other than an employee stock ownership plan) or a charity as an interest in an unrelated trade or business apply to the IRA with respect to its holding in the stock.

The Act also provides an exemption from prohibited transaction treatment for the sale by an IRA to the IRA beneficiary of bank stock held by the IRA on the date of enactment (October 22, 2004) of the provision. Under the Act, a sale is not a prohibited transaction if: (1) the sale is pursuant to an S corporation election by the bank; (2) the sale is for fair market value (as established by an independent appraiser) and is on terms at least as favorable to the IRA as the terms would be on a sale to an unrelated party; (3) the IRA incurs no commissions, costs, or other expenses in connection with the sale; and (4) the stock is sold in a single transaction for cash not later than 120 days after the S corporation election is made.

Effective Date

The provision takes effect on the date of enactment (October 22, 2004).

4. Disregard of unexercised powers of appointment in determining potential current beneficiaries of ESBT

Present and Prior Law

An electing small business trust ("ESBT") holding stock in an S corporation is taxed at the maximum individual tax rate on its ratable share of items of income, deduction, gain, or loss passing through from the S corporation. An ESBT generally is an electing trust all of whose beneficiaries are eligible S corporation shareholders. For purposes of determining the maximum number of shareholders, each person who is entitled to receive a distribution from the trust ("potential current beneficiary") is treated as a shareholder during the period the person may receive a distribution from the trust.

Under prior law, an ESBT had 60 days to dispose of the S corporation stock after an ineligible shareholder became a potential current beneficiary to avoid disqualification.

Explanation of Provision

Under the Act, powers of appointment to the extent not exercised are disregarded in determining the potential current beneficiaries of an electing small business trust.

The Act increases the period during which an ESBT can dispose of S corporation stock, after an ineligible shareholder becomes a potential current beneficiary, from 60 days to one year.

Effective Date

The provision applies to taxable years beginning after December 31, 2004.

5. Transfers of suspended losses incident to divorce, etc.

Present and Prior Law

Under prior law, any loss or deduction that was not allowed to a shareholder of an S corporation, because the loss exceeded the shareholder's basis in stock and debt of the corporation, was treated as incurred by the S corporation with respect to that shareholder in the subsequent taxable year.

Explanation of Provision

Under the Act, if a shareholder's stock in an S corporation is transferred to a spouse, or to a former spouse incident to a divorce, any suspended loss or deduction with respect to that stock is treated as incurred by the corporation with respect to the transferee in the subsequent taxable year.

Effective Date

The provision applies to transfers of stock after December 31, 2004.[323]

6. Use of passive activity loss and at-risk amounts by qualified subchapter S trust income beneficiaries

Present and Prior Law

Under present and prior law, the share of income of an S corporation, whose stock is held by a qualified subchapter S trust ("QSST") with respect to which the beneficiary makes an election, is taxed to the beneficiary. However, the trust, and not the beneficiary, is treated as the owner of the S corporation stock for purposes of determining the tax consequences of the disposition of the S corporation stock by the trust. A QSST generally is a trust with one individual income beneficiary for the life of the beneficiary.

Explanation of Provision

Under the Act, the beneficiary of a qualified subchapter S trust is generally allowed to deduct suspended losses under the at-risk rules and the passive loss rules when the trust disposes of the S corporation stock.

[323] A technical correction may be necessary so that the statute reflects this intent.

Effective Date

The provision applies to transfers made after December 31, 2004.

7. Exclusion of investment securities income from passive investment income test for bank S corporations

Present and Prior Law

An S corporation is subject to corporate-level tax, at the highest corporate tax rate, on its excess net passive income if the corporation has (1) accumulated earnings and profits at the close of the taxable year and (2) gross receipts more than 25 percent of which are passive investment income.

Excess net passive income is the net passive income for a taxable year multiplied by a fraction, the numerator of which is the amount of passive investment income in excess of 25 percent of gross receipts and the denominator of which is the passive investment income for the year. Net passive income is defined as passive investment income reduced by the allowable deductions that are directly connected with the production of that income. Passive investment income generally means gross receipts derived from royalties, rents, dividends, interest, annuities, and sales or exchanges of stock or securities (to the extent of gains). Passive investment income generally does not include interest on accounts receivable, gross receipts that are derived directly from the active and regular conduct of a lending or finance business, gross receipts from certain liquidations, or gain or loss from any section 1256 contract (or related property) of an options or commodities dealer.[324]

In addition, an S corporation election is terminated whenever the S corporation has accumulated earnings and profits at the close of each of three consecutive taxable years and has gross receipts for each of those years more than 25 percent of which are passive investment income.

Explanation of Provision

The Act provides that, in the case of a bank (as defined in section 581), a bank holding company (as defined in section 2(a) of the Bank Holding Company Act of 1956) or a financial holding company (as defined in section 2(p) of that Act), interest income and dividends on assets required to be held by the bank or holding company are not treated as passive investment income for purposes of the S corporation passive investment income rules.

Effective Date

The provision applies to taxable years beginning after December 31, 2004.

[324] Notice 97–5, 1997–1 C.B. 352, sets forth guidance relating to passive investment income on banking assets.

8. Relief from inadvertently invalid qualified subchapter S subsidiary elections and terminations

Present and Prior Law

Under present and prior law, inadvertent invalid subchapter S elections and terminations may be waived.

Explanation of Provision

The Act allows inadvertent invalid qualified subchapter S subsidiary elections and terminations to be waived by the IRS.

Effective Date

The provision applies to elections made and terminations made after December 31, 2004.

9. Information returns for qualified subchapter S subsidiaries

Present and Prior Law

A corporation all of whose stock is held by an S corporation is treated as a qualified subchapter S subsidiary if the S corporation so elects. The assets, liabilities, and items of income, deduction, and credit of the subsidiary are treated as assets, liabilities, and items of the parent S corporation.

Explanation of Provision

The Act provides authority to the Secretary to provide guidance regarding information returns of qualified subchapter S subsidiaries.

Effective Date

The provision applies to taxable years beginning after December 31, 2004.

10. Repayment of loans for qualifying employer securities

Present and Prior Law

An employee stock ownership plan (an "ESOP") is a defined contribution plan that is designated as an ESOP and is designed to invest primarily in qualifying employer securities. For purposes of ESOP investments, a "qualifying employer security" is defined as: (1) publicly traded common stock of the employer or a member of the same controlled group; (2) if there is no such publicly traded common stock, common stock of the employer (or member of the same controlled group) that has both voting power and dividend rights at least as great as any other class of common stock; or (3) noncallable preferred stock that is convertible into common stock described in (1) or (2) and that meets certain requirements. In some cases, an employer may design a class of preferred stock that meets these requirements and that is held only by the ESOP. Special rules apply to ESOPs that do not apply to other types of qualified retirement plans, including a special exemption from the prohibited transaction rules.

Certain transactions between an employee benefit plan and a disqualified person, including the employer maintaining the plan, are prohibited transactions that result in the imposition of an excise tax.[325] Prohibited transactions include, among other transactions, (1) the sale, exchange or leasing of property between a plan and a disqualified person, (2) the lending of money or other extension of credit between a plan and a disqualified person, and (3) the transfer to, or use by or for the benefit of, a disqualified person of the income or assets of the plan. However, certain transactions are exempt from prohibited transaction treatment, including certain loans to enable an ESOP to purchase qualifying employer securities.[326] In such a case, the employer securities purchased with the loan proceeds are generally pledged as security for the loan. Contributions to the ESOP and dividends paid on employer securities held by the ESOP are used to repay the loan. The employer securities are held in a suspense account and released for allocation to participants' accounts as the loan is repaid.

A loan to an ESOP is exempt from prohibited transaction treatment if the loan is primarily for the benefit of the participants and their beneficiaries, the loan is at a reasonable rate of interest, and the collateral given to a disqualified person consists of only qualifying employer securities. No person entitled to payments under the loan can have the right to any assets of the ESOP other than (1) collateral given for the loan, (2) contributions made to the ESOP to meet its obligations on the loan, and (3) earnings attributable to the collateral and the investment of contributions described in (2).[327] In addition, the payments made on the loan by the ESOP during a plan year cannot exceed the sum of those contributions and earnings during the current and prior years, less loan payments made in prior years.

An ESOP of a C corporation is not treated as violating the qualification requirements of the Code or as engaging in a prohibited transaction merely because, in accordance with plan provisions, a dividend paid with respect to qualifying employer securities held by the ESOP is used to make payments on a loan (including payments of interest as well as principal) that was used to acquire the employer securities (whether or not allocated to participants).[328] In the case of a dividend paid with respect to any employer security that is allocated to a participant, this relief does not apply unless the plan provides that employer securities with a fair market value of not less than the amount of the dividend are allocated to the participant for the year which the dividend would have been allocated to the participant.[329]

Explanation of Provision

Under the Act, an ESOP maintained by an S corporation is not treated as violating the qualification requirements of the Code or as engaging in a prohibited transaction merely because, in accord-

[325] Sec. 4975.

[326] Sec. 4975(d)(3). An ESOP that borrows money to purchase employer stock is referred to as a "leveraged" ESOP.

[327] Treas. Reg. sec. 54.4975–7(b)(5).

[328] Sec. 404(k)(5)(B).

[329] Sec. 404(k)(2)(B).

ance with plan provisions, a distribution made with respect to S corporation stock that constitutes qualifying employer securities held by the ESOP is used to repay a loan that was used to acquire the securities (whether or not allocated to participants). This relief does not apply in the case of a distribution with respect to S corporation stock that is allocated to a participant unless the plan provides that stock with a fair market value of not less than the amount of such distribution is allocated to the participant for the year which the distribution would have been allocated to the participant.

Effective Date

The provision is effective for distributions made with respect to S corporation stock after December 31, 1997.

E. Other Business Incentives

1. Repeal certain excise taxes on rail diesel fuel and inland waterway barge fuels (sec. 241 of the Act and secs. 4041, 4042, 6421, and 6427 of the Code)

Present and Prior Law

Diesel fuel used in trains is subject to a 4.4-cents-per-gallon excise tax. Revenues from 4.3 cents per gallon of this excise tax are retained in the General Fund of the Treasury. The remaining 0.1 cent per gallon is deposited in the Leaking Underground Storage Tank ("LUST") Trust Fund.

Similarly, fuels used in barges operating on the designated inland waterways system are subject to a 4.3-cents-per-gallon General Fund excise tax. This tax is in addition to the 20.1-cents-per-gallon tax rates that are imposed on fuels used in these barges to fund the Inland Waterways Trust Fund and the Leaking Underground Storage Tank Trust Fund.

Under prior law, the 4.3-cents-per-gallon excise tax rates were permanent. The LUST Trust Fund tax was scheduled to expire after March 31, 2005.[330]

Reasons for Change[331]

In 1993, the Congress enacted the present-law 4.3-cents-per-gallon excise tax on motor fuels as a deficit reduction measure, with the receipts payable to the General Fund. Since that time, the Congress has diverted the 4.3-cents-per-gallon excise tax for most uses to specified trust funds that provide benefits for those motor fuel users who ultimately bear the burden of these taxes. As a result, the Congress found that generally only rail and barge operators remain as motor fuel users subject to the 4.3-cents-per-gallon excise tax who receive no benefits from a dedicated trust fund as a result of their tax burden. The Congress observed that rail and barge operators compete with other transportation service providers who benefit from expenditures paid from dedicated trust funds. The

---

[330] On March 31, 2005, Pub. L. No. 109–6 extended the LUST Trust Fund tax through September 30, 2005.

[331] See H.R. 1537, the "Energy Tax Policy Act of 2003", which was reported by the House Committee on Ways and Means on April 9, 2003 (H.R. Rep. No. 108–67).

Congress concluded that it is inequitable and distortive of transportation decisions to continue to impose the 4.3-cents-per-gallon excise tax on diesel fuel used in trains and barges.

Explanation of Provision

The Act repeals the 4.3-cents-per-gallon General Fund excise tax rates on diesel fuel used in trains and fuels used in barges operating on the designated inland waterways system over a prescribed phase-out period. The 4.3-cent-per-gallon tax is reduced by 1 cent per gallon for the first six months of calendar year 2005 (January 1, 2005 through June 30, 2005). The reduction is 2 cents per gallon from July 1, 2005 through December 31, 2006, and 4.3 cents/gallon thereafter. Thus, the tax is fully repealed effective January 1, 2007. The 0.1 cent per gallon tax for the LUST Trust Fund is unchanged by the provision.

Effective Date

The provision is effective on January 1, 2005.

2. Modification of application of income forecast method of depreciation (sec. 242 of the Act and sec. 167 of the Code)

Present and Prior Law

In general

The modified accelerated cost recovery system ("MACRS") does not apply to certain property, including any motion picture film, video tape, or sound recording, or to any other property if the taxpayer elects to exclude such property from MACRS and the taxpayer properly applies a unit-of-production method or other method of depreciation not expressed in a term of years. Section 197 does not apply to certain intangible property, including property produced by the taxpayer or any interest in a film, sound recording, video tape, book or similar property not acquired in a transaction (or a series of related transactions) involving the acquisition of assets constituting a trade or business or substantial portion thereof. Thus, the recovery of the cost of a film, video tape, or similar property that is produced by the taxpayer or is acquired on a "standalone" basis by the taxpayer may not be determined under either the MACRS depreciation provisions or under the section 197 amortization provisions. The cost recovery of such property may be determined under section 167, which allows a depreciation deduction for the reasonable allowance for the exhaustion, wear and tear, or obsolescence of the property. A taxpayer is allowed to recover, through annual depreciation deductions, the cost of certain property used in a trade or business or for the production of income. Section 167(g) provides that the cost of motion picture films, sound recordings, copyrights, books, and patents are eligible to be recovered using the income forecast method of depreciation.

Income forecast method of depreciation

Under the income forecast method, a property's depreciation deduction for a taxable year is determined by multiplying the adjusted basis of the property by a fraction, the numerator of which is the income generated by the property during the year and the denominator of which is the total forecasted or estimated income expected to be generated prior to the close of the tenth taxable year after the year the property was placed in service. Any costs that are not recovered by the end of the tenth taxable year after the property was placed in service may be taken into account as depreciation in such year.

The adjusted basis of property that may be taken into account under the income forecast method only includes amounts that satisfy the economic performance standard of section 461(h). In addition, taxpayers that claim depreciation deductions under the income forecast method are required to pay (or receive) interest based on a recalculation of depreciation under a "look-back" method.

The "look-back" method is applied in any "recomputation year" by (1) comparing depreciation deductions that had been claimed in prior periods to depreciation deductions that would have been claimed had the taxpayer used actual, rather than estimated, total income from the property; (2) determining the hypothetical overpayment or underpayment of tax based on this recalculated depreciation; and (3) applying the overpayment rate of section 6621 of the Code. Except as provided in Treasury regulations, a "recomputation year" is the third and tenth taxable year after the taxable year the property was placed in service, unless the actual income from the property for each taxable year ending with or before the close of such years was within 10 percent of the estimated income from the property for such years.

Reasons for Change

The Congress was aware that taxpayers and the IRS have expended significant resources in auditing and litigating disputes regarding the proper treatment of participations and residuals for purposes of computing depreciation under the income forecast method of depreciation. The Congress understood that these issues related solely to the timing of deductions and not to whether such costs are valid deductions. In addition, the Congress was aware of other disagreements between taxpayers and the Treasury Department regarding the mechanics of the income forecast formula. The Congress believed expending taxpayer and government resources disputing these items was an unproductive use of economic resources. As such, the Act addressed the issues and eliminated any uncertainty as to the proper tax treatment of these items.

Explanation of Provision

The Act clarifies that, solely for purposes of computing the allowable deduction for property under the income forecast method of depreciation, participations and residuals may be included in the adjusted basis of the property beginning in the year such property is placed in service, but only if such participations and residuals relate to income to be derived from the property before the close of the tenth taxable year following the year the property is placed in service (as defined in section 167(g)(1)(A)). For purposes of the Act, participations and residuals are defined as costs the amount of which, by contract, varies with the amount of income earned in connection with such property. The Act also clarifies that the income from the property to be taken into account under the income forecast method is the gross income from such property.

The Act also grants authority to the Treasury Department to prescribe appropriate adjustments to the basis of property (and the look-back method) to reflect the treatment of participations and residuals under the Act.

In addition, the Act clarifies that, in the case of property eligible for the income forecast method that the holding in the *Associated Patentees*[332] decision will continue to constitute a valid method. Thus, rather than accounting for participations and residuals as a cost of the property under the income forecast method of depreciation, the taxpayer may deduct those payments as they are paid as under the *Associated Patentees* decision. This may be done on a property-by-property basis and shall be applied consistently with respect to a given property thereafter. The Act also clarifies that distribution costs are not taken into account for purposes of determining the taxpayer's current and total forecasted income with respect to a property.

Effective Date

The provision applies to property placed in service after date of enactment (October 22, 2004). No inference is intended as to the appropriate treatment under present and prior law. It is intended that the Treasury Department and the IRS expedite the resolution of open cases. In resolving these cases in an expedited and balanced manner, the Treasury Department and IRS are encouraged to take into account the principles of the provision.

3. Improvements related to real estate investment trusts (sec. 243 of the Act and secs. 856, 857 and 860 of the Code)

Present and Prior Law

In general

Under present and prior law, real estate investment trusts ("REITs") are treated, in substance, as pass through entities. Pass through status is achieved by allowing the REIT a deduction for dividends paid to its shareholders. The REIT's shareholders, in turn, include REIT dividends in their taxable income. REITs are generally restricted to investing in passive investments primarily in real estate and certain securities.

A REIT must satisfy four tests on a year-by-year basis: organizational structure, source of income, nature of its assets, and distribution of income. Whether the REIT meets the asset tests is generally measured each quarter.

Organizational structure requirements

Under present and prior law, to qualify as a REIT, an entity must be for its entire taxable year a corporation or a trust or asso-

---

[332] *Associated Patentees, Inc.* v. *Commissioner,* 4 T.C. 979 (1945).

ciation that would be taxable as a domestic corporation but for the REIT provisions, and must be managed by one or more trustees. The beneficial ownership of the entity must be evidenced by transferable shares or certificates of ownership. Except for the first taxable year for which an entity elects to be a REIT, the beneficial ownership of the entity must be held by 100 or more persons, and the entity may not be so closely held by individuals that it would be treated as a personal holding company if all its adjusted gross income constituted personal holding company income. A REIT is required to comply with regulations to ascertain the actual ownership of the REIT's outstanding shares.

Income requirements

In general

Under present and prior law, in order for an entity to qualify as a REIT, at least 95 percent of its gross income generally must be derived from certain passive sources (the "95-percent income test"). In addition, at least 75 percent of its income generally must be from certain real estate sources (the "75-percent income test"), including rents from real property (as defined) and gain from the sale or other disposition of real property, and income and gain derived from foreclosure property.

Qualified rental income

Under present and prior law, amounts received as impermissible "tenant services income" are not treated as rents from real property.[333] In general, such amounts are for services rendered to tenants that are not "customarily furnished" in connection with the rental of real property.[334]

Rents from real property, for purposes of the 95-percent and 75-percent income tests, generally do not include any amount received or accrued from any person in which the REIT owns, directly or indirectly, 10 percent or more of the vote or value.[335] An exception applies to rents received from a taxable REIT subsidiary ("TRS") (described further below) if at least 90 percent of the leased space of the property is rented to persons other than a TRS or certain related persons, and if the rents from the TRS are substantially comparable to unrelated party rents.[336]

Certain hedging instruments

Under prior law, except as provided in regulations, a payment to a REIT under an interest rate swap or cap agreement, option, futures contract, forward rate agreement, or any similar financial instrument, entered into by the trust in a transaction to reduce the

[333] A REIT is not treated as providing services that produce impermissible tenant services income if such services are provided by an independent contractor from whom the REIT does not derive or receive any income. An independent contractor is defined as a person who does not own, directly or indirectly, more than 35 percent of the shares of the REIT. Also, no more than 35 percent of the total shares of stock of an independent contractor (or of the interests in net assets or net profits, if not a corporation) can be owned directly or indirectly by persons owning 35 percent or more of the interests in the REIT.

[334] Rents for certain personal property leased in connection with the rental of real property are treated as rents from real property if the fair market value of the personal property does not exceed 15 percent of the aggregate fair market values of the real and personal property.

[335] Sec. 856(d)(2)(B).

[336] Sec. 856(d)(8).

interest rate risks with respect to any indebtedness incurred or to be incurred by the REIT to acquire or carry real estate assets, and any gain from the sale or disposition of any such investment, was treated as income qualifying for the 95-percent income test.

Tax if qualified income tests not met

Under present and prior law, if a REIT fails to meet the 95-percent or 75-percent income tests but has set out the income it did receive in a schedule and any error in the schedule is not due to fraud with intent to evade tax, then the REIT does not lose its REIT status provided that the failure to meet the 95-percent or 75-percent test is due to reasonable cause and not due to willful neglect. If the REIT qualifies for this relief, the REIT must pay a tax measured by the greater of the amount by which 90 percent under prior law[337] of the REIT's gross income exceeds the amount of items subject to the 95-percent test, or the amount by which 75 percent of the REIT's gross income exceeds the amount of items subject to the 75-percent test.[338]

Asset requirements

75-percent asset test

Under present and prior law, to satisfy the asset requirements to qualify for treatment as a REIT, at the close of each quarter of its taxable year, an entity must have at least 75 percent of the value of its assets invested in real estate assets, cash and cash items, and government securities (the "75-percent asset test"). The term real estate asset is defined to mean real property (including interests in real property and mortgages on real property) and interests in REITs.

Limitation on investment in other entities

Under present and prior law, a REIT is limited in the amount that it can own in other corporations. Specifically, a REIT cannot own securities (other than Government securities and certain real estate assets) in an amount greater than 25 percent of the value of REIT assets. In addition, it cannot own such securities of any one issuer representing more than 5 percent of the total value of REIT assets or more than 10 percent of the voting securities or 10 percent of the value of the outstanding securities of any one issuer. Securities for purposes of these rules are defined by reference to the Investment Company Act of 1940.

"Straight debt" exception

Under prior law, securities of an issuer that are within a safe-harbor definition of "straight debt" (as defined for purposes of sub-

[337] Prior to 1999, the rule had applied to the amount by which 95 percent of the income exceeded the items subject to the 95 percent test. Between 1999 and the effective date of the Act, the percent of income used in the fraction was reduced to 90 percent. The Act restored the 95 percent of income factor.

[338] The ratio of the REIT's net to gross income is applied to the excess amount, to determine the amount of tax (disregarding certain items otherwise subject to a 100-percent tax). In effect, the formula seeks to require that all of the REIT net income attributable to the failure of the income tests will be paid as tax. Sec. 857(b)(5).

chapter S)[339] were not taken into account in applying the limitation that a REIT may not hold more than 10 percent of the value of outstanding securities of a single issuer, if: (1) the issuer was an individual; (2) the only securities of such issuer held by the REIT or a taxable REIT subsidiary of the REIT were straight debt; or (3) the issuer was a partnership and the trust holds at least a 20 percent profits interest in the partnership.

Under prior law, straight debt for purposes of the REIT provision was defined as a written or unconditional promise to pay on demand or on a specified date a sum certain in money if (i) the interest rate (and interest payment dates) were not contingent on profits, the borrower's discretion, or similar factors, and (ii) there was no convertibility (directly or indirectly) into stock.

Certain subsidiary ownership permitted with income treated as income of the REIT

Under present and prior law, one exception to the rule limiting a REIT's securities holdings to no more than 10 percent of the vote or value of a single issuer allows a REIT to own 100 percent of the stock of a corporation, but in that case the income and assets of such corporation are treated as income and assets of the REIT.

Special rules for taxable REIT subsidiaries

Under present and prior law, another exception to the general rule limiting REIT securities ownership of other entities allows a REIT to own stock of a taxable REIT subsidiary ("TRS"), generally, a corporation other than a real estate investment trust[340] with which the REIT makes a joint election to be subject to special rules. A TRS can engage in active business operations that would produce income that would not be qualified income for purposes of the 95-percent or 75-percent income tests for a REIT, and that income is not attributed to the REIT. For example a TRS could provide noncustomary services to REIT tenants, or it could engage directly in the active operation and management of real estate (without use of an independent contractor); and the income the TRS derived from these nonqualified activities would not be treated as disqualified REIT income. Transactions between a TRS and a REIT are subject to a number of specified rules that are intended to prevent the TRS (taxable as a separate corporate entity) from shifting taxable income from its activities to the pass-through entity REIT or from absorbing more than its share of expenses. Under one rule, a 100-percent excise tax is imposed on rents to the extent that the amount of the rents would be reduced on distribution, apportionment, or allocation under section 482 to clearly reflect income as a result of services furnished by a TRS of the REIT to a tenant of the REIT.[341]

Under prior law, the 100-percent excise tax did not apply to amounts received directly or indirectly by a REIT from a TRS that

---

[339] Sec. 1361(c)(5), without regard to paragraph (B)(iii) thereof.

[340] Certain corporations are not eligible to be a TRS, such as a corporation which directly or indirectly operates or manages a lodging facility or a health care facility, or directly or indirectly provides to any other person rights to a brand name under which any lodging facility or health care facility is operated. Sec. 856(l)(3).

[341] If the excise tax applies, then the item is not reallocated back to the TRS under section 482.

would be excluded from unrelated taxable income if received by an organization described in section 511(a)(2). Such amounts are defined in section 512(b)(3). Also, the tax did not apply to income received by the REIT for services performed by the TRS that could have been performed directly by the REIT and produced qualified rental income, because they were customary services.

Under present and prior law, rents paid by a TRS to a REIT generally are treated as rents from real property if at least 90 percent of the leased space of the property is rented to persons other than the REIT's TRSs and other than persons related to the REIT. In such a case, the rent paid by the TRS to the REIT is treated as rent from real property only to the extent that it is substantially comparable to rents from other tenants of the REIT's property for comparable space.

Income distribution requirements

Under present and prior law, a REIT is generally required to distribute 90 percent of its income before the end of its taxable year, as deductible dividends paid to shareholders. This rule is similar to a rule for regulated investment companies ("RICs") that requires distribution of 90 percent of income. If a REIT declares certain dividends after the end of its taxable year but before the time prescribed for filing its return for that year and distributes those amounts to shareholders within the 12 months following the close of that taxable year, such distributions are treated as made during such taxable year for this purpose. As described further below, a REIT can also make certain "deficiency dividends" after the close of the taxable year after a determination that it has not distributed the correct amount for qualification as a REIT.

Consequences of failure to meet requirements

Under present and prior law, unless the REIT satisfies rules allowing the cure of a failure, a REIT loses its status as a REIT, and becomes subject to tax as a C corporation, if it fails to meet specified tests regarding the sources of its income, the nature and amount of its assets, its structure, and the amount of its income distributed to shareholders.

Under present and prior law, if a REIT fails to meet the source of income requirements, but has set out the income it did receive in a schedule and any error in the schedule is not due to fraud with intent to evade tax, then the REIT does not lose its REIT status, provided that the failure to meet the 95-percent or 75-percent test is due to reasonable cause and not to willful neglect. If the REIT qualifies for this relief, the REIT must pay the disallowed income as a tax to the Treasury.[342]

Failure to satisfy the asset test by reason of certain acquisitions during a quarter is excused if the REIT eliminates the discrepancy within 30 days. Failure to meet distribution requirements may also be excused if the REIT establishes to the satisfaction of the Secretary that it was unable to meet such requirement by reason of distributions previously made to meet the requirements of section 4981.

---

[342] Secs. 856(c)(6) and 857(b)(5).

Under prior law, there were no similar provisions that allow a REIT to pay a penalty and avoid disqualification in the case of other qualification failures.

Under present and prior law, a REIT may make a deficiency dividend after a determination is made that it has not distributed the correct amount of its income, and avoid disqualification. Under prior law, the Code provided only for determinations involving a controversy with or closing agreement or other allowed agreement with the IRS, and did not provide for a REIT to make such a distribution on its own initiative. Deficiency dividends could be declared on or after the date of "determination". A determination was defined to include only (i) a final decision by the Tax Court or other court of competent jurisdiction, (ii) a closing agreement under section 7121, or (iii) under Treasury regulations, an agreement signed by the Secretary and the REIT.

Reasons for Change

The Congress believed that a number of simplifying and conforming changes should be made to the "straight debt" provisions that exempt certain securities from the rule that a REIT may not hold more than 10 percent of the value of securities of a single issuer, as well as to the TRS rules, the rules relating to certain hedging arrangements, and the computation of tax liability when the 95-percent gross income test is not met.

The Congress also believed it was desirable to provide rules under which a REIT that inadvertently fails to meet certain REIT qualification requirements can correct such failure without losing REIT status.

Explanation of Provision

In general

The Act makes a number of modifications to the REIT rules.

Straight debt modification

In general

The Act modifies the definition of "straight debt" for purposes of the limitation that a REIT may not hold more than 10 percent of the value of the outstanding securities of a single issuer, to provide more flexibility than the present law rule. In addition, except as provided in regulations, neither such straight debt nor certain other types of securities are considered "securities" for purposes of this rule.

Straight debt securities

As under prior law, "straight-debt" is still defined by reference to section 1361(c)(5), without regard to subparagraph (B)(iii) thereof (limiting the nature of the creditor).

Special rules are provided permitting certain contingencies for purposes of the REIT provision. Any interest or principal shall not be treated as failing to satisfy section 1361(c)(5)(B)(i) solely by reason of the fact that the time of payment of such interest or principal is subject to a contingency, but only if (i) the contingency is one that does not have the effect of changing the effective yield to maturity, as determined under section 1272, other than a change in the annual yield to maturity that does not exceed the greater of ¼ of one percent or five percent of the annual yield to maturity, or (ii) neither the aggregate issue price nor the aggregate face amount of the issuer's debt instruments held by the REIT exceeds $1,000,000 and not more than 12 months of unaccrued interest can be required to be prepaid thereunder.

Also, the time or amount of any payment is permitted to be subject to a contingency upon a default or the exercise of a prepayment right by the issuer of the debt, provided that such contingency is consistent with customary commercial practice.[343]

The Act eliminates the prior law rule that straight debt securities are not counted if the REIT owns at least a 20 percent equity interest in a partnership. The Act instead provides new "look-through" rules determining a REIT partner's share of partnership securities, generally treating debt to the REIT as part of the REIT's partnership interest for this purpose, except in the case of otherwise qualifying debt of the partnership.[344]

Certain corporate or partnership issues that otherwise would be permitted to be held without limitation under the new special straight debt rules described above will not be so permitted if the REIT holding such securities, and any of its taxable REIT subsidiaries, holds any securities of the issuer which are not permitted securities (prior to the application of this rule) and have an aggregate value greater than one percent of the issuer's outstanding securities.

Other securities

Except as provided in regulations, the following also are not considered "securities" for purposes of the rule that a REIT cannot own more than 10 percent of the value of the outstanding securities of a single issuer: (i) any loan to an individual or an estate, (ii) any section 467 rental agreement, (as defined in section 467(d)), other than with a person described in section 856(d)(2)(B), (iii) any obligation to pay rents from real property, (iv) any security issued by a State or any political subdivision thereof, the District of Columbia, a foreign government, or any political subdivision thereof, or the Commonwealth of Puerto Rico, but only if the determination of any payment received or accrued under such security does not depend in whole or in part on the profits of any entity not described in this category, or payments on any obligation issued by such an entity, (v) any security issued by a real estate investment trust; and (vi) any other arrangement that, as determined by the Secretary, is excepted from the definition of a security.

In addition, any debt instrument issued by a partnership and not otherwise exempted from the definition of a "security" under the straight debt exception or under the categories listed above shall not be considered a security if at least 75 percent of the partner-

---

343 The prior law rules that limit qualified interest income to amounts the determination of which do not depend, in whole or in part, on the income or profits of any person, continue to apply to such contingent interest. See, e.g., secs. 856(c)(2)(G), 856(c)(3)(G) and 856(f).

344 Secs. 856(m)(3) and 856(m)(4)(A).

ship's gross income (excluding gross income from prohibited transactions) is derived from sources referred to in section 856(c)(3).[345]

Safe harbor testing date for certain rents

The Act provides specific safe-harbor rules regarding the dates for testing whether 90 percent of a REIT property is rented to unrelated persons and whether the rents paid by related persons are substantially comparable to unrelated party rents. These testing rules are provided solely for purposes of the special provision permitting rents received from a TRS to be treated as qualified rental income for purposes of the income tests.[346]

Customary services exception

The Act prospectively eliminates the safe harbor allowing rents received by a REIT to be exempt from the 100 percent excise tax if the rents are for customary services performed by the TRS[347] or are from a TRS and are described in section 512(b)(3). Instead, such payments are free of the excise tax if they satisfy the present law safe-harbor that applies if the REIT pays the TRS at least 150 percent of the cost to the TRS of providing any services.

Hedging rules

The rules governing the tax treatment of arrangements engaged in by a REIT to reduce certain interest rate risks are prospectively generally conformed to the rules included in section 1221. Also, the income of a REIT from such a hedging transaction is excluded from gross income for purposes of the 95-percent of gross income requirement to the extent the transaction hedges any indebtedness incurred or to be incurred by the REIT to acquire or carry real estate assets.

95-percent of gross income requirement

The Act prospectively amends the tax liability owed by a REIT when it fails to meet the 95-percent of gross income test by applying a taxable fraction based on 95 percent, rather than 90 percent, of the REIT's gross income.

Consequences of failure to meet REIT requirements

In general

Under the Act, a REIT may avoid disqualification in the event of certain failures of the requirements for REIT status, provided that (1) the failure was due to reasonable cause and not willful neglect, (2) the failure is corrected, and (3) except for certain failures not exceeding a specified de minimis amount, a penalty amount is paid.

---

[345] Sec. 856(m)(4)(B). Section 856(c)(3) describes the permitted real estate-related sources from which 75 percent of a qualified REIT's gross income must be derived.

[346] The Act does not modify any of the standards of section 482 as they apply to REITs and to TRSs.

[347] Although a REIT could itself provide such service and receive the income without receiving any disqualified income, in that case the REIT itself would be bearing the cost of providing the service. Under the prior law exception for a TRS providing such service, there was no explicit requirement that the TRS be reimbursed for the full cost of the service.

Certain de minimis asset failures of 5-percent or 10-percent tests

One requirement of present and prior law is that, with certain exceptions, (i) not more than 5 percent of the value of total REIT assets may be represented by securities of one issuer, and (ii) a REIT may not hold securities possessing more than 10 percent of the total voting power or 10 percent of the total value of the outstanding securities of any one issuer.[348] The requirements must be satisfied each quarter.

The Act provides that a REIT will not lose its REIT status for failing to satisfy these requirements in a quarter if the failure is due to the ownership of assets the total value of which does not exceed the lesser of (i) one percent of the total value of the REIT's assets at the end of the quarter for which such measurement is done or (ii) 10 million dollars; provided in either case that the REIT either disposes of the assets within six months after the last day of the quarter in which the REIT identifies the failure (or such other time period prescribed by the Treasury), or otherwise meets the requirements of those rules by the end of such time period.[349]

Other asset test failures (whether of 5-percent or 10-percent tests, or of 75-percent or other asset tests)

Under the Act, if a REIT fails to meet any of the asset test requirements for a particular quarter and the failure exceeds the de minimis threshold described above,[350] then the REIT still will be deemed to have satisfied the requirements if: (i) following the REIT's identification of the failure, the REIT files a schedule with a description of each asset that caused the failure, in accordance with regulations prescribed by the Treasury; (ii) the failure was due to reasonable cause and not to willful neglect, (iii) the REIT disposes of the assets within 6 months after the last day of the quarter in which the identification occurred or such other time period as is prescribed by the Treasury (or the requirements of the rules are otherwise met within such period), and (iv) the REIT pays a tax on the failure.

The tax that the REIT must pay on the failure is the greater of (i) $50,000, or (ii) an amount determined (pursuant to regulations) by multiplying the highest rate of tax for corporations under section 11, by the net income generated by the assets for the period beginning on the first date of the failure and ending on the date the REIT has disposed of the assets (or otherwise satisfies the requirements).

Such taxes are treated as excise taxes, for which the deficiency provisions of the excise tax subtitle of the Code (subtitle F) apply.

[348] Sec. 856(c)(4)(B)(iii). These rules do not apply to securities of a TRS, or to securities that qualify for the 75 percent asset test of section 856(c)(4)(A), such as real estate assets, cash items (including receivables), or Government securities.

[349] A REIT might satisfy the requirements without a disposition, for example, by increasing its other assets in the case of the 5 percent rule; or by the issuer modifying the amount or value of its total securities outstanding in the case of the 10 percent rule.

[350] It is intended that a REIT may also use the following procedure to cure de minimis failures of asset tests other than the 5-percent or 10-percent tests. A technical correction may be necessary so that the statute reflects this intent.

Conforming reasonable cause and reporting standard for failures of income tests

The Act conforms the reporting and reasonable cause standards for failure to meet the income tests to the new asset test standards. However, the Act does not change the rule under section 857(b)(5) that for income test failures, all of the net income attributed to the disqualified gross income is paid as tax.

Other failures

The Act adds a provision under which, if a REIT fails to satisfy one or more requirements for REIT qualification, other than the 95-percent and 75-percent gross income tests and other than the new rules provided for failures of the asset tests, the REIT may retain its REIT qualification if the failures are due to reasonable cause and not willful neglect, and if the REIT pays a penalty of $50,000 for each such failure.

Taxes and penalties paid deducted from amount required to be distributed

Any taxes or penalties paid under the Act are deducted from the net income of the REIT in determining the amount the REIT must distribute under the 90-percent distribution requirement.

Expansion of deficiency dividend procedure

The Act expands the circumstances in which a REIT may declare a deficiency dividend, by allowing such a declaration to occur after the REIT has attached a statement to its amendment or supplement to its tax return for the relevant tax year. Thus, the declaration need not await a decision of the Tax Court, a closing agreement, or an agreement signed by the Secretary of the Treasury.

Effective Date

The provision is generally effective for taxable years beginning after December 31, 2000.

However, some of the provisions are effective for taxable years beginning after the date of enactment (October 22, 2004). These are: the new "look through" rules determining a REIT partner's share of partnership securities for purposes of the "straight debt" rules; the provision changing the 90-percent of gross income reference to 95 percent, for purposes of the tax liability if a REIT fails to meet the 95-percent of gross income test; the new hedging definition;[351] the rule modifying the treatment of rents with respect to customary services; and the new rules for correction of certain failures to satisfy the REIT requirements.

[351] In light of the fact that the identification rules of the applicable Treasury Regulations require identification within 30 days of entering a hedge, the new hedging rules are intended to apply to hedges entered into in taxable years beginning after the date of enactment. A technical correction may be necessary so that the statute reflects this intent.

4. Special rules for certain film and television production (sec. 244 of the Act and new sec. 181 of the Code)

Present and Prior Law

The modified Accelerated Cost Recovery System ("MACRS") does not apply to certain property, including any motion picture film, video tape, or sound recording, or to any other property if the taxpayer elects to exclude such property from MACRS and the taxpayer properly applies a unit-of-production method or other method of depreciation not expressed in a term of years. Section 197 does not apply to certain intangible property, including property produced by the taxpayer or any interest in a film, sound recording, video tape, book or similar property not acquired in a transaction (or a series of related transactions) involving the acquisition of assets constituting a trade or business or substantial portion thereof. Thus, the recovery of the cost of a film, video tape, or similar property that is produced by the taxpayer or is acquired on a "stand-alone" basis by the taxpayer may not be determined under either the MACRS depreciation provisions or under the section 197 amortization provisions. The cost recovery of such property may be determined under section 167, which allows a depreciation deduction for the reasonable allowance for the exhaustion, wear and tear, or obsolescence of the property. A taxpayer is allowed to recover, through annual depreciation deductions, the cost of certain property used in a trade or business or for the production of income. Section 167(g) provides that the cost of motion picture films, sound recordings, copyrights, books, and patents are eligible to be recovered using the income forecast method of depreciation.

Reasons for Change

The Congress understood that over the past decade, production of American film projects has moved to foreign locations. Specifically, in recent years, a number of foreign governments have offered tax and other incentives designed to entice production of U.S. motion pictures and television programs to their countries. These governments have recognized that the benefits of hosting such productions do not flow only to the film and television industry. These productions create broader economic effects, with revenues and jobs generated in a variety of other local businesses. Hotels, restaurants, catering companies, equipment rental facilities, transportation vendors, and many others benefit from these productions.

This has become a significant trend affecting the film and television industry as well as the small businesses that they support. The Congress understood that a recent report by the U.S. Department of Commerce estimated that runaway production drains as much as $10 billion per year from the U.S. economy. These losses have been most pronounced in made-for-television movies and miniseries productions. According to the report, out of the 308 U.S.-developed television movies produced in 1998, 139 were produced abroad. This is a significant increase from the 30 produced abroad in 1990.

The Congress believed the report made a compelling case that runaway film and television production has eroded important segments of a vital American industry. According to official labor statistics, more than 270,000 jobs in the U.S. are directly involved in film production. By industry estimates, 70 to 80 percent of these workers are hired at the location where the production is filmed.

The Congress believed this legislation would encourage producers to bring feature film and television production projects to cities and towns across the United States, thereby decreasing the runaway production problem.

Explanation of Provision

The Act permits taxpayers to elect to deduct the cost of any qualifying film and television production in the year the expenditure is incurred in lieu of capitalizing the cost and recovering it through depreciation allowances.[352]

The Act does not apply to any qualified film or television production the aggregate cost of which exceeds $15 million.[353] The threshold is increased to $20 million if a significant amount of the production expenditures are incurred in areas eligible for designation as a low-income community or eligible for designation by the Delta Regional Authority as a distressed county or isolated area of distress.

The Act defines a qualified film or television production as any production of a motion picture (whether released theatrically or directly to video cassette or any other format); miniseries; scripted, dramatic television episode; or movie of the week if at least 75 percent of the total compensation expended on the production are for services performed in the United States.[354] With respect to property which is one or more episodes in a television series, only the first 44 episodes qualify under the provision.[355] Qualified property does not include sexually explicit productions as defined by section 2257 of title 18 of the U.S. Code.

The Congress intended that, for purposes of recapture under section 1245, any deduction allowed under this the Act shall be treated as if it were a deduction allowable for amortization.[356]

Effective Date

The provision is effective for qualified productions commencing after the date of enactment (October 22, 2004) and before January 1, 2009.[357]

---

[352] An election to deduct such costs shall be made in such manner as prescribed by the Secretary and by the due date (including extensions of time) for filing the taxpayer's return of tax for the taxable year in which production costs of such property are first incurred. An election may not be revoked without the consent of the Secretary. The Congress intends that, in the absence of specific guidance by the Secretary, deducting qualifying costs on the appropriate tax return shall constitute a valid election.

[353] A qualifying film or television production that is co-produced is eligible for the benefits of the provision only if its aggregate cost, regardless of funding source, does not exceed the threshold.

[354] The term compensation does not include participations and residuals.

[355] It is intended that, with respect to episodes in a television series, the aggregate cost threshold and the 75-percent-of-total-compensation test be applied on an episode-by-episode basis. A technical correction may be necessary so that the statute reflects this intent.

[356] A technical correction may be necessary so that the statute reflects this intent.

[357] For this purpose, a production is treated as commencing on the first date of principal photography.

5. Provide a tax credit for maintenance of railroad track (sec. 245 of the Act and new sec. 45G of the Code)

Present and Prior Law

Under prior law, there was no provision that provided for a railroad track maintenance tax credit.

Explanation of Provision

The Act provides a 50-percent business tax credit for qualified railroad track maintenance expenditures paid or incurred in a taxable year by eligible taxpayers. The credit is limited to the product of $3,500 times the number of miles of railroad track owned or leased by an eligible taxpayer as of the close of its taxable year. Each mile of railroad track may be taken into account only once, either by the owner of such mile or by the owner's assignee, in computing the per-mile limitation. Qualified railroad track maintenance expenditures are defined as amounts expended (whether or not chargeable to a capital account) for maintaining railroad track (including roadbed, bridges, and related track structures) owned or leased as of January 1, 2005, by a Class II or Class III railroad. An eligible taxpayer is defined as: (1) any Class II or Class III railroad; and (2) any person who transports property using the rail facilities of a Class II or Class III railroad or who furnishes railroad-related property or services to such person. The taxpayer's basis in railroad track is reduced by the amount of the credit allowed. No portion of the credit may be carried back to any taxable year beginning before January 1, 2005. Other rules apply.

This credit applies to qualified railroad track maintenance expenditures paid or incurred during taxable years beginning after December 31, 2004, and before January 1, 2008.

Effective Date

The provision is effective for taxable years beginning after December 31, 2004.

6. Suspension of occupational taxes relating to distilled spirits, wine, and beer (sec. 246 of the Act and new sec. 5148 of the Code)

Present and Prior Law

Special occupational taxes are imposed on producers and others engaged in the marketing of distilled spirits, wine, and beer. These excise taxes are imposed as part of a broader Federal tax and regulatory regime governing the production and marketing of alcoholic beverages. The special occupational taxes are payable annually, on July 1 of each year. The present tax rates are as follows:

Producers: [358]	
Distilled spirits and wines (sec. 5081)	$1,000 per year, per premise
Brewers (sec. 5091)	$1,000 per year, per premise

Wholesale dealers (sec. 5111)	
Liquors, wines, or beer	$500 per year
Retail dealers (sec. 5121)	
Liquors, wines, or beer	$250 per year
Nonbeverage use of distilled spirits (sec. 5131)	$500 per year
Industrial use of distilled spirits (sec. 5276)	$250 per year

[358] A reduced rate of tax in the amount of $500 is imposed on small proprietors. Secs. 5081(b), 5091(b).

The Code requires every wholesale or retail dealer in liquors, wine or beer to keep records of its transactions.[359] A delegate of the Secretary of the Treasury is authorized to inspect the records of any dealer during business hours.[360] There are penalties for failing to comply with the recordkeeping requirements.[361]

The Code limits the persons from whom dealers may purchase their liquor stock intended for resale. Under the Code, a dealer may only purchase from:

1. a wholesale dealer in liquors who has paid the special occupational tax as such dealer to cover the place where such purchase is made; or
2. a wholesale dealer in liquors who is exempt, at the place where such purchase is made, from payment of such tax under any provision of chapter 51 of the Code; or
3. a person who is not required to pay special occupational tax as a wholesale dealer in liquors.[362]

In addition, a limited retail dealer (such as a charitable organization selling liquor at a picnic) may lawfully purchase distilled spirits for resale from a retail dealer in liquors.[363]

Violation of this restriction is punishable by $1,000 fine, imprisonment of one year, or both.[364] A violation also makes the alcohol subject to seizure and forfeiture.[365]

Reasons for Change

The special occupational tax is not a tax on alcoholic products but rather operates as a license fee on businesses. The Congress believed that this tax places an unfair burden on business owners. However, the Congress recognized that the recordkeeping and registration requirements applicable to wholesalers and retailers engaged in such businesses are necessary enforcement tools to ensure the protection of the revenue arising from the excise taxes on these products. Thus, the Congress believed it appropriate to suspend the tax for a three-year period, while retaining present-law recordkeeping and registration requirements.

[359] Secs. 5114, 5124.
[360] Sec. 5146.
[361] Sec. 5603.
[362] Sec. 5117. For example, purchases from a proprietor of a distilled spirits plant at his principal business office would be covered under item (2) since such a proprietor is not subject to the special occupational tax on account of sales at his principal business office. Sec. 5113(a). Purchases from a State-operated liquor store would be covered under item (3). Sec. 5113(b).
[363] Sec. 5117(b).
[364] Sec. 5687.
[365] Sec. 7302.

Explanation of Provision

Under the Act, the special occupational taxes on producers and marketers of alcoholic beverages are suspended for a three-year period, July 1, 2005 through June 30, 2008. Present-law recordkeeping and registration requirements continue to apply, notwithstanding the suspension of the special occupation taxes. In addition, during the suspension period, it shall be unlawful for any dealer to purchase distilled spirits for resale from any person other than a wholesale dealer in liquors who is subject to the recordkeeping requirements, except that a limited retail dealer may purchase distilled spirits for resale from a retail dealer in liquors, as permitted under present law.

Effective Date

The provision is effective on the date of enactment (October 22, 2004).

7. Modification of unrelated business income limitation on investment in certain small business investment companies (sec. 247 of the Act and sec. 514 of the Code)

Present and Prior Law

In general, an organization that is otherwise exempt from Federal income tax is taxed on income from a trade or business regularly carried on that is not substantially related to the organization's exempt purposes. Certain types of income, such as rents, royalties, dividends, and interest, generally are excluded from unrelated business taxable income except when such income is derived from "debt-financed property." Debt-financed property generally means any property that is held to produce income and with respect to which there is acquisition indebtedness at any time during the taxable year.

In general, income of a tax-exempt organization that is produced by debt-financed property is treated as unrelated business income in proportion to the acquisition indebtedness on the income-producing property. Acquisition indebtedness generally means the amount of unpaid indebtedness incurred by an organization to acquire or improve the property and indebtedness that would not have been incurred but for the acquisition or improvement of the property. Under present and prior law, acquisition indebtedness does not include, however, (1) certain indebtedness incurred in the performance or exercise of a purpose or function constituting the basis of the organization's exemption, (2) obligations to pay certain types of annuities, (3) an obligation, to the extent it is insured by the Federal Housing Administration, to finance the purchase, rehabilitation, or construction of housing for low and moderate income persons, or (4) indebtedness incurred by certain qualified organizations to acquire or improve real property.

Special rules apply in the case of an exempt organization that owns a partnership interest in a partnership that holds debt-financed income-producing property. An exempt organization's share of partnership income that is derived from such debt-financed property generally is taxed as debt-financed income unless an exception provides otherwise.

Reasons for Change

Small business investment companies obtain financial assistance from the Small Business Administration in the form of equity or by incurring indebtedness that is held or guaranteed by the Small Business Administration pursuant to the Small Business Investment Act of 1958. Tax-exempt organizations that invest in small business investment companies who are treated as partnerships and who incur indebtedness that is held or guaranteed by the Small Business Administration may be subject to unrelated business income tax on their distributive shares of income from the small business investment company. Congress believed that the imposition of unrelated business income tax in such cases creates a disincentive for tax-exempt organizations to invest in small business investment companies, thereby reducing the amount of investment capital that may be provided by small business investment companies to the nation's small businesses. Congress believed, however, that ownership limitations on the percentage interests that may be held by exempt organizations are appropriate to prevent all or most of a small business investment company's income from escaping Federal income tax.

Explanation of Provision

The Act modifies the debt-financed property provisions by excluding from the definition of acquisition indebtedness any indebtedness incurred by a small business investment company licensed after the date of enactment (October 22, 2004) under the Small Business Investment Act of 1958 that is evidenced by a debenture (1) issued by such company under section 303(a) of said Act, and (2) held or guaranteed by the Small Business Administration. The exclusion does not apply during any period that any exempt organization (other than a governmental unit) owns more than 25 percent of the capital or profits interest in the small business investment company, or exempt organizations (including governmental units other than any agency or instrumentality of the United States) own, in the aggregate, 50 percent or more of the capital or profits interest in such company.

Effective Date

The provision is effective for debt incurred after the date of enactment (October 22, 2004) by small business investment companies licensed after the date of enactment (October 22, 2004).

8. Election to determine taxable income from certain international shipping activities using per ton rate (sec. 248 of the Act and new secs. 1352–1359 of the Code)

Present and Prior Law

The United States employs a "worldwide" tax system, under which domestic corporations generally are taxed on all income, including income from shipping operations, whether derived in the

United States or abroad. In order to mitigate double taxation, a foreign tax credit for income taxes paid to foreign countries is provided to reduce or eliminate the U.S. tax owed on such income, subject to certain limitations.

Generally, the United States taxes foreign corporations only on income that has a sufficient nexus to the United States. Thus, a foreign corporation is generally subject to U.S. tax only on income, including income from shipping operations, which is "effectively connected" with the conduct of a trade or business in the United States (sec. 882). Such "effectively connected income" generally is taxed in the same manner and at the same rates as the income of a U.S. corporation.

The United States imposes a four percent tax on the amount of a foreign corporation's U.S. gross transportation income (sec. 887). Transportation income includes income from the use (or hiring or leasing for use) of a vessel and income from services directly related to the use of a vessel. Fifty percent of the transportation income attributable to transportation that either begins or ends (but not both) in the United States is treated as U.S. source gross transportation income. The tax does not apply, however, to U.S. gross transportation income that is treated as income effectively connected with the conduct of a U.S. trade or business. U.S. gross transportation income is not treated as effectively connected income unless (1) the taxpayer has a fixed place of business in the United States involved in earning the income, and (2) substantially all the income is attributable to regularly scheduled transportation.

The taxes imposed by section 882 and 887 on income from shipping operations may be limited by an applicable U.S. income tax treaty or by an exemption of a foreign corporation's international shipping operations income in instances where a foreign country grants an equivalent exemption (sec. 883).

Under prior law, there was no provision that provided an alternative to the corporate income tax for taxable income attributable to international shipping activities.

Reasons for Change

In general, the Congress believed operators of U.S.-flag vessels in international trade were subject to higher taxes than their foreign-based competition. The uncompetitive U.S. taxation of shipping income caused a steady and substantial decline of the U.S. shipping industry. The Congress believed that the Act provides operators of U.S.-flag vessels in international trade the opportunity to be competitive with their tax-advantaged foreign competitors.

Explanation of Provision

In general

The Act generally allows corporations to elect a "tonnage tax" in lieu of the corporate income tax on taxable income from certain shipping activities. Accordingly, an electing corporation's gross income does not include its income from qualifying shipping activities, and electing corporations are only subject to tax on these activities at the maximum corporate income tax rate on their notional shipping income, which is based on the net tonnage of the corporation's qualifying vessels. An electing corporation is treated as a separate trade or business activity distinct from all other activities conducted by such corporation.

Notional shipping income

An electing corporation's notional shipping income for the taxable year is the sum of the products of the following amounts for each of the qualifying vessels it operates: (1) the daily notional shipping income[366] from the operation of the qualifying vessel in United States foreign trade,[367] and (2) the number of days during the taxable year that the electing corporation operated such vessel as a qualifying vessel in United States foreign trade.[368] However, in the case of a qualifying vessel any of the income of which is not included in gross income, the amount of notional shipping income from such vessel is equal to the notional shipping income from such vessel (determined without regard to this provision) that bears the same ratio as the gross income from the operation of such vessel in the United States foreign trade bears to the sum of such gross income and the income so excluded. Generally, a "qualifying vessel" is described as a self-propelled U.S.-flag vessel of not less than 10,000 deadweight tons used exclusively in U.S. foreign trade.

Items not subject to corporate income tax

Generally, a corporate member of an electing group[369] does not include in gross income its income from qualifying shipping activities. Qualifying shipping activities consist of (1) core qualifying activities, (2) qualifying secondary activities, and (3) qualifying incidental activities. All of an electing entity's core qualifying activities are excluded from gross income. However, only a portion of an electing corporation's secondary and incidental activities are treated as qualifying income and thus, are excluded from gross income.

Core qualifying activities consist of the operation of qualifying vessels.[370] Secondary activities generally consist of (1) the active management or operation of vessels in U.S. foreign trade; (2) the provision of vessels, barge, container or cargo-related facilities or services; and (3) other activities of the electing corporation and other members of its electing group that are an integral part of its business of operating qualifying vessels in United States foreign trade. Secondary activities do not include any core qualifying activities.[371] Incidental activities are activities that are incidental to

[366] The daily notional shipping income from the operation of a qualifying vessel is 40 cents for each 100 tons of the net tonnage of the vessel (up to 25,000 net tons), and 20 cents for each 100 tons of the net tonnage of the vessel, in excess of 25,000 net tons.

[367] "United States foreign trade" means the transportation of goods or passengers between a place in the United States and a foreign place or between foreign places. The temporary use in the United States domestic trade (i.e., the transportation of goods or passengers between places in the United States) of any qualifying vessel is deemed to be the use in the United States foreign trade of such vessel, if such use does not exceed 30 days in a taxable year.

[368] Special rules apply in the case of multiple operators of a vessel.

[369] An electing group means any group that would be treated as a single employer under subsection (a) or (b) of section 52 if paragraphs (1) and (2) of section 52(a) did not apply.

[370] It is intended that the operation of a lighter-aboard-ship be treated as the operation of a vessel and not the operation of a barge.

[371] The Act also provides any activities that would otherwise constitute core qualifying activities of a corporation, who is a member of an electing group but is not an electing corporation, are treated as qualifying secondary activities. A technical correction may be necessary so that the statute reflects this intent. See section 2(a)(3) of H.R. 5395 and S. 3019, the "Tax Technical Corrections Act of 2004," introduced November 19, 2004.

core qualifying activities and are not qualifying secondary activities.

Denial of credits, income and deductions

Each item of loss, deduction, or credit of any taxpayer is disallowed with respect to the income that is excluded from gross income under the Act. An electing corporation's interest expense is disallowed in the ratio that the fair market value of its qualifying vessels bears to the fair market value of its total assets; special rules apply for disallowing interest expense in the context of an electing group.

No deductions are allowed against the notional shipping income of an electing corporation, and no credit is allowed against the notional tax imposed under the tonnage tax regime. No deduction is allowed for any net operating loss attributable to the qualifying shipping activities of a corporation to the extent that such loss is carried forward by the corporation from a taxable year preceding the first taxable year for which such corporation was an electing corporation.

Dispositions of qualifying vessels

Generally, if a qualifying vessel operator sells or disposes of a qualifying vessel in an otherwise taxable transaction, at the election of the operator no gain is recognized if a replacement qualifying vessel is acquired during a limited replacement period except to the extent that the amount realized upon such sale or disposition exceeds the cost of the replacement qualifying vessel. Generally, in the case of the replacement of a qualifying vessel that results in the nonrecognition of any part of the gain under the rule above, the basis of the replacement vessel is the cost of such replacement property decreased in the amount of gain not recognized.

Generally, a qualifying vessel operator is a corporation that (1) operates one or more qualifying vessels and (2) meets certain requirements with respect to its shipping activities.[372] Special rules apply in determining whether corporate partners in pass-through entities are treated as qualifying vessel operators.

Election

Generally, any qualifying vessel operator may elect into the tonnage tax regime and such election is made in the form prescribed by Treasury. An election is only effective if made on or before the due date (including extensions) for filing the corporation's return for such taxable year.[373] However, a qualifying vessel operator, which is a member of a controlled group, may only make an election into the tonnage tax regime if all qualifying vessel operators that are members of the controlled group make such an election. Once made, an election is effective for the taxable year in which

[372] A person is generally treated as operating any vessel during a period if such vessel is owned by or chartered to such person (the term "charter" includes an operating agreement), and is in use as a qualifying vessel during such period. Special rules apply in the case of pass-through entities, and special rules apply in an instance in which an electing entity temporarily ceases to operate a qualifying vessel due to dry-docking, surveying, inspection, repairs and the like.

[373] A technical correction may be necessary so that the statute reflects this intent.

it was made and for all succeeding taxable years of the entity until the election is terminated.

Effective Date

The provision is effective for taxable years beginning after the date of enactment (October 22, 2004).

F. Exclusion of Incentive Stock Options and Employee Stock Purchase Plan Stock Options from Wages (sec. 251 of the Act and secs. 421(b), 423(c), 3121(a), 3231, and 3306(b) of the Code)

Present and Prior Law

Generally, when an employee exercises a compensatory option on employer stock, the difference between the option price and the fair market value of the stock (i.e., the "spread") is includible in income as compensation. In the case of an incentive stock option or an option to purchase stock under an employee stock purchase plan (collectively referred to as "statutory stock options"), the spread is not included in income at the time of exercise.[374]

If the statutory holding period requirements are satisfied with respect to stock acquired through the exercise of a statutory stock option, the spread, and any additional appreciation, will be taxed as capital gain upon disposition of such stock. Compensation income is recognized, however, if there is a disqualifying disposition (i.e., if the statutory holding period is not satisfied) of stock acquired pursuant to the exercise of a statutory stock option.

Federal Insurance Contribution Act ("FICA") and Federal Unemployment Tax Act ("FUTA") taxes (collectively referred to as "employment taxes") are generally imposed in an amount equal to a percentage of wages paid by the employer with respect to employment.[375] Under prior law, the applicable Code provisions[376] did not provide an exception from FICA and FUTA taxes for wages paid to an employee arising from the exercise of a statutory stock option.

There had been uncertainty in the past as to employer withholding obligations upon the exercise of statutory stock options. On June 25, 2002, the IRS announced that until further guidance is issued, it would not assess FICA or FUTA taxes, or impose Federal income tax withholding obligations, upon either the exercise of a statutory stock option or the disposition of stock acquired pursuant to the exercise of a statutory stock option.[377]

Reasons for Change

To provide taxpayers certainty, the Congress believed that it was appropriate to clarify the treatment of statutory stock options for employment tax and income tax withholding purposes. The Congress believed that, in the past, the IRS had been inconsistent in its treatment of taxpayers with respect to this issue and did not

[374] Sec. 421. For purposes of the individual alternative minimum tax, the transfer of stock pursuant to an incentive stock option is generally treated as the transfer of stock pursuant to a nonstatutory option. Sec. 56(b)(3).
[375] Secs. 3101, 3111 and 3301.
[376] Secs. 3121 and 3306.
[377] Notice 2002–47, 2002–28 I.R.B. 97.

uniformly challenge taxpayers who did not collect employment taxes and withhold income taxes on statutory stock options.

Until January 2001, the IRS had not published guidance with respect to the imposition of employment taxes and income tax withholding on statutory stock options. Many taxpayers relied on guidance published with respect to qualified stock options (the predecessor to incentive stock options) to take the position that no employment taxes or income tax withholding were required with respect to statutory stock options. It was the Congress' belief that a majority of taxpayers did not withhold employment and income taxes with respect to statutory stock options. Thus, proposed IRS regulations, if implemented, would have altered the treatment of statutory stock options for most employers.

Because there is a specific income tax exclusion with respect to statutory stock options, the Congress believed it was appropriate to clarify that there is a conforming exclusion for employment taxes and income tax withholding. Statutory stock options are required to meet certain Code requirements that do not apply to nonqualified stock options. The Congress believed that such requirements are intended to make statutory stock options a tool of employee ownership rather than a form of compensation subject to employment taxes. Furthermore, Congress believed that this clarification would ensure that, if further IRS guidance is issued, employees would not be faced with a tax increase that would reduce their net paychecks even though their total compensation had not changed.

The clarification would also eliminate the administrative burden and cost to employers who, in the absence of the Act, could be required to modify their payroll systems to provide for the withholding of income and employment taxes on statutory stock options that they were not currently required to withhold.

Explanation of Provision

The Act provides specific exclusions from FICA and FUTA wages for remuneration on account of the transfer of stock pursuant to the exercise of an incentive stock option or under an employee stock purchase plan, or any disposition of such stock. Thus, under the Act, FICA and FUTA taxes do not apply upon the exercise of a statutory stock option.[378] The Act also provides that such remuneration is not taken into account for purposes of determining Social Security benefits.

Additionally, the Act provides that Federal income tax withholding is not required on a disqualifying disposition, nor when compensation is recognized in connection with an employee stock purchase plan discount. Present law reporting requirements continue to apply.

Effective Date

The provision is effective for stock acquired pursuant to options exercised after the date of enactment (October 22, 2004).

---

[378] The Act also provides a similar exclusion under the Railroad Retirement Tax Act.

III. TAX RELIEF FOR AGRICULTURE AND SMALL MANUFACTURERS

A. Volumetric Ethanol Excise Tax Credit

1. Incentives for alcohol and biodiesel fuels (sec. 301 of the Act and secs. 4041, 4081, 4091, 6427, 9503 and new section 6426 of the Code)

Present and Prior Law

Alcohol fuels income tax credit

The alcohol fuels credit is the sum of three credits: the alcohol mixture credit, the alcohol credit, and the small ethanol producer credit. Generally, under prior law the alcohol fuels credit was scheduled to expire after December 31, 2007.[379]

A taxpayer (generally a petroleum refiner, distributor, or marketer) who mixes ethanol with gasoline (or a special fuel[380]) is an "ethanol blender." In 2004, ethanol blenders were eligible for an income tax credit of 52 cents per gallon of ethanol used in the production of a qualified mixture (the "alcohol mixture credit"). A qualified mixture means a mixture of alcohol and gasoline (or of alcohol and a special fuel) sold by the blender as fuel or used as fuel by the blender in producing the mixture. The term alcohol includes methanol and ethanol but does not include (1) alcohol produced from petroleum, natural gas, or coal (including peat), or (2) alcohol with a proof of less than 150. In 2004, businesses also may reduce their income taxes by 52 cents for each gallon of ethanol (not mixed with gasoline or other special fuel) that they sell at the retail level as vehicle fuel or use themselves as a fuel in their trade or business ("the alcohol credit"). Beginning on January 1, 2005, the credits are reduced to 51 cents per gallon.

A separate income tax credit is available for small ethanol producers (the "small ethanol producer credit"). A small ethanol producer is defined as a person whose ethanol production capacity does not exceed 30 million gallons per year. The small ethanol producer credit is 10 cents per gallon of ethanol produced during the taxable year for up to a maximum of 15 million gallons.

The credits that comprise the alcohol fuels tax credit are includible in income. The credit may not be used to offset alternative minimum tax liability. The credit is treated as a general business credit, subject to the ordering rules and carryforward/carryback rules that apply to business credits generally.

---

[379] The alcohol fuels credit is unavailable when, for any period before January 1, 2008, the tax rates for gasoline and diesel fuels drop to 4.3 cents per gallon.

[380] A special fuel includes any liquid (other than gasoline) that is suitable for use in an internal combustion engine.

Excise tax reductions for alcohol mixture fuels

In general

Generally, motor fuels tax rates are as follows:[381]

	Cents per gallon
Gasoline	18.3
Diesel fuel and kerosene	24.3
Special motor fuels	18.3

Under prior law, alcohol-blended fuels were subject to a reduced rate of tax. The benefits provided by the alcohol fuels income tax credit and the excise tax reduction were integrated such that the alcohol fuels credit was reduced to take into account the benefit of any excise tax reduction.

Gasohol

Under prior law, registered ethanol blenders could forgo the full income tax credit and instead pay reduced rates of excise tax on gasoline that they purchased for blending with ethanol. Most of the benefit of the alcohol fuels credit was claimed through the excise tax system.

The reduced excise tax rates applied to gasohol upon its removal or entry. Gasohol was defined as a gasoline/ethanol blend that contains 5.7 percent ethanol, 7.7 percent ethanol, or 10 percent ethanol. For the calendar year 2004, the following reduced rates applied to gasohol:[382]

	Cents per gallon
5.7 percent ethanol	15.436
7.7 percent ethanol	14.396
10.0 percent ethanol	13.200

Reduced excise tax rates also applied when gasoline was purchased for the production of "gasohol." When gasoline was purchased for blending into gasohol, the rates above were multiplied by a fraction (e.g., 10/9 for 10-percent gasohol) so that the increased volume of motor fuel will be subject to tax. The reduced tax rates applied if the person liable for the tax was registered with the IRS and (1) that person produced gasohol with gasoline within 24 hours of removing or entering the gasoline or (2) the gasoline was sold upon its removal or entry and the person liable for the

[381] These fuels are also subject to an additional 0.1 cent-per-gallon excise tax to fund the Leaking Underground Storage Tank Trust Fund. See secs. 4041(d) and 4081(a)(2)(B). In addition, the basic fuel tax rate will drop to 4.3 cents per gallon beginning on October 1, 2005.

[382] These rates include the additional 0.1 cent-per-gallon excise tax to fund the Leaking Underground Storage Tank Trust Fund. These special rates will terminate after September 30, 2007 (sec. 4081(c)(8)).

tax has an unexpired certificate from the buyer and has no reason to believe the certificate is false.[383]

Qualified methanol and ethanol fuels

Under prior law, qualified methanol or ethanol fuel was any liquid that contains at least 85 percent methanol or ethanol or other alcohol produced from a substance other than petroleum or natural gas. These fuels were taxed at reduced rates.[384] The rate of tax on qualified methanol was 12.35 cents per gallon. The rate on qualified ethanol in 2004 was 13.15 cents. From January 1, 2005, through September 30, 2007, the rate of tax on qualified ethanol was 13.25 cents.

Alcohol produced from natural gas

A mixture of methanol, ethanol, or other alcohol produced from natural gas that consists of at least 85 percent alcohol is also taxed at reduced rates.[385] For mixtures not containing ethanol, the applicable rate of tax is 9.25 cents per gallon before October 1, 2005. In all other cases, the rate is 11.4 cents per gallon. After September 30, 2005, the rate is reduced to 2.15 cents per gallon when the mixture does not contain ethanol and 4.3 cents per gallon in all other cases.

Blends of alcohol and diesel fuel or special motor fuels

A reduced rate of tax applied to diesel fuel or kerosene that was combined with alcohol as long as at least 10 percent of the finished mixture was alcohol. If none of the alcohol in the mixture was ethanol, the rate of tax is 18.4 cents per gallon. For alcohol mixtures containing ethanol, the rate of tax in 2004 was 19.2 cents per gallon and 19.3 cents per gallon for 2005 through September 30, 2007. Fuel removed or entered for use in producing a 10 percent diesel-alcohol fuel mixture (without ethanol), was subject to a tax of 20.44 cents per gallon. The rate of tax for fuel removed or entered for use to produce a 10 percent diesel-ethanol fuel mixture is 21.333 cents per gallon for 2004 and 21.444 cents per gallon for the period January 1, 2005, through September 30, 2007.[386]

Special motor fuel (nongasoline) mixtures with alcohol also were taxed at reduced rates.

Aviation fuel

Noncommercial aviation fuel is subject to a tax of 21.9 cents per gallon.[387] Fuel mixtures containing at least 10 percent alcohol were taxed at lower rates.[388] In the case of 10 percent ethanol mixtures, for any sale or use during 2004, the 21.9 cents was reduced by 13.2

[383] Treas. Reg. sec. 48.4081–6(c). A certificate from the buyer assures that the gasoline will be used to produce gasohol within 24 hours after purchase. A copy of the registrant's letter of registration cannot be used as a gasohol blender's certificate.

[384] These reduced rates terminate after September 30, 2007. Included in these rates is the 0.05–cent-per-gallon Leaking Underground Storage Tank Trust Fund tax imposed on such fuel. (sec. 4041(b)(2)).

[385] These rates include the additional 0.1 cent-per-gallon excise tax to fund the Leaking Underground Storage Tank Trust Fund (sec. 4041(d)(1)).

[386] These rates include the additional 0.1 cent-per-gallon excise tax to fund the Leaking Underground Storage Tank Trust Fund.

[387] This rate includes the additional 0.1 cent-per-gallon tax for the Leaking Underground Storage Tank Trust fund.

[388] Secs. 4041(k)(1) and 4091(c).

cents (for a tax of 8.7 cents per gallon), for 2005, 2006, and 2007 the reduction was 13.1 cents (for a tax of 8.8 cents per gallon) and was reduced by 13.4 cents in the case of any sale during 2008 or thereafter. For mixtures not containing ethanol, the 21.9 cents was reduced by 14 cents for a tax of 7.9 cents. These reduced rates were scheduled to expire after September 30, 2007.[389]

When aviation fuel was purchased for blending with alcohol, the rates above were multiplied by a fraction (10/9) so that the increased volume of aviation fuel will be subject to tax.

Refunds and payments

If fully taxed gasoline (or other taxable fuel) was used to produce a qualified alcohol mixture, the Code permitted the blender to file a claim for a quick excise tax refund. The refund was equal to the difference between the gasoline (or other taxable fuel) excise tax that was paid and the tax that would have been paid by a registered blender on the alcohol fuel mixture being produced. Generally, the IRS paid these quick refunds within 20 days. Interest accrued if the refund was paid more than 20 days after filing. A claim could be filed by any person with respect to gasoline, diesel fuel, or kerosene used to produce a qualified alcohol fuel mixture for any period for which $200 or more was payable and which was not less than one week.

Ethyl tertiary butyl ether (ETBE)

Ethyl tertiary butyl ether ("ETBE") is an ether that is manufactured using ethanol. Unlike ethanol, ETBE can be blended with gasoline before the gasoline enters a pipeline because ETBE does not result in contamination of fuel with water while in transport. Treasury regulations provide that gasohol blenders could claim (under prior law) the income tax credit and excise tax rate reductions for ethanol used in the production of ETBE. The regulations also provide a special election allowing refiners to claim the benefit of the prior-law excise-tax-rate reduction even though the fuel being removed from terminals did not contain the requisite percentages of ethanol for claiming the excise tax rate reduction.

Highway Trust Fund

With certain exceptions, the taxes imposed by section 4041 (relating to retail taxes on diesel fuels and special motor fuels) and section 4081 (relating to tax on gasoline, diesel fuel and kerosene) are credited to the Highway Trust Fund. Under prior law, in the case of alcohol fuels, 2.5 cents per gallon of the tax imposed was retained in the General Fund.[390] Under prior law, in the case of a taxable fuel taxed at a reduced rate upon removal or entry prior to mixing with alcohol, 2.8 cents of the reduced rate was retained in the General Fund.[391]

Biodiesel

If biodiesel is used in the production of blended taxable fuel, the Code imposes tax on the removal or sale of the blended taxable

---

[389] Sec. 4091(c)(1).
[390] Sec. 9503(b)(4)(E).
[391] Sec. 9503(b)(4)(F).

fuel.[392] In addition, the Code imposes tax on any liquid other than gasoline sold for use or used as a fuel in a diesel-powered highway vehicle or diesel-powered train unless tax was previously imposed and not refunded or credited.[393] If biodiesel that was not previously taxed or exempt is sold for use or used as a fuel in a diesel-powered highway vehicle or a diesel-powered train, tax is imposed.[394] There are no reduced excise tax rates for biodiesel.

Reasons for Change

Highway vehicles using alcohol-blended fuels contribute to the wear and tear of the same highway system used by gasoline or diesel vehicles. Therefore, the Congress believed that alcohol-blended fuels should be taxed at rates equal to gasoline or diesel. The Congress believed that prior law provided opportunities for fraud because individuals could buy gasoline at reduced tax rates for blending with alcohol, but never actually use the gasoline to make an alcohol fuel blend, The Congress believed that eliminating the reduced tax rate on gasoline prior to blending with alcohol would reduce such opportunities for fraud. The Congress also believed that providing a tax credit based on the gallons of alcohol used to make an alcohol fuel and eliminating the various blend tiers associated with reduced tax rates for alcohol-blended fuels would simplify present law.

Explanation of Provision

Overview

The Act eliminates reduced rates of excise tax for most alcohol-blended fuels. The Act imposes the full rate of excise tax on most alcohol-blended fuels (18.3 cents per gallon on gasoline blends and 24.3 cents per gallon of diesel blended fuel). In place of reduced rates, the Act creates two new excise tax credits: the alcohol fuel mixture credit and the biodiesel mixture credit. The sum of these credits may be taken against the tax imposed on taxable fuels (by section 4081). The Act allows taxpayers to file a claim for payment equal to the amount of these credits for biodiesel or alcohol used to produce an eligible mixture.

Under certain circumstances, a tax is imposed if an alcohol fuel mixture credit or biodiesel fuel mixture credit is claimed with respect to alcohol or biodiesel used in the production of any alcohol or biodiesel mixture, which is subsequently used for a purpose for which the credit is not allowed or changed into a substance that does not qualify for the credit.

The Act eliminates the General Fund retention of certain taxes on alcohol fuels, and credits these taxes to the Highway Trust

---

[392] Sec. 4081(b); Rev. Rul. 2002–76, 2002–46 I.R.B. 841 (2002). "Taxable fuels" are gasoline, diesel and kerosene (sec. 4083). Biodiesel, although suitable for use as a fuel in a diesel-powered highway vehicle or diesel-powered train, contains less than four percent normal paraffins and, therefore, is not treated as diesel fuel under the applicable Treasury regulations. Treas. Reg. secs. 48.4081–1(c)(2)(i) and (ii), and 48.4081–1(b); Rev. Rul. 2002–76, 2002–46 I.R.B. 841 (2002). As a result, biodiesel alone is not a taxable fuel for purposes of section 4081. As noted above, however, tax is imposed upon the removal or entry of blended taxable fuel made with biodiesel.

[393] Sec. 4041. The tax imposed under section 4041 also will not apply if an exemption from tax applies.

[394] Rev. Rul. 2002–76, 2002–46 I.R.B. 841 (2002).

Fund. The Highway Trust Fund is credited with the full amount of tax imposed on alcohol and biodiesel fuel mixtures.

The Act also extends the present-law alcohol fuels income tax credit through December 31, 2010.

Alcohol fuel mixture excise tax credit

The Act eliminates the reduced rates of excise tax for most alcohol-blended fuels.[395] Under the Act, the full rate of tax for taxable fuels is imposed on both alcohol fuel mixtures and the taxable fuel used to produce an alcohol fuel mixture.

In lieu of the reduced excise tax rates, the Act provides for an excise tax credit, the alcohol fuel mixture credit. The alcohol fuel mixture credit is 51 cents for each gallon of alcohol used by a person in producing an alcohol fuel mixture for sale or use in a trade or business of the taxpayer. For mixtures not containing ethanol (renewable source methanol), the credit is 60 cents per gallon.

For purposes of the alcohol fuel mixture credit, an "alcohol fuel mixture" is a mixture of alcohol and a taxable fuel that (1) is sold by the taxpayer producing such mixture to any person for use as a fuel or (2) is used as a fuel by the taxpayer producing the mixture. Alcohol for this purpose includes methanol, ethanol, and alcohol gallon equivalents of ETBE or other ethers produced from such alcohol. It does not include alcohol produced from petroleum, natural gas, or coal (including peat), or alcohol with a proof of less than 190 (determined without regard to any added denaturants). Taxable fuel is gasoline, diesel, and kerosene.[396] A mixture that includes ETBE or other ethers produced from alcohol produced by any person at a refinery prior to a taxable event is treated as sold at the time of its removal from the refinery (and only at such time) to another person for use as a fuel.

The excise tax credit is coordinated with the alcohol fuels income tax credit and is available through December 31, 2010.

Biodiesel mixture excise tax credit

The Act provides an excise tax credit for biodiesel mixtures.[397] The credit is 50 cents for each gallon of biodiesel used by the taxpayer in producing a qualified biodiesel mixture for sale or use in a trade or business of the taxpayer. A qualified biodiesel mixture is a mixture of biodiesel and diesel fuel that (1) is sold by the taxpayer producing such mixture to any person for use as a fuel, or (2) is used as a fuel by the taxpayer producing such mixture. In the case of agri-biodiesel, the credit is $1.00 per gallon. No credit is allowed unless the taxpayer obtains a certification (in such form and manner as prescribed by the Secretary) from the producer of the biodiesel that identifies the product produced and the percentage of biodiesel and agri-biodiesel in the product.

The credit is not available for any sale or use for any period after December 31, 2006. This excise tax credit is coordinated with the

---

[395] The Act does not change the present-law treatment of fuels blended with alcohol derived from natural gas (under sec. 4041(m)), or alcohol derived from coal or peat (under sec. 4041(b)(2)). The Act does not change the taxes imposed to fund the Leaking Underground Storage Tank Trust Fund.

[396] Sec. 4083(a)(1). Under present law, dyed fuels are taxable fuels that have been exempted from tax.

[397] The excise tax credit uses the same definitions as the biodiesel fuels income tax credit.

income tax credit for biodiesel such that credit for the same biodiesel cannot be claimed for both income and excise tax purposes.

Payments with respect to qualified alcohol and biodiesel fuel mixtures

To the extent the alcohol fuel mixture credit exceeds any section 4081 liability of a person, the Secretary is to pay such person an amount equal to the alcohol fuel mixture credit with respect to such mixture. Thus, if the person has no section 4081 liability, the credit is totally refundable. These payments are intended to provide an equivalent benefit to replace the partial exemption for fuels to be blended with alcohol and alcohol fuels being repealed by the provision. Similar rules apply to the biodiesel fuel mixture credit.

If claims for payment are not paid within 45 days, the claim is to be paid with interest. The provision also provides that in the case of an electronic claim, if such claim is not paid within 20 days, the claim is to be paid with interest. If claims are filed electronically, the claimant may make a claim for less than $200. The Secretary is to describe the electronic format for filing claims by December 31, 2004.

The payment provision does not apply with respect to alcohol fuel mixtures sold after December 31, 2010, and biodiesel fuel mixtures sold after December 31, 2006.

Alcohol and biodiesel fuel subsidies borne by General Fund

The Act eliminates the requirement that 2.5 and 2.8 cents per gallon of excise taxes be retained in the General Fund with the result that the full amount of tax on alcohol fuels is credited to the Highway Trust Fund. The Act also authorizes the full amount of fuel taxes to be appropriated to the Highway Trust Fund without reduction for amounts equivalent to the excise tax credits allowed for alcohol or biodiesel fuel mixtures and the Highway Trust Fund is not required to reimburse the General Fund for any credits or payments taken or made with respect to qualified alcohol fuel mixtures or biodiesel fuel mixtures.

Registration requirement

Every person producing or importing biodiesel or alcohol is required to register with the Secretary.

Alcohol fuels income tax credit

The Act extends the alcohol fuels income tax credit through December 31, 2010.[398]

Effective Dates

The provisions generally are effective for fuel sold or used after December 31, 2004. The repeal of the General Fund retention of the 2.5/2.8 cents per gallon regarding alcohol fuels is effective for fuel sold or used after September 30, 2004. The Secretary is to provide electronic filing instructions by December 31, 2004. The registration requirement is effective April 1, 2005.

---

[398] Sec. 40.

2. Biodiesel income tax credit (sec. 302 of the Act and new sec. 40A of the Code)

Present and Prior Law

Under prior law, no income tax credit was provided for biodiesel fuels. However, under present and prior law, a per-gallon income tax credit (the "alcohol fuels credit") is allowed for ethanol and methanol (derived from renewable sources) when the alcohol is used as a highway motor fuel.[399]

Reasons for Change

The Congress believed that providing a new income tax credit for biodiesel fuel will promote energy self-sufficiency.[400]

Explanation of Provision

In general

The Act provides a new income tax credit for biodiesel and qualified biodiesel mixtures, the biodiesel fuels credit. The biodiesel fuels credit is the sum of the biodiesel mixture credit plus the biodiesel credit and is treated as a general business credit. The amount of the biodiesel fuels credit is includable in gross income. The biodiesel fuels credit is coordinated to take into account benefits from the biodiesel excise tax credit and payment provisions created by the Act. The credit may not be carried back to a taxable year ending before or on December 31, 2004. The provision does not apply to fuel sold or used after December 31, 2006.

Biodiesel is monoalkyl esters of long chain fatty acids derived from plant or animal matter that meet (1) the registration requirements established by the Environmental Protection Agency under section 211 of the Clean Air Act and (2) the requirements of the American Society of Testing and Materials D6751. Agri-biodiesel is biodiesel derived solely from virgin oils including oils from corn, soybeans, sunflower seeds, cottonseeds, canola, crambe, rapeseeds, safflowers, flaxseeds, rice bran, mustard seeds, or animal fats.

Biodiesel may be taken into account for purposes of the credit only if the taxpayer obtains a certification (in such form and manner as prescribed by the Secretary) from the producer or importer of the biodiesel which identifies the product produced and the percentage of the biodiesel and agri-biodiesel in the product.

Biodiesel mixture credit

The biodiesel mixture credit is 50 cents for each gallon of biodiesel used by the taxpayer in the production of a qualified biodiesel mixture. For agri-biodiesel, the credit is $1.00 per gallon. A qualified biodiesel mixture is a mixture of biodiesel and diesel fuel that is (1) sold by the taxpayer producing such mixture to any person for use as a fuel, or (2) is used as a fuel by the taxpayer producing such mixture. The sale or use must be in the trade or business of the taxpayer and is to be taken into account for the taxable

[399] Sec. 40.

[400] See S. 1149, the "Energy Tax Incentives Act of 2003", which was reported by the Senate Committee on Finance on May 23, 2003 (S. Rep. No. 108–54).

year in which such sale or use occurs. No credit is allowed with respect to any casual off-farm production of a qualified biodiesel mixture.

Biodiesel credit

The biodiesel credit is 50 cents for each gallon of 100 percent biodiesel which is not in a mixture with diesel fuel and which during the taxable year is (1) used by the taxpayer as a fuel in a trade or business or (2) sold by the taxpayer at retail to a person and placed in the fuel tank of such person's vehicle. For agri-biodiesel, the credit is $1.00 per gallon.

Later separation or failure to use as fuel

In a manner similar to the treatment of alcohol fuels, a tax is imposed if a biodiesel fuels credit is claimed with respect to biodiesel that is subsequently used for a purpose for which the credit is not allowed or that is changed into a substance that does not qualify for the credit.

Effective Date

The provision is effective for fuel produced, and sold or used after December 31, 2004, in taxable years ending after such date.

3. Information reporting for persons claiming certain tax benefits (sec. 303 of the Act and new sec. 4104 of the Code)

Present and Prior Law

The Code provides an income tax credit for each gallon of ethanol and methanol derived from renewable sources (e.g., biomass) used or sold as a fuel, or used to produce a qualified alcohol fuel mixture, such as gasohol. The amount of the credit is equal to 51 cents per gallon (ethanol) and 60 cents per gallon (methanol).[401] This tax credit is provided to blenders of the alcohols with other taxable fuels, or to the retail sellers (or users) of unblended alcohol fuels. Under prior law, part or all of the benefits of the income tax credit could be claimed through reduced excise taxes paid, either in reduced-tax sales or by expedited blender refunds on fully taxed sales of gasoline to obtain the benefit of the reduced rates. The amount of the income tax credit determined with respect to any alcohol was reduced to take into account any benefit provided by the reduced excise tax rates. To obtain a partial refund on fully taxed gasoline, the following requirements applied: (1) the claim must be for gasohol sold or used during a period of at least one week, (2) the claim must be for at least $200, and (3) the claim must be filed by the last day of the first quarter following the earliest quarter included in the claim. If the blender could not meet these requirements, the blender was generally required to claim a credit on the blender's income tax return.

[401] Ethanol produced by certain "small producers" is eligible for an additional producer tax credit of 10 cents per gallon on up to 15 million gallons of ethanol production. Eligible small producers are defined as persons whose production capacity does not exceed 30 million gallons.

Explanation of Provision

The Act requires persons claiming the Code benefits (including those created by the Act[402]) related to alcohol fuels and biodiesel fuels to provide such information related to such benefits and the coordination of such benefits as the Secretary may require to ensure the proper administration and use of such benefits. The Secretary may deny, revoke or suspend the registration of any person to enforce this requirement. Persons claiming excise tax benefits are to file quarterly information returns.

Effective Date

The provision is effective January 1, 2005.

B. Agricultural Incentives

1. Special rules for livestock sold on account of weather-related conditions (sec. 311 of the Act and secs. 1033 and 451 of the Code)

Present and Prior Law

Generally, a taxpayer realizes gain to the extent the sales price (and any other consideration received) exceeds the taxpayer's basis in the property. The realized gain is subject to current income tax unless the gain is deferred or not recognized under a special tax provision.

Under section 1033, gain realized by a taxpayer from an involuntary conversion of property is deferred to the extent the taxpayer purchases property similar or related in service or use to the converted property within the applicable period. The taxpayer's basis in the replacement property generally is the cost of such property reduced by the amount of gain not recognized.

The applicable period for the taxpayer to replace the converted property begins with the date of the disposition of the converted property (or if earlier, the earliest date of the threat or imminence of requisition or condemnation of the converted property) and ends two years after the close of the first taxable year in which any part of the gain upon conversion is realized (the "replacement period"). Special rules extend the replacement period for certain real property and principal residences damaged by a Presidentially declared disaster to three years and four years, respectively, after the close of the first taxable year in which gain is realized.

Section 1033(e) provides that the sale of livestock (other than poultry) that is held for draft, breeding, or dairy purposes in excess of the number of livestock that would have been sold but for drought, flood, or other weather-related conditions is treated as an involuntary conversion. Consequently, gain from the sale of such livestock could be deferred by reinvesting the proceeds of the sale in similar property within a two-year period.

In general, cash-method taxpayers report income in the year it is actually or constructively received. However, section 451(e) provides that a cash-method taxpayer whose principal trade or busi-

---

[402] See secs. 301 and 302 of the Act (relating to the credit for alcohol and biodiesel fuel mixtures and outlay payments for such mixtures, and the biodiesel income tax credit).

ness is farming who is forced to sell livestock due to drought, flood, or other weather-related conditions may elect to include income from the sale of the livestock in the taxable year following the taxable year of the sale. This elective deferral of income is available only if the taxpayer establishes that, under the taxpayer's usual business practices, the sale would not have occurred but for drought, flood, or weather-related conditions that resulted in the area being designated as eligible for Federal assistance. This exception is generally intended to put taxpayers who receive an unusually high amount of income in one year in the position they would have been in absent the weather-related condition.

Reasons for Change

The Congress was aware of situations in which cattlemen sold livestock in excess of their usual business practice as a result of weather-related conditions, but were then unable to purchase replacement property because the weather-related conditions have continued. The Congress believed it was appropriate to extend the time period for cattlemen to purchase replacement property in such situations.

Explanation of Provision

The Act extends the applicable period for a taxpayer to replace livestock sold on account of drought, flood, or other weather-related conditions from two years to four years after the close of the first taxable year in which any part of the gain on conversion is realized. The extension is only available if the taxpayer establishes that, under the taxpayer's usual business practices, the sale would not have occurred but for drought, flood, or weather-related conditions that resulted in the area being designated as eligible for Federal assistance. In addition, the Secretary of the Treasury is granted authority to further extend the replacement period on a regional basis should the weather-related conditions continue longer than three years. Also, for property eligible for the extended replacement period, the Act provides that the taxpayer can make an election under section 451(e) until the period for reinvestment of such property under section 1033 expires.

The Act also permits the taxpayer to replace compulsorily or involuntarily converted livestock with other farm property if, due to drought, flood, or other weather-related conditions, it is not feasible for the taxpayer to reinvest the proceeds in property similar or related in use to the livestock so converted.

Effective Date

The provision is effective for any taxable year with respect to which the due date (without regard to extensions) for the return is after December 31, 2002.

2. Payment of dividends on stock of cooperatives without reducing patronage dividends (sec. 312 of the Act and sec. 1388 of the Code)

Present and Prior Law

Under present and prior law, cooperatives generally are entitled to deduct or exclude amounts distributed as patronage dividends in accordance with Subchapter T of the Code. In general, patronage dividends are comprised of amounts that are paid to patrons (1) on the basis of the quantity or value of business done with or for patrons, (2) under a valid and enforceable obligation to pay such amounts that was in existence before the cooperative received the amounts paid, and (3) which are determined by reference to the net earnings of the cooperative from business done with or for patrons.

Treasury Regulations provide that net earnings are reduced by dividends paid on capital stock or other proprietary capital interests (referred to as the "dividend allocation rule").[403] The dividend allocation rule has been interpreted to require that such dividends be allocated between a cooperative's patronage and nonpatronage operations, with the amount allocated to the patronage operations reducing the net earnings available for the payment of patronage dividends.

Reasons for Change

The Congress believed that the dividend allocation rule should not apply to the extent that the organizational documents of a cooperative provide that capital stock dividends do not reduce the amounts owed to patrons as patronage dividends. To the extent that capital stock dividends are in addition to amounts paid under the cooperative's organizational documents to patrons as patronage dividends, the Congress believed that those capital stock dividends are not being paid from earnings from patronage business.

In addition, the Congress believed cooperatives should be able to raise needed equity capital by issuing capital stock without dividends paid on such stock causing the cooperative to be taxed on a portion of its patronage income, and without preventing the cooperative from being treated as operating on a cooperative basis.

Explanation of Provision

The Act provides a special rule for dividends on capital stock of a cooperative. To the extent provided in organizational documents of the cooperative, dividends on capital stock do not reduce patronage income and do not prevent the cooperative from being treated as operating on a cooperative basis.

Effective Date

The provision is effective for distributions made in taxable years beginning after the date of enactment (October 22, 2004).

[403] Treas. Reg. sec. 1.1388–1(a)(1).

3. Small ethanol producer credit (sec. 313 of the Act and sec. 40 of the Code)

Present and Prior Law

Small ethanol producer credit

Present and prior law provides several tax benefits for ethanol and methanol produced from renewable sources (e.g., biomass) that are used as a motor fuel or that are blended with other fuels (e.g., gasoline) for such a use. In the case of ethanol, a separate 10–cents-per-gallon credit on up to 15 million gallons of ethanol production is provided for small producers, defined generally as persons whose production capacity does not exceed 30 million gallons per year (the "small ethanol producer credit"). The small ethanol producer credit is part of the alcohol fuels tax credit under section 40 of the Code. The alcohol fuels tax credit is includible in income. Under prior law, the alcohol fuels tax credit could not be used to offset alternative minimum tax liability.[404] The credit is treated as a general business credit, subject to the ordering rules and carryforward/carryback rules that apply to business credits generally. The alcohol fuels tax credit was scheduled to expire after December 31, 2007.[405]

Taxation of cooperatives and their patrons

Under present and prior law, cooperatives in essence are treated as pass-through entities in that the cooperative is not subject to corporate income tax to the extent the cooperative timely pays patronage dividends.

Reasons for Change

The Congress believed provisions allowing greater flexibility in utilizing the benefits of the small ethanol producer credit are consistent with the objective of increasing availability of alternative fuels.

Explanation of Provision

The Act allows cooperatives to elect to pass the small ethanol producer credit through to their patrons. Specifically, the credit is to be apportioned among patrons eligible to share in patronage dividends on the basis of the quantity or value of business done with or for such patrons for the taxable year. The election must be made on a timely filed return for the taxable year, and once made, is irrevocable for such taxable year.

The amount of the credit not apportioned to patrons is included in the organization's credit for the taxable year of the organization. The amount of the credit apportioned to patrons is to be included in the patron's credit for the first taxable year of each patron ending on or after the last day of the payment period for the taxable year of the organization, or, if earlier, for the taxable year of each

[404] Sec. 711 of the Act permits the alcohol fuels tax credit (which includes the small producer credit) to be allowed against the alternative minimum tax for taxable years beginning after December 31, 2004.

[405] Sec. 301 of the Act extends sec. 40 through December 31, 2010.

patron ending on or after the date on which the patron receives notice from the cooperative of the apportionment.

If the amount of the credit shown on the cooperative's return for a taxable year is in excess of the actual amount of the credit for that year, an amount equal to the excess of the reduction in the credit over the amount not apportioned to patrons for the taxable year is treated as an increase in the cooperative's tax. The increase is not treated as tax imposed for purposes of determining the amount of any tax credit or for purposes of the alternative minimum tax.

Effective Date

The provision is effective for taxable years ending after date of enactment (October 22, 2004).

4. Extend income averaging to fishermen; income averaging for farmers and fishermen not to increase alternative minimum tax (sec. 314 of the Act and sec. 55 of the Code)

Present and Prior Law

Under present and prior law, an individual taxpayer engaged in a farming business (as defined by section 263A(e)(4)) may elect to compute his or her current year regular tax liability by averaging, over the prior three-year period, all or portion of his or her taxable income from the trade or business of farming. Under prior law, because farmer income averaging reduced the regular tax liability, the AMT may have been increased. Thus, the benefits of farmer income averaging may have been reduced or eliminated for farmers subject to the AMT.

Reasons for Change

The Congress believed that farmers and fishermen should be allowed the full benefits of income averaging without incurring liability under the AMT.

Explanation of Provision

The Act extends the benefits of income averaging to fishermen.

The Act provides that, in computing AMT, a farmer or fisherman's regular tax liability is determined without regard to income averaging. Thus, a farmer or fisherman receives the full benefit of income averaging because averaging reduces the regular tax while the AMT (if any) remains unchanged.

Effective Date

The provision applies to taxable years beginning after December 31, 2003.

5. Capital gains treatment to apply to outright sales of timber by landowner (sec. 315 of the Act and sec. 631(b) of the Code)

Present and Prior Law

Under present and prior law, a taxpayer disposing of timber held for more than one year is eligible for capital gains treatment in the following situations. First, if the taxpayer sells or exchanges timber that is a capital asset (sec. 1221) or property used in the trade or business (sec. 1231), the gain generally is long-term capital gain; however, if the timber is held for sale to customers in the taxpayer's business, the gain will be ordinary income. Second, if the taxpayer disposes of the timber with a retained economic interest, the gain is eligible for capital gain treatment (sec. 631(b)). Third, if the taxpayer cuts standing timber, the taxpayer may elect to treat the cutting as a sale or exchange eligible for capital gains treatment (sec. 631(a)).

Reasons for Change

The Congress believed that the requirement that the owner of timber retain an economic interest in the timber in order to obtain capital gain treatment under section 631(b) resulted in poor timber management. Under prior law, the buyer, when cutting and removing timber, had no incentive to protect young or other uncut trees because the buyer only paid for the timber that was cut and removed. Therefore, the Act eliminates this requirement and provides for capital gain treatment under section 631(b) in the case of outright sales of timber.

Explanation of Provision

Under the Act, in the case of a sale of timber by the owner of the land from which the timber is cut, the requirement that a taxpayer retain an economic interest in the timber in order to treat gains as capital gain under section 631(b) does not apply. Outright sales of timber by the landowner will qualify for capital gains treatment in the same manner as sales with a retained economic interest qualify under prior law, except that the usual tax rules relating to the timing of the income from the sale of the timber will apply (rather than the special rule of section 631(b) treating the disposal as occurring on the date the timber is cut).

Effective Date

The provision is effective for sales of timber after December 31, 2004.

6. Modification to cooperative marketing rules to include value-added processing involving animals (sec. 316 of the Act and sec. 1388 of the Code)

Present and Prior Law

Under present and prior law, cooperatives generally are treated similarly to pass-through entities in that the cooperative is not subject to corporate income tax to the extent the cooperative timely pays patronage dividends. Farmers' cooperatives are tax-exempt and include cooperatives of farmers, fruit growers, and like organizations that are organized and operated on a cooperative basis for the purpose of marketing the products of members or other producers and remitting the proceeds of sales, less necessary marketing expenses, on the basis of either the quantity or the value of products furnished by them (sec. 521). Farmers' cooperatives may claim a limited amount of additional deductions for dividends on capital stock and patronage-based distributions of nonpatronage income.

In determining whether a cooperative qualified as a tax-exempt farmers' cooperative under prior law, the IRS apparently took the position that a cooperative is not marketing certain products of members or other producers if the cooperative adds value through the use of animals (e.g., farmers sell corn to a cooperative which is fed to chickens that produce eggs sold by the cooperative).

Reasons for Change

The Congress disagreed with the apparent IRS position concerning the marketing of certain products by cooperatives after the cooperative has added value to the products through the use of animals. Therefore, the Congress believed that the tax rules should be modified to clarify that cooperatives are permitted to market such products.

Explanation of Provision

The Act provides that marketing products of members or other producers includes feeding products of members or other producers to cattle, hogs, fish, chickens, or other animals and selling the resulting animals or animal products.

Effective Date

The provision is effective for taxable years beginning after the date of enactment (October 22, 2004).

7. Extension of declaratory judgment procedures to farmers' cooperative organizations (sec. 317 of the Act and sec. 7428 of the Code)

Present and Prior Law

In limited circumstances, the Code provides declaratory judgment procedures, which generally permit a taxpayer to seek judicial review of an IRS determination prior to the issuance of a notice of deficiency and prior to payment of tax. Examples of declaratory judgment procedures that are available include disputes involving the initial or continuing classification of a tax-exempt organization described in section 501(c)(3), a private foundation described in section 509(a), or a private operating foundation described in section 4942(j)(3), the qualification of retirement plans, the value of gifts, the status of certain governmental obligations, or eligibility of an estate to pay tax in installments under section 6166.[406] In such cases, taxpayers may challenge adverse administrative determinations by commencing a declaratory judgment action. For example, where the IRS denies an organization's application for recognition of exemption under section 501(c)(3) or fails to act on such application, or where the IRS informs a section 501(c)(3) organization that it is considering revoking or adversely modifying its tax-exempt status, the Code authorizes the organization to seek a declaratory judgment regarding its tax exempt status.

Declaratory judgment procedures were not available under prior law to a cooperative with respect to an IRS determination regarding its status as a farmers' cooperative under section 521.

Reasons for Change

The Congress believed that declaratory judgment procedures currently available to other organizations and in other situations also should be available to farmers' cooperative organizations with respect to an IRS determination regarding the status of an organization as a farmers' cooperative under section 521.

Explanation of Provision

The Act extends the declaratory judgment procedures to cooperatives. A declaratory judgment action may be commenced in the U.S. Tax Court, a U.S. district court, or the U.S. Court of Federal Claims, and such court would have jurisdiction to determine a cooperative's initial or continuing qualification as a farmers' cooperative described in section 521.

Effective Date

The provision is effective for pleadings filed after the date of enactment (October 22, 2004).

8. Certain expenses of rural letter carriers (sec. 318 of the Act and sec. 162(o) of the Code)

Prior Law

Under prior law, the deductible automobile expenses of rural letter carriers were deemed to be equal to the reimbursements that such carriers receive from the U.S. Postal Service. Carriers were not allowed to document their actual costs and claim itemized deductions for costs in excess of reimbursements,[407] nor were carriers required to include in income reimbursements in excess of their actual costs.

Explanation of Provision

If the reimbursements a rural letter carrier receives from the U.S. Postal Service fall short of the carrier's actual costs, the costs in excess of reimbursements qualify as a miscellaneous itemized

[406] For disputes involving the initial or continuing qualification of an organization described in sections 501(c)(3), 509(a), or 4942(j)(3), declaratory judgment actions may be brought in the U.S. Tax Court, a U.S. district court, or the U.S. Court of Federal Claims. For all other Federal tax declaratory judgment actions, proceedings may be brought only in the U.S. Tax Court.

[407] Section 162(o).

deduction subject to the two-percent floor. Reimbursements in excess of their actual costs continue not to be required to be included in gross income.

Effective Date

The provision is effective for taxable years beginning after December 31, 2003.

9. Treatment of certain income of electric cooperatives (sec. 319 of the Act and sec. 501 of the Code)

Present and Prior Law

In general

Under present and prior law, an entity must be operated on a cooperative basis in order to be treated as a cooperative for Federal income tax purposes. Although not defined by statute or regulation, the two principal criteria for determining whether an entity is operating on a cooperative basis are: (1) ownership of the cooperative by persons who patronize the cooperative; and (2) return of earnings to patrons in proportion to their patronage. The IRS requires that cooperatives must operate under the following principles: (1) subordination of capital in control over the cooperative undertaking and in ownership of the financial benefits from ownership; (2) democratic control by the members of the cooperative; (3) vesting in and allocation among the members of all excess of operating revenues over the expenses incurred to generate revenues in proportion to their participation in the cooperative (patronage); and (4) operation at cost (not operating for profit or below cost).[408]

In general, cooperative members are those who participate in the management of the cooperative and who share in patronage capital. As described below, income from the sale of electric energy by an electric cooperative may be member or non-member income to the cooperative, depending on the membership status of the purchaser. A municipal corporation may be a member of a cooperative.

For Federal income tax purposes, a cooperative generally computes its income as if it were a taxable corporation, with one exception—the cooperative may exclude from its taxable income distributions of patronage dividends. In general, patronage dividends are the profits of the cooperative that are rebated to its patrons pursuant to a pre-existing obligation of the cooperative to do so. The rebate must be made in some equitable fashion on the basis of the quantity or value of business done with the cooperative.

Except for tax-exempt farmers' cooperatives, cooperatives that are subject to the cooperative tax rules of subchapter T of the Code (sec. 1381, et seq.) are permitted a deduction for patronage dividends from their taxable income only to the extent of net income that is derived from transactions with patrons who are members of the cooperative.[409] The availability of such deductions from taxable income has the effect of allowing the cooperative to be treated like

---

[408] Announcement 96–24, "Proposed Examination Guidelines Regarding Rural Electric Cooperatives," 1996–16 I.R.B. 35.

[409] Sec. 1382.

a conduit with respect to profits derived from transactions with patrons who are members of the cooperative.

Cooperatives that qualify as tax-exempt farmers' cooperatives are permitted to exclude patronage dividends from their taxable income to the extent of all net income, including net income that is derived from transactions with patrons who are not members of the cooperative, provided the value of transactions with patrons who are not members of the cooperative does not exceed the value of transactions with patrons who are members of the cooperative.[410]

Taxation of electric cooperatives exempt from subchapter T

In general, the cooperative tax rules of subchapter T apply to any corporation operating on a cooperative basis (except mutual savings banks, insurance companies, other tax-exempt organizations, and certain utilities), including tax-exempt farmers' cooperatives (described in sec. 521(b)). However, subchapter T does not apply to an organization that is "engaged in furnishing electric energy, or providing telephone service, to persons in rural areas."[411] Instead, electric cooperatives are taxed under rules that were generally applicable to cooperatives prior to the enactment of subchapter T in 1962. Under these rules, an electric cooperative can exclude patronage dividends from taxable income to the extent of all net income of the cooperative, including net income derived from transactions with patrons who are not members of the cooperative.[412]

Tax exemption of rural electric cooperatives

Present and prior law generally provides an income tax exemption for rural electric cooperatives if at least 85 percent of the cooperative's income consists of amounts collected from members for the sole purpose of meeting losses and expenses of providing service to its members.[413] The IRS takes the position that rural electric cooperatives also must comply with the fundamental cooperative principles described above in order to qualify for tax exemption under section 501(c)(12).[414] Under present and prior law, the 85-percent test is determined without taking into account any income from qualified pole rentals and cancellation of indebtedness income from the prepayment of a loan under sections 306A, 306B, or 311 of the Rural Electrification Act of 1936 (as in effect on January 1, 1987). The exclusion for cancellation of indebtedness income applies to such income arising in 1987, 1988, or 1989 on debt that either originated with, or is guaranteed by, the Federal Government.

Rural electric cooperatives generally are subject to the tax on unrelated trade or business income under section 511.

Reasons for Change[415]

The Congress believed that the nature of an electric cooperative's activities does not change because it has income from open access transactions with non-members or from nuclear decommissioning

---

[410] Sec. 521.
[411] Sec. 1381(a)(2)(C).
[412] See Rev. Rul. 83–135, 1983–2 C.B. 149.
[413] Sec. 501(c)(12).
[414] Rev. Rul. 72–36, 1972–1 C.B. 151.
[415] See S. 1149, the "Energy Tax Incentives Act of 2003," which was reported by the Committee on Finance on May 23, 2003 (S. Rep. No. 108–54).

transactions. Accordingly, the Congress believed that the 85-percent test for tax exemption under present law should be applied without regard to such income.

For similar reasons, the Congress believed that the 85-percent test for tax exemption under present law should be applied without regard to income from certain asset exchange or conversion transactions that would otherwise qualify for deferred gain recognition under section 1031 or 1033.

The Congress further believed that electric energy sales to non-members should not result in a loss of tax-exempt status or cooperative status to the extent that such sales are necessary to replace lost sales of electric energy to members as a result of restructuring of the electric energy industry. Accordingly, the Congress believed that replacement electric energy sales to non-members (defined as "load loss transactions" in the Act) should be treated, for a limited period of time, as member income in applying the 85-percent test for tax exemption of rural electric cooperatives. The Congress believed that such treatment also should apply for purposes of determining whether tax-exempt and taxable electric cooperatives comply with the fundamental cooperative principles. Finally, the Congress believed that income from replacement electric energy sales should not be subject to the tax on unrelated trade or business income under Code section 511.

Explanation of Provision

Treatment of income from open access transactions

The Act provides that income received or accrued by a rural electric cooperative (other than income received or accrued directly or indirectly from a member of the cooperative) from the provision or sale of electric energy transmission services or ancillary services on a nondiscriminatory open access basis under an open access transmission tariff approved or accepted by the Federal Energy Regulatory Commission ("FERC") or under an independent transmission provider agreement approved or accepted by FERC (including an agreement providing for the transfer of control-but not ownership-of transmission facilities)[416] is excluded in determining whether a rural electric cooperative satisfies the 85-percent test for tax exemption under section 501(c)(12).

In addition, the Act provides that income is excluded for purposes of the 85-percent test if it is received or accrued by a rural electric cooperative (other than income received or accrued directly or indirectly from a member of the cooperative) from the provision or sale of electric energy distribution services or ancillary services, provided such services are provided on a nondiscriminatory open access basis to distribute electric energy not owned by the cooperative: (1) to end-users who are served by distribution facilities not owned by the cooperative or any of its members; or (2) generated by a generation facility that is not owned or leased by the cooperative or any of its members and that is directly connected to distribution facilities owned by the cooperative or any of its members.

[416] Under the provision, references to FERC are treated as including references to the Public Utility Commission of Texas.

Treatment of income from nuclear decommissioning transactions

The Act provides that income received or accrued by a rural electric cooperative from any "nuclear decommissioning transaction" also is excluded in determining whether a rural electric cooperative satisfies the 85-percent test for tax exemption under section 501(c)(12). The term "nuclear decommissioning transaction" is defined as (1) any transfer into a trust, fund, or instrument established to pay any nuclear decommissioning costs if the transfer is in connection with the transfer of the cooperative's interest in a nuclear powerplant or nuclear powerplant unit; (2) any distribution from a trust, fund, or instrument established to pay any nuclear decommissioning costs; or (3) any earnings from a trust, fund, or instrument established to pay any nuclear decommissioning costs.

Treatment of income from asset exchange or conversion transactions

The Act provides that gain realized by a tax-exempt rural electric cooperative from a voluntary exchange or involuntary conversion of certain property is excluded in determining whether a rural electric cooperative satisfies the 85-percent test for tax exemption under section 501(c)(12). This provision only applies to the extent that: (1) the gain would qualify for deferred recognition under section 1031 (relating to exchanges of property held for productive use or investment) or section 1033 (relating to involuntary conversions); and (2) the replacement property that is acquired by the cooperative pursuant to section 1031 or section 1033 (as the case may be) constitutes property that is used, or to be used, for the purpose of generating, transmitting, distributing, or selling electricity or natural gas.

Treatment of income from load loss transactions

Tax-exempt rural electric cooperatives

The Act provides that income received or accrued by a tax-exempt rural electric cooperative from a "load loss transaction" is treated under 501(c)(12) as income collected from members for the sole purpose of meeting losses and expenses of providing service to its members. Therefore, income from load loss transactions is treated as member income in determining whether a rural electric cooperative satisfies the 85-percent test for tax exemption under section 501(c)(12). The Act also provides that income from load loss transactions does not cause a tax-exempt electric cooperative to fail to be treated for Federal income tax purposes as a mutual or cooperative company under the fundamental cooperative principles described above.

The term "load loss transaction" is generally defined as any wholesale or retail sale of electric energy (other than to a member of the cooperative) to the extent that the aggregate amount of such sales during a seven-year period beginning with the "start-up year" does not exceed the reduction in the amount of sales of electric energy during such period by the cooperative to members. The "start-up year" is defined as the first year that the cooperative offers nondiscriminatory open access or, if later and at the election of the cooperative, the calendar year that includes the date of enactment of this provision.

The Act also excludes income received or accrued by rural electric cooperatives from load loss transactions from the tax on unrelated trade or business income.

Taxable electric cooperatives

The Act provides that the receipt or accrual of income from load loss transactions by taxable electric cooperatives is treated as income from patrons who are members of the cooperative. Thus, income from a load loss transaction is excludible from the taxable income of a taxable electric cooperative if the cooperative distributes such income pursuant to a pre-existing contract to distribute the income to a patron who is not a member of the cooperative. The Act also provides that income from load loss transactions does not cause a taxable electric cooperative to fail to be treated for Federal income tax purposes as a mutual or cooperative company under the fundamental cooperative principles described above.

Effective Date

The provision is effective for taxable years beginning after the date of enactment (October 22, 2004) and before January 1, 2007.

10. Exclusion from gross income for amounts paid under National Health Service Corps Loan Repayment Program (sec. 320 of the Act and sec. 108 of the Code)

Present and Prior Law

The National Health Service Corps Loan Repayment Program (the "NHSC Loan Repayment Program") provides education loan repayments to participants on condition that the participants provide certain services. The recipient of the loan repayment is obligated to provide medical services in a geographic area identified by the Public Health Service as having a shortage of health-care professionals. Loan repayments may be as much as $35,000 per year of service plus a tax assistance payment of 39 percent of the repayment amount.

States may also provide for education loan repayment programs for persons who agree to provide primary health services in health professional shortage areas. Under the Public Health Service Act, such programs may receive Federal grants with respect to such repayment programs if certain requirements are satisfied.

Generally, gross income means all income from whatever source derived including income for the discharge of indebtedness. However, gross income does not include discharge of indebtedness income if: (1) the discharge occurs in a Title 11 case; (2) the discharge occurs when the taxpayer is insolvent; (3) the indebtedness discharged is qualified farm indebtedness; or (4) except in the case of a C corporation, the indebtedness discharged is qualified real property business indebtedness.

Under prior law, because the loan repayments provided under the NHSC Loan Repayment Program or similar State programs under the Public Health Service Act were not specifically excluded from gross income, they were gross income to the recipient. There was also no exception from employment taxes (FICA and FUTA) for such loan repayments.

Reasons for Change[417]

The Congress believed that elimination of the tax on loan repayments provided under the NHSC Loan Repayment Program and similar State programs would free up NHSC resources which are currently being used to pay for services that will be provided by medical professionals as a condition of loan repayment and improve the ability of the NHSC to attract medical professionals to underserved areas.

Explanation of Provision

The Act excludes from gross income and employment taxes education loan repayments provided under the NHSC Loan Repayment Program and State programs eligible for funds under the Public Health Service Act. The Act also provides that such repayments are not taken into account as wages in determining benefits under the Social Security Act.

Effective Date

The provision is effective with respect to amounts received in taxable years beginning after December 31, 2003.

11. Modified safe harbor rules for timber REITs (sec. 321 of the Act and sec. 857 of the Code)

Present and Prior Law

In general

Under present law, real estate investment trusts ("REITs") are subject to a special taxation regime. Under this regime, a REIT is allowed a deduction for dividends paid to its shareholders. As a result, REITs generally do not pay tax on distributed income. REITs are generally restricted to earning certain types of passive income, primarily rents from real property and interests on mortgages secured by real property.

To qualify as a REIT, a corporation must satisfy a number of requirements, among which are four tests: organizational structure, source of income, nature of assets, and distribution of income.

Income or loss from prohibited transactions

A 100-percent tax is imposed on the net income of a REIT from "prohibited transactions". A prohibited transaction is the sale or other disposition of property held for sale in the ordinary course of a trade or business,[418] other than foreclosure property.[419] A safe harbor is provided for certain sales of land or improvements. To

---

[417] The reasons for change were included for a substantially similar provision in S. 2424, the "National Employee Savings and Trust Equity Guarantee Act," which was reported by the Senate Committee on Finance on May 14, 2004 (S. Rep. No. 108–266).

[418] Sec. 1221(a)(1).

[419] Thus, the 100-percent tax on prohibited transactions helps to ensure that the REIT is a passive entity and may not engage in ordinary retailing activities such as sales to customers of condominium units or subdivided lots in a development project.

qualify for the safe harbor, three criteria generally must be met. First, the REIT must have held the land or improvements for at least four years for the production of rental income.[420] Second, the aggregate expenditures made by the REIT during the four-year period prior to the date of the sale must not exceed 30 percent of the net selling price of the property. Third, either (i) the REIT must make seven or fewer sales of property during the taxable year or (ii) the aggregate adjusted basis of the property sold must not exceed 10 percent of the aggregate bases of all the REIT's assets at the beginning of the REIT's taxable year. In the latter case, substantially all of the marketing and development expenditures with respect to the property must be made through an independent contractor.

Certain timber income

Some REITs have been formed to hold land on which trees are grown. Upon maturity of the trees, the standing trees are sold by the REIT. The Internal Revenue Service has issued private letter rulings in particular instances stating that the income from the sale of the trees can qualify as REIT real property income because the uncut timber and the timberland on which the timber grew is considered real property and the sale of uncut trees can qualify as capital gain derived from the sale of real property.[421]

Limitation on investment in other entities

In general

A REIT is limited in the amount that it can own in other corporations. Specifically, a REIT cannot own securities (other than Government securities and certain real estate assets) in an amount greater than 25 percent of the value of REIT assets. In addition, it cannot own such securities of any one issuer representing more than five percent of the total value of REIT assets or more than 10 percent of the voting securities or 10 percent of the value of the outstanding securities of any one issuer. Securities for purposes of these rules are defined by reference to the Investment Company Act of 1940.[422]

Special rules for taxable REIT subsidiaries

Under an exception to the general rule limiting REIT securities ownership of other entities, a REIT can own stock of a taxable REIT subsidiary ("TRS"), generally, a corporation other than a REIT[423] with which the REIT makes a joint election to be subject to special rules. A TRS can engage in active business operations that would produce income that would not be qualified income for

[420] An exception to the requirement is provided for land or improvements acquired by foreclosure, deed in lieu of foreclosure, or lease termination. Sec. 857(b)(6)(C).

[421] See, e.g., PLR 200052021, PLR 199945055, PLR 19927021, PLR 8838016. A private letter ruling may be relied upon only by the taxpayer to which the ruling is issued. However, such rulings provide an indication of administrative practice.

[422] Certain securities that are within a safe-harbor definition of "straight debt" are not taken into account for purposes of the limitation to no more than 10 percent of the value of an issuer's outstanding securities.

[423] Certain corporations are not eligible to be a TRS, such as a corporation which directly or indirectly operates or manages a lodging facility or a health care facility or directly or indirectly provides to any other person rights to a brand name under which any lodging facility or health care facility is operated. Sec. 856(l)(3).

purposes of the 95-percent or 75-percent income tests for a REIT, and that income is not attributed to the REIT. Transactions between a TRS and a REIT are subject to a number of specified rules that are intended to prevent the TRS (taxable as a separate corporate entity) from shifting taxable income from its activities to the pass-through entity REIT or from absorbing more than its share of expenses. Under one rule, a 100-percent excise tax is imposed on rents, deductions, or interest paid by the TRS to the REIT to the extent such items would exceed an arm's length amount as determined under section 482.[424]

Reasons for Change

The Congress believed it was appropriate to provide a safe harbor from the prohibited transactions rules, to permit a REIT that holds timberland to make sales of timber property, provided there is not significant development of the property. A similar provision already exists for rental properties.

Explanation of Provision

The Act adds a new provision that a sale of a real estate asset by a REIT will not be a prohibited transaction if the following six requirements are met:

1. The asset must have been held for at least four years in the trade or business of producing timber;
2. The aggregate expenditures made by the REIT (or a partner of the REIT) during the four-year period preceding the date of sale that are includible in the basis of the property (other than timberland acquisition expenditures[425]) and that are directly related to the operation of the property for the production of timber or for the preservation of the property for use as timberland must not exceed 30 percent of the net selling price of the property;
3. The aggregate expenditures made by the REIT (or a partner of the REIT) during the four-year period preceding the date of sale that are includible in the basis of the property (other than timberland acquisition expenditures) and that are not directly related to the operation of the property for the production of timber or the preservation of the property for use as timberland must not exceed five percent of the net selling price of the property;
4. The REIT either (a) does not make more than seven sales of property (other than sales of foreclosure property or sales to which 1033 applies) or (b) the aggregate adjusted bases (as determined for purposes of computing earnings and profits) of property sold during the year (other than sales of foreclosure property or sales to which 1033 applies) does not exceed 10 percent of the aggregate bases (as determined for purposes of computing earnings and profits) of all assets of the REIT as of the beginning of the taxable year;

[424] If the excise tax applies, the item is not also reallocated back to the TRS under section 482.

[425] The timberland acquisition expenditures that are excluded for this purpose are those expenditures that are related to timberland other than the specific timberland that is being sold under the safe harbor, but costs of which may be combined with costs of such property in the same "managaement block" under Treas. Reg. sec. 1.611–3(d). Any specific timberland being sold must meet the requirement that it has been held for at least four years by the REIT in order to qualify for the safe harbor.

5. In the case that the seven property sales per year requirement is not met, substantially all of the marketing expenditures with respect to the property are made by persons who are independent contractors (as defined by section 856(d)(3)) with respect to the REIT and from whom the REIT does not derive or receive any income; and

6. The sales price on the sale of the property cannot be based in whole or in part on income or profits of any person, including income or profits derived from the sale or operation of such properties.

Capital expenditures counted towards the 30-percent limit are those expenditures that are includible in the basis of the property (other than timberland acquisition expenditures), and that are directly related to operation of the property for the production of timber, or for the preservation of the property for use as timberland. These capital expenditures are those incurred directly in the operation of raising timber (i.e., silviculture), as opposed to capital expenditures incurred in the ownership of undeveloped land. In general, these capital expenditures incurred directly in the operation of raising timber include capital expenditures incurred by the REIT to create an established stand of growing trees. A stand of trees is considered established when a target stand exhibits the expected growing rate and is free of non-target competition (e.g., hardwoods, grasses, brush, etc.) that may significantly inhibit or threaten the target stand survival. The costs commonly incurred during stand establishment are: (1) site preparation including manual or mechanical scarification, manual or mechanical cutting, disking, bedding, shearing, raking, piling, broadcast and windrow/pile burning (including slash disposal costs as required for stand establishment); (2) site regeneration including manual or mechanical hardwood coppice; (3) chemical application via aerial or ground to eliminate or reduce vegetation; (4) nursery operating costs including personnel salaries and benefits, facilities costs, cone collection and seed extraction, and other costs directly attributable to the nursery operations (to the extent such costs are allocable to seedlings used by the REIT); (5) seedlings including storage, transportation and handling equipment; (6) direct planting of seedlings; and (7) initial stand fertilization, up through stand establishment. Other examples of capital expenditures incurred directly in the operation of raising timber include construction costs of roads to be used for managing the timber land (including for removal of logs or fire protection), environmental costs (i.e., habitat conservation plans), and any other post stand establishment capital costs (e.g., "mid-term fertilization costs.)"

Capital expenditures counted towards the five-percent limit are those capital expenditures incurred in the ownership of undeveloped land that are not incurred in the direct operation of raising timber (i.e., silviculture). This category of capital expenditures includes: (1) expenditures to separate the REIT's holdings of land into separate parcels; (2) costs of granting leases or easements to cable, cellular or similar companies; (3) costs in determining the presence or quality of minerals located on the land; (4) costs incurred to defend changes in law that would limit future use of the land by the REIT or a purchaser from the REIT; (5) costs incurred to determine alternative uses of the land (e.g., recreational use); and (6) development costs of the property incurred by the REIT (e.g., engineering, surveying, legal, permit, consulting, road construction, utilities, and other development costs for use other than to grow timber).

Costs that are not includible in the basis of the property are not counted towards either the 30-percent or five-percent requirements.

Effective Date

The provision is effective for taxable years beginning after the date of enactment (October 22, 2004).

12. Expensing of reforestation expenditures (sec. 322 of the Act and secs. 48 and 194 of the Code)

Present and Prior Law

Section 194 permits a taxpayer to elect to amortize and deduct a limited amount of certain reforestation expenditures. No more than $10,000 of reforestation expenditures made by a taxpayer in any year can qualify for amortization.[426] Reforestation expenditures include direct costs incurred in connection with forestation or reforestation by planting or artificial or natural seeding, including costs for site preparation, seeds and seeding, labor and tools, and depreciation on equipment used in planting or seeding. Only reforestation expenditures that are included in the basis of qualified timber property qualify for amortization.[427] Qualified timber property means "a woodlot or other site located in the United States which will contain trees in significant commercial quantities and which is held by the taxpayer for the planting, cultivating, caring for, and cutting of trees for sale or use in the commercial production of timber products." If a taxpayer's otherwise qualifying reforestation expenditures exceed the amount permitted to be amortized under section 194 and are incurred with respect to more than one qualified timber property, the taxpayer may allocate the permitted amount between or among the properties in any manner the taxpayer chooses.[428]

Reforestation expenditures qualifying for amortization are deducted in 84 equal monthly installments starting with the seventh month of the taxable year during which the expenditures are paid or incurred.

Under prior law, section 48(b) allowed a tax credit of up to $10,000 each year for 10 percent of the costs eligible for amortization under section 194. The amount permitted to be amortized under section 194 was reduced by half the amount of the credit determined under section 48(b).

---

[426] The limit is reduced to $5,000 for married taxpayers filing separate returns. All members of a controlled group of corporations (as defined under section 1563(a) except that the 80-percent ownership requirement is reduced to a more than 50-percent requirement) must share a single $10,000 limit. If a partnership or S corporation incurs reforestation expenditures, the $10,000 limit applies separately to the partnership or S corporation and to each partner or shareholder. For an estate with reforestation expenditures, the $10,000 limit is apportioned between the estate and its beneficiaries. Section 194 does not apply to trusts.

[427] Section 194 applies only to costs required to be capitalized under the general rules of capitalization; costs that could be deducted in the absence of section 194 are not required to be amortized.

[428] Treas. Reg. sec. 1.194–2(b)(2).

Explanation of Provision

The Act amends section 194(b)(1) to permit a taxpayer to elect to deduct (expense) reforestation expenditures paid or incurred with respect to any qualified timber property. The amount permitted to be deducted with respect to each qualified timber property in any taxable year generally is $10,000 ($5,000 in the case of a married individual filing a separate return).[429] The prior law rules governing the allocation of the amortization limitation among partnerships, S corporations, and members of a controlled group of corporations now apply in allocating among those entities the limitation on the amount eligible for expensing.

The Act restricts the amount permitted to be amortized and deducted during the 84-month period described above to the amount not taken as a deduction under amended section 194(b)(1).

The Congress intended that, for purposes of recapture under section 1245, any deduction allowed under this provision shall be treated as if it were a deduction allowable for amortization.[430]

The section 194(b)(1) expensing election is not available for trusts. Reforestation expenditures incurred by a trust or estate are apportioned between the income beneficiaries and the fiduciary under regulations prescribed by the Secretary, and amounts apportioned to any beneficiary are treated as incurred by such beneficiary for purposes of applying section 194.[431]

The Act repeals the prior law section 48(b) reforestation credit.

Effective Date

The provision is effective for expenditures paid or incurred after the date of enactment (October 22, 2004).

C. Incentives for Small Manufacturers

1. Net income from publicly traded partnerships treated as qualifying income of regulated investment company (sec. 331 of the Act and secs. 851(b), 469(k), 7704(d) and new sec. 851(h) of the Code)

Present and Prior Law

Treatment of RICs

A regulated investment company ("RIC") generally is treated as a conduit for Federal income tax purposes. In computing its taxable income, a RIC deducts dividends paid to its shareholders to achieve conduit treatment.[432] In order to qualify for conduit treatment, a RIC must generally be a domestic corporation that, at all times during the taxable year, is registered under the Investment Company Act of 1940 as a management company or as a unit investment trust, or has elected to be treated as a business development

[429] The Act therefore changes the $10,000 ceiling from an aggregate to a per-property limit.
[430] A technical correction may be necessary so that the statute reflects this intent.
[431] A technical correction may be necessary so that the statute reflects this intent.
[432] Sec. 852(b).

company under that Act.[433] In addition, the corporation must elect RIC status, and must satisfy certain other requirements.[434]

One of the RIC qualification requirements is that at least 90 percent of the RIC's gross income is derived from dividends, interest, payments with respect to securities loans, and gains from the sale or other disposition of stock or securities or foreign currencies, or other income (including but not limited to gains from options, futures, or forward contracts) derived with respect to its business of investing in such stock, securities, or currencies.[435] Income derived from a partnership is treated as meeting this requirement only to the extent such income is attributable to items of income of the partnership that would meet the requirement if realized by the RIC in the same manner as realized by the partnership (the "look-through" rule for partnership income).[436] Under prior law, no distinction was made under this rule between a publicly traded partnership and any other partnership.

The RIC qualification rules include limitations on the ownership of assets and on the composition of the RIC's assets.[437] Under the ownership limitation, at least 50 percent of the value of the RIC's total assets must be represented by cash, government securities and securities of other RICs, and other securities; however, in the case of such other securities, the RIC may invest no more than five percent of the value of the total assets of the RIC in the securities of any one issuer, and may hold no more than 10 percent of the outstanding voting securities of any one issuer. Under the limitation on the composition of the RIC's assets, no more than 25 percent of the value of the RIC's total assets may be invested in the securities of any one issuer (other than Government securities or securities of other RICs), or in securities of two or more controlled issuers in the same or similar trades or businesses. These limitations generally are applied at the end of each quarter.[438]

Treatment of publicly traded partnerships

Present law provides that a publicly traded partnership means a partnership, interests in which are traded on an established securities market, or are readily tradable on a secondary market (or the substantial equivalent thereof). In general, a publicly traded partnership is treated as a corporation, but an exception to corporate treatment is provided if 90 percent or more of its gross income is interest, dividends, real property rents, or certain other types of qualifying income.[439]

A special rule for publicly traded partnerships applies under the passive loss rules. The passive loss rules limit deductions and credits from passive trade or business activities.[440] Deductions attributable to passive activities, to the extent they exceed income from passive activities, generally may not be deducted against other income. Deductions and credits that are suspended under these rules

[433] Sec. 851(a).
[434] Sec. 851(b).
[435] Sec. 851(b)(2).
[436] Sec. 851(b).
[437] Sec. 851(b)(3).
[438] Sec. 851(d).
[439] Sec. 7704(a), (c), and (d).
[440] Sec. 469.

are carried forward and treated as deductions and credits from passive activities in the next year. The suspended losses from a passive activity are allowed in full when a taxpayer disposes of his entire interest in the passive activity to an unrelated person. The special rule for publicly traded partnerships provides that the passive loss rules are applied separately with respect to items attributable to each publicly traded partnership.[441] Thus, income or loss from the publicly traded partnership is treated as separate from income or loss from other passive activities.

Reasons for Change

The Congress understood that publicly traded partnerships generally are treated as corporations under rules enacted to address Congress' view that publicly traded partnerships resemble corporations in important respects.[442] Publicly traded partnerships with specified types of income are not treated as corporations, however, for the reason that if the income is from sources that are commonly considered to be passive investments, then there is less reason to treat the publicly traded partnership as a corporation.[443] The Congress understood that these types of publicly traded partnerships may have improved access to capital markets if their interests were permitted investments of mutual funds. Therefore, the Act treats publicly traded partnership interests as permitted investments for mutual funds ("RICs").

Nevertheless, the Congress believed that permitting mutual funds to hold interests in a publicly traded partnership should not give rise to avoidance of unrelated business income tax or withholding of income tax that would apply if tax-exempt organizations or foreign persons held publicly traded partnership interests directly rather than through a mutual fund. Therefore, the Act requires that existing limitations on ownership and composition of assets of mutual funds apply to any investment in a publicly traded partnership by a mutual fund. The Congress believed that these limitations will serve to limit the use of mutual funds as conduits for avoidance of unrelated business income tax or withholding rules that would otherwise apply with respect to publicly traded partnership income.

Explanation of Provision

The Act modifies the 90-percent test with respect to income of a RIC to include net income derived from an interest in a publicly traded partnership. The Act also modifies the look-through rule for partnership income of a RIC so that it applies only to income from a partnership other than a publicly traded partnership.

In addition, the Act provides that net income from an interest in a publicly traded partnership is used for purposes of both the numerator and denominator of the 90-percent test. As under prior law with respect to other permitted investments, the Act also provides that gains from the sale or other disposition of interests in publicly

[441] Sec. 469(k).
[442] H.R. Rep. No. 100–391, pt. 2 of 2, at 1006 (1987)
[443] *Id.*

traded partnerships constitute qualifying income of regulated investment companies.

The Act provides that the limitation on ownership and the limitation on composition of assets that apply to other investments of a RIC also apply to RIC investments in publicly traded partnership interests.

The Act provides that the special rule for publicly traded partnerships under the passive loss rules (requiring separate treatment) applies to a RIC holding an interest in a publicly traded partnership, with respect to items attributable to the interest in the publicly traded partnership.

Effective Date

The provision is effective for taxable years beginning after the date of enactment (October 22, 2004).

2. Simplification of excise tax imposed on bows and arrows (sec. 332 of the Act and sec. 4161 of the Code)

Present and Prior Law

Under prior law, the Code imposed an excise tax of 11 percent on the sale by a manufacturer, producer or importer of any bow with a draw weight of 10 pounds or more.[444] An excise tax of 12.4 percent is imposed on the sale by a manufacturer or importer of any shaft, point, nock, or vane designed for use as part of an arrow which after its assembly (1) is over 18 inches long, or (2) is designed for use with a taxable bow (if shorter than 18 inches).[445] No tax is imposed on finished arrows. An 11-percent excise tax also is imposed on any part of an accessory for taxable bows and on quivers for use with arrows (1) over 18 inches long or (2) designed for use with a taxable bow (if shorter than 18 inches).[446]

Reasons for Change

Under prior law, foreign manufacturers and importers of arrows were able to avoid the 12.4 percent excise tax paid by domestic manufacturers because the tax was placed on arrow components rather than finished arrows. As a result, arrows assembled outside of the United States had a price advantage over domestically manufactured arrows. The Congress believed it was appropriate to close this loophole. The Congress also believed that adjusting the minimum draw weight for taxable bows from 10 pounds to 30 pounds would better target the excise tax to actual hunting use by eliminating the excise tax on instructional ("youth") bows.

Explanation of Provision

The Act increases the draw weight for a taxable bow from 10 pounds or more to a peak draw weight of 30 pounds or more.[447]

[444] Sec. 4161(b)(1)(A).

[445] Sec. 4161(b)(2).

[446] Sec. 4161(b)(1)(B).

[447] Draw weight is the maximum force required to bring the bowstring to a full-draw position not less than 26¼ inches, measured from the pressure point of the hand grip to the nocking position on the bowstring.

The Act subjects certain broadheads (a type of arrow point) to an excise tax equal to 11 percent of the sales price instead of 12.4 percent.

Section 332 of the Act included other provisions which were subsequently modified by Pub. L. No. 108–493. See Part Twenty-One for description of those provisions as modified.

Effective Date

The provisions of this section of the Act relating to the taxation of broadheads and bows are effective for articles sold by the manufacturer, producer or importer 30 days after the date of enactment (October 22, 2004) of the Act.

3. Reduce rate of excise tax on fishing tackle boxes to three percent (sec. 333 of the Act and sec. 4162 of the Code)

Present and Prior Law

A 10-percent manufacturer's excise tax is imposed on specified sport fishing equipment. Examples of taxable equipment include fishing rods and poles, fishing reels, artificial bait, fishing lures, line and hooks, and fishing tackle boxes. Revenues from the excise tax on sport fishing equipment are deposited in the Sport Fishing Account of the Aquatic Resources Trust Fund. Monies in the fund are spent, subject to an existing permanent appropriation, to support Federal-State sport fish enhancement and safety programs.

Reasons for Change

The Congress believed that fishing "tackle boxes" were little different in design and appearance from "tool boxes," yet the former were subject to a Federal excise tax at a rate of 10 percent, while the latter were not subject to Federal excise tax. This excise tax can create a sufficiently large price difference that some fishermen will choose to use a "tool box" to hold their hooks and lures rather than a traditional "tackle box." The Congress found that such a distortion of consumer choice placed an inappropriate burden on the manufacturers and purchasers of traditional tackle boxes, particularly in comparison to the modest amount of revenue raised by the excise tax, and that this burden warranted a reduction in the rate of tax.

Explanation of Provision

Under the Act, the rate of excise tax imposed on fishing tackle boxes is reduced to three percent.

Effective Date

The provision is effective for articles sold by the manufacturer, producer, or importer after December 31, 2004.

4. Repeal of excise tax on sonar devices suitable for finding fish (sec. 334 of the Act and secs. 4161 and 4162 of the Code)

Present and Prior Law

In general, the Code imposes a 10-percent tax on the sale by the manufacturer, producer, or importer of specified sport fishing equipment.[448] A three-percent rate, however, applies to the sale of electric outboard motors, and applied to the sale of sonar devices suitable for finding fish.[449] Further, the tax imposed on the sale of sonar devices suitable for finding fish was limited to $30. A sonar device suitable for finding fish did not include any device that was a graph recorder, a digital type, a meter readout, a combination graph recorder or combination meter readout.[450]

Revenues from the excise tax on sport fishing equipment are deposited in the Sport Fishing Account of the Aquatic Resources Trust Fund. Monies in the fund are spent, subject to an existing permanent appropriation, to support Federal-State sport fish enhancement and safety programs.

Reasons for Change

The Congress observed that the exemption for certain forms of sonar devices had the effect of exempting almost all of the devices currently on the market. The Congress understood that only one form of sonar device was not exempt from the tax, those units utilizing light-emitting diode ("LED") display technology. The Congress further understood that LED devices were not exempt from the tax because the technology was developed after the exemption for the other technologies was enacted. In the view of Congress, the application of the tax to LED display devices, and not to devices performing the same function with a different technology, created an unfair advantage for the exempt devices. Because most of the devices on the market were already exempt, the Congress believed it was appropriate to level the playing field by repealing the tax imposed on all sonar devices suitable for finding fish. The Congress believed that was a more suitable solution than exempting a device from the tax based on the type of technology used.

Explanation of Provision

The Act repeals the excise tax on all sonar devices suitable for finding fish.[451]

Effective Date

The provision is effective for articles sold by the manufacturer, producer, or importer after December 31, 2004.

---

[448] Sec. 4161(a)(1).
[449] Sec. 4161(a)(2).
[450] Sec. 4162(b).
[451] A clerical technical correction may be necessary to eliminate deadwood in connection with the provision. See section 2(g)(18) of H.R. 5395 and S. 3019, the "Tax Technical Corrections Act of 2004," introduced November 19, 2004.

5. Charitable contribution deduction for certain expenses in support of Native Alaskan subsistence whaling (sec. 335 of the Act and sec. 170 of the Code)

Present and Prior Law

In computing taxable income, individuals who do not elect the standard deduction may claim itemized deductions, including a deduction (subject to certain limitations) for charitable contributions or gifts made during the taxable year to a qualified charitable organization or governmental entity. Individuals who elect the standard deduction may not claim a deduction for charitable contributions made during the taxable year.

No charitable contribution deduction is allowed for a contribution of services. However, unreimbursed expenditures made incident to the rendition of services to an organization, contributions to which are deductible, may constitute a deductible contribution.[452] Specifically, section 170(j) provides that no charitable contribution deduction is allowed for traveling expenses (including amounts expended for meals and lodging) while away from home, whether paid directly or by reimbursement, unless there is no significant element of personal pleasure, recreation, or vacation in such travel.

Reasons for Change

Congress believes that subsistence bowhead whale hunting activities are important to certain native peoples of Alaska and further charitable purposes, and that certain expenses paid by individuals recognized as whaling captains by the Alaska Eskimo Whaling Commission in the conduct of sanctioned whaling activities conducted pursuant to the management plan of that Commission should be deductible expenses.

Explanation of Provision

The Act allows individuals to claim a deduction under section 170 not exceeding $10,000 per taxable year for certain expenses incurred in carrying out sanctioned whaling activities. The deduction is available only to an individual who is recognized by the Alaska Eskimo Whaling Commission as a whaling captain charged with the responsibility of maintaining and carrying out sanctioned whaling activities. The deduction is available for reasonable and necessary expenses paid by the taxpayer during the taxable year for: (1) the acquisition and maintenance of whaling boats, weapons, and gear used in sanctioned whaling activities; (2) the supplying of food for the crew and other provisions for carrying out such activities; and (3) the storage and distribution of the catch from such activities. Under the Act, the Secretary shall issue guidance regarding substantiation of amounts claimed as deductible whaling expenses, such as by maintaining appropriate written records that show, for example, the time, place, date, amount, and nature of the expense, as well as the taxpayer's eligibility for the deduction, and may require that such substantiation be provided as part of the taxpayer's income tax return.

---

[452] Treas. Reg. sec. 1.170A–1(g).

For purposes of the provision, the term "sanctioned whaling activities" means subsistence bowhead whale hunting activities conducted pursuant to the management plan of the Alaska Eskimo Whaling Commission.

Effective Date

The provision is effective for contributions made after December 31, 2004.

6. Extended placed in service date for bonus depreciation for certain aircraft (excluding aircraft used in the transportation industry) (sec. 336 of the Act and sec. 168 of the Code)

Present and Prior Law

In general

A taxpayer is allowed to recover, through annual depreciation deductions, the cost of certain property used in a trade or business or for the production of income. The amount of the depreciation deduction allowed with respect to tangible property for a taxable year is determined under the modified accelerated cost recovery system ("MACRS"). Under MACRS, different types of property generally are assigned applicable recovery periods and depreciation methods. The recovery periods applicable to most tangible personal property range from three to 25 years. The depreciation methods generally applicable to tangible personal property are the 200-percent and 150-percent declining balance methods, switching to the straight-line method for the taxable year in which the depreciation deduction would be maximized.

Thirty-percent additional first-year depreciation deduction

JCWAA allows an additional first-year depreciation deduction equal to 30 percent of the adjusted basis of qualified property.[453] The amount of the additional first-year depreciation deduction is not affected by a short taxable year. The additional first-year depreciation deduction is allowed for both regular tax and alternative minimum tax purposes for the taxable year in which the property is placed in service.[454] The basis of the property and the depreciation allowances in the placed-in-service year and later years are appropriately adjusted to reflect the additional first-year depreciation deduction. In addition, there are generally no adjustments to the allowable amount of depreciation for purposes of computing a taxpayer's alternative minimum taxable income with respect to property to which the provision applies. A taxpayer is allowed to elect out of the additional first-year depreciation for any class of property for any taxable year.[455]

---

[453] The additional first-year depreciation deduction is subject to the general rules regarding whether an item is deductible under section 162 or subject to capitalization under section 263 or section 263A.

[454] However, the additional first-year depreciation deduction is not allowed for purposes of computing earnings and profits.

[455] A taxpayer may elect out of the 50-percent additional first-year depreciation (discussed below) for any class of property and still be eligible for the 30-percent additional first-year depreciation.

In order for property to qualify for the additional first-year depreciation deduction, it must meet all of the following requirements. First, the property must be (1) property to which MACRS applies with an applicable recovery period of 20 years or less, (2) water utility property (as defined in section 168(e)(5)), (3) computer software other than computer software covered by section 197, or (4) qualified leasehold improvement property (as defined in section 168(k)(3)).[456] Second, the original use[457] of the property must commence with the taxpayer on or after September 11, 2001. Third, the taxpayer must acquire the property within the applicable time period. Finally, the property must be placed in service before January 1, 2005.

An extension of the placed-in-service date of one year (i.e., January 1, 2006) is provided for certain property with a recovery period of ten years or longer and certain transportation property.[458] Transportation property is defined as tangible personal property used in the trade or business of transporting persons or property.

The applicable time period for acquired property is (1) after September 10, 2001 and before January 1, 2005, but only if no binding written contract for the acquisition is in effect before September 11, 2001, or (2) pursuant to a binding written contract which was entered into after September 10, 2001, and before January 1, 2005.[459] With respect to property that is manufactured, constructed, or produced by the taxpayer for use by the taxpayer, the taxpayer must begin the manufacture, construction, or production of the property after September 10, 2001. For property eligible for the extended placed-in-service date, a special rule limits the amount of costs eligible for the additional first-year depreciation. With respect to such property, only the portion of the basis that is properly attributable to the costs incurred before January 1, 2005 ("progress expenditures") is eligible for the additional first-year depreciation.[460]

Fifty-percent additional first-year depreciation

JGTRRA provides an additional first-year depreciation deduction equal to 50 percent of the adjusted basis of qualified property. Qualified property is defined in the same manner as for purposes of the 30-percent additional first-year depreciation deduction provided by the JCWAA except that the applicable time period for acquisition (or self construction) of the property is modified. Property eligible for the 50-percent additional first-year depreciation deduction is not eligible for the 30-percent additional first-year depreciation deduction.

---

[456] A special rule precludes the additional first-year depreciation deduction for any property that is required to be depreciated under the alternative depreciation system of MACRS.

[457] The term "original use" means the first use to which the property is put, whether or not such use corresponds to the use of such property by the taxpayer.

If, in the normal course of its business, a taxpayer sells fractional interests in property to unrelated third parties, then the original use of such property begins with the first user of each fractional interest (i.e., each fractional owner is considered the original user of its proportionate share of the property).

[458] In order for property to qualify for the extended placed-in-service date, the property must be subject to section 263A and have an estimated production period exceeding two years or an estimated production period exceeding one year and a cost exceeding $1 million.

[459] Property does not fail to qualify for the additional first-year depreciation merely because a binding written contract to acquire a component of the property is in effect prior to September 11, 2001.

[460] For purposes of determining the amount of eligible progress expenditures, it is intended that rules similar to sec. 46(d)(3) as in effect prior to the Tax Reform Act of 1986 shall apply.

In order to qualify, the property must be acquired after May 5, 2003 and before January 1, 2005, and no binding written contract for the acquisition can be in effect before May 6, 2003.[461] With respect to property that is manufactured, constructed, or produced by the taxpayer for use by the taxpayer, the taxpayer must begin the manufacture, construction, or production of the property after May 5, 2003. For property eligible for the extended placed-in-service date (i.e., certain property with a recovery period of ten years or longer and certain transportation property), a special rule limits the amount of costs eligible for the additional first-year depreciation. With respect to such property, only progress expenditures properly attributable to the costs incurred before January 1, 2005 are eligible for the additional first-year depreciation.[462]

Reasons for Change

The Congress believed that certain non-commercial aircraft represent property having characteristics that should qualify for the extended placed-in-service date accorded for property having long production periods. This treatment should be available only if the purchaser makes a substantial deposit, the expected cost exceeds certain thresholds, and the production period is sufficiently long.

Explanation of Provision

Due to the extended production period, the Act provides criteria under which certain non-commercial aircraft can qualify for the extended placed-in-service date. Qualifying aircraft are eligible for the additional first-year depreciation deduction if placed in service before January 1, 2006. In order to qualify, the aircraft must:

1. be acquired by the taxpayer during the applicable time period as under present law;[463]
2. meet the appropriate placed-in-service date requirements;
3. not be tangible personal property used in the trade or business of transporting persons or property (except for agricultural or firefighting purposes);
4. be purchased[464] by a purchaser who, at the time of the contract for purchase, has made a nonrefundable deposit of the lesser of ten percent of the cost or $100,000; and
5. have an estimated production period exceeding four months and a cost exceeding $200,000.

The progress expenditures limitation does not apply to non-commercial aircraft which qualify under the provision.

[461] Property does not fail to qualify for the additional first-year depreciation merely because a binding written contract to acquire a component of the property is in effect prior to May 6, 2003. However, no 50-percent additional first-year depreciation is permitted on any such component. No inference is intended as to the proper treatment of components placed in service under the 30-percent additional first-year depreciation provided by the JCWAA.

[462] For purposes of determining the amount of eligible progress expenditures, it is intended that rules similar to sec. 46(d)(3) as in effect prior to the Tax Reform Act of 1986 shall apply.

[463] Property that is otherwise eligible for the extended placed-in-service rules, and that is acquired and placed in service during 2005 pursuant to a written binding contract which was entered into after May 5, 2003, and before January 1, 2005, is eligible for the 50-percent additional first-year depreciation deduction. A technical correction may be necessary so that the statute reflects this intent.

[464] For this purpose, it is intended that the term "purchase" be interpreted as it is defined in sec. 179(d)(2).

Effective Date

The provision is effective as if included in the amendments made by section 101 of JCWAA, which applies to property placed in service after September 10, 2001. However, because the property described by the provision qualifies for the additional first-year depreciation deduction under present law if placed in service prior to January 1, 2005, the provision will modify the treatment only of property placed in service during calendar year 2005.

7. Special placed in service rule for bonus depreciation for certain property subject to syndication (sec. 337 of the Act and sec. 168 of the Code)

Present and Prior Law

Section 101 of JCWAA provides generally for 30-percent additional first-year depreciation, and provides a binding contract rule in determining property that qualifies for it. In order for property to qualify, (1) the original use of the property must commence with the taxpayer on or after September 11, 2001, and (2) the taxpayer must acquire the property (i) after September 10, 2001 and before January 1, 2005, but only if no binding written contract for the acquisition is in effect before September 11, 2001, or (ii) pursuant to a binding contract which was entered into after September 10, 2001, and before January 1, 2005. In addition, JCWAA provides a special rule in the case of certain leased property. In the case of any property that is originally placed in service by a person and that is sold to the taxpayer and leased back to such person by the taxpayer within three months after the date that the property was placed in service, the property is treated as originally placed in service by the taxpayer not earlier than the date that the property is used under the leaseback. JCWAA did not specifically address the syndication of a lease by the lessor.

The Working Families Tax Relief Act of 2004 ("H.R. 1308") included a technical correction regarding the syndication of a lease by the lessor. The technical correction provides that if property is originally placed in service by a lessor (including by operation of the special rule for self-constructed property), such property is sold within three months after the date that the property was placed in service, and the user of such property does not change, then the property is treated as originally placed in service by the taxpayer not earlier than the date of such sale.

JGTRRA provides an additional first-year depreciation deduction equal to 50 percent of the adjusted basis of qualified property. Qualified property is defined in the same manner as for purposes of the 30-percent additional first-year depreciation deduction provided by the JCWAA except that the applicable time period for acquisition (or self construction) of the property is modified. Property with respect to which the 50-percent additional first-year depreciation deduction is claimed is not also eligible for the 30-percent additional first-year depreciation deduction. In order to qualify, the property must be acquired after May 5, 2003 and before January 1, 2005, and no binding written contract for the acquisition can be in effect before May 6, 2003. With respect to property that is manufactured, constructed, or produced by the taxpayer for use by the taxpayer, the taxpayer must begin the manufacture, construction, or production of the property after May 5, 2003.

Reasons for Change

The Congress was aware that certain syndication arrangements are entered into with respect to multiple units of property (such as rail cars) that, for logistical reasons, must be placed in service over a period of time that exceeds three months. In such cases, it would be impractical for the sale of the earlier produced units to occur within three months of its placed-in-service date. Thus, the Congress deemed it appropriate to provide a special rule with respect to the syndication of multiple units of property that will be placed in service over a period of up to twelve months.

Explanation of Provision

The Act provides a special rule in the case of multiple units of property subject to the same lease. In such cases, property will qualify as placed in service on the date of sale if it is sold within three months after the final unit is placed in service, so long as the period between the time the first and last units are placed in service does not exceed 12 months.

Effective Date

The provision applies to property sold after June 4, 2004.

8. Expensing of capital costs incurred for production in complying with Environmental Protection Agency sulfur regulations for small refiners (sec. 338 of the Act and new sec. 179B of the Code)

Present and Prior Law

Taxpayers generally may recover the costs of investments in refinery property through annual depreciation deductions.

Reasons for Change [465]

The Congress believed it was important for all refiners to meet applicable pollution control standards. However, the Congress was concerned that the cost of complying with the Highway Diesel Fuel Sulfur Control Requirement of the Environmental Protection Agency ("EPA") may force some small refiners out of business. To maintain this refining capacity and to foster compliance with pollution control standards the Congress believed it was appropriate to modify cost recovery provisions for small refiners to reduce their capital costs of complying with the Highway Diesel Fuel Sulfur Control Requirement of the EPA.

---

[465] These reasons for change were included for similar provisions included in H.R. 1531, the "Energy Tax Policy Act of 2003," which was reported by the House Committee on Ways and Means on April 9, 2003 (H.R. Rep. No. 108–67) and S. 1149, the "Energy Tax Incentive Act of 2003," which was reported by the Senate Committee on Finance on May 2, 2003 (S. Rep. No. 108–54). The two bills were conferenced to produce H.R. 6, the "Energy Policy Act of 2003," (H.R. Conf. Rep. 108–375).

Explanation of Provision

The Act permits small business refiners to immediately deduct as an expense up to 75 percent of the costs paid or incurred for the purpose of complying with the Highway Diesel Fuel Sulfur Control Requirements of the EPA. Costs qualifying for the deduction are those costs paid or incurred with respect to any facility of a small business refiner during the period beginning on January 1, 2003 and ending on the earlier of the date that is one year after the date on which the taxpayer must comply with the applicable EPA regulations or December 31, 2009.

For these purposes a small business refiner is a taxpayer who is in the business of refining petroleum products and employs not more than 1,500 employees directly in refining and has less than 205,000 barrels per day (average) of total refinery capacity. The deduction is reduced ratably for taxpayers with capacity between 155,000 barrels per day and 205,000 barrels per day. With respect to the definition of a small business refiner, the Congress intends that, in any case in which refinery through-put or retained production of the refinery differs substantially from its average daily output or refined product, capacity be measured by reference to the average daily output of refined product.

Effective Date

The provision is effective for expenses paid or incurred after December 31, 2002, in taxable years ending after that date.

9. Credit for small refiners for production of diesel fuel in compliance with Environmental Protection Agency sulfur regulations for small refiners (sec. 339 of the Act and new sec. 45H of the Code)

Present and Prior Law

Prior law did not provide a credit for the production of low-sulfur diesel fuel.

Reasons for Change [466]

The Congress believed it was important for all refiners to meet applicable pollution control standards. However, the Congress was concerned that the cost of complying with the Highway Diesel Fuel Sulfur Control Requirement of the Environmental Protection Agency ("EPA") may force some small refiners out of business. To maintain this refining capacity and to foster compliance with pollution control standards the Congress believed it was appropriate to modify cost recovery provisions for small refiners to reduce their capital costs of complying with the Highway Diesel Fuel Sulfur Control Requirement of the EPA.

[466] These reasons for change were included for similar provisions included in H.R. 1531, the "Energy Tax Policy Act of 2003," which was reported by the House Committee on Ways and Means on April 9, 2003 (H.R. Rep. No. 108–67) and S. 1149, the "Energy Tax Incentive Act of 2003," which was reported by the Senate Committee on Finance on May 2, 2003 (S. Rep. No. 108–54). The two bills were conferenced to produce H.R. 6, the "Energy Policy Act of 2003," (H.R. Conf. Rep. 108–375).

Explanation of Provision

The Act provides that a small business refiner may claim credit equal to five cents per gallon for each gallon of low sulfur diesel fuel produced during the taxable year that is in compliance with the Highway Diesel Fuel Sulfur Control Requirements of the EPA. The total production credit claimed by the taxpayer is limited to 25 percent of the capital costs incurred to come into compliance with the EPA diesel fuel requirements. Costs qualifying for the credit are those costs paid or incurred with respect to any facility of a small business refiner during the period beginning on January 1, 2003 and ending on the earlier of the date that is one year after the date on which the taxpayer must comply with the applicable EPA regulations or December 31, 2009. The taxpayer's basis in property with respect to which the credit applies is reduced by the amount of production credit claimed.

In the case of a qualifying small business refiner that is owned by a cooperative, the cooperative is allowed to elect to pass any production credits to patrons of the organization.

The Act makes the low sulfur diesel fuel credit a qualified business credit under section 169(c). Therefore, if any portion of the credit has not been allowed to the taxpayer as a general business credit (sec. 38) for any taxable year, an amount equal to that portion may be deducted by the taxpayer in the first taxable year following the last taxable year for which such portion could have been allowed as a credit under the carryback and carryforward rules (sec. 39).

For these purposes a small business refiner is a taxpayer who is in the business of refining petroleum products, employs not more than 1,500 employees directly in refining, and has less than 205,000 barrels per day (average) of total refinery capacity. The credit is reduced ratably for taxpayers with capacity between 155,000 barrels per day and 205,000 barrels per day. With respect to the definition of a small business refiner, the Congress intends that, in any case where refinery through-put or retained production of the refinery differs substantially from its average daily output of refined product, capacity be measured by reference to the average daily output of refined product.

Effective Date

The provision is effective for expenses paid or incurred after December 31, 2002, in taxable years ending after that date.

10. Modification to qualified small issue bonds (sec. 340 of the Act and sec. 144 of the Code)

Present and Prior Law

Qualified small-issue bonds are tax-exempt bonds issued by State and local governments to finance private business manufacturing facilities (including certain directly related and ancillary facilities) or the acquisition of land and equipment by certain farmers. In both instances, these bonds are subject to limits on the amount of financing that may be provided, both for a single borrowing and in the aggregate. In general, no more than $1 million of small-issue bond financing may be outstanding at any time for property of a business (including related parties) located in the same municipality or county. Generally, this $1 million limit may be increased to $10 million if in addition to outstanding bonds, all other capital expenditures of the business (including related parties) in the same municipality or county are counted toward the limit over a six-year period that begins three years before the issue date of the bonds and ends three years after such date. For example, assume that City, on October 22, 2003, issues $6 million principal amount of small issue bonds and loans the proceeds to Corporation to finance a manufacturing facility located in City. Further assume that Corporation incurred $4 million of capital expenditures on May 17, 2001, with respect to a separate facility also located in City. The capital expenditures incurred in 2001 must be taken into account for purposes of the $10 million limitation. Moreover, any additional capital expenditures Corporation (or any related party) incurred or incurs with respect to facilities located in City either three years before or three years after October 22, 2003, will cause the bonds issued on that date to lose the tax exemption.

Outstanding aggregate borrowing is limited to $40 million per borrower (including related parties) regardless of where the property is located.

Reasons for Change

The Congress believed it was appropriate to increase the $10 million capital expenditures limit for small-issue bonds because the limit had not been adjusted for many years.

Explanation of Provision

The Act increases the maximum allowable amount of total capital expenditures by an eligible business (or related party) in the same municipality or county from $10 million to $20 million for bonds issued after September 30, 2009.

Effective Date

The provision is effective for bonds issued after September 30, 2009.

11. Oil and gas production from marginal wells (sec. 341 of the Act and new sec. 45I of the Code)

Prior Law

Under prior law, there was no credit for the production of oil and gas from marginal wells. The costs of such production were recoverable under the Code's depreciation and depletion rules and in other cases as a deduction for ordinary and necessary business expenses.

Reasons for Change

The highly volatile price of oil and gas can result in lost production during periods when prices are low. The Congress learned that once a producing well is shut in, that source of supply may be forever lost. To increase domestic supply, the Congress determined that a tax credit will help ensure that supply is not lost as a result of low market prices.[467]

Explanation of Provision

The Act creates a new, $3-per-barrel credit for the production of crude oil and a $0.50 credit per 1,000 cubic feet of qualified natural gas production. In both cases, the credit is available only for production from a "qualified marginal well." A qualified marginal well is defined as a domestic well: (1) production from which is treated as marginal production for purposes of the Code percentage depletion rules; or (2) that during the taxable year had average daily production of not more than 25 barrel equivalents and produces water at a rate of not less than 95 percent of total well effluent. Under the Act, the maximum amount of production during any taxable year on which credit could be claimed is 1,095 barrels or barrel equivalents.

The credit is not available to production occurring if the reference price of oil exceeds $18 ($2.00 for natural gas). The credit is reduced proportionately as for reference prices between $15 and $18 ($1.67 and $2.00 for natural gas). Reference prices are determined on a one-year look-back basis.

In the case of production from a qualified marginal well which is eligible for the credit allowed under section 29 for the taxable year, no marginal well credit is allowable unless the taxpayer elects not to claim the credit under section 29 with respect to the well. Under the Act, the credit is treated as part of the general business credit; however, unused credits can be carried back for up to five years rather than the generally applicable carryback period of one year. The credit is indexed for inflation for taxable years beginning in a calendar year after 2005.

Effective Date

The provision is effective for production in taxable years beginning after December 31, 2004.

[467] See H.R. 1531, the "Energy Tax Policy of 2003," which was reported by the House Committee on Ways and Means on April 9, 2003 (H.R. Rep. No. 108–67).

IV. TAX REFORM AND SIMPLIFICATION FOR UNITED STATES BUSINESSES

A. Interest Expense Allocation Rules (sec. 401 of the Act and sec. 864 of the Code)

Present and Prior Law

In general

In order to compute the foreign tax credit limitation, a taxpayer must determine the amount of its taxable income from foreign sources. Thus, the taxpayer must allocate and apportion deductions between items of U.S.-source gross income, on the one hand, and items of foreign-source gross income, on the other.

In the case of interest expense, the rules generally are based on the approach that money is fungible and that interest expense is properly attributable to all business activities and property of a taxpayer, regardless of any specific purpose for incurring an obligation on which interest is paid.[468] For interest allocation purposes, the Code provides that all members of an affiliated group of corporations generally are treated as a single corporation (the so-called "one-taxpayer rule") and allocation must be made on the basis of assets rather than gross income.

Affiliated group

In general

The term "affiliated group" in this context generally is defined by reference to the rules for determining whether corporations are eligible to file consolidated returns. However, some groups of corporations are eligible to file consolidated returns yet are not treated as affiliated for interest allocation purposes, and other groups of corporations are treated as affiliated for interest allocation purposes even though they are not eligible to file consolidated returns. Thus, under the one-taxpayer rule, the factors affecting the allocation of interest expense of one corporation may affect the sourcing of taxable income of another related corporation even if the two corporations do not elect to file, or are ineligible to file, consolidated returns.

Definition of affiliated group—consolidated return rules

For consolidation purposes, the term "affiliated group" means one or more chains of includible corporations connected through stock ownership with a common parent corporation which is an includible corporation, but only if: (1) the common parent owns directly stock possessing at least 80 percent of the total voting power and

[468] However, exceptions to the fungibility principle are provided in particular cases, some of which are described below.

at least 80 percent of the total value of at least one other includible corporation; and (2) stock meeting the same voting power and value standards with respect to each includible corporation (excluding the common parent) is directly owned by one or more other includible corporations.

Generally, the term "includible corporation" means any domestic corporation except certain corporations exempt from tax under section 501 (for example, corporations organized and operated exclusively for charitable or educational purposes), certain life insurance companies, corporations electing application of the possession tax credit, regulated investment companies, real estate investment trusts, and domestic international sales corporations. A foreign corporation generally is not an includible corporation.

Definition of affiliated group—special interest allocation rules

Subject to exceptions, the consolidated return and interest allocation definitions of affiliation generally are consistent with each other.[469] For example, both definitions generally exclude all foreign corporations from the affiliated group. Thus, while debt generally is considered fungible among the assets of a group of domestic affiliated corporations, prior law did not apply such fungibility principles as between the domestic and foreign members of a group with the same degree of common control as the domestic affiliated group.

Banks, savings institutions, and other financial affiliates

The affiliated group for interest allocation purposes generally excludes what are referred to in the Treasury regulations as "financial corporations" (Treas. Reg. sec. 1.861–11T(d)(4)). These include any corporation, otherwise a member of the affiliated group for consolidation purposes, that is a financial institution (described in section 581 or section 591), the business of which is predominantly with persons other than related persons or their customers, and which is required by State or Federal law to be operated separately from any other entity which is not a financial institution (sec. 864(e)(5)(C)). The category of financial corporations also includes, to the extent provided in regulations, bank holding companies (including financial holding companies), subsidiaries of banks and bank holding companies (including financial holding companies), and savings institutions predominantly engaged in the active conduct of a banking, financing, or similar business (sec. 864(e)(5)(D)).

A financial corporation is not treated as a member of the regular affiliated group for purposes of applying the one-taxpayer rule to other non-financial members of that group. Instead, all such financial corporations that would be so affiliated are treated as a separate single corporation for interest allocation purposes.

Reasons for Change

The Congress observed that a U.S.-based multinational corporate group with a significant portion of its assets overseas would be required to allocate a significant portion of its interest expense to for-

[469] One such exception is that the affiliated group for interest allocation purposes includes section 936 corporations that are excluded from the consolidated group.

eign-source income, which would reduce the foreign tax credit limitation and thus the credits allowable, even though the interest expense incurred in the United States would not be deductible in computing the actual tax liability under foreign law. The Congress believed that this approach unduly limited such a taxpayer's ability to claim foreign tax credits and left it excessively exposed to double taxation of foreign-source income. The Congress observed that the United States was the only country to impose what it considered to be harsh and anti-competitive interest expense allocation rules on its businesses and workers. The Congress believed that the practical effect of these rules was to increase the cost for U.S. companies to borrow in the United States, and to make it more expensive to invest in the United States. The Congress believed that interest expense instead should be allocated using an elective "worldwide fungibility" approach, under which interest expense incurred in the United States is allocated against foreign-source income only if the debt-to-asset ratio is higher for U.S. than for foreign investments.

Explanation of Provision

In general

The Act modifies the interest expense allocation rules (which generally apply for purposes of computing the foreign tax credit limitation) by providing a one-time election under which the taxable income of the domestic members of an affiliated group from sources outside the United States generally is determined by allocating and apportioning interest expense of the domestic members of a worldwide affiliated group on a worldwide-group basis (i.e., as if all members of the worldwide group were a single corporation). If a group makes this election, the taxable income of the domestic members of a worldwide affiliated group from sources outside the United States is determined by allocating and apportioning the third-party interest expense of those domestic members to foreign-source income in an amount equal to the excess (if any) of (1) the worldwide affiliated group's worldwide third-party interest expense multiplied by the ratio which the foreign assets of the worldwide affiliated group bears to the total assets of the worldwide affiliated group,[470] over (2) the third-party interest expense incurred by foreign members of the group to the extent such interest would be allocated to foreign sources if the Act's principles were applied separately to the foreign members of the group.[471]

For purposes of the new elective rules based on worldwide fungibility, the worldwide affiliated group means all corporations in an affiliated group (as that term is defined under present law for

[470] For purposes of determining the assets of the worldwide affiliated group, neither stock in corporations within the group nor indebtedness (including receivables) between members of the group is taken into account. It is anticipated that the Treasury Secretary will adopt regulations addressing the allocation and apportionment of interest expense on such indebtedness that follow principles analogous to those of existing regulations. Income from holding stock or indebtedness of another group member is taken into account for all purposes under the present-law rules of the Code, including the foreign tax credit provisions.

[471] Although the interest expense of a foreign subsidiary is taken into account for purposes of allocating the interest expense of the domestic members of the electing worldwide affiliated group for foreign tax credit limitation purposes, the interest expense incurred by a foreign subsidiary is not deductible on a U.S. return.

interest allocation purposes)[472] as well as all controlled foreign corporations that, in the aggregate, either directly or indirectly,[473] would be members of such an affiliated group if section 1504(b)(3) did not apply (i.e., in which at least 80 percent of the vote and value of the stock of such corporations is owned by one or more other corporations included in the affiliated group). Thus, if an affiliated group makes this election, the taxable income from sources outside the United States of domestic group members generally is determined by allocating and apportioning interest expense of the domestic members of the worldwide affiliated group as if all of the interest expense and assets of 80-percent or greater owned domestic corporations (i.e., corporations that are part of the affiliated group under present-law section 864(e)(5)(A) as modified to include insurance companies) and certain controlled foreign corporations were attributable to a single corporation.

In addition, if an affiliated group elects to apply the new elective rules based on worldwide fungibility, the rules regarding the treatment of tax-exempt assets and the basis of stock in nonaffiliated 10–percent owned corporations apply on a worldwide affiliated group basis.

The common parent of the domestic affiliated group must make the worldwide affiliated group election. It must be made for the first taxable year beginning after December 31, 2008 in which a worldwide affiliated group exists that includes at least one foreign corporation that meets the requirements for inclusion in a worldwide affiliated group. Once made, the election applies to the common parent and all other members of the worldwide affiliated group for the taxable year for which the election was made and all subsequent taxable years, unless revoked with the consent of the Secretary of the Treasury.

Financial institution group election

The Act allows taxpayers to apply the bank group rules to exclude certain financial institutions from the affiliated group for interest allocation purposes under the worldwide fungibility approach. The Act also provides a one-time "financial institution group" election that expands the prior-law bank group. Under the Act, at the election of the common parent of the pre-election worldwide affiliated group, the interest expense allocation rules are applied separately to a subgroup of the worldwide affiliated group that consists of: (1) all corporations that are part of the prior-law bank group, and (2) all "financial corporations." For this purpose, a corporation is a financial corporation if at least 80 percent of its gross income is financial services income (as described in section 904(d)(2)(C)(i) and the regulations thereunder) that is derived from transactions with unrelated persons.[474] For these purposes, items of income or gain from a transaction or series of transactions are

[472] The Act expands the definition of an affiliated group for interest expense allocation purposes to include certain insurance companies that are generally excluded from an affiliated group under section 1504(b)(2) (without regard to whether such companies are covered by an election under section 1504(c)(2)).

[473] Indirect ownership is determined under the rules of section 958(a)(2) or through applying rules similar to those of section 958(a)(2) to stock owned directly or indirectly by domestic partnerships, trusts, or estates.

[474] See Treas. Reg. sec. 1.904–4(e)(2).

disregarded if a principal purpose for the transaction or transactions is to qualify any corporation as a financial corporation.

The common parent of the pre-election worldwide affiliated group must make the election for the first taxable year beginning after December 31, 2008 in which a worldwide affiliated group includes a financial corporation. Once made, the election applies to the financial institution group for the taxable year and all subsequent taxable years. In addition, the Act provides anti-abuse rules under which certain transfers from one member of a financial institution group to a member of the worldwide affiliated group outside of the financial institution group are treated as reducing the amount of indebtedness of the separate financial institution group. The Act provides regulatory authority with respect to the election to provide for the direct allocation of interest expense in circumstances in which such allocation is appropriate to carry out the purposes of the provision, prevent assets or interest expense from being taken into account more than once, or address changes in members of any group (through acquisitions or otherwise) treated as affiliated under this provision.

Effective Date

The provision is effective for taxable years beginning after December 31, 2008.

B. Recharacterize Overall Domestic Loss (sec. 402 of the Act and sec. 904 of the Code)

Present and Prior Law

The United States provides a credit for foreign income taxes paid or accrued. The foreign tax credit generally is limited to the U.S. tax liability on a taxpayer's foreign-source income, in order to ensure that the credit serves the purpose of mitigating double taxation of foreign-source income without offsetting the U.S. tax on U.S.-source income. This overall limitation is calculated by prorating a taxpayer's pre-credit U.S. tax on its worldwide income between its U.S.-source and foreign-source taxable income. The ratio (not exceeding 100 percent) of the taxpayer's foreign-source taxable income to worldwide taxable income is multiplied by its pre-credit U.S. tax to establish the amount of U.S. tax allocable to the taxpayer's foreign-source income and, thus, the upper limit on the foreign tax credit for the year.

In addition, this limitation is calculated separately for various categories of income, generally referred to as "separate limitation categories." The total amount of the foreign tax credit used to offset the U.S. tax on income in each separate limitation category may not exceed the proportion of the taxpayer's U.S. tax which the taxpayer's foreign-source taxable income in that category bears to its worldwide taxable income.

If a taxpayer's losses from foreign sources exceed its foreign-source income, the excess ("overall foreign loss," or "OFL") may offset U.S.-source income. Such an offset reduces the effective rate of U.S. tax on U.S.-source income.

In order to eliminate a double benefit (that is, the reduction of U.S. tax previously noted and, later, full allowance of a foreign tax credit with respect to foreign-source income), present and prior law includes an OFL recapture rule. Under this rule, a portion of foreign-source taxable income earned after an OFL year is recharacterized as U.S.-source taxable income for foreign tax credit purposes (and for purposes of the possessions tax credit). Unless a taxpayer elects a higher percentage, however, generally no more than 50 percent of the foreign-source taxable income earned in any particular taxable year is recharacterized as U.S.-source taxable income. The effect of the recapture is to reduce the foreign tax credit limitation in one or more years following an OFL year and, therefore, the amount of U.S. tax that can be offset by foreign tax credits in the later year or years.

Losses for any taxable year in separate foreign limitation categories (to the extent that they do not exceed foreign income for the year) are apportioned on a proportionate basis among (and operate to reduce) the foreign income categories in which the entity earns income in the loss year. A separate limitation loss recharacterization rule applies to foreign losses apportioned to foreign income pursuant to the above rule. If a separate limitation loss was apportioned to income subject to another separate limitation category and the loss category has income for a subsequent taxable year, then that income (to the extent that it does not exceed the aggregate separate limitation losses in the loss category not previously recharacterized) must be recharacterized as income in the separate limitation category that was previously offset by the loss. Such recharacterization must be made in proportion to the prior loss apportionment not previously taken into account.

A U.S.-source loss reduces pre-credit U.S. tax on worldwide income to an amount less than the hypothetical tax that would apply to the taxpayer's foreign-source income if viewed in isolation. The existence of foreign-source taxable income in the year of the U.S.-source loss reduces or eliminates any net operating loss carryover that the U.S.-source loss would otherwise have generated absent the foreign income. In addition, as the pre-credit U.S. tax on worldwide income is reduced, so is the foreign tax credit limitation. Moreover, any U.S.-source loss for any taxable year is apportioned among (and operates to reduce) foreign income in the separate limitation categories on a proportionate basis. As a result, some foreign tax credits in the year of the U.S.-source loss must be credited, if at all, in a carryover year. Tax on U.S.-source taxable income in a subsequent year may be offset by a net operating loss carryforward, but not by a foreign tax credit carryforward. Prior law provided no mechanism for recharacterizing such subsequent U.S.-source income as foreign-source income.

For example, suppose a taxpayer generates a $100 U.S.-source loss and earns $100 of foreign-source income in Year 1, and pays $30 of foreign tax on the $100 of foreign-source income. Because the taxpayer has no net taxable income in Year 1, no foreign tax credit can be claimed in Year 1 with respect to the $30 of foreign taxes. If the taxpayer then earns $100 of U.S.-source income and $100 of foreign-source income in Year 2, prior law did not recharacterize any portion of the $100 of U.S.-source income as foreign-source income to reflect the fact that the previous year's $100 U.S.-source loss reduced the taxpayer's ability to claim foreign tax credits.

Reasons for Change

The Congress believed that the overall foreign loss rules continue to represent sound tax policy, but that concerns of parity dictate that overall domestic loss rules be provided to address situations in which a domestic loss may restrict a taxpayer's ability to claim foreign tax credits. The Congress believed that it was important to create this parity in order to prevent the double taxation of income. The Congress believed that preventing double taxation would make U.S. businesses more competitive and lead to increased export sales. The Congress believed that this increase in export sales would increase production in the United States and increase jobs in the United States to support the increased exports.

Explanation of Provision

The Act applies a re-sourcing rule to U.S.-source income in cases in which a taxpayer's foreign tax credit limitation has been reduced as a result of an overall domestic loss. Under the Act, a portion of the taxpayer's U.S.-source income for each succeeding taxable year is recharacterized as foreign-source income in an amount equal to the lesser of: (1) the amount of the unrecharacterized overall domestic losses for years prior to such succeeding taxable year, and (2) 50 percent of the taxpayer's U.S.-source income for such succeeding taxable year.

The Act defines an overall domestic loss for this purpose as any domestic loss to the extent it offsets foreign-source taxable income for the current taxable year or for any preceding taxable year by reason of a loss carryback. For this purpose, a domestic loss means the amount by which the U.S.-source gross income for the taxable year is exceeded by the sum of the deductions properly apportioned or allocated thereto, determined without regard to any loss carried back from a subsequent taxable year. Under the Act, an overall domestic loss does not include any loss for any taxable year unless the taxpayer elected the use of the foreign tax credit for such taxable year.

Any U.S.-source income recharacterized under the Act is allocated among and increases the various foreign tax credit separate limitation categories in the same proportion that those categories were reduced by the prior overall domestic losses, in a manner similar to the recharacterization rules for separate limitation losses.

It is anticipated that situations may arise in which a taxpayer generates an overall domestic loss in a year following a year in which it had an overall foreign loss, or vice versa. In such a case, it would be necessary for ordering and other coordination rules to be developed for purposes of computing the foreign tax credit limitation in subsequent taxable years. The Act grants the Treasury Secretary authority to prescribe such regulations as may be necessary to coordinate the operation of the OFL recapture rules with the operation of the overall domestic loss recapture rules added by the Act.

Effective Date

The provision applies to losses incurred in taxable years beginning after December 31, 2006.

C. Apply Look-Through Rules for Dividends from Noncontrolled Section 902 Corporations (sec. 403 of the Act and sec. 904 of the Code)

Present and Prior Law

U.S. persons may credit foreign taxes against U.S. tax on foreign-source income. In general, the amount of foreign tax credits that may be claimed in a year is subject to a limitation that prevents taxpayers from using foreign tax credits to offset U.S. tax on U.S.-source income. Separate limitations are also applied to specific categories of income.

Prior law applied special foreign tax credit limitations in the case of dividends received from a foreign corporation in which the taxpayer owned at least 10 percent of the stock by vote and which was not a controlled foreign corporation (a so-called "10/50 company"). Dividends paid by a 10/50 company that was not a passive foreign investment company out of earnings and profits accumulated in taxable years beginning before January 1, 2003 were subject to a single foreign tax credit limitation for all 10/50 companies (other than passive foreign investment companies).[475] Dividends paid by a 10/50 company that was a passive foreign investment company out of earnings and profits accumulated in taxable years beginning before January 1, 2003 continued to be subject to a separate foreign tax credit limitation for each such 10/50 company. Dividends paid by a 10/50 company out of earnings and profits accumulated in taxable years after December 31, 2002 were treated as income in a foreign tax credit limitation category in proportion to the ratio of the 10/50 company's earnings and profits attributable to income in such foreign tax credit limitation category to its total earnings and profits (a "look-through" approach).

For these purposes, distributions were treated as made from the most recently accumulated earnings and profits. Regulatory authority was granted to provide rules regarding the treatment of distributions out of earnings and profits for periods prior to the taxpayer's acquisition of such stock.

Reasons for Change

The Congress believed that significant simplification could be achieved by eliminating the requirement that taxpayers segregate the earnings and profits of 10/50 companies on the basis of when such earnings and profits arose.

---

[475] Dividends paid by a 10/50 company in taxable years beginning before January 1, 2003 were subject to a separate foreign tax credit limitation for each 10/50 company.

Explanation of Provision

The Act generally applies the look-through approach to dividends paid by a 10/50 company regardless of the year in which the earnings and profits out of which the dividend is paid were accumulated.[476] If the Treasury Secretary determines that a taxpayer has inadequately substantiated that it assigned a dividend from a 10/50 company to the proper foreign tax credit limitation category, the dividend is treated as passive category income for foreign tax credit basketing purposes.[477]

Effective Date

The provision is effective for taxable years beginning after December 31, 2002. The provision also provides transition rules regarding the use of pre-effective-date foreign tax credits associated with a 10/50-company separate limitation category in post-effective-date years. Look-through principles similar to those applicable to post-effective-date dividends from a 10/50 company apply to determine the appropriate foreign tax credit limitation category or categories with respect to carrying forward foreign tax credits into future years. The provision allows the Treasury Secretary to issue regulations addressing the carryback of foreign tax credits associated with a dividend from a 10/50 company to pre-effective-date years.

D. Foreign Tax Credit Baskets and "Base Differences" (sec. 404 of the Act and sec. 904 of the Code)

Present and Prior Law

In general

The United States taxes its citizens and residents on their worldwide income. Because the countries in which income is earned also may assert their jurisdiction to tax the same income on the basis of source, foreign-source income earned by U.S. persons may be subject to double taxation. In order to mitigate this possibility, the United States provides a credit against U.S. tax liability for foreign income taxes paid, subject to a number of limitations. The foreign tax credit generally is limited to the U.S. tax liability on a taxpayer's foreign-source income, in order to ensure that the credit serves its purpose of mitigating double taxation of cross-border income without offsetting the U.S. tax on U.S.-source income.

Under prior law, the foreign tax credit limitation was applied separately to the following categories of income: (1) passive income; (2) high withholding tax interest; (3) financial services income; (4) shipping income; (5) certain dividends received from noncontrolled section 902 foreign corporations ("10/50 companies");[478] (6) certain

[476] This look-through treatment also applies to dividends that a controlled foreign corporation receives from a 10/50 company and then distributes to a U.S. shareholder.

[477] It is anticipated that the Treasury Secretary will reconsider the operation of the foreign tax credit regulations to ensure that the high-tax income rules apply appropriately to dividends treated as passive category income because of inadequate substantiation.

[478] Under prior law, subject to certain exceptions, dividends paid by a 10/50 company in taxable years beginning after December 31, 2002 were subject to either a look-through approach in which the dividend was attributed to a particular limitation category based on the underlying

Continued

dividends from a domestic international sales corporation or former domestic international sales corporation; (7) taxable income attributable to certain foreign trade income; (8) certain distributions from a foreign sales corporation or former foreign sales corporation; and (9) any other income not described in items (1) through (8) (so-called "general basket" income). In addition, a number of other provisions of the Code and U.S. tax treaties effectively create additional separate limitations in certain circumstances.[479]

Financial services income

In general, the term "financial services income" includes income received or accrued by a person predominantly engaged in the active conduct of a banking, insurance, financing, or similar business, if the income is derived in the active conduct of a banking, financing or similar business, or is derived from the investment by an insurance company of its unearned premiums or reserves ordinary and necessary for the proper conduct of its insurance business (sec. 904(d)(2)(C)). The Code also provides that financial services income includes income, received or accrued by a person predominantly engaged in the active conduct of a banking, insurance, financing, or similar business, of a kind which would generally be insurance income (as defined in section 953(a)), among other items.

Treasury regulations provide that a person is predominantly engaged in the active conduct of a banking, insurance, financing, or similar business for any year if for that year at least 80 percent of its gross income is "active financing income."[480] The regulations further provide that a corporation that is not predominantly engaged in the active conduct of a banking, insurance, financing, or similar business under the preceding definition can derive financial services income if the corporation is a member of an affiliated group (as defined in section 1504(a), but expanded to include foreign corporations) that, as a whole, meets the regulatory test of being "predominantly engaged."[481] In determining whether an affiliated group is "predominantly engaged," only the income of members of the group that are U.S. corporations, or controlled foreign corporations in which such U.S. corporations own (directly or indirectly) at least 80 percent of the total voting power and value of the stock, are counted.

"Base difference" items

Under Treasury regulations, foreign taxes are allocated and apportioned to the same limitation categories as the income to which they relate.[482] In cases in which foreign law imposes tax on an item of income that does not constitute income under U.S. tax prin-

---

earnings which gave rise to the dividend (for post-2002 earnings and profits), or a single-basket limitation approach for dividends from all 10/50 companies that were not passive foreign investment companies (for pre-2003 earnings and profits). Under the Act, these dividends are subject to a look-through approach, irrespective of when the underlying earnings and profits arose.

[479] See, e.g., sec. 56(g)(4)(C)(iii)(IV) (relating to certain dividends from corporations eligible for the sec. 936 credit); sec. 245(a)(10) (relating to certain dividends treated as foreign source under treaties); sec. 865(h)(1)(B) (relating to certain gains from stock and intangibles treated as foreign source under treaties); sec. 901(j)(1)(B) (relating to income from certain specified countries); and sec. 904(g)(10)(A) (relating to interest, dividends, and certain other amounts derived from U.S.-owned foreign corporations and treated as foreign source under treaties).

[480] Treas. Reg. sec. 1.904–4(e)(3)(i) and (2)(i).

[481] Treas. Reg. sec. 1.904–4(e)(3)(ii).

[482] Treas. Reg. sec. 1.904–6.

ciples (a "base difference" item), these regulations treat the tax as being imposed on income in the general limitation category.[483]

Reasons for Change

The Congress believed that requiring taxpayers to separate income and tax credits into nine separate tax baskets created some of the most complex tax reporting and compliance issues in the Code. The Congress believed that reducing the number of foreign tax credit baskets to two would greatly simplify the Code and undo much of the complexity created by the Tax Reform Act of 1986. The Congress believed that simplifying these rules would reduce double taxation, make U.S. businesses more competitive, and create jobs in the United States.

Explanation of Provision

In general

The Act generally reduces the number of foreign tax credit limitation categories to two: passive category income and general category income. Other income is included in one of the two categories, as appropriate. For example, shipping income generally falls into the general limitation category, whereas high withholding tax interest generally could fall into the passive income or the general limitation category, depending on the circumstances. Dividends from a domestic international sales corporation or former domestic international sales corporation, income attributable to certain foreign trade income, and certain distributions from a foreign sales corporation or former foreign sales corporation all are assigned to the passive income limitation category. The Act does not affect the separate computation of foreign tax credit limitations under special provisions of the Code relating to, for example, treaty-based sourcing rules or specified countries under section 901(j).

Financial services income

In the case of a member of a financial services group or any other person predominantly engaged in the active conduct of a banking, insurance, financing or similar business, the Act treats income meeting the definition of financial services income as general category income. Under the Act, a financial services group is an affiliated group that is predominantly engaged in the active conduct of a banking, insurance, financing or similar business. For this purpose, the definition of an affiliated group under section 1504(a) is applied, but expanded to include certain insurance companies (without regard to whether such companies are covered by an election under section 1504(c)(2)) and foreign corporations. In determining whether such a group is predominantly engaged in the active conduct of a banking, insurance, financing, or similar business, only the income of members of the group that are U.S. corporations or controlled foreign corporations in which such U.S. corporations own (directly or indirectly) at least 80 percent of total voting power and value of the stock are taken into account.

[483] Treas. Reg. sec. 1.904–6(a)(1)(iv).

The Act does not alter the existing interpretation of what it means to be a "person predominantly engaged in the active conduct of a banking, insurance, financing, or similar business."[484] Thus, other provisions of the Code that rely on this same concept of a "person predominantly engaged in the active conduct of a banking, insurance, financing, or similar business" are not affected by the provision. For example, under the "accumulated deficit rule" of section 952(c)(1)(B), subpart F income inclusions of a U.S. shareholder attributable to a "qualified activity" of a controlled foreign corporation may be reduced by the amount of the U.S. shareholder's pro rata share of certain prior year deficits attributable to the same qualified activity. In the case of a qualified financial institution, qualified activity consists of any activity giving rise to foreign personal holding company income, but only if the controlled foreign corporation was predominantly engaged in the active conduct of a banking, financing, or similar business in both the year in which the corporation earned the income and the year in which the corporation incurred the deficit. Similarly, in the case of a qualified insurance company, qualified activity consists of activity giving rise to insurance income or foreign personal holding company income, but only if the controlled foreign corporation was predominantly engaged in the active conduct of an insurance business in both the year in which the corporation earned the income and the year in which the corporation incurred the deficit. For this purpose, "predominantly engaged in the active conduct of a banking, insurance, financing, or similar business" is defined under present law by reference to the use of the term for purposes of the separate foreign tax credit limitations.[485] The existing meaning of "predominantly engaged" for purposes of section 952(c)(1)(B) remains unchanged under the provision.

The Act requires the Treasury Secretary to specify the treatment of financial services income received or accrued by pass-through entities that are not members of a financial services group. It is expected that these regulations will be generally consistent with regulations currently in effect.

"Base difference" items

Creditable foreign taxes that are imposed on amounts that do not constitute income under U.S. tax principles are treated as imposed on general limitation income.

Effective Date

The provision is effective for taxable years beginning after December 31, 2006. Taxes paid or accrued in a taxable year beginning before January 1, 2007, and carried to any subsequent taxable year are treated as if this provision were in effect on the date such taxes were paid or accrued. Thus, such taxes are assigned to one of the two foreign tax credit limitation categories, as appropriate. The Treasury Secretary is given authority to provide by regulations for the allocation of income with respect to taxes carried back to pre-

[484] See Treas. Reg. sec. 1.904–4(e).

[485] See H.R. Rep. No. 99–841, 99th Cong., 2d Sess. II–621 (1986); Staff of the Joint Committee on Taxation, 100th Cong., 1st Sess., General Explanation of the Tax Reform Act of 1986, at 984 (1987).

effective-date years (in which more than two limitation categories are in effect).

Creditable foreign taxes that are imposed on amounts that do not constitute income under U.S. tax principles are treated as imposed on general limitation income, as of the general effective date of the provision. Any such taxes arising in taxable years beginning after December 31, 2004, but before January 1, 2007 (when the number of limitation categories is reduced to two), are treated as imposed on either general limitation income or financial services income, at the taxpayer's election. Once made, this election applies to all such taxes for the taxable years described above and is revocable only with the consent of the Treasury Secretary.

E. Attribution of Stock Ownership Through Partnerships in Determining Section 902 and 960 Credits (sec. 405 of the Act and sec. 902 of the Code)

Present and Prior Law

Under section 902, a domestic corporation that receives a dividend from a foreign corporation in which it owns 10 percent or more of the voting stock is deemed to have paid a portion of the foreign taxes paid by such foreign corporation. Thus, such a domestic corporation is eligible to claim a foreign tax credit with respect to such deemed-paid taxes. The domestic corporation that receives a dividend is deemed to have paid a portion of the foreign corporation's post-1986 foreign income taxes based on the ratio of the amount of the dividend to the foreign corporation's post-1986 undistributed earnings and profits.

Foreign income taxes paid or accrued by lower-tier foreign corporations also are eligible for the deemed-paid credit if the foreign corporation falls within a qualified group (sec. 902(b)). A "qualified group" includes certain foreign corporations within the first six tiers of a chain of foreign corporations if, among other things, the product of the percentage ownership of voting stock at each level of the chain (beginning from the domestic corporation) equals at least five percent. In addition, in order to claim indirect credits for foreign taxes paid by certain fourth-, fifth-, and sixth-tier corporations, such corporations must be controlled foreign corporations (within the meaning of sec. 957) and the shareholder claiming the indirect credit must be a U.S. shareholder (as defined in sec. 951(b)) with respect to the controlled foreign corporations. The application of the indirect foreign tax credit below the third tier is limited to taxes paid in taxable years during which the payor is a controlled foreign corporation. Foreign taxes paid below the sixth tier of foreign corporations are ineligible for the indirect foreign tax credit.

Section 960 similarly permits a domestic corporation with subpart F inclusions from a controlled foreign corporation to claim deemed-paid foreign tax credits with respect to foreign taxes paid or accrued by the controlled foreign corporation on its subpart F income.

The foreign tax credit provisions in the Code under prior law did not specifically address whether a domestic corporation owning 10 percent or more of the voting stock of a foreign corporation through a partnership is entitled to a deemed-paid foreign tax credit.[486] In Rev. Rul. 71–141,[487] the IRS held that a foreign corporation's stock held indirectly by two domestic corporations through their interests in a domestic general partnership is attributed to such domestic corporations for purposes of determining the domestic corporations' eligibility to claim a deemed-paid foreign tax credit with respect to the foreign taxes paid by such foreign corporation. Accordingly, a general partner of a domestic general partnership is permitted to claim deemed-paid foreign tax credits with respect to a dividend distribution from the foreign corporation to the partnership.

However, in 1997, the Treasury Department issued final regulations under section 902, and the preamble to the regulations states that "[t]he final regulations do not resolve under what circumstances a domestic corporate partner may compute an amount of foreign taxes deemed paid with respect to dividends received from a foreign corporation by a partnership or other pass-through entity."[488] In recognition of the holding in Rev. Rul. 71–141, the preamble to the final regulations under section 902 states that a "domestic shareholder" for purposes of section 902 is a domestic corporation that "owns" the requisite voting stock in a foreign corporation rather than one that "owns directly" the voting stock. At the same time, the preamble states that the IRS is still considering under what other circumstances Rev. Rul. 71–141 should apply. Consequently, uncertainty remained regarding whether a domestic corporation owning 10 percent or more of the voting stock of a foreign corporation through a partnership was entitled to a deemed-paid foreign tax credit (other than through a domestic general partnership).

Reasons for Change

The Congress believed that a clarification was appropriate regarding the ability of a domestic corporation owning ten percent or more of the voting stock of a foreign corporation through a partnership to claim a deemed-paid foreign tax credit.

Explanation of Provision

The Act clarifies that a domestic corporation is entitled to claim deemed-paid foreign tax credits with respect to a foreign corporation that is held indirectly through a foreign or domestic partnership, provided that the domestic corporation owns (indirectly through the partnership) 10 percent or more of the foreign corporation's voting stock. No inference is intended as to the treatment of such deemed-paid foreign tax credits under prior law. The Act also clarifies that both individual and corporate partners (or estate or

[486] Under section 901(b)(5), an individual member of a partnership or a beneficiary of an estate or trust generally may claim a direct foreign tax credit with respect to the amount of his or her proportionate share of the foreign taxes paid or accrued by the partnership, estate, or trust. This rule does not specifically apply to corporations that are either members of a partnership or beneficiaries of an estate or trust. However, section 702(a)(6) provides that each partner (including individuals or corporations) of a partnership must take into account separately its distributive share of the partnership's foreign taxes paid or accrued. In addition, under section 703(b)(3), the election under section 901 (whether to credit the foreign taxes) is made by each partner separately.

[487] 1971–1 C.B. 211.

[488] T.D. 8708, 1997–1 C.B. 137.

trust beneficiaries) may claim direct foreign tax credits with respect to their proportionate shares of taxes paid or accrued by a partnership (or estate or trust).

Effective Date

The provision applies to taxes of foreign corporations for taxable years of such corporations beginning after the date of enactment (October 22, 2004).

F. Foreign Tax Credit Treatment of Deemed Payments Under Section 367(d) of the Code (sec. 406 of the Act and sec. 367(d) of the Code)

Present and Prior Law

In the case of transfers of intangible property to foreign corporations by means of contributions and certain other nonrecognition transactions, special rules apply that are designed to mitigate the tax avoidance that may arise from shifting the income attributable to intangible property offshore. Under section 367(d), the outbound transfer of intangible property is treated as a sale of the intangible for a stream of contingent payments. The amounts of these deemed payments must be commensurate with the income attributable to the intangible. The deemed payments are included in gross income of the U.S. transferor as ordinary income, and the earnings and profits of the foreign corporation to which the intangible was transferred are reduced by such amounts.

The Taxpayer Relief Act of 1997 (the "1997 Act") repealed a rule that treated all such deemed payments as giving rise to U.S.-source income. Because the foreign tax credit is generally limited to the U.S. tax imposed on foreign-source income, the pre-1997 Act rule reduced the taxpayer's ability to claim foreign tax credits. As a result of the repeal of the rule, the source of payments deemed received under section 367(d) is determined under general sourcing rules. These rules treat income from sales of intangible property for contingent payments the same as royalties, with the result that the deemed payments may give rise to foreign-source income.[489]

The 1997 Act did not address the characterization of the deemed payments for purposes of applying the foreign tax credit separate limitation categories.[490] If the deemed payments were treated like proceeds of a sale, then they could fall into the passive category; if the deemed payments were treated like royalties, then in many cases they could fall into the general category (under look-through rules applicable to payments of dividends, interest, rents, and royalties received from controlled foreign corporations).[491]

Reasons for Change

The Congress believed that it is appropriate to characterize deemed payments under section 367(d) as royalties for purposes of applying the separate limitation categories of the foreign tax credit,

[489] Secs. 865(d) and 862(a).
[490] Sec. 904(d).
[491] Sec. 904(d)(3).

and that this treatment should be effective for all transactions subject to the underlying provision of the 1997 Act.

Explanation of Provision

The Act specifies that deemed payments under section 367(d) are treated as royalties for purposes of applying the separate limitation categories of the foreign tax credit.

Effective Date

The provision is effective for amounts treated as received on or after August 5, 1997 (the effective date of the relevant provision of the 1997 Act).

G. United States Property Not to Include Certain Assets of Controlled Foreign Corporations (sec. 407 of the Act and sec. 956 of the Code)

Present and Prior Law

In general, the subpart F rules[492] require U.S. shareholders with a 10-percent or greater interest in a controlled foreign corporation ("U.S. 10-percent shareholders") to include in taxable income their pro rata shares of certain income of the controlled foreign corporation (referred to as "subpart F income") when such income is earned, whether or not the earnings are distributed currently to the shareholders. In addition, the U.S. 10-percent shareholders of a controlled foreign corporation are subject to U.S. tax on their pro rata shares of the controlled foreign corporation's earnings to the extent invested by the controlled foreign corporation in certain U.S. property in a taxable year.[493]

A shareholder's income inclusion with respect to a controlled foreign corporation's investment in U.S. property for a taxable year is based on the controlled foreign corporation's average investment in U.S. property for such year. For this purpose, the U.S. property held (directly or indirectly) by the controlled foreign corporation must be measured as of the close of each quarter in the taxable year.[494] The amount taken into account with respect to any property is the property's adjusted basis as determined for purposes of reporting the controlled foreign corporation's earnings and profits, reduced by any liability to which the property is subject. The amount determined for inclusion in each taxable year is the shareholder's pro rata share of an amount equal to the lesser of: (1) the controlled foreign corporation's average investment in U.S. property as of the end of each quarter of such taxable year, to the extent that such investment exceeds the foreign corporation's earnings and profits that were previously taxed on that basis; or (2) the controlled foreign corporation's current or accumulated earnings and profits (but not including a deficit), reduced by distributions during the year and by earnings that have been taxed previously as earnings invested in U.S. property.[495] An income inclusion is re-

[492] Secs. 951–964.
[493] Sec. 951(a)(1)(B).
[494] Sec. 956(a).
[495] Secs. 956 and 959.

quired only to the extent that the amount so calculated exceeds the amount of the controlled foreign corporation's earnings that have been previously taxed as subpart F income.[496]

For purposes of section 956, U.S. property generally is defined to include tangible property located in the United States, stock of a U.S. corporation, an obligation of a U.S. person, and certain intangible assets including a patent or copyright, an invention, model or design, a secret formula or process or similar property right which is acquired or developed by the controlled foreign corporation for use in the United States.[497]

Specified exceptions from the definition of U.S. property are provided for: (1) obligations of the United States, money, or deposits with certain financial institutions (as amended by section 837 of the Act); (2) certain export property; (3) certain trade or business obligations; (4) aircraft, railroad rolling stock, vessels, motor vehicles or containers used in transportation in foreign commerce and used predominantly outside of the United States; (5) certain insurance company reserves and unearned premiums related to insurance of foreign risks; (6) stock or debt of certain unrelated U.S. corporations; (7) moveable property (other than a vessel or aircraft) used for the purpose of exploring, developing, or certain other activities in connection with the ocean waters of the U.S. Continental Shelf; (8) an amount of assets equal to the controlled foreign corporation's accumulated earnings and profits attributable to income effectively connected with a U.S. trade or business; (9) property (to the extent provided in regulations) held by a foreign sales corporation and related to its export activities; (10) certain deposits or receipts of collateral or margin by a securities or commodities dealer, if such deposit is made or received on commercial terms in the ordinary course of the dealer's business as a securities or commodities dealer; and (11) certain repurchase and reverse repurchase agreement transactions entered into by or with a dealer in securities or commodities in the ordinary course of its business as a securities or commodities dealer.[498]

Reasons for Change

The Congress believed that the acquisition of securities by a controlled foreign corporation in the ordinary course of its business as a securities dealer generally should not give rise to an income inclusion as an investment in U.S. property under the provisions of subpart F. Similarly, the Congress believed that the acquisition by a controlled foreign corporation of obligations issued by unrelated U.S. noncorporate persons generally should not give rise to an income inclusion as an investment in U.S. property.

Explanation of Provision

The Act adds two new exceptions from the definition of U.S. property for determining current income inclusion by a U.S. 10-percent shareholder with respect to an investment in U.S. property by a controlled foreign corporation.

---

[496] Secs. 951(a)(1)(B) and 959.
[497] Sec. 956(c)(1).
[498] Sec. 956(c)(2).

The first exception generally applies to securities acquired and held by a controlled foreign corporation in the ordinary course of its trade or business as a dealer in securities. The exception applies only if the controlled foreign corporation dealer: (1) accounts for the securities as securities held primarily for sale to customers in the ordinary course of business; and (2) disposes of such securities (or such securities mature while being held by the dealer) within a period consistent with the holding of securities for sale to customers in the ordinary course of business.

The second exception generally applies to the acquisition by a controlled foreign corporation of obligations issued by a U.S. person that is not a domestic corporation and that is not (1) a U.S. 10-percent shareholder of the controlled foreign corporation, or (2) a partnership, estate or trust in which the controlled foreign corporation or any related person is a partner, beneficiary or trustee immediately after the acquisition by the controlled foreign corporation of such obligation.

Effective Date

The provision is effective for taxable years of foreign corporations beginning after December 31, 2004, and for taxable years of United States shareholders with or within which such taxable years of such foreign corporations end.

H. Election Not to Use Average Exchange Rate for Foreign Tax Paid Other Than in Functional Currency (sec. 408 of the Act and sec. 986 of the Code)

Prior Law

For taxpayers that take foreign income taxes into account when accrued, prior law provided that the amount of the foreign tax credit generally was determined by translating the amount of foreign taxes paid in foreign currencies into a U.S. dollar amount at the average exchange rate for the taxable year to which such taxes relate.[499] This rule applied to foreign taxes paid directly by U.S. taxpayers, which taxes were creditable in the year paid or accrued, and to foreign taxes paid by foreign corporations that are deemed paid by a U.S. corporation that is a shareholder of the foreign corporation, and hence creditable in the year that the U.S. corporation receives a dividend or has an income inclusion from the foreign corporation. This rule did not apply to any foreign income tax: (1) that was paid after the date that was two years after the close of the taxable year to which such taxes relate; (2) of an accrual-basis taxpayer that was actually paid in a taxable year prior to the year to which the tax relates; or (3) that was denominated in an inflationary currency (as defined by regulations).

Foreign taxes that were not eligible for translation at the average exchange rate generally were translated into U.S. dollar amounts using the exchange rates as of the time such taxes are paid. However, the Secretary was authorized to issue regulations that would allow foreign tax payments to be translated into U.S.

[499] Sec. 986(a)(1).

dollar amounts using an average exchange rate for a specified period.[500]

Reasons for Change

The Congress believed that taxpayers generally should be permitted to elect whether to translate foreign income tax payments using an average exchange rate for the taxable year or the exchange rate when the taxes are paid, provided the elected method does not provide opportunities for abuse and continues to be applied consistently unless revoked with the consent of the Treasury Secretary.

Explanation of Provision

For taxpayers that were required under prior law to translate foreign income tax payments at the average exchange rate, the Act provides an election to translate such taxes into U.S. dollar amounts using the exchange rates as of the time such taxes are paid, provided the foreign income taxes are denominated in a currency other than the taxpayer's functional currency.[501] Any election under the provision applies to the taxable year for which the election is made and to all subsequent taxable years unless revoked with the consent of the Secretary. The Act authorizes the Secretary to issue regulations that apply the election to foreign income taxes attributable to a qualified business unit.

The election does not apply to regulated investment companies that take into account income on an accrual basis. Instead, the Act provides that foreign income taxes paid or accrued by a regulated investment company with respect to such income are translated into U.S. dollar amounts using the exchange rate as of the date the income accrues.

Effective Date

The provision is effective with respect to taxable years beginning after December 31, 2004.

I. Eliminate Secondary Withholding Tax with Respect to Dividends Paid by Certain Foreign Corporations (sec. 409 of the Act and sec. 871 of the Code)

Present and Prior Law

Nonresident individuals who are not U.S. citizens and foreign corporations (collectively, foreign persons) are subject to U.S. tax on income that is effectively connected with the conduct of a U.S. trade or business; the U.S. tax on such income is calculated in the same manner and at the same graduated rates as the tax on U.S. persons (secs. 871(b) and 882). Foreign persons also are subject to a 30-percent gross basis tax, collected by withholding, on certain U.S.-source passive income (e.g., interest and dividends) that is not effectively connected with a U.S. trade or business. This 30-percent

[500] Sec. 986(a)(2).

[501] Electing taxpayers translate foreign income tax payments pursuant to the same prior-law rules that applied to taxpayers that were required to translate foreign income taxes using the exchange rates as of the time such taxes are paid.

withholding tax may be reduced or eliminated pursuant to an applicable tax treaty. Foreign persons generally are not subject to U.S. tax on foreign-source income that is not effectively connected with a U.S. trade or business.

In general, dividends paid by a domestic corporation are treated as being from U.S. sources and dividends paid by a foreign corporation are treated as being from foreign sources. Thus, dividends paid by foreign corporations to foreign persons generally are not subject to withholding tax because such income generally is treated as foreign-source income.

An exception from this general rule applies in the case of dividends paid by certain foreign corporations. If a foreign corporation derives 25 percent or more of its gross income as income effectively connected with a U.S. trade or business for the three-year period ending with the close of the taxable year preceding the declaration of a dividend, then a portion of any dividend paid by the foreign corporation to its shareholders is treated as U.S.-source income and, in the case of dividends paid to foreign shareholders, was subject under prior law to the 30-percent withholding tax (sec. 861(a)(2)(B)). This rule was sometimes referred to as the "secondary withholding tax." The portion of the dividend treated as U.S.-source income is equal to the ratio of the gross income of the foreign corporation that is effectively connected with its U.S. trade or business over the total gross income of the foreign corporation during the three-year period ending with the close of the preceding taxable year. The U.S.-source portion of the dividend paid by the foreign corporation to its foreign shareholders was subject to the 30-percent withholding tax.

Under the branch profits tax provisions of present and prior law, the United States taxes foreign corporations engaged in a U.S. trade or business on amounts of U.S. earnings and profits that are shifted out of the U.S. branch of the foreign corporation. The branch profits tax is comparable to the second-level taxes imposed on dividends paid by a domestic corporation to its foreign shareholders. The branch profits tax is 30 percent of the foreign corporation's "dividend equivalent amount," which generally is the earnings and profits of a U.S. branch of a foreign corporation attributable to its income effectively connected with a U.S. trade or business (secs. 884(a) and (b)).

Under prior law, if a foreign corporation was subject to the branch profits tax, then no secondary withholding tax would be imposed on dividends paid by the foreign corporation to its shareholders (sec. 884(e)(3)(A)). If a foreign corporation was a qualified resident of a tax treaty country and claimed an exemption from the branch profits tax pursuant to the treaty, the secondary withholding tax could apply with respect to dividends it paid to its shareholders. Several tax treaties (including treaties that prevent imposition of the branch profits tax), however, exempted dividends paid by the foreign corporation from the secondary withholding tax.

Reasons for Change

The Congress observed that the secondary withholding tax with respect to dividends paid by certain foreign corporations was largely superseded by the branch profits tax and applicable income tax treaties. Accordingly, the Congress believed that the tax should be repealed in the interest of simplification.

Explanation of Provision

The Act eliminates the secondary withholding tax with respect to dividends paid by certain foreign corporations.

Effective Date

The provision is effective for payments made after December 31, 2004.

J. Equal Treatment for Interest Paid by Foreign Partnership and Foreign Corporations (sec. 410 of the Act and sec. 861 of the Code)

Present and Prior Law

In general, interest income from bonds, notes or other interest-bearing obligations of noncorporate U.S. residents or domestic corporations is treated as U.S.-source income.[502] Other interest (e.g., interest on obligations of foreign corporations and foreign partnerships) generally is treated as foreign-source income. However, Treasury regulations provide that a foreign partnership is a U.S. resident for purposes of this rule if at any time during its taxable year it is engaged in a trade or business in the United States.[503] Therefore, any interest received from such a foreign partnership is U.S.-source income.

Notwithstanding the general rule described above, in the case of a foreign corporation engaged in a U.S. trade or business (or having gross income that is treated as effectively connected with the conduct of a U.S. trade or business), interest paid by such U.S. trade or business is treated as if it were paid by a domestic corporation (i.e., such interest is treated as U.S.-source income).[504]

Reasons for Change

The Congress believed that the source of interest income received from a foreign partnership or foreign corporation should be consistent. The Congress believed that interest payments from a foreign partnership engaged in a trade or business in the United States should be sourced in the same manner as interest payments from a foreign corporation engaged in a trade or business in the United States.

Explanation of Provision

The Act treats interest paid by foreign partnerships in a manner similar to the treatment of interest paid by foreign corporations. Thus, interest paid by a foreign partnership is treated as U.S.-source income only if the interest is paid by a U.S. trade or business conducted by the partnership or is allocable to income that is treated as effectively connected with the conduct of a U.S. trade or

[502] Sec. 861(a)(1).
[503] Treas. Reg. sec. 1.861–2(a)(2).
[504] Sec. 884(f)(1).

business. The Act applies only to foreign partnerships that are predominantly engaged in the active conduct of a trade or business outside the United States.

Effective Date

The provision is effective for taxable years beginning after December 31, 2003.

K. Treatment of Certain Dividends of Regulated Investment Companies (sec. 411 of the Act and secs. 871, 881, 897, and 2105 of the Code)

Present and Prior Law

Regulated investment companies

A regulated investment company ("RIC") is a domestic corporation that, at all times during the taxable year, is registered under the Investment Company Act of 1940 as a management company or as a unit investment trust, or has elected to be treated as a business development company under that Act.[505]

In addition, to qualify as a RIC, a corporation must elect such status and must satisfy certain tests.[506] These tests include a requirement that the corporation derive at least 90 percent of its gross income from dividends, interest, payments with respect to certain securities loans, and gains on the sale or other disposition of stock or securities or foreign currencies, or other income derived with respect to its business of investment in such stock, securities, or currencies.

Generally, a RIC pays no income tax because it is permitted to deduct dividends paid to its shareholders in computing its taxable income. The amount of any distribution generally is not considered as a dividend for purposes of computing the dividends paid deduction unless the distribution is pro rata, with no preference to any share of stock as compared with other shares of the same class.[507] However, for distributions by RICs to shareholders who made initial investments of at least $10,000,000, the distribution is not treated as non-pro rata or preferential solely by reason of an increase in the distribution due to reductions in administrative expenses of the company.

A RIC generally may pass through to its shareholders the character of its long-term capital gains. It does this by designating a dividend it pays as a capital gain dividend to the extent that the RIC has net capital gain (i.e., net long-term capital gain over net short-term capital loss). These capital gain dividends are treated as long-term capital gain by the shareholders. A RIC generally also can pass through to its shareholders the character of tax-exempt interest from State and local bonds, but only if, at the close of each quarter of its taxable year, at least 50 percent of the value of the total assets of the RIC consists of these obligations. In this case, the RIC generally may designate a dividend it pays as an exempt-interest dividend to the extent that the RIC has tax-exempt inter-

[505] Sec. 851(a).
[506] Sec. 851(b).
[507] Sec. 562(c).

est income. These exempt-interest dividends are treated as interest excludable from gross income by the shareholders.

U.S. source investment income of foreign persons

In general

The United States generally imposes a flat 30-percent tax, collected by withholding, on the gross amount of U.S.-source investment income payments, such as interest, dividends, rents, royalties or similar types of income, to nonresident alien individuals and foreign corporations ("foreign persons").[508] Under treaties, the United States may reduce or eliminate such taxes. However, even taking into account U.S. treaties, the tax on a dividend generally is not entirely eliminated. Instead, U.S.-source portfolio investment dividends received by foreign persons generally are subject to U.S. withholding tax at a rate of at least 15 percent.

Interest

Although payments of U.S.-source interest that is not effectively connected with a U.S. trade or business generally are subject to the 30-percent withholding tax, there are exceptions to this rule. For example, interest from certain deposits with banks and other financial institutions is exempt from tax.[509] Original issue discount on obligations maturing in 183 days or less from the date of original issue (without regard to the period held by the taxpayer) also is exempt from tax.[510] An additional exception is provided for certain interest paid on portfolio obligations.[511] "Portfolio interest" generally is defined as any U.S.-source interest (including original issue discount), not effectively connected with the conduct of a U.S. trade or business, (i) on an obligation that satisfies certain registration requirements or specified exceptions thereto (i.e., the obligation is "foreign targeted"), and (ii) that is not received by a 10-percent shareholder.[512] With respect to a registered obligation, a statement that the beneficial owner is not a U.S. person is required.[513] This exception is not available for any interest received either by a bank on a loan extended in the ordinary course of its business (except in the case of interest paid on an obligation of the United States), or by a controlled foreign corporation from a related person.[514] Moreover, this exception is not available for certain contingent interest payments.[515]

Capital gains

Foreign persons generally are not subject to U.S. tax on gain realized on the disposition of stock or securities issued by a U.S. person (other than a "U.S. real property holding corporation," as described below), unless the gain is effectively connected with the conduct of a trade or business in the United States. This exemption does not apply, however, if the foreign person is a nonresident alien

[508] Secs. 871(a), 881, 1441, and 1442.
[509] Secs. 871(i)(2)(A) and 881(d).
[510] Sec. 871(g).
[511] Secs. 871(h) and 881(c).
[512] Secs. 871(h)(3) and 881(c)(3).
[513] Secs. 871(h)(2), (5) and 881(c)(2).
[514] Sec. 881(c)(3).
[515] Secs. 871(h)(4) and 881(c)(4).

individual present in the United States for a period or periods aggregating 183 days or more during the taxable year.[516] A RIC may elect not to withhold on a distribution to a foreign person representing a capital gain dividend.[517]

Gain or loss of a foreign person from the disposition of a U.S. real property interest is subject to net basis tax as if the taxpayer were engaged in a trade or business within the United States and the gain or loss were effectively connected with such trade or business.[518] In addition to an interest in real property located in the United States or the Virgin Islands, U.S. real property interests include (among other things) any interest in a domestic corporation unless the taxpayer establishes that the corporation was not, during a 5-year period ending on the date of the disposition of the interest, a U.S. real property holding corporation (which is defined generally to mean a corporation the fair market value of whose U.S. real property interests equals or exceeds 50 percent of the sum of the fair market values of its real property interests and any other of its assets used or held for use in a trade or business).

Estate taxation

Decedents who were citizens or residents of the United States are generally subject to Federal estate tax on all property, wherever situated.[519] Nonresidents who are not U.S. citizens, however, are subject to estate tax only on their property which is within the United States. Property within the United States generally includes debt obligations of U.S. persons, including the Federal government and State and local governments,[520] but does not include either bank deposits or portfolio obligations, the interest on which would be exempt from U.S. income tax under section 871.[521] Stock owned and held by a nonresident who is not a U.S. citizen is treated as property within the United States only if the stock was issued by a domestic corporation.[522]

Treaties may reduce U.S. taxation on transfers by estates of nonresident decedents who are not U.S. citizens. Under recent treaties, for example, U.S. tax may generally be eliminated except insofar as the property transferred includes U.S. real property or business property of a U.S. permanent establishment.

Reasons for Change

Under prior law, a disparity existed between foreign persons who invest directly in certain interest-bearing and other securities and foreign persons who invest in such securities indirectly through U.S. mutual funds. In general, certain amounts received by the direct foreign investor (or a foreign investor through a foreign fund) could be exempt from the U.S. gross-basis withholding tax. In con-

[516] Sec. 871(a)(2).
[517] Treas. reg. sec. 1.1441–3(c)(2)(D).
[518] Sec. 897.
[519] The Economic Growth and Tax Relief Reconciliation Act of 2001 ("EGTRRA") repealed the estate tax for estates of decedents dying after December 31, 2009. However, EGTRRA included a "sunset" provision, pursuant to which EGTRRA's provisions (including estate tax repeal) do not apply to estates of decedents dying after December 31, 2010.
[520] Sec. 2104(c).
[521] Sec. 2105(b).
[522] Sec. 2104(a); Treas. Reg. sec. 20.2104–1(a)(5).

trast, distributions from a RIC generally were treated as dividends subject to the withholding tax, notwithstanding that the distributions may be attributable to amounts that otherwise could qualify for an exemption from withholding tax. U.S. financial institutions often responded to this disparate treatment by forming "mirror funds" outside the United States. The Congress believed that such disparate treatment should be eliminated so that U.S. financial institutions will be encouraged to form and operate their mutual funds within the United States rather than outside the United States.

Therefore, the Congress believed that, to the extent a RIC distributes to a foreign person a dividend attributable to amounts that would have been exempt from U.S. withholding tax had the foreign person received it directly (such as portfolio interest and capital gains, including short-term capital gains), such dividend similarly should be exempt from the U.S. gross-basis withholding tax. The Congress also believed that comparable treatment should be afforded for estate tax purposes to foreign persons who invest in certain assets through a RIC to the extent that such assets would not be subject to the estate tax if held directly.

Explanation of Provision

In general

Under the Act, a RIC that earns certain interest income that would not be subject to U.S. tax if earned by a foreign person directly may, to the extent of such income, designate a dividend it pays as derived from such interest income. A foreign person who is a shareholder in the RIC generally would treat such a dividend as exempt from gross-basis U.S. tax, as if the foreign person had earned the interest directly. Similarly, a RIC that earns an excess of net short-term capital gains over net long-term capital losses, which excess would not be subject to U.S. tax if earned by a foreign person, generally may, to the extent of such excess, designate a dividend it pays as derived from such excess. A foreign person who is a shareholder in the RIC generally would treat such a dividend as exempt from gross-basis U.S. tax, as if the foreign person had realized the excess directly. The Act also provides that the estate of a foreign decedent is exempt from U.S. estate tax on a transfer of stock in the RIC in the proportion that the assets held by the RIC are debt obligations, deposits, or other property that would generally be treated as situated outside the United States if held directly by the estate.

Interest-related dividends

Under the Act, a RIC may, under certain circumstances, designate all or a portion of a dividend as an "interest-related dividend" by written notice mailed to its shareholders not later than 60 days after the close of its taxable year. In addition, an interest-related dividend received by a foreign person generally is exempt from U.S. gross-basis tax under sections 871(a), 881, 1441 and 1442.

However, this exemption does not apply to a dividend on shares of RIC stock if the withholding agent does not receive a statement, similar to that required under the portfolio interest rules, that the beneficial owner of the shares is not a U.S. person. The exemption does not apply to a dividend paid to any person within a foreign country (or dividends addressed to, or for the account of, persons within such foreign country) with respect to which the Treasury Secretary has determined, under the portfolio interest rules, that exchange of information is inadequate to prevent evasion of U.S. income tax by U.S. persons.

In addition, the exemption generally does not apply to dividends paid to a controlled foreign corporation to the extent such dividends are attributable to income received by the RIC on a debt obligation of a person with respect to which the recipient of the dividend (i.e., the controlled foreign corporation) is a related person. Nor does the exemption generally apply to dividends to the extent such dividends are attributable to income (other than short-term original issue discount or bank deposit interest) received by the RIC on indebtedness issued by the RIC-dividend recipient or by any corporation or partnership with respect to which the recipient of the RIC dividend is a 10-percent shareholder. However, in these two circumstances the RIC remains exempt from its withholding obligation unless the RIC knows that the dividend recipient is such a controlled foreign corporation or 10-percent shareholder. To the extent that an interest-related dividend received by a controlled foreign corporation is attributable to interest income of the RIC that would be portfolio interest if received by a foreign corporation, the dividend is treated as portfolio interest for purposes of the de minimis rules, the high-tax exception, and the same country exceptions of subpart F.[523]

The aggregate amount designated as interest-related dividends for the RIC's taxable year (including dividends so designated that are paid after the close of the taxable year but treated as paid during that year as described in section 855) generally is limited to the qualified net interest income of the RIC for the taxable year. The qualified net interest income of the RIC equals the excess of: (1) the amount of qualified interest income of the RIC; over (2) the amount of expenses of the RIC properly allocable to such interest income.

Qualified interest income of the RIC is equal to the sum of its U.S.-source income with respect to: (1) bank deposit interest; (2) short term original issue discount that is currently exempt from the gross-basis tax under section 871; (3) any interest (including amounts recognized as ordinary income in respect of original issue discount, market discount, or acquisition discount under the provisions of sections 1271–1288, and such other amounts as regulations may provide) on an obligation which is in registered form, unless it is earned on an obligation issued by a corporation or partnership in which the RIC is a 10-percent shareholder or is contingent interest not treated as portfolio interest under section 871(h)(4); and (4) any interest-related dividend from another RIC.

If the amount designated as an interest-related dividend is greater than the qualified net interest income described above, the portion of the distribution so designated which constitutes an interest-

[523] See sec. 881(c)(5)(A).

related dividend will be only that proportion of the amount so designated as the amount of the qualified net interest income bears to the amount so designated.

Short-term capital gain dividends

Under the Act, a RIC also may, under certain circumstances, designate all or a portion of a dividend as a "short-term capital gain dividend," by written notice mailed to its shareholders not later than 60 days after the close of its taxable year. For purposes of the U.S. gross-basis tax, a short-term capital gain dividend received by a foreign person generally is exempt from U.S. gross-basis tax under sections 871(a), 881, 1441 and 1442. This exemption does not apply to the extent that the foreign person is a nonresident alien individual present in the United States for a period or periods aggregating 183 days or more during the taxable year. However, in this circumstance the RIC remains exempt from its withholding obligation unless the RIC knows that the dividend recipient has been present in the United States for such period.

The aggregate amount qualified to be designated as short-term capital gain dividends for the RIC's taxable year (including dividends so designated that are paid after the close of the taxable year but treated as paid during that year as described in sec. 855) is equal to the excess of the RIC's net short-term capital gains over net long-term capital losses. The short-term capital gain includes short-term capital gain dividends from another RIC. As provided under present law for purposes of computing the amount of a capital gain dividend, the amount is determined (except in the case where an election under sec. 4982(e)(4) applies) without regard to any net capital loss or net short-term capital loss attributable to transactions after October 31 of the year. Instead, that loss is treated as arising on the first day of the next taxable year. To the extent provided in regulations, this rule also applies for purposes of computing the taxable income of the RIC.

In computing the amount of short-term capital gain dividends for the year, no reduction is made for the amount of expenses of the RIC allocable to such net gains. In addition, if the amount designated as short-term capital gain dividends is greater than the amount of qualified short-term capital gain, the portion of the distribution so designated which constitutes a short-term capital gain dividend is only that proportion of the amount so designated as the amount of the excess bears to the amount so designated.

As under present and prior law for distributions from REITs, the Act provides that any distribution by a RIC to a foreign person shall, to the extent attributable to gains from sales or exchanges by the RIC of an asset that is considered a U.S. real property interest, be treated as gain recognized by the foreign person from the sale or exchange of a U.S. real property interest. The Act also extends the special rules for domestically-controlled REITs to domestically-controlled RICs.

Estate tax treatment

Under the Act, a portion of the stock in a RIC held by the estate of a nonresident decedent who is not a U.S. citizen is treated as property outside the United States. The portion so treated is based upon the proportion of the assets held by the RIC at the end of the quarter immediately preceding the decedent's death (or such other time as the Secretary may designate in regulations) that are "qualifying assets". Qualifying assets for this purpose are bank deposits of the type that are exempt from gross-basis income tax, portfolio debt obligations, certain original issue discount obligations, debt obligations of a domestic corporation that are treated as giving rise to foreign source income, and other property not within the United States.

Effective Date

The provision generally applies to dividends with respect to taxable years of RICs beginning after December 31, 2004, and before January 1, 2008. With respect to the treatment of a RIC for estate tax purposes, the provision applies to estates of decedents dying after December 31, 2004, and before January 1, 2008. With respect to the treatment of RICs under section 897 (relating to U.S. real property interests), the provision is effective after December 31, 2004, and before January 1, 2008.

L. Look-Through Treatment Under Subpart F for Sales of Partnership Interests (sec. 412 of the Act and sec. 954 of the Code)

Present and Prior Law

In general, the subpart F rules (secs. 951–964) require U.S. shareholders with a 10-percent or greater interest in a controlled foreign corporation to include in income currently for U.S. tax purposes certain types of income of the controlled foreign corporation, whether or not such income is actually distributed currently to the shareholders (referred to as "subpart F income"). Subpart F income includes foreign personal holding company income. Foreign personal holding company income generally consists of the following: (1) dividends, interest, royalties, rents, and annuities; (2) net gains from the sale or exchange of (a) property that gives rise to the preceding types of income, (b) property that does not give rise to income, and (c) interests in trusts, partnerships, and real estate mortgages investment conduits ("REMICs"); (3) net gains from commodities transactions; (4) net gains from foreign currency transactions; (5) income that is equivalent to interest; (6) income from notional principal contracts; and (7) payments in lieu of dividends. Thus, under prior law, if a controlled foreign corporation sold a partnership interest at a gain, regardless of the percentage of such interest, the gain generally constituted foreign personal holding company income and was included in the income of 10-percent U.S. shareholders of the controlled foreign corporation as subpart F income.

Reasons for Change

The Congress believed that the sale of a partnership interest by a controlled foreign corporation that owns a sufficiently large interest in the partnership should constitute subpart F income only to the extent that a proportionate sale of the underlying partnership assets attributable to the partnership interest would constitute subpart F income.

Explanation of Provision

The Act treats the sale by a controlled foreign corporation of a partnership interest as a sale of the proportionate share of partnership assets attributable to such interest for purposes of determining subpart F foreign personal holding company income. This rule applies only to partners owning directly, indirectly, or constructively at least 25 percent of a capital or profits interest in the partnership. Thus, the sale of a partnership interest by a controlled foreign corporation that meets this ownership threshold constitutes subpart F income under the Act only to the extent that a proportionate sale of the underlying partnership assets attributable to the partnership interest would constitute subpart F income. The Secretary is directed to prescribe such regulations as may be appropriate to prevent the abuse of this provision.

Effective Date

The provision is effective for taxable years of foreign corporations beginning after December 31, 2004, and taxable years of U.S. shareholders with or within which such taxable years of such foreign corporations end.

M. Repeal of Foreign Personal Holding Company Rules and Foreign Investment Company Rules (sec. 413 of the Act and secs. 542, 551–558, 954, 1246, and 1247 of the Code)

Present and Prior Law

Income earned by a foreign corporation from its foreign operations generally is subject to U.S. tax only when such income is distributed to any U.S. persons that hold stock in such corporation. Accordingly, a U.S. person that conducts foreign operations through a foreign corporation generally is subject to U.S. tax on the income from those operations when the income is repatriated to the United States through a dividend distribution to the U.S. person. The income is reported on the U.S. person's tax return for the year the distribution is received, and the United States imposes tax on such income at that time. The foreign tax credit may reduce the U.S. tax imposed on such income.

Several sets of anti-deferral rules impose current U.S. tax on certain income earned by a U.S. person through a foreign corporation. Detailed rules for coordination among the anti-deferral rules are provided to prevent the U.S. person from being subject to U.S. tax on the same item of income under multiple rules.

Prior law included the following anti-deferral rules: the controlled foreign corporation rules of subpart F (secs. 951–964); the passive foreign investment company rules (secs. 1291–1298); the foreign personal holding company rules (secs. 551–558); the personal holding company rules (secs. 541–547); the accumulated earnings tax rules (secs. 531–537); and the foreign investment company rules (secs. 1246–1247).

Reasons for Change

The Congress believed that the overlap among the various anti-deferral regimes resulted in significant complexity, usually with little or no ultimate tax consequences. These overlaps required the application of specific rules of priority for income inclusions among the regimes, as well as additional coordination provisions pertaining to other operational differences among the various regimes. The Congress believed that significant simplification would be achieved by streamlining these rules.

Explanation of Provision

The Act: (1) eliminates the rules applicable to foreign personal holding companies and foreign investment companies; (2) excludes foreign corporations from the application of the personal holding company rules; and (3) includes as subpart F foreign personal holding company income personal services contract income that was subject to the prior-law foreign personal holding company rules.

Effective Date

The provision is effective for taxable years of foreign corporations beginning after December 31, 2004, and taxable years of U.S. shareholders with or within which such taxable years of foreign corporations end.

N. Determination of Foreign Personal Holding Company Income with Respect to Transactions in Commodities (sec. 414 of the Act and sec. 954 of the Code)

Present and Prior Law

Subpart F foreign personal holding company income

Under the subpart F rules, U.S. shareholders with a 10-percent or greater interest in a controlled foreign corporation ("U.S. 10-percent shareholders") are subject to U.S. tax currently on certain income earned by the controlled foreign corporation, whether or not such income is distributed to the shareholders. The income subject to current inclusion under the subpart F rules includes, among other things, "foreign personal holding company income."

Foreign personal holding company income generally consists of the following: dividends, interest, royalties, rents and annuities; net gains from sales or exchanges of (1) property that gives rise to the foregoing types of income, (2) property that does not give rise to income, and (3) interests in trusts, partnerships, and real estate mortgage investment conduits ("REMICs"); net gains from commodities transactions; net gains from foreign currency transactions; income that is equivalent to interest; income from notional principal contracts; and payments in lieu of dividends.

With respect to transactions in commodities, prior law provided that foreign personal holding company income did not consist of gains or losses which arise out of bona fide hedging transactions that are reasonably necessary to the conduct of any business by a producer, processor, merchant, or handler of a commodity in the manner in which such business is customarily and usually conducted by others.[524] In addition, foreign personal holding company income did not consist of gains or losses which are comprised of active business gains or losses from the sale of commodities, but only if substantially all of the controlled foreign corporation's business is as an active producer, processor, merchant, or handler of commodities.[525]

Hedging transactions

Under present law, the term "capital asset" does not include any hedging transaction which is clearly identified as such before the close of the day on which it was acquired, originated, or entered into (or such other time as the Secretary may by regulations prescribe).[526] The term "hedging transaction" means any transaction entered into by the taxpayer in the normal course of the taxpayer's trade or business primarily: (1) to manage risk of price changes or currency fluctuations with respect to ordinary property which is held or to be held by the taxpayer; (2) to manage risk of interest rate or price changes or currency fluctuations with respect to borrowings made or to be made, or ordinary obligations incurred or to be incurred, by the taxpayer; or (3) to manage such other risks as the Secretary may prescribe in regulations.[527]

Reasons for Change

The Congress believed that exceptions from subpart F foreign personal holding company income for commodities hedging transactions and active business sales of commodities should be modified to better reflect current active business practices and, in the case of hedging transactions, to conform to recent tax law changes concerning hedging transactions generally.

Explanation of Provision

The Act modifies the requirements that must be satisfied for gains or losses from a commodities hedging transaction to qualify for exclusion from the definition of subpart F foreign personal holding company income. Under the Act, gains or losses from a transaction with respect to a commodity are not treated as foreign personal holding company income if the transaction satisfies the gen-

---

[524] For hedging transactions entered into on or after January 31, 2003, Treasury regulations provide that gains or losses from a commodities hedging transaction generally are excluded from the definition of foreign personal holding company income if the transaction is with respect to the controlled foreign corporation's business as a producer, processor, merchant or handler of commodities, regardless of whether the transaction is a hedge with respect to a sale of commodities in the active conduct of a commodities business by the controlled foreign corporation. The regulations also provide that, for purposes of satisfying the requirements for exclusion from the definition of foreign personal holding company income, a producer, processor, merchant or handler of commodities includes a controlled foreign corporation that regularly uses commodities in a manufacturing, construction, utilities, or transportation business (Treas. Reg. sec. 1.954–2(f)(2)(v)). However, the regulations provide that a controlled foreign corporation is not a producer, processor, merchant or handler of commodities (and therefore would not satisfy the requirements for exclusion) if its business is primarily financial (Treas. Reg. sec. 1.954–2(f)(2)(v)).

[525] Treasury regulations provide that substantially all of a controlled foreign corporation's business is as an active producer, processor, merchant or handler of commodities if: (1) the sum of its gross receipts from all of its active sales of commodities in such capacity and its gross receipts from all of its commodities hedging transactions that qualify for exclusion from the definition of foreign personal holding company income, equals or exceeds (2) 85 percent of its total receipts for the taxable year (computed as though the controlled foreign corporation was a domestic corporation). Treas. Reg. sec. 1.954–2(f)(2)(iii)(C).

[526] Sec. 1221(a)(7).

[527] Sec. 1221(b)(2)(A).

eral definition of a hedging transaction under section 1221(b)(2). For purposes of the Act, the general definition of a hedging transaction under section 1221(b)(2) is modified to include any transaction with respect to a commodity entered into by a controlled foreign corporation in the normal course of the controlled foreign corporation's trade or business primarily: (1) to manage risk of price changes or currency fluctuations with respect to ordinary property or property described in section 1231(b) which is held or to be held by the controlled foreign corporation; or (2) to manage such other risks as the Secretary may prescribe in regulations. Gains or losses from a transaction that satisfies the modified definition of a hedging transaction are excluded from the definition of foreign personal holding company income only if the transaction is clearly identified as a hedging transaction in accordance with the hedge identification requirements that apply generally to hedging transactions under section 1221(b)(2).[528]

The Act also changes the requirements that must be satisfied for active business gains or losses from the sale of commodities to qualify for exclusion from the definition of foreign personal holding company income. Under the Act, such gains or losses are not treated as foreign personal holding company income if substantially all of the controlled foreign corporation's commodities are comprised of: (1) stock in trade of the controlled foreign corporation or other property of a kind which would properly be included in the inventory of the controlled foreign corporation if on hand at the close of the taxable year, or property held by the controlled foreign corporation primarily for sale to customers in the ordinary course of the controlled foreign corporation's trade or business; (2) property that is used in the trade or business of the controlled foreign corporation and is of a character which is subject to the allowance for depreciation under section 167; or (3) supplies of a type regularly used or consumed by the controlled foreign corporation in the ordinary course of a trade or business of the controlled foreign corporation.[529]

For purposes of applying the requirements for active business gains or losses from commodities sales to qualify for exclusion from the definition of foreign personal holding company income, the Act also provides that commodities with respect to which gains or losses are not taken into account as foreign personal holding company income by a regular dealer in commodities (or financial instruments referenced to commodities) are not taken into account in determining whether substantially all of the dealer's commodities are comprised of the property described above.

Effective Date

The provision is effective with respect to transactions entered into after December 31, 2004.

[528] Sec. 1221(a)(7) and (b)(2)(B).

[529] For purposes of determining whether substantially all of the controlled foreign corporation's commodities are comprised of such property, it is intended that the 85-percent requirement provided in the current Treasury regulations (as modified to reflect the changes made by the provision) continue to apply.

O. Modifications to Treatment of Aircraft Leasing and Shipping Income (sec. 415 of the Act and sec. 954 of the Code)

Present and Prior Law

In general, the subpart F rules (secs. 951–964) require U.S. shareholders with a 10-percent or greater interest in a controlled foreign corporation ("CFC") to include currently in income for U.S. tax purposes certain income of the CFC (referred to as "subpart F income"), without regard to whether the income is distributed to the shareholders (sec. 951(a)(1)(A)). In effect, the Code treats the U.S. 10-percent shareholders of a CFC as having received a current distribution of their pro rata shares of the CFC's subpart F income. The amounts included in income by the CFC's U.S. 10-percent shareholders under these rules are subject to U.S. tax currently. The U.S. tax on such amounts may be reduced through foreign tax credits.

Under prior law, subpart F income included foreign base company shipping income (sec. 954(f)). Foreign base company shipping income generally included income derived from the use of an aircraft or vessel in foreign commerce, the performance of services directly related to the use of any such aircraft or vessel, the sale or other disposition of any such aircraft or vessel, and certain space or ocean activities (e.g., leasing of satellites for use in space). Foreign commerce generally involves the transportation of property or passengers between a port (or airport) in the U.S. and a port (or airport) in a foreign country, two ports (or airports) within the same foreign country, or two ports (or airports) in different foreign countries. In addition, foreign base company shipping income included dividends and interest that a CFC received from certain foreign corporations and any gains from the disposition of stock in certain foreign corporations, to the extent the dividends, interest, or gains were attributable to foreign base company shipping income. Foreign base company shipping income also included incidental income derived in the course of active foreign base company shipping operations (e.g., income from temporary investments in or sales of related shipping assets), foreign exchange gain or loss attributable to foreign base company shipping operations, and a CFC's distributive share of gross income of any partnership and gross income received from certain trusts to the extent that the income would have been foreign base company shipping income had it been realized directly by the corporation.

Subpart F income also includes foreign personal holding company income (sec. 954(c)). For subpart F purposes, foreign personal holding company income generally consists of the following: (1) dividends, interest, royalties, rents and annuities; (2) net gains from the sale or exchange of (a) property that gives rise to the preceding types of income, (b) property that does not give rise to income, and (c) interests in trusts, partnerships, and real estate mortgage investment conduits ("REMICs"); (3) net gains from commodities transactions; (4) net gains from foreign currency transactions; (5) income that is equivalent to interest; (6) income from notional principal contracts; and (7) payments in lieu of dividends.

Subpart F foreign personal holding company income does not include rents and royalties received by a CFC in the active conduct of a trade or business from unrelated persons (sec. 954(c)(2)(A)). The determination of whether rents or royalties are derived in the active conduct of a trade or business is based on all the facts and circumstances. However, the Treasury regulations provide certain types of rents are treated as derived in the active conduct of a trade or business. These include rents derived from property that is leased as a result of the performance of marketing functions by the lessor if the lessor (through its own officers or employees located in a foreign country) maintains and operates an organization in such country that regularly engages in the business of marketing, or marketing and servicing, the leased property and that is substantial in relation to the amount of rents derived from the leasing of such property. An organization in a foreign country is substantial in relation to rents if the active leasing expenses[530] equal at least 25 percent of the adjusted leasing profit.[531]

Also generally excluded from subpart F foreign personal holding company income are rents and royalties received by the CFC from a related corporation for the use of property within the country in which the CFC was organized (sec. 954(c)(3)). However, rent and royalty payments do not qualify for this exclusion to the extent that such payments reduce subpart F income of the payor.

Reasons for Change

In general, other countries do not tax foreign shipping income, whereas the United States imposed immediate U.S. tax on such income. The Congress believed that the uncompetitive U.S. taxation of shipping income directly caused a steady and substantial decline of the U.S. shipping industry. The Congress further believed that the provision provides U.S. shippers the opportunity to be competitive with their tax-advantaged foreign competitors.

In addition, the Congress believed that the prior-law exception from foreign base company income for rents and royalties received by a CFC in the active conduct of a trade or business from unrelated persons was too narrow in the context of the leasing of an aircraft or vessel in foreign commerce. The Congress believed that the income earned by a CFC in connection with an active foreign aircraft or vessel leasing business should be excluded from the anti-deferral rules of subpart F, provided that the CFC conducts substantial activities with respect to such business. The Congress also believed the provision of a safe harbor under the Act improves the competitiveness of U.S.-based multinationals engaging in these activities.

Explanation of Provision

The Act repeals the subpart F rules relating to foreign base company shipping income. The Act also amends the exception from for-

[530] "Active-leasing expenses" are section 162 expenses properly allocable to rental income other than (1) deductions for compensation for personal services rendered by the lessor's shareholders or a related person, (2) deductions for rents, (3) section 167 and 168 expenses, and (4) deductions for payments to independent contractors with respect to leased property. Treas. Reg. sec. 1.954–2(c)(2)(iii).

[531] Generally, "adjusted leasing profit" is rental income less the sum of (1) rents paid or incurred by the CFC with respect to such rental income; (2) section 167 and 168 expenses with respect to such rental income; and (3) payments to independent contractors with respect to such rental income. Treas. Reg. sec. 1.954–2(c)(2)(iv).

eign personal holding company income applicable to rents or royalties derived from unrelated persons in an active trade or business by providing a safe harbor for rents derived from leasing an aircraft or vessel in foreign commerce. Such rents are excluded from foreign personal holding company income if the active leasing expenses comprise at least 10 percent of the profit on the lease. The provision is to be applied in accordance with existing regulations under section 954(c)(2)(A) by comparing the lessor's "active leasing expenses" for its pool of leased assets to its "adjusted leasing profit."

The safe harbor will not prevent a lessor from otherwise showing that it actively carries on a trade or business. In this regard, the requirements of section 954(c)(2)(A) will be met if a lessor regularly and directly performs active and substantial marketing, remarketing, management and operational functions with respect to the leasing of an aircraft or vessel (or component engines).[532] This will be the case regardless of whether the lessor engages in marketing of the lease as a form of financing (versus marketing the property as such) or whether the lease is classified as a finance lease or operating lease for financial accounting purposes. If a lessor acquires, from an unrelated or related party, a vessel or aircraft subject to an existing lease, the requirements of section 954(c)(2)(A) will be satisfied if, following the acquisition, the lessor performs active and substantial management, operational, and remarketing functions with respect to the leased property. However, if an existing FSC or ETI lease is transferred to a CFC lessor, the lease will no longer be eligible for FSC or ETI benefits.

An aircraft or vessel is considered to be leased in foreign commerce if it is used for the transportation of property or passengers between a port (or airport) in the United States and one in a foreign country or between foreign ports (or airports), provided the aircraft or vessel is used predominantly outside the United States. An aircraft or vessel will be considered used predominantly outside the United States if more than 50 percent of the miles during the taxable year are traversed outside the United States or the aircraft or vessel is located outside the United States more than 50 percent of the time during such taxable year.

It is expected that the Secretary of the Treasury will issue timely guidance to make conforming changes to existing regulations, including guidance that aircraft or vessel leasing activity that satisfies the requirements of section 954(c)(2)(A) shall also satisfy the requirements for avoiding income inclusion under section 956 and section 367(a).

It is anticipated that taxpayers now eligible for the benefits of the ETI exclusion (or the FSC provisions pursuant to the FSC Repeal and Extraterritorial Income Exclusion Act of 2000), will find it appropriate, as a matter of sound business judgment, to restructure their business operations to take into account the tax law changes brought about by the Act. It is noted that courts have recognized the validity of structuring operations for the purpose of obtaining the benefit of tax regimes expressly intended by Congress.

[532] An "aircraft or vessel" also includes engines that are leased separately from an aircraft or vessel.

It is intended that structuring or restructuring of operations for the purposes of adapting to the repeal of the ETI exclusion (or the FSC regime) will be considered to serve a valid business purpose and will not constitute tax avoidance, where the restructured operations conform to the requirements expressly mandated by Congress for obtaining tax benefits that remain available. For example, it is intended that a restructuring undertaken to transfer aircraft subject to existing FSC or ETI leases to a CFC lessor, to take advantage of the amendments made by the Act, would serve a valid business purpose and would not constitute tax avoidance, for purposes of determining whether a particular tax treatment (such as nonrecognition of gain) applies to such restructuring. It is intended, for example, that if such a restructuring meets the other requirements necessary to qualify as a "reorganization" under section 368, the transaction will also be deemed to meet the "business purpose" requirements under section 368, and thus, qualify as a reorganization under that section.

Effective Date

The provision is effective for taxable years of foreign corporations beginning after December 31, 2004, and taxable years of U.S. shareholders with or within which such taxable years of such foreign corporations end.

P. Modification of Exceptions Under Subpart F for Active Financing (sec. 416 of the Act and sec. 954 of the Code)

Present and Prior Law

Under the subpart F rules, U.S. shareholders with a 10–percent or greater interest in a controlled foreign corporation ("CFC") are subject to U.S. tax currently on certain income earned by the CFC, whether or not such income is distributed to the shareholders. The income subject to current inclusion under the subpart F rules includes, among other things, foreign personal holding company income and insurance income. In addition, 10–percent U.S. shareholders of a CFC are subject to current inclusion with respect to their shares of the CFC's foreign base company services income (i.e., income derived from services performed for a related person outside the country in which the CFC is organized).

Foreign personal holding company income generally consists of the following: (1) dividends, interest, royalties, rents, and annuities; (2) net gains from the sale or exchange of (a) property that gives rise to the preceding types of income, (b) property that does not give rise to income, and (c) interests in trusts, partnerships, and real estate mortgage investment conduits ("REMICs"); (3) net gains from commodities transactions; (4) net gains from foreign currency transactions; (5) income that is equivalent to interest; (6) income from notional principal contracts; and (7) payments in lieu of dividends.

Insurance income subject to current inclusion under the subpart F rules includes any income of a CFC attributable to the issuing or reinsuring of any insurance or annuity contract in connection with risks located in a country other than the CFC's country of organization. Subpart F insurance income also includes income attributable to an insurance contract in connection with risks located within the CFC's country of organization, as the result of an arrangement under which another corporation receives a substantially equal amount of consideration for insurance of other country risks. Investment income of a CFC that is allocable to any insurance or annuity contract related to risks located outside the CFC's country of organization is taxable as subpart F insurance income.[533]

Temporary exceptions from foreign personal holding company income, foreign base company services income, and insurance income apply for subpart F purposes for certain income that is derived in the active conduct of a banking, financing, or similar business, or in the conduct of an insurance business (so-called "active financing income").[534]

With respect to income derived in the active conduct of a banking, financing, or similar business, a CFC is required to be predominantly engaged in such business and to conduct substantial activity with respect to such business in order to qualify for the exceptions. In addition, certain nexus requirements apply, which provide that income derived by a CFC or a qualified business unit ("QBU") of a CFC from transactions with customers is eligible for the exceptions if, among other things, substantially all of the activities in connection with such transactions are conducted directly by the CFC or QBU in its home country, and such income is treated as earned by the CFC or QBU in its home country for purposes of such country's tax laws. Moreover, the exceptions apply to income derived from certain cross-border transactions, provided that certain requirements are met. Additional exceptions from foreign personal holding company income apply for certain income derived by a securities dealer within the meaning of section 475 and for gain from the sale of active financing assets.

In the case of insurance, in addition to temporary exceptions from insurance income and from foreign personal holding company income for certain income of a qualifying insurance company with respect to risks located within the CFC's country of creation or organization, temporary exceptions from insurance income and from foreign personal holding company income apply for certain income of a qualifying branch of a qualifying insurance company with respect to risks located within the home country of the branch, provided certain requirements are met under each of the exceptions. Further, additional temporary exceptions from insurance income and from foreign personal holding company income apply for certain income of certain CFCs or branches with respect to risks located in a country other than the United States, provided that the requirements for these exceptions are met.

---

[533] Treas. Reg. sec. 1.953–1(a).

[534] Temporary exceptions from the subpart F provisions for certain active financing income applied only for taxable years beginning in 1998. Those exceptions were modified and extended for one year, applicable only for taxable years beginning in 1999. The Tax Relief Extension Act of 1999 (Pub. L. No. 106–170) clarified and extended the temporary exceptions for two years, applicable only for taxable years beginning after 1999 and before 2002. The Job Creation and Worker Assistance Act of 2002 (Pub L. No. 107–147) extended the temporary exceptions for five years, applicable only for taxable years beginning after 2001 and before 2007, with a modification relating to insurance reserves.

Reasons for Change

The Congress understood that banking and financial regulatory requirements in many foreign countries require different financial services activities to be conducted in separate entities, and that the interaction of these requirements with the prior-law rules regarding active financing income often required financial services firms to operate inefficiently. Therefore, the Congress believed that the rules for determining whether income earned by an eligible CFC or QBU is active financing income should be more consistent with the rules for determining whether a CFC or QBU is eligible to earn active financing income. In particular, the Congress believed that activities performed by employees of certain affiliates of a CFC or QBU should be taken into account in determining whether income of the CFC or QBU is active financing income in a manner similar to the rules for determining whether the CFC or QBU is eligible to earn active financing income.

Explanation of Provision

The Act modifies the temporary exceptions from subpart F foreign personal holding company income and foreign base company services income for income derived in the active conduct of a banking, financing, or similar business. For purposes of determining whether a CFC or QBU has conducted directly in its home country substantially all of the activities in connection with transactions with customers, the Act provides that an activity is treated as conducted directly by the CFC or QBU in its home country if the activity is performed by employees of a related person and: (1) the related person is itself an eligible CFC the home country of which is the same as that of the CFC or QBU; (2) the activity is performed in the home country of the related person; and (3) the related person is compensated on an arm's length basis for the performance of the activity by its employees and such compensation is treated as earned by such person in its home country for purposes of the tax laws of such country. For purposes of determining whether a CFC or QBU is eligible to earn active financing income, such activity may not be taken into account by any CFC or QBU (including the employer of the employees performing the activity) other than the CFC or QBU for which the activities are performed.

Effective Date

The provision is effective for taxable years of foreign corporations beginning after December 31, 2004, and taxable years of U.S. shareholders with or within which such taxable years of foreign corporations end.

Q. Ten-Year Foreign Tax Credit Carryover; One-Year Foreign Tax Credit Carryback (sec. 417 of the Act and sec. 904 of the Code)

Present and Prior Law

U.S. persons may credit foreign taxes against U.S. tax on foreign-source income. The amount of foreign tax credits that may be claimed in a year is subject to a limitation that prevents taxpayers from using foreign tax credits to offset U.S. tax on U.S.-source income. The amount of foreign tax credits generally is limited to a portion of the taxpayer's U.S. tax which portion is calculated by multiplying the taxpayer's total U.S. tax by a fraction, the numerator of which is the taxpayer's foreign-source taxable income (i.e., foreign-source gross income less allocable expenses or deductions) and the denominator of which is the taxpayer's worldwide taxable income for the year.[535]

In addition, this limitation is calculated separately for various categories of income, generally referred to as "separate limitation categories." The total amount of the foreign tax credit used to offset the U.S. tax on income in each separate limitation category may not exceed the proportion of the taxpayer's U.S. tax which the taxpayer's foreign-source taxable income in that category bears to its worldwide taxable income.

Under prior law, the amount of creditable taxes paid or accrued (or deemed paid) in any taxable year which exceeded the foreign tax credit limitation was permitted to be carried back to the two immediately preceding taxable years (to the earliest year first) and carried forward five taxable years (in chronological order) and credited (not deducted) to the extent that the taxpayer otherwise had excess foreign tax credit limitation for those years. Under present and prior law, excess credits that are carried back or forward are usable only to the extent that there is excess foreign tax credit limitation in the carryover or carryback year. Consequently, foreign tax credits arising in a taxable year are utilized before excess credits from another taxable year may be carried forward or backward. In addition, excess credits are carried forward or carried back on a separate limitation basis. Thus, if a taxpayer has excess foreign tax credits in one separate limitation category for a taxable year, those excess credits may be carried back and forward only as taxes allocable to that category, notwithstanding the fact that the taxpayer may have excess foreign tax credit limitation in another category for that year. If credits cannot be so utilized, they are permanently disallowed.

Reasons for Change

The Congress was concerned that excessive double taxation of foreign earnings could result from the expiration of foreign tax credits under prior law. The Congress believed that the purposes of the foreign tax credit would be better served by providing a larger window within which credits may be used, thereby reducing the likelihood that credits may expire.

Explanation of Provision

The Act extends the excess foreign tax credit carryforward period to ten years and limits the carryback period to one year.

[535] Sec. 904(a).

Effective Date

The extension of the carryforward period is effective for excess foreign tax credits that may be carried to any taxable years ending after the date of enactment (October 22, 2004) of the provision; the limited carryback period is effective for excess foreign tax credits arising in taxable years beginning after the date of enactment (October 22, 2004) of the provision.

R. Modify FIRPTA Rules for Real Estate Investment Trusts (sec. 418 of the Act and secs. 857 and 897 of the Code)

Present and Prior Law

A real estate investment trust ("REIT") is a U.S. entity that derives most of its income from passive real estate-related investments. A REIT must satisfy a number of tests on an annual basis that relate to the entity's organizational structure, the source of its income, the nature of its assets, and the distribution of its income. If an electing entity meets the requirements for REIT status, the portion of its income that is distributed to its investors each year generally is treated as a dividend deductible by the REIT and includible in income by its investors. In this manner, the distributed income of the REIT is not taxed at the entity level. The distributed income is taxed only at the investor level. A REIT generally is required to distribute 90 percent of its income to its investors before the end of its taxable year. A REIT may designate a dividend as a capital gain dividend under certain circumstances.

Special U.S. tax rules apply to gains of foreign persons attributable to dispositions of interests in U.S. real property, including certain transactions involving REITs. The rules governing the imposition and collection of tax on such dispositions are contained in a series of provisions that were enacted in 1980 and that are collectively referred to as the Foreign Investment in Real Property Tax Act ("FIRPTA").

In general, FIRPTA provides that gain or loss of a foreign person from the disposition of a U.S. real property interest is taken into account for U.S. tax purposes as if such gain or loss were effectively connected with a U.S. trade or business during the taxable year. Accordingly, foreign persons generally are subject to U.S. tax on any gain from a disposition of a U.S. real property interest at the same rates that apply to similar income received by U.S. persons. For these purposes, under prior law there was no exception to the rule that the receipt of a distribution from a REIT was treated as a disposition of a U.S. real property interest by the recipient, and thus as income effectively connected with a U.S, trade or business, to the extent that it is attributable to a sale or exchange of a U.S. real property interest by the REIT. Capital gains distributions from REITs treated in this manner generally are subject to withholding tax at a rate of 35 percent (or a lower treaty rate). In addition, the recipients of these capital gains distributions are required to file Federal income tax returns in the United States, since the recipients are treated as earning income effectively connected with a U.S. trade or business.

In addition, foreign corporations that have effectively connected income generally are subject to the branch profits tax at a 30-percent rate (or a lower treaty rate).

Reasons for Change

The Congress believed that it was appropriate to provide greater conformity in the tax consequences of REIT distributions and other corporate stock distributions.

Explanation of Provision

The Act removes from treatment as effectively connected income for a foreign investor a capital gain distribution from a REIT,[536] provided that (1) the distribution is received with respect to a class of stock that is regularly traded on an established securities market located in the United States and (2) the foreign investor does not own more than five percent of the class of stock at any time during the taxable year within which the distribution is received. Thus, a foreign investor is not required to file a U.S. Federal income tax return by reason of receiving such a distribution. The distribution is to be treated as a REIT dividend to that investor, taxed as a REIT dividend that is not a capital gain. Also, the branch profits tax no longer applies to such a distribution.

Effective Date

The provision applies to taxable years beginning after the date of enactment (October 22, 2004).[537]

S. Exclusion of Income Derived from Certain Wagers on Horse Races and Dog Races from Gross Income of Nonresident Aliens (sec. 419 of the Act and sec. 872 of the Code)

Present and Prior Law

Under section 871, certain items of gross income received by a nonresident alien from sources within the United States are subject to a flat 30-percent withholding tax. Gambling winnings received by a nonresident alien from wagers placed in the United States are U.S.-source and thus generally are subject to this withholding tax, unless exempted by treaty. Currently, several U.S. income tax treaties exempt U.S.-source gambling winnings of residents of the other treaty country from U.S. withholding tax. In addition, no withholding tax is imposed under section 871 on the non-business gambling income of a nonresident alien from wagers on the following games (except to the extent that the Secretary determines that collection of the tax would be administratively feasible): blackjack,

---

[536] It is not intended that regulated investment companies ("RICs") are eligible for this new exception from FIRPTA. A technical correction may be necessary so that the statute reflects this intent. See section 2(a)(6)(A) of H.R. 5395 and of S. 3019, the "Tax Technical Corrections Act of 2004," introduced November 19, 2004.

[537] It is intended that the provision applies to any distribution of a REIT that is treated as a deduction for a taxable year of the REIT beginning after the date of enactment. A technical correction may be necessary so that the statute reflects this intent. See sec. 2(a)(6)(B) of H.R. 5395 and of S. 3019, the "Tax Technical Corrections Act of 2004," introduced November 19, 2004.

baccarat, craps, roulette, and big-6 wheel. Various other (non-gambling-related) items of income of a nonresident alien are excluded from gross income under section 872(b) and are thereby exempt from the 30-percent withholding tax, without any authority for the Secretary to impose the tax by regulation. In cases in which a withholding tax on gambling winnings applies, section 1441(a) of the Code requires the party making the winning payout to withhold the appropriate amount and makes that party responsible for amounts not withheld.

Under prior law, with respect to gambling winnings of a nonresident alien resulting from a wager initiated outside the United States on a pari-mutuel[538] event taking place within the United States, the source of the winnings, and thus the applicability of the 30-percent U.S. withholding tax, depended on the type of wagering pool from which the winnings were paid. If the payout was made from a separate foreign pool, maintained completely in a foreign jurisdiction (e.g., a pool maintained by a racetrack or off-track betting parlor that was showing in a foreign country a simulcast of a horse race taking place in the United States), then the winnings paid to a nonresident alien generally would not be subject to withholding tax, because the amounts received generally would not be from sources within the United States. However, if the payout was made from a "merged" or "commingled" pool, in which betting pools in the United States and the foreign country were combined for a particular event, then the portion of the payout attributable to wagers placed in the United States could be subject to withholding tax. The party making the payment, in this case a racetrack or off-track betting parlor in a foreign country, would be responsible for withholding the tax.

Reasons for Change

The Congress believed that nonresident aliens should be able to wager outside the United States in pari-mutuel pools on live horse or dog races taking place within the United States without any resulting winnings being subjected to U.S. income tax, regardless of whether the foreign pool is merged with a U.S. pool.

Explanation of Provision

The Act provides an exclusion from gross income under section 872(b) for winnings paid to a nonresident alien resulting from a legal wager initiated outside the United States in a pari-mutuel pool on a live horse or dog race in the United States, regardless of whether the pool is a separate foreign pool or a merged U.S.-foreign pool.

[538] In pari-mutuel wagering (common in horse racing), odds and payouts are determined by the aggregate bets placed. The money wagered is placed into a pool, the party maintaining the pool takes a percentage of the total, and the bettors effectively bet against each other. Pari-mutuel wagering may be contrasted with fixed-odds wagering (common in sports wagering), in which odds (or perhaps a point spread) are agreed to by the bettor and the party taking the bet and are not affected by the bets placed by other bettors.

Effective Date

The provision is effective for wagers made after the date of enactment (October 22, 2004) of the provision.

T. Limitation of Withholding on U.S.-Source Dividends Paid to Puerto Rico Corporation (sec. 420 of the Act and secs. 881 and 1442 of the Code)

Present and Prior Law

In general, dividends paid by corporations organized in the United States[539] to corporations organized outside of the United States and its possessions are subject to U.S. income tax withholding at the flat rate of 30 percent. The rate may be reduced or eliminated under a tax treaty. Dividends paid by U.S. corporations to corporations organized in certain U.S. possessions are subject to different rules.[540] Corporations organized in the U.S. possessions of the Virgin Islands, Guam, American Samoa or the Northern Mariana Islands are not subject to withholding tax on dividends from corporations organized in the United States, provided that certain local ownership and activity requirements are met. Each of those possessions have adopted local internal revenue codes that provide a zero rate of withholding tax on dividends paid by corporations organized in the possession to corporations organized in the United States.

Under the tax laws of Puerto Rico, which is also a U.S. possession, a 10-percent withholding tax is imposed on dividends paid by Puerto Rico corporations to non-Puerto Rico corporations.[541] Under prior law, dividends paid by corporations organized in the United States to Puerto Rico corporations were subject to U.S. withholding tax at a 30-percent rate. Under Puerto Rico law, Puerto Rico corporations may elect to credit their U.S. income taxes against their Puerto Rico income taxes. Creditable income taxes include the dividend withholding tax and the underlying U.S. corporate tax attributable to the dividends. However, a Puerto Rico corporation's tax credit for U.S. income taxes may be limited because the sum of the U.S. withholding tax and the underlying U.S. corporate tax generally exceeds the amount of Puerto Rico corporate income tax imposed on the dividend. Consequently, Puerto Rico corporations with subsidiaries organized in the United States may be subject to some degree of double taxation on their U.S. subsidiaries' earnings.

Reasons for Change

The 30-percent withholding tax rate on U.S.-source dividends to Puerto Rico corporations placed such companies at an economic disadvantage relative to corporations organized in foreign countries with which the United States had a tax treaty, and relative to cor-

---

[539] The term "United States" does not include its possessions. Sec. 7701(a)(9).

[540] The usual method of effecting a mitigation of the flat 30 percent rate—an income tax treaty providing for a lower rate—is not possible in the case of a possession. See S. Rep. No. 1707, 89th Cong., 2d Sess. 34 (1966).

[541] The 10-percent withholding rate may be subject to exemption or elimination if the dividend is paid out of income that is subject to certain tax incentives offered by Puerto Rico. These tax incentives may also reduce the rate of underlying Puerto Rico corporate tax to a flat rate of between two and seven percent.

porations organized in other possessions. The Congress believed that creating and maintaining parity between U.S. and Puerto Rico dividend withholding tax rates would place Puerto Rico corporations on a more level playing field with corporations organized in treaty countries and other possessions.

Explanation of Provision

The Act lowers the withholding income tax rate on U.S. source dividends paid to a corporation created or organized in Puerto Rico from 30 percent to 10 percent, to create parity with the generally applicable 10-percent withholding tax imposed by Puerto Rico on dividends paid to U.S. corporations. The lower rate applies only if the same local ownership and activity requirements are met that are applicable to corporations organized in other possessions receiving dividends from corporations organized in the United States. If the generally applicable withholding tax rate imposed by Puerto Rico on dividends paid to U.S. corporations increases to greater than 10 percent, the U.S. withholding rate on dividends to Puerto Rico corporations reverts to 30 percent.

Effective Date

The provision is effective for dividends paid after the date of enactment (October 22, 2004).

U. Foreign Tax Credit Under Alternative Minimum Tax (sec. 421 of the Act and sec. 59 of the Code)

Present and Prior Law

In general

Under present and prior law, taxpayers are subject to an alternative minimum tax ("AMT"), which is payable, in addition to all other tax liabilities, to the extent that it exceeds the taxpayer's regular income tax liability. The tax is imposed at a flat rate of 20 percent, in the case of corporate taxpayers, on alternative minimum taxable income ("AMTI") in excess of a phased-out exemption amount. AMTI is the taxpayer's taxable income increased for certain tax preferences and adjusted by determining the tax treatment of certain items in a manner that limits the tax benefits resulting from the regular tax treatment of such items.

Foreign tax credit

Taxpayers are permitted to reduce their AMT liability by an AMT foreign tax credit. The AMT foreign tax credit for a taxable year is determined under principles similar to those used in computing the regular tax foreign tax credit, except that (1) the numerator of the AMT foreign tax credit limitation fraction is foreign source AMTI and (2) the denominator of that fraction is total AMTI. Taxpayers may elect to use as their AMT foreign tax credit limitation fraction the ratio of foreign source regular taxable income to total AMTI.

Under prior law, the AMT foreign tax credit for any taxable year generally could not offset a taxpayer's entire pre-credit AMT. Rather, the AMT foreign tax credit, under prior law, was limited to 90 percent of AMT computed without any AMT net operating loss deduction and the AMT foreign tax credit. For example, assume that a corporation has $10 million of AMTI, has no AMT net operating loss deduction, and has no regular tax liability. In the absence of the AMT foreign tax credit, the corporation's tax liability would be $2 million. Accordingly, the AMT foreign tax credit could not be applied to reduce the taxpayer's tax liability below $200,000. Any unused AMT foreign tax credit could be carried back two years and carried forward five years for use against AMT in those years under the principles of the foreign tax credit carryback and carryover rules set forth in section 904(c).

Reasons for Change

The Congress believed that taxpayers should be permitted full use of foreign tax credits in computing the AMT.

Explanation of Provision

The Act repeals the 90-percent limitation on the utilization of the AMT foreign tax credit.

Effective Date

The provision applies to taxable years beginning after December 31, 2004.

V. Incentives to Reinvest Foreign Earnings in the United States (sec. 422 of the Act and new sec. 965 of the Code)

Present and Prior Law

The United States employs a "worldwide" tax system, under which domestic corporations generally are taxed on all income, whether derived in the United States or abroad. Income earned by a domestic parent corporation from foreign operations conducted by foreign corporate subsidiaries generally is subject to U.S. tax when the income is distributed as a dividend to the domestic corporation. Until such repatriation, the U.S. tax on such income generally is deferred, and U.S. tax is imposed on such income when repatriated. However, under anti-deferral rules, the domestic parent corporation may be taxed on a current basis in the United States with respect to certain categories of passive or highly mobile income earned by its foreign subsidiaries, regardless of whether the income has been distributed as a dividend to the domestic parent corporation. The main anti-deferral provisions in this context are the controlled foreign corporation rules of subpart F [542] and the passive foreign investment company rules.[543] A foreign tax credit generally is available to offset, in whole or in part, the U.S. tax owed on foreign-source income, whether earned directly by the domestic corporation, repatriated as a dividend from a foreign subsidiary, or included in income under the anti-deferral rules.[544]

---

[542] Secs. 951–964.
[543] Secs. 1291–1298.
[544] Secs. 901, 902, 960, and 1291(g).

Reasons for Change

The Congress observed that the residual U.S. tax imposed on the repatriation of foreign earnings could serve as a disincentive to repatriate these earnings. The Congress believed that a temporary reduction in the U.S. tax on repatriated dividends would stimulate the U.S. domestic economy by triggering the repatriation of foreign earnings that otherwise would have remained abroad. The Congress emphasized that this tax reduction is a temporary economic stimulus measure, and that there is no intent to make the measure permanent, or to "extend" or enact it again in the future.

Explanation of Provision

Under the Act, certain dividends received by a U.S. corporation from controlled foreign corporations are eligible for an 85-percent dividends-received deduction. At the taxpayer's election, this deduction is available for dividends received either during the taxpayer's first taxable year beginning on or after the date of enactment of the bill, or during the taxpayer's last taxable year beginning before such date.[545] Dividends received after the election period will be taxed in the normal manner under present law.

The deduction applies only to cash dividends and other cash amounts included in gross income as dividends, such as cash amounts treated as dividends under Code sections 302 or 304 (but not to amounts treated as dividends under Code sections 78, 367, or 1248).[546] The deduction does not apply to items that are not included in gross income as dividends, such as subpart F inclusions or deemed repatriations under Code section 956. Similarly, the deduction does not apply to distributions of earnings previously taxed under subpart F, except to the extent that the subpart F inclusions result from the payment of a dividend by one controlled foreign corporation to another controlled foreign corporation within a certain chain of ownership during the election period, with the result that cash travels through a chain of controlled foreign corporations to the taxpayer within the election period. The amount of dividends eligible for the deduction is reduced by any increase in related-party indebtedness on the part of a controlled foreign corporation between October 3, 2004, and the close of the taxable year for which the deduction is being claimed, determined by treating all controlled foreign corporations with respect to which the taxpayer is a U.S. shareholder as one controlled foreign corporation.[547] This rule is intended to prevent a deduction from being claimed in cases in which the U.S. shareholder directly or indirectly (e.g., through a related party) finances the payment of a dividend from a controlled foreign corporation. In such a case, there may be no net re-

---

[545] The election is to be made on a timely filed return (including extensions) for the taxable year with respect to which the deduction is claimed.

[546] However, to the extent that the taxpayer actually receives cash in an inbound liquidation that is described in Code section 332 and treated as a dividend under Code section 367(b), such amount is treated as a dividend for these purposes. A deemed liquidation effectuated by means of a "check the box" election under the entity classification regulations will not involve an actual receipt of cash that is reinvested in the United States as required for purposes of this provision.

[547] Thus, indebtedness between such controlled foreign corporations is disregarded for purposes of this determination.

patriation of funds, and thus it would be inappropriate to provide the deduction.[548]

The deduction is subject to a number of general limitations. First, it applies only to cash repatriations in excess of the taxpayer's average repatriation level over three of the five most recent taxable years ending on or before June 30, 2003, determined by disregarding the highest-repatriation year and the lowest-repatriation year among such five years (the "base-period average"). If the taxpayer has fewer than five such years, then all taxable years ending on or before June 30, 2003 are included in the base period.[549] Repatriation levels are determined by reference to base-period tax returns as filed, including any amended returns that were filed on or before June 30, 2003. U.S. shareholders that file a consolidated tax return are treated as one U.S. shareholder for all purposes of this dividends-received deduction provision. Thus, all such shareholders are aggregated in determining the base-period average (as are all controlled foreign corporations). In addition to cash dividends, dividends of property, deemed repatriations under section 956, and distributions of earnings previously taxed under subpart F are included in the base-period average.

Second, the amount of dividends eligible for the deduction is limited to the greatest of: (1) $500 million; (2) the amount of earnings shown as permanently invested outside the United States on the taxpayer's "applicable financial statement" (generally, the most recent audited financial statement which is certified on or before June 30, 2003);[550] or (3) in the case of an applicable financial statement that does not show a specific amount of such earnings, but that does show a specific amount of tax liability attributable to such earnings, the amount of such earnings determined by grossing up the tax liability at a 35-percent rate. If there is no applicable financial statement, or if such statement does not show a specific earnings or tax liability amount, then the $500 million limit applies. This $500 million amount is divided among corporations that are members of a controlled group, using a 50-percent standard of common control. The two financial statement amounts described above are divided among the U.S. shareholders that are included on such statements.

---

[548] The Treasury Secretary has regulatory authority to prevent the avoidance of the purposes of this rule. Regulations issued pursuant to this authority may include rules to provide that cash dividends are not taken into account under Code section 965(a) to the extent attributable to the direct or indirect transfer of cash or other property from a related person to a controlled foreign corporation (including through the use of intervening entities or capital contributions). It is expected that this authority, which supplements existing principles relating to the treatment of circular flows of cash, will be used to prevent the application of the deduction in the case of a dividend that is effectively funded by the U.S. shareholder or its U.S. affiliates. A technical correction may be necessary so that the statute reflects this intent. See section 2(a)(7)(B) of H.R. 5395 and S. 3019, the "Tax Technical Corrections Act of 2004," introduced November 19, 2004.

[549] A corporation that was spun off from another corporation during the five-year period is treated for this purpose as having been in existence for the same period that such other corporation has been in existence. The pre-spin-off dividend history of the two corporations is generally allocated between them on the basis of their interests in the dividend-paying controlled foreign corporations immediately after the spin-off. In other cases involving companies entering and exiting corporate groups, rules similar to those of Code section 41(f)(3)(A) and (B) apply.

[550] This rule refers to elements of Accounting Principles Board Opinion 23 ("APB 23"), which provides an exception to the general rule of comprehensive recognition of deferred taxes for temporary book-tax differences. The exception is for temporary differences related to undistributed earnings of foreign subsidiaries and foreign corporate joint ventures that meet the indefinite reversal criterion in APB 23.

In the case of a U.S. shareholder that is required to file a financial statement with the Securities and Exchange Commission (or is included in such a statement filed by another person), the applicable financial statement is the most recent audited annual statement that was so filed and certified on or before June 30, 2003. For purposes of this rule, a restatement of a previously filed and certified financial statement that occurs after June 30, 2003 does not alter the statement's status as having been filed and certified on or before June 30, 2003. In addition, the term "applicable financial statement" includes the notes that form an integral part of the financial statement, but other materials, including work papers or materials that may be filed for some purposes with a financial statement but that do not form an integral part of such statement, may not be relied upon for purposes of producing an earnings or tax number under the provision. For example, if a note that is an integral part of an applicable financial statement states that the U.S. shareholder has not provided for deferred taxes on $1 billion of undistributed earnings of foreign subsidiaries because such earnings are intended to be reinvested permanently (or indefinitely) abroad, the U.S. shareholder's limit under Code section 965(b)(1) is $1 billion. If an applicable financial statement does not show a specific earnings or tax amount described in Code section 965(b)(1)(B) or (C), a taxpayer cannot rely on underlying work papers or other materials that are not a part of the financial statement to derive such an amount. If an applicable financial statement states that an earnings or tax amount is indeterminate (or that determination of a specific amount of earnings or taxes is not feasible), then the earnings or tax amount so described is treated as being zero.[551]

Third, in order to qualify for the deduction, dividends must be described in a domestic reinvestment plan approved by the taxpayer's senior management and board of directors. This plan must provide for the reinvestment of the repatriated dividends in the United States, including as a source for the funding of worker hiring and training, infrastructure, research and development, capital investments, and the financial stabilization of the corporation for the purposes of job retention or creation. This list of permitted uses is not exclusive. The reinvestment plan cannot, however, designate repatriated funds for use as payment for executive compensation. Dividends with respect to which the deduction is not being claimed are not required to be included in any domestic reinvestment plan.

Under Code section 965(d), no foreign tax credit (or deduction) is allowed for foreign taxes attributable to the deductible portion of any dividend.[552] For this purpose, the taxpayer may specifically identify which dividends are treated as carrying the deduction and which dividends are not.[553] In other words, the taxpayer is allowed to choose which of its dividends are treated as meeting the base-period repatriation level (and thus carry foreign tax credits, to the

[551] A technical correction may be necessary so that the statute reflects the intent described in this paragraph. See section 2(a)(7)(C) of H.R. 5395 and S. 3019, the "Tax Technical Corrections Act of 2004," introduced November 19, 2004.

[552] Foreign taxes that are not allowed as foreign tax credits by reason of Code section 965(d) also do not give rise to income inclusions under Code section 78. A technical correction may be necessary so that the statute reflects this intent. See section 2(a)(7)(E) of H.R. 5395 and S. 3019, the "Tax Technical Corrections Act of 2004," introduced November 19, 2004.

[553] In the absence of such a specification, a pro rata amount of foreign tax credits will be disallowed with respect to every dividend repatriated during the taxable year.

extent otherwise allowable), and which of its dividends are treated as comprising the excess eligible for the deduction (and thus entail proportional disallowance of any associated foreign tax credits). The deduction itself will have the effect of appropriately reducing the taxpayer's foreign tax credit limitation.

Deductions are disallowed for expenses that are directly allocable to the deductible portion of any dividend.[554]

The income attributable to the nondeductible portion of a qualifying dividend may not be offset by expenses, losses, or deductions, and the tax attributable to such income generally may not be offset by credits (other than foreign tax credits and AMT credits).[555] The only foreign tax credits that may be used to reduce the tax on the nondeductible portion of a dividend are credits for foreign taxes that are attributable to the nondeductible portion of the dividend. Credits for other foreign taxes cannot be used to reduce the tax on the nondeductible portion of the dividend.[556]

The tax on the income attributable to the nondeductible portion of a qualifying dividend also cannot reduce the alternative minimum tax that otherwise would be owed by the taxpayer. However, the deduction available under this provision is not treated as a preference item for purposes of computing the AMT. Thus, the deduction is allowed in computing alternative minimum taxable income notwithstanding the fact that it may not be deductible in computing earnings and profits. No deduction under sections 243 or 245 is allowed for any dividend for which a deduction is allowed under the provision.

Effective Date

The provision is effective only for a taxpayer's first taxable year beginning on or after the date of enactment (October 22, 2004) of the bill, or the taxpayer's last taxable year beginning before such date, at the taxpayer's election. The deduction available under the provision is not allowed for dividends received in any taxable year beginning one year or more after the date of enactment (October 22, 2004).

W. Delay in Effective Date of Final Regulations Governing Exclusion of Income from International Operations of Ships and Aircraft (sec. 423 of the Act and sec. 883 of the Code)

Present and Prior Law

Section 883 generally provides an exemption from gross income for earnings of a foreign corporation derived from the international operation of ships and aircraft if an equivalent exemption from tax is granted by the applicable foreign country to corporations organized in the United States.

---

[554] A technical correction may be necessary so that the statute reflects this intent. See section 2(a)(7)(D) of H.R. 5395 and S. 3019, the "Tax Technical Corrections Act of 2004," introduced November 19, 2004.

[555] These expenses, losses, and deductions may, however, have the effect of reducing other income of the taxpayer.

[556] A technical correction may be necessary so that the statute reflects this intent. See section 2(a)(7)(F) of H.R. 5395 and S. 3019, the "Tax Technical Corrections Act of 2004," introduced November 19, 2004.

The Treasury Department has issued regulations implementing the rules of section 883 that are effective for taxable years beginning 30 days or more after August 26, 2003. The regulations provide, in general, that a foreign corporation organized in a qualified foreign country and engaged in the international operation of ships or aircraft shall exclude qualified income from gross income for purposes of U.S. Federal income taxation, provided that the corporation can satisfy certain ownership and related documentation requirements. The proposed rules explain when a foreign country is a qualified foreign country and what income is considered to be qualified income.

Explanation of Provision

The Act delays the effective date for the Treasury regulations so that they apply to taxable years of foreign corporations seeking qualified foreign corporation status beginning after September 24, 2004.

Effective Date

The provision is effective after date of enactment (October 22, 2004).

X. Study of Earnings Stripping Provisions (sec. 424 of the Act and sec. 163(j) of the Code)

Present and Prior Law

The Code provides rules to limit the ability of U.S. corporations to reduce the U.S. tax on their U.S.-source income through certain earnings stripping transactions. These rules limit the deductibility of interest paid to certain related parties ("disqualified interest"), if the payor's debt-equity ratio exceeds 1.5 to 1 and the payor's net interest expense exceeds 50 percent of its "adjusted taxable income" (generally taxable income computed without regard to deductions for net interest expense, net operating losses, and depreciation, amortization, and depletion). Disqualified interest for these purposes also may include interest paid to unrelated parties in certain cases in which a related party guarantees the debt.

Explanation of Provision

The Act requires the Treasury Department to conduct a study of the earnings stripping rules, including a study of the effectiveness of these rules in preventing the shifting of income outside the United States, whether any deficiencies in these rules have the effect of placing U.S.-based businesses at a competitive disadvantage relative to foreign-based businesses, the impact of earnings stripping activities on the U.S. tax base, whether laws of foreign countries facilitate the stripping of earnings out of the United States, and whether changes to the earnings stripping rules would affect jobs in the United States. This study is to include specific recommendations for improving these rules and is to be submitted to the Congress not later than June 30, 2005.

Effective Date

The provision is effective on the date of enactment (October 22, 2004).

V. DEDUCTION OF STATE AND LOCAL GENERAL SALES TAXES

A. Deduction of State and Local General Sales Taxes (sec. 501 of the Act and sec. 164 of the Code)

Present and Prior Law

For purposes of determining regular tax liability, an itemized deduction is permitted for certain State and local taxes paid, including individual income taxes, real property taxes, and personal property taxes. The itemized deduction is not permitted for purposes of determining a taxpayer's alternative minimum taxable income. No itemized deduction is permitted for State or local general sales taxes.

Reasons for Change

The Congress recognized that not all States rely on income taxes as a primary source of revenue, and that allowing a deduction for State and local income taxes, but not sales taxes, created inequities across States and may also have created biases in the types of taxes that States and localities chose to impose. The Congress believed that the provision of an itemized deduction for State and local general sales taxes in lieu of the deduction for State and local income taxes would provide more equitable Federal tax treatment across States, and would cause the Federal tax laws to have a more neutral effect on the types of taxes that State and local governments utilize.

Explanation of Provision

The Act provides that, at the election of the taxpayer, an itemized deduction may be taken for State and local general sales taxes in lieu of the itemized deduction provided under present law for State and local income taxes. As is the case for State and local income taxes, the itemized deduction for State and local general sales taxes is not permitted for purposes of determining a taxpayer's alternative minimum taxable income.[557] Taxpayers have two options with respect to the determination of the sales tax deduction amount. Taxpayers may deduct the total amount of general State and local sales taxes paid by accumulating receipts showing general sales taxes paid. Alternatively, taxpayers may use tables created by the Secretary of the Treasury that show the allowable deduction. The tables are based on average consumption by taxpayers on a State-by-State basis taking into account filing status,

[557] A technical correction may be necessary so that the statute reflects this intent. See section 2(a)(8) of H.R. 5395 and S. 3019, the "Tax Technical Corrections Act of 2004," introduced November 19, 2004.

number of dependents, adjusted gross income and rates of State and local general sales taxation. Taxpayers who use the tables created by the Secretary may, in addition to the table amounts, deduct eligible general sales taxes paid with respect to the purchase of motor vehicles, boats and other items specified by the Secretary. Sales taxes for items that may be added to the tables are not reflected in the tables themselves.

The term "general sales tax" means a tax imposed at one rate with respect to the sale at retail of a broad range of classes of items. However, in the case of items of food, clothing, medical supplies, and motor vehicles, the fact that the tax does not apply with respect to some or all of such items is not taken into account in determining whether the tax applies with respect to a broad range of classes of items, and the fact that the rate of tax applicable with respect to some or all of such items is lower than the general rate of tax is not taken into account in determining whether the tax is imposed at one rate. Except in the case of a lower rate of tax applicable with respect to food, clothing, medical supplies, or motor vehicles, no deduction is allowed for any general sales tax imposed with respect to an item at a rate other than the general rate of tax. However, in the case of motor vehicles, if the rate of tax exceeds the general rate, such excess shall be disregarded and the general rate is treated as the rate of tax.

A compensating use tax with respect to an item is treated as a general sales tax, provided such tax is complementary to a general sales tax and a deduction for sales taxes is allowable with respect to items sold at retail in the taxing jurisdiction that are similar to such item.

Effective Date

The provision is effective for taxable years beginning after December 31, 2003, and prior to January 1, 2006.

VI. MISCELLANEOUS PROVISIONS

A. Brownfields Demonstration Program for Qualified Green Building and Sustainable Design Projects (sec. 701 of the Act and secs. 142 and 146 of the Code)

Present and Prior Law

In general

Interest on debt incurred by States or local governments is excluded from income if the proceeds of the borrowing are used to carry out governmental functions of those entities or the debt is repaid with governmental funds. Interest on bonds that nominally are issued by States or local governments, but the proceeds of which are used (directly or indirectly) by a private person and payment of which is derived from funds of such a private person is taxable unless the purpose of the borrowing is approved specifically in the Code or in a non-Code provision of a revenue Act. These bonds are called "private activity bonds." The term "private person" includes the Federal Government and all other individuals and entities other than States or local governments.

Private activities eligible for financing with tax-exempt private activity bonds

Present and prior law includes several exceptions permitting States or local governments to act as conduits providing tax-exempt financing for private activities. For example, interest on bonds issued to benefit section 501(c)(3) organizations is generally tax-exempt ("qualified 501(c)(3) bonds"). Both capital expenditures and limited working capital expenditures of section 501(c)(3) organizations may be financed with qualified 501(c)(3) bonds.

In addition, States or local governments may issue tax-exempt "exempt-facility bonds" to finance property for certain private businesses.[558] Business facilities eligible for this financing include transportation (airports, ports, local mass commuting, and high speed intercity rail facilities); privately owned and/or privately operated public works facilities (sewage, solid waste disposal, local district heating or cooling, hazardous waste disposal facilities, and public educational facilities); privately owned and/or operated low-income rental housing;[559] and certain private facilities for the local furnishing of electricity or gas. A further provision allows tax-exempt financing for "environmental enhancements of hydro-electric generating facilities." Tax-exempt financing also is authorized for capital expenditures for small manufacturing facilities and land and equipment for first-time farmers ("qualified small-issue

[558] Secs. 141(e) and 142(a).

[559] Residential rental projects must satisfy low-income tenant occupancy requirements for a minimum period of 15 years.

bonds"), local redevelopment activities ("qualified redevelopment bonds"), and eligible empowerment zone and enterprise community businesses. Tax-exempt private activity bonds also may be issued to finance limited non-business purposes: certain student loans and mortgage loans for owner-occupied housing ("qualified mortgage bonds" and "qualified veterans' mortgage bonds").

Generally, tax-exempt private activity bonds are subject to restrictions that do not apply to other bonds issued by State or local governments. For example, most tax-exempt private activity bonds are subject to annual volume limits on the aggregate face amount of such bonds that may be issued.[560]

Explanation of Provision

In general

The Act creates a new category of exempt-facility bond, the qualified green building and sustainable design project bond ("qualified green bond"). A qualified green bond is defined as any bond issued as part of an issue that finances a project designated by the Secretary, after consultation with the Administrator of the Environmental Protection Agency (the "Administrator"), as a green building and sustainable design project that meets the following eligibility requirements: (1) at least 75 percent of the square footage of the commercial buildings that are part of the project is registered for the U.S. Green Building Council's LEED[561] certification and is reasonably expected (at the time of designation) to meet such certification; (2) the project includes a brownfield site;[562] (3) the project receives at least $5 million in specific State or local resources; and (4) the project includes at least one million square feet of building or at least 20 acres of land.

Under the Act, qualified green bonds are not subject to the State bond volume limitations. Rather, there is a national limitation of $2 billion of qualified green bonds that the Secretary may allocate, in the aggregate, to qualified green building and sustainable design projects. Qualified green bonds may be currently refunded if certain conditions are met, but cannot be advance refunded. The authority to issue qualified green bonds terminates after September 30, 2009.

Application and designation process

The Act requires the submission of an application that meets certain requirements before a project may be designated for financing with qualified green bonds. In addition to the eligibility require-

---

[560] Sec. 146.

[561] The LEED ("Leadership in Energy and Environmental Design") Green Building Rating System is a voluntary, consensus-based national standard for developing high-performance sustainable buildings. Registration is the first step toward LEED certification. Actual certification requires that the applicant project satisfy a number of requirements. Commercial buildings, as defined by standard building codes, are eligible for certification. Commercial occupancies include, but are not limited to, offices, retail and service establishments, institutional buildings (e.g., libraries, schools, museums, churches, etc.), hotels, and residential buildings of four or more habitable stories.

[562] For this purpose, a brownfield site is defined by section 101(39) of the Comprehensive Environmental Response, Compensation, and Liability Act of 1980 (42 U.S.C. 9601), including a site described in subparagraph (D)(ii)(II)(aa) thereof (relating to a site that is contaminated by petroleum or a petroleum product excluded from the definition of "hazardous substance" under section 101).

ments listed above, each project application must demonstrate that the net benefit of the tax-exempt financing provided will be allocated for (i) the purchase, construction, integration or other use of energy efficiency, renewable energy and sustainable design features of the project, (ii) compliance with LEED certification standards, and/or (iii) the purchase, remediation, foundation construction, and preparation of the brownfield site. The application also must demonstrate that the project is expected, based on independent analysis, to provide the equivalent of at least 1,500 full-time permanent employees (150 full-time employees in rural States) when completed and the equivalent of at least 1,000 construction employees (100 full-time employees in rural States). In addition, each project application shall contain a description of: (1) the amount of electric consumption reduced as compared to conventional construction; (2) the amount of sulfur dioxide daily emissions reduced compared to coal generation; (3) the amount of gross installed capacity of the project's solar photovoltaic capacity measured in megawatts; and (4) the amount of the project's fuel cell energy generation, measured in megawatts.

Under the Act, each project must be nominated by a State or local government within 180 days of enactment of the Act and such State or local government must provide written assurances that the project will satisfy certain eligibility requirements. Within 60 days after the end of the application period, the Secretary, after consultation with the Administrator, will designate the qualified green building and sustainable design projects eligible for financing with qualified green bonds. At least one of the projects must be in or within a ten-mile radius of an empowerment zone (as defined under section 1391 of the Code) and at least one project must be in a rural State.[563] No more than one project is permitted in a State. A project shall not be designated for financing with qualified green bonds if such project includes a stadium or arena for professional sports exhibitions or games.

The Act requires the Secretary, after consultation with the Administrator, to ensure that the projects designated shall, in the aggregate: (1) reduce electric consumption by more than 150 megawatts annually as compared to conventional construction; (2) reduce daily sulfur dioxide emissions by at least 10 tons compared to coal generation power; (3) expand by 75 percent the domestic solar photovoltaic market in the United States (measured in megawatts) as compared to the expansion of that market from 2001 to 2002; and (4) use at least 25 megawatts of fuel cell energy generation.

Each project must certify to the Secretary, no later than 30 days after the completion of the project, that the net benefit of the tax-exempt financing was used for the purposes described in the project application. In addition, no bond proceeds can be used to provide any facility the principal business of which is the sale of food or alcoholic beverages for consumption on the premises.

[563] The term "rural State" means any State that has (1) a population of less than 4.5 million according to the 2000 census; (2) a population density of less than 150 people per square mile according to the 2000 census; and (3) increased in population by less than half the rate of the national increase between the 1990 and 2000 censuses.

Special rules

The Act requires each issuer to maintain, on behalf of each project, an interest bearing reserve account equal to one percent of the net proceeds of any qualified green bond issued for such project. Not later than five years after the date of issuance, the Secretary, after consultation with the Administrator, shall determine whether the project financed with the proceeds of qualified green bonds has substantially complied with the requirements and goals described in the project application. If the Secretary, after such consultation, certifies that the project has substantially complied with the requirements and goals, amounts in the reserve account, including all interest, shall be released to the project. If the Secretary determines that the project has not substantially complied with such requirements and goals, amounts in the reserve account, including all interest, shall be paid to the United States Treasury.

Effective Date

The provision is effective for bonds issued after December 31, 2004, and before October 1, 2009.

B. Exclusion of Gain or Loss on Sale or Exchange of Certain Brownfield Sites from Unrelated Business Taxable Income (sec. 702 of the Act and secs. 512 and 514 of the Code)

Present and Prior Law

In general, an organization that is otherwise exempt from Federal income tax is taxed on income from a trade or business regularly carried on that is not substantially related to the organization's exempt purposes. Gains or losses from the sale, exchange, or other disposition of property, other than stock in trade, inventory, or property held primarily for sale to customers in the ordinary course of a trade or business, generally are excluded from unrelated business taxable income. Gains or losses are treated as unrelated business taxable income, however, if derived from "debt-financed property." Debt-financed property generally means any property that is held to produce income and with respect to which there is acquisition indebtedness at any time during the taxable year.

In general, income of a tax-exempt organization that is produced by debt-financed property is treated as unrelated business income in proportion to the acquisition indebtedness on the income-producing property. Acquisition indebtedness generally means the amount of unpaid indebtedness incurred by an organization to acquire or improve the property and indebtedness that would not have been incurred but for the acquisition or improvement of the property. Acquisition indebtedness does not include: (1) certain indebtedness incurred in the performance or exercise of a purpose or function constituting the basis of the organization's exemption; (2) obligations to pay certain types of annuities; (3) an obligation, to the extent it is insured by the Federal Housing Administration, to finance the purchase, rehabilitation, or construction of housing for low and moderate income persons; or (4) indebtedness incurred by certain qualified organizations to acquire or improve real property.

Special rules apply in the case of an exempt organization that owns a partnership interest in a partnership that holds debt-financed property. An exempt organization's share of partnership income that is derived from debt-financed property generally is taxed as debt-financed income unless an exception provides otherwise.

Explanation of Provision

In general

The Act provides an exclusion from unrelated business taxable income for the gain or loss from the qualified sale, exchange, or other disposition of a qualifying brownfield property by an eligible taxpayer. The exclusion from unrelated business taxable income generally is available to an exempt organization that acquires, remediates, and disposes of the qualifying brownfield property. In addition, the Act provides an exception from the debt-financed property rules for such properties.

In order to qualify for the exclusions from unrelated business income and the debt-financed property rules, the eligible taxpayer is required to: (a) acquire from an unrelated person real property that constitutes a qualifying brownfield property; (b) pay or incur a minimum level of eligible remediation expenditures with respect to the property; and (c) transfer the remediated site to an unrelated person in a transaction that constitutes a sale, exchange, or other disposition for purposes of Federal income tax law.[564]

Qualifying brownfield properties

Under the Act, the exclusion from unrelated business taxable income applies only to real property that constitutes a qualifying brownfield property. A qualifying brownfield property means real property that is certified, before the taxpayer incurs any eligible remediation expenditures (other than to obtain a Phase I environmental site assessment), by an appropriate State agency (within the meaning of section 198(c)(4)) in the State in which the property is located as a brownfield site within the meaning of section 101(39) of the Comprehensive Environmental Response, Compensation, and Liability Act of 1980 (CERCLA) (as in effect on the date of enactment of the provision). The Act requires that the taxpayer's request for certification include a sworn statement of the taxpayer and supporting documentation of the presence of a hazardous substance, pollutant, or contaminant on the property that is complicating the expansion, redevelopment, or reuse of the property given the property's reasonably anticipated future land uses or capacity for uses of the property (including a Phase I environmental site assessment and, if applicable, evidence of the property's presence on a local, State, or Federal list of brownfields or contaminated property) and other environmental assessments prepared or obtained by the taxpayer.

---

[564] Under the Act, a person is related to another person if (1) such person bears a relationship to such other person that is described in section 267(b) (determined without regard to paragraph (9)), or section 707(b)(1), determined by substituting 25 percent for 50 percent each place it appears therein; or (2) if such other person is a nonprofit organization, if such person controls directly or indirectly more than 25 percent of the governing body of such organization.

Eligible taxpayer

An eligible taxpayer with respect to a qualifying brownfield property is an organization exempt from tax under section 501(a) that acquired such property from an unrelated person and paid or incurred a minimum amount of eligible remediation expenditures with respect to such property. The exempt organization (or the qualifying partnership of which it is a partner) is required to pay or incur eligible remediation expenditures with respect to a qualifying brownfield property in an amount that exceeds the greater of: (a) $550,000; or (b) 12 percent of the fair market value of the property at the time such property is acquired by the taxpayer, determined as if the property were not contaminated.

An eligible taxpayer does not include an organization that is: (1) potentially liable under section 107 of CERCLA with respect to the property; (2) affiliated with any other person that is potentially liable thereunder through any direct or indirect familial relationship or any contractual, corporate, or financial relationship (other than a contractual, corporate, or financial relationship that is created by the instruments by which title to a qualifying brownfield property is conveyed or financed by a contract of sale of goods or services); or (3) the result of a reorganization of a business entity which was so potentially liable.[565]

Qualified sale, exchange, or other disposition

Under the Act, a sale, exchange, or other disposition of a qualifying brownfield property shall be considered as qualified if such property is transferred by the eligible taxpayer to an unrelated person, and within one year of such transfer the taxpayer has received a certification (a "remediation certification") from the Environmental Protection Agency or an appropriate State agency (within the meaning of section 198(c)(4)) in the State in which the property is located that, as a result of the taxpayer's remediation actions, such property would not be treated as a qualifying brownfield property in the hands of the transferee. A taxpayer's request for a remediation certification shall be made no later than the date of the transfer and shall include a sworn statement by the taxpayer certifying that: (1) remedial actions that comply with all applicable or relevant and appropriate requirements (consistent with section 121(d) of CERCLA) have been substantially completed, such that there are no hazardous substances, pollutants or contaminants that complicate the expansion, redevelopment, or reuse of the property given the property's reasonably anticipated future land uses or capacity for uses of the property; (2) the reasonably anticipated future land uses or capacity for uses of the property are more economically productive or environmentally beneficial than the uses of

---

[565] In general, a person is potentially liable under section 107 of CERCLA if: (1) it is the owner and operator of a vessel or a facility; (2) at the time of disposal of any hazardous substance it owned or operated any facility at which such hazardous substances were disposed of; (3) by contract, agreement, or otherwise it arranged for disposal or treatment, or arranged with a transporter for transport for disposal or treatment, of hazardous substances owned or possessed by such person, by any other party or entity, at any facility or incineration vessel owned or operated by another party or entity and containing such hazardous substances; or (4) it accepts or accepted any hazardous substances for transport to disposal or treatment facilities, incineration vessels or sites selected by such person, from which there is a release, or a threatened release which causes the incurrence of response costs, of a hazardous substance. 42 U.S.C. sec. 9607(a) (2004).

the property in existence on the date the property was certified as a qualifying brownfield property;[566] (3) a remediation plan has been implemented to bring the property in compliance with all applicable local, State, and Federal environmental laws, regulations, and standards and to ensure that remediation protects human health and the environment; (4) the remediation plan, including any physical improvements required to remediate the property, is either complete or substantially complete, and if substantially complete,[567] sufficient monitoring, funding, institutional controls, and financial assurances have been put in place to ensure the complete remediation of the site in accordance with the remediation plan as soon as is reasonably practicable after the disposition of the property by the taxpayer; and (5) public notice and the opportunity for comment on the request for certification (in the same form and manner as required for public participation required under section 117(a) of CERCLA (as in effect on the date of enactment of the provision)) was completed before the date of such request. Public notice shall include, at a minimum, publication in a major local newspaper of general circulation.

A copy of each of the requests for certification that the property was a brownfield site, and that it would no longer be a qualifying brownfield property in the hands of the transferee, shall be included in the tax return of the eligible taxpayer (and, where applicable, of the qualifying partnership) for the taxable year during which the transfer occurs.

Eligible remediation expenditures

Under the Act, eligible remediation expenditures means, with respect to any qualifying brownfield property: (1) expenditures that are paid or incurred by the taxpayer to an unrelated person to obtain a Phase I environmental site assessment of the property; (2) amounts paid or incurred by the taxpayer after receipt of the certification that the property is a qualifying brownfield property for goods and services necessary to obtain the remediation certification; and (3) expenditures to obtain remediation cost-cap or stop-loss coverage, re-opener or regulatory action coverage, or similar coverage under environmental insurance policies,[568] or to obtain financial guarantees required to manage the remediation and monitoring of the property. Eligible remediation expenditures include expenditures to: (1) manage, remove, control, contain, abate, or otherwise remediate a hazardous substance, pollutant, or contaminant on the property; (2) obtain a Phase II environmental site assessment of the property, including any expenditure to monitor, sample, study, assess, or otherwise evaluate the release, threat of release, or presence of a hazardous substance, pollutant, or contaminant on the property; or (3) obtain environmental regulatory certifications and approvals required to manage the remediation and

---

[566] For this purpose, use of the property as a landfill or other hazardous waste facility shall not be considered more economically productive or environmentally beneficial.

[567] For these purposes, substantial completion means any necessary physical construction is complete, all immediate threats have been eliminated, and all long-term threats are under control.

[568] Cleanup cost-cap or stop-loss coverage is coverage that places an upper limit on the costs of cleanup that the insured may have to pay. Re-opener or regulatory action coverage is coverage for costs associated with any future government actions that require further site cleanup, including costs associated with the loss of use of site improvements.

monitoring of the hazardous substance, pollutant, or contaminant on the property. Eligible remediation expenditures do not include: (1) any portion of the purchase price paid or incurred by the eligible taxpayer to acquire the qualifying brownfield property; (2) environmental insurance costs paid or incurred to obtain legal defense coverage, owner/operator liability coverage, lender liability coverage, professional liability coverage, or similar types of coverage;[569] (3) any amount paid or incurred to the extent such amount is reimbursed, funded or otherwise subsidized by: (a) grants provided by the United States, a State, or a political subdivision of a State for use in connection with the property; (b) proceeds of an issue of State or local government obligations used to provide financing for the property, the interest of which is exempt from tax under section 103; or (c) subsidized financing provided (directly or indirectly) under a Federal, State, or local program in connection with the property; or (4) any expenditure paid or incurred before the date of enactment of the provision.[570]

Qualified gain or loss

The Act generally excludes from unrelated business taxable income the exempt organization's gain or loss from the sale, exchange, or other disposition of a qualifying brownfield property. Income, gain, or loss from other transfers does not qualify under the provision.[571] The amount of gain or loss excluded from unrelated business taxable income is not limited to or based upon the increase or decrease in value of the property that is attributable to the taxpayer's expenditure of eligible remediation expenditures. Further, the exclusion does not apply to an amount treated as gain that is ordinary income with respect to section 1245 or section 1250 property, including any amount deducted as a section 198 expense that is subject to the recapture rules of section 198(e), if the taxpayer had deducted such amount in the computation of its unrelated business taxable income.[572]

Special rules for qualifying partnerships

In general

In the case of a tax-exempt organization that is a partner of a qualifying partnership that acquires, remediates, and disposes of a qualifying brownfield property, the Act applies to the tax-exempt partner's distributive share of the qualifying partnership's gain or

[569] For this purpose, professional liability insurance is coverage for errors and omissions by public and private parties dealing with or managing contaminated land issues, and includes coverage under policies referred to as owner-controlled insurance. Owner/operator liability coverage is coverage for those parties that own the site or conduct business or engage in cleanup operations on the site. Legal defense coverage is coverage for lawsuits associated with liability claims against the insured made by enforcement agencies or third parties, including by private parties.

[570] The Act authorizes the Secretary of the Treasury to issue guidance regarding the treatment of government-provided funds for purposes of determining eligible remediation expenditures.

[571] For example, rent income from leasing the property does not qualify under the proposal.

[572] Depreciation or section 198 amounts that the taxpayer had not used to determine its unrelated business taxable income are not treated as gain that is ordinary income under sections 1245 or 1250 (secs. 1.1245–2(a)(8) and 1.1250–2(d)(6)), and are not recognized as gain or ordinary income upon the sale, exchange, or disposition of the property. Thus, an exempt organization would not be entitled to a double benefit resulting from a section 198 expense deduction and the proposed exclusion from gain with respect to any amounts it deducts under section 198.

loss from the disposition of the property.[573] A qualifying partnership is a partnership that: (1) has a partnership agreement that satisfies the requirements of section 514(c)(9)(B)(vi) at all times beginning on the date of the first certification received by the partnership that one of its properties is a qualifying brownfield property; (2) satisfies the requirements of the proposal if such requirements are applied to the partnership (rather than to the eligible taxpayer that is a partner of the partnership); and (3) is not an organization that would be prevented from constituting an eligible taxpayer by reason of it or an affiliate being potentially liable under CERCLA with respect to the property.

The exclusion is available to a tax-exempt organization with respect to a particular property acquired, remediated, and disposed of by a qualifying partnership only if the exempt organization is a partner of the partnership at all times during the period beginning on the date of the first certification received by the partnership that one of its properties is a qualifying brownfield property, and ending on the date of the disposition of the property by the partnership.[574]

Under the Act, the Secretary shall prescribe such regulations as are necessary to prevent abuse of the requirements of the provision, including abuse through the use of special allocations of gains or losses, or changes in ownership of partnership interests held by eligible taxpayers.

Certifications and multiple property elections

If the property is acquired and remediated by a qualifying partnership of which the exempt organization is a partner, it is intended that the certification as to status as a qualified brownfield property and the remediation certification will be obtained by the qualifying partnership, rather than by the tax-exempt partner, and that both the eligible taxpayer and the qualifying partnership will be required to make available such copies of the certifications to the IRS. Any elections or revocations regarding the application of the eligible remediation expenditure rules to multiple properties (as described below) acquired, remediated, and disposed of by a qualifying partnership must be made by the partnership. A tax-exempt partner is bound by an election made by the qualifying partnership of which it is a partner.

Special rules for multiple properties

The eligible remediation expenditure determinations generally are made on a property-by-property basis. An exempt organization (or a qualifying partnership of which the exempt organization is a partner) that acquires, remediates, and disposes of multiple qualifying brownfield properties, however, may elect to make the eligible remediation expenditure determinations on a multiple-property basis. In the case of such an election, the taxpayer satisfies the eligible remediation expenditures test with respect to all qualifying

---

[573] The Act's exclusions do not apply to a tax-exempt partner's gain or loss from the tax-exempt partner's sale, exchange, or other disposition of its partnership interest. Such transactions continue to be governed by present-law.

[574] The Act subjects a tax-exempt partner to tax on gain previously excluded by the partner (plus interest) if a property subsequently becomes ineligible for exclusion under the qualifying partnership's multiple-property election.

brownfield properties acquired during the election period if the average of the eligible remediation expenditures for all such properties exceeds the greater of: (a) $550,000; or (b) 12 percent of the average of the fair market value of the properties, determined as of the dates they were acquired by the taxpayer and as if they were not contaminated. If the eligible taxpayer elects to make the eligible remediation expenditure determination on a multiple property basis, then the election shall apply to all qualifying sales, exchanges, or other dispositions of qualifying brownfield properties the acquisition and transfer of which occur during the period for which the election remains in effect.[575]

An acquiring taxpayer makes a multiple-property election with its timely filed tax return (including extensions) for the first taxable year for which it intends to have the election apply. A timely filed election is effective as of the first day of the taxable year of the return in which the election is included or a later day in such taxable year selected by the taxpayer. An election remains effective until the earliest of a date selected by the taxpayer, the date which is eight years after the effective date of the election, the effective date of a revocation of the election, or, in the case of a partnership, the date of the termination of the partnership.

A taxpayer may revoke a multiple-property election by filing a statement of revocation with a timely filed tax return (including extensions). A revocation is effective as of the first day of the taxable year of the return in which the revocation is included or a later day in such taxable year selected by the eligible taxpayer or qualifying partnership. Once a taxpayer revokes the election, the taxpayer is ineligible to make another multiple-property election with respect to any qualifying brownfield property subject to the revoked election.[576]

Debt-financed property

The Act provides that debt-financed property, as defined by section 514(b), does not include any property the gain or loss from the sale, exchange, or other disposition of which is excluded by reason of the provisions of the proposal that exclude such gain or loss from computing the gross income of any unrelated trade or business of the taxpayer. Thus, gain or loss from the sale, exchange, or other disposition of a qualifying brownfield property that otherwise satisfies the requirements of the provision is not taxed as unrelated business taxable income merely because the taxpayer incurred debt to acquire or improve the site.

Termination date

The Act provides for a termination date of December 31, 2009, by applying to gain or loss on the sale, exchange, or other disposition of property that is acquired by the eligible taxpayer or qualifying partnership during the period beginning January 1, 2005, and ending December 31, 2009. Property acquired during the five-

[575] If the taxpayer fails to satisfy the averaging test for the properties subject to the election, then the taxpayer may not apply the exclusion on a separate property basis with respect to any of such properties.

[576] The Act subjects a taxpayer to tax on gain previously excluded (plus interest) in the event a site subsequently becomes ineligible for gain exclusion under the multiple-property election.

year acquisition period need not be disposed of by the termination date in order to qualify for the exclusion. For purposes of the multiple property election, gain or loss on property acquired after December 31, 2009, is not eligible for the exclusion from unrelated business taxable income, although properties acquired after the termination date (but during the election period) are included for purposes of determining average eligible remediation expenditures.

Effective Date

The provision applies to gain or loss on property that is acquired after December 31, 2004, subject to the December 31, 2009, termination date provision.

C. Civil Rights Tax Relief (sec. 703 of the Act and sec. 62 of the Code)

Present and Prior Law

Under present and prior law, gross income generally does not include the amount of any damages (other than punitive damages) received (whether by suit or agreement and whether as lump sums or as periodic payments) by individuals on account of personal physical injuries (including death) or physical sickness.[577] Expenses relating to recovering such damages are generally not deductible.[578]

Other damages are generally included in gross income. The related expenses to recover the damages, including attorneys' fees, are generally deductible as expenses for the production of income,[579] subject to the two-percent floor on itemized deductions.[580] Thus, such expenses are deductible only to the extent the taxpayer's total miscellaneous itemized deductions exceed two percent of adjusted gross income. Any amount allowable as a deduction is subject to reduction under the overall limitation of itemized deductions if the taxpayer's adjusted gross income exceeds a threshold amount.[581] For purposes of the alternative minimum tax, no deduction is allowed for any miscellaneous itemized deduction.

In some cases, claimants will engage an attorney to represent them on a contingent fee basis. That is, if the claimant recovers damages, a prearranged percentage of the damages will be paid to the attorney; if no damages are recovered, the attorney is not paid a fee. The proper tax treatment of contingent fee arrangements with attorneys has been litigated in recent years. Some courts[582] have held that the entire amount of damages is income and that the claimant is entitled to a miscellaneous itemized deduction subject to both the two-percent floor as an expense for the production

[577] Sec. 104(a)(2).
[578] Sec. 265(a)(1).
[579] Sec. 212.
[580] Sec. 67.
[581] Sec. 68.
[582] *Kenseth* v. *Commissioner,* 114 T.C. 399 (2000), aff'd 259 F.3d 881 (7th Cir. 2001); *Coady* v. *Commissioner,* 213 F.3d 1187 (9th Cir. 2000); *Benci-Woodward* v. *Commissioner,* 219 F.3d 941 (9th Cir. 2000); *Baylin* v. *United States,* 43 F.3d 1451 (Fed. Cir. 1995).

Subsequent to the October 22, 2004, enactment of the American Jobs Creation Act of 2004 ("AJCA"), the Supreme Court held that the contingent attorney fees portion of a taxpayer's settlement proceeds is an anticipatory assignment of income that is taxable income to the taxpayer. See *Commissioner* v. *Banks* and *Commissioner* v. *Banaitis,* 125 S.Ct. 826 (2005).

of income for the portion paid to the attorney and to the overall limitation on itemized deductions. Other courts have held that the portion of the recovery that is paid directly to the attorney is not income to the claimant, holding that the claimant has no claim of right to that portion of the recovery.[583]

Explanation of Provision

The Act provides an above-the-line deduction for attorneys' fees and costs paid by, or on behalf of, the taxpayer in connection with any action involving a claim of unlawful discrimination, certain claims against the Federal Government, or a private cause of action under the Medicare Secondary Payer statute. The amount that may be deducted above-the-line may not exceed the amount includible in the taxpayer's gross income for the taxable year on account of a judgment or settlement (whether by suit or agreement and whether as lump sum or periodic payments) resulting from such claim.

Under the Act, "unlawful discrimination" means an act that is unlawful under certain provisions of any of the following: the Civil Rights Act of 1991; the Congressional Accountability Act of 1995; the National Labor Relations Act; the Fair Labor Standards Act of 1938; the Age Discrimination in Employment Act of 1967; the Rehabilitation Act of 1973; the Employee Retirement Income Security Act of 1974; the Education Amendments of 1972; the Employee Polygraph Protection Act of 1988; the Worker Adjustment and Retraining Notification Act; the Family and Medical Leave Act of 1993; chapter 43 of Title 38 of the United States Code; the Revised Statutes; the Civil Rights Act of 1964; the Fair Housing Act; the Americans with Disabilities Act of 1990; any provision of Federal law (popularly known as whistleblower protection provisions) prohibiting the discharge of an employee, discrimination against an employee, or any other form of retaliation or reprisal against an employee for asserting rights or taking other actions permitted under Federal law; or any provision of Federal, State or local law, or common law claims permitted under Federal, State, or local law providing for the enforcement of civil rights or regulating any aspect of the employment relationship, including claims for wages, compensation, or benefits, or prohibiting the discharge of an employee, discrimination against an employee, or any other form of retaliation or reprisal against an employee for asserting rights or taking other actions permitted by law.

Effective Date

The provision applies to fees and costs paid after the date of enactment (October 22, 2004) with respect to any judgment or settlement occurring after such date.

---

[583] *Cotnam* v. *Commissioner,* 263 F.2d 119 (5th Cir. 1959); *Estate of Arthur Clarks* v. *United States,* 202 F.3d 854 (6th Cir. 2000); *Srivastava* v. *Commissioner,* 220 F.3d 353 (5th Cir. 2000). In some of these cases, such as Cotnam, State law has been an important consideration in determining that the claimant has no claim of right to the recovery.

As noted above, subsequent to the October 22, 2004, enactment of the AJCA, the Supreme Court held that the contingent attorney fees portion of a taxpayer's settlement proceeds is an anticipatory assignment of income that is taxable income to the taxpayer. See *Banks and Banaitis,* 125 S.Ct. 826.

D. Seven-Year Recovery Period for Certain Track Facilities (sec. 704 of the Act and sec. 168 of the Code)

Present and Prior Law

A taxpayer generally must capitalize the cost of property used in a trade or business and recover such cost over time through annual deductions for depreciation or amortization. Tangible property generally is depreciated under the modified accelerated cost recovery system ("MACRS"), which determines depreciation by applying specific recovery periods, placed-in-service conventions, and depreciation methods to the cost of various types of depreciable property (sec. 168). The cost of nonresidential real property is recovered using the straight-line method of depreciation and a recovery period of 39 years. Nonresidential real property is subject to the mid-month placed-in-service convention. Under the mid-month convention, the depreciation allowance for the first year property is placed in service is based on the number of months the property was in service, and property placed in service at any time during a month is treated as having been placed in service in the middle of the month. Land improvements (such as roads and fences) are recovered over 15 years. An exception exists for the theme and amusement park industry, whose assets are assigned a recovery period of seven years.

Explanation of Provision

The Act provides a statutory seven-year recovery period for permanent motorsports racetrack complexes. For this purpose, motorsports racetrack complexes include land improvements and support facilities but do not include transportation equipment, warehouses, administrative buildings, hotels, or motels.

Effective Date

The provision is effective for property placed in service after the date of enactment (October 22, 2004) and before January 1, 2008. The Act also excludes racetrack facilities placed in service after the date of enactment (October 22, 2004) from the definition of theme and amusement facilities classified under Asset Class 80.0. The Congress does not intend for this provision to create any inference as to the treatment of property placed in service on or before the date of enactment (October 22, 2004). Accordingly, the Congress does not intend for the provision to affect the interpretation of the scope of Asset Class 80.0 for assets placed in service prior to the date of enactment (October 22, 2004). The Congress strongly urges the Secretary to resolve expeditiously any taxpayer disputes with respect to the scope of Class 80.0.

E. Distributions to Shareholders From Policyholders Surplus Account of Life Insurance Companies (sec. 705 of the Act and sec. 815 of the Code)

Present and Prior Law

Under the law in effect from 1959 through 1983, a life insurance company was subject to a three-phase taxable income computation under Federal tax law. Under the three-phase system, a company was taxed on the lesser of its gain from operations or its taxable investment income (Phase I) and, if its gain from operations exceeded its taxable investment income, 50 percent of such excess (Phase II). Federal income tax on the other 50 percent of the gain from operations was deferred, and was accounted for as part of a policyholder's surplus account and, subject to certain limitations, taxed only when distributed to stockholders or upon corporate dissolution (Phase III). To determine whether amounts had been distributed, a company maintained a shareholders surplus account, which generally included the company's previously taxed income that would be available for distribution to shareholders. Distributions to shareholders were treated as being first out of the shareholders surplus account, then out of the policyholders surplus account, and finally out of other accounts.

The Deficit Reduction Act of 1984 included provisions that, for 1984 and later years, eliminated further deferral of tax on amounts (described above) that previously would have been deferred under the three-phase system. Although for taxable years after 1983, life insurance companies may not enlarge their policyholders surplus account, the companies are not taxed on previously deferred amounts unless the amounts are treated as distributed to shareholders or subtracted from the policyholders surplus account (sec. 815).

Any direct or indirect distribution to shareholders from an existing policyholders surplus account of a stock life insurance company is subject to tax at the corporate rate in the taxable year of the distribution. Present law (like prior law) provides that any distribution to shareholders is treated as made (1) first out of the shareholders surplus account, to the extent thereof, (2) then out of the policyholders surplus account, to the extent thereof, and (3) finally, out of other accounts.

Explanation of Provision

The Act suspends for a stock life insurance company's taxable years beginning after December 31, 2004, and before January 1, 2007, the application of the rules imposing income tax on distributions to shareholders from the policyholders surplus account of a life insurance company (sec. 815). The Act also reverses the order in which distributions reduce the various accounts, so that distributions are treated as first made out of the policyholders surplus account, to the extent thereof, and then out of the shareholders surplus account, and lastly out of other accounts.

Effective Date

The provision is effective for taxable years beginning after December 31, 2004.

F. Treat Certain Alaska Pipeline Property as Seven-Year Property (sec. 706 of the Act and sec. 168 of the Code)

Present and Prior Law

The applicable recovery period for assets placed in service under the Modified Accelerated Cost Recovery System is based on the "class life of the property." The class lives of assets placed in service after 1986 are generally set forth in Revenue Procedure 87–56.[584] Asset class 46.0, describing assets used in the private, commercial, and contract carrying of petroleum, gas and other products by means of pipes and conveyors, are assigned a class life of 22 years and a recovery period of 15 years.

Reasons for Change[585]

The Congress recognized that, on our present course, the nation will be ever more reliant on foreign governments, which do not always have America's interest at heart, for oil and natural gas. The Congress recognized that even with conservation efforts and alternative sources of energy our nation's long-term security depends on reducing our reliance on foreign energy sources. In light of this, the Congress believed it is appropriate to reduce the recovery period, and thus the cost of capital, for investment in natural gas pipeline systems in Alaska that meet certain requirements.

Explanation of Provision

The Act establishes a statutory seven-year recovery period and a class life of 22 years for any Alaska natural gas pipeline. The term "Alaska natural gas pipeline" is defined as any natural gas pipeline system (including the pipe, trunk lines, related equipment, and appurtenances used to carry natural gas, but not any gas processing plant) located in the State of Alaska that has a capacity of more than 500 billion Btu of natural gas per day and is placed in service after December 31, 2013. A taxpayer who places an otherwise qualifying system in service before January 1, 2014 may elect to treat the system as placed in service on January 1, 2014, thus qualifying for the seven-year recovery period.

Effective Date

The provision is effective for property placed in service after December 31, 2004.

G. Enhanced Oil Recovery Credit for Certain Gas Processing Facilities (sec. 707 of the Act and sec. 43 of the Code)

Present and Prior Law

The taxpayer may claim a credit equal to 15 percent of enhanced oil recovery costs. Qualified enhanced oil recovery costs include costs of depreciable tangible property that is part of an enhanced

---

[584] 1987–2 C.B. 674 (as clarified and modified by Rev. Proc. 88–22, 1988–1 C.B. 785).

[585] See S. 1149, the "Energy Tax Incentives Act of 2003," which was reported by the Committee on Finance on May 23, 2003 (S. Rep. No. 108–54).

oil recovery project, intangible drilling and development costs with respect to an enhanced oil recovery project, and tertiary injectant expenses incurred with respect to an enhanced oil recovery project. The credit is phased out when oil prices exceed a threshold amount.

Explanation of Provision

The Act provides that expenses in connection with the construction of any qualifying natural gas processing plant capable of processing two trillion British thermal units of Alaskan natural gas into a natural gas pipeline system on a daily basis are qualified enhanced oil recovery costs eligible for the enhanced oil recovery credit. A qualifying natural gas processing plant also must produce carbon dioxide for re-injection into a producing oil or gas field.

Effective Date

The provision is effective for costs paid or incurred in taxable years beginning after December 31, 2004.

H. Method of Accounting for Naval Shipbuilders (sec. 708 of the Act)

Present and Prior Law

Generally, taxpayers must use the percentage-of-completion method to determine taxable income from long-term contracts.[586] Under sec. 10203(b)(2)(B) of the Revenue Act of 1987,[587] an exception exists for certain ship construction contracts, which may be accounted for using the 40/60 percentage-of-completion/capitalized cost method ("PCCM"). Under the 40/60 PCCM, 60 percent of a taxpayer's long-term contract income is exempt from the requirement to use the percentage-of-completion method while 40 percent remains subject to the requirement. The exempt 60 percent of long-term contract income must be reported by consistently using the taxpayer's exempt contract method. Permissible exempt contract methods include the percentage-of-completion method, the exempt-contract percentage-of-completion method, and the completed contract method.[588]

Explanation of Provision

The Act provides that qualified naval ship contracts may be accounted for using the 40/60 PCCM during the five taxable year period beginning with the taxable year in which construction commences.[589] The cumulative reduction in tax resulting from the provision over the five-year period is recaptured and included in the taxpayer's tax liability in the sixth year. Qualified naval ship contracts are defined as any contract or portion thereof that is for the construction in the United States of one ship or submarine for the Federal Government if the taxpayer reasonably expects the acceptance date will occur no later than nine years after the construction

---

[586] Sec. 460(a).
[587] Pub. Law No. 100–203 (1987).
[588] Treas. Reg. sec. 1.460–4(c)(1).
[589] A technical correction may be necessary so that the statute reflect this intent.

commencement date.[590] The Act specifies that the construction commencement date is the date on which the physical fabrication of any section or component of the ship or submarine begins in the taxpayer's shipyard.

The Congress intended that section 481 not apply to any change of accounting method required by this provision.[591] Thus, a taxpayer who used a method other than the 40/60 PCCM in taxable years prior to the taxable year in which construction commences is not entitled to a section 481 adjustment when the taxpayer begins using the 40/60 PCCM. Likewise, upon reverting back to that prior method in the fifth year after the year in which construction commences, no section 481 adjustment is required because the recapture rule accomplishes a similar purpose.

Effective Date

The provision is effective for contracts with respect to which the construction commencement date occurs after date of enactment (October 22, 2004).

I. Minimum Cost Requirement for Excess Pension Asset Transfers (sec. 709 of the Act and sec. 420 of the Code)

Present and Prior Law

Defined benefit plan assets generally may not revert to an employer prior to termination of the plan and satisfaction of all plan liabilities. In addition, a reversion may occur only if the plan so provides. A reversion prior to plan termination may constitute a prohibited transaction and may result in plan disqualification. Any assets that revert to the employer upon plan termination are includible in the gross income of the employer and subject to an excise tax. The excise tax rate is 20 percent if the employer maintains a replacement plan or makes certain benefit increases in connection with the termination; if not, the excise tax rate is 50 percent. Upon plan termination, the accrued benefits of all plan participants are required to be 100-percent vested.

A pension plan may provide medical benefits to retired employees through a separate account that is part of such plan. A qualified transfer of excess assets of a defined benefit plan to such a separate account within the plan may be made in order to fund retiree health benefits.[592] A qualified transfer does not result in plan disqualification, is not a prohibited transaction, and is not treated as a reversion. Thus, transferred assets are not includible in the gross income of the employer and are not subject to the excise tax on reversions. No more than one qualified transfer may be made

---

[590] For example, if a taxpayer enters into a contract to construct three ships for the Federal government, and the taxpayer reasonably expects the acceptance date with respect to each ship will occur no later than nine years after the construction commencement date of such ship, then the taxpayer is treted as having entered into three separate qualified naval ship contracts. If the taxpayer meets the reasonable expectation standard with respect to only two of the three ships, then the taxpayer is treated as having entered into two separate qualified naval ship contracts, and the portion of the overall contract relating to the third ship is not treated as a qualified naval ship contract.

[591] A technical correction may be necessary so that the statute reflects this intent.

[592] Sec. 420.

in any taxable year. No qualified transfer may be made after December 31, 2013.

Excess assets generally means the excess, if any, of the value of the plan's assets[593] over the greater of (1) the accrued liability under the plan (including normal cost) or (2) 125 percent of the plan's current liability.[594] In addition, excess assets transferred in a qualified transfer may not exceed the amount reasonably estimated to be the amount that the employer will pay out of such account during the taxable year of the transfer for qualified current retiree health liabilities. No deduction is allowed to the employer for (1) a qualified transfer or (2) the payment of qualified current retiree health liabilities out of transferred funds (and any income thereon).

Transferred assets (and any income thereon) must be used to pay qualified current retiree health liabilities for the taxable year of the transfer. Transferred amounts generally must benefit pension plan participants, other than key employees, who are entitled upon retirement to receive retiree medical benefits through the separate account. Retiree health benefits of key employees may not be paid out of transferred assets.

Amounts not used to pay qualified current retiree health liabilities for the taxable year of the transfer are to be returned to the general assets of the plan. These amounts are not includible in the gross income of the employer, but are treated as an employer reversion and are subject to a 20-percent excise tax.

In order for a transfer to be qualified, accrued retirement benefits under the pension plan generally must be 100-percent vested as if the plan terminated immediately before the transfer (or in the case of a participant who separated in the one-year period ending on the date of the transfer, immediately before the separation).

In order for a transfer to be qualified, the transfer must meet the minimum cost requirement. To satisfy the minimum cost requirement, an employer generally must maintain retiree health benefits at the same level for the taxable year of the transfer and the following four years (referred to as the cost maintance period). The applicable employer cost during the cost maintenance period cannot be less than the higher of the applicable employer costs for each of the two taxable years preceding the taxable year of the transfer. The applicable employer cost is generally determined by dividing the current retiree health liabilities by the number of individuals provided coverage for applicable health benefits during the year. The Secretary is directed to prescribe regulations as may be necessary to prevent an employer who significantly reduces retiree health coverage during the period from being treated as satisfying the minimum cost requirement.

---

[593] The value of plan assets for this purpose is the lesser of fair market value or acturarial value.

[594] In the case of plan years beginning before January 1, 2004, excess assets generally means the excess, if any, of the value of the plan's assets over the greater of (1) the lesser of (a) the accrued liability under the plan (including normal cost) or (b) 170 percent of the plan's current liability (for 2003), or (2) 125 percent of the plan's current liability. The current liability full funding limit was repealed for years beginning after 2003. Under the general sunset provision of EGTRRA, the limit is reinstated for years after 2010.

Under Treasury regulations,[595] the minimum cost requirement is not satisfied if the employer significantly reduces retiree health coverage during the cost maintenance period. Under the regulations, an employer significantly reduces retiree health coverage for a year (beginning after 2001) during the cost maintenance period if either (1) the employer-initiated reduction percentage for that taxable year exceeds 10 percent, or (2) the sum of the employer-initiated reduction percentages for that taxable year and all prior taxable years during the cost maintenance period exceeds 20 percent.[596] The employer-initiated reduction percentage is the fraction, expressed as a percentage, of the number of individuals receiving coverage for applicable health benefits as of the day before the first day of the taxable year over the total number of such individuals whose coverage for applicable health benefits ended during the taxable year by reason of employer action.[597] Thus, under prior law, reductions in retiree health coverage would not cause a violation of section 420 only if the reduction was accomplished through a change in the number of individuals covered.

Reasons for Change[598]

The Congress believed that it was appropriate to provide greater flexibility in complying with the minimum cost requirement. The Congress believed that the requirement should not be violated if the reduction in health cost is not more than the allowable reduction in retiree health coverage.

Explanation of Provision

The Act provides that an eligible employer does not fail the minimum cost requirement if, in lieu of any reduction of health coverage permitted by Treasury regulations, the employer reduces applicable employer cost by an amount not in excess of the reduction in costs which would have occurred if the employer had made the maximum permissible reduction in retiree health coverage under such regulations. An employer is an eligible employer if, for the preceding taxable year, the qualified current retiree health liabilities of the employer were at least five percent of gross receipts.

In applying such regulations to any subsequent taxable year, any reduction in applicable employer cost under the proposal is treated as if it were an equivalent reduction in retiree health coverage.

Effective Date

The provision is effective for taxable years ending after the date of enactment (October 22, 2004).

---

[595] Treas. Reg. sec. 1.420–1(a).
[596] Treas. Reg. sec. 1.420–1(b)(1).
[597] Treas. Reg. sec. 1.420.
[598] See S. 2424, the "National Employee Savings and Trust Equity Guarantee Act," which was reported by the Senate Committee on Finance on May 14, 2004 (S. Rep. No. 108–266).

J. Credit for Electricity Produced from Certain Sources (sec. 710 of the Act and sec. 45 of the Code)

Present and Prior Law

An income tax credit is allowed for the production of electricity from either qualified wind energy, qualified "closed-loop" biomass, or qualified poultry waste facilities (sec. 45). The amount of the credit is 1.5 cents per kilowatt-hour (indexed for inflation) of electricity produced. The amount of the credit is 1.8 cents per kilowatt-hour for 2004. The credit is reduced for grants, tax-exempt bonds, subsidized energy financing, and other credits.

The credit applies to electricity produced by a wind energy facility placed in service after December 31, 1993, and before January 1, 2006, to electricity produced by a closed-loop biomass facility placed in service after December 31, 1992, and before January 1, 2006, and to a poultry waste facility placed in service after December 31, 1999, and before January 1, 2006. The credit is allowable for production during the 10-year period after a facility is originally placed in service. In order to claim the credit, a taxpayer must own the facility and sell the electricity produced by the facility to an unrelated party. In the case of a poultry waste facility, the taxpayer may claim the credit as a lessee/operator of a facility owned by a governmental unit.

Reasons for Change[599]

Based on the success of the section 45 credit in the development of wind power as an alternative source of electricity generation, the Congress believed the country will benefit from the expansion of the production credit to certain other "environmentally friendly" sources of electricity generation such as open-loop biomass, including agricultural livestock waste nutrients, geothermal power, solar power, small irrigation systems, landfill gas, and trash combustion. While not all of these additional facilities are pollution free, they do address environmental concerns related to waste disposal and, in the case of landfill gas, mitigate the release of methane gas into the atmosphere. In addition, these potential power sources further diversify the nation's energy supply.

The Congress also believed it is appropriate to include in qualifying facilities those facilities that co-fire closed-loop biomass fuels with coal, with other biomass, or with coal and other biomass.

The Congress also recognized that the credit for production of synthetic fuels from coal, provided by section 29 of the Code, has

[599] H.R. 4520, which was reported by the House Committee on Ways and Means on June 16, 2004 (H.R. Rep. No. 108–548) and passed the House of Representatives on June 17, 2004, provided for an extension of the placed in service date for certain qualified facilities, as explained in Part Fifteen, above, but did not contain provisions for the expansion of qualifying facilities. However, the conference agreement for H.R. 6, the "Energy Policy Act of 2003" (H.R. Rep. No. 108–375), contained provisions nearly identifical to S. 1637, the "Jumpstart Our Business Strength (JOBS) Act" (S. Rep. No. 108–192), as passed by the Senate on May 11, 2004.

These reasons for change were included for similar provisions included in H.R. 1531, the "Energy Tax Policy Act of 2003," which was reported by the House Committee on Ways and Means on April 9, 2003 (H.R. Rep. No. 108–67) and S. 1149, the "Energy Tax Incentive Act of 2003," which was reported by the Senate Committee on Finance on May 2, 2003 (S. Rep. No. 108–54). The two bills were conferenced to produce H.R. 6. The conference agreement for H.R. 6 provided tax benefits for "refined coal" as part of modifications to seciton 29 of the Code. The American Jobs Creation Act provided similar tax benefits as part of the expansion of section 45.

been interpreted to include fuels that are merely chemical changes to coal that do not necessarily enhance the value or environmental performance of the feedstock coal. Therefore, the Congress believed it is appropriate to provide a tax credit only to fuels produced from coal that achieve significant environmental and value-added improvements.

Lastly, the Congress believed that certain pre-existing facilities should qualify for the section 45 production credit, albeit at a reduced rate. These facilities previously received explicit subsidies, or implicit subsidies provided through rate regulation. In a deregulated electricity market, these facilities, and the environmental benefits they yield, may be uneconomic without additional economic incentive. The Congress believed the benefits provided by such existing facilities warrant their inclusion in the section 45 production credit.

Explanation of Provision

In general

The Act makes substantial modifications to sec. 45, primarily in defining additional qualified facilities eligible for the production tax credit.

Modification of placed in service date for existing facilities

The Act modifies the placed in service date with respect to qualifying closed-loop biomass facilities modified to use closed-loop biomass to co-fire with coal, to co-fire with other biomass, or to co-fire with coal and other biomass, but only if the modification is approved under the Biomass Power for Rural Development Programs or is part of a pilot project of the Commodity Credit Corporation. In the case of such a facility, a qualified facility must be originally placed in service and modified to co-fire the closed-loop biomass at any time before January 1, 2006. For such a facility, the 10–year credit period begins no earlier than October 22, 2004.

Additional qualifying resource and facilities

The Act also defines five new qualifying resources for the production of electricity: open-loop biomass (including agricultural livestock waste nutrients), geothermal energy, solar energy, small irrigation power, and municipal solid waste. Two different qualifying facilities use municipal solid waste as a qualifying resource: landfill gas facilities and trash combustion facilities. In addition, the Act defines refined coal as a qualifying resource.

Open-loop biomass (including agricultural livestock waste nutrients) facility

An open-loop biomass facility is a facility using open-loop biomass (including agricultural livestock waste nutrients) to produce electricity. Open-loop biomass is defined as any solid, nonhazardous, cellulosic waste material or any nonhazardous lignin waste material[600] which is segregated from other waste materials and which is derived from eligible forest-related resources, solid wood

[600] A technical correction may be necessary so that the statute reflects this intent.

waste materials, or agricultural sources. Eligible forest-related resources are mill residues, other than spent chemicals from pulp manufacturing, precommercial thinnings, slash, and brush. Solid wood waste materials include waste pallets, crates, dunnage, manufacturing and construction wood wastes (other than pressure-treated, chemically-treated, or painted wood wastes), and landscape or right-of-way tree trimmings. Agricultural sources include orchard tree crops, vineyard, grain, legumes, sugar, and other crop by-products or residues. However, qualifying open-loop biomass does not include municipal solid waste (garbage), gas derived from biodegradation of solid waste, or paper that is commonly recycled. In addition, open-loop biomass does not include closed-loop biomass or any biomass burned in conjunction with fossil fuel (cofiring) beyond such fossil fuel required for start up and flame stabilization.

Agricultural livestock waste nutrients are defined as agricultural livestock manure and litter, including bedding material for the disposition of manure. The installed capacity of a qualified agricultural livestock waste nutrient facility must be at least 150 kilowatts.

To be a qualified facility, an open-loop biomass facility must be placed in service after October 22, 2004 and before January 1, 2006, in the case of facility using agricultural livestock waste nutrients and must be placed in service at any time prior to January 1, 2006 in the case of a facility using other open-loop biomass.

Geothermal facility

A geothermal facility is a facility that uses geothermal energy to produce electricity. Geothermal energy is energy derived from a geothermal deposit which is a geothermal reservoir consisting of natural heat which is stored in rocks or in an aqueous liquid or vapor (whether or not under pressure). To be a qualified facility, a geothermal facility must be placed in service after the date of enactment (October 22, 2004) and before January 1, 2006. A qualifying geothermal energy facility may not have claimed any credit under sec. 48 of the Code.[601]

Solar facility

A solar facility is a facility that uses solar energy to produce electricity. To be a qualified facility, a solar facility must be placed in service after the date of enactment (October 22, 2004) and before January 1, 2006. A qualifying solar energy facility may not have claimed any credit under sec. 48 of the Code.[602]

Small irrigation facility

A small irrigation power facility is a facility that generates electric power through an irrigation system canal or ditch without any dam or impoundment of water. The installed capacity of a qualified facility must be at least 150 kilowatts and less than five megawatts. To be a qualified facility, a small irrigation facility

[601] If a geothermal facility claims credit for any year under section 45 of the Code, the facility is precluded from claiming any investment credit under section 48 of the Code in the future.

[602] If a solar facility claims credit for any year under section 45 of the Code, the facility is precluded from claiming any investment credit under section 48 of the Code in the future.

must be originally placed in service after the date of enactment and before January 1, 2006.

Landfill gas facility

A landfill gas facility is a facility that uses landfill gas to produce electricity. Landfill gas is defined as methane gas derived from the biodegradation of municipal solid waste. To be a qualified facility, a landfill gas facility must be placed in service after October 22, 2004 and before January 1, 2006.

Trash combustion facility

Trash combustion facilities are facilities that burn municipal solid waste (garbage) to produce steam to drive a turbine for the production of electricity. To be a qualified facility, a trash combustion facility must be placed in service after October 22, 2004 and before January 1, 2006.

Refined coal facility

A refined coal facility is a facility that produces refined coal. Refined coal is a qualifying liquid, gaseous, or solid synthetic fuel produced from coal (including lignite) or high-carbon fly ash, including such fuel used as a feedstock. A qualifying fuel is a fuel that when burned emits 20 percent less nitrogen oxides and either SO_2 or mercury than the burning of feedstock coal or comparable coal predominantly available in the marketplace as of January 1, 2003, and if the fuel sells at prices at least 50 percent greater than the prices of the feedstock coal or comparable coal. In addition, to be qualified refined coal the fuel must be sold by the taxpayer with the reasonable expectation that it will be used for the primary purpose of producing steam. A qualifying refined coal facility is a facility producing refined coal that is placed in service after October 22, 2004, and before January 1, 2009.

Credit period and credit rates

In general, the Act provides that taxpayers may claim the credit at a rate of 1.5 cents per kilowatt-hour (indexed for inflation and 1.8 cents per kilowatt-hour for 2004) for 10 years of production commencing on the date the facility is placed in service.

In the case of open-loop biomass (including agricultural livestock waste nutrients) facilities, geothermal energy facilities, solar energy facilities, small irrigation power facilities, landfill gas facilities, and trash combustion facilities the 10-year credit period is reduced to five years commencing on the date the facility is placed in service. In general, for facilities placed in service prior to January 1, 2005, the credit period commences on January 1, 2005.[603] In the case of closed-loop biomass facilities modified to co-fire with coal, to co-fire with other biomass, or to co-fire with coal and other biomass, the credit period shall begin no earlier than October 22, 2004.

In the case of open-loop biomass (including agricultural livestock waste nutrients) facilities, small irrigation power facilities, landfill

[603] A technical correction may be necessary so that the statute reflects this intent.

gas facilities, and trash combustion facilities, the otherwise allowable credit amount is reduced by one half.

An alternative credit applies for the production of refined coal. A qualified refined coal facility may claim credit at a rate of $4.375 per ton (indexed for inflation after 1992[604]) of refined coal sold to an unrelated person. As is the case for facilities that produce electricity, the credit a taxpayer may claim for the production of refined coal is phased out as the market price of refined coal exceeds certain threshold levels. The threshold is defined by reference to the price of feedstock fuel used to produce refined coal. Thus if a producer of refined coal uses Powder River Basin coal as a feedstock, the threshold price is determined by reference to prices of Powder River Basin coal. If the producer uses Appalachian coal, the threshold price is determined by reference to prices of Appalachian coal.

Credit claimants, treatment of other subsidies, and other provisions

The Act provides that a lessee or operator may claim the credit in lieu of the owner of the qualifying facility in the case of qualifying open-loop biomass facilities originally placed in service on or before the date of enactment and in the case of closed-loop biomass facilities modified to co-fire with coal, to co-fire with other biomass, or to co-fire with coal and other biomass.

In addition, for all qualifying facilities, other than closed-loop biomass facilities modified to co-fire with coal, to co-fire with other biomass, or to co-fire with coal and other biomass, the Act provides that any reduction in credit by reason of grants, tax-exempt bonds, subsidized energy financing, and other credits cannot exceed 50 percent. In the case of closed-loop biomass facilities modified to co-fire with coal, to co-fire with other biomass, or to co-fire with coal and other biomass, there is no reduction in credit by reason of grants, tax-exempt bonds, subsidized energy financing, and other credits.

The amendments made by the Act do not apply with respect to any poultry waste facility placed in service prior to January 1, 2005. Such facilities placed in service after December 31, 2004 generally may qualify for credit as animal livestock waste nutrient facilities.

The Act provides that no facility is a qualifying landfill gas facility for purposes of section 45 if the facility produces electricity from gas derived from the biodegradation of municipal solid waste if such gas is produced at a facility for which a credit under section 29 of the Code is allowed in the current year or was allowed in any prior taxable year.[605]

The Act provides that a taxpayer's tentative minimum tax is treated as being zero for purposes of determining the tax liability limitation with respect to the section 45 credit for electricity produced from a facility (placed in service after October 22, 2004) during the first four years of production beginning on the date the facility is placed in service.

---

[604] This amount would have equaled $5.350 per ton for 2004.

[605] A technical correction may be necessary so that the statute reflects this intent.

Effective Date

The provision is effective for electricity produced and sold from qualifying facilities after October 22, 2004 in taxable years ending after the date of enactment (October 22, 2004). With respect to open-loop biomass facilities placed in service prior to January 1, 2005, the provisions are effective for electricity produced and sold after December 31, 2004.

K. Allow Certain Business Energy Credits Against the Alternative Minimum Tax (sec. 711 of the Act and sec. 38 of the Code)

Present and Prior Law

Under prior law, generally, business tax credits may not exceed the excess of the taxpayer's income tax liability over the tentative minimum tax (or, if greater, 25 percent of the regular tax liability). Credits in excess of the limitation may be carried back one year and carried forward for up to 20 years.

The tentative minimum tax is an amount equal to specified rates of tax imposed on the excess of the alternative minimum taxable income over an exemption amount. To the extent the tentative minimum tax exceeds the regular tax, a taxpayer is subject to the alternative minimum tax.

Reasons for Change [606]

The alternative minimum tax limits the intended incentive effects of tax credits for some taxpayers. The Congress believed that the incentive effects of business energy credits should be available to taxpayers regardless of their alternative minimum tax status. Accordingly, the Act provides that certain business energy credits can be utilized by offsetting both the regular tax and the alternative minimum tax.

Explanation of Provision

The Act treats the tentative minimum tax as being zero for purposes of determining the tax liability limitation with respect to: (1) for taxable years beginning after December 31, 2004, the alcohol fuels credit determined under section 40; and (2) the section 45 credit for electricity produced from a facility (placed in service after the date of enactment) during the first four years of production beginning on the date the facility is placed in service.

Effective Date

The provision is effective for taxable years ending after the date of enactment (October 22, 2004).

[606] See H. R. 1531, the "Energy Tax Policy Act of 2003, which was reported by the House Committee on Ways and Means on April 9, 2003 (H.R. Rep. No. 108–67).

VII. REVENUE PROVISIONS

A. Provisions to Reduce Tax Avoidance Through Individual and Corporate Expatriation

1. Tax treatment of expatriated entities and their foreign parents (sec. 801 of the Act and new sec. 7874 of the Code)

Present and Prior Law

Determination of corporate residence

The U.S. tax treatment of a multinational corporate group depends significantly on whether the parent corporation of the group is domestic or foreign. For purposes of U.S. tax law, a corporation is treated as domestic if it is incorporated under the law of the United States or of any State. Other corporations (i.e., those incorporated under the laws of foreign countries) are treated as foreign.

U.S. taxation of domestic corporations

The United States employs a "worldwide" tax system, under which domestic corporations generally are taxed on all income, whether derived in the United States or abroad. In order to mitigate the double taxation that may arise from taxing the foreign-source income of a domestic corporation, a foreign tax credit for income taxes paid to foreign countries is provided to reduce or eliminate the U.S. tax owed on such income, subject to certain limitations.

Income earned by a domestic parent corporation from foreign operations conducted by foreign corporate subsidiaries generally is subject to U.S. tax when the income is distributed as a dividend to the domestic corporation. Until such repatriation, the U.S. tax on such income generally is deferred, and U.S. tax is imposed on such income when repatriated. However, certain anti-deferral regimes may cause the domestic parent corporation to be taxed on a current basis in the United States with respect to certain categories of passive or highly mobile income earned by its foreign subsidiaries, regardless of whether the income has been distributed as a dividend to the domestic parent corporation. The main anti-deferral regimes in this context are the controlled foreign corporation rules of subpart F (secs. 951–964) and the passive foreign investment company rules (secs. 1291–1298). A foreign tax credit is generally available to offset, in whole or in part, the U.S. tax owed on this foreign-source income, whether repatriated as an actual dividend or included under one of the anti-deferral regimes.

U.S. taxation of foreign corporations

The United States taxes foreign corporations only on income that has a sufficient nexus to the United States. Thus, a foreign corporation is generally subject to U.S. tax only on income that is "effectively connected" with the conduct of a trade or business in the United States. Such "effectively connected income" generally is taxed in the same manner and at the same rates as the income of a U.S. corporation. An applicable tax treaty may limit the imposition of U.S. tax on business operations of a foreign corporation to cases in which the business is conducted through a "permanent establishment" in the United States.

In addition, foreign corporations generally are subject to a gross-basis U.S. tax at a flat 30-percent rate on the receipt of interest, dividends, rents, royalties, and certain similar types of income derived from U.S. sources, subject to certain exceptions. The tax generally is collected by means of withholding by the person making the payment. This tax may be reduced or eliminated under an applicable tax treaty.

U.S. tax treatment of inversion transactions

A U.S. corporation may reincorporate in a foreign jurisdiction and thereby replace the U.S. parent corporation of a multinational corporate group with a foreign parent corporation. These transactions are commonly referred to as inversion transactions. Inversion transactions may take many different forms, including stock inversions, asset inversions, and various combinations of and variations on the two. Most of the known transactions to date have been stock inversions. In one example of a stock inversion, a U.S. corporation forms a foreign corporation, which in turn forms a domestic merger subsidiary. The domestic merger subsidiary then merges into the U.S. corporation, with the U.S. corporation surviving, now as a subsidiary of the new foreign corporation. The U.S. corporation's shareholders receive shares of the foreign corporation and are treated as having exchanged their U.S. corporation shares for the foreign corporation shares. An asset inversion reaches a similar result, but through a direct merger of the top-tier U.S. corporation into a new foreign corporation, among other possible forms. An inversion transaction may be accompanied or followed by further restructuring of the corporate group. For example, in the case of a stock inversion, in order to remove income from foreign operations from the U.S. taxing jurisdiction, the U.S. corporation may transfer some or all of its foreign subsidiaries directly to the new foreign parent corporation or other related foreign corporations.

In addition to removing foreign operations from the U.S. taxing jurisdiction, the corporate group may derive further advantage from the inverted structure by reducing U.S. tax on U.S.-source income through various earnings stripping or other transactions. This may include earnings stripping through payment by a U.S. corporation of deductible amounts such as interest, royalties, rents, or management service fees to the new foreign parent or other foreign affiliates. In this respect, the post-inversion structure enables the group to employ the same tax-reduction strategies that are available to other multinational corporate groups with foreign parents and U.S. subsidiaries, subject to the same limitations (e.g., secs. 163(j) and 482).

Inversion transactions may give rise to immediate U.S. tax consequences at the shareholder and/or the corporate level, depending on the type of inversion. In stock inversions, the U.S. shareholders generally recognize gain (but not loss) under section 367(a), based on the difference between the fair market value of the foreign corporation shares received and the adjusted basis of the domestic corporation stock exchanged. To the extent that a corporation's share value has declined, and/or it has many foreign or tax-exempt shareholders, the impact of this section 367(a) "toll charge" is reduced. The transfer of foreign subsidiaries or other assets to the foreign parent corporation also may give rise to U.S. tax consequences at the corporate level (e.g., gain recognition and earnings and profits inclusions under secs. 1001, 311(b), 304, 367, 1248 or other provisions). The tax on any income recognized as a result of these restructurings may be reduced or eliminated through the use of net operating losses, foreign tax credits, and other tax attributes.

In asset inversions, the U.S. corporation generally recognizes gain (but not loss) under section 367(a) as though it had sold all of its assets, but the shareholders generally do not recognize gain or loss, assuming the transaction meets the requirements of a reorganization under section 368.

Reasons for Change

The Congress believed that inversion transactions resulting in a minimal presence in a foreign country of incorporation were a means of avoiding U.S. tax and should be curtailed. In particular, these transactions permit corporations and other entities to continue to conduct business in the same manner as they did prior to the inversion, but with the result that the inverted entity avoids U.S. tax on foreign operations and may engage in earnings-stripping techniques to avoid U.S. tax on domestic operations. The Congress believed that corporate inversion transactions were a symptom of larger problems with our current system for taxing U.S.-based global businesses and were also indicative of the unfair advantages that our tax laws conveyed to foreign ownership.

The Act addressed the underlying problems with the U.S. system of taxing U.S.-based global businesses, and this provision removes the incentives for entering into inversion transactions. The Congress believed that certain inversion transactions have little or no non-tax effect or purpose and should be disregarded for U.S. tax purposes. The Congress believed that other inversion transactions may have sufficient non-tax effect and purpose to be respected, but warrant that any applicable corporate-level "toll charges" for establishing the inverted structure not be offset by tax attributes such as net operating losses or foreign tax credits.

Explanation of Provision

In general

The Act defines two different types of corporate inversion transactions and establishes a different set of consequences for each type. Certain partnership transactions also are covered.

Transactions involving at least 80 percent identity of stock ownership

The first type of inversion is a transaction in which, pursuant to a plan[607] or a series of related transactions: (1) a U.S. corporation becomes a subsidiary of a foreign-incorporated entity or otherwise transfers substantially all of its properties to such an entity in a transaction completed after March 4, 2003; (2) the former shareholders of the U.S. corporation hold (by reason of holding stock in the U.S. corporation) 80 percent or more (by vote or value) of the stock of the foreign-incorporated entity after the transaction; and (3) the foreign-incorporated entity, considered together with all companies connected to it by a chain of greater than 50 percent ownership (i.e., the "expanded affiliated group"), does not have substantial business activities in the entity's country of incorporation, compared to the total worldwide business activities of the expanded affiliated group. The Act denies the intended tax benefits of this type of inversion by deeming the top-tier foreign corporation to be a domestic corporation for all purposes of the Code.[608]

In determining whether a transaction meets the definition of an inversion under the provision, stock held by members of the expanded affiliated group that includes the foreign incorporated entity is disregarded. For example, if the former top-tier U.S. corporation receives stock of the foreign incorporated entity (e.g., so-called "hook" stock), that stock would not be considered in determining whether the transaction meets the definition. Similarly, if a U.S. parent corporation converts an existing wholly owned U.S. subsidiary into a new wholly owned controlled foreign corporation, all stock of the new foreign corporation would be disregarded, with the result that the transaction would not meet the definition of an inversion under the provision. Stock sold in a public offering related to the transaction also is disregarded for these purposes.

Transfers of properties or liabilities as part of a plan a principal purpose of which is to avoid the purposes of the provision are disregarded. In addition, the Treasury Secretary is to provide regulations to carry out the Act, including regulations to prevent the avoidance of the purposes of the provision, including avoidance through the use of related persons, pass-through or other noncorporate entities, or other intermediaries, and through transactions designed to qualify or disqualify a person as a related person or a member of an expanded affiliated group. Similarly, the Treasury Secretary is granted authority to treat certain non-stock instruments as stock, and certain stock as not stock, where necessary to carry out the purposes of the provision.

Transactions involving at least 60 percent but less than 80 percent identity of stock ownership

The second type of inversion is a transaction that would meet the definition of an inversion transaction described above, except that

---

[607] Acquisitions with respect to a domestic corporation or partnership are deemed to be "pursuant to a plan" if they occur within the four-year period beginning on the date which is two years before the ownership threshold under the provision is met with respect to such corporation or partnership.

[608] Since the top-tier foreign corporation is treated for all purposes of the Code as domestic, the shareholder-level "toll charge" of sec. 367(a) does not apply to these inversion transactions.

the 80-percent ownership threshold is not met. In such a case, if at least a 60-percent ownership threshold is met, then a second set of rules applies to the inversion. Under these rules, the inversion transaction is respected (i.e., the foreign corporation is treated as foreign), but any applicable corporate-level "toll charges" for establishing the inverted structure are not offset by tax attributes such as net operating losses or foreign tax credits. Specifically, any applicable corporate-level income or gain required to be recognized under sections 304, 311(b), 367, 1001, 1248, or any other provision with respect to the transfer of controlled foreign corporation stock or the transfer or license of other assets by a U.S. corporation as part of the inversion transaction or after such transaction to a related foreign person is taxable, without offset by any tax attributes (e.g., net operating losses or foreign tax credits). This rule does not apply to certain transfers of inventory and similar property. These measures generally apply for a 10-year period following the inversion transaction.

Under the Act, inversion transactions include certain partnership transactions. Specifically, the provision applies to transactions in which a foreign-incorporated entity acquires substantially all of the properties constituting a trade or business of a domestic partnership, if after the acquisition at least 60 percent of the stock of the entity is held by former partners of the partnership (by reason of holding their partnership interests), provided that the other terms of the basic definition are met. For purposes of applying this test, all partnerships that are under common control within the meaning of section 482 are treated as one partnership, except as provided otherwise in regulations. In addition, the modified "toll charge" proposals apply at the partner level.

A transaction otherwise meeting the definition of an inversion transaction is not treated as an inversion transaction if, on or before March 4, 2003, the foreign-incorporated entity had acquired directly or indirectly more than half of the properties held directly or indirectly by the domestic corporation, or more than half of the properties constituting the partnership trade or business, as the case may be.

Effective Date

The provision applies to taxable years ending after March 4, 2003.

2. Excise tax on stock compensation of insiders in expatriated corporations (sec. 802 of the Act and secs. 162(m), 275(a), and new sec. 4985 of the Code)

Present and Prior Law

The income taxation of a nonstatutory[609] compensatory stock option is determined under the rules that apply to property transferred in connection with the performance of services.[610] If a nonstatutory stock option does not have a readily ascertainable fair

[609] Nonstatutory stock options refer to stock options other than incentive stock options and employee stock purchase plans, the taxation of which is determined under sections 421–424.

[610] Sec. 83.

market value at the time of grant, which is generally the case unless the option is actively traded on an established market, no amount is included in the gross income of the recipient with respect to the option until the recipient exercises the option or disposes of the option in an arm's length transaction.[611] Upon exercise of such an option, the excess of the fair market value of the stock purchased over the option price is generally included in the recipient's gross income as ordinary income in such taxable year.[612]

The tax treatment of other forms of stock-based compensation (e.g., restricted stock and stock appreciation rights) is also determined under section 83. The excess of the fair market value over the amount paid (if any) for such property is generally includable in gross income in the first taxable year in which the rights to the property are transferable or are not subject to substantial risk of forfeiture.

Shareholders are generally required to recognize gain upon stock inversion transactions. An inversion transaction is generally not a taxable event for holders of stock options and other stock-based compensation.

Reasons for Change

The Congress believed that certain inversion transactions are a means of avoiding U.S. tax and should be curtailed. The Congress was concerned that, while shareholders are generally required to recognize gain upon stock inversion transactions, executives holding stock options and certain stock-based compensation are not taxed upon such transactions. Since such executives are often instrumental in deciding whether to engage in inversion transactions, the Congress believed that, upon certain inversion transactions, it was appropriate to impose an excise tax on certain executives holding stock options and stock-based compensation. Because shareholders are taxed at the capital gains rate upon inversion transactions, the Congress believed that it was appropriate to impose the excise tax at an equivalent rate.

Explanation of Provision

In general

Under the Act, specified holders of stock options and other stock-based compensation are subject to an excise tax upon certain inversion transactions. The Act imposes an excise tax on the value of specified stock compensation held (directly or indirectly) by or for the benefit of a disqualified individual, or a member of such individual's family, at any time during the 12-month period beginning six months before the corporation's expatriation date. Specified stock compensation is treated as held for the benefit of a disqualified individual if such compensation is held by an entity, e.g., a partnership or trust, in which the individual, or a member of the

[611] If an individual receives a grant of a nonstatutory option that has a readily ascertainable fair market value at the time the option is granted, the excess of the fair market value of the option over the amount paid for the option is included in the recipient's gross income as ordinary income in the first taxable year in which the option is either transferable or not subject to a substantial risk of forfeiture.

[612] Under section 83, such amount is includable in gross income in the first taxable year in which the rights to the stock are transferable or are not subject to substantial risk of forfeiture.

individual's family, has an ownership interest. The excise tax is imposed at a rate equal to the maximum rate of tax on the adjusted net capital gain of an individual (i.e., the rate of the excise tax would be 15 percent for 2005 through 2008 and 20 percent for taxable years beginning after December 31, 2008).

Disqualified individuals

A disqualified individual is any individual who, with respect to a corporation, is, at any time during the 12-month period beginning on the date which is six months before the expatriation date, subject to the requirements of section 16(a) of the Securities and Exchange Act of 1934 with respect to the corporation, or any member of the corporation's expanded affiliated group,[613] or would be subject to such requirements if the corporation (or member) were an issuer of equity securities referred to in section 16(a). Disqualified individuals generally include officers (as defined by section 16(a)),[614] directors, and 10-percent-or-greater owners of private and publicly-held corporations.

Application of excise tax

The excise tax is imposed on a disqualified individual of an expatriated corporation (as defined in the bill) only if gain (if any) is recognized in whole or part by any shareholder by reason of a corporate inversion transaction as previously defined in the bill.

Specified stock compensation

Specified stock compensation subject to the excise tax includes any payment[615] (or right to payment) granted by the expatriated corporation (or any member of the corporation's expanded affiliated group) to any person in connection with the performance of services by a disqualified individual for such corporation (or member of the corporation's expanded affiliated group) if the value of the payment or right is based on, or determined by reference to, the value or change in value of stock of such corporation (or any member of the corporation's expanded affiliated group). In determining whether such compensation exists and valuing such compensation, all restrictions, other than a non-lapse restriction, are ignored. Thus, the excise tax applies, and the value subject to the tax is determined, without regard to whether the specified stock compensation is subject to a substantial risk of forfeiture or is exercisable at the time of the inversion transaction.

Specified stock compensation includes compensatory stock and restricted stock grants, compensatory stock options, and other forms of stock-based compensation, including stock appreciation rights, phantom stock, and phantom stock options. Specified stock compensation also includes nonqualified deferred compensation

---

[613] An expanded affiliated group is an affiliated group (under section 1504) except that such group is determined without regard to the exceptions for certain corporations and is determined applying a greater than 50 percent threshold, in lieu of the 80–percent test.

[614] An officer is defined as the president, principal financial officer, principal accounting officer (or, if there is no such accounting officer, the controller), any vice-president in charge of a principal business unit, division or function (such as sales, administration or finance), any other officer who performs a policy-making function, or any other person who performs similar policy-making functions.

[615] Under the Act, any transfer of property is treated as a payment and any right to a transfer of property is treated as a right to a payment.

that is treated as though it were invested in stock or stock options of the expatriating corporation (or member). For example, the Act applies to a disqualified individual's nonqualified deferred compensation if company stock is one of the actual or deemed investment options under the nonqualified deferred compensation plan.

Specified stock compensation includes a compensation arrangement that gives the disqualified individual an economic stake substantially similar to that of a corporate shareholder. A payment directly tied to the value of the stock is specified stock compensation. The excise tax does not apply if a payment is simply triggered by a target value of the corporation's stock or where a payment depends on a performance measure other than the value of the corporation's stock. Similarly, the tax does not apply if the amount of the payment is not directly measured by the value of the stock or an increase in the value of the stock. For example, an arrangement under which a disqualified individual would be paid a cash bonus equal to $10,000 for every $1 increase in the share price of the corporation's stock is subject to the Act because the direct connection between the compensation amount and the value of the corporation's stock gives the disqualified individual an economic stake substantially similar to that of a shareholder. By contrast, an arrangement under which a disqualified individual would be paid a cash bonus of $500,000 if the corporation's stock increased in value by 25 percent over two years or $1,000,000 if the stock increased by 33 percent over two years is not specified stock compensation, even though the amount of the bonus generally is keyed to an increase in the value of the stock.

The excise tax applies to any specified stock compensation previously granted to a disqualified individual but cancelled or cashed-out within the six-month period ending with the expatriation date, and to any specified stock compensation awarded in the six-month period beginning with the expatriation date. As a result, for example, if a corporation cancels outstanding options three months before the inversion transaction and then reissues comparable options three months after the transaction, the tax applies both to the cancelled options and the newly granted options. It is intended that the Secretary issue guidance to avoid double counting with respect to specified stock compensation that is cancelled and then re-granted during the applicable 12-month period.

Specified stock compensation subject to the tax does not include a statutory stock option or any payment or right from a qualified retirement plan or annuity, tax-sheltered annuity, simplified employee pension, or SIMPLE. In addition, under the Act, the excise tax does not apply to any stock option that is exercised during the six-month period before the expatriation date or to any stock acquired pursuant to such exercise, if income is recognized under section 83 on or before the expatriation date with respect to the stock acquired pursuant to such exercise. The excise tax also does not apply to any specified stock compensation that is exercised, sold, exchanged, distributed, cashed out, or otherwise paid during such period in a transaction in which income, gain, or loss is recognized in full.

Determination of amount subject to tax

For specified stock compensation held on the expatriation date, the amount of the tax is determined based on the value of the compensation on such date. The tax imposed on specified stock compensation cancelled during the six-month period before the expatriation date is determined based on the value of the compensation on the day before such cancellation, while specified stock compensation granted after the expatriation date is valued on the date granted. Under the Act, the cancellation of a non-lapse restriction is treated as a grant.

The value of the specified stock compensation on which the excise tax is imposed is the fair value in the case of stock options (including warrants or other similar rights to acquire stock) and stock appreciation rights and the fair market value for all other forms of compensation. For purposes of the tax, the fair value of an option (or a warrant or other similar right to acquire stock) or a stock appreciation right is determined using an appropriate option-pricing model, as specified or permitted by the Secretary, that takes into account: (1) the stock price at the valuation date; (2) the exercise price under the option; (3) the remaining term of the option; (4) the volatility of the underlying stock and the expected dividends on it; and (5) the risk-free interest rate over the remaining term of the option. Options that have no intrinsic value (or "spread") because the exercise price under the option equals or exceeds the fair market value of the stock at valuation nevertheless have a fair value and are subject to tax under the Act. The value of other forms of compensation, such as phantom stock or restricted stock, is the fair market value of the stock as of the date of the expatriation transaction. The value of any deferred compensation that can be valued by reference to stock is the amount that the disqualified individual would receive if the plan were to distribute all such deferred compensation in a single sum on the date of the expatriation transaction (or the date of cancellation or grant, if applicable). It is expected that the Secretary issue guidance on valuation of specified stock compensation, including guidance similar to the guidance issued under section 280G, except that the guidance would not permit the use of a term other than the full remaining term and would be modified as necessary or appropriate to carry out the purposes of the Act. Pending the issuance of guidance, it is intended that taxpayers can rely on the guidance issued under section 280G (except that the full remaining term must be used and recalculation is not permitted).

Other rules

The excise tax also applies to any payment by the expatriated corporation or any member of the expanded affiliated group made to an individual, directly or indirectly, in respect of the tax. Whether a payment is made in respect of the tax is determined under all of the facts and circumstances. Any payment made to keep the individual in the same after-tax position that the individual would have been in had the tax not applied is a payment made in respect of the tax. This includes direct payments of the tax and payments to reimburse the individual for payment of the tax. It is expected that the Secretary issue guidance on determining when a payment is made in respect of the tax and that such guidance include certain factors that give rise to a rebuttable presumption that a payment is made in respect of the tax, including a rebuttable presumption that if the payment is contingent on the inversion transaction, it is made in respect to the tax. Any payment made in respect of the tax is includible in the income of the individual, but is not deductible by the corporation.

To the extent that a disqualified individual is also a covered employee under section 162(m), the $1,000,000 limit on the deduction allowed for employee remuneration for such employee is reduced by the amount of any payment (including reimbursements) made in respect of the tax under the Act. As discussed above, this includes direct payments of the tax and payments to reimburse the individual for payment of the tax.

The payment of the excise tax has no effect on the subsequent tax treatment of any specified stock compensation. Thus, the payment of the tax has no effect on the individual's basis in any specified stock compensation and no effect on the tax treatment for the individual at the time of exercise of an option or payment of any specified stock compensation, or at the time of any lapse or forfeiture of such specified stock compensation. The payment of the tax is not deductible and has no effect on any deduction that might be allowed at the time of any future exercise or payment.

Under the Act, the Secretary is authorized to issue regulations as may be necessary or appropriate to carry out the purposes of the Act.

Effective Date

The provision is effective as of March 4, 2003, except that periods before March 4, 2003, are not taken into account in applying the excise tax to specified stock compensation held or cancelled during the six-month period before the expatriation date.

3. Reinsurance of U.S. risks in foreign jurisdictions (sec. 803 of the Act and sec. 845(a) of the Code)

Present and Prior Law

In the case of a reinsurance agreement between two or more related persons, present and prior law provides the Treasury Secretary with authority to allocate among the parties or recharacterize income (whether investment income, premium or otherwise), deductions, assets, reserves, credits and any other items related to the reinsurance agreement, or make any other adjustment, in order to reflect the proper source and character of the items for each party.[616] For this purpose, related persons are defined as in section 482. Thus, persons are related if they are organizations, trades or businesses (whether or not incorporated, whether or not organized in the United States, and whether or not affiliated) that are owned or controlled directly or indirectly by the same interests. The provision may apply to a contract even if one of the related parties is

[616] Sec. 845(a).

not a domestic company.[617] In addition, the provision also permits such allocation, recharacterization, or other adjustments in a case in which one of the parties to a reinsurance agreement is, with respect to any contract covered by the agreement, in effect an agent of another party to the agreement, or a conduit between related persons.

Reason for Change

The Congress was concerned that reinsurance transactions were being used to allocate income, deductions, or other items inappropriately among U.S. and foreign related persons. The Congress was concerned that foreign related party reinsurance arrangements may be a technique for eroding the U.S. tax base. The Congress believed that the provision permitting the Treasury Secretary to allocate or recharacterize items related to a reinsurance agreement should be applied to prevent misallocation, improper characterization, or to make any other adjustment in the case of such reinsurance transactions between U.S. and foreign related persons (or agents or conduits). The Congress also wished to clarify that, in applying the authority with respect to reinsurance agreements, the amount, source or character of the items may be allocated, recharacterized or adjusted.

Explanation of Provision

The Act clarifies the rules of section 845, relating to authority for the Treasury Secretary to allocate items among the parties to a reinsurance agreement, recharacterize items, or make any other adjustment, in order to reflect the proper source and character of the items for each party. The Act authorizes such allocation, recharacterization, or other adjustment, in order to reflect the proper source, character or amount of the item. It is intended that this authority[618] be exercised in a manner similar to the authority under section 482 for the Treasury Secretary to make adjustments between related parties. It is intended that this authority be applied in situations in which the related persons (or agents or conduits) are engaged in cross-border transactions that require allocation, recharacterization, or other adjustments in order to reflect the proper source, character or amount of the item or items. No inference is intended that present and prior law does not provide this authority with respect to reinsurance agreements.

No regulations have been issued under section 845(a). It is expected that the Treasury Secretary will issue regulations under section 845(a) to address effectively the allocation of income (whether investment income, premium or otherwise) and other items, the recharacterization of such items, or any other adjustment necessary to reflect the proper amount, source or character of the item.

---

[617] See S. Rep. No. 97–494, 97th Cong., 2d Sess., 337 (1982) (describing provisions relating to the repeal of modified coinsurance provisions).

[618] The authority to allocate, recharacterize or make other adjustments was granted in connection with the repeal of provisions relating to modified coinsurance transactions.

Effective Date

The provision is effective for any risk reinsured after the date of enactment (October 22, 2004).

4. Revision of tax rules on expatriation of individuals (sec. 804 of the Act and secs. 877, 2107, 2501 and 6039G of the Code)

Present and Prior Law

In general

U.S. citizens and residents generally are subject to U.S income taxation on their worldwide income. The U.S. tax may be reduced or offset by a credit allowed for foreign income taxes paid with respect to foreign source income. Nonresident aliens are taxed at a flat rate of 30 percent (or a lower treaty rate) on certain types of passive income derived from U.S. sources, and at regular graduated rates on net profits derived from a U.S. trade or business. The estates of nonresident aliens generally are subject to estate tax on U.S.-situated property (e.g., real estate and tangible property located within the United States and stock in a U.S. corporation). Nonresident aliens generally are subject to gift tax on transfers by gift of U.S.-situated property (e.g., real estate and tangible property located within the United States, but excluding intangibles, such as stock, regardless of where they are located).

Income tax rules with respect to expatriates

For the 10 taxable years after an individual relinquishes his or her U.S. citizenship or terminates his or her U.S. residency[619] with a principal purpose of avoiding U.S. taxes, the individual is subject to an alternative method of income taxation than that generally applicable to nonresident aliens (the "alternative tax regime"). Generally, the individual is subject to income tax only on U.S.-source income[620] at the rates applicable to U.S. citizens for the 10-year period.

An individual who relinquishes citizenship or terminates residency is treated as having done so with a principal purpose of tax avoidance and is generally subject to the alternative tax regime if: (1) the individual's average annual U.S. Federal income tax liability for the five taxable years preceding citizenship relinquishment or residency termination exceeds $100,000; or (2) the individual's net worth on the date of citizenship relinquishment or residency termination equals or exceeds $500,000. These amounts are adjusted annually for inflation.[621] Certain categories of individuals (e.g., dual residents) may avoid being deemed to have a tax avoidance purpose for relinquishing citizenship or terminating residency by submitting a ruling request to the IRS regarding whether the

---

[619] Under prior law, an individual's U.S. residency is considered terminated for U.S. Federal tax purposes when the individual ceases to be a lawful permanent resident under the immigration law (or is treated as a resident of another country under a tax treaty and does not waive the benefits of such treaty).

[620] For this purpose, however, U.S.-source income has a broader scope than it does typically in the Code.

[621] The income tax liability and net worth thresholds under section 877(a)(2) for 2004 are $124,000 and $622,000, respectively. See Rev. Proc. 2003–85, 2003–49 I.R.B. 1184.

individual relinquished citizenship or terminated residency principally for tax reasons. Anti-abuse rules are provided to prevent the circumvention of the alternative tax regime.

Estate tax rules with respect to expatriates

Special estate tax rules apply to individuals who relinquish their citizenship or long-term residency within the 10 years prior to the date of death, unless he or she did not have a tax avoidance purpose (as determined under the test above). Under these special rules, certain closely-held foreign stock owned by the former citizen or former long-term resident is includible in his or her gross estate to the extent that the foreign corporation owns U.S.-situated assets.

Gift tax rules with respect to expatriates

Special gift tax rules apply to individuals who relinquish their citizenship or long-term residency within the 10 years prior to the date of death, unless he or she did not have a tax avoidance purpose (as determined under the rules above). The individual is subject to gift tax on gifts of U.S.-situated intangibles made during the 10 years following citizenship relinquishment or residency termination.

Information reporting

Under present and prior law, U.S. citizens who relinquish citizenship and long-term residents who terminate residency generally are required to provide information about their assets held at the time of expatriation. However, this information is only required once.

Reasons for Change

The Congress believed there were several difficulties in administering the prior-law alternative tax regime. One such difficulty was that the IRS was required to determine the subjective intent of taxpayers who relinquished citizenship or terminate residency. The prior-law presumption of a tax-avoidance purpose in cases in which objective income tax liability or net worth thresholds were exceeded mitigates this problem to some extent. However, the prior-law rules still required the IRS to make subjective determinations of intent in cases involving taxpayers who fell below these thresholds, as well as for certain taxpayers who exceeded these thresholds but were nevertheless allowed to seek a ruling from the IRS to the effect that they did not have a principal purpose of tax avoidance. The Congress believed that the replacement of the subjective determination of tax avoidance as a principal purpose for citizenship relinquishment or residency termination with objective rules result in easier administration of the tax regime for individuals who relinquish their citizenship or terminate residency.

Similarly, prior-law information-reporting and return-filing provisions did not provide the IRS with the information necessary to administer the alternative tax regime. Although individuals were required to file tax information statements upon the relinquishment of their citizenship or termination of their residency, difficulties were encountered in enforcing the requirement. The Congress believed that the tax benefits of citizenship relinquishment or residency termination should be denied an individual until he or she provides the information necessary for the IRS to enforce the alternative tax regime. The Congress also believed an annual report requirement and a penalty for the failure to comply with such requirement are needed to provide the IRS with sufficient information to monitor the compliance of former U.S. citizens and long-term residents.

Individuals who relinquish citizenship or terminate residency for tax reasons often do not want to fully sever their ties with the United States; they hope to retain some of the benefits of citizenship or residency without being subject to the U.S. tax system as a U.S. citizen or resident. Under prior law, these individuals generally could continue to spend significant amounts of time in the United States following citizenship relinquishment or residency termination—approximately four months every year—without being treated as a U.S. resident. The Congress believed that provisions in the Act that impose full U.S. taxation if the individual is present in the United States for more than 30 days in a calendar year substantially reduce the incentives to relinquish citizenship or terminate residency for individuals who desire to maintain significant ties to the United States.

With respect to the estate and gift tax rules, the Congress was concerned that prior-law did not adequately address opportunities for the avoidance of tax on the value of assets held by a foreign corporation whose stock the individual transfers. Thus, the provision imposes gift tax under the alternative tax regime in the case of gifts of certain stock of a closely held foreign corporation.

Explanation of Provision

In general

The Act provides: (1) objective standards for determining whether former citizens or former long-term residents are subject to the alternative tax regime; (2) tax-based (instead of immigration-based) rules for determining when an individual is no longer a U.S. citizen or long-term resident for U.S. Federal tax purposes; (3) the imposition of full U.S. taxation for individuals who are subject to the alternative tax regime and who return to the United States for extended periods; (4) imposition of U.S. gift tax on gifts of stock of certain closely-held foreign corporations that hold U.S.-situated property; and (5) an annual return-filing requirement for individuals who are subject to the alternative tax regime, for each of the 10 years following citizenship relinquishment or residency termination.[622]

Objective rules for the alternative tax regime

The Act replaces the subjective determination of tax avoidance as a principal purpose for citizenship relinquishment or residency termination under present law with objective rules. Under the Act, a former citizen or former long-term resident would be subject to the

[622] These provisions reflect recommendations contained in Joint Committee on Taxation, *Review of the Present Law Tax and Immigration Treatment of Relinquishment of Citizenship and Termination of Long-Term Residency*, (JCS–2–03), February 2003.

alternative tax regime for a 10-year period following citizenship relinquishment or residency termination, unless the former citizen or former long-term resident: (1) establishes that his or her average annual net income tax liability for the five preceding years does not exceed $124,000 (adjusted for inflation after 2004) and his or her net worth does not exceed $2 million, or alternatively satisfies limited, objective exceptions for dual citizens and minors who have had no substantial contact with the United States; and (2) certifies under penalties of perjury that he or she has complied with all U.S. Federal tax obligations for the preceding five years and provides such evidence of compliance as the Secretary of the Treasury may require.

The monetary thresholds under the Act replace the present-law inquiry into the taxpayer's intent. In addition, the Act eliminates the present-law process of IRS ruling requests.

If a former citizen exceeds the monetary thresholds, that person is excluded from the alternative tax regime if he or she falls within the exceptions for certain dual citizens and minors (provided that the requirement of certification and proof of compliance with Federal tax obligations is met). These exceptions provide relief to individuals who have never had substantial connections with the United States, as measured by certain objective criteria, and eliminate IRS inquiries as to the subjective intent of such taxpayers.

In order to be excepted from the application of the alternative tax regime under the Act, whether by reason of falling below the net worth and income tax liability thresholds or qualifying for the dual-citizen or minor exceptions, the former citizen or former long-term resident also is required to certify, under penalties of perjury, that he or she has complied with all U.S. Federal tax obligations for the five years preceding the relinquishment of citizenship or termination of residency and to provide such documentation as the Secretary of the Treasury may require evidencing such compliance (e.g., tax returns, proof of tax payments). Until such time, the individual remains subject to the alternative tax regime. It is intended that the IRS will continue to verify that the information submitted was accurate, and it is intended that the IRS will randomly audit such persons to assess compliance.

Termination of U.S. citizenship or long-term resident status for U.S. Federal income tax purposes

Under the Act, an individual continues to be treated as a U.S. citizen or long-term[623] resident for U.S. Federal tax purposes, including for purposes of section 7701(b)(10), until the individual: (1) gives notice of an expatriating act or termination of residency (with the requisite intent to relinquish citizenship or terminate residency) to the Secretary of State or the Secretary of Homeland Security, respectively; and (2) provides a statement in accordance with section 6039G (if such a statement is otherwise required under section 6039G).[624] This rule applies to all individuals losing U.S. citizenship or terminating long-term resident status, even if they are not subject to the alternative tax regime.

---

[623] A technical correction may be necessary so that the statute reflects this intent.
[624] A technical correction may be necessary so that the statute reflects this intent.

Sanction for individuals subject to the individual tax regime who return to the United States for extended periods

The alternative tax regime does not apply to any individual for any taxable year during the 10-year period following citizenship relinquishment or residency termination if such individual is present in the United States for more than 30 days in the calendar year ending in such taxable year. Such individual is treated as a U.S. citizen or resident for such taxable year and therefore is taxed on his or her worldwide income.

Similarly, if an individual subject to the alternative tax regime is present in the United States for more than 30 days in any calendar year ending during the 10-year period following citizenship relinquishment or residency termination, and the individual dies during that year, he or she is treated as a U.S. resident, and the individual's worldwide estate is subject to U.S. estate tax. Likewise, if an individual subject to the alternative tax regime is present in the United States for more than 30 days in any year during the 10-year period following citizenship relinquishment or residency termination, the individual is subject to U.S. gift tax on any transfer of his or her worldwide assets by gift during that taxable year.

For purposes of these rules, an individual is treated as present in the United States on any day if such individual is physically present in the United States at any time during that day. The present-law exceptions from being treated as present in the United States for residency purposes[625] generally do not apply for this purpose. However, for individuals with certain ties to countries other than the United States[626] and individuals with minimal prior physical presence in the United States,[627] a day of physical presence in the United States is disregarded if the individual is performing services in the United States on such day for an unrelated employer (within the meaning of sections 267 and 707(b)), who meets the requirements the Secretary of the Treasury may prescribe in regulations. No more than 30 days may be disregarded during any calendar year under this rule.

Imposition of gift tax with respect to stock of certain closely held foreign corporations

Gifts of stock of certain closely-held foreign corporations by a former citizen or former long-term resident who is subject to the alternative tax regime are subject to gift tax under this Act, if the gift is made within the 10-year period after citizenship relinquishment or residency termination. The gift tax rule applies if: (1) the

[625] Secs. 7701(b)(3)(D), 7701(b)(5) and 7701(b)(7)(B)–(D).

[626] An individual has such a relationship to a foreign country if the individual becomes a citizen or resident of the country in which (1) the individual becomes fully liable for income tax or (2) the individual was born, such individual's spouse was born, or either of the individual's parents was born.

[627] An individual has a minimal prior physical presence in the United States if the individual was physically present for no more than 30 days during each year in the ten-year period ending on the date of loss of United States citizenship or termination of residency. However, an individual is not treated as being present in the United States on a day if (1) the individual is a teacher or trainee, a student, a professional athlete in certain circumstances, or a foreign government-related individual or (2) the individual remained in the United States because of a medical condition that arose while the individual was in the United States. Sec. 7701(b)(3)(D). A technical correction may be necessary so that the statute reflects this intent.

former citizen or former long-term resident, before making the gift, directly or indirectly owns 10 percent or more of the total combined voting power of all classes of stock entitled to vote of the foreign corporation; and (2) directly or indirectly, is considered to own more than 50 percent of (a) the total combined voting power of all classes of stock entitled to vote in the foreign corporation, or (b) the total value of the stock of such corporation. If this stock ownership test is met, then taxable gifts of the former citizen or former long-term resident include that proportion of the fair market value of the foreign stock transferred by the individual, at the time of the gift, which the fair market value of any assets owned by such foreign corporation and situated in the United States (at the time of the gift) bears to the total fair market value of all assets owned by such foreign corporation (at the time of the gift).

This gift tax rule applies to a former citizen or former long-term resident who is subject to the alternative tax regime and who owns stock in a foreign corporation at the time of the gift, regardless of how such stock was acquired (e.g., whether issued originally to the donor, purchased, or received as a gift or bequest).

Annual return

The Act requires former citizens and former long-term residents to file an annual return for each year following citizenship relinquishment or residency termination in which they are subject to the alternative tax regime. The annual return is required even if no U.S. Federal income tax is due. The annual return requires certain information, including information on the permanent home of the individual, the individual's country of residence, the number of days the individual was present in the United States for the year, and detailed information about the individual's income and assets that are subject to the alternative tax regime. This requirement includes information relating to foreign stock potentially subject to the special estate tax rule of section 2107(b) and the gift tax rules of this Act.

If the individual fails to file the statement in a timely manner or fails correctly to include all the required information, the individual is required to pay a penalty of $5,000. The $5,000 penalty does not apply if it is shown that the failure is due to reasonable cause and not to willful neglect.

Effective Date

The provision applies to individuals who relinquish citizenship or terminate long-term residency after June 3, 2004.

5. Reporting of taxable mergers and acquisitions (sec. 805 of the Act and new sec. 6043A of the Code)

Present and Prior Law

Under section 6045 and the regulations thereunder, brokers (defined to include stock transfer agents) are required to make information returns and to provide corresponding payee statements as to sales made on behalf of their customers, subject to the penalty provisions of sections 6721–6724. Under the regulations issued under section 6045, this requirement generally does not apply with respect to taxable transactions other than exchanges for cash (e.g., stock inversion transactions taxable to shareholders by reason of section 367(a)).[628]

Reasons for Change

The Congress believed that administration of the tax laws would be improved by greater information reporting with respect to taxable non-cash transactions, and that the Treasury Secretary's authority to require such enhanced reporting should be made explicit in the Code.

Explanation of Provision

Under the Act, if gain or loss is recognized in whole or in part by shareholders of a corporation by reason of a second corporation's acquisition of the stock or assets of the first corporation, then the acquiring corporation (or the acquired corporation, if so prescribed by the Treasury Secretary) is required to make a return containing:

1. A description of the transaction;
2. The name and address of each shareholder of the acquired corporation that recognizes gain as a result of the transaction (or would recognize gain, if there was a built-in gain on the shareholder's shares);
3. The amount of money and the value of stock or other consideration paid to each shareholder described above; and
4. Such other information as the Treasury Secretary may prescribe.

Alternatively, a stock transfer agent who records transfers of stock in such transaction may make the return described above in lieu of the second corporation.

In addition, every person required to make a return described above is required to furnish to each shareholder (or the shareholder's nominee[629]) whose name is required to be set forth in such return a written statement showing:

1. The name, address, and phone number of the information contact of the person required to make such return;
2. The information required to be shown on that return; and
3. Such other information as the Treasury Secretary may prescribe.

This written statement is required to be furnished to the shareholder on or before January 31 of the year following the calendar year during which the transaction occurred.

The present-law penalties for failure to comply with information reporting requirements are extended to failures to comply with the requirements set forth under the Act.

---

[628] Recently issued temporary regulations under section 6043 (relating to information reporting with respect to liquidations, recapitalizations, and changes in control) impose information reporting requirements with respect to certain taxable inversion transactions, and proposed regulations would expand these requirements more generally to taxable transactions occurring after the proposed regulations are finalized.

[629] In the case of a nominee, the nominee must furnish the information to the shareholder in the manner prescribed by the Treasury Secretary.

Effective Date

The provision is effective for acquisitions after the date of enactment (October 22, 2004).

6. Studies (sec. 806 of the Act)

Present and Prior Law

Due to the variation in tax rates and tax systems among countries, a multinational enterprise, whether U.S.-based or foreign-based, may have an incentive to shift income, deductions, or tax credits in order to arrive at a reduced overall tax burden. Such a shifting of items could be accomplished by establishing artificial, non-arm's-length prices for transactions between group members.

Under section 482, the Treasury Secretary is authorized to reallocate income, deductions, or credits between or among two or more organizations, trades, or businesses under common control if he determines that such a reallocation is necessary to prevent tax evasion or to clearly reflect income. Treasury regulations adopt the arm's-length standard as the standard for determining whether such reallocations are appropriate. Thus, the regulations provide rules to identify the respective amounts of taxable income of the related parties that would have resulted if the parties had been uncontrolled parties dealing at arm's length. Transactions involving intangible property and certain services may present particular challenges to the administration of the arm's-length standard, because the nature of these transactions may make it difficult or impossible to compare them with third-party transactions.

In addition to the statutory rules governing the taxation of foreign income of U.S. persons and U.S. income of foreign persons, bilateral income tax treaties limit the amount of income tax that may be imposed by one treaty partner on residents of the other treaty partner. For example, treaties often reduce or eliminate withholding taxes imposed by a treaty country on certain types of income (e.g., dividends, interest and royalties) paid to residents of the other treaty country. Treaties also contain provisions governing the creditability of taxes imposed by the treaty country in which income was earned in computing the amount of tax owed to the other country by its residents with respect to such income. Treaties further provide procedures under which inconsistent positions taken by the treaty countries with respect to a single item of income or deduction may be mutually resolved by the two countries.

Explanation of Provision

The Act requires the Treasury Secretary to conduct and submit to the Congress three studies. The first study will examine the effectiveness of the transfer pricing rules of section 482, with an emphasis on transactions involving intangible property. The second study will examine income tax treaties to which the United States is a party, with a view toward identifying any inappropriate reductions in withholding tax or opportunities for abuse that may exist. The third study will examine the impact of the provisions of this Act on inversion transactions.

Effective Date

The tax treaty study required under the provision is due no later than June 30, 2005. The transfer pricing study required under the provision is due no later than June 30, 2005. The inversions study required under the provision is due no later than December 31, 2006.

B. Provisions Relating to Tax Shelters

1. Penalty for failure to disclose reportable transactions (sec. 811 of the Act and new sec. 6707A of the Code)

Present and Prior Law

Regulations under section 6011 require a taxpayer to disclose with its tax return certain information with respect to each "reportable transaction" in which the taxpayer participates.[630]

There are six categories of reportable transactions. The first category is any transaction that is the same as (or substantially similar to)[631] a transaction that is specified by the Treasury Department as a tax avoidance transaction whose tax benefits are subject to disallowance (referred to as a "listed transaction").[632]

The second category is any transaction that is offered under conditions of confidentiality. In general, a transaction is considered to be offered to a taxpayer under conditions of confidentiality if the advisor who is paid a minimum fee places a limitation on disclosure by the taxpayer of the tax treatment or tax structure of the transaction and the limitation on disclosure protects the confidentiality of that advisor's tax strategies (irrespective of whether terms are legally binding).[633]

The third category of reportable transactions is any transaction for which (1) the taxpayer has the right to a full or partial refund of fees if the intended tax consequences from the transaction are not sustained or, (2) the fees are contingent on the intended tax consequences from the transaction being sustained.[634]

The fourth category of reportable transactions relates to any transaction resulting in a taxpayer claiming a loss (under section 165) of at least (1) $10 million in any single year or $20 million in any combination of years by a corporate taxpayer or a partnership with only corporate partners; (2) $2 million in any single year or $4 million in any combination of years by all other partnerships, S corporations, trusts, and individuals; or (3) $50,000 in any single

---

[630] On February 27, 2003, the Treasury Department and the IRS released final regulations regarding the disclosure of reportable transactions. In general, the regulations are effective for transactions entered into on or after February 28, 2003.

The discussion of present and prior law refers to the final regulations. The rules that apply with respect to transactions entered into on or before February 28, 2003, are contained in Treas. Reg. sec. 1.6011–4T in effect on the date the transaction was entered into.

[631] The regulations clarify that the term "substantially similar" includes any transaction that is expected to obtain the same or similar types of tax consequences and that is either factually similar or based on the same or similar tax strategy. Further, the term must be broadly construed in favor of disclosure. Treas. Reg. sec. 1.6011–4(c)(4).

[632] Treas. Reg. sec. 1.6011–4(b)(2).

[633] Treas. Reg. sec. 1.6011–4(b)(3).

[634] Treas. Reg. sec. 1.6011–4(b)(4). Rev. Proc. 2004–65, 2004–50 I.R.B. 965, exempts certain types of transactions from this reportable transaction category.

year for individuals or trusts if the loss arises with respect to foreign currency transaction losses.[635]

The fifth category of reportable transactions refers to any transaction done by certain taxpayers[636] in which the tax treatment of the transaction differs (or is expected to differ) by more than $10 million from its treatment for book purposes (using generally accepted accounting principles) in any year.[637]

The final category of reportable transactions is any transaction that results in a tax credit exceeding $250,000 (including a foreign tax credit) if the taxpayer holds the underlying asset for less than 45 days.[638]

Under prior law, there was no specific penalty for failing to disclose a reportable transaction; however, such a failure could jeopardize a taxpayer's ability to claim that any income tax understatement attributable to such undisclosed transaction is due to reasonable cause, and that the taxpayer acted in good faith.[639]

Reasons for Change

The Congress believed that the best way to combat tax shelters is to be aware of them. The Treasury Department, using the tools available, issued regulations requiring disclosure of certain transactions and requiring organizers and promoters of tax-engineered transactions to maintain customer lists and make these lists available to the IRS. Nevertheless, the Congress believed that legislation was needed to provide the Treasury Department with additional tools to assist its efforts to curtail abusive transactions. Moreover, the Congress believed that a penalty for failing to make the required disclosures, when the imposition of such penalty is not dependent on the tax treatment of the underlying transaction ultimately being sustained, would provide an additional incentive for taxpayers to satisfy their reporting obligations under the new disclosure provisions.

Explanation of Provision

In general

The Act creates a new penalty for any person who fails to include with any return or statement any required information with respect to a reportable transaction. The new penalty applies without

[635] Treas. Reg. sec. 1.6011–4(b)(5). Rev. Proc. 2004–66, 2004–50 I.R.B. 966, modifying and superseding Rev. Proc. 2003–24, 2003–11 I.R.B. 599, exempts certain types of losses from this reportable transaction category.

[636] The significant book-tax category applies only to taxpayers that are reporting companies under the Securities Exchange Act of 1934 or business entities that have $250 million or more in gross assets. Rev. Proc. 2004–45, 2004–31 I.R.B. 140, provides alternative disclosure procedures for certain taxpayers with respect to this reportable transaction category.

[637] Treas. Reg. sec. 1.6011–4(b)(6). Rev. Proc. 2004–67, 2004–50 I.R.B. 967, modifying and superseding Rev. Proc. 2003–25, 2003–11 I.R.B. 601, exempts certain types of transactions from this reportable transaction category.

[638] Treas. Reg. sec. 1.6011–4(b)(7). Rev. Proc. 2004–68, 2004–50 I.R.B. 969, modifying and superseding 2003–11 I.R.B. 601, exempts certain types of transactions from this reportable transaction category.

[639] Section 6664(c) provides that a taxpayer can avoid the imposition of a section 6662 accuracy-related penalty in cases where the taxpayer can demonstrate that there was reasonable cause for the underpayment and that the taxpayer acted in good faith. Regulations under sections 6662 and 6664 provide that a taxpayer's failure to disclose a reportable transaction is a strong indication that the taxpayer failed to act in good faith, which would bar relief under section 6664(c). Treas. Reg. sec. 1.6664–4(d).

regard to whether the transaction ultimately results in an understatement of tax, and applies in addition to any accuracy-related penalty that may be imposed.

Transactions to be disclosed

The Act does not define the terms "listed transaction"[640] or "reportable transaction," nor does it explain the type of information that must be disclosed in order to avoid the imposition of a penalty. Rather, the Act authorizes the Treasury Department to define a "listed transaction" and a "reportable transaction" under section 6011.

Penalty rate

The penalty for failing to disclose a reportable transaction is $10,000 in the case of a natural person and $50,000 in any other case. The amount is increased to $100,000 and $200,000, respectively, if the failure is with respect to a listed transaction. The penalty cannot be waived with respect to a listed transaction. As to reportable transactions, the IRS Commissioner or his delegate can rescind (or abate) the penalty only if rescinding the penalty would promote compliance with the tax laws and effective tax administration.[641] The decision to rescind a penalty must be accompanied by a record describing the facts and reasons for the action and the amount rescinded. There will be no taxpayer right to judicially appeal a refusal to rescind a penalty.[642] The IRS also is required to submit an annual report to Congress summarizing the application of the disclosure penalties and providing a description of each penalty rescinded under this provision and the reasons for the rescission.

In addition, the Act provides that a public entity that is required to pay a penalty for failing to disclose a listed transaction (or is subject to an understatement penalty attributable to a non-disclosed listed transaction or a non-disclosed reportable avoidance transaction) must disclose the imposition of the penalty in reports to the Securities and Exchange Commission for such period as the Secretary shall specify. This requirement applies without regard to whether the taxpayer determines the amount of the penalty to be material to the reports in which the penalty must appear, and treats any failure to disclose a transaction in such reports as a failure to disclose a listed transaction. A taxpayer must disclose a penalty in reports to the Securities and Exchange Commission once the taxpayer has exhausted its administrative and judicial rem-

[640] The Act provides that, except as provided in regulations, a listed transaction means a reportable transaction, which is the same as, or substantially similar to, a transaction specifically identified by the Secretary as a tax avoidance transaction for purposes of section 6011. For this purpose, it is expected that the definition of "substantially similar" will be the definition used in Treas. Reg. sec. 1.6011–4(c)(4). However, the Secretary may modify this definition (as well as the definitions of "listed transaction" and "reportable transactions") as appropriate.

[641] In determining whether to rescind (or abate) the penalty for failing to disclose a reportable transaction on the grounds that doing so would promote compliance with the tax laws and effective tax administration, it is intended that the IRS Commissioner take into account whether: (1) the person on whom the penalty is imposed has a history of complying with the tax laws; (2) the violation is due to an unintentional mistake of fact; and (3) imposing the penalty would be against equity and good conscience.

[642] This does not limit the ability of a taxpayer to challenge whether a penalty is appropriate (e.g., a taxpayer may litigate the issue of whether a transaction is a reportable transaction (and thus subject to the penalty if not disclosed) or not a reportable transaction (and thus not subject to the penalty)).

edies with respect to the penalty (or if earlier, when paid). However, the taxpayer is only required to report the penalty one time. The Act further provides that this requirement also applies to a public entity that is subject to a gross valuation misstatement penalty under section 6662(h) attributable to a non-disclosed listed transaction or non-disclosed reportable avoidance transaction.

Effective Date

The provision is effective for returns and statements the due date for which is after the date of enactment (October 22, 2004).[643]

2. Modifications to the accuracy-related penalties for listed transactions and reportable transactions having a significant tax avoidance purpose (sec. 812 of the Act and new sec. 6662A of the Code)

Present and Prior Law

A 20-percent accuracy-related penalty applies to the portion of any underpayment that is attributable to: (1) negligence; (2) any substantial understatement of income tax; (3) any substantial valuation misstatement; (4) any substantial overstatement of pension liabilities; or (5) any substantial estate or gift tax valuation understatement.[644] The amount of any understatement generally is reduced by any portion attributable to an item if: (1) the treatment of the item is or was supported by substantial authority, or (2) facts relevant to the tax treatment of the item were adequately disclosed and there was a reasonable basis for its tax treatment.[645]

Special rules apply with respect to tax shelters.[646] For understatements by non-corporate taxpayers attributable to tax shelters, prior law provided that the accuracy-related penalty could be avoided only if the taxpayer established that, in addition to having substantial authority for the position, the taxpayer reasonably believed that the treatment claimed was more likely than not the proper treatment of the item. Under present and prior law, this reduction in the penalty is unavailable to corporate tax shelters.

The understatement penalty generally is abated (even with respect to tax shelters) in cases in which the taxpayer can demonstrate that there was "reasonable cause" for the underpayment and that the taxpayer acted in good faith.[647] The relevant regulations provide that reasonable cause exists where the taxpayer "reasonably relies in good faith on an opinion based on a professional tax advisor's analysis of the pertinent facts and authorities [that] . . . unambiguously concludes that there is a greater than 50-per-

[643] It is intended that the provision be effective for returns and statements the original or extended due date for which is after the date of enactment, as well as delinquent returns and statements the original or extended due date for which is before the date of enactment but that are filed after the date of enactment. A technical correction may be necessary so that the statute reflects this intent.

[644] Sec. 6662(a) and (b). As amended by section 819 of the Act, a "substantial understatement" for non-corporate taxpayers exists if the amount of the understatement for the taxable year exceeds the greater of 10 percent of the correct tax or $5,000 ($10,000 in the case of most corporations), while a substantial understatement for corporate taxpayers exists if the amount of the understatement for the taxable year exceeds the lesser of 10 percent of the correct tax (or, if greater, $10,000) or $10 million. Sec. 6662(d)(1).

[645] Sec. 6662(d)(2)(B).

[646] Sec. 6662(d)(2)(C).

[647] Sec. 6664(c).

cent likelihood that the tax treatment of the item will be upheld if challenged" by the IRS.[648]

Reasons for Change

Disclosure is vital to combating abusive tax avoidance transactions, and the shelter initiatives undertaken by the Treasury Department emphasize combating abusive tax avoidance transactions by requiring increased disclosure of such transactions by all parties involved. Therefore, the Congress believed that taxpayers should be subject to a strict liability penalty on an understatement of tax that is attributable to non-disclosed listed transactions or non-disclosed reportable transactions that have a significant purpose of tax avoidance. Furthermore, in order to deter taxpayers from entering into tax avoidance transactions, the Congress believe that a more meaningful (but not a strict liability) accuracy-related penalty should apply to such transactions even when disclosed.

Explanation of Provision

In general

In general

The Act augments the present-law accuracy related penalty with a new accuracy-related penalty that applies to listed transactions and reportable transactions with a significant tax avoidance purpose (hereinafter referred to as a "reportable avoidance transaction").[649] The penalty rate and defenses available to avoid the penalty vary depending on whether the transaction was adequately disclosed.

Disclosed transactions

In general, a 20-percent accuracy-related penalty is imposed on any understatement attributable to an adequately disclosed listed transaction or reportable avoidance transaction. The only exception to the penalty is if the taxpayer satisfies a more stringent reasonable cause and good faith exception (hereinafter referred to as the "strengthened reasonable cause exception"), which is described below. The strengthened reasonable cause exception is available only if the relevant facts affecting the tax treatment are adequately disclosed, there is or was substantial authority for the claimed tax treatment, and the taxpayer reasonably believed that the claimed tax treatment was more likely than not the proper treatment.

Undisclosed transactions

If the taxpayer does not adequately disclose the transaction, the strengthened reasonable cause exception is not available (i.e., a strict-liability penalty applies), and the taxpayer is subject to an increased penalty equal to 30 percent of the understatement.

---

[648] Treas. Reg. sec. 1.6662–4(g)(4)(i)(B); Treas. Reg. sec. 1.6664–4(c).

[649] The terms "reportable transaction" and "listed transaction" have the same meanings as used for purposes of the penalty under new section 6707A for failing to disclose reportable transactions.

Determination of the understatement amount

The penalty is applied to the amount of any understatement attributable to the listed or reportable avoidance transaction without regard to other items on the tax return. For purposes of this provision, the amount of the understatement is determined as the sum of (1) the product of the highest corporate or individual tax rate (as appropriate) and the increase in taxable income resulting from the difference between the taxpayer's treatment of the item and the proper treatment of the item (without regard to other items on the tax return),[650] and (2) the amount of any decrease in the aggregate amount of credits which results from a difference between the taxpayer's treatment of an item and the proper tax treatment of such item.

Except as provided in regulations, a taxpayer's treatment of an item shall not take into account any amendment or supplement to a return if the amendment or supplement is filed after the earlier of when the taxpayer is first contacted regarding an examination of the return or such other date as specified by the Secretary.

Strengthened reasonable cause exception

In general

A penalty is not imposed under the Act with respect to any portion of an understatement if it shown that there was reasonable cause for such portion and the taxpayer acted in good faith. Such a showing requires (1) adequate disclosure of the facts affecting the transaction in accordance with the regulations under section 6011,[651] (2) that there is or was substantial authority for such treatment, and (3) that the taxpayer reasonably believed that such treatment was more likely than not the proper treatment. For this purpose, a taxpayer will be treated as having a reasonable belief with respect to the tax treatment of an item only if such belief (1) is based on the facts and law that exist at the time the tax return (that includes the item) is filed, and (2) relates solely to the taxpayer's chances of success on the merits and does not take into account the possibility that (a) a return will not be audited, (b) the treatment will not be raised on audit, or (c) the treatment will be resolved through settlement if raised.

A taxpayer may (but is not required to) rely on an opinion of a tax advisor in establishing its reasonable belief with respect to the tax treatment of the item. However, a taxpayer may not rely on an opinion of a tax advisor for this purpose if the opinion (1) is provided by a "disqualified tax advisor," or (2) is a "disqualified opinion."

---

[650] For this purpose, any reduction in the excess of deductions allowed for the taxable year over gross income for such year, and any reduction in the amount of capital losses which would (without regard to section 1211) be allowed for such year, shall be treated as an increase in taxable income.

[651] See the previous discussion regarding the penalty under new section 6707A for failing to disclose a reportable transaction.

Disqualified tax advisor

A disqualified tax advisor is any advisor who (1) is a material advisor[652] and who participates in the organization, management, promotion or sale of the transaction or is related (within the meaning of section 267(b) or 707(b)(1)) to any person who so participates, (2) is compensated directly or indirectly[653] by a material advisor with respect to the transaction, (3) has a fee arrangement with respect to the transaction that is contingent on all or part of the intended tax benefits from the transaction being sustained, or (4) as determined under regulations prescribed by the Secretary, has a disqualifying financial interest with respect to the transaction.

Organization, management, promotion or sale of a transaction.— A material advisor is considered as participating in the "organization" of a transaction if the advisor performs acts relating to the development of the transaction. This may include, for example, preparing documents (1) establishing a structure used in connection with the transaction (such as a partnership agreement), (2) describing the transaction (such as an offering memorandum or other statement describing the transaction), or (3) relating to the registration of the transaction with any Federal, State or local government body.[654] Participation in the "management" of a transaction means involvement in the decision-making process regarding any business activity with respect to the transaction. Participation in the "promotion or sale" of a transaction means involvement in the marketing or solicitation of the transaction to others. Thus, an advisor who provides information about the transaction to a potential participant is involved in the promotion or sale of a transaction, as is any advisor who recommends the transaction to a potential participant.

Disqualified opinion

An opinion may not be relied upon if the opinion: (1) is based on unreasonable factual or legal assumptions (including assumptions as to future events); (2) unreasonably relies upon representations, statements, finding or agreements of the taxpayer or any other person; (3) does not identify and consider all relevant facts; or (4) fails to meet any other requirement prescribed by the Secretary.

---

[652] Under the Act, the term "material advisor" (defined below in connection with the new information filing requirements for material advisors) means any person who provides any material aid, assistance, or advice with respect to organizing, managing, promoting, selling, implementing, insuring, or carrying out any reportable transaction, and who derives gross income in excess of $50,000 in the case of a reportable transaction substantially all of the tax benefits from which are provided to natural persons ($250,000 in any other case).

[653] This situation could arise, for example, when an advisor has an arrangement or understanding (oral or written) with an organizer, manager, or promoter of a reportable transaction that such party will recommend or refer potential participants to the advisor for an opinion regarding the tax treatment of the transaction.

[654] An advisor should not be treated as participating in the organization of a transaction if the advisor's only involvement with respect to the organization of the transaction is the rendering of an opinion regarding the tax consequences of such transaction. However, such an advisor may be a "disqualified tax advisor" with respect to the transaction if the advisor participates in the management, promotion or sale of the transaction (or if the advisor is compensated by a material advisor, has a fee arrangement that is contingent on the tax benefits of the transaction, or as determined by the Secretary, has a disqualifying financial interest with respect to the transaction).

Coordination with other penalties

Any portion of an underpayment upon which a penalty is imposed under the Act is not subject to the penalties under section 6662 for substantial understatements of income tax or, in general, substantial valuation misstatements.[655] However, the understatement to which such portion is attributable is included for purposes of determining whether an understatement (as defined in sec. 6662(d)(2)) is a substantial understatement (as defined under section 6662(d)(1)) subject to the penalty under section 6662 for substantial understatements of income tax.

Any portion of an underpayment attributable to a substantial valuation misstatement upon which a penalty under section 6662 is imposed is not subject to the penalty under the Act if the penalty amount is increased under section 6662(h) because the substantial valuation misstatement is determined to be a gross valuation misstatement.

The penalty imposed under the Act shall not apply to any portion of an underpayment to which a fraud penalty is applied under section 6663.

Effective Date

The provision is effective for taxable years ending after the date of enactment (October 22, 2004).[656]

3. Tax shelter exception to confidentiality privileges relating to taxpayer communications (sec. 813 of the Act and sec. 7525 of the Code)

Present and Prior Law

In general, a common law privilege of confidentiality exists for communications between an attorney and client with respect to the legal advice the attorney gives the client. The Code provides that, with respect to tax advice, the same common law protections of confidentiality that apply to a communication between a taxpayer and an attorney also apply to a communication between a taxpayer and a federally authorized tax practitioner to the extent the communication would be considered a privileged communication if it were between a taxpayer and an attorney. This rule is inapplicable to communications regarding corporate tax shelters.

Reasons for Change

The Congress believed that the rule previously applicable only to corporate tax shelters should be applied to all tax shelters, regardless of whether or not the participant is a corporation.

---

[655] With regard to the section 6662 penalties for underpayments attributable to negligence, substantial overstatement of pension liabilities or substantial estate or gift tax valuation understatements, a technical correction may be necessary to more clearly reflect the intent that such penalties are not to be imposed upon the portion of any underpayment upon which a penalty is imposed under the Act.

[656] It is not intended that the provision relating to disqualified opinions apply generally on a retroactive basis. Therefore, a technical correction may be necessary to clarify that this provision does not apply to opinions provided to taxpayers before the date of enactment with respect to transactions that were entered into before the date of enactment and at least a portion of the tax consequences of which were reported on a return or statement that was filed before the date of enactment.

Explanation of Provision

The Act modifies the rule relating to corporate tax shelters by making it applicable to all tax shelters, whether entered into by corporations, individuals, partnerships, tax-exempt entities, or any other entity. Accordingly, communications with respect to tax shelters are not subject to the confidentiality provision of the Code that otherwise applies to a communication between a taxpayer and a federally authorized tax practitioner.

Effective Date

The provision is effective with respect to communications made on or after the date of enactment (October 22, 2004).

4. Statute of limitations for unreported listed transactions (sec. 814 of the Act and sec. 6501 of the Code)

Present and Prior Law

In general, the Code requires that taxes be assessed within three years[657] after the date a return is filed.[658] If there has been a substantial omission of items of gross income that totals more than 25 percent of the amount of gross income shown on the return, the period during which an assessment must be made is extended to six years.[659] If an assessment is not made within the required time periods, the tax generally cannot be assessed or collected at any future time. Tax may be assessed at any time if the taxpayer files a false or fraudulent return with the intent to evade tax or if the taxpayer does not file a tax return at all.[660]

Reasons for Change

The Congress observed that some taxpayers and their advisors have been employing dilatory tactics and failing to cooperate with the IRS in an attempt to avoid liability through the expiration of the statute of limitations. The Congress accordingly believed that it was appropriate to extend the statute of limitations for unreported listed transactions, which will encourage taxpayers to provide the required disclosure and will afford the IRS additional time to discover the transaction if the taxpayer does not disclose it.

Explanation of Provision

The Act extends the statute of limitations with respect to a listed transaction if a taxpayer fails to include on any return or statement for any taxable year any information with respect to a listed transaction[661] which is required to be included (under section 6011) with such return or statement. The statute of limitations with respect to such a transaction will not expire before the date which is one year after the earlier of: (1) the date on which the Sec-

[657] Sec. 6501(a).

[658] For this purpose, a return that is filed before the date on which it is due is considered to be filed on the required due date (sec. 6501(b)(1)).

[659] Sec. 6501(e).

[660] Sec. 6501(c).

[661] The term "listed transaction" has the same meaning as described in a previous provision regarding the penalty for failure to disclose reportable transactions.

retary is furnished the information so required; or (2) the date that a material advisor (as defined in 6111) satisfies the list maintenance requirements (as defined by section 6112) with respect to a request by the Secretary.[662] For example, if a taxpayer engaged in a transaction in 2005 that becomes a listed transaction in 2007 and the taxpayer fails to disclose such transaction in the manner required by Treasury regulations, then the transaction is subject to the extended statute of limitations.[663]

Effective Date

The provision is effective for taxable years with respect to which the period for assessing a deficiency did not expire before the date of enactment (October 22, 2004).

5. Disclosure of reportable transactions by material advisors (secs. 815 and 816 of the Act and secs. 6111 and 6707 of the Code)

Present and Prior Law

Registration of tax shelter arrangements

Under prior law, an organizer of a tax shelter was required to register the shelter with the Secretary not later than the day on which the shelter was first offered for sale.[664] A "tax shelter" was defined as any investment with respect to which the tax shelter ratio[665] for any investor as of the close of any of the first five years ending after the investment was offered for sale may be greater than two to one and which was: (1) required to be registered under Federal or State securities laws; (2) sold pursuant to an exemption from registration requiring the filing of a notice with a Federal or State securities agency; or (3) a substantial investment (greater than $250,000 and involving at least five investors).[666]

Other promoted arrangements were treated as tax shelters for purposes of the prior-law registration requirement if: (1) a significant purpose of the arrangement was the avoidance or evasion of Federal income tax by a corporate participant; (2) the arrangement

[662] It is intended that the term "material advisor" for this purpose includes either a material advisor as defined in section 6111(b)(1) or, in the case of material aid, assistance, or advice rendered on or before the date of enactment, a material advisor as defined in Treasury regulations under section 6112. See Treas. Reg. sec. 301.6112–1(c)(2). It also is intended that the date on which a material advisor satisfies the list maintenance requirements for this purpose applies to both (1) material advisors with respect to reportable transactions under present-law section 6112, (2) and organizers and sellers of potentially abusive tax shelters under prior-law section 6112. Technical corrections may be necessary so that the statute reflects this intent.

[663] If the Treasury Department lists a transaction in a year subsequent to the year in which a taxpayer entered into such transaction and the taxpayer's tax return for the year the transaction was entered into is closed by the statute of limitations prior to the date the transaction became a listed transaction, this provision does not re-open the statute of limitations with respect to such transaction for such year. However, if the purported tax benefits of the transaction are recognized over multiple tax years, the provision's extension of the statute of limitations shall apply to such tax benefits in any subsequent tax year in which the statute of limitations had not closed prior to the date the transaction became a listed transaction.

[664] Sec. 6111(a).

[665] The tax shelter ratio was, with respect to any year, the ratio that the aggregate amount of the deductions and 350 percent of the credits, which were represented to be potentially allowable to any investor, bears to the investment base (money plus basis of assets contributed) as of the close of the tax year.

[666] Sec. 6111(c).

was offered under conditions of confidentiality; and (3) the promoter may receive fees in excess of $100,000 in the aggregate.[667]

In general, a transaction had a "significant purpose of avoiding or evading Federal income tax" under prior law if the transaction: (1) was the same as or substantially similar to a "listed transaction,"[668] or (2) was structured to produce tax benefits that constituted an important part of the intended results of the arrangement and the promoter reasonably expected to present the arrangement to more than one taxpayer.[669] Certain exceptions were provided with respect to the second category of transactions.[670]

An arrangement was treated as offered under conditions of confidentiality if: (1) an offeree had an understanding or agreement to limit the disclosure of the transaction or any significant tax features of the transaction; or (2) the promoter knew, or had reason to know, that the offeree's use or disclosure of information relating to the transaction was limited in any other manner.[671]

Failure to register tax shelter

Under prior law, the penalty for failing to timely register a tax shelter (or for filing false or incomplete information with respect to the tax shelter registration) generally was the greater of one percent of the aggregate amount invested in the shelter or $500.[672] However, if the tax shelter involved an arrangement offered to a corporation under conditions of confidentiality, the penalty was the greater of $10,000 or 50 percent of the fees payable to any promoter with respect to offerings prior to the date of late registration. Intentional disregard of the requirement to register increased the penalty to 75 percent of the applicable fees.

Prior-law section 6707 also imposed (1) a $100 penalty on the promoter for each failure to furnish the investor with the required tax shelter identification number, and (2) a $250 penalty on the investor for each failure to include the tax shelter identification number on a return.

Reasons for Change

The Congress understood that the prior-law promoter registration rules were not proving particularly helpful, primarily because the rules were not appropriate for the kinds of abusive transactions now prevalent, and because the limitations regarding confidential corporate arrangements had proven easy to circumvent.

The Congress believed that providing a single, clear definition regarding the types of transactions that must be disclosed by taxpayers and material advisors, coupled with more meaningful penalties for failing to disclose such transactions, are necessary tools

---

[667] Sec. 6111(d).

[668] Treas. Reg. sec. 301.6111–2(b)(2).

[669] Treas. Reg. sec. 301.6111–2(b)(3).

[670] Treas. Reg. sec. 301.6111–2(b)(4).

[671] The regulations provide that the determination of whether an arrangement is offered under conditions of confidentiality is based on all the facts and circumstances surrounding the offer. If an offeree's disclosure of the structure or tax aspects of the transaction is limited in any way by an express or implied understanding or agreement with or for the benefit of a tax shelter promoter, an offer is considered made under conditions of confidentiality, whether or not such understanding or agreement is legally binding. Treas. Reg. sec. 301.6111–2(c)(1).

[672] Sec. 6707.

if the effort to curb the use of abusive tax avoidance transactions is to be effective.

Explanation of Provision[673]

Disclosure of reportable transactions by material advisors

The Act repeals the present law rules with respect to registration of tax shelters. Instead, the Act requires each material advisor with respect to any reportable transaction (including any listed transaction)[674] to timely file an information return with the Secretary (in such form and manner as the Secretary may prescribe). The return must be filed on such date as specified by the Secretary.

The information return will include: (1) information identifying and describing the transaction; (2) information describing any potential tax benefits expected to result from the transaction; and (3) such other information as the Secretary may prescribe. It is expected that the Secretary may seek from the material advisor the same type of information that the Secretary may request from a taxpayer in connection with a reportable transaction.[675]

A "material advisor" means any person: (1) who provides material aid, assistance, or advice with respect to organizing, managing, promoting, selling, implementing, insuring, or carrying out any reportable transaction; and (2) who directly or indirectly derives gross income for such aid, assistance or advice in excess of $250,000 ($50,000 in the case of a reportable transaction substantially all of the tax benefits from which are provided to natural persons) or such other amount as may be prescribed by the Secretary.

The Secretary may prescribe regulations which provide (1) that only one material advisor has to file an information return in cases in which two or more material advisors would otherwise be required to file information returns with respect to a particular reportable transaction, (2) exemptions from the requirements of this section, and (3) other rules as may be necessary or appropriate to carry out the purposes of this section (including, for example, rules regarding the aggregation of fees in appropriate circumstances).

Penalty for failing to furnish information regarding reportable transactions

The Act repeals the present-law penalty for failure to register tax shelters. Instead, the Act imposes a penalty on any material advisor who fails to file an information return, or who files a false or incomplete information return, with respect to a reportable transaction (including a listed transaction).[676] The amount of the penalty is $50,000. If the penalty is with respect to a listed transaction, the amount of the penalty is increased to the greater of (1) $200,000, or (2) 50 percent of the gross income of such person with respect to aid, assistance, or advice which is provided with respect

[673] Notice 2004–80, 2004–50 I.R.B. 963, Notice 2005–17, 2005–8 I.R.B. 1, and Notice 2005–22, 2005–12 IRB 756 provide interim guidance concerning the application of this provision.

[674] The terms "reportable transaction" and "listed transaction" have the same meaning as previously described in connection with the taxpayer-related provisions.

[675] See the previous discussion regarding the disclosure requirements under new section 6707A.

[676] The terms "reportable transaction" and "listed transaction" have the same meaning as previously described in connection with the taxpayer-related provisions.

to the transaction before the date the information return that includes the transaction is filed. Intentional disregard by a material advisor of the requirement to disclose a listed transaction increases the penalty to 75 percent of the gross income.

The penalty cannot be waived with respect to a listed transaction. As to reportable transactions, the penalty can be rescinded (or abated) only in exceptional circumstances.[677] All or part of the penalty may be rescinded only if rescinding the penalty would promote compliance with the tax laws and effective tax administration. The decision to rescind a penalty must be accompanied by a record describing the facts and reasons for the action and the amount rescinded. There will be no right to judicially appeal a refusal to rescind a penalty. The IRS also is required to submit an annual report to Congress summarizing the application of the disclosure penalties and providing a description of each penalty rescinded under this provision and the reasons for the rescission.

Effective Date

The provision requiring disclosure of reportable transactions by material advisors applies to transactions with respect to which material aid, assistance or advice is provided after the date of enactment (October 22, 2004).

The provision imposing a penalty for failing to disclose reportable transactions applies to returns the due date for which is after the date of enactment (October 22, 2004).

6. Investor lists and modification of penalty for failure to maintain investor lists (secs. 815 and 817 of the Act and secs. 6112 and 6708 of the Code)

Present and Prior Law

Investor lists

Under prior law, any organizer or seller of a potentially abusive tax shelter was required to maintain a list identifying each person who was sold an interest in any such tax shelter with respect to which registration was required under section 6111 (even though the particular party may not have been subject to confidentiality restrictions).[678] Recently issued regulations under section 6112 contain rules regarding the list maintenance requirements.[679] In general, the regulations apply to transactions that are potentially abusive tax shelters entered into, or acquired after, February 28, 2003.[680]

The regulations provide that a person is an organizer or seller of a potentially abusive tax shelter if the person is a material advisor with respect to that transaction.[681] A material advisor is defined as any person who is required to register the transaction

[677] The Secretary's present-law authority to postpone certain tax-related deadlines because of Presidentially-declared disasters (sec. 7508A) will also encompass the authority to postpone the reporting deadlines established by the provision.

[678] Sec. 6112.

[679] Treas. Reg. sec. 301.6112–1.

[680] A special rule applies the list maintenance requirements to transactions entered into after February 28, 2000 if the transaction becomes a listed transaction (as defined in Treas. Reg. 1.6011–4) after February 28, 2003.

[681] Treas. Reg. sec. 301.6112–1(c)(1).

under section 6111, or expects to receive a minimum fee of (1) $250,000 for a transaction that is a potentially abusive tax shelter if all participants are corporations, or (2) $50,000 for any other transaction that is a potentially abusive tax shelter.[682] For listed transactions (as defined in the regulations under section 6011), the minimum fees are reduced to $25,000 and $10,000, respectively.

A potentially abusive tax shelter is any transaction that (1) is required to be registered under section 6111, (2) is a listed transaction (as defined under the regulations under section 6011), or (3) any transaction that a potential material advisor, at the time the transaction is entered into, knows is or reasonably expects will become a reportable transaction (as defined under the new regulations under section 6011).[683]

Under prior law, the Secretary was required to prescribe regulations which provide that, in cases in which two or more persons are required to maintain the same list, only one person would be required to maintain the list.[684]

Penalty for failing to maintain investor lists

Under prior law, the penalty for failing to maintain the list required under prior law section 6112 was $50 for each name omitted from the list (with a maximum penalty of $100,000 per year).[685]

Reasons for Change

The Congress had been advised that the prior-law penalties for failure to maintain customer lists were not meaningful and that promoters often have refused to provide requested information to the IRS. The Congress believed that requiring material advisors to maintain a list of advisees with respect to each reportable transaction, coupled with more meaningful penalties for failing to maintain an investor list, are important tools in the ongoing efforts to curb the use of abusive tax avoidance transactions.

Explanation of Provision [686]

Investor lists

Each material advisor[687] with respect to a reportable transaction (including a listed transaction)[688] is required to maintain a list that (1) identifies each person with respect to whom the advisor acted as a material advisor with respect to the reportable transaction, and (2) contains other information as may be required by the Secretary. In addition, the Act authorizes (but does not require) the Secretary to prescribe regulations which provide that, in cases in which two or more persons are required to maintain the same list, only one person would be required to maintain the list.

---

[682] Treas. Reg. sec. 301.6112–1(c)(2) and (3).

[683] Treas. Reg. sec. 301.6112–1(b).

[684] Sec. 6112(c)(2).

[685] Sec. 6708.

[686] Notice 2004–80, 2004–50 I.R.B. 963, provides interim guidance concerning the application of this provision.

[687] The term “material advisor” has the same meaning as when used in connection with the requirement to file an information return under section 6111, as amended by the Act.

[688] The terms “reportable transaction” and “listed transaction” have the same meaning as previously described in connection with the taxpayer-related provisions.

Penalty for failing to maintain investor lists

The Act modifies the penalty for failing to maintain the required list by making it a time-sensitive penalty.[689] Thus, a material advisor who is required to maintain an investor list and who fails to make the list available upon written request by the Secretary within 20 business days after the request will be subject to a $10,000 per day penalty. The penalty applies to a person who fails to maintain a list, maintains an incomplete list, or has in fact maintained a list but does not make the list available to the Secretary. The penalty can be waived if the failure to make the list available is due to reasonable cause.[690]

Effective Date

The provision requiring a material advisor to maintain an investor list applies to transactions with respect to which material aid, assistance or advice is provided after the date of enactment (October 22, 2004). The provision imposing a penalty for failing to maintain investor lists applies to requests made after the date of enactment (October 22, 2004).

7. Penalty on promoters of tax shelters (sec. 818 of the Act and sec. 6700 of the Code)

Present and Prior Law

A penalty is imposed on any person who organizes, assists in the organization of, or participates in the sale of any interest in, a partnership or other entity, any investment plan or arrangement, or any other plan or arrangement, if in connection with such activity the person makes or furnishes a qualifying false or fraudulent statement or a gross valuation overstatement.[691] A qualified false or fraudulent statement is any statement with respect to the allowability of any deduction or credit, the excludability of any income, or the securing of any other tax benefit by reason of holding an interest in the entity or participating in the plan or arrangement which the person knows or has reason to know is false or fraudulent as to any material matter. A "gross valuation overstatement" means any statement as to the value of any property or services if the stated value exceeds 200 percent of the correct valuation, and the value is directly related to the amount of any allowable income tax deduction or credit.

Under present and prior law, the amount of the penalty is $1,000 (or, if the person establishes that it is less, 100 percent of the gross income derived or to be derived by the person from such activity). A penalty attributable to a gross valuation misstatement can be waived on a showing that there was a reasonable basis for the valuation and it was made in good faith.

---

[689] It is intended that the modified penalty for failing to comply with the list maintenance requirements applies to both (1) material advisors with respect to reportable transactions under present-law section 6112, (2) and organizers and sellers of potentially abusive tax shelters under prior-law section 6112. A technical correction may be necessary so that the statute reflects this intent.

[690] In no event will failure to maintain a list be considered reasonable cause for failing to make a list available to the Secretary.

[691] Sec. 6700.

Reasons for Change

The Congress believed that the present-law $1,000 penalty for tax shelter promoters was insufficient to deter tax shelter activities. The Congress believed that the increased penalties for tax shelter promoters are meaningful and will help deter the promotion of tax shelters.

Explanation of Provision

The Act modifies the penalty amount to equal 50 percent of the gross income derived by the person from the activity for which the new penalty is imposed. The new penalty rate applies to any activity that involves a statement regarding the tax benefits of participating in a plan or arrangement if the person knows or has reason to know that such statement is false or fraudulent as to any material matter. The enhanced penalty does not apply to a gross valuation overstatement.

Effective Date

The provision is effective for activities occurring after the date of enactment (October 22, 2004).

8. Modifications of substantial understatement penalty for nonreportable transactions (sec. 819 of the Act and sec. 6662 of the Code)

Present and Prior Law

An accuracy-related penalty equal to 20 percent applies to any substantial understatement of tax. Under prior law, a "substantial understatement" for both corporate and noncorporate taxpayers existed if the correct income tax liability for a taxable year exceeded that reported by the taxpayer by the greater of 10 percent of the correct tax or $5,000 ($10,000 in the case of most corporations).[692]

The amount of any understatement generally is reduced by any portion attributable to an item if (1) the treatment of the item is or was supported by substantial authority, or (2) facts relevant to the tax treatment of the item were adequately disclosed and there was a reasonable basis for its tax treatment.[693] Under prior law, the Secretary was required to prescribe (and revise at least annually) a list of positions for which the Secretary believes there is not substantial authority and which affect a significant number of taxpayers. Such list was required to be published in the Federal Register.

Reasons for Change

The Congress believed that the prior-law definition of substantial understatement allowed large corporate taxpayers to avoid the accuracy-related penalty on questionable transactions of a significant size. The Congress believed that an understatement of more than $10 million is substantial in and of itself, regardless of the proportion it represents of the taxpayer's total tax liability.

---

[692] Sec. 6662(a) and (d)(1)(A).
[693] Sec. 6662(d)(2)(B).

Explanation of Provision

The Act modifies the definition of "substantial" for corporate taxpayers. Under the Act, a corporate taxpayer has a substantial understatement if the amount of the understatement for the taxable year exceeds the lesser of (1) 10 percent of the tax required to be shown on the return for the taxable year (or, if greater, $10,000), or (2) $10 million.

The Act also modifies the requirement of the Secretary to prescribe a list of positions that do not have substantial authority, and authorizes (but does not require) the Secretary to publish such list in either the Federal Register or the Internal Revenue Bulletin. The Act also authorizes (but does not require) the Secretary to publish (in either the Federal Register or Internal Revenue Bulletin) a list of positions that do not have a realistic possibility of being sustained on the merits for purposes of the income tax return preparer penalty under section 6694.

Effective Date

The provision is effective for taxable years beginning after date of enactment (October 22, 2004).

9. Modification of actions to enjoin certain conduct related to tax shelters and reportable transactions (sec. 820 of the Act and sec. 7408 of the Code)

Present and Prior Law

The Code authorizes civil actions to enjoin any person from promoting abusive tax shelters or aiding or abetting the understatement of tax liability.[694]

Reasons for Change

The Congress believed that expanding the authority to obtain injunctions against promoters and material advisors that (1) fail to file an information return with respect to a reportable transaction or (2) fail to maintain, or to timely furnish upon written request by the Secretary, a list of investors with respect to reportable transactions would discourage tax shelter activity and encourage compliance with the tax shelter disclosure requirements.

The Congress similarly believed that expanding the authority to obtain injunctions against violations of the rules under Circular 230 would encourage compliance with such rules.

Explanation of Provision

The Act expands this rule so that injunctions may also be sought with respect to the requirements relating to the reporting of reportable transactions[695] and the keeping of lists of investors by material advisors.[696] Thus, under the Act, an injunction may be sought against a material advisor to enjoin the advisor from (1) failing to file an information return with respect to a reportable transaction,

---

[694] Sec. 7408.
[695] Sec. 6707, as amended by other provisions of the Act.
[696] Sec. 6708, as amended by other provisions of the Act.

or (2) failing to maintain, or to timely furnish upon written request by the Secretary, a list of investors with respect to each reportable transaction.

The Act further expands this rule to permit injunctions to be sought with respect to violations of any of the rules under Circular 230, which regulates the practice of representatives of persons before the Department of the Treasury.

Effective Date

The provision is effective on the day after the date of enactment (October 22, 2004).

10. Penalty on failure to report interests in foreign financial accounts (sec. 821 of the Act and sec. 5321 of Title 31, United States Code)

Present and Prior Law

The Secretary must require citizens, residents, or persons doing business in the United States to keep records and file reports when that person makes a transaction or maintains an account with a foreign financial entity.[697] In general, individuals must fulfill this requirement by answering questions regarding foreign accounts or foreign trusts that are contained in Part III of Schedule B of the IRS Form 1040. Taxpayers who answer "yes" in response to the question regarding foreign accounts must then file Treasury Department Form TD F 90–22.1. This form must be filed with the Department of the Treasury, and not as part of the tax return that is filed with the IRS.

The Secretary may impose a civil penalty on any person who willfully violates this reporting requirement. Under prior law, the civil penalty was the amount of the transaction or the value of the account at the time of the violation, up to a maximum of $100,000; the minimum amount of the penalty was $25,000.[698] In addition, any person who willfully violates this reporting requirement is subject to a criminal penalty. The criminal penalty is a fine of not more than $250,000 or imprisonment for not more than five years (or both); if the violation is part of a pattern of illegal activity, the maximum amount of the fine is increased to $500,000 and the maximum length of imprisonment is increased to 10 years.[699]

On April 26, 2002, the Secretary submitted to the Congress a report on these reporting requirements.[700] This report, which was statutorily required,[701] studies methods for improving compliance with these reporting requirements. It makes several administrative recommendations, but no legislative recommendations. A further report was required to be submitted by the Secretary to the Congress by October 26, 2002.

---

[697] 31 U.S.C. sec. 5314.

[698] 31 U.S.C. sec. 5321(a)(5).

[699] 31 U.S.C. sec. 5322.

[700] *A Report to Congress in Accordance with Sec. 361(b) of the Uniting and Strengthening America by Providing Appropriate Tools Required to Intercept and Obstruct Terrorism Act of 2001,* April 26, 2002.

[701] Sec. 361(b) of the USA PATRIOT Act of 2001 (Pub. L. No. 107–56).

Reasons for Change

The Congress understood that the number of individuals using offshore bank accounts to engage in abusive tax scams has grown significantly in recent years. For one scheme alone, the IRS estimates that there may be hundreds of thousands of taxpayers with offshore bank accounts attempting to conceal income from the IRS. The Congress was concerned about this activity and believed that improving compliance with this reporting requirement is vitally important to sound tax administration, to combating terrorism, and to preventing the use of abusive tax schemes and scams. The Congress believed that increasing the prior-law penalty for willful noncompliance with this requirement and imposing a new civil penalty that applies without regard to willfulness in such noncompliance will improve the reporting of foreign financial accounts.

Explanation of Provision

The Act adds an additional civil penalty that may be imposed on any person who violates this reporting requirement (without regard to willfulness). This new civil penalty is up to $10,000. This penalty may be waived if any income from the account was properly reported on the person's income tax return and there was reasonable cause for the failure to report.

In addition, the Act increases the prior-law penalty for willful behavior to the greater of $100,000 or 50 percent of the amount of the transaction or account.

Effective Date

The provision is effective with respect to failures to report occurring on or after the date of enactment (October 22, 2004).

11. Regulation of individuals practicing before the Department of the Treasury (sec. 822 of the Act and sec. 330 of Title 31, United States Code)

Present and Prior Law

The Secretary is authorized to regulate the practice of representatives of persons before the Department of the Treasury.[702] The Secretary also is authorized to suspend or disbar from practice before the Department a representative who is incompetent, who is disreputable, who violates the rules regulating practice before the Department, or who (with intent to defraud) willfully and knowingly misleads or threatens the person being represented (or a person who may be represented). The rules promulgated by the Secretary pursuant to this provision are contained in Circular 230.[703]

---

[702] 31 U.S.C. sec. 330.

[703] On December 20, 2004, the Treasury Department and the IRS published proposed and final regulations amending Circular 230. 69 Fed. Reg. 75887; T.D. 9165, 69 Fed. Reg. 75839. The final regulations do not reflect amendments made by the Act, although the preamble to the final regulations states that the Treasury Department and the IRS expect to propose additional regulations implementing the provisions of the Act.

Reasons for Change

The Congress believed that it was critical that the Secretary have the authority to censure tax advisors as well as to impose monetary sanctions against tax advisors because of the important role of tax advisors in our tax system. Use of these sanctions is expected to curb the participation of tax advisors in both tax shelter activity and any other activity that is contrary to Circular 230 standards.

Explanation of Provision

The Act makes two modifications to expand the sanctions that the Secretary may impose pursuant to these statutory provisions. First, the Act expressly permits censure as a sanction. Second, the Act permits the imposition of a monetary penalty as a sanction. If the representative is acting on behalf of an employer or other entity, the Secretary may impose a monetary penalty on the employer or other entity if it knew, or reasonably should have known, of the conduct. This monetary penalty on the employer or other entity may be imposed in addition to any monetary penalty imposed directly on the representative. These monetary penalties are not to exceed the gross income derived (or to be derived) from the conduct giving rise to the penalty. These monetary penalties may be in addition to, or in lieu of, any suspension, disbarment, or censure of such individual.

The Act also confirms the authority of the Secretary to impose standards applicable to written advice with respect to an entity, transaction, plan, or arrangement that is of a type that the Secretary determines as having a potential for tax avoidance or evasion.

Effective Date

The modifications to expand the sanctions that the Secretary may impose are effective for actions taken after the date of enactment (October 22, 2004).

12. Treatment of stripped bonds to apply to stripped interests in bond and preferred stock funds (sec. 831 of the Act and secs. 305 and 1286 of the Code)

Present and Prior Law

Assignment of income in general

In general, an "income stripping" transaction involves a transaction in which the right to receive future income from income-producing property is separated from the property itself. In such transactions, it may be possible to generate artificial losses from the disposition of certain property or to defer the recognition of taxable income associated with such property.

Common law has developed a rule (referred to as the "assignment of income" doctrine) whereby if the right to receive income is transferred without an accompanying transfer of the underlying property, the transfer is not respected. A leading judicial decision relating to the assignment of income doctrine involved a case in which a taxpayer made a gift of detachable interest coupons before their due date while retaining the bearer bond. The U.S. Supreme Court ruled that the donor was taxable on the entire amount of interest when paid to the donee on the grounds that the transferor had "assigned" to the donee the right to receive the income.[704]

In addition to general common law assignment of income principles, specific statutory rules have been enacted to address certain specific types of stripping transactions, such as transactions involving stripped bonds and stripped preferred stock (which are discussed below).[705] Under prior law, however, there were no specific statutory rules that addressed stripping transactions with respect to common stock or other equity interests (other than preferred stock).[706]

Stripped bonds

Special rules are provided with respect to the purchaser and "stripper" of stripped bonds.[707] A "stripped bond" is defined as a debt instrument in which there has been a separation in ownership between the underlying debt instrument and any interest coupon that has not yet become payable.[708] In general, upon the disposition of either the stripped bond or the detached interest coupons, the retained portion and the portion that is disposed of each is treated as a new bond that is purchased at a discount and is payable at a fixed amount on a future date. Accordingly, section 1286 treats both the stripped bond and the detached interest coupons as individual bonds that are newly issued with original issue discount ("OID") on the date of disposition. Consequently, section 1286 effectively subjects the stripped bond and the detached interest coupons to the general OID periodic income inclusion rules.

A taxpayer who purchases a stripped bond or one or more stripped coupons is treated as holding a new bond that is issued on the purchase date with OID in an amount that is equal to the excess of the stated redemption price at maturity (or in the case of a coupon, the amount payable on the due date) over the ratable share of the purchase price of the stripped bond or coupon, determined on the basis of the respective fair market values of the stripped bond and coupons on the purchase date.[709] The OID on the stripped bond or coupon is includible in gross income under the general OID periodic income inclusion rules.

A taxpayer who strips a bond and disposes of either the stripped bond or one or more stripped coupons must allocate the taxpayer's basis, immediately before the disposition, in the bond (with the

---

[704] *Helvering* v. *Horst*, 311 U.S. 112 (1940).

[705] Depending on the facts, the IRS also could determine that a variety of other Code-based and common law-based authorities could apply to income stripping transactions, including: (1) sections 269, 382, 446(b), 482, 701, or 704 and the regulations thereunder; (2) authorities that recharacterize certain assignments or accelerations of future payments as financings; (3) business purpose, economic substance, and sham transaction doctrines; (4) the step transaction doctrine; and (5) the substance-over-form doctrine. See Notice 95–53, 1995–2 C.B. 334 (accounting for lease strips and other stripping transactions).

[706] However, in *Estate of Stranahan* v. *Commissioner*, 472 F.2d 867 (6th Cir. 1973), the court held that where a taxpayer sold a carved-out interest of stock dividends, with no personal obligation to produce the income, the transaction was treated as a sale of an income interest.

[707] Sec. 1286.

[708] Sec. 1286(e).

[709] Sec. 1286(a).

coupons attached) between the retained and disposed items.[710] Special rules apply to require that interest or market discount accrued on the bond prior to such disposition must be included in the taxpayer's gross income (to the extent that it had not been previously included in income) at the time the stripping occurs, and the taxpayer increases the basis in the bond by the amount of such accrued interest or market discount. The adjusted basis (as increased by any accrued interest or market discount) is then allocated between the stripped bond and the stripped interest coupons in relation to their respective fair market values. Amounts realized from the sale of stripped coupons or bonds constitute income to the taxpayer only to the extent such amounts exceed the basis allocated to the stripped coupons or bond. With respect to retained items (either the detached coupons or stripped bond), to the extent that the price payable on maturity, or on the due date of the coupons, exceeds the portion of the taxpayer's basis allocable to such retained items, the difference is treated as OID that is required to be included under the general OID periodic income inclusion rules.[711]

Stripped preferred stock

"Stripped preferred stock" is defined as preferred stock in which there has been a separation in ownership between such stock and any dividend on such stock that has not become payable.[712] A taxpayer who purchases stripped preferred stock is required to include in gross income, as ordinary income, the amounts that would have been includible if the stripped preferred stock were a bond issued on the purchase date with OID equal to the excess of the redemption price of the stock over the purchase price.[713] This treatment is extended to any taxpayer whose basis in the stock is determined by reference to the basis in the hands of the purchaser. A taxpayer who strips and disposes the future dividends is treated as having purchased the stripped preferred stock on the date of such disposition for a purchase price equal to the taxpayer's adjusted basis in the stripped preferred stock.[714]

Reasons for Change

The Congress was concerned that taxpayers are entering into tax avoidance transactions to generate artificial losses, or defer the recognition of ordinary income and convert such income into capital gains, by selling or purchasing stripped interests that are not subject to the present-law rules relating to stripped bonds and preferred stock but that represent interests in bonds or preferred stock. Therefore, the Congress believed that it is appropriate to provide Treasury with regulatory authority to apply such rules to interests that do not constitute bonds or preferred stock but never-

---

[710] Sec. 1286(b). Similar rules apply in the case of any person whose basis in any bond or coupon is determined by reference to the basis in the hands of a person who strips the bond.

[711] Special rules are provided with respect to stripping transactions involving tax-exempt obligations that treat OID (computed under the stripping rules) in excess of OID computed on the basis of the bond's coupon rate (or higher rate if originally issued at a discount) as income from a non-tax-exempt debt instrument (sec. 1286(d)).

[712] Sec. 305(e)(5).

[713] Sec. 305(e)(1).

[714] Sec. 305(e)(3).

theless derive their economic value and characteristics exclusively from underlying bonds or preferred stock.

Explanation of Provision

The Act authorizes the Treasury Department to promulgate regulations that, in appropriate cases, apply rules that are similar to the present-law rules for stripped bonds and stripped preferred stock to direct or indirect interests in an entity or account substantially all of the assets of which consist of bonds (as defined in section 1286(e)(1)), preferred stock (as defined in section 305(e)(5)(B)), or any combination thereof. The Act applies only to cases in which the present-law rules for stripped bonds and stripped preferred stock do not already apply to such interests.

For example, such Treasury regulations could apply to a transaction in which a person effectively strips future dividends from shares in a money market mutual fund (and disposes of either the stripped shares or stripped future dividends) by contributing the shares (with the future dividends) to a custodial account through which another person purchases rights to either the stripped shares or the stripped future dividends. However, it is intended that Treasury regulations issued under the Act would not apply to certain transactions involving direct or indirect interests in an entity or account substantially all the assets of which consist of tax-exempt obligations (as defined in section 1275(a)(3)), such as a tax-exempt bond partnership described in Rev. Proc. 2002–68,[715] *modifying and superseding* Rev. Proc. 2002–16.[716]

No inference is intended as to the treatment under the rules for stripped bonds and stripped preferred stock, or under any other provisions or doctrines of law, of interests in an entity or account substantially all of the assets of which consist of bonds, preferred stock, or any combination thereof. The Treasury regulations, when issued, would be applied prospectively, except in cases to prevent abuse.

Effective Date

The provision is effective for purchases and dispositions occurring after the date of enactment (October 22, 2004).

13. Minimum holding period for foreign tax credit with respect to withholding taxes on income other than dividends (sec. 832 of the Act and sec. 901 of the Code)

Present and Prior Law

In general, U.S. persons may credit foreign taxes against U.S. tax on foreign-source income. The amount of foreign tax credits that may be claimed in a year is subject to a limitation that prevents taxpayers from using foreign tax credits to offset U.S. tax on U.S.-source income. Separate limitations are applied to specific categories of income.

---

[715] 2002–43 I.R.B. 753.
[716] 2002–9 I.R.B. 572.

As a consequence of the foreign tax credit limitations of the Code, certain taxpayers are unable to utilize their creditable foreign taxes to reduce their U.S. tax liability. U.S. taxpayers that are tax-exempt receive no U.S. tax benefit for foreign taxes paid on income that they receive.

The Code denies a U.S. shareholder the foreign tax credits normally available with respect to a dividend from a corporation or a regulated investment company ("RIC") if the shareholder has not held the stock for more than 15 days (within a 30-day testing period) in the case of common stock or more than 45 days (within a 90-day testing period) in the case of preferred stock (sec. 901(k)). The disallowance applies both to foreign tax credits for foreign withholding taxes that are paid on the dividend where the dividend-paying stock is held for less than these holding periods, and to indirect foreign tax credits for taxes paid by a lower-tier foreign corporation or a RIC where any of the required stock in the chain of ownership is held for less than these holding periods. Periods during which a taxpayer is protected from risk of loss (e.g., by purchasing a put option or entering into a short sale with respect to the stock) generally are not counted toward the holding period requirement. In the case of a bona fide contract to sell stock, a special rule applies for purposes of indirect foreign tax credits. The disallowance does not apply to foreign tax credits with respect to certain dividends received by active dealers in securities. If a taxpayer is denied foreign tax credits because the applicable holding period is not satisfied, the taxpayer is entitled to a deduction for the foreign taxes for which the credit is disallowed.

Reasons for Change

The Congress believed that the holding period requirement for claiming foreign tax credits with respect to dividends is too narrow in scope and, in general, should be extended to apply to items of income or gain other than dividends, such as interest.

Explanation of Provision

The Act expands the disallowance of foreign tax credits to include credits for gross-basis foreign withholding taxes with respect to any item of income or gain from property if the taxpayer who receives the income or gain has not held the property for more than 15 days (within a 31-day testing period), exclusive of periods during which the taxpayer is protected from risk of loss. The Act does not apply to foreign tax credits that are subject to the disallowance with respect to dividends. The Act also does not apply to certain income or gain that is received with respect to property held by active dealers.[717] Rules similar to the disallowance for foreign tax credits with respect to dividends apply to foreign tax credits that are subject to the Act. In addition, the Act authorizes the Treasury Department to issue regulations providing that the provision does not apply in appropriate cases.

[717] It is intended that the exception for certain withholding taxes paid by registered or licensed brokers and dealers on income and gain from securities also apply to gain from the sale of stock. A technical correction may be necessary so that the statute reflects this intent.

It is intended that the Secretary will prescribe regulations to adapt the holding period and hedging rules of section 901(k) to property other than stock. It is anticipated that such regulations will provide that credits are not disallowed merely because a taxpayer eliminates its risk of loss from interest rate or currency fluctuations. In addition, it is intended that such regulations might permit other hedging activities, such as hedging of credit risk, provided that the taxpayer does not hedge most of its risk of loss with respect to the property unless there has been a meaningful and unanticipated change in circumstances.

Effective Date

The provision is effective for amounts that are paid or accrued more than 30 days after the date of enactment (October 22, 2004).

14. Treatment of partnership loss transfers and partnership basis adjustments (sec. 833 of the Act and secs. 704, 734, 743, and 754 of the Code)

Present and Prior Law

Contributions of property

If a partner contributes property to a partnership, generally no gain or loss is recognized to the contributing partner at the time of contribution.[718] The partnership takes the property at an adjusted basis equal to the contributing partner's adjusted basis in the property.[719] The contributing partner increases its basis in its partnership interest by the adjusted basis of the contributed property.[720] Any items of partnership income, gain, loss and deduction with respect to the contributed property are allocated among the partners to take into account any built-in gain or loss at the time of the contribution.[721] This rule is intended to prevent the transfer of built-in gain or loss from the contributing partner to the other partners by generally allocating items to the noncontributing partners based on the value of their contributions and by allocating to the contributing partner the remainder of each item.[722]

If the contributing partner transfers its partnership interest, the built-in gain or loss will be allocated to the transferee partner as it would have been allocated to the contributing partner.[723] If the contributing partner's interest is liquidated, there is no specific guidance preventing the allocation of the built-in loss to the remaining partners. Thus, it appears that losses can be "transferred" to other partners where the contributing partner no longer remains a partner.

---

[718] Sec. 721.
[719] Sec. 723.
[720] Sec. 722.
[721] Sec. 704(c)(1)(A).
[722] If there is an insufficient amount of an item to allocate to the noncontributing partners, Treasury regulations allow for curative or remedial allocations to remedy this insufficiency. Treas. Reg. sec. 1.704–3(c) and (d).
[723] Treas. Reg. sec. 1.704–3(a)(7).

Transfers of partnership interests

A partnership does not adjust the basis of partnership property following the transfer of a partnership interest unless the partnership has made a one-time election under section 754 to make basis adjustments.[724] If an election is in effect, adjustments are made with respect to the transferee partner to account for the difference between the transferee partner's proportionate share of the adjusted basis of the partnership property and the transferee's basis in its partnership interest.[725] These adjustments are intended to adjust the basis of partnership property to approximate the result of a direct purchase of the property by the transferee partner. Under these rules, if a partner purchases an interest in a partnership with an existing built-in loss and no election under section 754 is in effect, the transferee partner may be allocated a share of the loss when the partnership disposes of the property (or depreciates the property).

Distributions of partnership property

With certain exceptions, partners may receive distributions of partnership property without recognition of gain or loss by either the partner or the partnership.[726] In the case of a distribution in liquidation of a partner's interest, the basis of the property distributed in the liquidation is equal to the partner's adjusted basis in its partnership interest (reduced by any money distributed in the transaction).[727] In a distribution other than in liquidation of a partner's interest, the distributee partner's basis in the distributed property is equal to the partnership's adjusted basis in the property immediately before the distribution, but not to exceed the partner's adjusted basis in the partnership interest (reduced by any money distributed in the same transaction).[728]

The determination of the basis of individual properties distributed by a partnership is dependent on the adjusted basis of the properties in the hands of the partnership.[729] If a partnership interest is transferred to a partner and the partnership has not elected to adjust the basis of partnership property, a special basis rule provides for the determination of the transferee partner's basis of properties that are later distributed by the partnership.[730] Under this rule, in determining the basis of property distributed by a partnership within 2 years following the transfer of the partnership interest, the transferee may elect to determine its basis as if the partnership had adjusted the basis of the distributed property under section 743(b) on the transfer. The special basis rule also applies to distributed property if, at the time of the transfer, the fair market value of partnership property other than money exceeds 110 percent of the partnership's basis in such property and a liquidation of the partnership interest immediately after the transfer

[724] Sec. 743(a).
[725] Sec. 743(b).
[726] Sec. 731(a) and (b).
[727] Sec. 732(b).
[728] Sec. 732(a).
[729] Sec. 732(a)(1) and (c).
[730] Sec. 732(d).

would have resulted in a shift of basis to property subject to an allowance of depreciation, depletion or amortization.[731]

Adjustments to the basis of the partnership's undistributed properties are not required unless the partnership has made the election under section 754 to make basis adjustments.[732] If an election is in effect under section 754, adjustments are made by a partnership to increase or decrease the remaining partnership assets to reflect any increase or decrease in the adjusted basis of the distributed properties in the hands of the distributee partner (or gain or loss recognized by the distributee partner).[733] To the extent the adjusted basis of the distributed properties increases (or loss is recognized) the partnership's adjusted basis in its properties is decreased by a like amount; likewise, to the extent the adjusted basis of the distributed properties decreases (or gain is recognized), the partnership's adjusted basis in its properties is increased by a like amount. Under these rules, a partnership with no election in effect under section 754 may distribute property with an adjusted basis lower than the distributee partner's proportionate share of the adjusted basis of all partnership property and leave the remaining partners with a smaller net built-in gain or a larger net built-in loss than before the distribution.

Reasons for Change

The Congress believed that the partnership rules allowed for the inappropriate transfer of losses among partners. This has allowed partnerships to be created and used to aid tax-shelter transactions. The Act limits the ability to transfer losses among partners, while preserving the simplification aspects of the current partnership rules for transactions involving smaller amounts. The Congress was made aware that certain types of investment partnerships would incur administrative difficulties in making partnership-level basis adjustments in the event of a transfer of a partnership interest, as evidenced by the present practice of a number of investment partnerships not to elect partnership basis adjustments even when the adjustments would be upward adjustments to the basis of partnership property. Accordingly, the Act provides a partner-level loss limitation as an alternative to the partnership basis adjustments otherwise required under the Act in the case of transfers of interests in certain investment partnerships that are engaged in investment activities rather than in any trade or business activity.

Explanation of Provision

Contributions of property

Under the Act, a built-in loss may be taken into account only by the contributing partner and not by other partners. Except as provided in regulations, in determining the amount of items allocated to partners other than the contributing partner, the basis of the contributed property is treated as the fair market value at the time of contribution. Thus, if the contributing partner's partnership interest is transferred or liquidated, the partnership's adjusted basis

[731] Treas. Reg. sec. 1.732–1(d)(4).
[732] Sec. 734(a).
[733] Sec. 734(b).

in the property is based on its fair market value at the time of contribution, and the built-in loss is eliminated.[734]

Transfers of partnership interests

The Act provides generally that the basis adjustment rules under section 743 are mandatory in the case of the transfer of a partnership interest with respect to which there is a substantial built-in loss (rather than being elective as under prior law). For this purpose, a substantial built-in loss exists if the partnership's adjusted basis in its property exceeds by more than $250,000 the fair market value of the partnership property.

Thus, for example, assume that partner A sells his 25-percent partnership interest to B for its fair market value of $1 million. Also assume that, immediately after the transfer, the fair market value of partnership assets is $4 million and the partnership's adjusted basis in the partnership assets is $4.3 million. Under the bill, section 743(b) applies, so that an adjustment is required to the adjusted basis of the partnership assets with respect to B. As a result, B would recognize no gain or loss if the partnership immediately sold all its assets for their fair market value.

The Act provides that an electing investment partnership is not treated as having a substantial built-in loss, and thus is not required to make basis adjustments to partnership property, in the case of a transfer of a partnership interest. In lieu of the partnership basis adjustments, a partner-level loss limitation rule applies. Under this rule, the transferee partner's distributive share of losses (determined without regard to gains) from the sale or exchange of partnership property is not allowed, except to the extent it is established that the partner's share of such losses exceeds the loss recognized by the transferor partner. In the event of successive transfers, the transferee partner's distributive share of such losses is not allowed, except to the extent that it is established that such losses exceed the loss recognized by the transferor (or any prior transferor to the extent not fully offset by a prior disallowance under this rule). Losses disallowed under this rule do not decrease the transferee partner's basis in its partnership interest. Thus, on subsequent disposition of its partnership interest, the partner's gain is reduced (or loss increased) because the basis of the partnership interest has not been reduced by such losses. The Act is applied without regard to any termination of a partnership under section 708(b)(1)(B). In the case of a basis reduction to property distributed to the transferee partner in a nonliquidating distribution, the amount of the transferor's loss taken into account under this rule is reduced by the amount of the basis reduction.

For this purpose, an electing investment partnership means a partnership that satisfies the following requirements: (1) it makes an election under the provision that is irrevocable except with the consent of the Secretary; (2) it would be an investment company under section 3(a)(1)(A) of the Investment Company Act of 1940[735]

---

[734] It is intended that a corporation succeeding to attributes of the contributing corporate partner under section 381 shall be treated in the same manner as the contributing partner.

[735] Section 3(a)(1)(A) of the Investment Company Act of 1940 provides, "when used in this title, 'investment company' means any issuer which is or holds itself out as being engaged pri-

Continued

but for an exemption under paragraph (1) or (7) of section 3(c) of that Act; (3) it has never been engaged in a trade or business; (4) substantially all of its assets are held for investment; (5) at least 95 percent of thc assets contributed to it consist of money; (6) no assets contributed to it had an adjusted basis in excess of fair market value at the time of contribution; (7) all partnership interests are issued by the partnership pursuant to a private offering prior to the date that is 24 months after the date of the first capital contribution to the partnership (the Congress intends that "dry" closings in which partnership interests are issued without the contribution of capital not start the running of the 24-month period); (8) the partnership agreement has substantive restrictions on each partner's ability to cause a redemption of the partner's interest; and (9) the partnership agreement provides for a term that is not in excess of 15 years.

It is intended that in applying the requirement (with respect to electing investment partnerships) that the partnership agreement have substantive restrictions on each partner's ability to cause a redemption, the following are illustrative examples of substantive restrictions (i.e., redemption is permitted under the partnership agreement only if the following would result absent the redemption): A violation of Federal or State law (such as ERISA or the Bank Holding Company Act); and imposition of a Federal excise tax on, or a change in the Federal tax-exempt status of, a tax-exempt partner.

The Congress understands that electing investment partnerships will generally include venture capital funds, buyout funds, and funds of funds. These funds are formed to raise capital from investors pursuant to a private offering and to make investments during the limited term of the partnership with the intention of holding the investments for capital appreciation.

The Act requires an electing investment partnership to furnish to any transferee partner the information necessary to enable the partner to compute the amount of losses disallowed under this rule. With respect to this requirement, it is expected that in some cases the transferor of the partnership interest will furnish information relating to the amount of its loss to the transferee partner. It is intended that the requirement that the electing investment partnership furnish necessary information to the transferee partner be administered by the Treasury Secretary in a manner that (to the greatest extent feasible) minimizes the need for the partnership to furnish information to the transferee partner that the transferee partner has obtained from the transferor.

Distributions of partnership property

The Act provides that a basis adjustment under section 734(b) is required in the case of a distribution with respect to which there is a substantial basis reduction. A substantial basis reduction means a downward adjustment of more than $250,000 that would be made to the basis of partnership assets if a section 754 election were in effect.

---

marily, or proposes to engage primarily, in the business of investing, reinvesting, or trading in securities."

Thus, for example, assume that A and B each contributed $2.5 million to a newly formed partnership and C contributed $5 million, and that the partnership purchased LMN stock for $3 million and XYZ stock for $7 million. Assume that the value of each stock declined to $1 million. Assume LMN stock is distributed to C in liquidation of its partnership interest. Under prior law, the basis of LMN stock in C's hands is $5 million. Under prior law, C would recognize a loss of $4 million if the LMN stock were sold for $1 million.

Under the Act, there is a substantial basis adjustment because the $2 million increase in the adjusted basis of LMN stock (described in section 734(b)(2)(B)) is greater than $250,000. Thus, the partnership is required to decrease the basis of XYZ stock (under section 734(b)(2)) by $2 million (the amount by which the basis of LMN stock was increased), leaving a basis of $5 million. If the XYZ stock were then sold by the partnership for $1 million, A and B would each recognize a loss of $2 million.

Other rules

The Act adds an exception for securitization partnerships to the rules requiring partnership basis adjustments in the case of transfers of partnership interests and distributions of property to a partner. The exceptions provide that a securitization partnership is not treated as having a substantial built-in loss in the case of a transfer of a partnership interest, or as having a substantial basis reduction in the case of a partnership distribution, and thus is not required to make basis adjustments to partnership property. Partnership basis adjustments remain elective for such a partnership. Unlike in the case of an electing investment partnership, the partner-level loss limitation rule does not apply in the case of a securitization partnership. For this purpose, a securitization partnership is any partnership the sole business activity of which is to issue securities that provide for a fixed principal (or similar) amount and that are primarily serviced by the cash flows of a discrete pool (either fixed or revolving) of receivables or other financial assets that by their terms convert into cash in a finite period, but only if the sponsor of the pool reasonably believes that the receivables and other financial assets comprising the pool are not acquired so as to be disposed of. It is intended that rules similar to those applicable to sponsors of REMICs apply in determining whether the sponsor's belief is reasonable.[736] It is not intended that the rules requiring partnership basis adjustments on transfers or distributions be avoided through dispositions of pool assets.

It is intended that an electing investment partnership or securitization partnership that subsequently fails to meet the definition of an electing investment partnership or of a securitization partnership will be subject to the partnership basis adjustment rules of the provision with respect to the first transfer of a partnership interest (and, in the case of a securitization partnership, the first distribution) that occurs after the partnership ceases to meet

[736] See Treas. Reg. sec. 1.860G–2(a)(3), providing that a sponsor's belief is not reasonable if the sponsor actually knows or has reason to know that the requirement is not met, or if the requirement is later discovered not to have been met.

the applicable definition and to each subsequent transfer (and distribution, in the case of a securitization partnership).

It is not intended that the rules of the provision be avoided through the use of tiered partnerships.

It is not intended that the provision relating to contributions of built-in loss property limit the ability of master-feeder structures to apply an aggregate method for making allocations under section 704(c) to the extent the aggregate method is permitted under prior law.[737]

Effective Date

The provision applies to contributions, distributions and transfers (as the case may be) after the date of enactment (October 22, 2004).

In the case of an electing investment partnership in existence on June 4, 2004, the requirement that the partnership agreement have substantive restrictions on redemptions does not apply, and the requirement that the partnership agreement provide for a term not exceeding 15 years is modified to permit a term not exceeding 20 years.

15. No reduction of basis under section 734 in stock held by partnership in corporate partner (sec. 834 of the Act and sec. 755 of the Code)

Present and Prior Law

In general

Generally, a partner and the partnership do not recognize gain or loss on a contribution of property to the partnership.[738] Similarly, a partner and the partnership generally do not recognize gain or loss on the distribution of partnership property.[739] This includes current distributions and distributions in liquidation of a partner's interest.

Basis of property distributed in liquidation

The basis of property distributed in liquidation of a partner's interest is equal to the partner's tax basis in its partnership interest (reduced by any money distributed in the same transaction).[740] Thus, the partnership's tax basis in the distributed property is adjusted (increased or decreased) to reflect the partner's tax basis in the partnership interest.

---

[737] See. Rev. Proc. 2001–36, 2001–1 C.B. 1326. Definitional requirements of a master-feeder structure include that there is a portfolio of assets that is treated as a partnership for Federal tax purposes and that is registered as an investment company under the Investment Company Act of 1940, each partner of which is a feeder fund that is a regulated investment company (RIC) for Federal tax purposes, or is an investment advisor, principal underwriter, or manager of the portfolio. The Congress believes that these restrictions (and other applicable restrictions) serve to limit potential avoidance of the section 704(c) provision through use of the aggregate method in the case of master-feeder structures.

[738] Sec. 721(a).

[739] Sec. 731(a) and (b).

[740] Sec. 732(b).

Election to adjust basis of partnership property

When a partnership distributes partnership property, the basis of partnership property generally is not adjusted to reflect the effects of the distribution or transfer. However, the partnership is permitted to make an election (referred to as a 754 election) to adjust the basis of partnership property in the case of a distribution of partnership property.[741] The effect of the 754 election is that the partnership adjusts the basis of its remaining property to reflect any change in basis of the distributed property in the hands of the distributee partner resulting from the distribution transaction. Such a change could be a basis increase due to gain recognition, or a basis decrease due to the partner's adjusted basis in its partnership interest exceeding the adjusted basis of the property received. If the 754 election is made, it applies to the taxable year with respect to which such election was filed and all subsequent taxable years.

In the case of a distribution of partnership property to a partner with respect to which the 754 election is in effect, the partnership increases the basis of partnership property by (1) any gain recognized by the distributee partner and (2) the excess of the adjusted basis of the distributed property to the partnership immediately before its distribution over the basis of the property to the distributee partner, and decreases the basis of partnership property by (1) any loss recognized by the distributee partner and (2) the excess of the basis of the property to the distributee partner over the adjusted basis of the distributed property to the partnership immediately before the distribution.

The allocation of the increase or decrease in basis of partnership property is made in a manner that has the effect of reducing the difference between the fair market value and the adjusted basis of partnership properties.[742] In addition, the allocation rules require that any increase or decrease in basis be allocated to partnership property of a like character to the property distributed. For this purpose, the two categories of assets are (1) capital assets and depreciable and real property used in the trade or business held for more than one year, and (2) any other property.[743]

Reasons for Change

The Joint Committee on Taxation staff's investigative report of Enron Corporation[744] revealed that certain transactions were being undertaken that purported to use the interaction of the partnership basis adjustment rules and the rules protecting a corporation from recognizing gain on its stock to obtain unintended tax results. These transactions generally purported to increase the tax basis of depreciable assets and to decrease, by a corresponding amount, the tax basis of the stock of a partner. Because the tax rules protect a corporation from gain on the sale of its stock (including through a partnership), the transactions enable taxpayers

[741] Sec. 754.
[742] Sec. 755(a).
[743] Sec. 755(b).
[744] See Joint Committee on Taxation, *Report of Investigation of Enron Corporation and Related Entities Regarding Federal Tax and Compensation Issues, and Policy Recommendations* (JCS–3–03), February 2003.

to duplicate tax deductions at no economic cost. The provision precludes the ability to reduce the basis of corporate stock of a partner (or related party) in certain transactions.

Explanation of Provision

The Act provides that in applying the basis allocation rules to a distribution in liquidation of a partner's interest, a partnership is precluded from decreasing the basis of corporate stock of a partner or a related person. Any decrease in basis that, absent the provision, would have been allocated to the stock is allocated to other partnership assets. If the decrease in basis exceeds the basis of the other partnership assets, then gain is recognized by the partnership in the amount of the excess.

Effective Date

The provision applies to distributions after the date of enactment (October 22, 2004).

16. Repeal of special rules for FASITs (sec. 835 of the Act and secs. 860H through 860L of the Code)

Present and Prior Law

Financial asset securitization investment trusts

In general

In 1996 Congress created a new type of statutory entity called a "financial asset securitization investment trust" ("FASIT") that facilitates the securitization of debt obligations such as credit card receivables, home equity loans, and auto loans.[745] A FASIT generally was not taxable; the FASIT's taxable income or net loss flowed through to the owner of the FASIT.

The ownership interest of a FASIT generally was required to be entirely held by a single domestic C corporation. In addition, a FASIT generally could hold only qualified debt obligations, and certain other specified assets, and was subject to certain restrictions on its activities. An entity that qualified as a FASIT could issue one or more classes of instruments that met certain specified requirements and treat those instruments as debt for Federal income tax purposes. Instruments issued by a FASIT bearing yields to maturity over five percentage points above the yield to maturity on specified United States government obligations (i.e., "high-yield interests") were required to be held, directly or indirectly, only by domestic C corporations that are not exempt from income tax.

Qualification as a FASIT

To qualify as a FASIT, an entity was required to: (1) make an election to be treated as a FASIT for the year of the election and all subsequent years;[746] (2) have assets substantially all of which

[745] Sections 860H through 860L.

[746] Once an election to be a FASIT was made, the election applied from the date specified in the election and all subsequent years until the entity ceased to be a FASIT. If an election to be a FASIT was made after the initial year of an entity, all of the assets in the entity at the time of the FASIT election were deemed contributed to the FASIT at that time and, accordingly, any gain (but not loss) on such assets would be recognized at that time.

(including assets that the FASIT was treated as owning because they support regular interests) were specified types called "permitted assets;" (3) have non-ownership interests be certain specified types of debt instruments called "regular interests"; (4) have a single ownership interest which was held by an "eligible holder"; and (5) not qualify as a regulated investment company ("RIC"). Any entity, including a corporation, partnership, or trust could be treated as a FASIT. In addition, a segregated pool of assets could qualify as a FASIT.

An entity ceased to qualify as a FASIT if the entity's owner ceased being an eligible corporation. Loss of FASIT status was treated as if all of the regular interests of the FASIT were retired and then reissued without the application of the rule that deems regular interests of a FASIT to be debt.

Permitted assets

For an entity or arrangement to qualify as a FASIT, substantially all of its assets were required to consist of the following "permitted assets": (1) cash and cash equivalents; (2) certain permitted debt instruments; (3) certain foreclosure property; (4) certain instruments or contracts that represent a hedge or guarantee of debt held or issued by the FASIT; (5) contract rights to acquire permitted debt instruments or hedges; and (6) a regular interest in another FASIT. Permitted assets could be acquired at any time by a FASIT, including any time after its formation.

"Regular interests" of a FASIT

"Regular interests" of a FASIT were treated as debt for Federal income tax purposes, regardless of whether instruments with similar terms issued by non-FASITs might be characterized as equity under general tax principles. To be treated as a "regular interest", an instrument was required to have fixed terms and was required to: (1) unconditionally entitle the holder to receive a specified principal amount; (2) pay interest that was based on (a) fixed rates, or (b) except as provided by regulations issued by the Treasury Secretary, variable rates permitted with respect to REMIC interests under section 860G(a)(1)(B)(i); (3) have a term to maturity of no more than 30 years, except as permitted by Treasury regulations; (4) be issued to the public with a premium of not more than 25 percent of its stated principal amount; and (5) have a yield to maturity determined on the date of issue of less than five percentage points above the applicable Federal rate ("AFR") for the calendar month in which the instrument was issued.

Permitted ownership holder

A permitted holder of the ownership interest in a FASIT generally was a non-exempt (i.e., taxable) domestic C corporation, other than a corporation that qualified as a RIC, REIT, REMIC, or cooperative.

Transfers to FASITs

In general, gain (but not loss) was recognized immediately by the owner of the FASIT upon the transfer of assets to a FASIT. Where property was acquired by a FASIT from someone other than the

FASIT's owner (or a person related to the FASIT's owner), the property was treated as being first acquired by the FASIT's owner for the FASIT's cost in acquiring the asset from the non-owner and then transferred by the owner to the FASIT.

Valuation rules.—In general, except in the case of debt instruments, the value of FASIT assets was their fair market value. Similarly, in the case of debt instruments that are traded on an established securities market, the market price was used for purposes of determining the amount of gain realized upon contribution of such assets to a FASIT. However, in the case of debt instruments which are not traded on an established securities market, special valuation rules applied for purposes of computing gain on the transfer of such debt instruments to a FASIT. Under these rules, the value of such debt instruments was the sum of the present values of the reasonably expected cash flows from such obligations discounted over the weighted average life of such assets. The discount rate was 120 percent of the AFR, compounded semiannually, or such other rate that the Treasury Secretary shall prescribe by regulations.

Taxation of a FASIT

A FASIT generally was not subject to tax. Instead, all of the FASIT's assets and liabilities were treated as assets and liabilities of the FASIT's owner and any income, gain, deduction or loss of the FASIT was allocable directly to its owner. Accordingly, income tax rules applicable to a FASIT (e.g., related party rules, sec. 871(h), sec. 165(g)(2)) were to be applied in the same manner as they applied to the FASIT's owner. The taxable income of a FASIT was calculated using an accrual method of accounting. The constant yield method and principles that apply for purposes of determining original issue discount ("OID") accrual on debt obligations whose principal is subject to acceleration applied to all debt obligations held by a FASIT to calculate the FASIT's interest and discount income and premium deductions or adjustments.

Taxation of holders of FASIT regular interests

In general, a holder of a regular interest was taxed in the same manner as a holder of any other debt instrument, except that the regular interest holder was required to account for income relating to the interest on an accrual method of accounting, regardless of the method of accounting otherwise used by the holder.

Taxation of holders of FASIT ownership interests

Because all of the assets and liabilities of a FASIT were treated as assets and liabilities of the holder of a FASIT ownership interest, the ownership interest holder took into account all of the FASIT's income, gain, deduction, or loss in computing its taxable income or net loss for the taxable year. The character of the income to the holder of an ownership interest was the same as its character to the FASIT, except tax-exempt interest was included in the income of the holder as ordinary income.

Although the recognition of losses on assets contributed to the FASIT was not allowed upon contribution of the assets, such losses were allowed to the FASIT owner upon their disposition by the

FASIT. Furthermore, the holder of a FASIT ownership interest was not permitted to offset taxable income from the FASIT ownership interest (including gain or loss from the sale of the ownership interest in the FASIT) with other losses of the holder. In addition, any net operating loss carryover of the FASIT owner was computed by disregarding any income arising by reason of a disallowed loss. Where the holder of a FASIT ownership interest was a member of a consolidated group, this rule applied to the consolidated group of corporations of which the holder was a member as if the group were a single taxpayer.

Real estate mortgage investment conduits

In general, a real estate mortgage investment conduit ("REMIC") is a self-liquidating entity that holds a fixed pool of mortgages and issues multiple classes of investor interests. A REMIC is not treated as a separate taxable entity. Rather, the income of the REMIC is allocated to, and taken into account by, the holders of the interests in the REMIC under detailed rules.[747] In order to qualify as a REMIC, substantially all of the assets of the entity must consist of qualified mortgages and permitted investments as of the close of the third month beginning after the startup day of the entity. A "qualified mortgage" generally includes any obligation which is principally secured by an interest in real property, and which is either transferred to the REMIC on the startup day of the REMIC in exchange for regular or residual interests in the REMIC or purchased by the REMIC within three months after the startup day pursuant to a fixed-price contract in effect on the startup day. A "permitted investment" generally includes any intangible property that is held for investment and is part of a reasonably required reserve to provide for full payment of certain expenses of the REMIC or amounts due on regular interests.

All of the interests in the REMIC must consist of one or more classes of regular interests and a single class of residual interests. A "regular interest" is an interest in a REMIC that is issued with a fixed term, designated as a regular interest, and unconditionally entitles the holder to receive a specified principal amount (or other similar amount) with interest payments that are either based on a fixed rate (or, to the extent provided in regulations, a variable rate) or consist of a specified portion of the interest payments on qualified mortgages that does not vary during the period such interest is outstanding. In general, a "residual interest" is any interest in the REMIC other than a regular interest, and which is so designated by the REMIC, provided that there is only one class of such interest and that all distributions (if any) with respect to such interests are pro rata. Holders of residual REMIC interests are subject to tax on the portion of the income of the REMIC that is not allocated to the regular interest holders.

---

[747] See secs. 860A–860G.

Reasons for Change

The Joint Committee on Taxation staff's investigative report of Enron Corporation[748] described two structured tax-motivated transactions—Projects Apache and Renegade—that Enron undertook in which the use of a FASIT was a key component in the structure of the transactions. The Congress was aware that FASITs were not being used widely in the manner envisioned by the Congress and, consequently, the FASIT rules had not served the purpose for which they originally were intended. Moreover, the Joint Committee staff's report and other information indicated that FASITs were particularly prone to abuse and likely were being used primarily to facilitate tax avoidance transactions.[749] Therefore, the Congress believed that the potential for abuse that was inherent in FASITs far outweighed any beneficial purpose that the FASIT rules may have served. Accordingly, the Congress believed that these rules should be repealed, with appropriate transition relief for existing FASITs and appropriate modifications to the REMIC rules to permit the use of REMICs by taxpayers that have relied upon FASITs to securitize certain obligations secured by interests in real property.

Explanation of Provision

The Act repeals the special rules for FASITs. The Act provides a transition period for existing FASITs, pursuant to which the repeal of the FASIT rules generally does not apply to any FASIT in existence on the date of enactment to the extent that regular interests issued by the FASIT prior to such date continue to remain outstanding in accordance with their original terms.

For purposes of the REMIC rules, the Act also modifies the definitions of REMIC regular interests, qualified mortgages, and permitted investments so that certain types of real estate loans and loan pools can be transferred to, or purchased by, a REMIC. Specifically, the Act modifies the definition of a REMIC "regular interest" to provide that an interest in a REMIC does not fail to qualify as a regular interest solely because the specified principal amount of such interest or the amount of interest accrued on such interest could be reduced as a result of the nonoccurrence of one or more contingent payments with respect to one or more reverse mortgages loans, as defined below, that are held by the REMIC, provided that on the startup day for the REMIC, the REMIC sponsor reasonably believes that all principal and interest due under the interest will be paid at or prior to the liquidation of the REMIC. For this purpose, a reasonable belief concerning ultimate payment of all amounts due under an interest is presumed to exist if, as of the startup day, the interest receives an investment grade rating from at least one nationally recognized statistical rating agency.

---

[748] See Joint Committee on Taxation, Report of Investigation of Enron Corporation and Related Entities Regarding Federal Tax and Compensation Issues, and Policy Recommendations (JCS–3–03), February 2003.

[749] For example, the Congress was aware that FASITs also had been used to facilitate the issuance of certain tax-advantaged cross-border hybrid instruments that were treated as indebtedness in the United States but equity in the foreign country of the holder of the instruments. The Congress did not intend such use of FASITs when it enacted the FASIT rules.

In addition, the Act makes three modifications to the definition of a "qualified mortgage." First, the Act modifies the definition to include an obligation principally secured by real property which represents an increase in the principal amount under the original terms of an obligation, provided such increase: (1) is attributable to an advance made to the obligor pursuant to the original terms of the obligation; (2) occurs after the REMIC startup day; and (3) is purchased by the REMIC pursuant to a fixed price contract in effect on the startup day. Second, the Act modifies the definition to generally include reverse mortgage loans and the periodic advances made to obligors on such loans. For this purpose, a "reverse mortgage loan" is defined as a loan that: (1) is secured by an interest in real property; (2) provides for one or more advances of principal to the obligor (each such advance giving rise to a "balance increase"), provided such advances are principally secured by an interest in the same real property as that which secures the loan; (3) may provide for a contingent payment at maturity based upon the value or appreciation in value of the real property securing the loan; (4) provides for an amount due at maturity that cannot exceed the value, or a specified fraction of the value, of the real property securing the loan; (5) provides that all payments under the loan are due only upon the maturity of the loan; and (6) matures after a fixed term or at the time the obligor ceases to use as a personal residence the real property securing the loan. Third, the Act modifies the definition to provide that, if more than 50 percent of the obligations transferred to, or purchased by, the REMIC are: (1) originated by the United States or any State (or any political subdivision, agency, or instrumentality of the United States or any State); and (2) principally secured by an interest in real property, then each obligation transferred to, or purchased by, the REMIC shall be treated as principally secured by an interest in real property.[750]

In addition, the Act modifies the present-law definition of a "permitted investment" to include intangible investment property held as part of a reasonably required reserve to provide a source of funds for the purchase of obligations described above as part of the modified definition of a "qualified mortgage."

Effective Date

Except as provided by the transition period for existing FASITs, the provision is effective January 1, 2005.

[750] It is intended that, if more than 50 percent of the obligations transferred to, or purchased by, a REMIC are originated by a Government entity and are principally secured by an interest in real property, then each obligation originated by a Government entity and transferred to, or purchased by, the REMIC is treated as principally secured by an interest in real property. Thus, it is intended that this rule align with the "principally secured" standard that generally is provided by the definition of a qualified mortgage, and that the treatment of obligations as principally secured by an interest in real property under this rule does not extend to obligations that are not originated by a Government entity. Technical corrections may be necessary to reflect this intent.

17. Limitation on transfer and importation of built-in losses (sec. 836 of the Act and secs. 362 and 334 of the Code)

Present and Prior Law

Generally, no gain or loss is recognized when one or more persons transfer property to a corporation in exchange for stock and immediately after the exchange such person or persons control the corporation.[751] Under present and prior law, the transferor's basis in the stock of the controlled corporation generally is the same as the basis of the property contributed to the controlled corporation, increased by the amount of any gain (or dividend) recognized by the transferor on the exchange, and reduced by the amount of any money or property received, and by the amount of any loss recognized by the transferor.[752]

Under present and prior law, the basis of property received by a corporation, whether from domestic or foreign transferors, in a tax-free incorporation, reorganization, or liquidation of a subsidiary corporation generally is the same as the adjusted basis in the hands of the transferor, adjusted for gain or loss recognized by the transferor.[753]

Reasons for Change

The Joint Committee on Taxation staff's investigative report of Enron Corporation[754] and other information revealed that taxpayers are engaging in various tax motivated transactions to duplicate a single economic loss and, subsequently, are deducting such loss more than once. Congress has previously taken actions to limit the ability of taxpayers to engage in specific transactions that purport to duplicate a single economic loss. However, new schemes that purport to duplicate losses have continued to proliferate. In furtherance of the overall tax policy objective of accurately measuring taxable income, the Congress believed that a single economic loss should not be deducted more than once. Thus, the Congress believed that it generally is appropriate to limit a corporation's basis in property acquired in a tax-free transfer to the fair market value of such property. In addition, the Congress believed that it is appropriate to prevent the importation of economic losses into the U.S. tax system if such losses arose before the assets became subject to the U.S. tax system.

Explanation of Provision

Importation of built-in losses

The Act provides that if property with a net built-in loss is transferred in a tax-free organization or reorganization, the basis of certain property so transferred is adjusted to its fair market value in the hands of the transferee. The property that receives a fair market value adjusted basis under this rule is property with respect to

[751] Sec. 351.
[752] Sec. 358.
[753] Secs. 334(b) and 362(a) and (b).
[754] See Joint Committee on Taxation, Report of Investigation of Enron Corporation and Related Entities Regarding Federal Tax and Compensation Issues, and Policy Recommendations (JCS–3–03), February 2003.

which any gain or loss would not be subject to U.S. income tax in the hands of the transferor immediately before the transfer but would be subject to U.S. income tax in the hands of the transferee immediately after the transfer. A similar rule applies in the case of the tax-free liquidation by a domestic corporation of its foreign subsidiary.[755]

Under the Act, transferred property has a net built-in loss if the aggregate adjusted basis of property received by a transferee corporation exceeds the fair market value of the property. Thus, for example, if in a tax-free incorporation some properties are received by a corporation from U.S. persons subject to tax, and some properties are received from foreign persons not subject to U.S. tax, the Act adjusts the basis of each property received from the foreign persons to its fair market value at the time of the transfer. In the case of a transfer by a partnership (either domestic or foreign), the Act applies as if the properties had been transferred by each of the partners in proportion to their interests in the partnership.

Limitation on transfer of built-in losses in section 351 transactions

Separately, the Act also provides that if the aggregate adjusted basis of property contributed by a transferor to a corporation in a tax-free incorporation exceeds the aggregate fair market value of the transferred property, the transferee's aggregate basis of the transferred property generally is limited to the aggregate fair market value of the property. Under the Act, any required basis reduction is allocated among the transferred properties in proportion to their respective built-in losses immediately before the transaction.

In lieu of limiting the basis of the transferred property in a transaction to which this provision applies, the Act permits the transferor and transferee to jointly elect to limit the basis in the stock received by the transferor to the aggregate fair market value of the transferred property. Such election shall be included with the tax returns of the transferor and transferee for the taxable year in which the transaction occurs and, once made, shall be irrevocable.

Effective Date

The provision applies to transactions and liquidations after the date of enactment (October 22, 2004).

[755] As is the case with non-liquidation transactions to which this provision applies, it is intended that the adjustment to the basis of property that is transferred in a liquidation to which this provision applies occurs only with respect to property the gain or loss on which would not have U.S. income tax consequences in the hands of the transferor immediately before the transfer but would have U.S. income tax consequences in the hands of the transferee immediately after the transfer. A technical correction may be necessary so that the statute reflects this intent.

18. Clarification of banking business for purposes of determining investment of earnings in U.S. property (sec. 837 of the Act and sec. 956 of the Code)

Present and Prior Law

In general, the subpart F rules[756] require the U.S. 10-percent shareholders of a controlled foreign corporation to include in income currently their pro rata shares of certain income of the controlled foreign corporation (referred to as "subpart F income"), whether or not such earnings are distributed currently to the shareholders. In addition, the U.S. 10-percent shareholders of a controlled foreign corporation are subject to U.S. tax currently on their pro rata shares of the controlled foreign corporation's earnings to the extent invested by the controlled foreign corporation in certain U.S. property.[757]

A shareholder's current income inclusion with respect to a controlled foreign corporation's investment in U.S. property for a taxable year is based on the controlled foreign corporation's average investment in U.S. property for such year. For this purpose, the U.S. property held (directly or indirectly) by the controlled foreign corporation must be measured as of the close of each quarter in the taxable year.[758] The amount taken into account with respect to any property is the property's adjusted basis as determined for purposes of reporting the controlled foreign corporation's earnings and profits, reduced by any liability to which the property is subject. The amount determined for current inclusion is the shareholder's pro rata share of an amount equal to the lesser of: (1) the controlled foreign corporation's average investment in U.S. property as of the end of each quarter of such taxable year, to the extent that such investment exceeds the foreign corporation's earnings and profits that were previously taxed on that basis; or (2) the controlled foreign corporation's current or accumulated earnings and profits (but not including a deficit), reduced by distributions during the year and by earnings that have been taxed previously as earnings invested in U.S. property.[759] An income inclusion is required only to the extent that the amount so calculated exceeds the amount of the controlled foreign corporation's earnings that have been previously taxed as subpart F income.[760]

For purposes of section 956, U.S. property generally is defined to include tangible property located in the United States, stock of a U.S. corporation, an obligation of a U.S. person, and certain intangible assets including a patent or copyright, an invention, model or design, a secret formula or process or similar property right which is acquired or developed by the controlled foreign corporation for use in the United States.[761]

Specified exceptions from the definition of U.S. property are provided for: (1) obligations of the United States or money; (2) certain export property; (3) certain trade or business obligations; (4) air-

[756] Secs. 951–964.
[757] Sec. 951(a)(1)(B).
[758] Sec. 956(a).
[759] Secs. 956 and 959.
[760] Secs. 951(a)(1)(B) and 959.
[761] Sec. 956(c)(1).

craft, railroad rolling stock, vessels, motor vehicles or containers used in transportation in foreign commerce and used predominantly outside of the United States; (5) certain insurance company reserves and unearned premiums related to insurance of foreign risks; (6) stock or debt of certain unrelated U.S. corporations; (7) moveable property (other than a vessel or aircraft) used for the purpose of exploring, developing, or certain other activities in connection with the ocean waters of the U.S. Continental Shelf; (8) an amount of assets equal to the controlled foreign corporation's accumulated earnings and profits attributable to income effectively connected with a U.S. trade or business; (9) property (to the extent provided in regulations) held by a foreign sales corporation and related to its export activities; (10) certain deposits or receipts of collateral or margin by a securities or commodities dealer, if such deposit is made or received on commercial terms in the ordinary course of the dealer's business as a securities or commodities dealer; and (11) certain repurchase and reverse repurchase agreement transactions entered into by or with a dealer in securities or commodities in the ordinary course of its business as a securities or commodities dealer.[762] Under prior law, an additional exception from the definition of U.S. property was provided for deposits with persons carrying on the banking business.

With regard to the exception for deposits with persons carrying on the banking business, the U.S. Court of Appeals for the Sixth Circuit in *The Limited, Inc.* v. *Commissioner*[763] concluded that a U.S. subsidiary of a U.S. shareholder was "carrying on the banking business" even though its operations were limited to the administration of the private label credit card program of the U.S. shareholder. Therefore, the court held that a controlled foreign corporation of the U.S. shareholder could make deposits with the subsidiary (e.g., through the purchase of certificates of deposit) under this exception, and avoid taxation of the deposits under section 956 as an investment in U.S. property.

Reasons for Change

The Congress believed that further guidance was necessary under the U.S. property investment provisions of subpart F with regard to the treatment of deposits with persons carrying on the banking business. In particular, the Congress believed that the transaction at issue in The Limited case was not contemplated or intended by Congress when it excepted from the definition of U.S. property deposits with persons carrying on the banking business. Therefore, the Congress believed that it was appropriate and necessary to clarify the scope of this exception so that it applies only to deposits with regulated banking businesses and their affiliates.

Explanation of Provision

The Act provides that the exception from the definition of U.S. property under section 956 for deposits with persons carrying on the banking business is limited to deposits with: (1) any bank (as defined by section 2(c) of the Bank Holding Company Act of 1956

[762] Sec. 956(c)(2).
[763] 286 F.3d 324 (6th Cir. 2002), *rev'g* 113 T.C. 169 (1999).

(12 U.S.C. 1841(c), without regard to paragraphs (C) and (G) of paragraph (2) of such section); or (2) any other corporation with respect to which a bank holding company (as defined by section 2(a) of such Act) or financial holding company (as defined by section 2(p) of such Act) owns directly or indirectly more than 80 percent by vote or value of the stock of such corporation.

No inference is intended as to the meaning of the phrase "carrying on the banking business" under prior law.

Effective Date

The provision is effective on the date of enactment (October 22, 2004).

19. Denial of deduction for interest on underpayments attributable to nondisclosed reportable transactions (sec. 838 of the Act and sec. 163 of the Code)

Present and Prior Law

In general, corporations may deduct interest paid or accrued within a taxable year on indebtedness.[764] Interest on indebtedness to the Federal government attributable to an underpayment of tax generally may be deducted pursuant to this provision.

Reasons for Change

The Congress believed that it was inappropriate for corporations to deduct interest paid to the Government with respect to certain tax shelter transactions.

Explanation of Provision

The Act disallows any deduction for interest paid or accrued within a taxable year on any portion of an underpayment of tax that is attributable to an understatement arising from an undisclosed listed transaction or from an undisclosed reportable avoidance transaction (other than a listed transaction).[765]

Effective Date

The provision is effective for underpayments attributable to transactions entered into in taxable years beginning after the date of enactment (October 22, 2004).

20. Clarification of rules for payment of estimated tax for certain deemed asset sales (sec. 839 of the Act and sec. 338 of the Code)

Present and Prior Law

In certain circumstances, taxpayers can make an election under section 338(h)(10) to treat a qualifying purchase of 80 percent of the stock of a target corporation by a corporation from a corpora-

[764] Sec. 163(a).

[765] The definitions of these transactions are the same as those previously described in connection with the provision elsewhere in this Act to modify the accuracy-related penalty for listed and certain reportable transactions.

tion that is a member of an affiliated group (or a qualifying purchase of 80 percent of the stock of an S corporation by a corporation from S corporation shareholders) as a sale of the assets of the target corporation, rather than as a stock sale. The election must be made jointly by the buyer and seller of the stock and is due by the 15th day of the ninth month beginning after the month in which the acquisition date occurs. An agreement for the purchase and sale of stock often may contain an agreement of the parties to make a section 338(h)(10) election.

Section 338(a) also permits a unilateral election by a buyer corporation to treat a qualified stock purchase of a corporation as a deemed asset acquisition, whether or not the seller of the stock is a corporation (or an S corporation is the target). In such a case, the seller or sellers recognize gain or loss on the stock sale (including any estimated taxes with respect to the stock sale), and the target corporation recognizes gain or loss on the deemed asset sale.

Section 338(h)(13) provides that, for purposes of section 6655 (relating to additions to tax for failure by a corporation to pay estimated income tax), tax attributable to a deemed asset sale under section 338(a)(1) shall not be taken into account.

Reasons for Change

The Congress was concerned that some taxpayers might inappropriately be taking the position that estimated tax and the penalty (computed in the amount of an interest charge) under section 6655 applies neither to the stock sale nor to the asset sale in the case of a section 338(h)(10) election. The Congress believed that estimated tax should not be avoided merely because an election may be made under section 338(h)(10). Furthermore, the Congress understood that parties typically negotiate a sale with an understanding as to whether or not an election under section 338(h)(10) will be made. In the event there is a contingency in this regard, the parties may provide for adjustments to the price to reflect the effect of the election.

Explanation of Provision

The Act clarifies section 338(h)(13) to provide that the exception for estimated tax purposes with respect to tax attributable to a deemed asset sale does not apply with respect to a qualified stock purchase for which an election is made under section 338(h)(10).

Under the Act if a transaction eligible for the election under section 338(h)(10) occurs, estimated tax would be determined based on the stock sale unless and until there is an agreement of the parties to make a section 338(h)(10) election.

If at the time of the sale there is an agreement of the parties to make a section 338(h)(10) election, then estimated tax is computed based on an asset sale, computed from the date of the sale.

If the agreement to make a section 338(h)(10) election is concluded after the stock sale, such that the original computation was based on a stock sale, estimated tax is recomputed based on the asset sale election.

No inference is intended as to prior law.

Effective Date

The provision is effective for qualified stock purchase transactions that occur after the date of enactment (October 22, 2004).

21. Exclusion of like-kind exchange property from nonrecognition treatment on the sale or exchange of a principal residence (sec. 840 of the Act)

Present and Prior Law

A taxpayer may exclude up to $250,000 ($500,000 if married filing a joint return) of gain realized on the sale or exchange of a principal residence. Under prior law, there were no special rules relating to the sale or exchange of a principal residence that was acquired in a like-kind exchange within the prior five years.

Reasons for Change

The Congress believed that the present-law exclusion of gain allowable upon the sale or exchange of principal residences serves an important role in encouraging home ownership. The Congress did not believe that this exclusion was appropriate for properties that were recently acquired in like-kind exchanges. Under the like-kind exchange rules, a taxpayer that exchanges property that was held for productive use or investment for like-kind property may acquire the replacement property on a tax-free basis. Because the replacement property generally has a low carry-over tax basis, the taxpayer will have taxable gain upon the sale or exchange of the replacement property. However, when the taxpayer converts the replacement property into the taxpayer's principal residence, the taxpayer may shelter some or all of this gain from income taxation. The Congress believed that this proposal balances the concerns associated with these provisions to reduce this tax shelter concern without unduly limiting the exclusion on sales or exchanges of principal residences.

Explanation of Provision

The Act provides that the exclusion for gain on the sale or exchange of a principal residence does not apply if the principal residence was acquired in a like-kind exchange in which any gain was not recognized within the prior five years.

Effective Date

The provision is effective for sales or exchanges of principal residences after the date of enactment (October 22, 2004).

22. Prevention of mismatching of interest and original issue discount deductions and income inclusions in transactions with related foreign persons (sec. 841 of the Act and secs. 163 and 267 of the Code)

Present and Prior Law

Income earned by a foreign corporation from its foreign operations generally is subject to U.S. tax only when such income is distributed to any U.S. person that holds stock in such corporation. Accordingly, a U.S. person that conducts foreign operations through a foreign corporation generally is subject to U.S. tax on the income from such operations when the income is repatriated to the United States through a dividend distribution to the U.S. person. The income is reported on the U.S. person's tax return for the year the distribution is received, and the United States imposes tax on such income at that time. However, certain anti-deferral regimes may cause the U.S. person to be taxed on a current basis in the United States with respect to certain categories of passive or highly mobile income earned by the foreign corporations in which the U.S. person holds stock. The main anti-deferral regimes have been the controlled foreign corporation rules of subpart F (secs. 951–964), the passive foreign investment company rules (secs. 1291–1298), and the prior-law foreign personal holding company rules (secs. 551–558).

As a general rule, there is allowed as a deduction all interest paid or accrued within the taxable year with respect to indebtedness, including the aggregate daily portions of original issue discount ("OID") of the issuer for the days during such taxable year.[766] However, if a debt instrument is held by a related foreign person, any portion of such OID is not allowable as a deduction to the payor of such instrument until paid ("related-foreign-person rule"). This related-foreign-person rule does not apply to the extent that the OID is effectively connected with the conduct by such foreign related person of a trade or business within the United States (unless such OID is exempt from taxation or is subject to a reduced rate of taxation under a treaty obligation).[767] Treasury regulations further modified the related-foreign-person rule by providing that in the case of a debt owed to a foreign personal holding company ("FPHC"), controlled foreign corporation ("CFC") or passive foreign investment company ("PFIC"), a deduction was allowed for OID as of the day on which the amount was includible in the income of the FPHC, CFC or PFIC, respectively.[768]

In the case of unpaid stated interest and expenses of related persons, where, by reason of a payee's method of accounting, an amount is not includible in the payee's gross income until it is paid but the unpaid amounts are deductible currently by the payor, the amount generally is allowable as a deduction when such amount is includible in the gross income of the payee.[769] With respect to stated interest and other expenses owed to related foreign corporations, Treasury regulations provide a general rule that requires a taxpayer to use the cash method of accounting with respect to the deduction of amounts owed to such related foreign persons (with an exception for income of a related foreign person that is effectively connected with the conduct of a U.S. trade or business and that is not exempt from taxation or subject to a reduced rate of taxation

[766] Sec. 163(e)(1).
[767] Sec. 163(e)(3).
[768] Treas. Reg. sec. 1.163–12(b)(3). In the case of a PFIC, the regulations further require that the person owing the amount at issue have in effect a qualified electing fund election pursuant to section 1295 with respect to the PFIC.
[769] Sec. 267(a)(2).

under a treaty obligation).[770] As in the case of OID, the Treasury regulations additionally provided that in the case of stated interest owed to a FPHC, CFC, or PFIC, a deduction was allowed as of the day on which the amount was includible in the income of the FPHC, CFC or PFIC.[771]

Reasons for Change

The special rules in the Treasury regulations for FPHCs, CFCs and PFICs were exceptions to the general rule that OID and unpaid interest owed to a related foreign person are deductible when paid (i.e., under the cash method). These special rules were deemed appropriate in the case of FPHCs, CFCs and PFICs because it was thought that there would be little material distortion in matching of income and deductions with respect to amounts owed to a related foreign corporation that is required to determine its taxable income and earnings and profits for U.S. tax purposes pursuant to the FPHC, subpart F or PFIC provisions. The Congress believed that this premise failed to take into account the situation where amounts owed to the related foreign corporation were included in the income of the related foreign corporation but were not currently included in the income of the related foreign corporation's U.S. shareholder. Consequently, under the Treasury regulations, both the U.S. payors and U.S.-owned foreign payors were able to accrue deductions for amounts owed to related FPHCs, CFCs or PFICs without the U.S. owners of such related entities taking into account for U.S. tax purposes a corresponding amount of income. These deductions could be used to reduce U.S. income or, in the case of a U.S.-owned foreign payor, to reduce earnings and profits which could reduce a CFC's income that would be currently taxable to its U.S. shareholders under subpart F.

Explanation of Provision

The Act provides that deductions for amounts accrued but unpaid (whether by U.S. or foreign persons) to related FPHCs, CFCs, or PFICs are allowable only to the extent that the amounts accrued by the payor are, for U.S. tax purposes, currently includible in the income of the direct or indirect U.S. owners of the related foreign corporation under the relevant inclusion rules.[772] Deductions that have accrued but are not allowable under this provision are allowed when the amounts are paid.

For purposes of determining the amount of the deduction allowable, the extent that an amount attributable to OID or an item is includible in the income of a U.S. person is determined without regard to (1) properly allocable deductions of the related foreign corporation, and (2) qualified deficits of the related foreign corporation under section 952(c)(1)(B). Properly allocable deductions of the related foreign corporation are those expenses, losses, and other deductible amounts of the related foreign corporation that are properly allocated or apportioned, under the principles of section

[770] Treas. Reg. sec. 1.267(a)–3(b)(1), –3(c).

[771] Treas. Reg. sec. 1.267(a)–3(c)(4).

[772] Section 413 of the Act repeals the foreign personal holding company regime, effective for taxable years of foreign corporations beginning after December 31, 2004, and taxable years of U.S. shareholders with or within which such taxable years of foreign corporations end.

954(b)(5), to the relevant income item of the related foreign corporation.

The following examples illustrate the operation of the Act. Assume the following facts. A U.S. parent corporation owns 60 percent of the stock of a CFC. An unrelated foreign corporation owns the remaining 40 percent interest in the CFC. The U.S. parent accrues an expense item of 100 to the CFC. The parent would be entitled to a current deduction of 100 for the accrued amount, before taking into account the Act. The item constitutes gross foreign base company income in the hands of the CFC. The item is the only gross income item of the CFC that has the potential to result in the CFC having subpart F income, and has not been paid by the end of the taxable year of the parent. The CFC has deductions of 60 that are properly allocated or apportioned to the 100 of gross foreign base company income under the principles of section 954(b)(5), resulting in 40 (100 − 60) of net foreign base company income. The CFC has earnings and profits for its taxable year in excess of 40, and has 40 of subpart F income. Under these facts, the U.S. parent is allowed a current deduction of 60 (100 × 60%).

If, in the example above, the CFC has deductions of 100 (or more) properly allocated or apportioned to the sole item of 100 of gross foreign base company income under the principles of section 954(b)(5), and has no other income or deductions, the same deduction is allowed to the U.S. parent. Under these circumstances, the parent is allowed a deduction of 60, whether the CFC has positive earnings and profits for its taxable year or has a deficit in earnings and profits for such year.

If the CFC's item of net foreign base company income is positive, and the earnings and profits limitation of section 952(c)(1)(A) reduces what would otherwise be a U.S. shareholder's pro rata share of the CFC's subpart F income, then the deduction will also be reduced under the provision. For example, assume the facts in the first example above, in which the CFC has deductions of 60 that are properly allocated or apportioned to the item of 100 of gross foreign base company income under the principles of section 954(b)(5), resulting in 40 of net foreign base company income. Further assume that, due solely to other losses, the CFC's earnings and profits for its taxable year are 10 instead of 40. In that case, the CFC's subpart F income is limited to 10, and only six is includible in the gross income of the U.S. parent as its pro rata share of subpart F income. Under the Act, the U.S. parent is allowed a current deduction in that case of 42 ((10+60)×60%). If, as a result of such other losses, the CFC has no earnings and profits for its taxable year or has a deficit in earnings and profits for such year, the U.S. parent is instead allowed a current deduction of 36 ((0+60)×60%).

The Act grants the Secretary regulatory authority to exempt transactions from these rules, including any transactions entered into by the payor in the ordinary course of a trade or business in which the payor is predominantly engaged, and (in the case of items other than OID) in which the payment of the accrued amounts occurs shortly after its accrual.

Effective Date

The provision is effective for payments accrued on or after the date of enactment (October 22, 2004).

23. Deposits made to suspend the running of interest on potential underpayments (sec. 842 of the Act and new sec. 6603 of the Code)

Present and Prior Law

Generally, interest on underpayments and overpayments continues to accrue during the period that a taxpayer and the IRS dispute a liability. The accrual of interest on an underpayment is suspended if the IRS fails to notify an individual taxpayer in a timely manner, but interest will begin to accrue once the taxpayer is properly notified. No similar suspension is available for other taxpayers.

A taxpayer that wants to limit its exposure to underpayment interest has a limited number of options. The taxpayer can continue to dispute the amount owed and risk paying a significant amount of interest. If the taxpayer continues to dispute the amount and ultimately loses, the taxpayer will be required to pay interest on the underpayment from the original due date of the return until the date of payment.

In order to avoid the accrual of underpayment interest, the taxpayer may choose to pay the disputed amount and immediately file a claim for refund. Payment of the disputed amount will prevent further interest from accruing if the taxpayer loses (since there is no longer any underpayment) and the taxpayer will earn interest on the resultant overpayment if the taxpayer wins. However, the taxpayer will generally lose access to the Tax Court if it follows this alternative. Amounts paid generally cannot be recovered by the taxpayer on demand, but must await final determination of the taxpayer's liability. Even if an overpayment is ultimately determined, overpaid amounts may not be refunded if they are eligible to be offset against other liabilities of the taxpayer.

The taxpayer may also make a deposit in the nature of a cash bond. The procedures for making a deposit in the nature of a cash bond are provided in Rev. Proc. 84–58.[773]

A deposit in the nature of a cash bond will stop the running of interest on an amount of underpayment equal to the deposit, but the deposit does not itself earn interest. A deposit in the nature of a cash bond is not a payment of tax and is not subject to a claim for credit or refund. A deposit in the nature of a cash bond may be made for all or part of the disputed liability and generally may be recovered by the taxpayer prior to a final determination. However, a deposit in the nature of a cash bond need not be refunded to the extent the Secretary determines that the assessment or collection of the tax determined would be in jeopardy, or that the deposit should be applied against another liability of the taxpayer in the same manner as an overpayment of tax. If the taxpayer recovers the deposit prior to final determination and a deficiency is later determined, the taxpayer will not receive credit for the period in

[773] 1984–2 C.B. 501.

which the funds were held as a deposit. The taxable year to which the deposit in the nature of a cash bond relates must be designated, but the taxpayer may request that the deposit be applied to a different year under certain circumstances.

Reasons for Change

The Congress believed that taxpayers should be able to limit their underpayment interest exposure in a tax dispute. An improved deposit system will help taxpayers better manage their exposure to underpayment interest without requiring them to surrender access to their funds or requiring them to make a potentially indefinite-term investment in a non-interest bearing account. The Congress believed that an improved deposit system that allows for the payment of interest on amounts that are not ultimately needed to offset tax liability when the taxpayer's position is upheld, as well as allowing for the offset of tax liability when the taxpayer's position fails, will provide an effective way for taxpayers to manage their exposure to underpayment interest. However, the Congress believed that such an improved deposit system should be reserved for the issues that are known to both parties, either through IRS examination or voluntary taxpayer disclosure.

Explanation of Provision

In general

The Act allows a taxpayer to deposit cash with the IRS that may subsequently be used to pay an underpayment of income, gift, estate, generation-skipping, or certain excise taxes. Interest will not be charged on the portion of the underpayment that is deposited for the period that the amount is on deposit. Generally, deposited amounts that have not been used to pay a tax may be withdrawn at any time if the taxpayer so requests in writing. The withdrawn amounts will earn interest at the applicable Federal rate to the extent they are attributable to a disputable tax.

The Secretary may issue rules relating to the making, use, and return of the deposits.

Use of a deposit to offset underpayments of tax

Any amount on deposit may be used to pay an underpayment of tax that is ultimately assessed. If an underpayment is paid in this manner, the taxpayer will not be charged underpayment interest on the portion of the underpayment that is so paid for the period the funds were on deposit.

For example, assume a calendar year individual taxpayer deposits $20,000 on May 15, 2005, with respect to a disputable item on its 2004 income tax return. On April 15, 2007, an examination of the taxpayer's year 2004 income tax return is completed, and the taxpayer and the IRS agree that the taxable year 2004 taxes were underpaid by $25,000. The $20,000 on deposit is used to pay $20,000 of the underpayment, and the taxpayer also pays the remaining $5,000. In this case, the taxpayer will owe underpayment interest from April 15, 2005 (the original due date of the return) to the date of payment (April 15, 2007) only with respect to the $5,000 of the underpayment that is not paid by the deposit. The taxpayer will owe underpayment interest on the remaining $20,000 of the underpayment only from April 15, 2005, to May 15, 2005, the date the $20,000 was deposited.

Withdrawal of amounts

A taxpayer may request the withdrawal of any amount on deposit at any time. The Secretary must comply with the withdrawal request unless the amount has already been used to pay tax or the Secretary properly determines that collection of tax is in jeopardy. Interest will be paid on deposited amounts that are withdrawn at a rate equal to the short-term applicable Federal rate for the period from the date of deposit to a date not more than 30 days preceding the date of the check paying the withdrawal. Interest is not payable to the extent the deposit was not attributable to a disputable tax.

For example, assume a calendar year individual taxpayer receives a 30-day letter showing a deficiency of $20,000 for taxable year 2004 and deposits $20,000 on May 15, 2006. On April 15, 2007, an administrative appeal is completed, and the taxpayer and the IRS agree that the 2004 taxes were underpaid by $15,000. $15,000 of the deposit is used to pay the underpayment. In this case, the taxpayer will owe underpayment interest from April 15, 2005 (the original due date of the return) to May 15, 2006, the date the $20,000 was deposited. Simultaneously with the use of the $15,000 to offset the underpayment, the taxpayer requests the return of the remaining amount of the deposit (after reduction for the underpayment interest owed by the taxpayer from April 15, 2005, to May 15, 2006). This amount must be returned to the taxpayer with interest determined at the applicable Federal short-term rate from the May 15, 2006, to a date not more than 30 days preceding the date of the check repaying the deposit to the taxpayer.

Limitation on amounts for which interest may be allowed

Interest on a deposit that is returned to a taxpayer shall be allowed for any period only to the extent attributable to a disputable item for that period. A disputable item is any item for which the taxpayer (1) has a reasonable basis for the treatment used on its return and (2) reasonably believes that the Secretary also has a reasonable basis for disallowing the taxpayer's treatment of such item.

All items included in a 30-day letter issued to a taxpayer are deemed disputable for this purpose. Thus, once a 30-day letter has been issued, the disputable amount cannot be less than the amount of the proposed deficiency shown in the 30-day letter. A 30-day letter is the first letter of proposed deficiency that allows the taxpayer an opportunity for administrative review in the Internal Revenue Service Office of Appeals.

Deposits are not payments of tax

A deposit is not a payment of tax prior to the time the deposited amount is used to pay a tax. Similarly, withdrawal of a deposit will not establish a period for which interest was allowable at the short-term applicable Federal rate for the purpose of establishing a net zero interest rate on a similar amount of underpayment for the same period.

Effective Date

The provision is effective for deposits made after date of enactment (October 22, 2004).

24. Authorize IRS to enter into installment agreements that provide for partial payment (sec. 843 of the Act and sec. 6159 of the Code)

Present and Prior Law

The Code authorizes the IRS to enter into written agreements with any taxpayer under which the taxpayer is allowed to pay taxes owed, as well as interest and penalties, in installment payments if the IRS determines that doing so will facilitate collection of the amounts owed (sec. 6159). An installment agreement does not reduce the amount of taxes, interest, or penalties owed. Generally, during the period installment payments are being made, other IRS enforcement actions (such as levies or seizures) with respect to the taxes included in that agreement are held in abeyance.

Prior to 1998, the IRS administratively entered into installment agreements that provided for partial payment (rather than full payment) of the total amount owed over the period of the agreement. In that year, the IRS Chief Counsel issued a memorandum concluding that partial payment installment agreements were not permitted.

Reasons for Change

According to the Department of the Treasury, at the end of fiscal year 2003, the IRS had not pursued 2.25 million cases totaling more than $16.5 billion in delinquent taxes. The Congress believed that clarifying that the IRS is authorized to enter into installment agreements with taxpayers that do not provide for full payment of the taxpayer's liability over the life of the agreement will improve effective tax administration.

The Congress recognized that some taxpayers are unable or unwilling to enter into a realistic offer-in-compromise. The Congress believed that these taxpayers should be encouraged to make partial payments toward resolving their tax liability, and that providing for partial payment installment agreements will help facilitate this.

Explanation of Provision

The Act clarifies that the IRS is authorized to enter into installment agreements with taxpayers which do not provide for full payment of the taxpayer's liability over the life of the agreement. The Act also requires the IRS to review partial payment installment agreements at least every two years. The primary purpose of this review is to determine whether the financial condition of the taxpayer has significantly changed so as to warrant an increase in the value of the payments being made.

Effective Date

The provision is effective for installment agreements entered into on or after the date of enactment (October 22, 2004).

25. Affirmation of consolidated return regulation authority (sec. 844 of the Act and sec. 1502 of the Code)

Present and Prior Law

An affiliated group of corporations may elect to file a consolidated return in lieu of separate returns. A condition of electing to file a consolidated return is that all corporations that are members of the consolidated group must consent to all the consolidated return regulations prescribed under section 1502 prior to the last day prescribed by law for filing such return.[774]

Section 1502 states:

> The Secretary shall prescribe such regulations as he may deem necessary in order that the tax liability of any affiliated group of corporations making a consolidated return and of each corporation in the group, both during and after the period of affiliation, may be returned, determined, computed, assessed, collected, and adjusted, in such manner as clearly to reflect the income-tax liability and the various factors necessary for the determination of such liability, and in order to prevent the avoidance of such tax liability.[775]

Under this authority, the Treasury Department has issued extensive consolidated return regulations.[776]

In the recent case of *Rite Aid Corp.* v. *United States,*[777] the Federal Circuit Court of Appeals addressed the application of a particular provision of certain consolidated return loss disallowance regulations, and concluded that the provision was invalid.[778] The

[774] Sec. 1501.

[775] Sec. 1502.

[776] Regulations issued under the authority of section 1502 are considered to be "legislative" regulations rather than "interpretative" regulations, and as such are usually given greater deference by courts in case of a taxpayer challenge to such a regulation. See, S. Rep. No. 960, 70th Cong., 1st Sess. at 15 (1928), describing the consolidated return regulations as "legislative in character". The Supreme Court has stated that ". . . legislative regulations are given controlling weight unless they are arbitrary, capricious, or manifestly contrary to the statute." *Chevron, U.S.A., Inc.* v. *Natural Resources Defense Council, Inc.*, 467 U.S. 837, 844 (1984) (involving an environmental protection regulation). For examples involving consolidated return regulations, see, e.g., *Wolter Construction Company* v. *Commissioner,* 634 F.2d 1029 (6th Cir. 1980); *Garvey, Inc.* v. *United States,* 1 Ct. Cl. 108 (1983), *aff'd* 726 F.2d 1569 (Fed. Cir. 1984), *cert. denied,* 469 U.S. 823 (1984). *Compare, e.g., Audrey J. Walton* v. *Commissioner,* 115 T.C. 589 (2000), describing different standards of review. The case did not involve a consolidated return regulation.

[777] 255 F.3d 1357 (Fed. Cir. 2001), *reh'g denied,* 2001 U.S. App. LEXIS 23207 (Fed. Cir. Oct. 3, 2001).

[778] Prior to this decision, there had been a few instances involving prior laws in which certain consolidated return regulations were held to be invalid. See, e.g., *American Standard, Inc.* v. *United States,* 602 F.2d 256 (Ct. Cl. 1979), discussed in the text *infra. See also Union Carbide Corp.* v. *United States,* 612 F.2d 558 (Ct. Cl. 1979), and *Allied Corporation* v. *United States,* 685 F. 2d 396 (Ct. Cl. 1982), all three cases involving the allocation of income and loss within a consolidated group for purposes of computation of a deduction allowed under prior law by the Code for Western Hemisphere Trading Corporations. See also *Joseph Weidenhoff* v. *Commissioner,* 32 T.C. 1222, 1242–1244 (1959), involving the application of certain regulations to the excess profits tax credit allowed under prior law, and concluding that the Commissioner had applied a particular regulation in an arbitrary manner inconsistent with the wording of the regulation and inconsistent with even a consolidated group computation. *Cf. Kanawha Gas & Utilities Co.* v. *Commissioner,* 214 F.2d 685 (1954), concluding that the substance of a transaction was an acquisition of assets rather than stock. Thus, a regulation governing basis of the assets of consolidated subsidiaries did not apply to the case. See also *General Machinery Corporation*

particular provision, known as the "duplicated loss" provision,[779] would have denied a loss on the sale of stock of a subsidiary by a parent corporation that had filed a consolidated return with the subsidiary, to the extent the subsidiary corporation had assets that had a built-in loss, or had a net operating loss, that could be recognized or used later.[780]

The Federal Circuit Court opinion contained language discussing the fact that the regulation produced a result different than the result that would have obtained if the corporations had filed separate returns rather than consolidated returns.[781]

The Federal Circuit Court opinion cited a 1928 Senate Finance Committee Report to legislation that authorized consolidated return regulations, which stated that "many difficult and complicated problems, . . . have arisen in the administration of the provisions permitting the filing of consolidated returns" and that the committee "found it necessary to delegate power to the commissioner to prescribe regulations legislative in character covering them."[782] The Court's opinion also cited a previous decision of the Court of Claims for the proposition, interpreting this legislative history, that section 1502 grants the Secretary "the power to conform the applicable income tax law of the Code to the special, myriad problems resulting from the filing of consolidated income tax returns;" but that section 1502 "does not authorize the Secretary to choose a

v. *Commissioner,* 33 B.T.A. 1215 (1936); *Lefcourt Realty Corporation,* 31 B.T.A. 978 (1935); *Helvering* v. *Morgans, Inc.,* 293 U.S. 121 (1934), interpreting the term "taxable year."

[779] Treas. Reg. sec. 1.1502–20(c)(1)(iii).

[780] Treasury Regulation section 1.1502–20, generally imposing certain "loss disallowance" rules on the disposition of subsidiary stock, contained other limitations besides the "duplicated loss" rule that could limit the loss available to the group on a disposition of a subsidiary's stock. Treasury Reg sec. 1.1502–20 as a whole was promulgated in connection with regulations issued under section 337(d), principally in connection with the so-called *General Utilities* repeal of 1986 (referring to the case of *General Utilities & Operating Company* v. *Helvering,* 296 U.S. 200 (1935)). Such repeal generally required a liquidating corporation, or a corporation acquired in a stock acquisition treated as a sale of assets, to pay corporate level tax on the excess of the value of its assets over the basis. Treasury regulation section 1.1502–20 principally reflected an attempt to prevent corporations filing consolidated returns from offsetting income with a loss on the sale of subsidiary stock. Such a loss could result from the unique upward adjustment of a subsidiary's stock basis required under the consolidated return regulations for subsidiary income earned in consolidation, an adjustment intended to prevent taxation of both the subsidiary and the parent on the same income or gain. As one example, absent a denial of certain losses on a sale of subsidiary stock, a consolidated group could obtain a loss deduction with respect to subsidiary stock, the basis of which originally reflected the subsidiary's value at the time of the purchase of the stock, and that had then been adjusted upward on recognition of any built-in income or gain of the subsidiary reflected in that value. The regulations also contained the duplicated loss factor addressed by the court in *Rite Aid.* The preamble to the regulations stated: "it is not administratively feasible to differentiate between loss attributable to built-in gain and duplicated loss." T.D. 8364, 1991–2 C.B. 43, 46 (Sept. 13, 1991). The government also argued in the *Rite Aid* case that duplicated loss was a separate concern of the regulations. 255 F.3d at 1360.

[781] For example, the court stated: "The duplicated loss factor . . . addresses a situation that arises from the sale of stock regardless of whether corporations file separate or consolidated returns. With I.R.C. secs. 382 and 383, Congress has addressed this situation by limiting the subsidiary's potential future deduction, not the parent's loss on the sale of stock under I.R.C. sec. 165." 255 F.3d 1357, 1360 (Fed. Cir. 2001).

[782] S. Rep. No. 960, 70th Cong., 1st Sess. 15 (1928). Though not quoted by the court in *Rite Aid,* the same Senate report also indicated that one purpose of the consolidated return authority was to permit treatment of the separate corporations as if they were a single unit, stating "The mere fact that by legal fiction several corporations owned by the same shareholders are separate entities should not obscure the fact that they are in reality one and the same business owned by the same individuals and operated as a unit." S. Rep. No. 960, 70th Cong., 1st Sess. 29 (1928).

method that imposes a tax on income that would not otherwise be taxed."[783]

The Federal Circuit Court construed these authorities and applied them to invalidate Treas. Reg. Sec. 1.1502–20(c)(1)(iii), stating that:

> The loss realized on the sale of a former subsidiary's assets after the consolidated group sells the subsidiary's stock is not a problem resulting from the filing of consolidated income tax returns. The scenario also arises where a corporate shareholder sells the stock of a non-consolidated subsidiary. The corporate shareholder could realize a loss under I.R.C. sec. 1001, and deduct the loss under I.R.C. sec. 165. The subsidiary could then deduct any losses from a later sale of assets. The duplicated loss factor, therefore, addresses a situation that arises from the sale of stock regardless of whether corporations file separate or consolidated returns. With I.R.C. secs. 382 and 383, Congress has addressed this situation by limiting the subsidiary's potential future deduction, not the parent's loss on the sale of stock under I.R.C. sec. 165.[784]

The Treasury Department has announced that it will not continue to litigate the validity of the duplicated loss provision of the regulations, and has issued interim regulations that permit taxpayers for all years to elect a different treatment, though they may apply the provision for the past if they wish.[785]

Reasons for Change

The Congress was concerned that Treasury Department resources might be unnecessarily devoted to defending challenges to consolidated return regulations on the mere assertion by a taxpayer that the result under the consolidated return regulations is different than the result for separate taxpayers. The consolidated return regulations offer many benefits that are not available to separate taxpayers, including generally rules that tax income re-

---

[783] *American Standard, Inc.* v. *United States*, 602 F.2d 256, 261 (Ct. Cl. 1979). That case did not involve the question of separate returns as compared to a single return approach. It involved the computation of a Western Hemisphere Trade Corporation ("WHTC") deduction under prior law (which deduction would have been computed as a percentage of each WHTC's taxable income if the corporations had filed separate returns), in a case where a consolidated group included several WHTCs as well as other corporations. The question was how to apportion income and losses of the admittedly consolidated WHTCs and how to combine that computation with the rest of the group's consolidated income or losses. The court noted that the new, changed regulations approach varied from the approach taken to a similar problem involving public utilities within a group and previously allowed for WHTCs. The court objected that the allocation method adopted by the regulation allowed non-WHTC losses to reduce WHTC income. However, the court did not disallow a method that would net WHTC income of one WHTC with losses of another WHTC, a result that would not have occurred under separate returns. Nor did the court expressly disallow a different fractional method that would net both income and losses of the WHTCs with those of other corporations in the consolidated group. The court also found that the regulation had been adopted without proper notice.

[784] *Rite Aid*, 255 F.3d at 1360.

[785] See Temp. Treas. Reg. sec. 1.1502–20T(i)(2), Temp. Treas. Reg. sec. 1.337(d)–2T, and Temp. Treas. Reg. sec. 1.1502–35T. The Treasury Department has also indicated its intention to continue to study all the issues that the original loss disallowance regulations addressed (including issues of furthering single entity principles) and possibly issue different regulations (not including the particular approach of Treas. Reg. Sec. 1.1502–20(c)(1)(iii)) on the issues in the future. See, e.g. Notice 2002–11, 2002–7 I.R.B. 526 (Feb. 19, 2002); T.D. 8984, 67 F.R. 11034 (March 12, 2002); REG–102740–02, 67 F.R. 11070 (March 12, 2002); see also Notice 2002–18, 2002–12 I.R.B. 644 (March 25, 2002); REG–131478–02, 67 F.R. 65060 (October 18, 2002); T.D. 9048, 68 F.R. 12287 (March 14, 2003); and T.D. 9118, REG–153172–03 (March 17, 2004).

ceived by the group once and attempt to avoid a second tax on that same income when stock of a subsidiary is sold.

Explanation of Provision

The Act confirms that, in exercising its authority under section 1502 to issue consolidated return regulations, the Treasury Department may provide rules treating corporations filing consolidated returns differently from corporations filing separate returns.

Thus, under the statutory authority of section 1502, the Treasury Department is authorized to issue consolidated return regulations utilizing either a single taxpayer or separate taxpayer approach or a combination of the two approaches, as Treasury deems necessary in order that the tax liability of any affiliated group of corporations making a consolidated return, and of each corporation in the group, both during and after the period of affiliation, may be determined and adjusted in such manner as clearly to reflect the income-tax liability and the various factors necessary for the determination of such liability, and in order to prevent avoidance of such liability.

Rite Aid is thus overruled to the extent it suggests that the Secretary is required to identify a problem created from the filing of consolidated returns in order to issue regulations that change the application of a Code provision. The Secretary may promulgate consolidated return regulations to change the application of a tax code provision to members of a consolidated group, provided that such regulations are necessary to clearly reflect the income tax liability of the group and each corporation in the group, both during and after the period of affiliation.

The Act nevertheless allows the result of the *Rite Aid* case to stand with respect to the type of factual situation presented in the case. That is, the Act provides for the override of the regulatory provision that took the approach of denying a loss on a deconsolidating disposition of stock of a consolidated subsidiary[786] to the extent the subsidiary had net operating losses or built in losses that could be used later outside the group.[787]

Retaining the result in the *Rite Aid* case with respect to the particular regulation section 1.1502–20(c)(1)(iii) as applied to the factual situation of the case does not in any way prevent or invalidate the various approaches Treasury has announced it will apply or that it intends to consider in lieu of the approach of that regulation, including, for example, the denial of a loss on a stock sale if inside losses of a subsidiary may also be used by the consolidated group, and the possible requirement that inside attributes be adjusted when a subsidiary leaves a group.[788]

---

[786] Treas. Reg. Sec. 1.1502–20(c)(1)(iii).

[787] The Act is not intended to overrule the current Treasury Department regulations, which allow taxpayers in certain circumstances for the past to follow Treasury Regulations section 1.1502–20(c)(1)(iii), if they choose to do so. Temp. Treas. Reg. sec. 1.1502–20T(i)(2).

[788] See, e.g., Notice 2002–11, 2002–7 I.R.B. 526 (February 19, 2002); Temp. Treas. Reg. sec. 1.337(d)–2T, (T.D. 8984, 67 F.R. 11034 (March 12, 2002) and T.D. 8998, 67 F.R. 37998 (May 31, 2002)); REG–102740–02, 67 F.R. 11070 (March 12, 2002); see also Notice 2002–18, 2002–12 I.R.B. 644 (March 25, 2002); REG–131478–02, 67 F.R. 65060 (October 18, 2002); Temp. Reg. sec. 1.1502–35T (T.D. 9048, 68 F.R. 12287 (March 14, 2003)); and T.D. 9118, REG–153172–03 (March 17, 2004). In exercising its authority under section 1502, the Secretary is also authorized to prescribe rules that protect the purpose of *General Utilities* repeal using presumptions and other simplifying conventions.

Effective Date

The provision is effective for all years, whether beginning before, on, or after the date of enactment (October 22, 2004). No inference is intended that the results following from this provision are not the same as the results under present law.

26. Expanded disallowance of deduction for interest on convertible debt (sec. 845 of the Act and sec. 163 of the Code)

Present and Prior Law

Whether an instrument qualifies for tax purposes as debt or equity is determined under all the facts and circumstances based on principles developed in case law. If an instrument qualifies as equity, the issuer generally does not receive a deduction for dividends paid and the holder generally includes such dividends in income (although individual holders generally may pay tax on the income at capital gains rates, and corporate holders generally may obtain a dividends-received deduction of at least 70 percent of the amount of the dividend). If an instrument qualifies as debt, the issuer may receive a deduction for accrued interest and the holder generally includes interest in income, subject to certain limitations.

Original issue discount ("OID") on a debt instrument is the excess of the stated redemption price at maturity over the issue price of the instrument. An issuer of a debt instrument with OID generally accrues and deducts the discount as interest over the life of the instrument even though interest may not be paid until the instrument matures. The holder of such a debt instrument also generally includes the OID in income as it accrues.

Under present and prior law, no deduction is allowed for interest or OID on a debt instrument issued by a corporation (or issued by a partnership to the extent of its corporate partners) that is payable in equity of the issuer or a related party (within the meaning of sections 267(b) and 707(b)), including a debt instrument a substantial portion of which is mandatorily convertible or convertible at the issuer's option into equity of the issuer or a related party.[789] In addition, a debt instrument is treated as payable in equity if a substantial portion of the principal or interest is required to be determined, or may be determined at the option of the issuer or related party, by reference to the value of equity of the issuer or related party.[790] A debt instrument also is treated as payable in equity if it is part of an arrangement that is designed to result in the payment of the debt instrument with or by reference to such equity, such as in the case of certain issuances of a forward contract in connection with the issuance of debt, nonrecourse debt that is secured principally by such equity, or certain debt instruments that are paid in, converted to, or determined with reference to the value of equity if it may be so required at the option of the holder or a related party and there is a substantial certainty that option will be exercised.[791]

---

[789] Sec. 163(l), enacted in the Taxpayer Relief Act of 1997, Pub. L. No. 105–34, sec. 1005(a).
[790] Sec. 163(l)(3)(B).
[791] Sec. 163(l)(3)(C).

Reasons for Change

The Joint Committee on Taxation staff's investigative report on Enron Corporation[792] described two structured financing transactions that Enron undertook in 1995 and 1999 involving what the report referred to as "investment unit securities." In substance, these securities featured principal repayment that was not unconditional in amount, as generally is required in order for debt characterization to be respected for tax purposes. Instead, principal on the securities was payable upon maturity in stock of an Enron affiliate (or in cash equivalent to the value of such stock).

The Congress believed that the financing activities undertaken by Enron in 1995 and 1999 using investment unit securities cast doubt upon the tax policy rationale for excluding stock ownership interests of 50 percent or less (by virtue of the prior-law related party threshold) from the application of the interest expense disallowance rules for certain convertible equity-linked debt instruments. With regard to the securities issued by Enron, the fact that Enron owned more than 50 percent of the affiliate stock at the time of the 1995 issuance but owned less than 50 percent of such stock at the time of the 1999 issuance (or shortly thereafter) had no discernible bearing on the intent or economic consequences of either transaction. In each instance, the transaction did not involve a borrowing by Enron in substance for which an interest deduction is appropriate. Rather, these transactions had the purpose and effect of carrying out a monetization of the affiliate stock. Nevertheless, the tax consequences of the 1995 issuance likely would have been different from those of the 1999 issuance if the prior-law rules had been in effect at the time of both transactions, rather than only at the time of the 1999 transaction (to which the interest expense disallowance rules did not apply because of the prior-law 50-percent related party threshold). Therefore, the Congress believed that eliminating the related party threshold for the application of these rules would further the tax policy objective of similar tax treatment of economically equivalent transactions. The Congress further believed that disallowed interest under the Act should increase the basis of the equity to which the equity is linked in a manner similar to that contemplated under currently proposed Treasury regulations.[793]

Explanation of Provision

The Act expands the disallowance of interest deductions on certain convertible or equity-linked corporate debt that is payable in, or by reference to the value of, equity. Under the Act, the disallowance is expanded to include interest on corporate debt that is payable in, or by reference to the value of, any equity held by the issuer (or by any related party) in any other person, without regard to whether such equity represents more than a 50-percent ownership interest in such person. However, the Act does not apply to debt that is issued by an active dealer in securities (or by a related

---

[792] See Joint Committee on Taxation, *Report of Investigation of Enron Corporation and Related Entities Regarding Federal Tax and Compensation Issues, and Policy Recommendations* (JCS–3–03), February 2003.

[793] Prop. Treas. Reg. sec. 1.263(g)–4.

party) if the debt is payable in, or by reference to the value of, equity that is held by the securities dealer in its capacity as a dealer in securities.

Effective Date

The provision applies to debt instruments that are issued after October 3, 2004.

27. Reform of tax treatment of certain leasing arrangements and limitation on deductions allocable to property used by governments or other tax-exempt entities (secs. 847 through 849 of the Act and secs. 167 and 168 of the Code, and new sec. 470 of the Code)

Present and Prior Law

Overview of depreciation

A taxpayer is allowed to recover, through annual depreciation deductions, the cost of certain property used in a trade or business or for the production of income. The amount of the depreciation deduction allowed with respect to tangible property for a taxable year is determined under the modified accelerated cost recovery system ("MACRS"). Under MACRS, different types of property generally are assigned applicable recovery periods and depreciation methods based on such property's class life. The recovery periods applicable to most tangible personal property (generally tangible property other than residential rental property and nonresidential real property) range from three to 25 years and are significantly shorter than the property's class life, which is intended to approximate the economic useful life of the property. In addition, the depreciation methods generally applicable to tangible personal property are the 200-percent and 150-percent declining balance methods, switching to the straight-line method for the taxable year in which the depreciation deduction would be maximized.

Characterization of leases for tax purposes

In general, a taxpayer is treated as the tax owner and is entitled to depreciate property leased to another party if the taxpayer acquires and retains significant and genuine attributes of a traditional owner of the property, including the benefits and burdens of ownership. No single factor is determinative of whether a lessor will be treated as the owner of the property. Rather, the determination is based on all the facts and circumstances surrounding the leasing transaction.

A sale-leaseback transaction is respected for Federal tax purposes if "there is a genuine multiple-party transaction with economic substance which is compelled or encouraged by business or regulatory realities, is imbued with tax-independent considerations, and is not shaped solely by tax-avoidance features that have meaningless labels attached." [794]

[794] *Frank Lyon Co. v. United States, 435 U.S. 561, 583–84 (1978).*

Recovery period for tax-exempt use property

Under present and prior law, "tax-exempt use property" must be depreciated on a straight-line basis over a recovery period equal to the longer of the property's class life or 125 percent of the lease term.[795] For purposes of this rule, "tax-exempt use property" is tangible property that is leased (other than under a short-term lease) to a tax-exempt entity.[796] For this purpose, the term "tax-exempt entity" includes Federal, State and local governmental units, charities, and, foreign entities or persons.[797]

In determining the length of the lease term for purposes of the 125-percent calculation, several special rules apply. In addition to the stated term of the lease, the lease term includes options to renew the lease or other periods of time during which the lessee could be obligated to make rent payments or assume a risk of loss related to the leased property.

Tax-exempt use property does not include property that is used by a taxpayer to provide a service to a tax-exempt entity. So long as the relationship between the parties is a bona fide service contract, the taxpayer will be allowed to depreciate the property used in satisfying the contract under normal MACRS rules, rather than the rules applicable to tax-exempt use property.[798] In addition, property is not treated as tax-exempt use property merely by reason of a short-term lease. In general, a short-term lease means any lease the term of which is less than three years and less than the greater of one year or 30 percent of the property's class life.[799]

Also, tax-exempt use property generally does not include qualified technological equipment that meets the exception for leases of high technology equipment to tax-exempt entities with lease terms of five years or less.[800] The recovery period for qualified technological equipment that is treated as tax-exempt use property, but is not subject to the high technology equipment exception, is five years.[801]

The term "qualified technological equipment" is defined as computers and related peripheral equipment, high technology telephone station equipment installed on a customer's premises, and high technology medical equipment.[802] In addition, tax-exempt use property does not include computer software because it is intangible property.

[795] Sec. 168(g)(3)(A). Under present law, section 168(g)(3)(C) states that the recovery period of "qualified technological equipment" is five years.

[796] Sec. 168(h)(1).

[797] Sec. 168(h)(2).

[798] Sec. 7701(e) provides that a service contract will not be respected, and instead will be treated as a lease of property, if such contract is properly treated as a lease taking into account all relevant factors. The relevant factors include, among others, the service recipient controls the property, the service recipient is in physical possession of the property, the service provider does not bear significant risk of diminished receipts or increased costs if there is nonperformance, the property is not used to concurrently provide services to other entities, and the contract price does not substantially exceed the rental value of the property.

[799] Sec. 168(h)(1)(C).

[800] Sec. 168(h)(3). However, the exception does not apply if part or all of the qualified technological equipment is financed by a tax-exempt obligation, is sold by the tax-exempt entity (or related party) and leased back to the tax-exempt entity (or related party), or the tax-exempt entity is the United States or any agency or instrumentality of the United States.

[801] Sec. 168(g)(3)(C).

[802] Sec. 168(i)(2).

Reasons for Change

The special rules applicable to the depreciation of tax-exempt use property were enacted to prevent tax-exempt entities from using leasing arrangements to transfer the tax benefits of accelerated depreciation on property they used to a taxable entity. The Congress was concerned that some taxpayers were attempting to circumvent this policy through the creative use of service contracts with the tax-exempt entities.

More generally, the Congress believed that certain ongoing leasing activity with tax-exempt entities and foreign governments indicated that the prior-law tax rules were not effective in curtailing the ability of a tax-exempt entity to transfer certain tax benefits to a taxable entity. The Congress was concerned about this activity and the continual development of new structures that purported to minimize or neutralize the effect of these rules. In addition, the Congress also was concerned about the increasing use of certain leasing structures involving property purported to be qualified technological equipment. Although the Congress recognized that leasing plays an important role in ensuring the availability of capital to businesses, it believed that certain transactions of which it recently had become aware did not serve this role. These transactions resulted in little or no accumulation of capital for financing or refinancing but, instead, essentially involved an accommodation fee paid by a U.S. taxpayer to a tax indifferent party.

In discussing the reasons for the enactment of rules in 1984 that were intended to limit the transfer of tax benefits to taxable entities with respect to property used by tax-exempt entities, Congress at the time stated that: (1) the Federal budget was in no condition to sustain substantial and growing revenue losses by making additional tax benefits (in excess of tax exemption itself) available to tax-exempt entities through leasing transactions; (2) there were concerns about possible problems of accountability of governments to their citizens, and of tax-exempt organizations to their clientele, if substantial amounts of their property came under the control of outside parties solely because the Federal tax system made leasing more favorable than owning; (3) the tax system should not encourage tax-exempt entities to dispose of assets they own or to forego control over the assets they use; (4) there were concerns about waste of Federal revenues because in some cases a substantial portion of the tax savings was retained by lawyers, investment bankers, lessors, and investors and, thus, the Federal revenue loss became more of a gain to financial entities than to tax-exempt entities; (5) providing aid to tax-exempt entities through direct appropriations was more efficient and appropriate than providing such aid through the Code; and (6) popular confidence in the tax system must be sustained by ensuring that the system generally is working correctly and fairly.[803]

The Congress believed that the reasons stated above for the enactment in 1984 of the present-law rules are as important today as they were in 1984. Unfortunately, the prior-law rules did not adequately deter taxpayers from engaging in transactions that at-

[803] See H.R. Rep. No. 98–432, Pt. 2, pp. 1140–1141 (1984) and S. Prt. No. 98–169, Vol. I, pp. 125–127 (1984).

tempted to circumvent the rules enacted in 1984. Therefore, the Congress believed that changes to prior law were essential to ensure the attainment of the aforementioned Congressional intentions, provided such changes did not inhibit legitimate commercial leasing transactions that involve a significant and genuine transfer of the benefits and burdens of tax ownership between the taxpayer and the tax-exempt lessee.

Explanation of Provision

Overview

The Act expands the prior-law definition of tax-exempt entity for purposes of this provision, modifies the recovery period of certain property leased to a tax-exempt entity, alters the definition of lease term for all property leased to a tax-exempt entity, expands the short-term lease exception for qualified technological equipment, and establishes rules to limit deductions associated with leases to tax-exempt entities if the leases do not satisfy specified criteria.

Definition of tax-exempt entity

The Act expands the definition of tax-exempt entity for purposes of this provision to include certain Indian tribal governments in addition to Federal, State, local, and foreign governmental units, charities, foreign entities or persons.

Modify the recovery period of certain property leased to a tax-exempt entity

The Act modifies the recovery period for qualified technological equipment, computer software and certain intangibles leased to a tax-exempt entity to be the longer of the property's assigned class life[804] or 125 percent of the lease term. This provision does not apply to short-term leases, as defined under present and prior law with a modification described below for short-term leases of qualified technological equipment.

Modify definition of lease term

In determining the length of the lease term for purposes of the 125-percent calculation, the Act provides that the lease term includes all service contracts (whether or not treated as a lease under section 7701(e)) and other similar arrangements that follow a lease of property to a tax-exempt entity and that are part of the same transaction (or series of transactions) as the lease.[805]

Under the Act, service contracts and other similar arrangements include arrangements by which services are provided using the property in exchange for fees that provide a source of repayment of the capital investment in the property.[806]

---

[804] In the case of computer software and intangible assets, this rule is applied by substituting useful life and amortization period, respectively, for class life.

[805] A service contract involving property that previously was leased to the tax-exempt entity is not part of the same transaction as the preceding leasing arrangement (and, thus, is not included in the lease term of such arrangement) if the service contract was not included in the terms and conditions, or contemplated at the inception, of the preceding leasing arrangement.

[806] For purposes of this provision, a service contract does not include an arrangement for the provision of services if the leased property or substantially similar property is not utilized to provide such services. For example, if at the conclusion of a lease term, a tax-exempt lessee pur-

Continued

This requirement applies to all leases of property to a tax-exempt entity.

Expand short-term lease exception for qualified technological equipment

For purposes of determining whether a lease of qualified technological equipment to a tax-exempt entity satisfies the five-year short-term lease exception for leases of qualified technological equipment, the Act provides that the term of the lease does not include an option or options of the lessee to renew or extend the lease, provided the rents under the renewal or extension are based upon fair market value determined at the time of the renewal or extension. The aggregate period of such renewals or extensions not included in the lease term under this provision may not exceed 24 months. In addition, this provision does not apply to any period following the failure of a tax-exempt lessee to exercise a purchase option if the result of such failure is that the lease renews automatically at fair market value rents.

Limit deductions for certain leases of property to tax-exempt parties

The Act also provides that if a taxpayer leases property to a tax-exempt entity, the taxpayer may not claim deductions for a taxable year from the lease transaction in excess of the taxpayer's gross income from the lease for that taxable year. The deduction limitation provision does not apply to certain transactions involving property with respect to which the low-income housing credit or the rehabilitation credit is allowable.

The deduction limitation provision applies to deductions or losses related to a lease to a tax-exempt entity and the leased property.[807] Any disallowed deductions are carried forward and treated as deductions related to the lease in the following taxable year subject to the same limitations. Under rules similar to those applicable to passive activity losses (including the treatment of dispositions of property in which less than all of the gain or loss from the disposition is recognized),[808] a taxpayer generally is permitted to deduct previously disallowed deductions and losses when the taxpayer completely disposes of its interest in the property.

A lease of property to a tax-exempt party is not subject to the deduction limitations of this provision if the lease satisfies all of the following requirements:[809]

chases property from the taxpayer and enters into an agreement pursuant to which the taxpayer maintains the property, the maintenance agreement will not be included in the lease term for purposes of the 125-percent computation.

[807] Deductions related to a lease of tax-exempt use property include any depreciation or amortization expense, maintenance expense, taxes or the cost of acquiring an interest in, or lease of, property. In addition, this provision applies to interest that is properly allocable to tax-exempt use property, including interest on any borrowing by a related person, the proceeds of which were used to acquire an interest in the property, whether or not the borrowing is secured by the leased property or any other property.

[808] See Sec. 469(g).

[809] Even if a transaction satisfies each of the following requirements, the taxpayer will be treated as the owner of the leased property only if the taxpayer acquires and retains significant and genuine attributes of an owner of the property under the present-law tax rules, including the benefits and burdens of ownership.

1. Tax-exempt lessee does not monetize its lease obligations

In general, the tax-exempt lessee may not monetize its lease obligations (including any purchase option) in an amount that exceeds 20 percent of the taxpayer's adjusted basis[810] in the leased property at the time the lease is entered into.[811] Specifically, a lease does not satisfy this requirement if the tax-exempt lessee monetizes such excess amount pursuant to an arrangement, set-aside, or expected set-aside, that is to or for the benefit of the taxpayer or any lender, or is to or for the benefit of the tax-exempt lessee, in order to satisfy the lessee's obligations or options under the lease. This determination shall be made at all times during the lease term and shall include the amount of any interest or other income or gain earned on any amount set aside or subject to an arrangement described in this provision. For purposes of determining whether amounts have been set aside or are expected to be set aside, amounts are treated as set aside or expected to be set aside only if a reasonable person would conclude that the facts and circumstances indicate that such amounts are set aside or expected to be set aside.[812]

The Secretary may provide by regulations that this requirement is satisfied, even if a tax-exempt lessee monetizes its lease obligations or options in an amount that exceeds 20 percent of the taxpayer's adjusted basis in the leased property, in cases in which the creditworthiness of the tax-exempt lessee would not otherwise satisfy the taxpayer's customary underwriting standards. Such credit support would not be permitted to exceed 50 percent of the taxpayer's adjusted basis in the property. In addition, if the lease provides the tax-exempt lessee an option to purchase the property for a fixed purchase price (or for other than the fair market value of the property determined at the time of exercise of the option), such credit support at the time that such option may be exercised would not be permitted to exceed 50 percent of the purchase option price.

Certain lease arrangements that involve circular cash flows or insulation of the taxpayer's equity investment from the risk of loss fail this requirement without regard to the amount in which the tax-exempt lessee monetizes its lease obligations or options. Thus, a lease does not satisfy this requirement if the tax-exempt lessee enters into an arrangement to monetize in any amount its lease obligations or options if such arrangement involves (1) a loan (other than an amount treated as a loan under section 467 with respect to a section 467 rental agreement) from the tax-exempt lessee to the taxpayer or a lender, (2) a deposit that is received, a letter of

[810] For purposes of this requirement, the adjusted basis of property acquired by the taxpayer in a like-kind exchange or involuntary conversion to which section 1031 or section 1033 applies is equal to the lesser of (1) the fair market value of the property as of the beginning of the lease term, or (2) the amount that would be the taxpayer's adjusted basis if section 1031 or section 1033 did not apply to such acquisition.

[811] Arrangements to monetize lease obligations include defeasance arrangements, loans by the tax-exempt entity (or an affiliate) to the taxpayer (or an affiliate) or any lender, deposit agreements, letters of credit collateralized with cash or cash equivalents, payment undertaking agreements, prepaid rent (within the meaning of the regulations under section 467), sinking fund arrangements, guaranteed investment contracts, financial guaranty insurance, or any similar arrangements.

[812] It is anticipated under the Act that the customary and budgeted funding by tax-exempt entities of current obligations under a lease through unrestricted accounts or funds for general working capital needs will not be considered arrangements, set-asides, or expected set-asides under this requirement.

credit that is issued, or a payment undertaking agreement that is entered into by a lender otherwise involved in the transaction, or (3) in the case of a transaction that involves a lender, any credit support made available to the taxpayer in which any such lender does not have a claim that is senior to the taxpayer.

2. Taxpayer makes and maintains a substantial equity investment in the leased property

The taxpayer must make and maintain a substantial equity investment in the leased property. For this purpose, a taxpayer generally does not make or maintain a substantial equity investment unless (1) at the time the lease is entered into, the taxpayer initially makes an unconditional at-risk equity investment in the property of at least 20 percent of the taxpayer's adjusted basis[813] in the leased property at that time,[814] (2) the taxpayer maintains such equity investment throughout the lease term, and (3) at all times during the lease term, the fair market value of the property at the end of the lease term is reasonably expected to be equal to at least 20 percent of such basis.[815] For this purpose, the fair market value of the property at the end of the lease term is reduced to the extent that a person other than the taxpayer bears a risk of loss in the value of the property.

This requirement does not apply to leases with lease terms of five years or less.

3. Tax-exempt lessee does not bear more than a minimal risk of loss

The tax-exempt lessee generally may not assume or retain more than a minimal risk of loss, other than the obligation to pay rent and insurance premiums, to maintain the property, or other similar conventional obligations of a net lease.[816] For this purpose, a tax-exempt lessee assumes or retains more than a minimal risk of loss if, as a result of obligations assumed or retained by, on behalf of, or pursuant to an agreement with the tax-exempt lessee, the taxpayer is protected from either (1) any portion of the loss that would occur if the fair market value of the leased property were 25 percent less than the leased property's reasonably expected fair market value at the time the lease is terminated, or (2) an aggregate loss that is greater than 50 percent of the loss that would occur if the fair market value of the leased property were zero at lease ter-

[813] For purposes of this requirement, the adjusted basis of property acquired by the taxpayer in a like-kind exchange or involuntary conversion to which section 1031 or section 1033 applies is equal to the lesser of (1) the fair market value of the property as of the beginning of the lease term, or (2) the amount that would be the taxpayer's adjusted basis if section 1031 or section 1033 did not apply to such acquisition.

[814] The taxpayer's at-risk equity investment shall include only consideration paid, and personal liability incurred, by the taxpayer to acquire the property. Cf. Rev. Proc. 2001–28, 2001–2 C.B. 1156.

[815] Cf. Rev. Proc. 2001–28, sec. 4.01(2), 2001–1 C.B. 1156. The fair market value of the property must be determined without regard to inflation or deflation during the lease term and after subtracting the cost of removing the property.

[816] Examples of arrangements by which a tax-exempt lessee might assume or retain a risk of loss include put options, residual value guarantees, residual value insurance, and service contracts. However, leases do not fail to satisfy this requirement solely by reason of lease provisions that require the tax-exempt lessee to pay a contractually stipulated loss value to the taxpayer in the event of an early termination due to a casualty loss, a material default by the tax-exempt lessee (excluding the failure by the tax-exempt lessee to enter into an arrangement described above), or other similar extraordinary events that are not reasonably expected to occur at lease inception.

mination.[817] In addition, the Secretary may provide by regulations that this requirement is not satisfied where the tax-exempt lessee otherwise retains or assumes more than a minimal risk of loss. Such regulations shall be prospective only.

This requirement does not apply to leases with lease terms of 5 years or less.

4. Lease of certain property does not include a fixed-price purchase option of the tax-exempt lessee

The tax-exempt lessee may not have an option to purchase the leased property for any stated purchase price other than the fair market value of the property (as determined at the time of exercise of the option). This requirement does not apply to (1) property with a class life (as defined in section 168(i)(1)) of seven years or less, or (2) any fixed-wing aircraft or vessels (i.e., ships).

Coordination with like-kind exchange and involuntary conversion rules

Under the deduction limitation provision, neither the like-kind exchange rules (sec. 1031) nor the involuntary conversion rules (sec. 1033) apply if either (1) the exchanged or converted property is tax-exempt use property subject to a lease that was entered into prior to the effective date of the provision and the lease would not have satisfied the requirements of the provision had such requirements been in effect when the lease was entered into, or (2) the replacement property is tax-exempt use property subject to a lease that does not meet the requirements of the provision.

Other rules

The deduction limitation provision continues to apply throughout the lease term to property that initially was tax-exempt use property, even if the property ceases to be tax-exempt use property during the lease term.[818] In addition, the deduction limitation provision is applied before the application of the passive activity loss rules under section 469.

The deduction limitation provision does not alter the treatment of any Qualified Motor Vehicle Operating Agreement within the meaning of section 7701(h). In the case of any such agreement, the second and third requirements provided by the provision (relating to taxpayer equity investment and tax-exempt lessee risk of loss, respectively) shall be applied without regard to any terminal rental adjustment clause.

[817] For purposes of this requirement, residual value protection provided to the taxpayer by a manufacturer or dealer of the leased property is not treated as borne by the tax-exempt lessee if the manufacturer or dealer provides such residual value protection to customers in the ordinary course of its business.

[818] Conversely, however, a lease of property that is not tax-exempt use property does not become subject to this provision solely by reason of requisition or seizure by the Federal government in national emergency circumstances.

Effective Date

The provision generally is effective for leases[819] entered into after March 12, 2004.[820] However, the provision does not apply to property located in the United States that is subject to a lease with respect to which a formal application (1) was submitted for approval to the Federal Transit Administration (an agency of the Department of Transportation) after June 30, 2003, and before March 13, 2004, (2) is approved by the Federal Transit Administration before January 1, 2006, and (3) includes a description and the fair market value of such property.

The provisions relating to intangible assets and Indian tribal governments are effective for leases entered into after October 3, 2004.

The provisions relating to coordination with the like-kind exchange and involuntary conversion rules are effective with respect to property that is exchanged or converted after the date of enactment (October 22, 2004).

No inference is intended regarding the appropriate prior-law tax treatment of transactions entered into prior to the effective date of the Act. In addition, it is intended that the Act shall not be construed as altering or supplanting the present-law tax rules providing that a taxpayer is treated as the owner of leased property only if the taxpayer acquires and retains significant and genuine attributes of an owner of the property, including the benefits and burdens of ownership. The Act also is not intended to affect the scope of any other present-law or prior-law tax rules or doctrines applicable to purported leasing transactions.

C. Reduction of Fuel Tax Evasion

1. Exemption from certain excise taxes for mobile machinery vehicles and modification of definition of off-highway vehicle (secs. 851 and 852 of the Act and secs. 4053, 4072, 4082, 4483, 6421, and 7701 of the Code)

Present and Prior Law

The definition of a "highway vehicle" affects the application of the retail tax on heavy vehicles, the heavy vehicle use tax, the tax on tires, and fuel taxes.[821] Section 4051 of the Code provides for a 12-percent retail sales tax on tractors, heavy trucks with a gross vehicle weight ("GVW") over 33,000 pounds, and trailers with a GVW over 26,000 pounds. Section 4071 provides for a tax on certain highway vehicle tires.[822] Section 4481 provides for an annual

[819] While the effective date of the provision refers specifically to leases, it is intended that the deduction limitation provision applies without regard to whether the tax-exempt use property is treated as such by reason of a lease or otherwise (e.g., by virtue of section 168(h)(6) because the property is owned by a partnership that has a tax-exempt partner and provides for certain special allocations). A technical correction, effective for transactions involving property that is acquired after March 12, 2004, may be necessary to reflect this intent. On March 10, 2005, the IRS issued Notice 2005–29, 2005–13 I.R.B. 796, which provides temporary transition relief from the Act to partnerships and other pass-through entities that are treated as holding tax-exempt use property by virtue of section 168(h)(6).

[820] If a lease entered into on or before March 12, 2004, is transferred in a transaction that does not materially alter the terms of such lease, the Act shall not apply to the lease as a result of such transfer.

[821] Secs. 4051, 4071, 4481, 4041 and 4081.

[822] This tax was modified by section 869 of the Act.

use tax on heavy vehicles with a GVW of 55,000 pounds or more, with higher rates of tax on heavier vehicles. All of these excise taxes are paid into the Highway Trust Fund.

Federal excise taxes are also levied on the motor fuels used in highway vehicles. Gasoline is subject to a tax of 18.4 cents per gallon, of which 18.3 cents per gallon is paid into the Highway Trust Fund and 0.1 cent per gallon is paid into the Leaking Underground Storage Tank ("LUST") Trust Fund. Highway diesel fuel is subject to a tax of 24.4 cents per gallon, of which 24.3 cents per gallon is paid into the Highway Trust Fund and 0.1 cent per gallon is paid into the LUST Trust Fund.

The Code does not define a "highway vehicle." For purposes of these taxes, Treasury regulations define a highway vehicle as any self-propelled vehicle or trailer or semitrailer designed to perform a function of transporting a load over the public highway, whether or not also designed to perform other functions. Excluded from the definition of highway vehicle are (1) certain specially designed mobile machinery vehicles for non-transportation functions (the "mobile machinery exception"); (2) certain vehicles specially designed for off-highway transportation for which the special design substantially limits or impairs the use of such vehicle to transport loads over the highway (the "off-highway transportation vehicle" exception); and (3) certain trailers and semi-trailers specially designed to function only as an enclosed stationary shelter for the performance of non-transportation functions off the public highways.[823]

Under prior law, the mobile machinery exception applied if three tests were met: (1) the vehicle consists of a chassis to which jobsite machinery (unrelated to transportation) has been permanently mounted; (2) the chassis has been specially designed to serve only as a mobile carriage and mount for the particular machinery; and (3) by reason of such special design, the chassis could not, without substantial structural modification, be used to transport a load other than the particular machinery. An example of a mobile machinery vehicle is a crane mounted on a truck chassis that meets the foregoing factors.

On June 6, 2002, the Treasury Department put forth proposed regulations that would eliminate the mobile machinery exception.[824] The other exceptions from the definition of highway vehicle would continue to apply with some modifications. Under the proposed regulations, the chassis of a mobile machinery vehicle would be subject to the retail sales tax on heavy vehicles unless the vehicle qualified under the off-highway transportation vehicle exception. Also, under the proposed regulations, mobile machinery vehicles may be subject to the heavy vehicle use tax. In addition, the tax credits, refunds, and exemptions from tax may not be available for the fuel used in these vehicles.

The proposed regulations also would modify the off-highway transportation vehicle exception.[825] Under the proposed regulations, a vehicle is not treated as a highway vehicle if it is specially designed for the primary function of transporting a particular type of load other than over the public highway and because of this spe-

---

823 See Treas. Reg. sec. 48.4061–1(d)).

824 Prop. Treas. Reg. sec. 48.4051–1(a), 67 Fed. Reg. 38913, 38914–38915 (2002).

825 Prop. Treas. Reg. sec. 48.4051–1(a)(2)(i).

cial design its capability to transport a load over the public highway is substantially limited or impaired. A vehicle's design is determined solely on the basis of its physical characteristics. In determining whether substantial limitation or impairment exists, account may be taken of factors such as the size of the vehicle, whether it is subject to the licensing, safety, and other requirements applicable to highway vehicles, and whether it can transport a load at a sustained speed of at least 25 miles per hour. Under the proposed regulation, it is not material that a vehicle can transport a greater load off the public highway than it is permitted to transport over the public highway.

The proposed regulation provides an exception to the definition of a highway vehicle for nontransportation trailers and semitrailers.[826] Under the proposed regulation, a trailer or semitrailer is not treated as a highway vehicle if it is specially designed to function only as an enclosed stationary shelter for the carrying on of an off-highway function at an off-highway site. For example, a trailer that is capable only of functioning as an office for an off-highway construction operation is not a highway vehicle.

Reasons for Change

The Treasury Department delayed issuance of final regulations regarding mobile machinery to allow Congressional action on a statutory definition of mobile machinery vehicle. The Highway Trust Fund is supported by taxes related to the use of vehicles on the public highways. The Congress understood that a mobile machinery exemption was created by Treasury regulation because the Treasury Department believed that mobile machinery used the public highways only incidentally to get from one job site to another. However, it had come to the attention of the Congress that certain vehicles are taking advantage of the mobile machinery exemption even though they spend a significant amount of time on public highways and, therefore, cause wear and tear to such highways. Because the mobile machinery exemption is based on incidental use of the public highways, the Congress believed it was appropriate to add a use-based test to the design-based test that exists under current regulation. The Congress believed that a use-based test was practical to administer only for purposes of the fuel excise tax.

Explanation of Provision

The Act codifies the three-part mobile machinery exemption for purposes of three taxes: the retail tax on heavy vehicles, the heavy vehicle use tax, and the tax on tires. Thus, if a vehicle can satisfy the three-part design test, it will not be treated as a highway vehicle and will be exempt from these taxes.

For purposes of the fuel excise tax, the three-part design test is codified and a use test is added by the provision. Specifically, in addition to the three-part design test, the vehicle must not have traveled more than 7,500 miles over public highways during the owner's taxable year. Refunds of fuel taxes are permitted on an annual

[826] Prop. Treas. Reg. sec. 48.4051–1(a)(2)(ii).

basis only. For purposes of this rule, a person's taxable year is his taxable year for income tax purposes. Vehicles owned by an organization described in section 501(c), exempt from tax under section 501(a), need only satisfy the three-part design test to recover taxes paid with respect to such vehicles.

The Act also adopts the definition of an off-highway transportation vehicle and a nontransportation trailer and semitrailer described in Proposed Treasury Regulation section 48.4051–1(a)(2).

For example, as provided in the proposed regulations,[827] Vehicle C consists of a truck chassis on which an oversize body designed to transport and apply liquid agricultural chemicals on farms has been installed. It is capable of transporting a load over the public highway. It is 132 inches in width, which is considerably in excess of standard highway vehicle width. For travel on uneven and soft terrain, it is equipped with oversize wheels with high-flotation tires, and nonstandard axles, brakes, and transmission. It has a special fuel and carburetor air filtration system that enable it to perform efficiently in an environment of dirt and dust. It is not able to maintain a speed of 25 miles per hour for more than one mile while fully loaded. Because Vehicle C is a self-propelled vehicle capable of transporting a load over the public highway, it would meet the general definition of a highway vehicle. However, its considerable physical characteristics for transporting its load other than over the public highway, when compared with its physical characteristics for transporting the load over the public highway, establish that it is specially designed for the primary function of transporting its load other than over the public highway. Further, the physical characteristics for transporting its load other than over the public highway substantially limit its capability to transport a load over the public highway. Therefore, Vehicle C is an off-highway vehicle and is not treated as a highway vehicle.

Effective Date

The provisions are generally effective after the date of enactment (October 22, 2004). As to the fuel taxes, the provisions are effective for taxable years beginning after the date of enactment.

2. Taxation of aviation-grade kerosene (sec. 853 of the Act and secs. 4041, 4081, 4082, 4083, 4091, 4092, 4093, 4101, and 6427 of the Code)

Present and Prior Law

In general

Under prior law, aviation fuel was defined as kerosene and any liquid (other than any product taxable under section 4081) that is suitable for use as a fuel in an aircraft.[828] Unlike other fuels that generally are taxed upon removal from a terminal rack,[829] under prior law, aviation fuel was taxed upon sale of the fuel by a pro-

[827] Prop. Treas. Reg. sec. 48.4051–1(c), Example (3).

[828] Sec. 4093(a). All references to sections 4091, 4092, and 4093 are to such sections as in effect prior to enactment of the Act, which repealed such sections.

[829] A rack is a mechanism capable of delivering taxable fuel into a means of transport other than a pipeline or vessel. Treas. Reg. sec. 48.4081–1(b).

ducer or importer.[830] Sales by a registered producer to another registered producer were exempt from tax, with the result that, as a practical matter, aviation fuel was not taxed under prior law until the fuel was used at the airport (or sold to an unregistered person). Use of untaxed aviation fuel by a producer was treated as a taxable sale.[831] The producer or importer was liable for the tax. The rate of tax on aviation fuel under present and prior law is 21.9 cents per gallon.[832]

Under present and prior law, the tax on aviation fuel is reported by filing Form 720—Quarterly Federal Excise Tax Return. Generally, semi-monthly deposits are required using Form 8109B—Federal Tax Deposit Coupon or by depositing the tax by electronic funds transfer.

Partial exemptions

In general, under present and prior law aviation fuel sold for use or used in commercial aviation is taxed at a reduced rate of 4.4 cents per gallon.[833] Commercial aviation means any use of an aircraft in a business of transporting persons or property for compensation or hire by air (unless the use is allocable to any transportation exempt from certain excise taxes).[834]

Under prior law, in order to qualify for the 4.4-cents-per-gallon rate, the person engaged in commercial aviation was required to be registered with the Secretary[835] and to provide the seller with a written exemption certificate stating the airline's name, address, taxpayer identification number, registration number, and intended use of the fuel. A person that was registered as a buyer of aviation fuel for use in commercial aviation generally was assigned a registration number with a "Y" suffix (a "Y" registrant), which entitled the registrant to purchase aviation fuel at the 4.4-cents-per-gallon rate.

Large commercial airlines that also are producers of aviation fuel qualify for registration numbers with an "H" suffix. Under prior law, as producers of aviation fuel, "H" registrants could buy aviation fuel tax free pursuant to a full exemption that applied to sales of aviation fuel by a registered producer to a registered producer. If the "H" registrant ultimately used such untaxed fuel in domestic commercial aviation, the H registrant was liable for the aviation fuel tax at the 4.4-cents-per-gallon rate.

Exemptions

Under prior law, aviation fuel sold by a producer or importer for use by the buyer in a nontaxable use was exempt from the excise

[830] Sec. 4091(a)(1).

[831] Sec. 4091(a)(2).

[832] Sec. 4081(a)(2)(A)(iv); sec. 4091(b). This rate includes a 0.1 cent per gallon Leaking Underground Storage Tank ("LUST") Trust Fund tax. The LUST Trust Fund is set to expire after September 30, 2005, with the result that on October 1, 2005, the tax rate is scheduled to be 21.8 cents per gallon.

[833] Sec. 4081(a)(2)(C); sec. 4092(b). The 4.4-cent rate includes 0.1 cent per gallon that is attributable to the LUST Trust Fund financing rate. A full exemption, discussed below, applies to aviation fuel that is sold for use in commercial aviation as fuel supplies for vessels or aircraft, which includes use by certain foreign air carriers and for the international flights of domestic carriers.

[834] Sec. 4083(b).

[835] Notice 88–132, sec. III(D). See also, Form 637—Application for Registration (For Certain Excise Tax Activities). A bond may be required as a condition of registration.

tax on sales of aviation fuel.[836] To qualify for the exemption, the buyer had to provide the seller with a written exemption certificate stating the buyer's name, address, taxpayer identification number, registration number (if applicable), and intended use of the fuel.

Under present and prior law, nontaxable uses include: (1) use other than as fuel in an aircraft (such as use in heating oil); (2) use on a farm for farming purposes; (3) use in a military aircraft owned by the United States or a foreign country; (4) use in a domestic air carrier engaged in foreign trade or trade between the United States and any of its possessions;[837] (5) use in a foreign air carrier engaged in foreign trade or trade between the United States and any of its possessions (but only if the foreign carrier's country of registration provides similar privileges to United States carriers); (6) exclusive use of a State or local government; (7) sales for export, or shipment to a United States possession; (8) exclusive use by a nonprofit educational organization; (9) use by an aircraft museum exclusively for the procurement, care, or exhibition of aircraft of the type used for combat or transport in World War II; and (10) use as a fuel in a helicopter or a fixed-wing aircraft for purposes of providing transportation with respect to which certain requirements are met.[838]

Under prior law, a producer that was registered with the Secretary could sell aviation fuel tax free to another registered producer.[839] Producers included refiners, blenders, wholesale distributors of aviation fuel, dealers selling aviation fuel exclusively to producers of aviation fuel, the actual producer of the aviation fuel, and with respect to fuel purchased at a reduced rate, the purchaser of such fuel.

Refunds and credits

Under prior law, a claim for refund of taxed aviation fuel held by a registered aviation fuel producer was allowed[840] (without interest) if: (1) the aviation fuel tax was paid by an importer or producer (the "first producer") and the tax was not otherwise credited or refunded; (2) the aviation fuel was acquired by a registered aviation fuel producer (the "second producer") after the tax was paid; (3) the second producer filed a timely refund claim with the proper information; and (4) the first producer and any other person that owned the fuel after its sale by the first producer and before its purchase by the second producer met certain reporting requirements.[841] Refund claims had to contain the volume and type of aviation fuel, the date on which the second producer acquired the fuel, the amount of tax that the first producer paid, a statement by the claimant that the amount of tax was not collected nor included in the sales price of the fuel by the claimant when the fuel was sold to a subsequent purchaser, the name, address, and employer identification number of the first producer, and a copy of any required statement of a subsequent seller (subsequent to the

---

[836] Sec. 4092(a).

[837] "Trade" includes the transportation of persons or property for hire. Treas. Reg. sec. 48.4221–4(b)(8).

[838] Secs. 4041(f)(2), 4041(g), 4041(h), 4041(l), and 4092.

[839] Sec. 4092(c).

[840] Sec. 4091(d).

[841] Treas. Reg. sec. 48.4091–3(b).

first producer but prior to the second producer) that the second producer received. A claim for refund was filed on Form 8849, Claim for Refund of Excise Taxes, and could not be combined with any other refunds.[842]

Under prior law, a payment was allowable to the ultimate purchaser of taxed aviation fuel if the aviation fuel was used in a nontaxable use. A claim for payment could be made on Form 8849 or on Form 720, Schedule C. A claim made on Form 720, Schedule C, could be netted against the claimant's excise tax liability. Claims for payment not so taken could be allowed as income tax credits on Form 4136, Credit for Federal Tax Paid on Fuels.

Reasons for Change

The Congress believed that the prior law rules for taxation of aviation fuel created opportunities for widespread abuse and evasion of fuels excise taxes. In general, aviation fuel was taxed on its sale, whereas other fuel generally is taxed on its removal from a refinery or terminal rack. Because the incidence of tax on aviation fuel was sale and not removal, under prior law, aviation fuel could be removed from a refinery or terminal rack tax free if such fuel was intended for use in aviation purposes. The Congress was aware that unscrupulous persons were removing fuel tax free, purportedly for aviation use, but then were selling the fuel for highway use, charging their customer the full rate of tax that would be owed on highway fuel, and keeping the amount of the tax.

In order to prevent such fraud, the Congress believed that it was appropriate to conform the tax treatment of all taxable fuels by shifting the incidence of taxation on aviation fuel from the sale of aviation fuel to the removal of such fuel from a refinery or terminal rack. In general, all removals of aviation fuel are fully taxed at the time of removal, therefore minimizing the cost to the government of the fraudulent diversion of aviation fuel for non-aviation uses. If fuel is later used for an aviation use to which a reduced rate of tax applies, refunds are available. The Congress noted that when the incidence of tax for other fuels (for example, gasoline or diesel) was shifted to the rack, collection of the tax increased significantly indicating that fraud had been occurring.

The Act provides exceptions to the general rule in cases where the opportunities for fraud are insignificant. For example, if fuel is removed from an airport terminal directly into the wing of a commercial aircraft by a hydrant system, it is clear that the fuel will be used in commercial aviation and that the reduced rate of tax for commercial aviation should apply. In addition, if a terminal is located within a secure airport and, except in exigent circumstances, does not fuel highway vehicles, then the Congress believed it was appropriate to permit certain airline refueling vehicles to transport fuel from the terminal rack directly to the wing of an aircraft and have the applicable rate of tax (reduced or otherwise) apply upon removal from the refueling vehicle.

[842] Treas. Reg. sec. 48.4091–3(d)(1).

Explanation of Provision

The Act changes the incidence of taxation of aviation fuel from the sale of aviation fuel to the removal of aviation fuel from a refinery or terminal, or the entry into the United States of aviation fuel. Sales of not previously taxed aviation fuel to an unregistered person also are subject to tax.

Under the Act, the full rate of tax—21.9 cents per gallon—is imposed upon removal of aviation fuel from a refinery or terminal (or entry into the United States). Aviation fuel may be removed at a reduced rate—either 4.4 or zero cents per gallon—only if the aviation fuel is: (1) removed directly into the wing of an aircraft (i) that is registered with the Secretary as a buyer of aviation fuel for use in commercial aviation (e.g., a "Y" registrant), (ii) that is a foreign airline entitled to the present law exemption for aviation fuel used in foreign trade, or (iii) for a tax-exempt use; or (2) removed or entered as part of an exempt bulk transfer.[843] An exempt bulk transfer is a removal or entry of aviation fuel transferred in bulk by pipeline or vessel to a terminal or refinery if the person removing or entering the aviation fuel, the operator of such pipeline or vessel, and the operator of such terminal or refinery are registered with the Secretary.

Under a special rule, the Act treats certain refueler trucks, tankers, and tank wagons as part of a terminal if certain requirements are met. For the special rule to apply, a qualifying truck, tanker, or tank wagon must be loaded with aviation fuel from a terminal: (1) that is located within a secured area of an airport, and (2) from which no vehicle licensed for highway use is loaded with aviation fuel, except in exigent circumstances identified by the Secretary in regulations. The Act requires the Secretary to publish, by December 15, 2004, and maintain a list of airports that include a secured area in which a terminal is located.[844] It is intended that an exi-

[843] See sec. 4081(a)(1)(B).

[844] It is intended that the following airports, subject to verification by the Secretary, be included on the Secretary's initial list of airports that include a secured area in which a terminal is located. The airports are listed by airport name, and the terminal with respect to the airport is identified by terminal control number. In maintaining the list of qualified airports, the Secretary has the discretion to add or remove airports from the list. Ted Stevens International Airport, T–91–AK–4520; William B. Hartsfield Atlanta International Airport, T–58–GA–2512; William B. Hartsfield Atlanta International Airport, T–58–GA–2513; William B. Hartsfield Atlanta International Airport, T–58–GA–2536; Bradley International Airport, T–06–CT–1271; Nashville Metropolitan Airport, T–62–TN–2222; Logan International Airport, T–04–MA–1171; Baltimore/Washington International Airport, T–52–MD–1569; Cleveland Hopkins International Airport, T–31–OH–3109; Charlotte/Douglas International Airport, T–56–NC–2032; Colorado Springs Airport, T–84–CO–4108; Cincinnati/Northern Kentucky International Airport, T–61–KY–3277; Dallas Love Field Airport, T–75–TX–2663; Ronald Reagan National Airport, T–54–VA–1686; Denver International Airport, T–84–CO–4111; Dallas Fort Worth International Airport, T–75–TX–2673; Wayne County Metropolitan Airport, T–38–MI–3018; Newark Liberty International Airport, T–22–NJ–1532; Fort Lauderdale/Hollywood International Airport; T–65–FL–2158; Piedmont Triad International Airport, T–56–NC–2038; Honolulu International Airport, T–91–HI–4570; Dulles International Airport, T–54–VA–1676; George Bush Intercontinental Airport, T–76–TX–2818; Mid Continent Airport, T–43–KS–3653; John F. Kennedy International Airport, T–11–NY–1334; McCarren International Airport, T–86–NV–4355; Kansas City International Airport, T–43–MO–3723; Orlando International Airport, T–59–FL–2111; Midway Airport, T–36–IL–3376; Memphis International Airport, T–62–TN–2212; General Mitchell International Airport, T–39–WI–3092; Minneapolis-St. Paul International Airport, T–41–MN–3419; Minneapolis-St. Paul International Airport, T–41–MN–3420; Minneapolis-St. Paul International Airport, T–41–MN–3421; Louis Armstrong New Orleans International Airport, T–72–LA–2356; Oakland International Airport, T–94–CA–4702; Eppley Airfield, T–47–NE–3608; Ontario International Airport, T–33–CA–4792; O'Hare International Airport, T–36–IL–3325; Portland International Airport, T–91–OR–4450; Philadelphia International Airport, T–23–PA–1770; Sky Harbor International Airport, T–86–

Continued

gent circumstance under which loading a vehicle registered for highway use with fuel would not disqualify a terminal under the special rule would include, for example, the unloading of fuel from bulk storage tanks into highway vehicles in order to repair the storage tanks.

In order to qualify for the special rule, a refueler truck, tanker, or tank wagon must: (1) be loaded with aviation fuel for delivery into aircraft at the airport where the terminal is located; (2) have storage tanks, hose, and coupling equipment designed and used for the purposes of fueling aircraft; (3) not be registered for highway use; and (4) be operated by the terminal operator (who operates the terminal rack from which the fuel is unloaded) or by a person that makes a daily accounting to such terminal operator of each delivery of fuel from such truck, tanker, or tank wagon.[845]

The Act does not change the applicable rates of tax—21.9 cents per gallon for use in noncommercial aviation, 4.4 cents per gallon for use in commercial aviation, and zero cents per gallon for use by domestic airlines in an international flight, by foreign airlines, or other nontaxable use. The Act imposes liability for the tax on aviation fuel removed from a refinery or terminal directly into the wing of an aircraft for use in commercial aviation on the person receiving the fuel, in which case, such person self-assesses the tax on a return. The Act does not change the nontaxable uses of aviation fuel, or change the persons or the qualifications of persons who are entitled to purchase fuel at a reduced rate, except that a producer is not permitted to purchase aviation fuel at a reduced rate by reason of such person's status as a producer.

Under the Act, a refund is allowable to the ultimate vendor of aviation fuel if such ultimate vendor purchases fuel tax paid and subsequently sells the fuel to a person qualified to purchase at a reduced rate and who waives the right to a refund. In such a case, the Act permits an ultimate vendor to net refund claims against any excise tax liability of the ultimate vendor, in a manner similar to the present and prior law treatment of ultimate purchaser payment claims.[846]

As under prior law, if previously taxed aviation fuel is used for a nontaxable use, the ultimate purchaser may claim a refund for the tax previously paid. If previously taxed aviation fuel is used for a taxable nonaircraft use, the fuel is subject to the tax imposed on kerosene (24.4 cents per gallon) and a refund of the previously paid aviation fuel tax is allowed. Claims by the ultimate vendor or the purchaser that are not taken as refund claims may be allowable as income tax credits.

AZ–4302; Pittsburgh International Airport, T–23–PA–1766; Raleigh/Durham International Airport, T–56–NC–2045; Reno Cannon International Airport, T–86–NV–4352; San Diego International Airport, T–33–CA–4788; San Antonio International Airport, pending; Seattle Tacoma International Airport, T–91–WA–4425; San Francisco International Airport, T–94–CA–4701; San Jose Municipal Airport, T–77–CA–4650; Salt Lake City International Airport, T–84–UT–4207; John Wayne Airport/Orange County, T–33–CA–4772; Lambert International Airport, T–43–MO–3722; Tampa/St. Petersburg International Airport, T–59–FL–2110.

[845] The Act requires that if such delivery of information is provided to a terminal operator (or if a terminal operator collects such information), the terminal operator must provide such information to the Secretary.

[846] For example, X is a commercial airline subsidiary of airline Y. If Y sells fuel to X, X can waive its right to a refund to Y as the ultimate vendor. Y would then be entitled to file for a refund or net the refund against its excise tax liability.

For example, for an airport that is not served by a pipeline, aviation fuel generally is removed from a terminal and transported to an airport storage facility for eventual use at the airport. In such a case, the aviation fuel will be taxed at 21.9 cents per gallon upon removal from the terminal. At the airport, if the fuel is purchased from a vendor by a person registered with the Secretary to use fuel in commercial aviation, the purchaser may buy the fuel at a reduced rate (generally, 4.4 cents per gallon for domestic flights and zero cents per gallon for international flights) and waive the right to a refund. The ultimate vendor generally may claim a refund for the difference between 21.9 cents per gallon of tax paid upon removal and the rate of tax paid to the vendor by the purchaser. To obtain a zero rate upon purchase, a registered domestic airline must certify to the vendor at the time of purchase that the fuel is for use in an international flight; otherwise, the airline must pay the 4.4 cents per gallon rate and file a claim for refund to the Secretary if the fuel is used for international aviation. If a zero rate is paid and the fuel subsequently is used in domestic and not international travel, the domestic airline is liable for tax at 4.4 cents per gallon. A foreign airline eligible under present law to purchase aviation fuel tax free would continue to purchase such fuel tax free.

As another example, for an airport that is served by a pipeline, aviation fuel generally is delivered to the wing of an aircraft either by a refueling truck or by a "hydrant" that runs directly from the pipeline to the airplane wing. If a refueling truck that is not licensed for highway use loads fuel from a terminal located within the airport (and the other requirements of the provision for such truck and terminal are met), and delivers the fuel directly to the wing of an aircraft for use in commercial aviation, the aviation fuel is taxed at 4.4 cents per gallon upon delivery to the wing and the person receiving the fuel is liable for the tax, which such person would be able to self-assess on a return.[847] If fuel is loaded into a refueling truck that does not meet the requirements of the provision, then the fuel is treated as removed from the terminal into the refueling truck and tax of 21.9 cents per gallon is paid on such removal. The ultimate vendor is entitled to a refund of the difference between 21.9 cents per gallon paid on removal and the rate paid by a commercial airline purchaser (assuming the purchaser waived the refund right). If fuel is removed from a terminal directly to the wing of an aircraft registered to use fuel in commercial aviation by a hydrant or similar device, the person receiving the aviation fuel is liable for a tax of 4.4 cents per gallon (or zero in the case of an international flight or qualified foreign airline) and may self-assess such tax on a return.

Under the Act, a floor stocks tax applies to aviation fuel held by a person (if title for such fuel has passed to such person) on January 1, 2005. The tax is equal to the amount of tax that would have been imposed before January 1, 2005, if the provision was in effect at all times before such date, reduced by (1) the tax imposed by section 4091, as in effect on the day before such date and, (2) in the case of kerosene held exclusively for the holder's own use, the

[847] Alternatively, if the aviation fuel in the example is for use in noncommercial aviation, the fuel is taxed at 21.9 cents per gallon upon delivery into the wing. Self-assessment of the tax would not apply in such case.

amount which such holder would reasonably expect under the provision to be paid as a refund for a nontaxable use with respect to the kerosene. The tax does not apply to kerosene held in the fuel tank of an aircraft on January 1, 2005. The Secretary shall determine the time and manner for payment of the tax, including the nonapplication of the tax on de minimis amounts of aviation fuel. Under the provision, 0.1 cents per gallon of such tax is transferred to the LUST Trust Fund. The remainder is transferred to the Airport and Airway Trust Fund.

The Congress expects the Secretary to delay the due date of the excise tax return with respect to aviation fuel for the quarter beginning on January 1, 2005. It is intended that the requirement of semi-monthly deposits of aviation fuel taxes continue unchanged.

Effective Date

The provision is effective for aviation-grade kerosene removed, entered, or sold after December 31, 2004.

3. Mechanical dye injection and related penalties (secs. 854, 855, and 856 of the Act and secs. 4082 and 6715 and new sec. 6715A of the Code)

Present and Prior Law

Statutory rules

Gasoline, diesel fuel and kerosene are generally subject to excise tax upon removal from a refinery or terminal, upon importation into the United States, and upon sale to unregistered persons unless there was a prior taxable removal or importation of such fuels.[848] However, a tax is not imposed upon diesel fuel or kerosene if all of the following are met: (1) the Secretary determines that the fuel is destined for a nontaxable use, (2) the fuel is indelibly dyed in accordance with regulations prescribed by the Secretary,[849] and (3) the fuel meets marking requirements prescribed by the Secretary.[850] A nontaxable use is defined as (1) any use that is exempt from the tax imposed by section 4041(a)(1) other than by reason of a prior imposition of tax, (2) any use in a train, or (3) certain uses in buses for public and school transportation, as described in section 6427(b)(1) (after application of section 6427(b)(3)).[851]

The Secretary is required to prescribe necessary regulations relating to dyeing, including specifically the labeling of retail diesel fuel and kerosene pumps.[852]

---

[848] Sec. 4081(a)(1)(A). If such fuel is used for a nontaxable purpose, the purchaser is entitled to a refund of tax paid, or in some cases, an income tax credit. See sec. 6427.

[849] Dyeing is not a requirement, however, for certain fuels under certain conditions, i.e., diesel fuel or kerosene exempted from dyeing in certain States by the EPA under the Clean Air Act, aviation-grade kerosene as determined under regulations prescribed by the Secretary, kerosene received by pipeline or vessel and used by a registered recipient to produce substances (other than gasoline, diesel fuel or special fuels), kerosene removed or entered by a registrant to produce such substances or for resale, and (under regulations) kerosene sold by a registered distributor who sells kerosene exclusively to ultimate vendors that resell it (1) from a pump that is not suitable for fueling any diesel-powered highway vehicle or train, or (2) for blending with heating oil to be used during periods of extreme or unseasonable cold. Sec. 4082(c), (d).

[850] Sec. 4082(a).

[851] Sec. 4082(b).

[852] Sec. 4082(e).

A person who sells dyed fuel (or holds dyed fuel for sale) for any use that such person knows (or has reason to know) is a taxable use, or who willfully alters or attempts to alter the dye in any dyed fuel, is subject to a penalty.[853] The penalty also applies to any person who uses dyed fuel for a taxable use (or holds dyed fuel for such a use) and who knows (or has reason to know) that the fuel is dyed.[854] The penalty is the greater of $1,000 per act or $10 per gallon of dyed fuel involved. In determining the amount of the penalty, the $1,000 is increased by the product of $1,000 and the number of prior penalties imposed upon such person (or a related person or predecessor of such person or related person).[855] The penalty may be imposed jointly and severally on any business entity and on each officer, employee, or agent of such entity who willfully participated in any act giving rise to such penalty.[856] For purposes of the penalty, the term "dyed fuel" means any dyed diesel fuel or kerosene, whether or not the fuel was dyed pursuant to section 4082.[857]

Regulations

The Secretary has prescribed certain regulations under this provision, including regulations that specify the allowable types and concentration of dye, that the person claiming the exemption must be a taxable fuel registrant, that the terminal must be an approved terminal (in the case of a removal from a terminal rack), and the contents of the notice to posted on diesel fuel and kerosene pumps.[858] However, the regulations do not prescribe the time or method of adding the dye to taxable fuel.[859] Diesel fuel is usually dyed at a terminal rack by either manual dyeing or mechanical injection. The regulations also provide that a terminal operator is jointly and severally liable for unpaid tax if undyed diesel fuel or kerosene is removed and the terminal operator provides any person with documentation that such fuel is dyed.[860]

Reasons for Change

The Federal government, State governments, and various segments of the petroleum industry have long been concerned with the problem of diesel fuel tax evasion. To address this problem, the Congress changed the law to require that untaxed diesel fuel be indelibly dyed. The Congress remained concerned, however, that tax could still be evaded through removals at a terminal of undyed fuel that had been designated as dyed.

Manual dyeing was inherently difficult to monitor. It occurred after diesel fuel had been withdrawn from a terminal storage tank, generally required the work of several people, was imprecise, and

---

[853] Sec. 6715(a).
[854] Sec. 6715(a).
[855] Sec. 6715(b).
[856] Sec. 6715(d).
[857] Sec. 6715(c)(1).
[858] Treas. Reg. secs. 48.4082–1,–2.
[859] In March 2000, the IRS withdrew its Notice of Proposed Rulemaking PS–6–95 (61 F.R. 10490 (1996)) relating to dye injection systems. Announcement 2000–42, 2000–1 C.B. 949. The proposed regulation established standards for mechanical dye injection equipment and required terminal operators to report nonconforming dyeing to the IRS. See also Treas. Reg. sec. 48.4082–1(c), (d).
[860] Treas. Reg. sec. 48.4081–2(c).

did not automatically create a reliable record. The Congress believed that requiring that untaxed diesel fuel be dyed only by mechanical injection will significantly reduce the opportunities for diesel fuel tax evasion.

The Congress further believed that security of such mechanical dyeing systems will be enhanced by the establishment of standards for making such systems tamper resistant, and by the addition of new penalties for tampering with such mechanical dyeing systems and for failing to maintain the established security standards for such systems. In furtherance of the enforcement of these penalties in the case of business entities, it was appropriate to impose joint and several liability for such penalties upon natural persons who willfully participate in any act giving rise to these penalties and upon the parent corporation of an affiliated group of which the business entity is a member.

Explanation of Provision

With respect to terminals that offer dyed fuel, the Act eliminates manual dyeing of fuel and requires dyeing by a mechanical system. Not later than 180 days after the date of enactment, the Secretary of the Treasury is to prescribe regulations establishing standards for tamper resistant mechanical injector dyeing. Such standards shall be reasonable, cost-effective, and establish levels of security commensurate with the applicable facility.

The Act adds an additional set of penalties for violation of the new rules. A penalty, equal to the greater of $25,000 or $10 for each gallon of fuel involved, applies to each act of tampering with a mechanical dye injection system. The person committing the act is also responsible for any unpaid tax on removed undyed fuel. A penalty of $1,000 is imposed upon the operator of a mechanical dye injection system for each failure to maintain the security standards for such system.[861] An additional penalty of $1,000 is imposed upon such operator for each day any such violation remains uncorrected after the first day such violation has been or reasonably should have been discovered. For purposes of the daily penalty, a violation may be corrected by shutting down the portion of the system causing the violation. If any of these penalties are imposed on any business entity, each officer, employee, or agent of such entity or other contracting party who willfully participated in any act giving rise to such penalty is jointly and severally liable with such entity for such penalty. If such business entity is part of an affiliated group, the parent corporation of such entity is jointly and severally liable with such entity for the penalty.

The Act also denies administrative appeal or review for repeat offenders (persons found, after a chemical analysis of the fuel, to be subject to more than two penalties after October 22, 2004), except in the case of a claim regarding fraud or mistake in the chemical analysis or error in the mathematical calculation of the amount of penalty.

The Act also extends present-law penalties to any person who knows that the strength or composition of any dye or marking in

[861] The operator remains liable under current Treas. Reg. sec. 48.4081–2(c) for any unpaid tax on removed undyed fuel.

any dyed fuel has been altered, chemically or otherwise, and who sells (or holds for sale) such fuel for any use that the person knows or has reason to know is a taxable use of such fuel.

Effective Date

Penalties relating to mechanical dyeing systems are effective 180 days after the required regulations are issued. The Secretary must issue such regulations no later than 180 days after the date of enactment (October 22, 2004). The prohibition on certain administrative review is effective for penalties assessed after the date of enactment (October 22, 2004). The extension of present-law penalties is effective on the date of enactment (October 22, 2004).

4. Terminate dyed diesel use by intercity buses (sec. 857 of the Act and secs. 4082 and 6427 of the Code)

Present and Prior Law

A manufacturer's tax of 24.4 cents per gallon applies to diesel fuel.[862] Diesel fuel that is to be used for a nontaxable purpose will not be taxed upon removal from the terminal if it is dyed to indicate its nontaxable purpose. Under prior law, use in an intercity bus was a nontaxable use for purposes of the manufacturers tax on diesel fuel. However, diesel fuel was subject to a retail backup tax. The retail tax was 7.4 cents per gallon for intercity buses, but only applied if no tax was imposed on the diesel under the manufacturers tax. Thus, dyed diesel removed from the terminal was exempt from the manufacturers tax but a tax of 7.3 cents per gallon (plus 0.1 cents per gallon for LUST) was imposed on the delivery of the dyed fuel into the fuel supply tank of the intercity bus. The operator of the bus was liable for the tax.

Under present and prior law, intercity bus operators may buy fully taxed undyed diesel and seek a refund of the difference between the 24.4-cents-per-gallon rate and the 7.4-cents-per-gallon rate.

Explanation of Provision

The Act eliminates the ability of intercity buses to buy dyed diesel and self-assess the 7.4 cents per gallon. Under the Act, operators of such buses must buy clear fuel and seek a refund of the difference between 24.4 and 7.4 cents per gallon of tax on diesel fuel. The Act also permits ultimate vendors to make such refund claims if the bus operator assigns its right to claim a refund to the ultimate vendor. The Act permits refund claimants to obtain interest if they file their refund claims electronically and the Secretary does not pay such claims within 20 days (45 days for paper claims).

Effective Date

The provision is effective for fuel sold after January 1, 2005.

[862] Sec. 4081.

5. Authority to inspect on-site records (sec. 858 of the Act and sec. 4083 of the Code)

Present and Prior Law [863]

The IRS is authorized to inspect any place where taxable fuel [864] is produced or stored (or may be stored). As part of the inspection, the IRS is authorized to: (1) examine the equipment used to determine the amount or composition of the taxable fuel and the equipment used to store the fuel; and (2) take and remove samples of taxable fuel.[865] Places of inspection include, but are not limited to, terminals, fuel storage facilities, retail fuel facilities or any designated inspection site.[866]

In conducting the inspection, the IRS may detain any receptacle that contains or may contain any taxable fuel, or detain any vehicle or train to inspect its fuel tanks and storage tanks. The scope of the inspection includes the books and records kept at the place of inspection to determine the excise tax liability under section 4081.[867]

Reasons for Change

The Congress believed it was appropriate to expand the authority of the IRS to make on-site inspections of books and records. The Congress believed that such expanded authority will aid in the detection of fuel tax evasion and the enforcement of Federal fuel taxes.

Explanation of Provision

The Act expands the scope of the inspection to include any books, records, or shipping papers pertaining to taxable fuel located in any authorized inspection location.

Effective Date

The provision is effective on the date of enactment (October 22, 2004).

6. Assessable penalty for refusal of entry (sec. 859 of the Act and new sec. 6717 of the Code)

Present and Prior Law [868]

The IRS is authorized to inspect any place where taxable fuel is produced or stored (or may be stored). As part of the inspection, the IRS is authorized to: (1) examine the equipment used to determine the amount or composition of the taxable fuel and the equipment used to store the fuel; and (2) take and remove samples of taxable fuel.[869] Places of inspection, include, but are not limited to, termi-

---

[863] Code references are those in effect immediately before the enactment of the Act.
[864] "Taxable fuel" means gasoline, diesel fuel, and kerosene. Sec. 4083(a).
[865] Sec. 4083(c)(1)(A).
[866] Treas. Reg. sec. 48.4083–1(b).
[867] Treas. Reg. sec. 48.4083–1(c)(1).
[868] Code references are those in effect immediately before the enactment of the Act.
[869] Sec. 4083(c)(1)(A).

nals, fuel storage facilities, retail fuel facilities or any designated inspection site.[870]

In conducting the inspection, the IRS may detain any receptacle that contains or may contain any taxable fuel, or detain any vehicle or train to inspect its fuel tanks and storage tanks. The scope of the inspection includes the books and records kept to determine the excise tax liability under section 4081.[871] The IRS is authorized to establish inspection sites. A designated inspection site includes any State highway inspection station, weigh station, agricultural inspection station, mobile station or other location designated by the IRS.[872]

Any person that refuses to allow an inspection is subject to a penalty in the amount of $1,000 for each refusal.[873] The IRS is not able to assess this penalty in the same manner as it would a tax. It must first seek the assistance of the Department of Justice to obtain a judgment. Assessable penalties are payable upon notice and demand by the Secretary and are assessed and collected in the same manner as taxes.[874]

Explanation of Provision

In addition to the $1,000 non-assessable penalty under present and prior law, the Act imposes an assessable penalty with respect to the refusal of entry. The assessable penalty is $1,000 for such refusal. The penalty will not apply if it is shown that such failure is due to reasonable cause. If the penalty is imposed on a business entity, the Act provides for joint and several liability with respect to each officer, employee, or agent of such entity or other contracting party who willfully participated in the act giving rise to the penalty. If the business entity is part of an affiliated group, the parent corporation also will be jointly and severally liable for the penalty.

Effective Date

The provision is effective on January 1, 2005.

7. Registration of pipeline or vessel operators required for exemption of bulk transfers to registered terminals or refineries (sec. 860 of the Act and sec. 4081 of the Code)

Present and Prior Law

In general, under present and prior law, gasoline, diesel fuel, and kerosene ("taxable fuel") are taxed upon removal from a refinery or a terminal.[875] Tax also is imposed on the entry into the United States of any taxable fuel for consumption, use, or warehousing. The tax does not apply to any removal or entry of a taxable fuel transferred in bulk (a "bulk transfer") to a terminal or refinery if both the person removing or entering the taxable fuel and the oper-

---

[870] Treas. Reg. sec. 48.4083–1(b).
[871] Treas. Reg. sec. 48.4083–1(b)(2).
[872] Sec. 4083(c); Treas. Reg. sec. 48.4083–1(b)(1).
[873] Secs. 4083(c)(3) and 7342.
[874] Sec. 6671.
[875] Sec. 4081(a)(1)(A).

ator of such terminal or refinery are registered with the Secretary.[876]

Prior law did not require that the vessel or pipeline operator that transfers fuel as part of a bulk transfer be registered in order for the transfer to be exempt. For example, under prior law if a registered refiner transferred fuel to an unregistered vessel or pipeline operator who in turn transferred fuel to a registered terminal operator, the transfer was exempt despite the intermediate transfer to an unregistered person.

In general, under present and prior law, the owner of the fuel is liable for payment of tax with respect to bulk transfers not received at an approved terminal or refinery.[877] The refiner is liable for payment of tax with respect to certain taxable removals from the refinery.[878]

Under present and prior law, disclosure of excise tax registration information is permitted to the extent the Secretary determines that such disclosure is needed for effective excise tax administration.[879]

Reasons for Change

The Congress was concerned that unregistered pipeline and vessel operators were receiving bulk transfers of taxable fuel, and then diverting the fuel to retailers or end users without the tax ever being paid. The Congress believed that requiring that a pipeline or vessel operator be registered with the IRS in order for a bulk transfer exemption to be valid, in combination with other provisions that impose penalties relating to registration, would help to ensure that transfers of fuel in bulk are delivered as intended to approved refineries and terminals and taxed appropriately.

Explanation of Provision

The Act requires that for a bulk transfer of a taxable fuel to be exempt from tax, any pipeline or vessel operator that is a party to the bulk transfer be registered with the Secretary. Transfer to an unregistered party will subject the transfer to tax.

Under the authority of section 6103(k)(7), the Secretary is required to publish periodically a list of all registered persons that are required to register.

Effective Date

The provision is effective on March 1, 2005, except that the Secretary is required to publish the list of persons required to register beginning on January 1, 2005.

---

[876] Sec. 4081(a)(1)(B). The sale of a taxable fuel to an unregistered person prior to a taxable removal or entry of the fuel is subject to tax. Sec. 4081(a)(1)(A).

[877] Treas. Reg. sec. 48.4081–3(e)(2).

[878] Treas. Reg. sec. 48.4081–3(b).

[879] Sec. 6103(k)(7).

8. Display of registration and penalties for failure to display registration and to register (secs. 861 of the Act and secs. 4101, 7232, 7272 and new secs. 6718 and 6719 of the Code)

Present and Prior Law

Under present and prior law, blenders, enterers, pipeline operators, position holders, refiners, terminal operators, and vessel operators are required to register with the Secretary with respect to fuels taxes imposed by sections 4041(a)(1) and 4081.[880]

Under prior law, a non-assessable penalty for failure to register was $50.[881] Under prior law, a criminal penalty of $5,000, or imprisonment of not more than five years, or both, together with the costs of prosecution also applied to a failure to register and to certain false statements made in connection with a registration application.[882]

Reasons for Change

Registration with the Secretary is a critical component of enabling the Secretary to regulate the movement and use of taxable fuels and ensure that the appropriate excise taxes are being collected. The Congress believed that prior law penalties were not severe enough to ensure that persons that are required to register in fact register. Accordingly, the Congress believed it was appropriate to increase prior law penalties significantly and to add a new assessable penalty for failure to register. In addition, the Congress believed that persons that do business with vessel operators should be able easily to verify whether the vessel operator is registered. Thus, the Congress required that vessel operators display proof of registration on their vessels and imposed an attendant penalty for failure to display such proof.

Explanation of Provision

The Act requires that every operator of a vessel who is required to register with the Secretary display on each vessel used by the operator to transport fuel, proof of registration through an identification device prescribed by the Secretary. A failure to display such proof of registration results in a penalty of $500 per month per vessel. The amount of the penalty is increased for multiple prior violations. No penalty is imposed upon a showing by the taxpayer of reasonable cause.

The Act imposes a new assessable penalty for failure to register of $10,000 for each initial failure, plus $1,000 per day that the failure continues. No penalty is imposed upon a showing by the taxpayer of reasonable cause. In addition, the Act increases the non-assessable penalty for failure to register from $50 to $10,000 and the criminal penalty for failure to register from $5,000 to $10,000.

---

[880] Sec. 4101; Treas. Reg. sec. 48.4101–1(a) and (c)(1).
[881] Sec. 7272(a).
[882] Sec. 7232.

Effective Date

The provision requiring display of registration is effective on January 1, 2005. The provision relating to penalties is effective for penalties imposed after December 31, 2004.

9. Registration of persons within foreign trade zones (sec. 862 of the Act and sec. 4101 of the Code)

Present and Prior Law

Under present and prior law, blenders, enterers, pipeline operators, position holders, refiners, terminal operators, and vessel operators are required to register with the Secretary with respect to fuels taxes imposed by sections 4041(a)(1) and 4081.[883]

Explanation of Provision

The Secretary shall require registration by any person that operates a terminal or refinery within a foreign trade zone or within a customs bonded storage facility, or holds an inventory position with respect to a taxable fuel in such a terminal. It is intended that the Secretary shall establish a date by which persons required to register under the provision must be registered.

Effective Date

The provision is effective on January 1, 2005.

10. Penalties for failure to report (sec. 863 of the Act and new sec. 6725 of the Code)

Present and Prior Law

Under present and prior law, a fuel information reporting program, the Excise Summary Terminal Activity Reporting System ("ExSTARS"), requires terminal operators and bulk transport carriers to report monthly on the movement of any liquid product into or out of an approved terminal.[884] Terminal operators file Form 720–TO—Terminal Operator Report, which shows the monthly receipts and disbursements of all liquid products to and from an approved terminal.[885] Bulk transport carriers (barges, vessels, and pipelines) that receive liquid product from an approved terminal or deliver liquid product to an approved terminal file Form 720–CS—Carrier Summary Report, which details such receipts and disbursements. In general, under prior law, the only penalty for failure to file a report or a failure to furnish all of the required information in a report was $50 per report.[886]

Reasons for Change

The Congress believed that the proper and timely reporting of the disbursements of taxable fuels under the ExSTARs system was

---

[883] Sec. 4101; Treas. Reg. sec. 48.4101–1(a) and (c)(1).

[884] Sec. 4010(d); Treas. Reg. sec. 48.4101–2. The reports are required to be filed by the end of the month following the month to which the report relates.

[885] An approved terminal is a terminal that is operated by a taxable fuel registrant that is a terminal operator. Treas. Reg. sec. 48.4081–1(b).

[886] Sec. 6721(a).

essential to the Treasury Department's ability to monitor and enforce the fuels excise taxes. Accordingly, the Congress believed it was appropriate to provide for significant penalties if required information is not provided accurately, completely, and on a timely basis.

Explanation of Provision

The Act imposes a new assessable penalty for failure to file a report required by the ExSTARS system or for filing a report with incomplete or inaccurate information. The penalty is $10,000 per failure with respect to each vessel or facility (e.g., a terminal or other facility) for which information is required to be furnished. No penalty is imposed upon a showing by the taxpayer of reasonable cause.

Effective Date

The provision is effective for penalties imposed after December 31, 2004.

11. Electronic filing of required information reports (sec. 864 of the Act and sec. 4010 of the Code)

Present and Prior Law

Under present and prior law, a fuel information reporting program, the Excise Summary Terminal Activity Reporting System ("ExSTARS"), requires terminal operators and bulk transport carriers to report monthly on the movement of any liquid product into or out of an approved terminal.[887] Terminal operators file Form 720–TO—Terminal Operator Report, which shows the monthly receipts and disbursements of all liquid products to and from an approved terminal.[888] Bulk transport carriers (barges, vessels, and pipelines) that receive liquid product from an approved terminal or deliver liquid product to an approved terminal file Form 720–CS—Carrier Summary Report, which details such receipts and disbursements.

Explanation of Provision

The Act requires that any person who must report under the ExSTARs systems and who has 25 or more reportable transactions in a month to report in electronic format.

Effective Date

The provision is effective on January 1, 2006.

---

[887] Sec. 4101(d); Treas. Reg. sec. 48.4101–2. The reports are required to be filed by the end of the month following the month to which the report relates.

[888] An approved terminal is a terminal that is operated by a taxable fuel registrant that is a terminal operator. Treas. Reg. sec. 48.4081–1(b).

12. Taxable fuel refunds for certain ultimate vendors (sec. 865 of the Act and secs. 6416 and 6427 of the Code)

Present and Prior Law

Under prior law, a wholesale distributor that sold gasoline on which tax had been paid for an exempt purpose was treated as the only person who paid the tax, and thereby was the proper claimant for a credit or refund of the tax paid. Relevant exempt purposes were gasoline: sold to a State or local government for its exclusive use; sold to a nonprofit educational organization for its exclusive use; used or sold for use as supplies for vessels or aircraft; exported; or used or sold for use in the production of special fuels. In the case of undyed diesel fuel or kerosene used on a farm for farming purposes or by a State or local government, a credit or payment is allowable only to the ultimate, registered vendors ("ultimate vendors") of such fuels.

In general, refunds of such taxes were paid without interest. However, in the case of refunds of tax due ultimate vendors of diesel fuel or kerosene used on a farm for farming purposes or by a State or local government, the Secretary is required to pay interest on certain refunds. Under present and prior law, the Secretary must pay interest on such refunds of $200 or more ($100 or more in the case of kerosene) due to the taxpayer arising from sales over any period of a week or more, if the Secretary does not make payment within a prescribed period. Under prior law, the prescribed period was 20 days.

Reasons for Change

The Congress observed that refund procedures for gasoline differ from those for diesel fuel and kerosene. The Congress believed that simplification of administration can be achieved for both taxpayers and the IRS by providing a more uniform refund procedure applicable to all taxed highway fuels. The Congress further believed that compliance can be increased and administration made less costly by increased use of electronic filing.

Explanation of Provision

The Act provides that for sales of gasoline, on which tax has been paid, to a State or local government or to a nonprofit educational organization for its exclusive use, the refund procedure conforms to the procedure in the case of diesel fuel or kerosene. That is, the ultimate vendor (if registered) is the only person entitled to claim the refund. The Act provides that the special rules for refunds to ultimate vendors of diesel fuel or kerosene used on a farm for farming purposes or by a State or local government apply to claims made under this provision. In addition, under the Act, interest is paid on such refunds of $200 or more arising from sales over any period of a week or more if the Secretary does not make payment within 45 days from the date of the filing of such claim. That period is shortened to 20 days in the case of an electronic claim, except that such shortened period does not apply unless the ultimate vendor has certified to the Secretary for the most recent quarter of the taxable year that all ultimate purchasers of the vendor are certified and entitled to a refund as State or local governments or nonprofit educational organizations purchasing for their exclusive use.

Effective Date

The provision is effective on January 1, 2005.

13. Two party exchanges (sec. 866 of the Act and new sec. 4105 of the Code)

Present and Prior Law

Most fuel is taxed when it is removed from a registered terminal.[889] The party liable for payment of this tax is the "position holder." The position holder is the person reflected on the records of the terminal operator as holding the inventory position in the fuel.[890]

It is common industry practice for oil companies to serve customers of other oil companies under exchange agreements, *e.g.*, where Company A's terminal is more conveniently located for wholesale or retail customers of Company B. In such cases, the exchange agreement party (Company B in the example) owns the fuel when the motor fuel is removed from the terminal and sold to B's customer.

Reasons for Change

The Congress believed it was appropriate to recognize industry practice under exchange agreements by relieving the original position holder of tax liability for the removal of a taxable fuel from a terminal if certain circumstances are met.

Explanation of Provision

The Act permits two registered parties to switch position holder status in fuel within a registered terminal (thereby relieving the person originally owning the fuel[891] of tax liability as the position holder) if all of the following occur:

1. The transaction includes a transfer from the original owner, i.e., the person who holds the original inventory position for taxable fuel in the terminal as reflected in the records of the terminal operator prior to the transaction.
2. The exchange transaction occurs before or at the same time as completion of removal across the rack from the terminal by the receiving person or its customer.
3. The terminal operator in its books and records treats the receiving person as the person that removes the product across a terminal rack for purposes of reporting the transaction to the Internal Revenue Service.
4. The transaction is the subject of a written contract.

---

[889] A "terminal" is a storage and distribution facility that is supplied by pipeline or vessel, and from which fuel may be removed at a rack. A "rack" is a mechanism capable of delivering taxable fuel into a means of transport other than a pipeline or vessel.

[890] Such person has a contractual agreement with the terminal operator to store and provide services with respect to the fuel. A "terminal operator" is any person who owns, operates, or otherwise controls a terminal. A terminal operator can also be a position holder if that person owns fuel in its terminal.

[891] In the provision, this person is referred to as the "delivering person."

Effective Date

The provision is effective on the date of enactment (October 22, 2004).

14. Modification of the use tax on heavy highway vehicles (sec. 867 of the Act and secs. 4481, 4483, and 6165 of the Code)

Present and Prior Law

An annual use tax is imposed on heavy highway vehicles, at the rates below.[892]

Under 55,000 pounds	No tax
55,000–75,000 pounds	$100 plus $22 per 1,000 pounds over 55,000
Over 75,000 pounds	$550

The annual use tax is imposed for a taxable period of July 1 through June 30. Generally, the tax is paid by the person in whose name the vehicle is registered. Under prior law, in certain cases, taxpayers were allowed to pay the tax in installments.[893] State governments are required to receive proof of payment of the use tax as a condition of vehicle registration.

Exemptions and reduced rates are provided for certain "transit-type buses," trucks used for fewer than 5,000 miles on public highways (7,500 miles for agricultural vehicles), and logging trucks.[894] Any highway motor vehicle that is issued a base plate by Canada or Mexico and is operated on U.S. highways is subject to the annual use tax whether or not the vehicles are required to be registered in the United States. Under prior law, the tax rate for Canadian and Mexican vehicles was 75 percent of the rate that would otherwise be imposed.[895]

Reasons for Change

The Congress noted that in the case of taxpayers that elect quarterly installment payments, the IRS had no procedure for ensuring that installments subsequent to the first one actually are paid. Thus, it was possible for taxpayers to receive State registrations when only the first quarterly installment is paid with the return. Similarly, it was possible for taxpayers repeatedly to pay the first quarterly installment and continue to receive State registrations because the IRS has no computerized system for checking past compliance when it issues certificates of payment for the current year. In the case of taxpayers owning only one or a few vehicles, it was not cost effective for the IRS to monitor and enforce compliance. Thus, the Congress believed it was appropriate to eliminate the ability of taxpayers to pay the use tax in installments. The Congress also believed that Canadian and Mexican vehicles operating on U.S. highways should be subject to the full amount of use tax, as such vehicles contribute to the wear and tear on U.S. highways.

---

[892] Sec. 4481.
[893] Sec. 6156.
[894] See generally, sec. 4483.
[895] Sec. 4483(f): Treas. Reg. sec. 41.4483–7(a).

Explanation of Provision

The Act eliminates the ability to pay the tax in installments. It also eliminates the reduced rates for Canadian and Mexican vehicles. The Act requires taxpayers with 25 or more vehicles for any taxable period to file their returns electronically. Finally, the Act permits proration of tax for vehicles sold during the taxable period.

Effective Date

The provision is effective for taxable periods beginning after the date of enactment (October 22, 2004).

15. Dedication of revenue from certain penalties to the Highway Trust Fund (sec. 868 of the Act and sec. 9503 of the Code)

Prior Law

Prior law did not dedicate to the Highway Trust Fund any penalties assessed and collected by the Secretary.

Reasons for Change

The Congress believed it was appropriate to dedicate to the Highway Trust Fund penalties associated with the administration and enforcement of taxes supporting the Highway Trust Fund.

Explanation of Provision

The Act dedicates to the Highway Trust Fund amounts equivalent to the penalties paid under sections 6715 (relating to dyed fuel sold for use or used in taxable use), 6715A (penalty for tampering with or failing to maintain security requirements for mechanical dye injection systems), 6717 (assessable penalty for refusal of entry), 6718 (penalty for failing to display tax registration on vessels), 6719 (assessable penalty for failure to register), 6725 (penalty for failing to report information required by the Secretary), 7232 (penalty for failing to register and false representations of registration status), and 7272 (but only with regard to penalties related to failure to register under section 4101).

Effective Date

The provision is effective for penalties assessed on or after the date of enactment (October 22, 2004).

16. Simplification of tax on tires (sec. 869 of the Act and sec. 4071 of the Code)

Present and Prior Law

Under prior law, a graduated excise tax was imposed on the sale by a manufacturer (or importer) of tires designed for use on highway vehicles (sec. 4071). The tire tax rates were as follows:

Tire Weight	Tax Rate
Not more than 40 lbs.	No tax
More than 40 lbs., but not more than 70 lbs..	15 cents/lb. in excess of 40 lbs.
More than 70 lbs., but not more than 90 lbs.	$4.50 plus 30 cents/lb. in excess of 70 lbs.
More than 90 lbs.	$10.50 plus 50 cents/lb. in excess of 90 lbs.

No tax is imposed on the recapping of a tire that previously has been subject to tax. Tires of extruded tiring with internal wire fastening also are exempt.

The tax expires after September 30, 2005.

Reasons for Change

Under prior law, the tire excise tax was based on the weight of each tire. This forced tire manufacturers to weigh sample batches of every type of tire made and collect the tax based on that weight. This regime also made it difficult for the IRS to measure and enforce compliance with the tax, as the IRS likewise must weigh sample batches of tires to ensure compliance. The Congress believed significant administrative simplification for both tire manufacturers and the IRS would be achieved if the tax were based on the weight carrying capacity of the tire, rather than the weight of the tire, because the Department of Transportation requires the load rating to be stamped on the side of highway tires. Thus, both the manufacturer and the IRS will know immediately whether a tire is taxable and how much tax should be paid.

Explanation of Provision

The Act modifies the excise tax applicable to tires. The Act replaces the present-law tax rates based on the weight of the tire with a tax rate based on the load capacity of the tire. In general, the tax is 9.45 cents for each 10 pounds of tire load capacity in excess of 3,500 pounds. In the case of a biasply tire, the tax rate is 4.725 cents for each 10 pounds of tire load capacity in excess of 3,500 pounds. The Act also imposes tax at a rate of is 4.725 cents for each 10 pounds of tire load capacity in excess of 3,500 pounds on any super single tire. The Act also exempts from tax any tire sold for the exclusive use of the United States Department of Defense or the United States Coast Guard.

The Act modifies the definition of tires for use on highway vehicles to include any tire marked for highway use pursuant to certain regulations promulgated by the Secretary of Transportation. A super single tire is a single tire greater than 13 inches in cross section width designed to replace two tires in a dual fitment. The Act provides that a biasply tire means a pneumatic tire on which the ply cords that extend to the beads are laid at alternate angles substantially less than 90 degrees to the centerline of the tread. Tire load capacity is the maximum load rating labeled on the tire pursuant to regulations promulgated by the Secretary of Transportation.

Nothing in the Act is to be construed to have any effect on subsection (d) of section 48.4701–1 of Title 26, Code of Federal Regulations (relating to recapped and retreaded tires). The Secretary is to prescribe regulations implementing the amendment to section 4071 but that such regulations will not affect subsection (d). No tax is to be imposed on the recapping of a tire that previously has been subject to tax.

Effective Date

The provision is effective for sales in calendar years beginning more than 30 days after the date of enactment (October 22, 2004).

17. Taxation of transmix and diesel fuel blend stocks and Treasury study on fuel tax compliance (secs. 870 and 871 of the Act and sec. 4083 of the Code)

Present and Prior Law [896]

Definition of taxable fuels

A "taxable fuel" is gasoline, diesel fuel (including any liquid, other than gasoline, which is suitable for use as a fuel in a diesel-powered highway vehicle or train), and kerosene.[897]

Under the regulations, "gasoline" includes all products commonly or commercially known or sold as gasoline and suited for use as a motor fuel, and that have an octane rating of 75 or more. Gasoline also includes, to the extent provided in regulations, gasoline blendstocks and products commonly used as additives in gasoline. The term "gasoline blendstocks" does not include any product that cannot be blended into gasoline without further processing or fractionation ("off-spec gasoline").[898]

Diesel fuel is any liquid (other than gasoline) that is suitable for use as a fuel in a diesel-powered highway vehicle or diesel-powered train.[899] By regulation, diesel fuel does not include kerosene, gasoline, No. 5 and No. 6 fuel oils (as described in ASTM Specification D 396), or F–76 (Fuel Naval Distillates MIL-F–16884), any liquid that contains less than four percent normal paraffins, or any liquid that has a distillation range of 125 degrees Fahrenheit or less, sulfur content of 10 ppm or less, and minimum color of +27 Saybolt (these are known as "excluded liquids").[900]

By regulation, kerosene is defined as the kerosene described in ASTM Specification D 3699 (No. 1–K and No. 2–K), ASTM Specification D 1655 (kerosene-type jet fuel), and military specifications MIL–DTL–5624T (Grade JP–5) and MIL–DTL–83133E (Grade JP–

---

[896] All Code references are with respect to those in effect immediately prior to the enactment of the Act.

[897] Sec. 4083(a).

[898] Treas. Reg. sec. 48.4081–1(c)(3)(ii). The term "gasoline blendstocks" means alkylate; butane; catalytically cracked gasoline; coker gasoline; ethyl tertiary butyl ether (ETBE); hexane; hydrocrackate; isomerate; methyl tertiary butyl ether (MTBE); mixed xylene (not including any separated isomer of xylene); natural gasoline; pentane; pentane mixture; polymer gasoline; raffinate; reformate; straight-run gasoline; straight-run naphtha; tertiary amyl methyl ether (TAME); tertiary butyl alcohol (gasoline grade) (TBA); thermally cracked gasoline; toluene; and transmix containing gasoline. Treas. Reg. sec. 48.4081–1(c)(3)(i).

[899] Sec. 4083(a)(3).

[900] Treas. Reg. sec. 48.4081–1(c)(2)(ii).

8). Kerosene does not include any liquid that is an excluded liquid.[901]

Taxable events and exemptions

In general

An excise tax is imposed upon (1) the removal of any taxable fuel from a refinery or terminal, (2) the entry of any taxable fuel into the United States, or (3) the sale of any taxable fuel to any person who is not registered with the IRS to receive untaxed fuel, unless there was a prior taxable removal or entry.[902] The tax does not apply to any removal or entry of taxable fuel transferred in bulk to a terminal or refinery if the person removing or entering the taxable fuel and the operator of such terminal or refinery are registered with the Secretary.[903]

Gasoline exemptions

If certain conditions are met, the removal, entry, or sale of gasoline blendstocks is not taxable. Generally, the exemption from tax applies if a gasoline blendstock is not used to produce finished gasoline or is received at an approved terminal or refinery. No tax is imposed on nonbulk removals from a terminal or refinery, or nonbulk entries into the United States or on any gasoline blendstocks if the person liable for the tax is a gasoline registrant, has an unexpired notification certificate, and knows of no false information in the certificate. The sale of a gasoline blendstock that was not subject to tax on nonbulk removal or entry is taxable unless the seller has an unexpired certificate from the buyer and has no reason to believe that any information in the certificate is false. No tax is imposed on, or purchaser certification required for, off-spec gasoline.

Diesel fuel and kerosene exemptions

Diesel fuel or kerosene that is to be used for a nontaxable purpose will not be taxed upon removal from the terminal if it is dyed to indicate its nontaxable purpose. Undyed aviation-grade kerosene also is exempt from tax at the rack if it is destined for use as a fuel in an aircraft. The tax does not apply to diesel fuel asserted to be "not suitable for use" or kerosene asserted to qualify as an excluded liquid.

Feedstock kerosene that a registered industrial user receives by pipeline or vessel also is exempt from the dyeing requirement. A kerosene feedstock user is defined as a person that receives kerosene by bulk transfer for its own use in the manufacture or production of any substance (other than gasoline, diesel fuel or special fuels subject to tax). Thus, for example, kerosene is used for a feedstock purpose when it is used as an ingredient in the production of paint and is not used for a feedstock purpose when it is used to power machinery at a factory where paint is produced. The person receiving the kerosene must be registered with the IRS and provide

[901] Treas. Reg. sec. 48.4081–1(b).
[902] Sec. 4081(a)(1).
[903] Sec. 4081(a)(1)(B).

a certificate noting that the kerosene will be used for a feedstock purpose in order for the exemption to apply.

Information and tax return reporting

The IRS collects data under the ExSTARS reporting system that tracks all removals across the terminal rack regardless of whether or not the product is technically excluded from the definition of gasoline, diesel or blendstocks. ExSTARS reporting identifies the position holder at the time of removal. Below the rack, no information is gathered for exempt or excluded products or uses.

Taxpayers file quarterly excise tax returns showing only net taxable gallons.[904] Taxpayers do not account for gallons they claim to be exempt on such returns. Although the return is a quarterly return, the excise taxes are paid in semimonthly deposits.[905] If deposits are not made as required, a taxpayer may be required to file returns on a monthly or semimonthly basis instead of quarterly.[906]

Explanation of Provision

The Act adds two additional categories to the definition of diesel fuel. Under the Act, diesel fuel means: (1) any liquid (other than gasoline) which is suitable for use as a fuel in a diesel-powered highway vehicle, or a diesel-powered train; (2) transmix; and (3) diesel fuel blend stocks as identified by the Secretary. Transmix means a by-product of refined products pipeline operations created by the mixing of different specification products during pipeline transportation. Transmix generally results when one fuel, such as diesel fuel, is placed in a pipeline followed by another taxable fuel, such as kerosene. The mixture created between the two fuels when it is neither all diesel fuel nor all kerosene, is an example of a transmix. Under the provision, all transmix is taxable as diesel fuel, regardless of whether it contains gasoline.

Under the Act, it is intended that the re-refining of tax-paid transmix into gasoline, diesel fuel or kerosene qualify as a nontaxable off-highway business use of such transmix, for purposes of the refund and payment provisions relating to nontaxable uses of diesel fuel.

Not later than January 31, 2005, the Secretary shall submit to the Committee on Finance of the Senate and the Committee on Ways and Means of the House of Representatives a report regarding fuel tax compliance, which shall include information, and analysis as specified below, and recommendations to address the issues identified.

The Secretary is to identify chemical products that should be added to the list of blendstocks. The Secretary is to identify those chemical products, as identified by lab analysis of fuel samples taken by the IRS, that have been blended with taxable fuel but are not currently treated as a blendstock. The report should indicate, to the extent possible, any statistics as to the frequency in which such chemical product has been discovered, and whether the samples contained above-normal concentrations of such chemical prod-

[904] Treas. Reg. sec. 406011(a)–1(a); Form 720, Quarterly Federal Excise Tax Return.
[905] Treas. Reg. sec. 40.6302(c)–1(a).
[906] Treas. Reg. sec. 40.6011(a)–1(b).

uct. The report also shall include a discussion of IRS findings regarding the addition of waste products to taxable fuel and any recommendations to address the taxation of such products. The report shall include a discussion of IRS findings regarding sales of taxable fuel to entities claiming exempt status as a State or local government. Such discussion shall include the frequency of erroneous certifications as to exempt status determined on audit. The Secretary shall consult with representatives of State and local governments in providing recommendations to address this issue, including the feasibility of State maintained lists of their exempt governmental entities.

Effective Date

The provision regarding the taxation of transmix and diesel fuel blendstocks is effective for fuel removed, sold, or used after December 31, 2004. The requirement for a Treasury study is effective on the date of enactment (October 22, 2004).

D. Other Revenue Provisions

1. Permit private sector debt collection companies to collect tax debts (sec. 881 of the Act and new sec. 6306 of the Code)

Present and Prior Law

In fiscal years 1996 and 1997, the Congress earmarked $13 million for IRS to test the use of private debt collection companies. There were several constraints on this pilot project. First, because both IRS and OMB considered the collection of taxes to be an inherently governmental function, only government employees were permitted to collect the taxes.[907] The private debt collection companies were utilized to assist the IRS in locating and contacting taxpayers, reminding them of their outstanding tax liability, and suggesting payment options. If the taxpayer agreed at that point to make a payment, the taxpayer was transferred from the private debt collection company to the IRS. Second, the private debt collection companies were paid a flat fee for services rendered; the amount that was ultimately collected by the IRS was not taken into account in the payment mechanism.

The pilot program was discontinued because of disappointing results. GAO reported[908] that the IRS collected $3.1 million attributable to the private debt collection company efforts; expenses were also $3.1 million. In addition, there were lost opportunity costs of $17 million to the IRS because collection personnel were diverted from their usual collection responsibilities to work on the pilot. The pilot program results were disappointing because "IRS' efforts to design and implement the private debt collection pilot program were hindered by limitations that affected the program's results." The limitations included the scope of work permitted to the private debt collection companies, the number and type of cases referred to the private debt collection companies, and the ability of IRS' com-

---

[907] Sec. 7801(a).

[908] GOA/GGD–97–129R *Issues Affecting IRS' Collection Pilot* (July 18, 1997).

puter systems to identify, select, and transmit collection cases to the private debt collectors.

The IRS has in the last several years expressed renewed interest in the possible use of private debt collection companies; for example, IRS recently revised its extensive Request for Information concerning its possible use of private debt collection companies.[909] GAO recently reviewed IRS' planning and preparation for the use of private debt collection companies.[910] GAO identified five broad factors critical to the success of using private debt collection companies to collect taxes. GAO concluded: "If Congress does authorize PCA[911] use, IRS's planning and preparations to address the critical success factors for PCA contracting provide greater assurance that the PCA program is headed in the right direction to meet its goals and achieve desired results. Nevertheless, much work and many challenges remain in addressing the critical success factors and helping to maximize the likelihood that a PCA program would be successful."[912]

In general, Federal agencies are permitted to enter into contracts with private debt collection companies for collection services to recover indebtedness owed to the United States.[913] That provision does not apply to the collection of debts under the Internal Revenue Code.[914]

The President's fiscal year 2004 and 2005 budget proposals proposed the use of private debt collection companies to collect Federal tax debts.

Reasons for Change

The Congress believed that the use of private debt collection agencies will help facilitate the collection of taxes that are owed to the Government. The Congress also believed that safeguards it has incorporated will protect taxpayers' rights and privacy.

Explanation of Provision

The Act permits the IRS to use private debt collection companies to locate and contact taxpayers owing outstanding tax liabilities of any type[915] and to arrange payment of those taxes by the taxpayers. There must be an assessment pursuant to section 6201 in order for there to be an outstanding tax liability. An assessment is the formal recording of the taxpayer's tax liability that fixes the amount payable. An assessment must be made before the IRS is permitted to commence enforcement actions to collect the amount

[909] TIRNO–03–H–0001 (February 14, 2003), at www.procurement.irs.treas.gov. The basic request for information is 104 pages, and there are 16 additional attachments.

[910] GAO–04–492 *Tax Debt Collection: IRS Is Addressing Critical Success Factors for Contracting Out but Will Need to Study the Best Use of Resources* (May 2004).

[911] Private collection agencies.

[912] Page 19 of the May 2004 GAO report.

[913] 31 U.S.C. sec. 3718.

[914] 31 U.S.C. sec. 3718(f).

[915] The Act generally applies to any type of tax imposed under the Internal Revenue Code. It is anticipated that the focus in implementing the provision will be: (a) taxpayers who have filed a return showing a balance due but who have failed to pay that balance in full; and (b) taxpayers who have been assessed additional tax by the IRS and who have made several voluntary payments toward satisfying their obligation but have not paid in full.

payable. In general, an assessment is made at the conclusion of all examination and appeals processes within the IRS.[916]

Several steps are involved in the deployment of private debt collection companies. First, the private debt collection company contacts the taxpayer by letter.[917] If the taxpayer's last known address is incorrect, the private debt collection company searches for the correct address. Second, the private debt collection company telephones the taxpayer to request full payment.[918] If the taxpayer cannot pay in full immediately, the private debt collection company offers the taxpayer an installment agreement providing for full payment of the taxes over a period of as long as five years. If the taxpayer is unable to pay the outstanding tax liability in full over a five-year period, the private debt collection company obtains financial information from the taxpayer and will provide this information to the IRS for further processing and action by the IRS.

The Act specifies several procedural conditions under which the provision would operate. First, provisions of the Fair Debt Collection Practices Act apply to the private debt collection company. Second, taxpayer protections that are statutorily applicable to the IRS are also made statutorily applicable to the private sector debt collection companies. In addition, taxpayer protections that are statutorily applicable to IRS employees are made statutorily applicable to employees of private sector debt collection companies. Third, subcontractors are prohibited from having contact with taxpayers, providing quality assurance services, and composing debt collection notices; any other service provided by a subcontractor must receive prior approval from the IRS. In addition, it is intended that the IRS require the private sector debt collection companies to inform every taxpayer they contact of the availability of assistance from the Taxpayer Advocate.

The Act creates a revolving fund from the amounts collected by the private debt collection companies. The private debt collection companies will be paid out of this fund. The Act prohibits the payment of fees for all services in excess of 25 percent of the amount collected under a tax collection contract.[919]

The Act also provides that up to 25 percent of the amount collected may be used for IRS collection enforcement activities. The Act requires Treasury to provide a biennial report to Congress. The Congress expected that, consistent with best management practices and sound tax administration principles, the Secretary will utilize this new debt collection provision to the maximum extent feasible.

---

[916] An amount of tax reported as due on the taxpayer's tax return is considered to be self-assessed. If the IRS determines that the assessment or collection of tax will be jeopardized by delay, it has the authority to assess the amount immediately (sec. 6861), subject to several procedural safeguards.

[917] Several portions of the Act require that the IRS disclose confidential taxpayer information to the private debt collection company. Section 6103(n) permits disclosure of returns and return information for "the providing of other services . . . for purposes of tax administration." Accordingly, no amendment to section 6103 is necessary to implement the provision. It is intended, however, that the IRS vigorously protect the privacy of confidential taxpayer information by disclosing the least amount of information possible to contractors consistent with the effective operation of the Act.

[918] The private debt collection company is not permitted to accept payment directly. Payments are required to be processed by IRS employees.

[919] It is assumed that there will be competitive bidding for these contracts by private sector tax collection agencies and that vigorous bidding will drive the overhead costs down.

The Congress expected that activities conducted by any person under a qualified tax collection contract will be in compliance with the Fair Debt Collection Practices Act, as required by new section 6306(e) of the Code. Accordingly, the Congress anticipated that the Secretary will not impose requirements that would violate this provision of the Code. The Congress believed that this new debt collection provision will protect both taxpayers' rights and the confidentiality of tax information.

Effective Date

The provision is effective on the date of enactment (October 22, 2004).

2. Modify charitable contribution rules for donations of patents and other intellectual property (sec. 882 of the Act and secs. 170 and 6050L of the Code)

Present and Prior Law

In general, under present and prior law, a deduction is permitted for charitable contributions, subject to certain limitations that depend on the type of taxpayer, the property contributed, and the donee organization.[920] In the case of non-cash contributions, the amount of the deduction generally equals the fair market value of the contributed property on the date of the contribution.

Under present and prior law, for certain contributions of property, the taxpayer is required to reduce the deduction amount by any gain, generally resulting in a deduction equal to the taxpayer's basis. This rule applies to contributions of: (1) property that, at the time of contribution, would not have resulted in long-term capital gain if the property was sold by the taxpayer on the contribution date; (2) tangible personal property that is used by the donee in a manner unrelated to the donee's exempt (or governmental) purpose; and (3) property to or for the use of a private foundation (other than a foundation defined in section 170(b)(1)(E)).

Charitable contributions of capital gain property generally are deductible at fair market value. Capital gain property means any capital asset or property used in the taxpayer's trade or business the sale of which at its fair market value, at the time of contribution, would have resulted in gain that would have been long-term capital gain. Contributions of capital gain property are subject to different percentage limitations than other contributions of property. Under present and prior law, certain copyrights are not considered capital assets, in which case the charitable deduction for such copyrights generally is limited to the taxpayer's basis.[921]

In general, a charitable contribution deduction is allowed only for contributions of the donor's entire interest in the contributed property, and not for contributions of a partial interest.[922] If a taxpayer sells property to a charitable organization for less than the property's fair market value, the amount of any charitable contribution deduction is determined in accordance with the bargain sale

---

[920] Charitable deductions are provided for income, estate, and gift tax purposes. Secs. 170, 2055, and 2522, respectively.

[921] See sec. 1221(a)(3), 1231(b)(1)(C).

[922] Sec. 170(f)(3).

rules.[923] In general, if a donor receives a benefit or quid pro quo in return for a contribution, any charitable contribution deduction is reduced by the amount of the benefit received. For contributions of $250 or more, no charitable contribution deduction is allowed unless the donee organization provides a contemporaneous written acknowledgement of the contribution that describes and provides a good faith estimate of the value of any goods or services provided by the donee organization in exchange for the contribution.[924]

In general, taxpayers are required to obtain a qualified appraisal for donated property with a value of $5,000 or more, and to attach the appraisal to the tax return in certain cases. Under Treasury regulations, a qualified appraisal means an appraisal document that, among other things, (1) relates to an appraisal that is made not earlier than 60 days prior to the date of contribution of the appraised property and not later than the due date (including extensions) of the return on which a deduction is first claimed under section 170;[925] (2) is prepared, signed, and dated by a qualified appraiser; (3) includes (a) a description of the property appraised; (b) the fair market value of such property on the date of contribution and the specific basis for the valuation; (c) a statement that such appraisal was prepared for income tax purposes; (d) the qualifications of the qualified appraiser; and (e) the signature and taxpayer identification number ("TIN") of such appraiser; and (4) does not involve an appraisal fee that violates certain prescribed rules.[926]

Reasons for Change

The Congress believed that the value of certain intellectual property, such as patents, copyrights, trademarks, trade names, trade secrets, know-how, software, similar property, or applications or registrations of such property, that is contributed to a charity often is highly speculative. Some donated intellectual property may prove to be worthless, or the initial promise of worth may be diminished by future inventions, marketplace competition, or other factors. Although in theory, such intellectual property may promise significant monetary benefits, the benefits generally will not materialize if the charity does not make the appropriate investments, have the right personnel and equipment, or even have sufficient sustained interest to exploit the intellectual property. The Congress understood that valuation is made yet more difficult in the charitable contribution context because the transferee does not provide full, if any, consideration in exchange for the transferred property pursuant to arm's length negotiations, and there may not be a comparable sales market for such property to use as a benchmark for valuations.

The Congress was concerned that taxpayers with intellectual property were taking advantage of the inherent difficulties in valuing such property and were preparing or obtaining erroneous valuations. In such cases, the charity would receive an asset of questionable value, while the taxpayer received a significant tax

[923] Sec. 1011(b) and Treas. Reg. sec. 1.1011–2.
[924] Sec. 170(f)(8).
[925] In the case of a deduction first claimed or reported on an amended return, the deadline is the date on which the amended return is filed.
[926] Treas. Reg. sec. 1.170A–13(c)(3).

benefit. The Congress believed that the excessive charitable contribution deductions enabled by inflated valuations were best addressed by ensuring that the amount of the deduction for charitable contributions of such property may not exceed the taxpayer's basis in the property. The Congress noted that for other types of charitable contributions for which valuation is especially problematic—charitable contributions of property created by the personal efforts of the taxpayer and charitable contributions to certain private foundations—a basis deduction generally is the result under present and prior law.

Although the Congress believed that a deduction of basis was appropriate in this context, the Congress recognized that some contributions of intellectual property may be proven to be of economic benefit to the charity and that donors may need an economic incentive to make such contributions. Accordingly, the Congress believed that it was appropriate to permit donors of intellectual property to receive certain additional charitable contribution deductions in the future but only if the contributed property generates qualified income for the charitable organization.

Explanation of Provision

The Act provides that if a taxpayer contributes a patent or other intellectual property (other than certain copyrights or inventory) to a charitable organization, the taxpayer's initial charitable deduction is limited to the lesser of the taxpayer's basis in the contributed property or the fair market value of the property. In addition, the taxpayer is permitted to deduct, as a charitable deduction, certain additional amounts in the year of contribution or in subsequent taxable years based on a specified percentage of the qualified donee income received or accrued by the charitable donee with respect to the contributed property. For this purpose, "qualified donee income" includes net income received or accrued by the donee that properly is allocable to the intellectual property itself (as opposed to the activity in which the intellectual property is used).

The amount of any additional charitable deduction is calculated as a sliding-scale percentage of qualified donee income received or accrued by the charitable donee that properly is allocable to the contributed property to the applicable taxable year of the donor, determined as follows:

Taxable Year of Donor	Deduction Permitted for Such Taxable Year
1st year ending on or after contribution.	100 percent of qualified donee income
2nd year ending on or after contribution.	100 percent of qualified donee income
3rd year ending on or after contribution.	90 percent of qualified donee income
4th year ending on or after contribution.	80 percent of qualified donee income
5th year ending on or after contribution.	70 percent of qualified donee income

Taxable Year of Donor	Deduction Permitted for Such Taxable Year
6th year ending on or after contribution.	60 percent of qualified donee income
7th year ending on or after contribution.	50 percent of qualified donee income
8th year ending on or after contribution.	40 percent of qualified donee income
9th year ending on or after contribution.	30 percent of qualified donee income
10th year ending on or after contribution.	20 percent of qualified donee income
11th year ending on or after contribution.	10 percent of qualified donee income
12th year ending on or after contribution.	10 percent of qualified donee income
Taxable years thereafter	No deduction permitted

An additional charitable deduction is allowed only to the extent that the aggregate of the amounts that are calculated pursuant to the sliding-scale exceed the amount of the deduction claimed upon the contribution of the patent or intellectual property.

No charitable deduction is permitted with respect to any revenues or income received or accrued by the charitable donee after the expiration of the legal life of the patent or intellectual property, or after the tenth anniversary of the date the contribution was made by the donor.

The taxpayer is required to inform the donee at the time of the contribution that the taxpayer intends to treat the contribution as a contribution subject to the additional charitable deduction provisions of the provision. In addition, the taxpayer must obtain written substantiation from the donee of the amount of any qualified donee income properly allocable to the contributed property during the charity's taxable year.[927] The donee is required to file an annual information return that reports the qualified donee income and other specified information relating to the contribution. In instances where the donor's taxable year differs from the donee's taxable year, the donor bases its additional charitable deduction on the qualified donee income of the charitable donee properly allocable to the donee's taxable year that ends within the donor's taxable year.

Under the Act, additional charitable deductions are not available for patents or other intellectual property contributed to a private foundation (other than a private operating foundation or certain other private foundations described in section 170(b)(1)(E)).

Under the Act, the Secretary may prescribe regulations or other guidance to carry out the purposes of the provision, including providing for the determination of amounts to be treated as qualified donee income in certain cases where the donee uses the donated

[927] The net income taken into account by the taxpayer may not exceed the amount of qualified donee income reported by the donee to the taxpayer and the IRS under the provision's substantiation and reporting requirements.

property to further its exempt activities or functions, or as may be necessary or appropriate to prevent the avoidance of the purposes of the Act.

Effective Date

The provision is effective for contributions made after June 3, 2004.

3. Require increased reporting for noncash charitable contributions (sec. 883 of the Act and sec. 170 of the Code)

Present and Prior Law

In general, under present and prior law, a deduction is permitted for charitable contributions, subject to certain limitations that depend on the type of taxpayer, the property contributed, and the donee organization.[928] In the case of noncash contributions, the amount of the deduction generally equals the fair market value of the contributed property on the date of the contribution.

In general, under present and prior law, if the total charitable deduction claimed for non-cash property exceeds $500, the taxpayer must file IRS Form 8283 (Noncash Charitable Contributions) with the IRS. Under present and prior law, C corporations (other than personal service corporations and closely-held corporations) are required to file Form 8283 only if the deduction claimed exceeds $5,000.

In general, under present and prior law, certain taxpayers are required to obtain a qualified appraisal for donated property (other than money and publicly traded securities) with a value of more than $5,000.[929] Under prior law, corporations (other than a closely-held corporation, a personal service corporation, or an S corporation) were not required to obtain a qualified appraisal. Under prior law, taxpayers were not required to attach a qualified appraisal to the taxpayer's return, except in the case of contributed art-work valued at more than $20,000.

Under Treasury regulations, a qualified appraisal means an appraisal document that, among other things, (1) relates to an appraisal that is made not earlier than 60 days prior to the date of contribution of the appraised property and not later than the due date (including extensions) of the return on which a deduction is first claimed under section 170;[930] (2) is prepared, signed, and

---

[928] Charitable deductions are provided for income, estate, and gift tax purposes. Secs. 170, 2055, and 2522, respectively.

[929] Pub. L. No. 98–369, sec. 155(a)(1) through (6) (1984) (providing that not later than December 31, 1984, the Secretary shall prescribe regulations requiring an individual, a closely held corporation, or a personal service corporation claiming a charitable deduction for property (other than publicly traded securities) to obtain a qualified appraisal of the property contributed and attach an appraisal summary to the taxpayer's return if the claimed value of such property (plus the claimed value of all similar items of property donated to one or more donees) exceeds $5,000). Under Pub. L. No. 98–369, a qualified appraisal means an appraisal prepared by a qualified appraiser that includes, among other things, (1) a description of the property appraised; (2) the fair market value of such property on the date of contribution and the specific basis for the valuation; (3) a statement that such appraisal was prepared for income tax purposes; (4) the qualifications of the qualified appraiser; (5) the signature and taxpayer identification number of such appraiser; and (6) such additional information as the Secretary prescribes in such regulations.

[930] In the case of a deduction first claimed or reported on an amended return, the deadline is the date on which the amended return is filed.

dated by a qualified appraiser; (3) includes (a) a description of the property appraised; (b) the fair market value of such property on the date of contribution and the specific basis for the valuation; (c) a statement that such appraisal was prepared for income tax purposes; (d) the qualifications of the qualified appraiser; and (e) the signature and taxpayer identification number of such appraiser; and (4) does not involve an appraisal fee that violates certain prescribed rules.[931]

Reasons for Change

Under present and prior law, an individual who contributes property to a charity and claims a deduction in excess of $5,000 must obtain a qualified appraisal, but, under prior law, a C corporation (other than a closely-held corporation or a personal services corporation) that donated property in excess of $5,000 was not required to obtain such an appraisal. Prior law did not require that appraisals, even for large gifts, be attached to a taxpayer's return. The Congress believed that requiring C corporations to obtain a qualified appraisal for charitable contributions of certain property in excess of $5,000, and requiring that appraisals be attached to a taxpayer's return for large gifts, would reduce valuation abuses.

Explanation of Provision

The Act requires increased donor reporting for certain charitable contributions of property other than cash, inventory, or publicly traded securities. The Act extends to all C corporations the present and prior law requirement, applicable to an individual, closely-held corporation, personal service corporation, partnership, or S corporation, that the donor must obtain a qualified appraisal of the property if the amount of the deduction claimed exceeds $5,000. The Act also provides that if the amount of the contribution of property other than cash, inventory, or publicly traded securities exceeds $500,000, then the donor (whether an individual, partnership, or corporation) must attach the qualified appraisal to the donor's tax return. For purposes of the dollar thresholds under the provision, property and all similar items of property donated to one or more donees are treated as one property. Taxpayers contributing artwork valued at more than $20,000 are still required to attach a copy of the qualified appraisal to the taxpayer's return.

Appraisals are not required for charitable contributions of certain vehicles that are sold by the donee organization without a significant intervening use or material improvement of the vehicle by such organization, and for which the organization provides an acknowledgement to the donor containing a certification that the vehicle was sold in an arm's length transaction between unrelated parties, and providing the gross sales proceeds from the sale, and a statement that the donor's deductible amount may not exceed the amount of such gross proceeds.

The Act provides that a donor that fails to substantiate a charitable contribution of property, as required by the Secretary, is denied a charitable contribution deduction. If the donor is a partner-

[931] Treas. Reg. sec. 1.170A–13(c)(3).

ship or S corporation, the deduction is denied at the partner or shareholder level. The denial of the deduction does not apply if it is shown that such failure is due to reasonable cause and not to willful neglect.

The Act provides that the Secretary may prescribe such regulations as may be necessary or appropriate to carry out the purposes of the Act, including regulations that may provide that some or all of the requirements of the Act do not apply in appropriate cases.

Effective Date

The provision is effective for contributions made after June 3, 2004.

4. Limit deduction for charitable contributions of vehicles (sec. 884 of the Act and new sec. 6720 and sec. 170 of the Code)

Present and Prior Law

In general, under present and prior law, a deduction is permitted for charitable contributions, subject to certain limitations that depend on the type of taxpayer, the property contributed, and the donee organization.[932] In the case of non-cash contributions, the amount of the deduction generally equals the fair market value of the contributed property on the date of the contribution.

Under present and prior law, for certain contributions of property, the taxpayer is required to determine the deductible amount by subtracting any gain from fair market value, generally resulting in a deduction equal to the taxpayer's basis. This rule applies to contributions of: (1) property that, at the time of contribution, would not have resulted in long-term capital gain if the property was sold by the taxpayer on the contribution date; (2) tangible personal property that is used by the donee in a manner unrelated to the donee's exempt (or governmental) purpose; and (3) property to or for the use of a private foundation (other than a foundation defined in section 170(b)(1)(E)).

Under present and prior law, charitable contributions of capital gain property generally are deductible at fair market value. Capital gain property means any capital asset or property used in the taxpayer's trade or business the sale of which at its fair market value, at the time of contribution, would have resulted in gain that would have been long-term capital gain. Contributions of capital gain property are subject to different percentage limitations than other contributions of property.

Under prior law, a taxpayer who donated a used automobile to a charitable donee generally deducted the fair market value (rather than the taxpayer's basis) of the automobile. A taxpayer who donated a used automobile generally was permitted to use an established used car pricing guide to determine the fair market value of the automobile, but only if the guide listed a sales price for an automobile of the same make, model and year, sold in the same area, and in the same condition as the donated automobile. Similar

---

[932] Charitable deductions are provided for income, estate, and gift tax purposes. Secs. 170, 2055, and 2522, respectively.

rules applied to contributions of other types of vehicles and property, such as boats.

Under present and prior law, charities are required to provide donors with written substantiation of donations of $250 or more. Taxpayers are required to report non-cash contributions totaling $500 or more and the method used for determining fair market value.

In general, under present and prior law, taxpayers are required to obtain a qualified appraisal for donated property with a value of $5,000 or more, and to attach the appraisal to the tax return in certain cases. Under Treasury regulations, a qualified appraisal means an appraisal document that, among other things, (1) relates to an appraisal that is made not earlier than 60 days prior to the date of contribution of the appraised property and not later than the due date (including extensions) of the return on which a deduction is first claimed under section 170;[933] (2) is prepared, signed, and dated by a qualified appraiser; (3) includes (a) a description of the property appraised; (b) the fair market value of such property on the date of contribution and the specific basis for the valuation; (c) a statement that such appraisal was prepared for income tax purposes; (d) the qualifications of the qualified appraiser; and (e) the signature and taxpayer identification number ("TIN") of such appraiser; and (4) does not involve an appraisal fee that violates certain prescribed rules.[934]

Under present and prior law, appraisal fees paid by an individual to determine the fair market value of donated property are deductible as miscellaneous expenses subject to the 2 percent of adjusted gross income limit.[935]

Explanation of Provision

Under the Act, the amount of deduction for charitable contributions of vehicles (generally including automobiles, boats, and airplanes for which the claimed value exceeds $500 and excluding inventory property) depends upon the use of the vehicle by the donee organization. If the donee organization sells the vehicle without any significant intervening use or material improvement of such vehicle by the organization, the amount of the deduction shall not exceed the gross proceeds received from the sale.

The Act imposes new substantiation requirements for contributions of vehicles for which the claimed value exceeds $500 (excluding inventory). A deduction is not allowed unless the taxpayer substantiates the contribution by a contemporaneous written acknowledgement by the donee. The acknowledgement must contain the name and taxpayer identification number of the donor and the vehicle identification number (or similar number) of the vehicle. In addition, if the donee sells the vehicle without performing a significant intervening use or material improvement of such vehicle, the acknowledgement must provide a certification that the vehicle was sold in an arm's length transaction between unrelated parties, and state the gross proceeds from the sale and that the deductible

[933] In the case of a deduction first claimed or reported on an amended return, the deadline is the date on which the amended return is filed.
[934] Treas. Reg. sec. 1.170A–13(c)(3).
[935] Rev. Rul. 67–461, 1967–2 C.B. 125.

amount may not exceed such gross proceeds. In all other cases, the acknowledgement must contain a certification of the intended use or material improvement of the vehicle and the intended duration of such use, and a certification that the vehicle will not be transferred in exchange for money, other property, or services before completion of such use or improvement. The donee must notify the Secretary of the information contained in an acknowledgement, in a time and manner provided by the Secretary. An acknowledgement is considered contemporaneous if provided within 30 days of sale of a vehicle that is not significantly improved or materially used by the donee, or, in all other cases, within 30 days of the contribution.

A penalty applies if a donee organization knowingly furnishes a false or fraudulent acknowledgement, or knowingly fails to furnish an acknowledgement in the manner, at the time, and showing the required information. In the case of an acknowledgement provided within 30 days of sale of a vehicle which is not significantly used or materially improved by the donee, the penalty is the greater of the gross proceeds from the sale of the vehicle or the product of the highest rate of tax specified in section 1 and the sales price stated on the acknowledgement. For all other acknowledgements, the penalty is the greater of $5,000 or the product of the highest rate of tax specified in section 1 and the claimed value of the vehicle.

The Act provides that the Secretary shall prescribe such regulations or other guidance as may be necessary to carry out the purposes of the proposal. The Secretary may prescribe regulations or other guidance that exempts sales of vehicles that are in direct furtherance of the donee's charitable purposes from the requirement that the donor may not deduct an amount in excess of the gross proceeds from the sale, and the requirement that the donee certify that the vehicle will not be transferred in exchange for money, other property, or services before completion of a significant use or material improvement by the donee. It is intended that such guidance may be appropriate, for example, if an organization directly furthers its charitable purposes by selling automobiles to needy persons at a price significantly below fair market value.

It is intended that in providing guidance on the provision, the Secretary shall strictly construe the requirement of significant use or material improvement. To meet the significant use test, an organization must actually use the vehicle to substantially further the organization's regularly conducted activities and the use must be significant. A donee will not be considered to significantly use a qualified vehicle if, under the facts and circumstances, the use is incidental or not intended at the time of the contribution. Whether a use is significant also depends on the frequency and duration of use. With respect to the material improvement test, it is intended that a material improvement would include major repairs to a vehicle, or other improvements to the vehicle that improve the condition of the vehicle in a manner that significantly increases the vehicle's value. Cleaning the vehicle, minor repairs, and routine maintenance are not considered a material improvement.

Example 1.—As part of its regularly conducted activities, an organization delivers meals to needy individuals. The use requirement would be met if the organization actually used a donated qualified vehicle to deliver food to the needy. Use of the vehicle to deliver meals substantially furthers a regularly conducted activity of the organization. However, the use also must be significant, which depends on the nature, extent, and frequency of the use. If the organization used the vehicle only once or a few times to deliver meals, the use would not be considered significant. If the organization used the vehicle to deliver meals every day for one year the use would be considered significant. If the organization drove the vehicle 10,000 miles while delivering meals, such use likely would be considered significant. However, use of a vehicle in such an activity for one week or for several hundreds of miles generally would not be considered a significant use.

Example 2.—An organization uses a donated qualified vehicle to transport its volunteers. The use would not be significant merely because a volunteer used the vehicle over a brief period of time to drive to or from the organization's premises. On the other hand, if at the time the organization accepts the contribution of a qualified vehicle, the organization intends to use the vehicle as a regular and ongoing means of transport for volunteers of the organization, and such vehicle is so used, then the significant use test likely would be met.

Example 3.—The following example is a general illustration of the Act. A taxpayer makes a charitable contribution of a used automobile in good running condition and that needs no immediate repairs to a charitable organization that operates an elder care facility. The donee organization accepts the vehicle and immediately provides the donor a written acknowledgment containing the name and TIN of the donor, the vehicle identification number, a certification that the donee intends to retain the vehicle for a year or longer to transport the facility's residents to community and social events and deliver meals to the needy, and a certification that the vehicle will not be transferred in exchange for money, other property, or services before completion of such use by the organization. A few days after receiving the vehicle, the donee organization commences to use the vehicle three times a week to transport some of its residents to various community events, and twice a week to deliver food to needy individuals. The organization continues to regularly use the vehicle for these purposes for approximately one year and then sells the vehicle. Under the Act, the donee's use of the vehicle constitutes a significant intervening use prior to the sale by the organization, and the donor's deduction is not limited to the gross proceeds received by the organization.

Effective Date

The provision is effective for contributions made after December 31, 2004.

5. Treatment of nonqualified deferred compensation plans (sec. 885 of the Act secs. 6040 and 6051 and new sec. 409A of the Code)

Present and Prior Law

In general

Under present and prior law, the determination of when amounts deferred under a nonqualified deferred compensation arrangement are includible in the gross income of the individual earning the compensation depends on the facts and circumstances of the arrangement. A variety of tax principles and Code provisions may be relevant in making this determination, including the doctrine of constructive receipt, the economic benefit doctrine,[936] the provisions of section 83 relating generally to transfers of property in connection with the performance of services, and provisions relating specifically to nonexempt employee trusts (sec. 402(b)) and nonqualified annuities (sec. 403(c)). Under prior law, the Code did not include rules specifically governing nonqualified deferred compensation.

In general, the time for income inclusion of nonqualified deferred compensation depends on whether the arrangement is unfunded or funded. If the arrangement is unfunded, then the compensation is generally includible in income when it is actually or constructively received. If the arrangement is funded, then income is includible for the year in which the individual's rights are transferable or not subject to a substantial risk of forfeiture.

Nonqualified deferred compensation is generally subject to social security and Medicare taxes when the compensation is earned (i.e., when services are performed), unless the nonqualified deferred compensation is subject to a substantial risk of forfeiture. If nonqualified deferred compensation is subject to a substantial risk of forfeiture, it is subject to social security and Medicare tax when the risk of forfeiture is removed (i.e., when the right to the nonqualified deferred compensation vests). Amounts deferred under a nonaccount balance plan that are not reasonably ascertainable are not required to be taken into account as wages subject to social security and Medicare taxes until the first date that such amounts are reasonably ascertainable. Social security and Medicare tax treatment is not affected by whether the arrangement is funded or unfunded, which is relevant in determining when amounts are includible in income (and subject to income tax withholding).

In general, an arrangement is considered funded if there has been a transfer of property under section 83. Under that section, a transfer of property occurs when a person acquires a beneficial ownership interest in such property. The term "property" is defined very broadly for purposes of section 83.[937] Property includes real and personal property other than money or an unfunded and unsecured promise to pay money in the future. Property also includes a beneficial interest in assets (including money) that are trans-

[936] See, e.g., *Sproull v. Commissioner*, 16 T.C. 244 (1951), aff'd, *per curiam*, 194 F.2d 541 (6th Cir. 1952); Rev. Rul. 60–31, 1960–1 C.B. 174.

[937] Treas. Reg. sec. 1.83–3(e). This definition, in part, reflects previous IRS rulings on nonqualified deferred compensation.

ferred or set aside from claims of the creditors of the transferor; for example, in a trust or escrow account. Accordingly, if, in connection with the performance of services, vested contributions are made to a trust on an individual's behalf and the trust assets may be used solely to provide future payments to the individual, the payment of the contributions to the trust constitutes a transfer of property to the individual that is taxable under section 83. On the other hand, deferred amounts are generally not includible in income if nonqualified deferred compensation is payable from general corporate funds that are subject to the claims of general creditors, as such amounts are treated as unfunded and unsecured promises to pay money or property in the future.

As discussed above, if the arrangement is unfunded, then the compensation is generally includible in income when it is actually or constructively received under section 451.[938] Income is constructively received when it is credited to an individual's account, set apart, or otherwise made available so that it may be drawn on at any time. Income is not constructively received if the taxpayer's control of its receipt is subject to substantial limitations or restrictions. A requirement to relinquish a valuable right in order to make withdrawals is generally treated as a substantial limitation or restriction.

Rabbi trusts

Arrangements have developed in an effort to provide employees with security for nonqualified deferred compensation, while still allowing deferral of income inclusion. A "rabbi trust" is a trust or other fund established by the employer to hold assets from which nonqualified deferred compensation payments will be made. The trust or fund is generally irrevocable and does not permit the employer to use the assets for purposes other than to provide nonqualified deferred compensation, except that the terms of the trust or fund provide that the assets are subject to the claims of the employer's creditors in the case of insolvency or bankruptcy.

As discussed above, for purposes of section 83, property includes a beneficial interest in assets set aside from the claims of creditors, such as in a trust or fund, but does not include an unfunded and unsecured promise to pay money in the future. In the case of a rabbi trust, terms providing that the assets are subject to the claims of creditors of the employer in the case of insolvency or bankruptcy have been the basis for the conclusion that the creation of a rabbi trust does not cause the related nonqualified deferred compensation arrangement to be funded for income tax purposes.[939] As a result, no amount is included in income by reason of the rabbi trust; generally income inclusion occurs as payments are made from the trust.

The IRS has issued guidance setting forth model rabbi trust provisions.[940] Revenue Procedure 92–64 provides a safe harbor for taxpayers who adopt and maintain grantor trusts in connection with

[938] Treas. Reg. secs. 1.451–1 and 1.451–2.

[939] This conclusion was first provided in a 1980 private ruling issued by the IRS with respect to an arrangement covering a rabbi; hence, the popular name "rabbi trust." Priv. Ltr. Rul. 8113107 (Dec. 31, 1980).

[940] Rev. Proc. 92–64, 1992–2 C.B. 422, modified in part by Notice 2000–56, 2000–2 C.B. 393.

unfunded deferred compensation arrangements. The model trust language requires that the trust provide that all assets of the trust are subject to the claims of the general creditors of the company in the event of the company's insolvency or bankruptcy.

Since the concept of rabbi trusts was developed, arrangements have developed which attempt to protect the assets from creditors despite the terms of the trust. Arrangements also have developed which attempt to allow deferred amounts to be available to individuals, while still purporting to meet the safe harbor requirements set forth by the IRS.

Reasons for Change

The Congress was aware of the popular use of deferred compensation arrangements by executives to defer current taxation of substantial amounts of income. Many nonqualified deferred compensation arrangements had developed which allowed improper deferral of income. Executives often used arrangements that allowed deferral of income, but also provided security of future payment and control over amounts deferred. For example, nonqualified deferred compensation arrangements often contained provisions that allowed participants to receive distributions upon request, subject to forfeiture of a minimal amount (i.e., a "haircut" provision).

The Congress was aware that since the concept of a rabbi trust was developed, techniques had been used that attempted to protect the assets from creditors despite the terms of the trust. For example, the trust or fund would be located in a foreign jurisdiction, making it difficult or impossible for creditors to reach the assets.

While the general tax principles governing deferred compensation were well established, the determination whether a particular arrangement effectively allowed deferral of income was generally made on a facts and circumstances basis. There was limited specific guidance with respect to common deferral arrangements. The Congress believed that it was appropriate to provide specific rules regarding whether deferral of income inclusion should be permitted.

The Congress believed that certain arrangements that allow participants inappropriate levels of control or access to amounts deferred should not result in deferral of income inclusion. The Congress also believed that certain arrangements, such as offshore trusts, which effectively protect assets from creditors, should be treated as funded and not result in deferral of income inclusion.[941]

[941] The staff of the Joint Committee on Taxation made recommendations similar to the new provision in the report on their investigation on Enron Corporation, which detailed how executives deferred millions of dollars in Federal income taxes through nonqualified deferred compensation arrangements. See Joint Committee on Taxation, *Report of Investigation of Enron Corporation and Related Entities Regarding Federal Tax and Compensation Issues, and Policy Recommendations* (JCS–3–03), February 2003.

Explanation of Provision

In general

Under the Act, all amounts deferred under a nonqualified deferred compensation plan[942] for all taxable years are currently includible in gross income to the extent not subject to a substantial risk of forfeiture[943] and not previously included in gross income, unless certain requirements are satisfied.[944] If the requirements of the Act are not satisfied, in addition to current income inclusion, interest at the underpayment rate plus one percentage point is imposed on the underpayments that would have occurred had the compensation been includible in income when first deferred, or if later, when not subject to a substantial risk of forfeiture. The amount required to be included in income is also subject to a 20-percent additional tax.[945]

Current income inclusion, interest, and the additional tax apply only with respect to the participants with respect to whom the requirements of the Act are not met. For example, suppose a plan covering all executives of an employer (including those subject to section 16(a) of the Securities and Exchange Act of 1934) allows distributions to individuals subject to section 16(a) upon a distribution event that is not permitted under the Act. The individuals subject to section 16(a), rather than all participants of the plan, would be required to include amounts deferred in income and would be subject to interest and the 20-percent additional tax.

Permissible distributions

In general

Under the Act, distributions from a nonqualified deferred compensation plan may be allowed only upon separation from service (as determined by the Secretary), death, a specified time (or pursuant to a fixed schedule), change in control of a corporation (to the extent provided by the Secretary), occurrence of an unforeseeable emergency, or if the participant becomes disabled. A nonqualified deferred compensation plan may not allow distributions other than upon the permissible distribution events and, except as provided in regulations by the Secretary, may not permit acceleration of a distribution.

Separation from service

In the case of a specified employee who separates from service, distributions may not be made earlier than six months after the

---

[942] A plan includes an agreement or arrangement, including an agreement or arrangement that includes one person. Amounts deferred also include actual or notional earnings.

[943] As under section 83, the rights of a person to compensation are subject to a substantial risk of forfeiture if the person's rights to such compensation are conditioned upon the performance of substantial services by an individual.

[944] It is inteded that Treasury regulations will provide guidance regarding when an amount is deferred. It is intended that timing of an election to defer is not determinative of when the deferral is made.

[945] These consequences apply under the Act to amounts deferred after the effective date of the provision. The additional tax and interest are not treated as payments of regular tax for alternative minimum tax purposes. A technical correction may be necessary so that the statute reflects this intent. See section 2(a)(10)(A) of H.R. 5395 and S. 3019, the "Tax Technical Corrections Act of 2004," introduced November 19, 2004.

date of the separation from service or upon death. Specified employees are key employees[946] of publicly-traded corporations.

Specified time

Amounts payable at a specified time or pursuant to a fixed schedule must be specified under the plan at the time of deferral. Amounts payable upon the occurrence of an event are not treated as amounts payable at a specified time. For example, amounts payable when an individual attains age 65 are payable at a specified time, while amounts payable when an individual's child begins college are payable upon the occurrence of an event.

Change in control

Distributions upon a change in the ownership or effective control of a corporation, or in the ownership of a substantial portion of the assets of a corporation, may only be made to the extent provided by the Secretary. It is intended that the Secretary use a similar, but more restrictive, definition of change in control as is used for purposes of the golden parachute provisions of section 280G consistent with the purposes of the Act. The Act requires the Secretary to issue guidance defining change of control within 90 days after the date of enactment.

Unforeseeable emergency

An unforeseeable emergency is defined as a severe financial hardship to the participant: (1) resulting from an illness or accident of the participant, the participant's spouse, or a dependent (as defined in sec. 152(a)); (2) loss of the participant's property due to casualty; or (3) other similar extraordinary and unforeseeable circumstances arising as a result of events beyond the control of the participant. The amount of the distribution must be limited to the amount needed to satisfy the emergency plus taxes reasonably anticipated as a result of the distribution. Distributions may not be allowed to the extent that the hardship may be relieved through reimbursement or compensation by insurance or otherwise, or by liquidation of the participant's assets (to the extent such liquidation would not itself cause a severe financial hardship).

Disability

A participant is considered disabled if he or she (1) is unable to engage in any substantial gainful activity by reason of any medically determinable physical or mental impairment which can be expected to result in death or can be expected to last for a continuous period of not less than 12 months; or (2) is, by reason of any medically determinable physical or mental impairment which can be expected to result in death or can be expected to last for a continuous period of not less than 12 months, receiving income replacement benefits for a period of not less than three months under an accident and health plan covering employees of the participant's employer.

---

[946] Key employees are defined in section 416(i) and generally include officers having annual compensation greater than $130,000 (adjusted for inflation and limited to 50 employees), five percent owners, and one percent owners having annual compensation from the employer greater than $150,000.

Prohibition on acceleration of distributions

As mentioned above, except as provided in regulations by the Secretary, no accelerations of distributions may be allowed. In general, changes in the form of distribution that accelerate payments are subject to the rule prohibiting acceleration of distributions. However, it is intended that the rule against accelerations is not violated merely because a plan provides a choice between cash and taxable property if the timing and amount of income inclusion is the same regardless of the medium of distribution. For example, the choice between a fully taxable annuity contract and a lump-sum payment may be permitted. It is also intended that the Secretary provide rules under which the choice between different forms of actuarially equivalent life annuity payments is permitted.

It is intended that the Secretary will provide other, limited, exceptions to the prohibition on accelerated distributions, such as when the accelerated distribution is required for reasons beyond the control of the participant and the distribution is not elective. For example, it is anticipated that an exception could be provided if a distribution is needed in order to comply with Federal conflict of interest requirements or a court-approved settlement incident to divorce. It is intended that Treasury regulations provide that a plan would not violate the prohibition on accelerations by providing that withholding of an employee's share of employment taxes will be made from the employee's interest in the nonqualified deferred compensation plan. It is also intended that Treasury regulations provide that a plan would not violate the prohibition on accelerations by providing for a distribution to a participant to pay income taxes due upon a vesting event subject to section 457(f), provided that such amount is not more than an amount equal to the income tax withholding that would have been remitted by the employer if there had been a payment of wages equal to the income includible by the participant under section 457(f). It is also intended that Treasury regulations provide that a plan would not violate the prohibition on accelerations by providing for automatic distributions of minimal interests in a deferred compensation plan upon permissible distribution events for purposes of administrative convenience. For example, a plan could provide that upon separation from service of a participant, account balances less than $10,000 will be automatically distributed (except in the case of specified employees).

Requirements with respect to elections

The Act requires that a plan must provide that compensation for services performed during a taxable year may be deferred at the participant's election only if the election to defer is made no later than the close of the preceding taxable year, or at such other time as provided in Treasury regulations.[947] In the case of any performance-based compensation based on services performed over a period of at least 12 months, such election may be made no later than six months before the end of the service period. It is not intended that

[947] Under the Act, in the first year that an employee becomes eligible for participation in a nonqualified deferred compensation plan, the election may be made within 30 days after the date that the employee is initially eligible.

the Act override the constructive receipt doctrine, as constructive receipt rules continue to apply. It is intended that the term "performance-based compensation" will be defined by the Secretary to include compensation to the extent that an amount is: (1) variable and contingent on the satisfaction of pre-established organizational or individual performance criteria and (2) not readily ascertainable at the time of the election. For the purposes of the Act, it is intended that performance-based compensation may be required to meet certain requirements similar to those under section 162(m), but would not be required to meet all requirements under that section. For example, it is expected that the Secretary will provide that performance criteria would be considered pre-established if it is established in writing no later than 90 days after the commencement of the service period, but the requirement of determination by the compensation committee of the board of directors would not be required. It is expected that the Secretary will issue guidance providing coordination rules, as appropriate, regarding the timing of elections in the case when the fiscal year of the employer and the taxable year of the individual are different. It is expected that Treasury regulations will not permit any election to defer any bonus or other compensation if the timing of such election would be inconsistent with the purposes of the Act.

The time and form of distributions must be specified at the time of initial deferral. A plan could specify the time and form of payments that are to be made as a result of a distribution event (e.g., a plan could specify that payments upon separation of service will be paid in lump sum within 30 days of separation from service) or could allow participants to elect the time and form of payment at the time of the initial deferral election. If a plan allows participants to elect the time and form of payment, such election is subject to the rules regarding initial deferral elections under the Act. It is intended that multiple payout events are permissible. For example, a participant could elect to receive 25 percent of their account balance at age 50 and the remaining 75 percent at age 60. A plan could also allow participants to elect different forms of payment for different permissible distribution events. For example, a participant could elect to receive a lump-sum distribution upon disability, but an annuity at age 65.

Under the Act, a plan may allow changes in the time and form of distributions subject to certain requirements. A nonqualified deferred compensation plan may allow a subsequent election to delay the timing or form of distributions only if: (1) the plan requires that such election cannot be effective for at least 12 months after the date on which the election is made; (2) except in the case of elections relating to distributions on account of death, disability or unforeseeable emergency, the plan requires that the additional deferral with respect to which such election is made is for a period of not less than five years from the date such payment would otherwise have been made[948]; and (3) the plan requires that an election related to a distribution to be made upon a specified time may not be made less than 12 months prior to the date of the first

[948] A technical correction may be necessary so that the statute reflects this intent. See section 2(a)(10)(B) of H.R. 5395 and S. 3019, the "Tax Technical Corrections Act of 2004," introduced November 19, 2004.

scheduled payment. It is expected that in limited cases, the Secretary will issue guidance, consistent with the purposes of the Act, regarding to what extent elections to change a stream of payments are permissible. The Secretary may issue regulations regarding elections with respect to payments under nonelective, supplemental retirement plans.

Foreign trusts

Under the Act, in the case of assets set aside (directly or indirectly) in a trust (or other arrangement determined by the Secretary) for purposes of paying nonqualified deferred compensation, such assets are treated as property transferred in connection with the performance of services under section 83 (whether or not such assets are available to satisfy the claims of general creditors) at the time set aside if such assets (or trust or other arrangement) are located outside of the United States or at the time transferred if such assets (or trust or other arrangement) are subsequently transferred outside of the United States. Any subsequent increases in the value of, or any earnings with respect to, such assets are treated as additional transfers of property. Interest at the underpayment rate plus one percentage point is imposed on the underpayments that would have occurred had the amounts set aside been includible in income for the taxable year in which first deferred or, if later, the first taxable year not subject to a substantial risk of forfeiture. The amount required to be included in income is also subject to an additional 20-percent tax.

It is expected that the Secretary will provide rules for identifying the deferrals to which assets set aside are attributable, for situations in which assets equal to less than the full amount of deferrals are set aside. The Act does not apply to assets located in a foreign jurisdiction if substantially all of the services to which the nonqualified deferred compensation relates are performed in such foreign jurisdiction. The Act is specifically intended to apply to foreign trusts and arrangements that effectively shield from the claims of general creditors any assets intended to satisfy nonqualified deferred compensation arrangements. The Secretary has authority to exempt arrangements from the Act if the arrangements do not result in an improper deferral of U.S. tax and will not result in assets being effectively beyond the reach of creditors.

Triggers upon financial health

Under the Act, a transfer of property in connection with the performance of services under section 83 also occurs with respect to compensation deferred under a nonqualified deferred compensation plan if the plan provides that upon a change in the employer's financial health, assets will be restricted to the payment of nonqualified deferred compensation. An amount is treated as restricted even if the assets are available to satisfy the claims of general creditors. For example, the Act applies in the case of a plan that provides that upon a change in financial health, assets will be transferred to a rabbi trust.

The transfer of property occurs as of the earlier of when the assets are so restricted or when the plan provides that assets will be restricted. It is intended that the transfer of property occurs to the extent that assets are restricted or will be restricted with respect to such compensation. For example, in the case of a plan that provides that upon a change in the employer's financial health, a trust will become funded to the extent of all deferrals, all amounts deferred under the plan are treated as property transferred under section 83. If a plan provides that deferrals of certain individuals will be funded upon a change in financial health, the transfer of property would occur with respect to compensation deferred by such individuals. The Act is not intended to apply when assets are restricted for a reason other than change in financial health (e.g., upon a change in control) or if assets are periodically restricted under a structured schedule and scheduled restrictions happen to coincide with a change in financial status. Any subsequent increases in the value of, or any earnings with respect to, restricted assets are treated as additional transfers of property. Interest at the underpayment rate plus one percentage point is imposed on the underpayments that would have occurred had the amounts been includible in income for the taxable year in which first deferred or, if later, the first taxable year not subject to a substantial risk of forfeiture. The amount required to be included in income is also subject to an additional 20-percent tax.

Definition of nonqualified deferred compensation plan

A nonqualified deferred compensation plan is any plan that provides for the deferral of compensation other than a qualified employer plan or any bona fide vacation leave, sick leave, compensatory time, disability pay, or death benefit plan.[949] A qualified employer plan means a qualified retirement plan, tax-deferred annuity, simplified employee pension, and SIMPLE.[950] A qualified governmental excess benefit arrangement (sec. 415(m)) is a qualified employer plan. An eligible deferred compensation plan (sec. 457(b)) is also a qualified employer plan under the Act. A tax-exempt or governmental deferred compensation plan that is not an eligible deferred compensation plan is not a qualified employer plan. The application of the Act is not limited to arrangements between an employer and employee.

For purposes of the Act, it is not intended that the term "nonqualified deferred compensation plan" include an arrangement taxable under section 83 providing for the grant of an option on employer stock with an exercise price that is not less than the fair market value of the underlying stock on the date of grant if such arrangement does not include a deferral feature other than the feature that the option holder has the right to exercise the option in the future. The Act is not intended to change the tax treatment of incentive stock options meeting the requirements of 422 or options granted under an employee stock purchase plan meeting the requirements of section 423.

[949] The Act does not apply to a plan meeting the requirements of section 457(e)(12) if the plan was in existence as of May 1, 2004, was providing nonelective deferred compensation described in section 457(e)(12) on such date, and is established or maintained by an organization incorporated on July 2, 1974. If the plan has a material change in the class of individuals eligible to participate in the plan after May 1, 2004, the Act applies to compensation provided under the plan after the date of such change.

[950] A qualified employer plan also includes a section 501(c)(18) trust.

It is intended that the Act does not apply to annual bonuses or other annual compensation amounts paid within 2½ months after the close of the taxable year in which the relevant services required for payment have been performed.

Other rules

Interest imposed under the Act is treated as interest on an underpayment of tax. Income (whether actual or notional) attributable to nonqualified deferred compensation is treated as additional deferred compensation and is subject to the Act. The Act is not intended to prevent the inclusion of amounts in gross income under any provision or rule of law earlier than the time provided in the Act. Any amount included in gross income under the Act is not required to be included in gross income under any provision of law later than the time provided in the Act. The Act does not affect the rules regarding the timing of an employer's deduction for nonqualified deferred compensation.

Treasury regulations

The Act provides the Secretary authority to prescribe regulations as are necessary to carry out the purposes of Act, including regulations: (1) providing for the determination of amounts of deferral in the case of defined benefit plans; (2) relating to changes in the ownership and control of a corporation or assets of a corporation; (3) exempting from the provisions providing for transfers of property arrangements that will not result in an improper deferral of U.S. tax and will not result in assets being effectively beyond the reach of creditors; (4) defining financial health; and (5) disregarding a substantial risk of forfeiture. It is intended that substantial risk of forfeitures may not be used to manipulate the timing of income inclusion. It is intended that substantial risks of forfeiture should be disregarded in cases in which they are illusory or are used in a manner inconsistent with the purposes of the Act. For example, if an executive is effectively able to control the acceleration of the lapse of a substantial risk of forfeiture, such risk of forfeiture should be disregarded and income inclusion should not be postponed on account of such restriction. The Secretary may also address in regulations issues relating to stock appreciation rights.

Aggregation rules

Under the Act, except as provided by the Secretary, employer aggregation rules apply. It is intended that the Secretary issue guidance providing aggregation rules as are necessary to carry out the purposes of the Act. For example, it is intended that aggregation rules would apply in the case of separation from service so that the separation from service from one entity within a controlled group, but continued service for another entity within the group, would not be a permissible distribution event. It is also intended that aggregation rules would not apply in the case of a change in control so that the change in control of one member of a controlled group would not be a permissible distribution event for participants of a deferred compensation plan of another member of the group.

Reporting requirements

Amounts required to be included in income under the Act are subject to reporting and Federal income tax withholding requirements. Amounts required to be includible in income are required to be reported on an individual's Form W–2 (or Form 1099) for the year includible in income.

The Act also requires annual reporting to the IRS of amounts deferred. Such amounts are required to be reported on an individual's Form W–2 (or Form 1099) for the year deferred even if the amount is not currently includible in income for that taxable year. It is expected that annual reporting of annual amounts deferred will provide the IRS greater information regarding such arrangements for enforcement purposes. It is intended that the information reported would provide an indication of what arrangements should be examined and challenged. Under the Act, the Secretary is authorized, through regulations, to establish a minimum amount of deferrals below which the reporting requirement does not apply. The Secretary may also provide that the reporting requirement does not apply with respect to amounts of deferrals that are not reasonably ascertainable. It is intended that the exception for amounts not reasonable ascertainable only apply to nonaccount balance plans and that amounts be required to be reported when they first become reasonably ascertainable.[951]

Effective Date

In general

The provision is generally effective for amounts deferred in taxable years beginning after December 31, 2004. Earnings on amounts deferred before the effective date are subject to the provision to the extent that such amounts deferred are subject to the provision.

Amounts deferred in taxable years beginning before January 1, 2005, are subject to the provision if the plan under which the deferral is made is materially modified after October 3, 2004. The addition of any benefit, right or feature is a material modification. The exercise or reduction of an existing benefit, right, or feature is not a material modification. For example, an amendment to a plan on November 1, 2004, to add a provision that distributions may be allowed upon request if participants are required to forfeit 10 percent of the amount of the distribution (i.e., a "haircut") would be a material modification to the plan so that the rules of the provision would apply to the plan. Similarly, accelerating vesting under a plan after October 3, 2004, would be a material modification. A change in the plan administrator would not be a material modification. As another example, amending a plan to remove a distribution provision (e.g., to remove a "haircut") would not be considered a material modification.

Operating under the terms of a deferred compensation arrangement that complies with prior law and is not materially modified after October 3, 2004, with respect to amounts deferred before Jan-

[951] It is intended that the exception be similar to that under Treas. Reg. sec. 31.3121(v)(2)–1(e)(4).

uary 1, 2005, is permissible, as such amounts would not be subject to the requirements of the provision. For example, subsequent deferrals with respect to amounts deferred before January 1, 2005, under a plan that is not materially modified after October 3, 2004, would be subject to prior law and would not be subject to the provision.[952] No inference is intended that all deferrals before the effective date are permissible under prior law. It is expected that the IRS will challenge pre-effective date deferral arrangements that do not comply with prior law.

For purposes of the effective date, an amount is considered deferred before January 1, 2005, if the amount is earned and vested before such date. To the extent there is no material modification after October 3, 2004, prior law applies with respect to vested rights.

No later than 60 days after the date of enactment, the Secretary shall issue guidance providing a limited period of time during which a nonqualified deferred compensation plan adopted before January 1, 2005,[953] may, without violating the requirements of the provision relating to distributions, accelerations, and elections be amended (1) to provide that a participant may terminate participation in the plan, or cancel an outstanding deferral election with respect to amounts deferred after December 31, 2004, if such amounts are includible in income of the participant as earned, or if later, when not subject to a substantial risk of forfeiture, and (2) to conform with the provision with respect to amounts deferred after December 31, 2004. It is expected that the Secretary may provide exceptions to certain requirements of the provision during the transition period (e.g., the rules regarding timing of elections) for plans coming into compliance with the provision. Moreover, it is expected that the Secretary will provide a reasonable time, during the transition period but after the issuance of guidance, for plans to be amended and approved by the appropriate parties in accordance with this provision.

Funding provisions

Notwithstanding the general effective date, the effective date of the funding provisions relating to offshore trusts and financial triggers is January 1, 2005.[954] Thus, for example, amounts set aside in an offshore trust before such date for the purpose of paying deferred compensation and plans providing for the restriction of assets in connection with a change in the employer's financial health are subject to the funding provisions on January 1, 2005.

---

[952] There is no inference that all subsequent deferral elections under plans that are not materially modified are permissible under prior law.

[953] A technical correction may be necessary so that the statute reflects this intent. See section 2(1)(10)(D) of H.R. 5395 and S. 3019, the "Tax Technical Corrections Act of 2004," introduced November 19, 2004.

[954] A technical correction may be necessary so that the statute reflects this intent. See section 2(a)(10)(C) of H.R. 5395 and S. 3019, the "Tax Technical Corrections Act of 2004," introduced November 19, 2004.

6. Extend the present-law intangible amortization provisions to acquisitions of sports franchises (sec. 886 of the Act and sec. 197 of the Code)

Present and Prior Law

The purchase price allocated to intangible assets (including franchise rights) acquired in connection with the acquisition of a trade or business generally must be capitalized and amortized over a 15-year period.[955] These rules were enacted in 1993 to minimize disputes regarding the proper treatment of acquired intangible assets. The rules do not apply to a franchise to engage in professional sports and any intangible asset acquired in connection with such a franchise.[956] However, other special rules apply to certain of these intangible assets.

Under section 1056, when a franchise to conduct a sports enterprise is sold or exchanged, the basis of a player contract acquired as part of the transaction is generally limited to the adjusted basis of such contract in the hands of the transferor, increased by the amount of gain, if any, recognized by the transferor on the transfer of the contract. Moreover, not more than 50 percent of the consideration from the transaction may be allocated to player contracts unless the transferee establishes to the satisfaction of the Commissioner that a specific allocation in excess of 50 percent is proper. However, these basis rules may not apply if a sale or exchange of a franchise to conduct a sports enterprise is effected through a partnership.[957] Basis allocated to the franchise or to other valuable intangible assets acquired with the franchise may not be amortizable if these assets lack a determinable useful life.

In general, section 1245 provides that gain from the sale of certain property is treated as ordinary income to the extent depreciation or amortization was allowed on such property. Section 1245(a)(4) provides special rules for recapture of depreciation and deductions for losses taken with respect to player contracts. The special recapture rules apply in the case of the sale, exchange, or other disposition of a sports franchise. Under the special recapture rules, the amount recaptured as ordinary income is the amount of gain not to exceed the greater of (1) the sum of the depreciation taken plus any deductions taken for losses (i.e., abandonment losses) with respect to those player contracts which are initially acquired as a part of the original acquisition of the franchise or (2) the amount of depreciation taken with respect to those player contracts which are owned by the seller at the time of the sale of the sports franchise.

Reasons for Change

Section 197 was enacted to minimize disputes regarding the measurement of acquired intangible assets. Prior to the enactment of section 197, there were many disputes regarding the value and useful life of various intangible assets acquired together in a business acquisition. Furthermore, in the absence of a showing of a rea-

[955] Sec. 197.
[956] Sec. 197(e)(6).
[957] *P.D.B. Sports, Ltd.* v. *Comm.*, 109 T.C. 423 (1997).

sonably determinable useful life, an asset could not be amortized. Taxpayers tended to identify and allocate large amounts of purchase price to assets said to have short useful lives, while the IRS would allocate a large amount of value to intangible value for which no determinable useful life could be shown (e.g., goodwill), and would deny amortization for that amount of purchase price.

The prior-law rules for acquisitions of sports franchises did not eliminate the potential for disputes, because they addressed only player contracts, while a sports franchise acquisition can involve many intangibles other than player contracts. In addition, disputes could arise regarding the appropriate period for amortization of particular player contracts. The Congress believed expending taxpayer and government resources disputing these items was an unproductive use of economic resources. The Congress further believed that the section 197 rules should apply to all types of businesses regardless of the nature of their assets.

Explanation of Provision

The Act extends the 15-year recovery period for intangible assets to franchises to engage in professional sports and any intangible asset acquired in connection with the acquisition of such a franchise (including player contracts). Thus, the same rules for amortization of intangibles that apply to other acquisitions also apply to acquisitions of sports franchises. The Act also repeals the special rules under section 1245(a)(4) and makes other conforming changes.

Effective Date

The provision is effective for property acquired after the date of enactment (October 22, 2004). The amendment to section 1245(a)(4) applies to franchises acquired after the date of enactment (October 22, 2004).

7. Increase continuous levy for certain Federal payments (sec. 887 of the Act and sec. 6331(h) of the Code)

Present and Prior Law

Under present and prior law, if any person is liable for any internal revenue tax and does not pay it within 10 days after notice and demand[958] by the IRS, the IRS may, after providing notice of collection due process rights, collect the tax by levy upon all property and rights to property belonging to the person,[959] unless there is an explicit statutory restriction on doing so. A levy is the seizure of the person's property or rights to property. Property that is not cash is sold pursuant to statutory requirements.[960]

A continuous levy is applicable to specified Federal payments.[961] This includes any Federal payment for which eligibility is not

[958] Notice and demand is the notice given to a person liable for tax stating that the tax has been assessed and demanding that payment be made. The notice and demand must be mailed to the person's last known address or left at the person's dwelling or usual place of business (sec. 6303).

[959] Sec. 6331.

[960] Secs. 6335–6343.

[961] Sec. 6331(h).

based on the income and/or assets of a payee. Thus, a Federal payment to a vendor of goods or services to the government is subject to continuous levy. Under prior law, this continuous levy attached up to 15 percent of any specified Federal payment due the taxpayer.

Reasons for Change

There had recently been reports of abuses of the Federal tax system by some Federal contractors. Consequently, the Congress believed that it was appropriate to increase the permissible percentage of specified Federal payments subject to levy.

Explanation of Provision

The Act permits a levy of up to 100 percent of a Federal payment to a vendor of goods or services to the Federal Government.

Effective Date

The provision is effective on the date of enactment (October 22, 2004).

8. Modification of straddle rules (sec. 888 of the Act and sec. 1092 of the Code)

Present and Prior Law

Straddle rules

In general

A "straddle" generally refers to offsetting positions (sometimes referred to as "legs" of the straddle) with respect to actively traded personal property. Positions are offsetting if there is a substantial diminution in the risk of loss from holding one position by reason of holding one or more other positions in personal property. A "position" is an interest (including a futures or forward contract or option) in personal property. When a taxpayer realizes a loss with respect to a position in a straddle, the taxpayer may recognize that loss for any taxable year only to the extent that the loss exceeds the unrecognized gain (if any) with respect to offsetting positions in the straddle.[962] Deferred losses are carried forward to the succeeding taxable year and are subject to the same limitation with respect to unrecognized gain in offsetting positions.

Positions in stock

Under prior law, the straddle rules generally did not apply to positions in stock. However, the straddle rules did apply where one of the positions was stock and at least one of the offsetting positions was: (1) an option with respect to the stock, (2) a securities futures contract (as defined in section 1234B) with respect to the stock, or (3) a position with respect to substantially similar or related property (other than stock) as defined in Treasury regulations. In addition, the straddle rules applied to stock of a corpora-

[962] Sec. 1092.

tion formed or availed of to take positions in personal property that offset positions taken by any shareholder.

Although the straddle rules apply to offsetting positions that consist of stock and an option with respect to stock, the straddle rules generally do not apply if the option is a "qualified covered call option" written by the taxpayer.[963] In general, a qualified covered call option is defined as an exchange-listed option that is not deep-in-the-money and is written by a non-dealer more than 30 days before expiration of the option.

The prior-law stock exception from the straddle rules largely had been curtailed by statutory amendment and regulatory interpretation. Under proposed Treasury regulations, the application of the stock exception essentially would be limited to offsetting positions involving direct ownership of stock and short sales of stock.[964]

Unbalanced straddles

When one position with respect to personal property offsets only a portion of one or more other positions ("unbalanced straddles"), prior law directed the Secretary to prescribe by regulations the method for determining the portion of such other positions that is to be taken into account for purposes of the straddle rules.[965] To date, no such regulations have been promulgated.

Unbalanced straddles can be illustrated with the following example: Assume the taxpayer holds two shares of stock (i.e., is long) in XYZ corporation—share A with a $30 basis and share B with a $40 basis. When the value of the XYZ stock is $45 per share, the taxpayer pays a $5 premium to purchase a put option on one share of the XYZ stock with an exercise price of $40. The issue arises as to whether the purchase of the put option creates a straddle with respect to share A, share B, or both. Assume that, when the value of the XYZ stock is $100, the put option expires unexercised. Taxpayer incurs a loss of $5 on the expiration of the put option, and sells share B for a $60 gain. On a literal reading of the straddle rules, the $5 loss would be deferred because the loss ($5) does not exceed the unrecognized gain ($70) in share A, which is also an offsetting position to the put option-notwithstanding that the taxpayer recognized more gain than the loss through the sale of share B. This problem is exacerbated when the taxpayer has a large portfolio of actively traded personal property that may be offsetting the loss leg of the straddle.

Although Treasury has not issued regulations to address unbalanced straddles, the IRS issued a private letter ruling in 1999 that addressed an unbalanced straddle situation.[966] Under the facts of the ruling, a taxpayer entered into a costless collar with respect to a portion of the shares of a particular stock held by the tax-

---

[963] However, if the option written by the taxpayer is a qualified covered call option that is in-the-money, then (1) any loss with respect to such option is treated as long-term capital loss if, at the time such loss is realized, gain on the sale or exchange of the offsetting stock held by the taxpayer would be treated as long-term capital gain, and (2) the holding period of such stock does not include any period during which the taxpayer is the grantor of the option (sec. 1092(f)).

[964] Prop. Treas. Reg. sec. 1.1092(d)–2(c).

[965] Prior-law sec. 1092(c)(2)(B).

[966] Priv. Ltr. Rul. 199925044 (Feb. 3, 1999).

payer.[967] Other shares were held in an account as collateral for a loan and still other shares were held in excess of the shares used as collateral and the number of shares specified in the collar. The ruling concluded that the collar offset only a portion of the stock (i.e., the number of shares specified in the costless collar) because that number of shares determined the payoff under each option comprising the collar. The ruling further concluded that:

> In the absence of regulations under section 1092(c)(2)(B), we conclude that it is permissible for Taxpayer to identify which shares of Corporation stock are part of the straddles and which shares are used as collateral for the loans using appropriately modified versions of the methods of section 1.1012–1(c)(2) and (3) [providing rules for adequate identification of shares of stock sold or transferred by a taxpayer] or section 1.1092(b)–3T(d)(4) [providing requirements and methods for identification of positions that are part of a section 1092(b)(2) identified mixed straddle].

Holding period for dividends-received deduction

If an instrument issued by a U.S. corporation is classified for tax purposes as stock, a corporate holder of the instrument generally is entitled to a dividends-received deduction for dividends received on that instrument.[968] The dividends-received deduction is allowed to a corporate shareholder only if the shareholder satisfies a 46-day holding period for the dividend-paying stock (or a 91-day holding period for certain dividends on preferred stock).[969] The holding period must be satisfied for each dividend over a period that is immediately before and immediately after the taxpayer becomes entitled to receive the dividend. The 46- or 91-day holding period generally does not include any time during which the shareholder is protected (other than by writing a qualified covered call) from the risk of loss that is otherwise inherent in the ownership of any equity interest.[970]

Reasons for Change

The Congress believed that the straddle rules should be modified in several respects. While the prior-law rules provided authority for the Secretary to issue guidance concerning unbalanced straddles, the Congress was of the view that such guidance was not forthcoming. Therefore, the Congress believed that it was necessary to provide such guidance by statute. The Congress further believed that it was appropriate to repeal the general exception from the straddle rules for positions in stock, particularly in light of statutory changes in the straddle rules and elsewhere in the Code that

[967] A costless collar generally is comprised of the purchase of a put option and the sale of a call option with the same trade dates and maturity dates and set such that the premium paid substantially equals the premium received. The collar can be considered as economically similar to a short position in the stock.

[968] Sec. 243. The amount of the deduction is 70 percent of dividends received if the recipient owns less than 20 percent (by vote and value) of stock of the payor. If the recipient owns 20 percent or more of the stock, the deduction is increased to 80 percent. If the recipient owns 80 percent or more of the stock, the deduction is further increased to 100 percent for qualifying dividends.

[969] Sec. 246(c).

[970] Sec. 246(c)(4).

have significantly diminished the continuing utility of the exception. In addition, the Congress believed that the treatment of physically settled positions under the straddle rules required clarification.

Explanation of Provision

Straddle rules

In general

The Act modifies the straddle rules in three respects: (1) permits taxpayers to identify offsetting positions of a straddle; (2) provides a special rule to clarify the treatment of certain physically settled positions of a straddle; and (3) repeals the stock exception from the straddle rules.

Identified straddles

Under the Act, taxpayers generally are permitted to identify the offsetting positions that are components of a straddle at the time the taxpayer enters into a transaction that creates a straddle, including an unbalanced straddle.[971] Taxpayers are not permitted to identify offsetting positions of a straddle that itself is part of a larger straddle. However, this prohibition does not preclude the identification of a straddle involving offsetting positions merely because the offsetting positions comprise an unbalanced straddle.[972]

If there is a loss with respect to any identified position that is part of an identified straddle, the general straddle loss deferral rules do not apply to such loss. Instead, the basis of each of the identified positions that offset the loss position in the identified straddle is increased by an amount that bears the same ratio to the loss as the unrecognized gain (if any) with respect to such offsetting position bears to the aggregate unrecognized gain with respect to all positions that offset the loss position in the identified straddle.[973] Any loss with respect to an identified position that is part of an identified straddle cannot otherwise be taken into account by the taxpayer or any other person to the extent that the loss increases the basis of any identified positions that offset the loss position in the identified straddle.

In addition, the Act provides the Secretary authority to issue regulations that would specify (1) the proper methods for clearly identifying a straddle as an identified straddle (and identifying positions as positions in an identified straddle), (2) the application of

---

[971] However, to the extent provided by Treasury regulations, taxpayers are not permitted to identify offsetting positions of a straddle if the fair market value of the straddle position already held by the taxpayer at the creation of the straddle is less than its adjusted basis in the hands of the taxpayer.

[972] The Act preserves a special rule that also applied to prior-law identified straddles, which provides that any position that is not part of an identified straddle shall not be treated as offsetting with respect to any position which is part of an identified straddle. Sec. 1092(c)(2)(B). For example, if a taxpayer holds an unbalanced straddle comprised of 100 shares of XYZ corporation and a put option on 50 shares of XYZ corporation, the taxpayer may identify 50 of the shares and the put option as an identified straddle under the Act. The identified straddle is not considered part of a larger straddle merely by virtue of the remaining (unidentified) 50 shares held by the taxpayer because such shares (which are not part of the identified straddle) are not treated as offsetting with respect to the put option (which is part of the identified straddle).

[973] For this purpose, "unrecognized gain" is the excess of the fair market value of an identified position that is part of an identified straddle at the time the taxpayer incurs a loss with respect to another identified position in the identified straddle, over the fair market value of such position when the taxpayer identified the position as a position in the identified straddle.

the identified straddle rules to a taxpayer that fails to properly identify the positions of an identified straddle,[974] and (3) provide an ordering rule for dispositions of less than an entire position that is part of an identified straddle.

Physically settled straddle positions

The Act also clarifies the straddle rules with respect to taxpayers that settle a position that is part of a straddle by delivering property to which the position relates. Specifically, the Act clarifies that the straddle loss deferral rules treat as a two-step transaction the physical settlement of a straddle position that, if terminated, would result in the realization of a loss. With respect to the physical settlement of such a position, the taxpayer is treated as having terminated the position for its fair market value immediately before the settlement. The taxpayer then is treated as having sold at fair market value the property used to physically settle the position.

Stock exception repeal

The Act also eliminates the exception from the straddle rules for stock (other than the exception relating to qualified covered call options). Thus, offsetting positions comprised of actively traded stock and a position with respect to such stock or substantially similar or related property generally constitute a straddle.[975]

Dividends-received deduction holding period

The Act also modifies the required 46- or 91-day holding period for the dividends-received deduction by providing that the holding period does not include any time during which the shareholder is protected from the risk of loss otherwise inherent in the ownership of any equity interest if the shareholder obtains such protection by writing an in-the-money call option on the dividend-paying stock.

Effective Date

The provision is effective for positions established on or after the date of enactment (October 22, 2004) that substantially diminish the risk of loss from holding offsetting positions (regardless of when such offsetting positions were established).

9. Add vaccines against Hepatitis A to the list of taxable vaccines (sec. 889 of the Act and sec. 4132 of the Code)

Present and Prior Law

A manufacturers' excise tax is imposed at the rate of 75 cents per dose[976] on the following vaccines routinely recommended for ad-

---

[974] For example, although the Act does not require taxpayers to identify any positions of a straddle as an identified straddle, it may be necessary to provide rules requiring all balanced offsetting positions to be included in an identified straddle if a taxpayer elects to identify any of the offsetting positions as an identified straddle.

[975] It is intended that Treasury regulations defining substantially similar or related property for this purpose will continue to apply subsequent to repeal of the stock exception and generally will constitute the exclusive definition of a straddle with respect to offsetting positions involving stock. See Prop. Treas. Reg. sec. 1.1092(d)-2(b). However, the general straddles rules regarding substantial diminution in risk of loss will continue to apply to stock of corporations formed or availed of to take positions in personal property that offset positions taken by the shareholder.

[976] Sec. 4131.

ministration to children: diphtheria, pertussis, tetanus, measles, mumps, rubella, polio, HIB (haemophilus influenza type B), hepatitis B, varicella (chicken pox), rotavirus gastroenteritis, and streptococcus pneumoniae. The tax applies to any vaccine that is a combination of vaccine components equals 75 cents times the number of components in the combined vaccine.

Amounts equal to net revenues from this excise tax are deposited in the Vaccine Injury Compensation Trust Fund to finance compensation awards under the Federal Vaccine Injury Compensation Program for individuals who suffer certain injuries following administration of the taxable vaccines. This program provides a substitute Federal, "no fault" insurance system for the State-law tort and private liability insurance systems otherwise applicable to vaccine manufacturers. All persons immunized after September 30, 1988, with covered vaccines must pursue compensation under this Federal program before bringing civil tort actions under State law.

Reasons for Change

The Congress was aware that the Centers for Disease Control and Prevention have recommended that children in 17 highly endemic States be inoculated with a hepatitis A vaccine. The population of children in the affected States exceeds 20 million. Several of the affected States mandate childhood vaccination against hepatitis A. The Congress was aware that the Advisory Commission on Childhood Vaccines has recommended that the vaccine excise tax be extended to cover vaccines against hepatitis A. For these reasons, the Congress believed it was appropriate to include vaccines against hepatitis A as part of the Vaccine Injury Compensation Program. Making the hepatitis A vaccine taxable is a first step.[977] In the unfortunate event of an injury related to this vaccine, families of injured children are eligible for the no-fault arbitration system established under the Vaccine Injury Compensation Program rather than going to Federal Court to seek compensatory redress.

Explanation of Provision

The Act adds any vaccine against hepatitis A to the list of taxable vaccines.

Effective Date

The provision is effective for vaccines sold on or after the first day of the first month beginning more than four weeks after the date of enactment (October 22, 2004).

[977] The Congress recognized that, to become covered under the Vaccine Injury Compensation Program, the Secretary of Health and Human Services also must list the hepatitis A vaccine on the Vaccine Injury Table. In addition, after the Secretary of Health and Human Service lists the vaccine on the Vaccine Injury Table, the Congress must make a revision to the Trust Fund expenditure purposes under Code sec. 9510.

10. Add vaccines against influenza to the list of taxable vaccines (sec. 890 of the Act and sec. 4132 of the Code)

Present and Prior Law

A manufacturers' excise tax is imposed at the rate of 75 cents per dose[978] on the following vaccines routinely recommended for administration to children: diphtheria, pertussis, tetanus, measles, mumps, rubella, polio, HIB (haemophilus influenza type B), hepatitis B, varicella (chicken pox), rotavirus gastroenteritis, and streptococcus pneumoniae. The tax applies to any vaccine that is a combination of vaccine components equals 75 cents times the number of components in the combined vaccine.

Amounts equal to net revenues from this excise tax are deposited in the Vaccine Injury Compensation Trust Fund to finance compensation awards under the Federal Vaccine Injury Compensation Program for individuals who suffer certain injuries following administration of the taxable vaccines. This program provides a substitute Federal, "no fault" insurance system for the State-law tort and private liability insurance systems otherwise applicable to vaccine manufacturers. All persons immunized after September 30, 1988, with covered vaccines must pursue compensation under this Federal program before bringing civil tort actions under State law.

Reasons for Change

The Congress understood that on October 15, 2003, the Advisory Committee on Immunization Practices of the Centers for Disease Control and Prevention issued a recommendation for the routine annual vaccination of infants six to 23 months of age with an inactivated influenza vaccine licensed by the FDA. This is the first recommendation for "routine use" in children although trivalent influenza vaccine products have long been available and approved for use in children of varying ages and these vaccines have long been recommended for use by seniors. For these reasons, the Congress believed it was appropriate to include trivalent vaccines against influenza as part of the Vaccine Injury Compensation Program. Making an influenza vaccine taxable is a first step.[979] In the unfortunate event of an injury related to these vaccines, an injured individual is eligible for the no-fault arbitration system established under the Vaccine Injury Compensation Program rather than going to Federal Court to seek compensatory redress.

Explanation of Provision

The Act adds any trivalent vaccine against influenza to the list of taxable vaccines.

---

[978] Sec. 4131.

[979] The Committee recognizes that, to become covered under the Vaccine Injury Compensation Program, the Secretary of Health and Human Services also must list each trivalent vaccine against influenza on the Vaccine Injury Table. In addition, after the Secretary of Health and Human Service lists the vaccine on the Vaccine Injury Table, the Congress must make a revision to the Trust Fund expenditure purposes under Code sec. 9510.

Effective Date

The provision is effective for vaccines sold or used on or after the later of the first day of the first month beginning more than four weeks after the date of enactment (October 22, 2004) or the date on which the Secretary of Health and Human Services lists any such vaccine for purposes of compensation for any vaccine-related injury or death through the Vaccine Injury Compensation Trust Fund.

11. Extension of IRS user fees (sec. 891 of the Act and sec. 7528 of the Code)

Present and Prior Law

The IRS generally charges a fee for requests for a letter ruling, determination letter, opinion letter, or other similar ruling or determination.[980] Under prior law, these user fees were authorized by statute through December 31, 2004.

Reasons for Change

The Congress believed that it was appropriate to provide a further extension of the applicability of these user fees.

Explanation of Provision

The Act extends the statutory authorization for these user fees through September 30, 2014.

Effective Date

The provision is effective for requests made after the date of enactment (October 22, 2004).

12. Extension of Customs user fees (sec. 892 of the Act)

Present and Prior Law

Section 13031 of the Consolidated Omnibus Budget Reconciliation Act of 1985 ("COBRA")[981] authorized the Secretary of the Treasury to collect certain service fees. Section 412 of the Homeland Security Act of 2002[982] authorized the Secretary of the Treasury to delegate such authority to the Secretary of Homeland Security. Provided for under 19 U.S.C. 58c, these fees include: processing fees for air and sea passengers, commercial trucks, rail cars, private aircraft and vessels, commercial vessels, dutiable mail packages, barges and bulk carriers, merchandise, and Customs broker permits. COBRA was amended on several occasions but most recently by Pub. L. No. 108–121, which extended authorization for the collection of these fees through March 1, 2005.[983]

---

[980] Sec. 7528.

[981] Pub. L. No. 99-272.

[982] Pub. L. No. 107–296.

[983] Sec. 201, 117 Stat. 1335.

Reasons for Change

The Congress believed it was important to extend these fees to cover the expenses of the services provided. However, the Congress also believed it was important that any fee imposed be a true user fee. That is, the Congress believed that when the Congress authorizes the executive branch to assess user fees, those fees must be determined to reflect only the cost of providing the service for which the fee is assessed.

Explanation of Provision

The Act extends the passenger and conveyance processing fees and the merchandise processing fees authorized under COBRA through September 30, 2014. For fiscal years after September 30, 2005, the Secretary is to charge fees in amounts that are reasonably related to the costs of providing customs services in connection with the activity or item for which the fee is charged.

The Act also includes a sense of the Congress regarding the extent to which fees are related to the costs of providing customs services in connection with the activities or items for which the fees have been charged under such paragraphs. The Act further provides that the Secretary conduct a study of all the fees collected by the Department of Homeland Security.

Effective Date

The provision is effective on the date of enactment (October 22, 2004).

13. Prohibition on nonrecognition of gain through complete liquidation of holding company (sec. 893 of the Act and sec. 332 of the Code)

Present and Prior Law

A U.S. corporation owned by foreign persons is subject to U.S. income tax on its net income. In addition, the earnings of the U.S. corporation are subject to a second tax, when dividends are paid to the corporation's shareholders.

In general, dividends paid by a U.S. corporation to nonresident alien individuals and foreign corporations that are not effectively connected with a U.S. trade or business are subject to a U.S. withholding tax on the gross amount of such income at a rate of 30 percent. The 30-percent withholding tax may be reduced pursuant to an income tax treaty between the United States and the foreign country where the foreign person is resident.

In addition, the United States imposes a branch profits tax on U.S. earnings of a foreign corporation that are shifted out of a U.S. branch of the foreign corporation. The branch profits tax is comparable to the second-level taxes imposed on dividends paid by a U.S. corporation to foreign shareholders. The branch profits tax is 30 percent (subject to possible income tax treaty reduction) of a foreign corporation's dividend equivalent amount. The "dividend equivalent amount" generally is the earnings and profits of a U.S. branch of a foreign corporation attributable to its income effectively connected with a U.S. trade or business.

In general, U.S. withholding tax is not imposed with respect to a distribution of a U.S. corporation's earnings to a foreign corporation in complete liquidation of the subsidiary, because the distribution is treated as made in exchange for stock and not as a dividend. In addition, detailed rules apply for purposes of exempting foreign corporations from the branch profits tax for the year in which it completely terminates its U.S. business conducted in branch form. The exemption from the branch profits tax generally applies if, among other things, for three years after the termination of the U.S. branch, the foreign corporation has no income effectively connected with a U.S. trade or business, and the U.S. assets of the terminated branch are not used by the foreign corporation or a related corporation in a U.S. trade or business.

Regulations under section 367(e) provide that the Commissioner may require a domestic liquidating corporation to recognize gain on distributions in liquidation made to a foreign corporation if a principal purpose of the liquidation is the avoidance of U.S. tax. Avoidance of U.S. tax for this purpose includes, but is not limited to, the distribution of a liquidating corporation's earnings and profits with a principal purpose of avoiding U.S. tax.

Reasons for Change

The Congress was concerned that foreign corporations were establishing a U.S. holding company to receive tax-free dividends from U.S. operating companies, liquidating the U.S. holding company to distribute the U.S. earnings free of U.S. withholding taxes, and then reestablishing another U.S. holding company, with the intention of escaping U.S. withholding taxes. The Congress believed that instances of such withholding tax abuse will be significantly restricted by imposing U.S. withholding taxes on a liquidating distribution to foreign corporate shareholders of earnings and profits of a U.S. holding company created within five years of the liquidation.

Explanation of Provision

The Act treats as a dividend any distribution of earnings by a U.S. holding company to a foreign corporation in a complete liquidation, if the U.S. holding company was in existence for less than five years.

Effective Date

The provision is effective for distributions occurring on or after the date of enactment (October 22, 2004).

14. Effectively connected income to include certain foreign source income (sec. 894 of the Act and sec. 864 of the Code)

Present and Prior Law

Nonresident alien individuals and foreign corporations (collectively, foreign persons) are subject to U.S. tax on income that is effectively connected with the conduct of a U.S. trade or business; the U.S. tax on such income is calculated in the same manner and at the same graduated rates as the tax on U.S. persons.[984] Foreign persons also are subject to a 30-percent gross-basis tax, collected by withholding, on certain U.S.-source income, such as interest, dividends and other fixed or determinable annual or periodical ("FDAP") income, that is not effectively connected with a U.S. trade or business. This 30-percent withholding tax may be reduced or eliminated pursuant to an applicable tax treaty. Foreign persons generally are not subject to U.S. tax on foreign-source income that is not effectively connected with a U.S. trade or business.

Detailed rules apply for purposes of determining whether income is treated as effectively connected with a U.S. trade or business (so-called "U.S.-effectively connected income").[985] The rules differ depending on whether the income at issue is U.S-source or foreign-source income. Under these rules, U.S.-source FDAP income, such as U.S.-source interest and dividends, and U.S.-source capital gains are treated as U.S.-effectively connected income if such income is derived from assets used in or held for use in the active conduct of a U.S. trade or business, or from business activities conducted in the United States. All other types of U.S.-source income are treated as U.S.-effectively connected income (sometimes referred to as the "force of attraction rule").

In general, foreign-source income is not treated as U.S.-effectively connected income.[986] However, foreign-source income, gain, deduction, or loss generally is considered to be effectively connected with a U.S. business only if the person has an office or other fixed place of business within the United States to which such income, gain, deduction, or loss is attributable and such income falls into one of three categories described below.[987] For these purposes, income generally is not considered attributable to an office or other fixed place of business within the United States unless such office or fixed place of business is a material factor in the production of the income, and such office or fixed place of business regularly carries on activities of the type that generate such income.[988]

The first category consists of rents or royalties for the use of patents, copyrights, secret processes, or formulas, good will, trademarks, trade brands, franchises, or other similar intangible properties derived in the active conduct of the U.S. trade or business.[989] The second category consists of interest or dividends derived in the active conduct of a banking, financing, or similar business within the United States, or received by a corporation whose principal business is trading in stocks or securities for its own account.[990] Notwithstanding the foregoing, foreign-source income consisting of dividends, interest, or royalties is not treated as effectively connected if the items are paid by a foreign corporation in which the recipient owns, directly, indirectly, or constructively, more than 50 percent of the total combined voting power of the stock.[991] The third category consists of income, gain, deduction, or loss derived

[984] Secs. 871(b) and 882.
[985] Sec. 864(c).
[986] Sec. 864(c)(4).
[987] Sec. 864(c)(4)(B).
[988] Sec. 864(c)(5).
[989] Sec. 864(c)(4)(B)(i).
[990] Sec. 864(c)(4)(B)(ii).
[991] Sec. 864(c)(4)(D)(i).

from the sale or exchange of inventory or property held by the taxpayer primarily for sale to customers in the ordinary course of the trade or business where the property is sold or exchanged outside the United States through the foreign person's U.S. office or other fixed place of business.[992] Such amounts are not treated as effectively connected if the property is sold or exchanged for use, consumption, or disposition outside the United States and an office or other fixed place of business of the taxpayer in a foreign country materially participated in the sale or exchange.

The Code provides sourcing rules for enumerated types of income, including interest, dividends, rents, royalties, and personal services income.[993] For example, interest income generally is sourced based on the residence of the obligor. Dividend income generally is sourced based on the residence of the corporation paying the dividend. Thus, interest paid on obligations of foreign persons and dividends paid by foreign corporations generally are treated as foreign-source income.

Other types of income are not specifically covered by the Code's sourcing rules. For example, fees for accepting or confirming letters of credit have been sourced under principles analogous to the interest sourcing rules.[994] In addition, under regulations, payments in lieu of dividends and interest derived from securities lending transactions are sourced in the same manner as interest and dividends, including for purposes of determining whether such income is effectively connected with a U.S. trade or business.[995] Moreover, income from notional principal contracts (such as interest rate swaps) generally is sourced based on the residence of the recipient of the income, but is treated as U.S.-source effectively connected income if it arises from the conduct of a United States trade or business.[996]

Reasons for Change

The Congress believed that prior law created arbitrary distinctions between economically similar transactions that were equally related to a U.S. trade of business. The Congress believed that the rules for determining whether foreign-source income (e.g., interest and dividends) is U.S.-effectively connected income should be the same as the rules for determining whether income that is economically equivalent to such foreign-source income is U.S.-effectively connected income.

Explanation of Provision

Under the Act, each category of foreign-source income that is treated as effectively connected with a U.S. trade or business is expanded to include economic equivalents of such income (i.e., economic equivalents of certain foreign-source (1) rents and royalties, (2) dividends and interest, and (3) income on sales or exchanges of goods in the ordinary course of business). Thus, such economic equivalents are treated as U.S.-effectively connected income in the same circumstances that foreign-source rents, royalties, dividends,

[992] Sec. 864(c)(4)(B)(iii).
[993] Secs. 861—865.
[994] See *Bank of America* v. *United States*, 680 F.2d 142 (Ct. Cl. 1982).
[995] Treas. Reg. sec. 1.864–5(b)(2)(ii).
[996] Treas. Reg. sec. 1.863–7(b)(3).

interest, or certain inventory sales are treated as U.S.-effectively connected income. For example, foreign-source interest and dividend equivalents are treated as U.S.-effectively connected income if the income is attributable to a U.S. office of the foreign person, and such income is derived by such foreign person in the active conduct of a banking, financing, or similar business within the United States, or the foreign person is a corporation whose principal business is trading in stocks or securities for its own account.

Effective Date

The provision is effective for taxable years beginning after the date of enactment (October 22, 2004).

15. Recapture of overall foreign losses on sale of controlled foreign corporation stock (sec. 895 of the Act and sec. 904 of the Code)

Present and Prior Law

U.S. persons may credit foreign taxes against U.S. tax on foreign-source income. The amount of foreign tax credits that may be claimed in a year is subject to a limitation that prevents taxpayers from using foreign tax credits to offset U.S. tax on U.S.-source income. The amount of foreign tax credits generally is limited to a portion of the taxpayer's U.S. tax which portion is calculated by multiplying the taxpayer's total U.S. tax by a fraction, the numerator of which is the taxpayer's foreign-source taxable income (i.e., foreign-source gross income less allocable expenses or deductions) and the denominator of which is the taxpayer's worldwide taxable income for the year.[997] Separate limitations are applied to specific categories of income.[998]

Special recapture rules apply in the case of foreign losses for purposes of applying the foreign tax credit limitation.[999] Under these rules, losses for any taxable year in a limitation category which exceed the aggregate amount of foreign income earned in other limitation categories (a so-called "overall foreign loss") are recaptured by resourcing foreign-source income earned in a subsequent year as U.S.-source income.[1000] The amount resourced as U.S.-source income generally is limited to the lesser of the amount of the overall foreign losses not previously recaptured, or 50 percent of the taxpayer's foreign-source income in a given year (the "50-percent limit"). Taxpayers may elect to recapture a larger percentage of such losses.

A special recapture rule applies to ensure the recapture of an overall foreign loss where property which was used in a trade or business predominantly outside the United States is disposed of prior to the time the loss has been recaptured.[1001] In this regard, dispositions of trade or business property used predominantly outside the United States are treated as resulting in the recognition

[997] Sec. 904(a).

[998] Section 404 of the Act reduces the number of limitation categories from nine to two, effective for taxable years beginning after December 31, 2006.

[999] Sec. 904(f).

[1000] Sec. 904(f)(1).

[1001] Sec. 904(f)(3).

of foreign-source income (regardless of whether gain would otherwise be recognized upon disposition of the assets), in an amount equal to the lesser of the excess of the fair market value of such property over its adjusted basis, or the amount of unrecaptured overall foreign losses. Such foreign-source income is resourced as U.S.-source income without regard to the 50-percent limit. For example, if a U.S. corporation transfers its foreign branch business assets to a foreign corporation in a nontaxable section 351 transaction, the taxpayer would be treated for purposes of the recapture rules as having recognized foreign-source income in the year of the transfer in an amount equal to the excess of the fair market value of the property disposed over its adjusted basis (or the amount of unrecaptured foreign losses, if smaller). Such income would be recaptured as U.S.-source income to the extent of any prior unrecaptured overall foreign losses.[1002]

Detailed rules apply in allocating and apportioning deductions and losses for foreign tax credit limitation purposes. In the case of interest expense, such amounts generally are apportioned to all gross income under an asset method, under which the taxpayer's assets are characterized as producing income in statutory or residual groupings (i.e., foreign-source income in the various limitation categories or U.S.-source income).[1003] Interest expense is apportioned among these groupings based on the relative asset values in each. Taxpayers may elect to value assets based on either tax book value or fair market value.

Each corporation that is a member of an affiliated group is required to apportion its interest expense using apportionment fractions determined by reference to all assets of the affiliated group. For this purpose, an affiliated group generally is defined to include only domestic corporations. Stock in a foreign subsidiary, however, is treated as a foreign asset that may attract the allocation of U.S. interest expense for these purposes.[1004] If tax basis is used to value assets, the adjusted basis of the stock of certain 10-percent or greater owned foreign corporations or other non-affiliated corporations must be increased by the amount of earnings and profits of such corporation accumulated during the period the U.S. shareholder held the stock, for purposes of the interest apportionment.

Reasons for Change

The Congress believed that dispositions of corporate stock should be subject to the special recapture rules for overall foreign losses. Ownership of stock in a foreign subsidiary can lead to, or increase, an overall foreign loss as a result of interest expenses allocated against foreign-source income under the interest expense allocation rules. The recapture of overall foreign losses created by such interest expense allocations may be avoided if, for example, the stock of the foreign subsidiary subsequently were transferred to unaffiliated parties in non-taxable transactions. The Congress believed that

[1002] Coordination rules apply in the case of losses recaptured under the branch loss recapture rules. Sec. 367(a)(3)(C).

[1003] Sec. 864(e) and Temp. Treas. Reg. sec. 1.861–9T.

[1004] Under section 401 of the Act, effective for taxable years beginning after December 31, 2008, a taxpayer may elect to apportion interest expense on the basis of the assets of the worldwide affiliated group. For purposes of determining the assets of such group, stock of group members is not taken into account.

overall foreign losses should be recaptured when stock of a controlled foreign corporation is disposed of regardless of whether such stock is disposed of in a nontaxable transaction.

Explanation of Provision

Under the Act, the special recapture rule for overall foreign losses that currently applies to dispositions of foreign trade or business assets applies to the disposition of stock in a controlled foreign corporation controlled by the taxpayer. Thus, a disposition of controlled foreign corporation stock by a controlling shareholder results in the recognition of foreign-source income in an amount equal to the lesser of the fair market value of the stock over its adjusted basis, or the amount of prior unrecaptured overall foreign losses. Such income is resourced as U.S.-source income for foreign tax credit limitation purposes without regard to the 50-percent limit.

Although the Act generally extends to all dispositions of such stock, regardless of whether gain or loss is recognized on the transfer, exceptions are made for certain internal restructurings. Contributions to corporations or partnerships under sections 351 and 721, respectively, and certain stock and asset reorganizations do not trigger recapture of overall foreign losses, provided that the transferor's underlying indirect interest in the disposed controlled foreign corporation does not change. In addition, a disposition of controlled foreign corporation stock in a transaction in which the taxpayer or a member of its consolidated group acquires the assets of the controlled foreign corporation in a liquidation under section 332 or a reorganization does not trigger the recapture of overall foreign losses. However, any gain recognized in connection with a transaction meeting any of these exceptions, such as boot, triggers recapture of overall foreign losses to the extent of such gain.

Effective Date

The provision applies to dispositions after the date of enactment (October 22, 2004).

16. Recognition of cancellation of indebtedness income realized on satisfaction of debt with partnership interest (sec. 896 of the Act and sec. 108 of the Code)

Present and Prior Law

A corporation that transfers shares of its stock in satisfaction of its debt must recognize cancellation of indebtedness income in the amount that would be realized if the debt were satisfied with money equal to the fair market value of the stock.[1005] Prior to enactment of this provision in 1993, case law provided that a corporation did not recognize cancellation of indebtedness income when it transferred stock to a creditor in satisfaction of debt (referred to as the "stock-for-debt exception").[1006]

[1005] Sec. 108(e)(8).

[1006] E.g., *Motor Mart Trust* v. *Commissioner*, 4 T.C. 931 (1945), aff'd, 156 F.2d 122 (1st Cir. 1946), acq. 1947–1 C.B. 3; *Capento Sec. Corp.* v. *Commissioner*, 47 B.T.A. 691 (1942), nonacq.

Continued

When cancellation of indebtedness income is realized by a partnership, it generally is allocated among the partners in accordance with the partnership agreement, provided the allocations under the agreement have substantial economic effect. A partner who is allocated cancellation of indebtedness income is entitled to exclude it if the partner qualifies for one of the various exceptions to recognition of such income, including the exception for insolvent taxpayers or that for qualified real property business indebtedness of taxpayers other than subchapter C corporations.[1007] The availability of each of these exceptions is determined at the partner, rather than the partnership, level.

In the case of a partnership that transfers to a creditor a capital or profits interest in the partnership in satisfaction of its debt, no prior-law Code provision expressly required the partnership to realize cancellation of indebtedness income. Thus, it was unclear whether the partnership was required to recognize cancellation of indebtedness income under either the case law that established the stock-for-debt exception or the statutory repeal of the stock-for-debt exception. It also was unclear whether any requirement to recognize cancellation of indebtedness income was affected if the cancelled debt is nonrecourse indebtedness.[1008]

Reasons for Change

The Congress believed that further guidance was necessary with regard to the application of the stock-for-debt exception in the context of transfers of partnership interests in satisfaction of partnership debt. In particular, the Congress believed that it was necessary to clarify that the treatment of corporate indebtedness that is satisfied with transfers of stock of the debtor corporation also applies to partnership indebtedness that is satisfied with transfers of capital or profits interests in the debtor partnership.

Explanation of Provision

The Act provides that when a partnership transfers a capital or profits interest in the partnership to a creditor in satisfaction of partnership debt, the partnership generally recognizes cancellation of indebtedness income in the amount that would be recognized if the debt were satisfied with money equal to the fair market value of the partnership interest. The Act applies without regard to whether the cancelled debt is recourse or nonrecourse indebtedness. Any cancellation of indebtedness income recognized under the Act is allocated solely among the partners who held interests in the partnership immediately prior to the satisfaction of the debt.

Under the Act, no inference is intended as to the treatment under prior law of the transfer of a partnership interest in satisfaction of partnership debt.

1943 C.B. 28, aff'd, 140 F.2d 382 (1st Cir. 1944); *Tower Bldg. Corp.* v. *Commissioner*, 6 T.C. 125 (1946), acq. 1947–1 C.B. 4; *Alcazar Hotel, Inc.* v. *Commissioner*, 1 T.C. 872 (1943), acq. 1943 C.B. 1.

[1007] Sec. 108(a).

[1008] See, e.g., *Fulton Gold Corp.* v. *Commissioner*, 31 B.T.A. 519 (1934); *American Seating Co.* v. *Commissioner*, 14 B.T.A. 328, aff'd in part and rev'd in part, 50 F.2d 681 (7th Cir. 1931); *Hiatt* v. *Commissioner*, 35 B.T.A. 292 (1937); *Hotel Astoria, Inc.* v. *Commissioner*, 42 B.T.A. 759 (1940); Rev. Rul. 91–31, 1991–1 C.B. 19.

Effective Date

The provision is effective for cancellations of indebtedness occurring on or after the date of enactment (October 22, 2004).

17. Denial of installment sale treatment for all readily tradable debt (sec. 897 of the Act and sec. 453 of the Code)

Present and Prior Law

Taxpayers are permitted to recognize as gain on a disposition of property only that proportion of payments received in a taxable year which is the same as the proportion that the gross profit bears to the total contract price (the "installment method").[1009] However, the installment method is not available if the taxpayer sells property in exchange for a readily tradable evidence of indebtedness that is issued by a corporation or a government or political subdivision.[1010]

No similar provision under prior law prohibited the use of the installment method where the taxpayer sells property in exchange for readily tradable indebtedness issued by a partnership or an individual.

Reasons for Change

The Congress believed that the prior-law exception from the installment method for dispositions of property in exchange for readily tradable debt was too narrow in scope and, in general, should be extended to apply to all dispositions in exchange for readily tradable debt, regardless of the nature of the issuer of such debt.

Explanation of Provision

The Act denies installment sale treatment with respect to all sales in which the taxpayer receives indebtedness that is readily tradable regardless of the nature of the issuer. For example, if the taxpayer receives readily tradable debt of a partnership in a sale, the partnership debt is treated as payment on the installment note, and the installment method is unavailable to the taxpayer.

Effective Date

The provision is effective for sales occurring on or after date of enactment (October 22, 2004).

18. Modify treatment of transfers to creditors in divisive reorganizations (sec. 898 of the Act and secs. 357 and 361 of the Code)

Present and Prior Law

Section 355 of the Code permits a corporation ("distributing") to separate its businesses by distributing a controlled subsidiary ("controlled") tax-free, if certain conditions are met. In cases where the distributing corporation contributes property to the controlled

[1009] Sec. 453.
[1010] Sec. 453(f)(3). Instead, the receipt of such indebtedness is treated as a receipt of payment.

corporation that is to be distributed, no gain or loss is recognized if the property is contributed solely in exchange for stock or securities of the controlled corporation (which are subsequently distributed to distributing's shareholders). The contribution of property to a controlled corporation that is followed by a distribution of its stock and securities may qualify as a reorganization described in section 368(a)(1)(D). That section also applies to certain transactions that do not involve a distribution under section 355 and that are considered 'acquisitive" rather than "divisive" reorganizations.

The contribution in the course of either a divisive or an acquisitive section 368(a)(1)(D) reorganization was subject to the rules of section 357(c) under prior law. That section provides that the transferor corporation will recognize gain if the amount of liabilities assumed by controlled exceeds the basis of the property transferred to it.

Because the contribution transaction in connection with a section 355 distribution is a reorganization under section 368(a)(1)(D), it also was subject to certain other rules applicable to both divisive and acquisitive reorganizations under prior law. One such rule, in section 361(b), stated generally under prior law that a transferor corporation will not recognize gain if it receives money or other property and distributes that money or other property to its shareholders or creditors. The amount of property that may be distributed to creditors without gain recognition was unlimited under this provision for both divisive and acquisitive reorganizations.

Reasons for Change

The Congress was concerned that taxpayers engaged in section 355 transactions could effectively avoid the rules that require gain recognition if the controlled corporation assumes liabilities of the transferor that exceed the basis of the assets transferred to such corporation. This could occur because of the rules of section 361(b), which state that the transferor can receive money or other property from the transferee without gain recognition, so long as the money or property is distributed to creditors of the transferor. For example, a transferor corporation could receive money from the transferee corporation (e.g., money obtained from a borrowing by the transferee) and use that money to pay the transferor's creditors, without gain recognition. Such a transaction is economically similar to the actual assumption by the transferee of the transferor's liabilities, but was taxed differently under prior law because section 361(b) did not contain a limitation on the amount that can be distributed to creditors.

The Congress also believed that it was appropriate to liberalize the treatment of acquisitive reorganizations that are included under section 368(a)(1)(D). The Congress believed that in these cases, the transferor should be permitted to assume liabilities of the transferee without application of the rules of section 357(c). This is because in an acquisitive reorganization under section 368(a)(1)(D), the transferor must generally transfer substantially all its assets to the acquiring corporation and then go out of existence. Assumption of its liabilities by the acquiring corporation thus does not enrich the transferor corporation, which ceases to exist and whose liability was limited to its assets in any event, by corporate form. The Congress believed that it was appropriate to conform the treatment of acquisitive reorganizations under section 368(a)(1)(D) to that of other acquisitive reorganizations.

Explanation of Provision

The Act limits the amount of money plus the fair market value of other property that a distributing corporation can distribute to its creditors without gain recognition under section 361(b) in a divisive reorganization under section 368(a)(1)(D) to the amount of the basis of the assets contributed to a controlled corporation in the divisive reorganization.[1011] In addition, the Act provides that acquisitive reorganizations under section 368(a)(1)(D) are no longer subject to the liabilities assumption rules of section 357(c).

Effective Date

The provision is effective for transactions on or after the date of enactment (October 22, 2004).

19. Clarify definition of nonqualified preferred stock (sec. 899 of the Act and sec. 351(g) of the Code)

Present and Prior Law

The Taxpayer Relief Act of 1997 amended sections 351, 354, 355, 356, and 1036 to treat "nonqualified preferred stock" as boot in corporate transactions, subject to certain exceptions. For this purpose, preferred stock is defined as stock that is "limited and preferred as to dividends and does not participate in corporate growth to any significant extent." Nonqualified preferred stock is defined as any preferred stock if (1) the holder has the right to require the issuer or a related person to redeem or purchase the stock, (2) the issuer or a related person is required to redeem or purchase, (3) the issuer or a related person has the right to redeem or repurchase, and, as of the issue date, it is more likely than not that such right will be exercised, or (4) the dividend rate varies in whole or in part (directly or indirectly) with reference to interest rates, commodity prices, or similar indices, regardless of whether such varying rate is provided as an express term of the stock (as in the case of an adjustable rate stock) or as a practical result of other aspects of the stock (as in the case of auction stock). For this purpose, clauses (1), (2), and (3) apply if the right or obligation may be exercised within 20 years of the issue date and is not subject to a contingency which, as of the issue date, makes remote the likelihood of the redemption or purchase.

Reasons for Change

The Congress was concerned that taxpayers may attempt to avoid characterization of an instrument as nonqualified preferred

[1011] It is not intended that basis may be double counted both for this purpose and for purposes of section 357(c). It is intended that the basis against which the amount of money plus the fair market value of property distributed to creditors is measured under this provision will be reduced by amounts treated as assumed liabilities under section 357. A technical correction may be necessary so that the statute reflects this intent.

stock by including illusory participation rights or including terms that taxpayers argue create an "unlimited" dividend.

Clarification was desirable to conserve IRS resources that otherwise might have to be devoted to this area.

Explanation of Provision

The Act clarifies the definition of nonqualified preferred stock to ensure that stock for which there is not a real and meaningful likelihood of actually participating in the earnings and profits of the corporation is not considered to be outside the definition of stock that is limited and preferred as to dividends and does not participate in corporate growth to any significant extent.[1012]

As one example, instruments that are preferred on liquidation and that are entitled to the same dividends as may be declared on common stock do not escape being nonqualified preferred stock by reason of that right if the corporation does not in fact pay dividends either to its common or preferred stockholders. As another example, stock that entitles the holder to a dividend that is the greater of seven percent or the dividends common shareholders receive does not avoid being preferred stock if the common shareholders are not expected to receive dividends greater than seven percent.

No inference is intended as to the characterization of stock under prior law that has terms providing for unlimited dividends or participation rights but, based on all the facts and circumstances, is limited and preferred as to dividends and does not participate in corporate growth to any significant extent.

Effective Date

The provision is effective for transactions after May 14, 2003.

20. Modify definition of controlled group of corporations (sec. 900 of the Act and sec. 1563 of the Code)

Present and Prior Law

Under present law, a tax is imposed on the taxable income of corporations. The rates are as follows:

MARGINAL FEDERAL CORPORATE INCOME TAX RATES

If taxable income is:	Then the income tax rate is:
$0–$50,000	15 percent of taxable income
$50,001–$75,000	25 percent of taxable income
$75,001–$10,000,000	34 percent of taxable income
Over $10,000,000	35 percent of taxable income

[1012] It is also intended that stock that by its terms appears not to be limited or preferred as to dividends will be treated as limited or preferred as to dividends if there is not a real and meaningful likelihood that the stock will participate in earnings beyond a limited or preference dividend. A technical correction may be necessary so that the statute reflects this intent.

The first two graduated rates described above are phased out by a five-percent surcharge for corporations with taxable income between $100,000 and $335,000. Also, the application of the 34-percent rate is phased out by a three-percent surcharge for corporations with taxable income between $15 million and $18,333,333.

The component members of a controlled group of corporations are limited to one amount in each of the taxable income brackets shown above.[1013] For this purpose, a controlled group of corporations means a parent-subsidiary controlled group and a brother-sister controlled group.

A brother-sister controlled group under prior law meant two or more corporations if five or fewer persons who are individuals, estates or trusts own (or constructively own) stock possessing (1) at least 80 percent of the total combined voting power of all classes of stock entitled to vote and at least 80 percent of the total value of all stock, and (2) more than 50 percent of percent of the total combined voting power of all classes of stock entitled to vote or more than 50 percent of the total value of all stock, taking into account the stock ownership of each person only to the extent the stock ownership is identical with respect to each corporation.[1014]

Reasons for Change

The Congress was concerned that taxpayers may be able to obtain benefits, such as multiple lower-bracket corporate tax rates, through the use of corporations that are effectively under common control even though the 80-percent test of present law is not satisfied. The Congress believed it was appropriate to eliminate the 80-percent test for purposes of the currently effective provisions under section 1561 (corporate tax brackets, the accumulated earnings credit, and the minimum tax).

Explanation of Provision

Under the Act, a brother-sister controlled group means two or more corporations if five or fewer persons who are individuals, estates or trusts own (or constructively own) stock possessing more than 50 percent of the total combined voting power of all classes of stock entitled to vote, or more than 50 percent of the total value of all stock, taking into account the stock ownership of each person only to the extent the stock ownership is identical with respect to each corporation.

The Act applies only for purposes of section 1561, currently relating to corporate tax brackets, the accumulated earnings credit, and

[1013] Component members are also limited to one alternative minimum tax exemption and one accumulated earnings credit.

[1014] Sec. 1563(a)(2). The Supreme Court held in *United States* v. *Vogel Fertilizer,* 455 U.S. 16 (1982), that Treas. Reg. sec. 1.1563–1(a)(3), as it was then written, was invalid insofar as it would require an individual's stock to be taken into account, for purposes of the 80-percent brother-sister corporation ownership test, where that individual did not own stock in each of the corporations in the asserted controlled group. In that case, one corporation was owned 77.49 percent by one shareholder and 22.51 by an unrelated shareholder. The 77.49 percent shareholder of that first corporation also owned 87.5 percent of the voting stock and more than 90 percent of the value of the stock of a second corporation. The Supreme Court held the corporations were not a controlled group, even though they would have been one had the then applicable Treasury regulations been considered valid in their application to the case. The Treasury regulations were subsequently changed to conform to the Supreme Court decision. T.D. 8179, 53 F.R. 6603 (March 2, 1988).

the minimum tax. The Act does not affect other Code sections or other provisions that utilize or refer to the section 1563 brother-sister corporation controlled group test for other purposes.[1015]

Effective Date

The provision applies to taxable years beginning after the date of enactment (October 22, 2004).

21. Establish specific class lives for utility grading costs (sec. 901 of the Act and sec. 168 of the Code)

Present and Prior Law

A taxpayer is allowed a depreciation deduction for the exhaustion, wear and tear, and obsolescence of property that is used in a trade or business or held for the production of income. For most tangible property placed in service after 1986, the amount of the depreciation deduction is determined under the modified accelerated cost recovery system ("MACRS") using a statutorily prescribed depreciation method, recovery period, and placed in service convention. For some assets, the recovery period for the asset is provided in section 168. In other cases, the recovery period of an asset is determined by reference to its class life. The class lives of assets placed in service after 1986 are generally set forth in Revenue Procedure 87–56.[1016] If no class life is provided, the asset is allowed a seven-year recovery period under MACRS.

Assets that are used in the transmission and distribution of electricity for sale are included in asset class 49.14, with a class life of 30 years and a MACRS recovery period of 20 years. The cost of initially clearing and grading land improvements are specifically excluded from asset class 49.14. Prior to adoption of the accelerated cost recovery system, the IRS ruled that an average useful life of 84 years for the initial clearing and grading relating to electric transmission lines and 46 years for the initial clearing and grading relating to electric distribution lines, would be accepted. However, the result in this ruling was not incorporated in the asset classes included in Rev. Proc. 87–56 or its predecessors. Accordingly, such costs are depreciated over a seven-year recovery period under MACRS as assets for which no class life is provided.

A similar situation exists with regard to gas utility trunk pipelines and related storage facilities. Such assets are included in asset class 49.24, with a class life of 22 years and a MACRS recovery period of 15 years. Initial clearing and grade improvements are specifically excluded from the asset class, and no separate asset class is provided for such costs. Accordingly, such costs are depreciated over a seven-year recovery period under MACRS as assets for which no class life is provided.

Reasons for Change

The Congress believed the clearing and grading costs in question are incurred for the purpose of installing the transmission lines or

[1015] As one example, the Act does not change the present-law standards relating to deferred compensation, contained in subchapter D of the Code, that refer to section 1563.
[1016] 1987–2 C.B. 674 (as clarified and modified by Rev. Proc. 88–22, 1988–1 C.B. 785).

pipelines and are properly seen as part of the cost of installing such lines or pipelines and their cost should be recovered in the same manner. The clearing and grading costs are not expected to have a useful life other than the useful life of the transmission line or pipeline to which they relate.

Explanation of Provision

The Act assigns a class life to depreciable electric and gas utility clearing and grading costs incurred to locate transmission and distribution lines and pipelines. The Act includes these assets in the asset classes of the property to which the clearing and grading costs relate (generally, asset class 49.14 for electric utilities and asset class 49.24 for gas utilities, giving these assets a recovery period of 20 years and 15 years, respectively).

Effective Date

The provision is effective for property placed in service after the date of enactment (October 22, 2004).

22. Provide consistent amortization period for intangibles (sec. 902 of the Act and secs. 195, 248, and 709 of the Code)

Present and Prior Law

At the election of the taxpayer, start-up expenditures[1017] and organizational expenditures[1018] may be amortized over a period of not less than 60 months, beginning with the month in which the trade or business begins. Start-up expenditures are amounts that would have been deductible as trade or business expenses, had they not been paid or incurred before business began. Organizational expenditures are expenditures that are incident to the creation of a corporation (sec. 248) or the organization of a partnership (sec. 709), are chargeable to capital, and that would be eligible for amortization had they been paid or incurred in connection with the organization of a corporation or partnership with a limited or ascertainable life.

Treasury regulations[1019] require that a taxpayer file an election to amortize start-up expenditures no later than the due date for the taxable year in which the trade or business begins. The election must describe the trade or business, indicate the period of amortization (not less than 60 months), describe each start-up expenditure incurred, and indicate the month in which the trade or business began. Similar requirements apply to the election to amortize organizational expenditures. A revised statement may be filed to include start-up and organizational expenditures that were not included on the original statement, but a taxpayer may not include as a start-up expenditure any amount that was previously claimed as a deduction.

Section 197 requires most acquired intangible assets (such as goodwill, trademarks, franchises, and patents) that are held in con-

[1017] Sec. 195
[1018] Secs. 248 and 709.
[1019] Treas. Reg. sec. 1.195–1.

nection with the conduct of a trade or business or an activity for the production of income to be amortized over 15 years beginning with the month in which the intangible was acquired.

Reasons for Change

The Congress believed that allowing a fixed amount of start-up and organizational expenditures to be deductible, rather than requiring their amortization, may help encourage the formation of new businesses that do not require significant start-up or organizational costs to be incurred. In addition, the Congress believed a consistent amortization period for intangibles was appropriate.

Explanation of Provision

The Act modifies the treatment of start-up and organizational expenditures. A taxpayer is allowed to elect to deduct up to $5,000 of start-up and $5,000 of organizational expenditures in the taxable year in which the trade or business begins. However, each $5,000 amount is reduced (but not below zero) by the amount by which the cumulative cost of start-up or organizational expenditures exceeds $50,000, respectively. Start-up and organizational expenditures that are not deductible in the year in which the trade or business begins would be amortized over a 15-year period consistent with the amortization period for section 197 intangibles.

Effective Date

The provision is effective for start-up and organizational expenditures incurred after the date of enactment (October 22, 2004). Start-up and organizational expenditures that are incurred on or before the date of enactment (October 22, 2004) continue to be eligible to be amortized over a period not to exceed 60 months. However, all start-up and organizational expenditures related to a particular trade or business, whether incurred before or after the date of enactment (October 22, 2004), are considered in determining whether the cumulative cost of start-up or organizational expenditures exceeds $50,000.

23. Freeze of provision regarding suspension of interest where Secretary fails to contact taxpayer (sec. 903 of the Act and sec. 6404(g) of the Code)

Present and Prior Law

In general, interest and penalties accrue during periods for which taxes were unpaid without regard to whether the taxpayer was aware that there was tax due. The Code suspends the accrual of certain penalties and interest after 1 year after the filing of the tax return[1020] if the IRS has not sent the taxpayer a notice specifically stating the taxpayer's liability and the basis for the liability within the specified period.[1021] With respect to taxable years beginning before January 1, 2004, the one-year period is increased to 18

[1020] If the return is filed before the due date, for this purpose it is considered to have been filed on the due date.

[1021] Sec. 6404(g). This provision was added to the Code by sec. 3305 of the IRS Restructuring and Reform Act of 1998 (Pub. L. No. 105–206, July 22,1998).

months. Interest and penalties resume 21 days after the IRS sends the required notice to the taxpayer. The provision is applied separately with respect to each item or adjustment. The provision does not apply where a taxpayer has self-assessed the tax. The suspension only applies to taxpayers who file a timely tax return. The provision applies only to individuals and does not apply to the failure to pay penalty, in the case of fraud, or with respect to criminal penalties.

Explanation of Provision

The Act makes the 18-month rule the permanent rule. The Act also adds gross misstatements[1022] and listed and reportable avoidance transactions[1023] to the list of provisions to which the suspension of interest rules do not apply.

Effective Date

The provision is effective for taxable years beginning after December 31, 2003,[1024] except that the addition of listed and reportable avoidance transactions applies to interest accruing after October 3, 2004.

24. Increase in withholding from supplemental wage payments in excess of $1 million (sec. 904 of the Act and sec. 13273 of the Revenue Reconciliation Act of 1993)

Present and Prior Law

An employer must withhold income taxes from wages paid to employees; there are several possible methods for determining the amount of income tax to be withheld. The IRS publishes tables (Publication 15, "Circular E") to be used in determining the amount of income tax to be withheld. The tables generally reflect the income tax rates under the Code so that withholding approximates the ultimate tax liability with respect to the wage payments. In some cases, "supplemental" wage payments (e.g., bonuses or commissions) may be subject to withholding at a flat rate,[1025] based on the third lowest income tax rate under the Code (25 percent for 2005).[1026] Under prior law, special rules did not apply to wages in excess of $1 million.

[1022] This includes any substantial omission of items to which the six-year statute of limitations applies (sec. 6051(e)), gross valuation misstatements (sec. 6662(h)), and similar provisions.

[1023] A reportable avoidance transaction is a reportable transaction with a significant tax avoidance purpose.

[1024] It is intended that this provision apply retroactively to the period beginning January 1, 2004 and ending on the date of enactment. The due date for returns for the taxable period beginning January 1, 2004 is generally April 15, 2005; April 15, 2005 is therefore the date from which the 12–month period that must pass under present-law prior to the commencement of suspension is calculated. Consequently, suspension of interest would generally not begin until April 15, 2006. Accordingly, the provision has no actual retroactive effect.

[1025] Sec. 13273 of the Revenue Reconciliation Act of 1993.

[1026] Sec. 101(c)(11) of the Economic Growth and Tax Relief Reconciliation Act of 2001.

Reasons for Change[1027]

The Congress believed that because most employees who receive annual supplemental wage payments in excess of $1 million will ultimately be taxed at the highest marginal rate, it is appropriate to raise the withholding rate on such payments so that withholding more closely approximates the ultimate tax liability with respect to these payments.

Explanation of Provision

Under the Act, once annual supplemental wage payments to an employee exceed $1 million, any additional supplemental wage payments to the employee in that year are subject to withholding at the highest income tax rate (e.g., 35 percent for 2004 and 2005), regardless of any other withholding rules and regardless of the employee's Form W–4.

This rule applies only for purposes of wage withholding; other types of withholding (such as pension withholding and backup withholding) are not affected.

Effective Date

The provision is effective for payments made after December 31, 2004.

25. Capital gain treatment on sale of stock acquired from exercise of statutory stock options to comply with conflict of interest requirements (sec. 905 of the Act and sec. 421 of the Code)

Present and Prior Law

Statutory stock options

Generally, when an employee exercises a compensatory option on employer stock, the difference between the option price and the fair market value of the stock (i.e., the "spread") is includible in income as compensation. Upon such exercise, an employer is allowed a corresponding compensation deduction. In the case of an incentive stock option or an option to purchase stock under an employee stock purchase plan (collectively referred to as "statutory stock options"), the spread is not included in income at the time of exercise.[1028]

If an employee disposes of stock acquired upon the exercise of a statutory option, the employee generally is taxed at capital gains rates with respect to the excess of the fair market value of the stock on the date of disposition over the option price, and no compensation expense deduction is allowable to the employer, unless the employee fails to meet a holding period requirement. The employee fails to meet this holding period requirement if the disposition occurs within two years after the date the option is granted or one year after the date the option is exercised. The gain upon a disposition that occurs prior to the expiration of the applicable

---

[1027] See S. 2424, the "National Employee Savings and Trust Equity Guarantee Act," which was reported by the Senate Committee on Finance on May 14, 2004 (S. Rep. No. 108–266).

[1028] Sec. 421.

holding period(s) (a "disqualifying disposition") does not qualify for capital gains treatment. In the event of a disqualifying disposition, the income attributable to the disposition is treated by the employee as income received in the taxable year in which the disposition occurs, and a corresponding deduction is allowable to the employer for the taxable year in which the disposition occurs.

Sale of property to comply with conflict of interest requirements

The Code provides special rules for recognizing gain on sales of property which are required in order to comply with certain conflict of interest requirements imposed by the Federal Government.[1029] Certain executive branch Federal employees (and their spouses and minor or dependent children) who are required to divest property in order to comply with conflict of interest requirements may elect to postpone the recognition of resulting gains by investing in certain replacement property within a 60-day period. The basis of the replacement property is reduced by the amount of the gain not recognized. Permitted replacement property is limited to any obligation of the United States or any diversified investment fund approved by regulations issued by the Office of Government Ethics. The rule applies only to sales under certificates of divestiture issued by the President or the Director of the Office of Government Ethics.

Reasons for Change[1030]

To comply with Federal conflict of interest requirements, executive branch personnel may be required, before the statutory holding period requirements have been satisfied, to divest holdings of stock acquired pursuant to the exercise of statutory stock options. Because Federal conflict of interest requirements mandate the sale of such shares, the Congress believed that such individuals should be afforded the tax treatment that would be allowed had the individual held the stock for the required holding period.

Explanation of Provision

Under the Act, an eligible person who, in order to comply with Federal conflict of interest requirements, is required to sell shares of stock acquired pursuant to the exercise of a statutory stock option is treated as satisfying the statutory holding period requirements, regardless of how long the stock was actually held. An eligible person generally includes an officer or employee of the executive branch of the Federal Government (and any spouse or minor or dependent children whose ownership in property is attributable to the officer or employee). Because the sale is not treated as a disqualifying disposition, the individual is afforded capital gain treatment on any resulting gains. Such gains are eligible for deferral treatment under section 1043.

The employer granting the option is not allowed a deduction upon the sale of the stock by the individual.

[1029] Sec. 1043.

[1030] See S. 2424, the "National Employee Savings and Trust Equity Guarantee Act," which was reported by the Senate Committee on Finance on May 14, 2004 (S. Rep. No. 108–266).

Effective Date

The provision is effective for sales after the date of enactment (October 22, 2004).

26. Application of basis rules to nonresident aliens (sec. 906 of the Act sec. 83 and new sec. 72(w) of the Code)

Present and Prior Law

Distributions from retirement plans

Distributions from retirement plans are includible in gross income under the rules relating to annuities[1031] and, thus, are generally includible in income, except to the extent the amount received represents investment in the contract (i.e., the participant's basis). The participant's basis includes amounts contributed by the participant on an after-tax basis, together with certain amounts contributed by the employer, minus the aggregate amount (if any) previously distributed to the extent that such amount was excludable from gross income. Amounts contributed by the employer are included in the calculation of the participant's basis only to the extent that such amounts were includible in the gross income of the participant, or to the extent that such amounts would have been excludable from the participant's gross income if they had been paid directly to the participant at the time they were contributed.[1032]

Employer contributions to retirement plans and other payments for labor or personal services performed outside the United States by a nonresident alien generally are not treated as U.S. source income. Such contributions, therefore, generally would not be includible in the nonresident alien's gross income if they had been paid directly to the nonresident alien at the time they were contributed. Consequently, the amounts of such contributions generally are includible in the employee's basis and are not taxed by the United States if a distribution is made when the employee is a U.S. citizen or resident.[1033]

Earnings on contributions are not included in basis unless previously includible in income. In general, in the case of a nonexempt trust, earnings are includible in income when distributed or made available.[1034] In the case of highly compensated employees, the amount of the vested accrued benefit under the trust (other than the employee's investment in the contract) is generally required to be included in income annually (to the extent not previously includible). That is, earnings, as well as contributions, that are part of the vested accrued benefit are currently includible in income.[1035]

Property transferred in connection with the performance of services

The Code contains rules governing the amount and timing of income and deductions attributable to transfers of property in con-

[1031] Secs. 72 and 402.
[1032] Sec. 72(f).
[1033] Rev. Rul. 58–236, 1958–1 C.B. 37.
[1034] Sec. 402(b)(2).
[1035] Sec. 402(b)(4).

nection with the performance of services. If, in connection with the performance of services, property is transferred to any person other than the person for whom such services are performed, in general, an amount is includible in the gross income of the person performing the services (the "service provider") for the taxable year in which the property is first vested (i.e., transferable or not subject to a substantial risk of forfeiture).[1036] The amount includible in the service provider's income is the excess of the fair market value of the property over the amount (if any) paid for the property. Basis in such property includes any amount that is included in income as a result of the transfer.[1037]

U.S. income tax treaties

Under the 1996 U.S. Model Income Tax Treaty ("U.S. Model") and some U.S. income tax treaties in force, retirement plan distributions beneficially owned by a resident of a treaty country in consideration for past employment generally are taxable only by the individual recipient's country of residence. Under the U.S. Model treaty and some U.S. income tax treaties, this exclusive residence-based taxation rule is limited to the taxation of amounts that were not previously included in taxable income in the other country. For example, if a treaty country had imposed tax on a resident individual with respect to some portion of a retirement plan's earnings, subsequent distributions to that person while a resident of the United States would not be taxable in the United States to the extent the distributions were attributable to such previously taxed amounts.

Compensation of employees of foreign governments or international organizations

Under section 893, wages, fees, and salaries of any employee of a foreign government or international organization (including a consular or other officer or a nondiplomatic representative) received as compensation for official services to the foreign government or international organization generally are excluded from gross income when (1) the employee is not a citizen of the United States, or is a citizen of the Republic of the Philippines (whether or not a citizen of the United States); (2) in the case of an employee of a foreign government, the services are of a character similar to those performed by employees of the United States in foreign countries; and (3) in the case of an employee of a foreign government, the foreign government grants an equivalent exemption to employees of the United States performing similar services in such foreign country. The Secretary of State certifies the names of the foreign countries which grant an equivalent exclusion to employees of the United States performing services in those countries, and the character of those services.

The exclusion does not apply to employees of controlled commercial entities or employees of foreign governments whose services are primarily in connection with commercial activity (whether within or outside the United States) of the foreign government.

[1036] Sec. 83(a).

[1037] Treas. Reg. sec. 1.61–2(d)(i).

Reasons for Change

The Congress believed the rules which governed the calculation of basis provided an inflated basis in assets in retirement and similar arrangements for many individuals who became U.S. residents after accruing benefits under such arrangements. The Congress believed the ability of former nonresident aliens to receive tax-free distributions from such arrangements of amounts which had not been previously taxed was inconsistent with the taxation of benefits paid to individuals who both accrue and receive distributions of benefits from such arrangements as U.S. residents (i.e., basis generally includes only previously-taxed amounts). The Congress believed that the rule which allowed basis in contributions to such arrangements for individuals who became U.S. residents after they accrued benefits was inappropriate. While there was no comparable statutory provision providing basis for earnings, the Congress was aware that some taxpayers took the position that there was basis in the earnings on such contributions, even though such amounts had not been subject to tax. The Congress believed it was appropriate to provide more equitable taxation with respect to the distributions of both contributions and earnings from such arrangements.

Explanation of Provision

Employee or employer contributions are not included in basis (under sec. 72) if: (1) the employee was a nonresident alien at the time the services were performed with respect to which the contribution was made; (2) the contribution is with respect to compensation for labor or personal services from sources without the United States; and (3) the contribution was not subject to income tax (and would have been subject to income tax if paid as cash compensation when the services were rendered) under the laws of the United States or any foreign country.

Additionally, earnings on employer or employee contributions are not included in basis if: (1) the earnings are paid or accrued with respect to any employer or employee contributions which were made with respect to compensation for labor or personal services; (2) the employee was a nonresident alien at the time the earnings were paid or accrued; and (3) the earnings were not subject to income tax under the laws of the United States or any foreign country.

The Act does not change the rules applicable to calculation of basis with respect to contributions or earnings while an employee is a U.S. resident.

There is no inference that the Act applies in any case to create tax jurisdiction with respect to wages, fees, and salaries otherwise exempt under section 893. Similarly, there is no inference that the Act applies where contrary to an agreement of the United States that has been validly authorized by Congress (or in the case of a treaty, ratified by the Senate), and which provides an exemption for income.

Most U.S. tax treaties specifically address the taxation of pension distributions. The U.S. Model treaty provides for exclusive residence-based taxation of pension distributions to the extent such distributions were not previously included in taxable income in the other country. For purposes of the U.S. Model treaty, the United States treats any amount that has increased the recipient's basis (as defined in sec. 72) as having been previously included in taxable income. The following example illustrates how the Act could affect the amount of a distribution that may be taxed by the United States pursuant to a tax treaty.

Assume the following facts. A, a nonresident alien individual, performs services outside the United States, in A's country of residence, country Z. A's employer makes contributions on behalf of A to a pension plan established in country Z. For U.S. tax purposes, no portion of the contributions or earnings are included in A's income (and would not be included in income if the amounts were paid as cash compensation when the services were performed) because such amounts relate to services performed without the United States.[1038] Later in time, A retires and becomes a permanent resident of the United States.

Under the Act, the employer contributions to the pension plan would not be taken into account in determining A's basis if A was not subject to income tax on the contributions by a foreign country and the contributions would have been subject to tax by a foreign country if the contributions had been paid to A as cash compensation when the services were performed. Thus, in those circumstances, A would be subject to U.S. tax on the distribution of all of the contributions, as such distributions are made. However, if the contributions would not have been subject to tax in the foreign country if they had been paid to A as cash compensation when the services were performed, under the provision, the contributions would be included in A's basis. Earnings that accrued while A was a nonresident alien would not result in basis if not taxed under U.S. or foreign law. Earnings that accrued while A was a permanent resident of the United States would be subject to the existing rules. This result generally is consistent with the treatment of pension distributions under the U.S. Model treaty.

The Act authorizes the Secretary of the Treasury to issue regulations to carry out the purposes of the Act, including regulations treating contributions as not subject to income tax under the laws of any foreign country under appropriate circumstances. For example, Treasury could provide that foreign income tax that was merely nominal would not satisfy the "subject to income tax" requirement.

The Act also changes the rules for determining basis in property received in connection with the performance of services in the case of an individual who was a nonresident alien at the time of the performance of services, if the property is treated as income from sources outside the United States. In that case, the individual's basis in the property does not include any amount that was not subject to income tax (and would have been subject to income tax if paid as cash compensation when the services were performed) under the laws of the United States or any foreign country.

[1038] Sec. 872.

Effective Date

.e provision is effective for distributions occurring on or after . . date of enactment (October 22, 2004). No inference is intended that the earnings subject to the provision are included in basis under the law in effect before the date of enactment (October 22, 2004).

27. Deduction for personal use of company aircraft and other entertainment expenses (sec. 907 of the Act and sec. 274(e) of the Code)

Present and Prior Law

Under present and prior law, no deduction is allowed with respect to (1) an activity generally considered to be entertainment, amusement or recreation, unless the taxpayer establishes that the item was directly related to (or, in certain cases, associated with) the active conduct of the taxpayer's trade or business, or (2) a facility (e.g., an airplane) used in connection with such activity.[1039] The Code includes a number of exceptions to the general rule disallowing deductions of entertainment expenses. Under one exception, the deduction disallowance rule does not apply to expenses for goods, services, and facilities to the extent that the expenses are reported by the taxpayer as compensation and wages to an employee.[1040] The deduction disallowance rule also does not apply to expenses paid or incurred by the taxpayer for goods, services, and facilities to the extent that the expenses are includible in the gross income of a recipient who is not an employee (e.g., a nonemployee director) as compensation for services rendered or as a prize or award.[1041] The exceptions apply only to the extent that amounts are properly reported by the company as compensation and wages or otherwise includible in income. In no event can the amount of the deduction exceed the amount of the actual cost, even if a greater amount is includible in income.

Except as otherwise provided, gross income includes compensation for services, including fees, commissions, fringe benefits, and similar items. In general, an employee or other service provider must include in gross income the amount by which the fair value of a fringe benefit exceeds the amount paid by the individual. Treasury regulations provide rules regarding the valuation of fringe benefits, including flights on an employer-provided aircraft.[1042] In general, the value of a non-commercial flight is determined under the base aircraft valuation formula, also known as the Standard Industry Fare Level formula or "SIFL".[1043] If the SIFL valuation rules do not apply, the value of a flight on a company-provided aircraft is generally equal to the amount that an individual would have to pay in an arm's-length transaction to charter the same or a comparable aircraft for that period for the same or a comparable flight.[1044]

[1039] Sec. 274(a).
[1040] Sec. 274(e)(2).
[1041] Sec. 274(e)(9).
[1042] Treas. Reg. sec. 1.61–21.
[1043] Treas. Reg. sec. 1.61–21(g).
[1044] Treas. Reg. sec. 1.61–21(b)(6).

In the context of an employer providing an aircraft to employees for nonbusiness (e.g., vacation) flights, the exception for expenses treated as compensation was interpreted by the Tax Court in 2000, as not limiting the company's deduction for operation of the aircraft to the amount of compensation reportable to its employees,[1045] which can result in a deduction multiple times larger than the amount required to be included in income. In many cases, the individual including amounts attributable to personal travel in income directly benefits from the enhanced deduction, resulting in a net deduction for the personal use of the company aircraft.

Explanation of Provision

Under the Act, in the case of specified individuals, the exceptions to the general entertainment expense disallowance rule for expenses treated as compensation or includible in income apply only to the extent of the amount of expenses treated as compensation or includible in income. Specified individuals include individuals who, with respect to an employer or other service recipient, are subject to the requirements of section 16(a) of the Securities and Exchange Act of 1934, or would be subject to such requirements if the employer or service recipient were an issuer of equity securities referred to in section 16(a). Such individuals generally include officers (as defined by section 16(a)),[1046] directors, and 10–percent-or-greater owners of private and publicly-held companies. No deduction is allowed with respect to expenses for (1) a nonbusiness activity generally considered to be entertainment, amusement or recreation, or (2) a facility (e.g., an airplane) used in connection with such activity to the extent that such expenses exceed the amount treated as compensation or includible in income to the specified individuals. For example, a company's deduction attributable to aircraft operating costs for a specified individual's vacation use of a company aircraft is limited to the amount reported as compensation to the individual. As under present and prior law, the amount of the deduction cannot exceed the actual cost.

The Act is intended to overturn *Sutherland Lumber-Southwest, Inc. v. Commissioner* with respect to specified individuals. As under present and prior law, the exceptions apply only if amounts are properly reported by the company as compensation and wages or otherwise includible in income.

Effective Date

The provision is effective for expenses incurred after the date of enactment (October 22, 2004).

[1045] *Sutherland Lumber-Southwest, Inc.* v. *Comm.*, 114 T.C. 197 (2000), *aff'd*, 255 F.3d 495 (8th Cir. 2001), acq., AOD 2002–02 (Feb. 11, 2002).

[1046] An officer is defined as the president, principal financial officer, principal accounting officer (or, if there is no such accounting officer, the controller), any vice-president in charge of a principal business unit, division or function (such as sales, administration or finance), any other officer who performs a policy-making function, or any other person who performs similar policy-making functions.

28. Residence and source rules related to a United States possession (sec. 908 of the Act and new sec. 937 of the Code)

Present and Prior Law

In general

Generally, U.S. citizens are subject to U.S. income taxation on their worldwide income. Thus, all income earned by U.S. citizens is subject to U.S. income tax, regardless of its source.

The U.S. income taxation of alien individuals varies depending on whether they are resident or non-resident aliens. A resident alien is generally taxed in the same manner as a U.S. citizen.[1047] In contrast, a nonresident alien is generally subject to U.S. tax only on certain gross U.S. source income at a flat 30 percent rate (unless such rate is eliminated or reduced by treaty) and on net income that has a sufficient nexus to the United States at the graduated rates applicable to U.S. citizens and residents under section 1.

An alien is considered a resident of the United States if the individual: (1) has entered the United States as a lawful permanent resident and is such a resident at any time during the calendar year, (2) is present in the United States for a substantial period of time (the so-called "substantial presence test"), or (3) makes an election to be treated as a resident of the United States (sec. 7701(b)). An alien who does not meet the definition of a "resident alien" is considered to be a non-resident alien for U.S. income tax purposes.

Under the substantial presence test, an alien individual is generally treated as a resident alien if he or she is present in the United States for 31 days during the taxable year and the sum of the number of days on which such individual was present in the United States (when multiplied by the applicable multiplier) during the current year and the preceding two calendar years equals or exceeds 183 days. The applicable multiplier for the current year is one; the first preceding year is one-third; and the second preceding year is one-sixth.

An alien individual who meets the above test may nevertheless be a nonresident if he or she (1) is present in the United States for fewer than 183 days during the current year; (2) has a tax home in a foreign country during the year; and (3) has a closer connection to that country than to the United States.

For purposes of the substantial presence test, the United States includes the states and the District of Columbia, but does not include U.S. possessions. An individual is present in the United States for a particular day if he or she is physically present in the United States during any time during such day. However, in certain circumstances an individual's presence in the United States is ignored, including presence in the United States as a result of certain medical emergencies.

[1047] Section 7701(a)(30) defines a citizen or resident of the United States as "U.S. persons."

U.S. income taxation of residents of U.S. possessions

Generally, special U.S. income tax rules apply with respect to U.S. persons who are bona fide residents of certain U.S. possessions (i.e., Puerto Rico, Virgins Islands, Guam, Northern Mariana Islands and American Samoa) and who have possession source income or income effectively connected to the conduct of a trade or business within a possession.

Generally under prior law, a bona fide resident of a U.S. possession (regardless of whether the individual is a U.S. citizen or alien) was determined using the principles of a subjective, facts-and-circumstances test set forth in the regulations under section 871. Prior to the adoption of present-law section 7701(b), this subjective test was used to determine whether an alien individual was a resident of the United States. Under these rules, an individual is generally a resident of the United States if an individual (1) is actually present in the United States, and (2) is not a mere transient or sojourner.[1048] Whether individuals are transients is determined by their intentions with regard to the length and nature of their stay. However, the regulations provide that section 7701(b) (discussed above) provides the basis for determining whether an alien individual is a resident of a U.S. possession with a mirror income tax code.[1049]

The principles that generally apply for determining income from sources within and without the United States also generally applied in determining income from sources within and without a U.S. possession.[1050] Under prior law, the Code and regulations did not indicate how to determine whether income was effectively connected with the conduct of a trade or business within a U.S. possession. However, section 864(c) provides rules for determining whether income is effectively connected to a trade or business conducted within the United States.

Information reporting

Section 7654(e) provides that Treasury may require information reporting with respect to individuals that may take advantage of certain special U.S. income tax rules with respect to U.S. possessions. Section 6688 provides that an individual may be subject to a $100 penalty if the individual fails to furnish the information required by regulations issued pursuant to section 7654(e).

Explanation of Provision

The Congress understood that certain U.S. citizens and residents were claiming that they were exempt from U.S. income tax on their worldwide income based on a position that they were bona fide residents of the Virgin Islands or another possession. However, these individuals often did not spend a significant amount of time in the particular possession during a taxable year and, in some cases, continued to live and work in the United States. Under the

---

[1048] Treas. Reg. sec. 1.871–2(b).

[1049] A U.S. possession with a mirror income tax code is "a United States possession . . . that administers income tax laws that are identical (except for the substitution of the name of the possession or territory for the term 'United States' where appropriate) to those in the United States." Treas. Reg. sec. 7701(b)–1(d)(1).

[1050] Treas. Reg. sec. 1.863–6.

Virgin Island's Economic Development Program, many of these same individuals secured a reduction of up to 90 percent of their Virgin Islands income tax liability on income they took the position was Virgin Islands source or effectively connected with the conduct of a Virgin Islands trade or business. The Congress was also aware that taxpayers were taking the position that income earned for services performed in the United States was Virgin Islands source or that their U.S. activities generated income effectively connected with the conduct of a Virgin Islands trade or business.

The Congress believed that the various exemptions from U.S. tax provided to residents of possessions should not be available to individuals who continue to live and work in the United States. The Congress also believed that the special U.S. income tax rules applicable to residents in a possession needed to be rationalized. The Congress was further concerned that the general rules for determining whether income was effectively connected with the conduct of a trade or business in a possession presented numerous opportunities for erosion of the U.S. tax base.

Generally, the Act provides that the term "bona fide resident" means a person who meets a two-part test with respect to Guam, American Samoa, the Northern Mariana Islands, Puerto Rico, or the Virgin Islands, as the case may be, for the taxable year. First, an individual must be present in the possession for at least 183 days in the taxable year. Second, an individual must (i) not have a tax home outside such possession during the taxable year and (ii) not have a closer connection to the United States or a foreign country during such year.

The Act also grants authority to Treasury to create exceptions to these general rules as appropriate. The Congress intends for such exceptions to cover, in particular, persons whose presence outside a possession for extended periods of time lacks a tax avoidance purpose, such as military personnel, workers in the fisheries trade, and retirees who travel outside the possession for certain personal reasons.

An individual is present in a possession for a particular day if he is physically present in such possession during any time during such day. In certain circumstances an individual's presence outside a possession is ignored (e.g., certain medical emergencies) as provided under the principles of section 7701(b).

The Act provides that a taxpayer must file a notice in the first taxable year they claim bona fide residence in a possession. The Act imposes a penalty of $1000 for the failure to file such notice or to comply with any filing required by regulation under section 7654(e).

The Act generally codifies the existing rules for determining when income is considered to be from sources within a possession by providing that, as a general rule, for all purposes of the Code, the principles for determining whether income is U.S. source are applicable for purposes of determining whether income is possession source. In addition, the Act provides that the principles for determining whether income is effectively connected with the conduct of a U.S. trade or business are applicable for purposes of determining whether income is effectively connected to the conduct of a possession trade or business. However, the Act further provides that, except as provided in regulations, any income treated as U.S. source income or as effectively connected with the conduct of a U.S. trade or business is not treated as income from within any possession or as effectively connected with a trade or business within any such possession.

The Act also grants authority to the Secretary to create exceptions to these general rules regarding possession source income and income effectively connected with a possession trade or business as appropriate. It is anticipated that this authority will be used to continue the existing treatment of income from the sale of goods manufactured in a possession. It also is intended for this authority to be used to prevent abuse, for example, to prevent U.S. persons from avoiding U.S. tax on appreciated property by acquiring residence in a possession prior to its disposition.

No inference is intended as to the prior-law rules for determining (1) bona fide residence in a possession, (2) whether income is possession source, and (3) whether income is effectively connected with the conduct of a trade or business within a possession.

Effective Date

Generally, the provision is effective for taxable years ending after the date of enactment (October 22, 2004). The first prong of the two-part residency test (i.e., the 183–day test) is effective for taxable years beginning after date of enactment (October 22, 2004). The general effective date applies with respect to the second prong of such test. The rule providing that income treated as U.S. source income or as effectively connected with the conduct of a U.S. trade or business is not treated as income from within any possession or as effectively connected with the conduct of a trade or business within any such possession is effective for income earned after the date of enactment (October 22, 2004).

29. Dispositions of transmission property to implement Federal Energy Regulatory Commission restructuring policy (sec. 909 of the Act and sec. 451 of the Code)

Present and Prior Law

Generally, a taxpayer recognizes gain to the extent the sales price (and any other consideration received) exceeds the seller's basis in the property. The recognized gain is subject to current income tax unless the gain is deferred or not recognized under a special tax provision.

Reasons for Change [1051]

The Congress recognized that electric deregulation has been occurring, and is continuing to occur, at both the Federal and State level. Federal and State energy regulators are calling for the "unbundling" of electric transmission assets held by vertically integrated utilities, with the transmission assets ultimately placed under the ownership or control of independent transmission providers (or other similarly-approved operators). This policy is in-

[1051] See H.R. 1531, the "Energy Tax Policy Act of 2003," which was reported by the Committee on Ways and Means on April 9, 2003 (H.R. Rep. No. 108–67).

tended to improve transmission management and facilitate the formation of competitive markets. To facilitate the implementation of these policy objectives, the Congress believed it was appropriate to assist taxpayers in moving forward with industry restructuring by providing a tax deferral for gain associated with certain dispositions of electric transmission assets.

Explanation of Provision

The Act permits taxpayers to elect to recognize gain from qualifying electric transmission transactions ratably over an eight-year period beginning in the year of sale if the amount realized from such sale is used to purchase exempt utility property within the applicable period[1052] (the "reinvestment property"). If the amount realized exceeds the amount used to purchase reinvestment property, any realized gain shall be recognized to the extent of such excess in the year of the qualifying electric transmission transaction. Any remaining realized gain is recognized ratably over the eight-year period.

A qualifying electric transmission transaction is the sale or other disposition of property used by the taxpayer in the trade or business of providing electric transmission services, or an ownership interest in such an entity, to an independent transmission company prior to January 1, 2007. In general, an independent transmission company is defined as: (1) an independent transmission provider[1053] approved by the FERC; (2) a person (i) who the FERC determines under section 203 of the Federal Power Act (or by declaratory order) is not a "market participant" and (ii) whose transmission facilities are placed under the operational control of a FERC-approved independent transmission provider before the close of the period specified in such authorization, but not later than January 1, 2007;[1054] or (3) in the case of facilities subject to the jurisdiction of the Public Utility Commission of Texas, (i) a person which is approved by that Commission as consistent with Texas State law regarding an independent transmission organization, or (ii) a political subdivision, or affiliate thereof, whose transmission facilities are under the operational control of an organization described in (i).

Exempt utility property is defined as: (1) property used in the trade or business of generating, transmitting, distributing, or selling electricity or producing, transmitting, distributing, or selling natural gas, or (2) stock in a controlled corporation whose principal trade or business consists of the activities described in (1).

If a taxpayer is a member of an affiliated group of corporations filing a consolidated return, the proposal permits the reinvestment property to be purchased by any member of the affiliated group (in lieu of the taxpayer).

If a taxpayer elects the application of the provision, then the statutory period for the assessment of any deficiency, for any taxable year in which any part of the gain eligible for the provision

---

[1052] The applicable period for a taxpayer to reinvest the proceeds is four years after the close of the taxable year in which the qualifying electric transmission transaction occurs.

[1053] For example, a regional transmission organization, an independent system operator, or and independent transmission company.

[1054] A technical correction may be necessary so that the statute reflects this intent.

is realized, attributable to such gain shall not expire prior to the expiration of three years from the date the Secretary of the Treasury is notified by the taxpayer of the reinvestment property or an intention not to reinvest.

An electing taxpayer is required to attach a statement to that effect in the tax return for the taxable year in which the transaction takes place in the manner as the Secretary shall prescribe. The election shall be binding for that taxable year and all subsequent taxable years.[1055] In addition, an electing taxpayer is required to attach a statement that identifies the reinvestment property in the manner as the Secretary shall prescribe.

Effective Date

The provision is effective for transactions occurring after the date of enactment (October 22, 2004), in taxable years ending after such date.

30. Expansion of limitation on expensing of certain passenger automobiles (sec. 910 of the Act and sec. 179 of the Code)

Present and Prior Law

A taxpayer is allowed to recover, through annual depreciation deductions, the cost of certain property used in a trade or business or for the production of income. The amount of the depreciation deduction allowed with respect to tangible property for a taxable year is determined under the modified accelerated cost recovery system ("MACRS"). Under MACRS, passenger automobiles generally are recovered over five years. However, section 280F limits the annual depreciation deduction with respect to certain passenger automobiles.[1056]

For purposes of the depreciation limitation, passenger automobiles are defined broadly to include any four-wheeled vehicles that are manufactured primarily for use on public streets, roads, and highways and which are rated at 6,000 pounds unloaded gross vehicle weight or less.[1057] In the case of a truck or a van, the depreciation limitation applies to vehicles that are rated at 6,000 pounds gross vehicle weight or less. Sports utility vehicles are treated as a truck for the purpose of applying the section 280F limitation.

In lieu of depreciation, a taxpayer with a sufficiently small amount of annual investment may elect to expense such investment (sec. 179). The Jobs and Growth Tax Relief Reconciliation Act

---

[1055] The Act also provides that the installment sale rules shall not apply to any qualifying electric transmission transaction for which a taxpayer elects the application of this provision.

[1056] The limitation is commonly referred to as the "luxury automobile depreciation limitation." For passenger automobiles (subject to the such limitation) placed in service in 2002, the maximum amount of allowable depreciation is $7,660 for the year in which the vehicle was placed in service, $4,900 for the second year, $2,950 for the third year, and $1,775 for the fourth and later years. This limitation applies to the combined depreciation deduction provided under present law for depreciation, including section 179 expensing and the temporary 30 percent additional first year depreciation allowance. For luxury automobiles eligible for the 50 percent additional first depreciation allowance, the first year limitation is increased by an additional $3,050.

[1057] Sec. 280F(d)(5). Exceptions are provided for any ambulance, hearse, or any vehicle used by the taxpayer directly in the trade or business of transporting persons or property for compensation or hire.

("JGTRRA") of 2003[1058] increased the amount a taxpayer may deduct, for taxable years beginning in 2003 through 2005, to $100,000 of the cost of qualifying property placed in service for the taxable year.[1059] In general, qualifying property is defined as depreciable tangible personal property that is purchased for use in the active conduct of a trade or business. The $100,000 amount is reduced (but not below zero) by the amount by which the cost of qualifying property placed in service during the taxable year exceeds $400,000. Prior to the enactment of JGTRRA (and for taxable years beginning in 2006 and thereafter), a taxpayer with a sufficiently small amount of annual investment may elect to deduct up to $25,000 of the cost of qualifying property placed in service for the taxable year. The $25,000 amount is reduced (but not below zero) by the amount by which the cost of qualifying property placed in service during the taxable year exceeds $200,000. Passenger automobiles subject to section 280F are eligible for section 179 expensing only to the extent of the applicable limits contained in section 280F.

Reasons for Change

The Congress believed that section 179 expensing provides two important benefits for small business. First, it lowers the cost of capital for property used in a trade or business. With a lower cost of capital, the Congress believed small business would invest in more equipment and employ more workers. Second, it eliminates depreciation recordkeeping requirements with respect to expensed property. However, the Congress understood that some taxpayers were using section 179 to lower the cost of purchasing certain types of vehicles (1) that are not subject to the luxury automobile limitations imposed by Congress and (2) for which the specific features of such vehicle are not necessary for purposes of conducting the taxpayer's business. The Congress was concerned about such market distortions and did not believe that the United States taxpayers should subsidize a portion of such purchase. The provision places new restrictions on the ability of certain vehicles to qualify for the expensing provisions of section 179.

Explanation of Provision

The Act limits the ability of taxpayers to claim deductions under section 179 for certain vehicles not subject to section 280F to $25,000. The Act applies to sport utility vehicles rated at 14,000 pounds gross vehicle weight or less (in place of the present law 6,000 pound rating). For this purpose, a sport utility vehicle is defined to exclude any vehicle that: (1) is designed for more than nine individuals in seating rearward of the driver's seat; (2) is equipped with an open cargo area, or a covered box not readily accessible from the passenger compartment, of at least six feet in interior length; or (3) has an integral enclosure, fully enclosing the driver compartment and load carrying device, does not have seating rear-

---

[1058] Pub. L. No. 108–27, sec. 202 (2003).

[1059] Additional section 179 incentives are provided with respect to a qualified property used by a business in the New York Liberty Zone (sec. 1400L(f)), an empowerment zone (sec. 1397A), or a renewal community (sec. 1400J).

ward of the driver's seat, and has no body section protruding more than 30 inches ahead of the leading edge of the windshield.

The following example illustrates the operation of the Act.

Example.—Assume that during 2004, on a date which is after the date of enactment, a calendar year taxpayer acquires and places in service a sport utility vehicle subject to the Act that costs $70,000. In addition, assume that the property otherwise qualifies for the expensing election under section 179. Under the Act, the taxpayer is first allowed a $25,000 deduction under section 179. The taxpayer is also allowed an additional first-year depreciation deduction (sec. 168(k)) of $22,500 based on $45,000 ($70,000 original cost less the section 179 deduction of $25,000) of adjusted basis. Finally, the remaining adjusted basis of $22,500 ($45,000 adjusted basis less $22,500 additional first-year depreciation) is eligible for an additional depreciation deduction of $4,500 under the general depreciation rules (automobiles are five-year recovery property). The remaining $18,000 of cost ($70,000 original cost less $52,000 deductible currently) is recovered in 2005 and subsequent years pursuant to the general depreciation rules.

Effective Date

The provision is effective for property placed in service after the date of enactment (October 22, 2004).

PART EIGHTEEN: THE REVENUE PROVISIONS OF THE RONALD W. REAGAN NATIONAL DEFENSE AUTHORIZATION ACT FOR FISCAL YEAR 2005 (PUBLIC LAW 108–375) [1060]

A. Exclusion from Gross Income of Travel Benefits under Operation Hero Miles (sec. 585(b) of the Act and sec. 134 of the Code)

Present and Prior Law

Qualified military benefits are not included in gross income. Generally, a qualified military benefit is any allowance or in-kind benefit (other than personal use of a vehicle) which: (1) is received by any member or former member of the uniformed services of the United States or any dependent of such member by reason of such member's status or service as a member of such uniformed services; and (2) was excludable from gross income on September 9, 1986, under any provision of law, regulation, or administrative practice which was in effect on such date. Generally, other than certain cost of living adjustments, no modification or adjustment of any qualified military benefit after September 9, 1986, is taken into account for purposes of this exclusion from gross income.

Explanation of Provision

Under the Act, qualified military benefits include a travel benefit provided under a Department of Defense program under which travel benefits donated to the Department of Defense from various sources (including members of the public) are used to: (1) facilitate the travel while on leave of a member of the armed forces who is serving on active duty outside the United States; or (2) facilitate the travel of the family of a member of the armed forces who is recuperating from a service-related injury or illness, in order for the family to be reunited with the member.[1061] For this purpose, travel benefit means frequent traveler miles, credits for tickets, or tickets for air or surface transportation issued by an air carrier or a surface carrier, respectively, that serves the public.

Effective Date

The provision applies to travel benefits provided after the date of the enactment of the Act (October 28, 2004).

[1060] H.R. 4200. The House Committee on Armed Services reported the bill on May 14, 2004 (H.R. Rep. No. 108–491). The House passed the bill on May 20, 2004. The Senate Committee on Armed Services reported S. 2400 on May 11, 2004 (S. Rep. No. 108–260). The Senate passed H. R. 4200, as amended by the provisions of S. 2400, on June 23, 2004. The conference report was filed on October 8, 2004 (H.R. Rep. No. 108–767), and was passed by the House on October 9, 2004, and the Senate on October 9, 2004. The President signed the bill on October 28, 2004.

[1061] 10 U.S.C. section 2613. Authorization for this program, referred to as "Operation Hero Miles," is provided by section 585(a) of the Act.

PART NINETEEN: THE REVENUE PROVISIONS OF THE CONSOLIDATED APPROPRIATIONS ACT, 2005 (PUBLIC LAW 108–447) [1062]

A. Application of the ERISA Anticutback Rules to Certain Multiemployer Plan Amendments (Division J, sec. 110 of the Act and sec. 204(g) of ERISA)

Present and Prior Law

Under the Code and the Employee Retirement Income Security Act of 1974 ("ERISA"), a participant's accrued benefit under a qualified retirement plan must become vested (or nonforfeitable) in accordance with one of two alternative minimum vesting schedules.[1063] For this purpose, an accrued benefit under a multiemployer plan is not treated as forfeitable solely because the plan provides that benefit payments are suspended for the period that the employee is employed, after benefits commence, in the same industry, in the same trade or craft, and in the same geographic area covered by the plan as when payments commenced.

Under the "anticutback" rule of the Code and ERISA, a plan amendment may not reduce participants' accrued benefits.[1064] An amendment also violates the anticutback rule if, with respect to benefits accrued before the amendment is adopted, the amendment has the effect of either: (1) eliminating or reducing an early retirement benefit or a retirement-type subsidy; or (2) except as provided by Treasury regulations, eliminating an optional form of benefit.

On June 7, 2004, the Supreme Court held that an amendment to a multiemployer plan that expanded the circumstances in which a participant's benefit payments were suspended and that applied to previously accrued benefits violated the anticutback rule.[1065]

Explanation of Provision

The Act limits the application of the anticutback rule of ERISA to a plan amendment adopted before June 7, 2004, by a multiemployer pension plan covering primarily employees working in the State of Alaska. Under the Act, the anticutback rule of ERISA does not apply at any time (whether before or after enactment of the provision) to the extent that the plan amendment: (1) provides for the suspension of the payment of benefits, modifies the conditions

---

[1062] H.R. 4818. The House Committee on Appropriations reported the bill as an original measure on July 13, 2004 (H.R. Rep. No. 108–599). The House passed the bill on July 15, 2004. The Senate passed the bill in lieu of S. 2812 with an amendment on September 23, 2004. The conference report was filed on November 20, 2004 (H.R. Rep. No. 108–792) and was passed by the House and the Senate on November 20, 2004. The bill was signed by the President on December 8, 2004.

[1063] Code sec. 411; ERISA sec. 203.

[1064] Code sec. 411(d)(6); ERISA sec. 204(g).

[1065] *Central Laborers' Pension Fund* v. *Heinz,* 541 U.S. 739 (2004).

under which the payment of benefits is suspended, or suspends certain actuarial adjustments in benefit payments; and (2) applies to participants who have not retired before the adoption of the amendment. The Act does not change the application of the anticutback rule of the Code to such a plan amendment.

Effective Date

The provision is effective on the date of enactment (October 22, 2004).

PART TWENTY: AN ACT TO TREAT CERTAIN ARRANGEMENTS MAINTAINED BY THE YMCA RETIREMENT FUND AS CHURCH PLANS FOR PURPOSES OF CERTAIN PROVISIONS OF THE INTERNAL REVENUE CODE OF 1986, AND FOR OTHER PURPOSES (PUBLIC LAW 108–476)[1066]

A. Certain Arrangements Maintained by the YMCA Retirement Fund Treated as Church Plans (sec. 1 of the Act and secs. 401(a), 403(b), and 7702(j) of the Code)

Present and Prior Law

Special retirement plan rules for church plans

In general

Tax-favored retirement plans are subject to various requirements under the Code. However, church plans are exempt from some of these requirements or are subject to special rules. In general, a church plan is a plan established and maintained for its employees by a church or by a convention or association of churches that is exempt from tax.[1067] In addition, the term "church plan" includes a plan established or maintained by an organization: (1) that is controlled by or associated with a church and (2) the principal purpose or function of which is the administration or funding of a retirement or welfare benefit plan or program for church employees. Such organizations are referred to here as "church-associated organizations."

Retirement plans are generally subject to the requirements of the Employee Retirement Income Security Act of 1974 ("ERISA"), as well as to the requirements of the Code. However, church plans generally are exempt from ERISA.

Tax-sheltered annuities

Favorable tax treatment applies to annuity contracts purchased for an employee by an employer that is a tax-exempt charitable organization or an educational institution and that meet certain requirements ("tax-sheltered annuities").[1068] For this purpose, a "retirement income account" is treated as an annuity contract. A retirement income account means a defined contribution program established or maintained by a church or a convention or association of churches or a church-associated organization. Subject to certain exceptions, the same rules apply to retirement income accounts

---

[1066] H.R. 5365. The House passed the bill on a motion to suspend the rules and pass the bill on November 19, 2004. The Senate passed the bill without amendment by unanimous consent on December 7, 2004. The President signed the bill on December 21, 2004.
[1067] Sec. 414(e).
[1068] Sec. 403(b).

that apply to tax-sheltered annuities, except that the purchase of an annuity contract is not required.

Tax-sheltered annuity contracts must be purchased under a plan that meets certain nondiscrimination requirements. The nondiscrimination requirements do not apply to an annuity contract purchased by a church, a convention or association of churches, or certain church-controlled organizations.[1069] Contributions to a tax-sheltered annuity are generally subject to limitations, but a higher limitation may apply to a tax-sheltered annuity maintained by a church.[1070]

Minimum distribution rules apply to tax-favored retirement arrangements, including tax-sheltered annuities.[1071] Special minimum distribution rules apply to payments from an annuity contract purchased with an employee's benefit by a plan from an insurance company.[1072] Annuity payments from a retirement income account may be eligible for these special minimum distribution rules even though the payments are not made under an annuity contract purchased from an insurance company.[1073]

Qualified retirement plans

Church plans are exempt from many of the rules that apply to qualified retirement plans, unless the church elects to have the requirements apply.[1074] For example, unless such an election has been made, a church plan is exempt from: (1) the prohibition on assignment or alienation of benefits (sec. 401(a)(13)); (2) joint and survivor annuity requirements (sec. 401(a)(11)); (3) vesting requirements and anti-cutback protections (sec. 411); (4) funding requirements (sec. 412); and (5) prohibited transaction rules (sec. 4975).

Under the joint and survivor annuity rules, a plan is generally required to provide benefits in the form of a qualified joint and survivor annuity ("QJSA") unless the participant and his or her spouse consent to another form of benefit. A QJSA is an annuity for the life of the participant, with a survivor annuity for the life of the spouse that is not less than 50 percent (and not more than 100 percent) of the amount of the annuity payable during the joint lives of the participant and his or her spouse.

The joint and survivor annuity requirements generally do not apply to defined contribution plans other than money purchase pension plans. A money purchase pension plan is a type of defined contribution plan that provides for a set level of required employer contributions, generally as a specified percentage of participants' compensation, and for the distribution of benefits in the form of an annuity.

Special life insurance rule for church plans

The Code contains a definition of the term "life insurance contract," which applies for purposes of the Code, including the exclu-

[1069] For purposes of the exemption from the nondiscrimination rules, church and church-controlled organization are defined as in section 3121(w)(3). This definition generally applies to a narrower class of organizations than the definition of church plan in section 414(e).

[1070] Sec. 415(c)(7).

[1071] Secs. 401(a)(9) and 403(b)(10).

[1072] Treas. Reg. sec. 1.401(a)(9)-6, A–4.

[1073] Treas. Reg. sec. 1.403(b)-3, A–1(c)(3).

[1074] Sec. 410(d). A church plan with respect to which such an election has been made is referred to as an "electing" church plan. Electing church plans are subject to ERISA.

sion from gross income for the proceeds of a life insurance contract paid by reason of the death of the insured.[1075] This definition generally requires the contract to be a life insurance contract under applicable law. However, this requirement does not apply to a plan or arrangement that provides for the payment of benefits by reason of the death of individuals covered under the plan or arrangement and that is provided by a church for the benefit of its employees and their beneficiaries, either directly or through a church-associated organization.

Retirement plans maintained by the YMCA Retirement Fund

Employees of the Young Men's Christian Association ("YMCA") are covered by two plans maintained by the YMCA Retirement Fund.[1076] The YMCA Retirement Plan provides for employer contributions and after-tax employee contributions and is designed to be a qualified money purchase pension plan. The YMCA Tax-Deferred Contribution Plan allows employees to make pretax contributions under salary reduction agreements and is designed to be a tax-sheltered annuity arrangement. Contributions under both plans are maintained in accounts under the YMCA Retirement Fund. Benefits under the plans are payable in the form of annuities without the purchase of commercial annuity contracts. Besides retirement benefits, the plans provide benefits in the case of death or disability.

Explanation of Provision

The Act specifies the treatment of the retirement plans maintained by the YMCA Retirement Fund for certain purposes of the Code. In general, under the Act, for purposes of the rules governing qualified retirement plans and tax-sheltered annuities, any retirement plan maintained by the YMCA Retirement Fund as of January 1, 2003 (a "YMCA retirement plan"), is treated as a church plan maintained by a church-associated organization.

In the case of a YMCA retirement plan that allows contributions to be made under a salary reduction agreement (i.e., the YMCA Tax-Deferred Contribution Plan), church plan treatment does not apply for purposes of the special contribution limit applicable to tax-sheltered annuities maintained by churches. In addition, any account maintained for a participant or beneficiary of the plan is treated for purposes of the Code as a retirement income account. However, an account is not treated as an annuity contract purchased by a church for purposes of the nondiscrimination rules applicable to tax-sheltered annuities.

In the case of a YMCA retirement plan that is subject to the qualification requirements of the Code (i.e., the YMCA Retirement Plan), the plan (but not any reserves held by the YMCA Retirement Fund) is treated for purposes of the Code as a defined contribution plan that is a money purchase pension plan. In addition, the plan is treated as having made an election under section 410(d) for plan years beginning after December 31, 2005. Thus, the plan

[1075] Sec. 101(a).

[1076] The YMCA Retirement Fund is a corporation created by an Act of the State of New York that became law on April 30, 1921 (1921 New York Laws, Chapter 459).

is treated as an electing church plan for plan years beginning after December 31, 2005. Notwithstanding the election, nothing in ERISA or the Code shall prohibit the YMCA Retirement Fund from commingling for investment purposes the assets of the electing plan with the assets of the Fund and with the assets of any employee benefit plan maintained by the Fund. In addition, nothing in the Act is to be construed as subjecting any commingled assets, other than the assets of the electing plan, to any provision of ERISA. The Act also allows the plan, notwithstanding the joint and survivor annuity rules of the Code and ERISA, to offer a lump-sum distribution option to participants who have not attained age 55 without offering such participants an annuity option. In addition, any account maintained for a participant or beneficiary of the plan is treated as a retirement income account for purposes of the minimum distribution rules.

For purposes of the definition of life insurance contract under the Code, a YMCA retirement plan is treated as an arrangement that provides for the payment of benefits by reason of the death of individuals covered under the arrangement and that is provided by a church for the benefit of its employees and their beneficiaries, directly or through a church-associated organization.

Effective Date

The provision is effective for plan years beginning after December 31, 2003.

PART TWENTY-ONE: AN ACT TO MODIFY THE TAXATION OF ARROW COMPONENTS (PUBLIC LAW 108–493) [1077]

A. Excise Tax on Arrows (sec. 1 of the Act and sec. 4161 of the Code)

Present and Prior Law

Under prior law, section 332(b) of the AJCA imposed a 12-percent tax on the sale by the manufacturer, importer or producer of arrows generally. An arrow for this purpose was defined as a taxable arrow shaft to which additional components are attached. In the case of any arrow comprised of a shaft or any other component upon which tax has been imposed, the amount of the arrow tax was equal to the excess of (1) the arrow tax that would have been imposed but for this exception, over (2) the amount of tax paid with respect to such components.[1078]

Present and prior law also imposes an 11-percent excise tax on the sale by the manufacturer, importer or producer of any part of an accessory for taxable bows, and any quivers or broadheads for use with arrows (1) over 18 inches long or (2) designed for use with a taxable bow (if shorter than 18 inches).

Prior law imposed a 12.4 percent excise tax on the sale by the manufacturer, importer or producer of certain arrow components. Under prior law points (other than broadheads) were taxed at 12.4 percent as arrow components.

Explanation of Provision [1079]

The Act repealed the 12-percent excise tax on arrows imposed by section 332(b) of AJCA and required that the law be administered as if that provision was never enacted. In addition, after March 31, 2005, the 12.4-percent tax on arrow components is repealed and replaced with a tax equal to 39 cents per arrow shaft on the first sale of such shaft (whether sold separately or incorporated as part of a finished or unfinished product). Points are subject to the 11-percent excise tax imposed on accessories. A 39-cent amount is adjusted for inflation after 2005.

[1077] H.R. 5394 was introduced on November 19, 2004. It was passed by the House under suspension of the rules on December 6, 2004. The Senate passed the measure by unanimous consent on December 8, 2004. The President signed the measure on December 23, 2004.

[1078] Under present and prior law, a credit or refund may be obtained when an item was taxed and it is used in the manufacture or production of another taxable item. Sec. 6416(b)(3). As arrow components and finished arrows are both taxable, in lieu of a refund of the tax paid on components, the provision suspended the application of sec. 6416(b)(3) and permitted the taxpayer to reduce the tax due on the finished arrow by the amount of the previous tax paid on the components used in the manufacture of such arrow.

[1079] Section 332 of AJCA made two changes unaffected by Pub. L. No. 108–493: (1) increased the draw weight for a taxable bow from 10 pounds or more to a peak draw weight of 30 pounds or more; and (2) subjected certain broadheads (a type of arrow point) to an excise tax equal to 11 percent of the sales price instead of 12.4 percent.

Effective Dates

The provisions relating to the tax on shafts and points are effective for articles sold by the manufacturer, producer or importer after March 31, 2005.

APPENDIX:
ESTIMATED BUDGET EFFECTS OF TAX LEGISLATION ENACTED IN THE 108TH CONGRESS

APPENDIX:
ESTIMATED BUDGET EFFECTS OF TAX LEGISLATION ENACTED IN THE 108TH CONGRESS
Fiscal Years 2003–2014

[Millions of dollars]

Provision	Effective	2003	2004	2005	2006	2007	2008	2009	2010	2011	2012	2013	2014	2003–14
PART ONE: JOBS AND GROWTH TAX RELIEF RECONCILIATION ACT OF 2003 ("JGTRRA") (P.L. 108–27, signed into law by the President on May 28, 2003)														
I. Acceleration of Certain Previously Enacted Tax Reductions														
1. Expand the child credit to $1,000 for 2003 through 2004; revert to present-law phase in for 2005 (1)	tyba 12/31/02	−13,712	−5,820	−12,956										−32,488
2. Accelerate the expansion of the 15% individual income tax rate bracket and the increase in the standard deduction for married taxpayers filing joint returns; revert to present-law phase in for 2005	tyba 12/31/02	−4,936	−24,904	−5,234										−35,074
3. Accelerate the expansion of the 10% bracket; revert to present-law phase in for 2005	tyba 12/31/02	−1,549	−8,445	−1,912										−11,906
4. Accelerate the 2006 rate schedule	tyba 12/31/02	−9,531	−38,809	−19,930	−5,915									−74,185
5. Increase individual AMT exemption amount by $4,500 single and $9,000 joint for 2003 and 2004	tyba 12/31/02	−1,176	−10,346	−6,260										−17,782
Total of Acceleration of Certain Previously Enacted Tax Reductions		**−30,904**	**−88,324**	**−46,292**	**−5,915**									**−171,435**

II. Growth Incentives for Business													
1. Increase bonus depreciation to 50% and extend through 12/31/04	ppisa 5/5/03 (2)	−9,918	−33,298	−11,684	9,414	9,300	8,112	6,648	4,987	3,586	2,212	1,447	−9,194
2. Increase section 179 expensing—increase the amount that can be expensed from $25,000 to $100,000 and increase the phaseout threshold amount from $200,000 to $400,000; include software in section 179 property; and index both the deduction limit and the phaseout threshold after 2003 (sunset after 2005)	tyba 12/31/02	−1,647	−2,681	−3,690	−1,027	2,724	1,842	1,290	937	647	410	243	−952
Total of Growth Incentives for Business		**−11,565**	**−35,979**	**−15,374**	**8,387**	**12,024**	**9,954**	**7,938**	**5,924**	**4,233**	**2,622**	**1,690**	**−10,146**
III. Reductions in Taxes on Dividends and Capital Gains													
1. Tax capital gains with a 15%/5% rate structure for 2003 through 2007, and 15%/0% in 2008 (sunset 12/31/08)	so/a 5/6/03	−62	−928	−1,335	−3,042	−4,454	−3,544	509	−9,532				−22,386
2. Tax dividends with a 15%/5% rate structure for 2003 through 2007, and 15%/0% in 2008 (sunset 12/31/08) (3)	dri tyba 12/31/02	−4,250	−17,506	−19,215	−20,081	−21,263	−23,203	−19,689	−493				−125,700
Total of Reductions in Taxes on Dividends and Capital Gains		**−4,312**	**−18,434**	**−20,550**	**−23,123**	**−25,717**	**−26,747**	**−19,180**	**−10,025**				**−148,086**
IV. Temporary State Fiscal Relief Fund (outlay effects) (4)	**DOE**						***No Revenue Effect***						
V. Special Estimated Tax Rules for Certain Corporate Estimated Tax Payments (25% of estimated payments otherwise due on September 15, 2003 are payable on October 1, 2003)	**DOE**	**−6,325**	**6,325**										

APPENDIX:—Continued

ESTIMATED BUDGET EFFECTS OF TAX LEGISLATION ENACTED IN THE 108TH CONGRESS

Fiscal Years 2003–2014

[Millions of dollars]

Provision	Effective	2003	2004	2005	2006	2007	2008	2009	2010	2011	2012	2013	2014	2003–14
TOTAL OF PART ONE: JOBS AND GROWTH TAX RELIEF RECONCILIATION ACT OF 2003		−53,106	−136,412	−82,216	−20,651	−13,693	−16,793	−11,242	−4,101	4,233	2,622	1,690		−329,667
PART TWO: SURFACE TRANSPORTATION EXTENSION ACT OF 2003—Extension of Highway Trust Fund and Aquatic Resources Trust Fund Expenditure Authority (P.L. 108–88, signed into law by the President on September 30, 2003)	DOE	*No Revenue Effect*												
PART THREE: EXTEND THE TEMPORARY ASSISTANCE FOR NEEDY FAMILIES BLOCK GRANT PROGRAM, AND CERTAIN TAX AND TRADE PROGRAMS (P.L. 108–89, signed into law by the President on October 1, 2003)														
I. Disclosure of Return Information Relating to Student Loans (4)	DOE	*The Congressional Budget Office Did Not Estimate This Provision*												
II. Extension of IRS User Fees (through 12/31/04) (4).	rma DOE		33	8										41
III. Extension of Customs User Fees (through 3/31/04) (4)	DOE		698											698

TOTAL OF PART THREE: EXTEND THE TEMPORARY ASSISTANCE FOR NEEDY FAMILIES BLOCK GRANT PROGRAM, AND CERTAIN TAX AND TRADE PROGRAMS			**731**	**8**									**739**
PART FOUR: MILITARY FAMILY TAX RELIEF ACT OF 2003 (P.L. 108–121, signed into law by the President on November 11, 2003)													
I. Provisions to Improve Tax Equity for Military Personnel													
1. Exclusion of gain on sale of a principal residence by a member of the uniformed and foreign services	soea 5/6/97		−68	−14	−14	−15	−15	−16	−17	−17	−18	−18	−212
2. Treatment of death gratuities payable with respect to deceased members of the armed forces:													
a. Increase the death gratuity benefit for members of the armed forces to $12,000 (outlays)	Doo/a 9/11/01		−33	−9	−9	−9	−9	−8	−8	−8	−8	−8	−112
b. Exclusion from gross income of certain death gratuity payments	doa 9/10/01		−2	−1	−1	−1	−1	−1	−1	−1	−1	−1	−10
3. Exclusion for amounts received under Department of Defense Homeowners Assistance Program	pma DOE		(5)	−2	−2	−2	−2	−2	−2	−2	−2	−2	−19
4. Expansion of combat zone filing rules to contingency operations	(6)		−9	(5)	(5)	(5)	−1	−1	−1	−1	−1	−1	−13
5. Modification of membership requirement for exemption from tax for certain veterans' organizations	tyba DOE		(5)	−1	−1	−2	−2	−2	−2	−2	−2	−2	−17
6. Clarification of treatment of certain dependent care assistance programs provided to members of the uniformed services of the United States	tyba 12/31/02							*No Revenue Effect*					

APPENDIX:—Continued

ESTIMATED BUDGET EFFECTS OF TAX LEGISLATION ENACTED IN THE 108TH CONGRESS

Fiscal Years 2003–2014

[Millions of dollars]

Provision	Effective	2003	2004	2005	2006	2007	2008	2009	2010	2011	2012	2013	2014	2003–14
7. Treatment of service academy appointments as scholarships for purposes of qualified tuition programs and Coverdell Education Savings Accounts	tyba 12/31/02	....	(5)	(5)	(5)	(5)	(5)	(5)	(5)	(5)	(5)	(5)	....	−2
8. Suspension of tax-exempt status of terrorist organizations	dmbo/a DOE	*Negligible Revenue Effect*												
9. Above-the-line deduction for overnight travel expenses (not exceeding per diem levels) of National Guard and reserve members traveling more than 100 miles from home	apoi tyba 12/31/02	....	−90	−77	−78	−80	−82	−84	−87	−89	−91	−93	....	−851
10. Tax relief and assistance for families of astronauts who lose their lives in the line of duty	(7)	....	(5)	(5)	(5)	(5)	(5)	(5)	(5)	(5)	(5)	(5)	....	(5)
Total of Provisions to Improve Tax Equity for Military Personnel	....	....	**−202**	**−104**	**−105**	**−109**	**−112**	**−114**	**−118**	**−120**	**−123**	**−125**	....	**−1,236**
II. Extension of Customs User Fees														
1. Passenger and conveyance processing fee (through 3/1/05) (4)	DOE	....	75	206	....									281
2. Merchandise processing fee (through 3/1/05) (4)	DOE	....	545	480	....									1,025
Total of Extension of Customs User Fees	....	....	**619**	**686**	....									**1,305**
TOTAL OF PART FOUR: MILITARY FAMILY TAX RELIEF ACT OF 2003	....	....	**417**	**582**	**−105**	**−109**	**−112**	**−114**	**−118**	**−120**	**−123**	**−125**	....	**69**

Provision	Effective													
PART FIVE: CERTAIN PROVISIONS CONTAINED IN THE MEDICARE PRESCRIPTION DRUG, IMPROVEMENT, AND MODERNIZATION ACT OF 2003 (P.L. 108–173, signed into law by the President on December 8, 2003)														
A. Disclosure of Return Information for Purposes of Providing Transitional Assistance Under Medicare Discount Card Program	DMa DOE						*No Revenue Effect*							
B. Disclosure of Return Information Relating to Income-Related Reduction in Part B Premium Subsidy	(8)						*No Revenue Effect*							
C. Health Savings Accounts	tyba 12/31/03		−160	−474	−533	−597	−650	−704	−754	−801	−849	−897		−6,419
D. Indirect Tax Effects of Reductions in Employer Costs for Prescription Drug Insurance and Medicare Subsidies to Employers (4) (9)	(10)		2	4	1,580	2,301	2,648	2,903	3,264	3,569	4,102	4,571		24,944
E. Tax Exclusion for Certain Subsidies to Employers (4) (11)	tyba DOE				−1,130	−1,644	−1,889	−2,070	−2,322	−2,540	−2,923	−3,257		−17,775
F. Exception to Form 1099 Information Reporting Requirements for Certain Health Arrangements	pma 12/31/02		−23	−24	−24	−25	−26	−27	−27	−28	−29	−30		−263
TOTAL OF PART FIVE: CERTAIN PROVISIONS CONTAINED IN THE MEDICARE PRESCRIPTION DRUG, IMPROVEMENT, AND MODERNIZATION ACT OF 2003			**−181**	**−494**	**−107**	**35**	**83**	**102**	**161**	**200**	**301**	**387**		**487**
PART SIX: VISION 100—CENTURY OF AVIATION REAUTHORIZATION ACT (P.L. 108–176, signed into law by the President on December 12, 2003)	**(12)**						***The Joint Committee on Taxation Did Not Estimate This Provision***							
PART SEVEN: SERVICE MEMBERS CIVIL RELIEF ACT (P.L. 108–189, signed into law by the President on December 19, 2003)	**DOE**						***No Revenue Effect***							

APPENDIX:—Continued
ESTIMATED BUDGET EFFECTS OF TAX LEGISLATION ENACTED IN THE 108TH CONGRESS
Fiscal Years 2003–2014

[Millions of dollars]

Provision	Effective	2003	2004	2005	2006	2007	2008	2009	2010	2011	2012	2013	2014	2003–14
PART EIGHT: SURFACE TRANSPORTATION EXTENSION ACT OF 2004—EXTENSION OF HIGHWAY TRUST FUND AND AQUATIC RESOURCES TRUST FUND EXPENDITURE AUTHORITY (P.L. 108–202, signed into law by the President on February 29, 2004)	**DOE**						***No Revenue Effect***							
PART NINE: REVENUE PROVISIONS OF THE SOCIAL SECURITY PROTECTION ACT OF 2004 (P.L. 108–203, signed into law by the President on March 2, 2004)														
A. Technical Amendment Clarifying Treatment for Certain Purposes of Individual Work Plans Under the Ticket to Work and Self-Sufficiency Program	aiiiTWWIIA		(5)	(5)	(5)	(5)	(5)	(5)	(5)	(5)	(5)	(5)	(5)	(5)
B. Clarification Respecting the FICA and SECA Tax Exemptions for an Individual Whose Earnings are Subject to the Laws of a Totalization Agreement Partner (4)	DOE						*Negligible or No Revenue Effect*							
C. Technical Amendments (4)	various						*Negligible or No Revenue Effect*							
TOTAL OF PART NINE: REVENUE PROVISIONS OF THE SOCIAL SECURITY PROTECTION ACT OF 2004			**(5)**	**(5)**	**(5)**	**(5)**	**(5)**	**(5)**	**(5)**	**(5)**	**(5)**	**(5)**	**(5)**	**(5)**

PART TEN: PENSION FUNDING EQUITY ACT OF 2004 (13) (P.L. 108–218, signed into law by the President on April 10, 2004)

I. Pension Funding													
A. Temporary replacement of interest rate used for purposes of pension funding and PBGC variable rate premiums for 2004 and 2005; employers may elect whether to use temporary replacement interest rate in applying deduction limits; allow the use of 5.5% for purposes of applying section 415 to lump sums in 2004 and 2005 (14)	pyba 12/31/03	....	3,299	5,563	1,247	−1,261	−1,004	−2,216	−2,737	−1,888	−1,160	−828	−985
B. Partially waive deficit reduction contributions for 2 years for plans of certain employers not subject to the deficit reduction contributions rules in 2000; additional required contribution would generally be the greater of: (1) 20 percent of the otherwise applicable additional contribution or (2) the amount of the excess, if any, of (i) the expected increase in current liability due to current year accruals, over (ii) the regular funding contribution for the year; applies to passenger airlines, steel and iron ore pellets industries, and a certain tax-exempt organization (sunset plan years beginning after 12/27/05) (14) (15)	pyba 12/27/03	....	14	44	32	−46	−72	−47	−31	−33	−28	−20	−187
C. Multiemployer plan funding notices (16)	pyba 12/31/04	*No Revenue Effect*											

APPENDIX:—Continued
ESTIMATED BUDGET EFFECTS OF TAX LEGISLATION ENACTED IN THE 108TH CONGRESS
Fiscal Years 2003–2014

[Millions of dollars]

Provision	Effective	2003	2004	2005	2006	2007	2008	2009	2010	2011	2012	2013	2014	2003–14
D. Provide deferral for up to 2 years of up to 80% of certain charges to funding standard account of eligible multiemployer plans; applies to charges attributable to net experience loss for first plan year beginning after 12/31/01, that would otherwise be made for plan years beginning after 6/30/03, and before 7/1/05	DOE	....	1	4	3	−5	−4	(17)	(17)	(17)	(17)	(17)	....	−1
Total of Pension Funding	....	....	**3,314**	**5,611**	**1,282**	**−1,312**	**−1,080**	**−2,263**	**−2,768**	**−1,921**	**−1,188**	**−848**	....	**−1,173**
II. Other Provisions														
A. 2-year extension of transition rule to pension funding requirements	pyba 12/31/03	....	2	6	2	−3	−2	−2	−2	−1	−1	(5)	....	−1
B. Procedures applicable to disputes involving pension plan withdrawal liability (18)	(19)						*Negligible Revenue Effect*							
C. Sense of Congress Regarding Defined Benefit Pension System Reform	DOE						*No Revenue Effect*							
D. Allow employers to transfer excess defined benefit plan assets to a special account for health benefits of retirees (sunset 12/31/13)	DOE	....	....	....	18	38	40	40	40	40	40	40	....	298
E. Repeal of section 809 related to the reduction in policyholder dividends	tyba 12/31/04	....	....	−25	−33	−43	−47	−43	−38	−39	−39	−39	....	−347

F. Limit 501(c)(15) to organizations with gross receipts of $600,000 and premiums at least 50% of gross receipts; and to mutual insurance companies with gross receipts less than $150,000 and premium income at least 35% of gross receipts; and modify definition of insurance company. Transition relief for insurance companies in receivership or liquidation on April 1, 2004, limited to lesser of four years or time spent in receivership	tyba 12/31/03	....	47	105	118	120	127	134	137	141	146	152	....	1,228
Total of Other Provisions	....	....	**49**	**86**	**105**	**112**	**118**	**129**	**137**	**141**	**146**	**153**	....	**1,178**
TOTAL OF PART TEN: PENSION FUNDING EQUITY ACT OF 2004	....	....	**3,363**	**5,697**	**1,387**	**−1,200**	**−962**	**−2,134**	**−2,631**	**−1,780**	**−1,042**	**−695**	....	**5**
PART ELEVEN: SURFACE TRANSPORTATION EXTENSION ACT OF 2004, PART II—EXTENSION OF HIGHWAY TRUST FUND AND AQUATIC RESOURCES TRUST FUND EXPENDITURE AUTHORITY (P.L. 108–224, signed into law by the President on April 30, 2004)	**DOE**						***No Revenue Effect***							
PART TWELVE: SURFACE TRANSPORTATION EXTENSION ACT OF 2004, PART III—EXTENSION OF HIGHWAY TRUST FUND AND AQUATIC RESOURCES TRUST FUND EXPENDITURE AUTHORITY (P.L. 108–263, signed into law by the President on June 30, 2004)	**DOE**						***No Revenue Effect***							

APPENDIX:—Continued

ESTIMATED BUDGET EFFECTS OF TAX LEGISLATION ENACTED IN THE 108TH CONGRESS

Fiscal Years 2003–2014

[Millions of dollars]

Provision	Effective	2003	2004	2005	2006	2007	2008	2009	2010	2011	2012	2013	2014	2003–14
PART THIRTEEN: SURFACE TRANSPORTATION EXTENSION ACT OF 2004, PART IV—EXTENSION OF HIGHWAY TRUST FUND AND AQUATIC RESOURCES TRUST FUND EXPENDITURE AUTHORITY (P.L. 108–280, signed into law by the President on July 30, 2004)	**DOE**						***No Revenue Effect***							
PART FOURTEEN: SURFACE TRANSPORTATION EXTENSION ACT OF 2004, PART V—EXTENSION OF HIGHWAY TRUST FUND AND AQUATIC RESOURCES TRUST FUND EXPENDITURE AUTHORITY (P.L. 108–310, signed into law by the President on September 30, 2004)	**DOE**						***No Revenue Effect***							
PART FIFTEEN: WORKING FAMILIES TAX RELIEF ACT OF 2004 (P.L. 108–311, signed into law by the President on October 4, 2004)														
I. Tax Reduction Provisions:														
1. Extension of Family Tax Provisions:														
a. Extend $1,000 child tax credit through 12/31/09	tyba 12/31/04			−2,638	−13,193	−13,198	−13,227	−12,376	−6,942					−61,574
b. Extend marriage penalty relief through 12/31/08	tyba 12/31/04			−5,415	−5,412	−3,050	−1,493	−323						−15,693
c. Extend 10% bracket through 12/31/10	tyba 12/31/04			−4,262	−6,423	−6,796	−4,330	−3,229	−3,315	−1,006				−29,361

2. Accelerate refundability of child credit to 2004	tyba 12/31/03		−1,993									−1,993
3. Extend individual AMT relief through 12/31/05	tyba 12/31/04		−9,031	−13,546								−22,577
4. Inclusion of combat pay in earned income for purposes of the child tax credit and for purposes of earned income credit at taxpayer's election	([20])		−49	−50	−24	−21	−18	−19	−17			−199
Total of Tax Reduction Provisions			**−23,388**	**−38,624**	**−23,068**	**−19,071**	**−15,946**	**−10,276**	**−1,023**			**−131,396**
II. Uniform Definition of a Qualifying Child for the Dependency Exemption, the Child Credit, the EIC, the Dependent Care Credit, and Head-of-Household Filing Status	**tyba 12/31/04**		**−84**	**−206**	**−209**	**−218**	**−225**	**−229**	**−183**	**−75**	**−75**	**−76**	**−1,580**
III. Extension of Certain Expiring Provisions												
1. Extension of the R&E credit (sunset 12/31/05)	epoia 6/30/04		−3,480	−1,986	−936	−678	−390	−90				−7,560
2. Parity in the application of certain limits to mental health benefits (sunset 12/31/05)([21])	DOE		−4	−43	−10							−57
3. Work opportunity tax credit (sunset 12/31/05)	wpoifibwa 12/31/03		−278	−181	−81	−39	−23	−9	−1			−614
4. Welfare-to-work tax credit (sunset 12/31/05)	wpoifibwa 12/31/03		−35	−39	−28	−14	−7	−4	−1	([5])		−127
5. Qualified zone academy bonds (sunset 12/31/05)	oia 12/31/03		−3	−10	−20	−27	−28	−28	−28	−28	−28	−28	−231
6. Increase in limit on cover over of rum excise tax revenues (from $10.50 to $13.25 per proof gallon) to Puerto Rico and the Virgin Islands (sunset 12/31/05)	abiUSa 12/31/03		−151	−18								−169
7. Extension of enhanced deduction for qualified computer contributions (sunset for taxable years beginning after 12/31/05)	cmd tyba 12/31/03		−198	−62								−260

APPENDIX:—Continued
ESTIMATED BUDGET EFFECTS OF TAX LEGISLATION ENACTED IN THE 108TH CONGRESS
Fiscal Years 2003–2014

[Millions of dollars]

Provision	Effective	2003	2004	2005	2006	2007	2008	2009	2010	2011	2012	2013	2014	2003–14
8. Above-the-line deduction for teacher classroom expenses capped at $250 annually (sunset 12/31/05)	tyba 12/31/03			−227	−192									−419
9. Expensing of "Brownfields" environmental remediation costs (sunset 12/31/05)	epoia 12/31/03			−409	−93	32	38	39	34	30	26	22	20	−261
10. New York Liberty Zone bond provisions (22):														
a. Extend authority to issue Liberty Zone bonds (sunset 12/31/09); add municipal assistance corporation to eligible advance refunding bonds	generally DOE			−4	−18	−34	−47	−58	−65	−65	−65	−65	−65	−486
b. Extend authority to issue advance refunding bonds (sunset 12/31/05)	generally DOE			−6	−15	−16	−15	−12	−10	−8	−6	−4	−2	−93
11. Tax incentives for investment in the District of Columbia (sunset 12/31/05)	(23)			−161	−56	−18	−12	−17	−62	−74	−42	−42	−37	−522
12. Combined employment tax reporting (sunset 12/31/05)	do/a DOE	No Revenue Effect												
13. Treatment of nonrefundable personal credits under the individual alternative minimum tax (sunset 12/31/05) (24)	tyba 12/31/03			−332	−260									−592
14. Tax credit for electricity production from wind, closed-loop biomass, and poultry litter—facilities placed in service date (sunset 12/31/05)	fpisa 12/31/03			−44	−75	−97	−111	−127	−139	−144	−149	−151	−126	−1,163
15. Extension of suspension of 100% of taxable income limit with respect to marginal production (sunset 12/31/05)	tyba 12/31/03			−78	−16									−94

16. Indian employment tax credit (sunset 12/31/05)	DOE	....	−25	−34	−10								−68
17. Accelerated depreciation for business property on Indian reservation (sunset 12/31/05)	DOE	....	−150	−261	−97	21	71	111	90	48	5	−10	−173
18. Disclosure of tax return information to carry out administration of income contingent repayment of student loans (sunset 12/31/05) (4)	DOE	....			*No Revenue Effect*								
19. Tax credit for qualified electric vehicles (100% benefit through 12/31/05)	ppisa 12/31/03	....	−5	−1	(25)	(25)	(25)	(25)	(25)	(25)			−5
20. Deduction for clean-fuel vehicles (100% benefit through 12/31/05)	ppisa 12/31/03	....	−119	−16	25	16	12	7	2				−72
21. Disclosures relating to terrorist activities (sunset 12/31/05):													
a. Extension of authority to make disclosures regarding terrorist activities	dmo/a DOE	....					*No Revenue Effect*						
b. Technical correction regarding disclosure of taxpayer identity to law enforcement officials investigating terrorist activities	(26)	....					*No Revenue Effect*						
22. Joint Committee on Taxation report and joint hearing on IRS strategic plans (sunset 12/31/05)	DOE	....					*No Revenue Effect*						
23. Availability of Archer medical savings accounts (sunset 12/31/05)	1/1/04	....					*Negligible Revenue Effect*						
Total of Extension of Certain Expiring Provisions	....	....	**−5,709**	**−3,376**	**−1,290**	**−868**	**−540**	**−255**	**−199**	**−216**	**−263**	**−248**	**−12,966**
IV. Tax Technical Correction Provisions	**DOE**	....					***No Revenue Effect***						
TOTAL OF PART FIFTEEN: WORKING FAMILIES TAX RELIEF ACT OF 2004	....	....	**−29,181**	**−42,206**	**−24,567**	**−20,157**	**−16,711**	**−10,760**	**−1,405**	**−291**	**−338**	**−324**	**−145,942**

APPENDIX:—Continued
ESTIMATED BUDGET EFFECTS OF TAX LEGISLATION ENACTED IN THE 108TH CONGRESS
Fiscal Years 2003–2014

[Millions of dollars]

Provision	Effective	2003	2004	2005	2006	2007	2008	2009	2010	2011	2012	2013	2014	2003–14
PART SIXTEEN: CLARIFY TAX TREATMENT OF BONDS AND OTHER OBLIGATIONS ISSUED BY THE GOVERNMENT OF AMERICAN SAMOA (P.L. 108–326, signed into law by the President on October 16, 2004)	oia DOE	*Negligible Revenue Effect*												
PART SEVENTEEN: AMERICAN JOBS CREATION ACT OF 2004 (P.L. 108–357, signed into law by the President on October 22, 2004)														
I. Provisions Relating to Repeal of Exclusion for Extraterritorial Income														
1. Repeal of exclusion for extraterritorial income (27)	ta 12/31/04			354	1,317	3,528	5,475	5,737	5,985	6,275	6,562	6,840	7,126	49,199
2. Deduction relating to income attributable to United States production activities	tyba 12/31/04			−2,054	−3,052	−4,396	−6,241	−6,722	−8,841	−10,741	−11,122	−11,525	−11,815	−76,509
Total of Provisions Relating to Repeal of Exclusion for Extraterritorial Income				**−1,700**	**−1,735**	**−868**	**−766**	**−985**	**−2,856**	**−4,466**	**−4,560**	**−4,685**	**−4,689**	**−27,310**

II. Business Tax Incentives												
A. Small Business Expensing—increase section 179 expensing from $25,000 to $100,000 and increase the phaseout threshold amount from $200,000 to $400,000; include software in section 179 property; and extend indexing of both the deduction limit and the phaseout threshold (sunset after 2007)	tyba 12/31/05		−3,814	−6,636	−488	3,786	2,416	1,665	1,116	609	249	−1,095
B. Depreciation												
1. 15-year straight-line cost recovery for qualified leasehold improvements (sunset after 2005)	ppisa DOE	−65	−147	−185	−181	−174	−158	−151	−159	−156	−149	−1,523
2. 15-year straight-line cost recovery for qualified restaurant improvements (sunset after 2005)	ppisa DOE	−141	−33	−40	−40	−40	−40	−40	−40	−40	−40	−494
C. Community Revitalization												
1. Modification of targeted areas and low-income communities designated for new markets tax credit	DMA DOE	*No Revenue Effect*										
2. Expansion of designated renewal community area based on 2000 census data	(28)	−35	−10	−10	−9	−9	(29)	8	9	9	8	−37
3. Modification of income requirement for census tracts within high migration rural counties	(30)	*No Revenue Effect*										
D. S Corporation Reform and Simplification												
1. Treat members of family as one shareholder (6 generations; multiple families per S corporation) (includes interaction with line 2. below)	generally tyba 12/31/04	−1	−4	−6	−8	−9	−9	−10	−10	−10	−10	−76
2. Increase in number of eligible shareholders to 100	tyba 12/31/04	−18	−43	−56	−66	−74	−79	−82	−83	−84	−84	−669
3. Expansion of bank S corporation eligible shareholders to include IRAs	DOE	−23	−34	−36	−37	−39	−41	−43	−45	−47	−49	−394
4. Disregard unexercised powers of appointment in determining potential current beneficiaries of ESBT.	tyba 12/31/04	*Negligible Revenue Effect*										
5. Transfer of suspended losses incident to divorce	tosa 12/31/04	−1	−2	−2	−2	−3	−3	−3	−3	−3	−3	−25

APPENDIX:—Continued
ESTIMATED BUDGET EFFECTS OF TAX LEGISLATION ENACTED IN THE 108TH CONGRESS
Fiscal Years 2003–2014

[Millions of dollars]

Provision	Effective	2003	2004	2005	2006	2007	2008	2009	2010	2011	2012	2013	2014	2003–14
6. Use of passive activity loss by subchapter S trust income beneficiaries	tma 12/31/04			−1	−1	−1	−1	−1	−1	−1	−1	−1	−1	−7
7. Exclusion of investment securities income from passive income test for bank S corporations	tyba 12/31/04	Negligible Revenue Effect												
8. Relief from inadvertently invalid qualified subchapter S subsidiary elections and terminations	ematma 12/31/04			−2	−1	−1	−1	−1	−1	−1	−1	−1	−1	−14
9. Information returns for qualified subchapter S subsidiaries	tyba 12/31/04	No Revenue Effect												
10. Repayment of loan for qualifying employer securities held by an ESOP	dma 12/31/97			−1	(5)	(5)	(5)	(5)	(5)	(5)	−1	−1	−1	−5
E. Other Business Incentives														
1. Repeal of 4.3-cent General Fund excise taxes on railroad diesel fuel and inland waterway fuel (reduce excise taxes by 1 cent/gallon from 1/1/05 through 6/30/05, 2 cents/gallon from 7/1/05 through 12/31/06, and 4.3 cents/gallon thereafter)	1/1/05			−33	−74	−139	−170	−174	−179	−184	−189	−193	−198	−1,532
2. Modification of application of the income forecast method of accounting	ppisa DOE			−182	−139	−81	−32	−24	−24	−28	−31	−35	−39	−615
3. Improvements related to real estate investment trusts	tyba 12/31/00 & tyba DOE	Negligible Revenue Effect												
4. Special rules for certain film and television production (sunset taxable years beginning after 12/31/08)	pca DOE			−82	−99	−94	−60	−1	62	93	81	40	18	−42

5. Provide a 50% tax credit for certain expenditures for maintaining railroad tracks (sunset 12/31/07)	epoid tyba 12/31/04		−63	−121	−109	−88	−59	−38	−21	−4	(5)	(5)	−501
6. Suspension of the occupational taxes relating to distilled spirits, wine, and beer (sunset 6/30/08)	7/1/05		−66	−78	−78	−12							−234
7. Modification of unrelated business income limitation on investment in certain debt-financed properties of SBICs	(31)		−1	−1	−1	−1	−1	−1	−1	−1	−1	−1	−9
8. Tonnage tax election for income from international shipping	tyba DOE		−2	−4	−5	−6	−6	−6	−6	−7	−7	−8	−57
F. Exclusion of Incentive Stock Options and Employee Stock Purchase Plan Stock Options From Wages	saptoea DOE						*No Revenue Effect*						
Total of Business Tax Incentives			**−717**	**−4,605**	**−7,480**	**−1,203**	**3,171**	**1,898**	**1,196**	**631**	**79**	**−309**	**−7,329**
III. Provisions Relating to Tax Relief for Agriculture and Small Manufacturers													
A. Volumetric Ethanol Excise Tax Credit													
1. Provide excise tax credit (in lieu of reduced tax rate on gasoline) to certain blenders of alcohol fuel mixtures (sunset 12/31/10)	fsoua 12/31/04						*No Revenue Effect*						
2. Provide that all alcohol fuels excise tax credits and payments are paid from the General Fund (32) (33)	fsoua 12/31/04								1,131	1,559	1,586	1,614	5,890
3. Repeal reduced-rate sales of gasoline for blending with alcohol and reduced-rate sales of alcohol fuel blends	fsoua 12/31/04		16	23	23	23	23	23	23	22	22	22	220
4. Provide outlay payments (in lieu of excise tax credits and refunds) to producers of alcohol fuel mixtures	fsoua 12/31/04						*No Revenue Effect*						

APPENDIX:—Continued
ESTIMATED BUDGET EFFECTS OF TAX LEGISLATION ENACTED IN THE 108TH CONGRESS
Fiscal Years 2003–2014

[Millions of dollars]

Provision	Effective	2003	2004	2005	2006	2007	2008	2009	2010	2011	2012	2013	2014	2003–14
5. Transfer full amount of alcohol fuel excise taxes to the Highway Trust Fund (i.e., repeal 2.5/2.8 cents transfer to General Fund)	fsoua 9/30/04	*No Revenue Effect*												
6. Provide excise tax credits for biodiesel used to produce a qualified fuel mixture [34] ($1.00/gallon for agribiodiesel and $0.50/gallon for biodiesel) and provide that the excise tax credits are paid from the General Fund (sunset 12/31/06) [35]	fsoua 12/31/04			−33	−57	−16								−107
7. Provide outlay payments (in lieu of excise tax credits and refunds) to producers of biodiesel fuel mixtures	fsoua 12/31/04	*Negligible Revenue Effect*												
8. Extension of section 40 alcohol fuels income tax credit (sunset 12/31/10)	DOE						−2	−6	−8	−8	−6	−3		−34
9. Biodiesel income tax credit—provide income tax credits for biodiesel fuel and biodiesel used to produce a qualified fuel mixture ($1.00/gallon for agribiodiesel and $0.50/gallon for biodiesel) (sunset 12/31/06).	fpasoua 12/31/04	*Estimate Included in Item 6. Above*												
10. Information reporting for persons claiming ethanol and biodiesel tax benefits	1/1/05	*Negligible Revenue Effect*												
B. Agricultural Incentives														
1. Special rules for livestock sold on account of weather-related conditions	trda 12/31/02			−18	−7	−4	−3	−3	−3	4	6	2	(29)	−27

Provision	Effective												
2. Payment of dividends on stock of cooperatives without reducing patronage dividends	di tyba DOE		(5)	(5)	−1	−1	−1	−1	−2	−2	−3	−4	−15
3. Allow small ethanol producer cooperatives to pass the small producer credit through to cooperative members	tyea DOE		−8	−8	−9	−10	−11	−12	−10	−6	−3		−77
4. Extend income averaging to fishermen and provide that income averaging for farmers and fishermen will not increase AMT liability	tyba 12/31/03		−3	−3	−4	−5	−6	−7	−7	−8	−9	−10	−61
5. Capital gains treatment to apply to outright sales of timber by landowner	sota 12/31/04		*Negligible Revenue Effect*										
6. Modify cooperative marketing to include value-added processing involving animals	tyba DOE		−1	−2	−4	−5	−6	−7	−9	−10	−11	−12	−68
7. Extend declaratory judgment relief to farm cooperatives	pfa DOE		*Estimate Included in Line Above*										
8. Certain expenses of rural letter carriers	tyba 12/31/03		−2	−3	−3	−3	−3	−3	−4	−4	−4	−4	−33
9. Treatment of certain income of electric cooperatives (sunset 12/31/06)	tyba DOE		−10	−19	−8								−38
10. Exclude from gross income and employment taxes payments made to individuals under NHSC Loan Repayment Program and certain State loan repayment programs	tyba 12/31/03		−2	−2	−2	−4	−5	−6	−8	−11	−14	−18	−72
11. Modified safe-harbor rules for timber REITs	tyba DOE		(5)	(5)	−1	−1	−2	−2	−3	−4	−5	−5	−23
12. Deduction of the first $10,000 of qualified reforestation costs	epoia DOE		−55	−37	−25	−11	−1	2	8	13	20	22	−64
C. Incentive for Small Manufacturers													
1. Net income from publicly traded partnerships treated as qualifying income for regulated investment company	tyba DOE		−1	−2	−3	−5	−5	−6	−6	−7	−7	−7	−49
2. Simplification of excise tax imposed on bows and arrows (36)	asbmpoi 30da DOE		−1	−1	−1	−1	−1	−1	−1	−1	−1	−1	−9

APPENDIX:—Continued

ESTIMATED BUDGET EFFECTS OF TAX LEGISLATION ENACTED IN THE 108TH CONGRESS

Fiscal Years 2003–2014

[Millions of dollars]

Provision	Effective	2003	2004	2005	2006	2007	2008	2009	2010	2011	2012	2013	2014	2003–14
3. Reduce excise tax on fishing tackle boxes to 3 percent (37)	asbmpoia 12/31/04			−1	−1	−1	−1	−1	−1	−1	−1	−1	−1	−11
4. Repeal excise tax on sonar devices suitable for finding fish (38)	asbmpoia 12/31/04			(5)	(5)	(5)	(5)	(5)	(5)	−1	−1	−1	−1	−4
5. Charitable contribution deduction for certain expenses in support of Native Alaska subsistence whaling	cma 12/31/04			(5)	(5)	(5)	(5)	(5)	(5)	(5)	(5)	(5)	(5)	−4
6. Extended placed in service date for bonus depreciation for certain aircraft (excluding aircraft used in the transportation industry)	ppisa 9/10/01 (39)			−1,265	−175	576	346	271	194	54				
7. Special placed in service rule for bonus depreciation for certain property subject to syndication	sa 6/4/04			−27	8	6	4	4	4	2	1			
8. Expensing of capital costs incurred for production in complying with Environmental Protection Agency sulfur regulations for small refiners	epoia 12/31/02			−16	−8	−12	−28	−53	−21	3	4	5	6	−119
9. Credit for small refiners for production for diesel fuel in compliance with Environmental Protection Agency sulfur regulations for small refiners	epoia 12/31/02	*Estimate Included in Line Above*												
10. Modification to small issue bonds—increase capital expenditure limit from $10 million to $20 million (maximum bond limit remains at $10 million)	bia 9/30/09								−6	−14	−22	−30	−38	−110

11. Oil and gas from marginal wells	pi tyba 12/31/04						*No Revenue Effect*						
Total of Provisions Relating to Tax Relief for Agriculture and Small Manufacturers			**−1,427**	**−294**	**511**	**293**	**194**	**139**	**1,151**	**1,522**	**1,543**	**1,563**	**5,185**
IV. Tax Reform and Simplification for United States Businesses													
1. Interest expense allocation rules	tyba 12/31/08						−908	−2,487	−2,586	−2,689	−2,797	−2,909	−14,376
2. Recharacterize overall domestic loss	lii tyba 12/31/06				−57	−680	−713	−756	−793	−829	−862	−895	−5,585
3. Apply look-through rules for dividends from noncontrolled section 902 corporations	tyba 12/31/02		−662	−51	−23	−6	−1	(40)	(40)	(40)	(40)	(40)	−743
4. Base differences and reduction to 2 foreign tax credit baskets	(41)		−8	−13	−615	−900	−927	−1,002	−1,039	−1,078	−1,119	−1,161	−7,862
5. Attribution of stock ownership through partnerships in determining section 902 and 960 credits	tyba DOE		−1	−3	−3	−3	−3	−3	−3	−3	−3	−3	−28
6. Foreign tax credit treatment of deemed payments under section 367(d)	ataro/a 8/5/97		−26	−5	−5	−5	−5	−5	−5	−5	−5	−5	−71
7. United States property not to include certain assets of controlled foreign corporations	(42)		−3	−20	−21	−22	−23	−24	−25	−27	−29	−31	−225
8. Translation of foreign taxes	tyba 12/31/04						*Negligible Revenue Effect*						
9. Eliminate secondary withholding tax with respect to dividends paid by certain foreign corporations	pma 12/31/04		−2	−3	−3	−3	−3	−3	−3	−3	−3	−3	−29
10. Provide equal treatment for interest paid by foreign partnerships and foreign corporations doing business in the U.S	tyba 12/31/03		−3	−2	−2	−2	−2	−2	−2	−3	−3	−3	−24
11. Treatment of certain dividends of regulated investment companies (sunset after 3 years)	(43)		−7	−59	−63	−57							−186
12. Look-through treatment under subpart F for sales of partnership interests	(42)		−39	−91	−96	−101	−106	−111	−116	−122	−129	−137	−1,048

APPENDIX:—Continued
ESTIMATED BUDGET EFFECTS OF TAX LEGISLATION ENACTED IN THE 108TH CONGRESS
Fiscal Years 2003–2014

[Millions of dollars]

Provision	Effective	2003	2004	2005	2006	2007	2008	2009	2010	2011	2012	2013	2014	2003–14
13. Repeal of rules applicable to foreign personal holding companies and foreign investment companies, personal holding company rules as they apply to foreign corporations, and include in subpart F personal service contract income, as defined under the foreign personal holding company rules	(42)			−25	−65	−73	−81	−91	−102	−114	−128	−143	−162	−984
14. Determination of foreign personal holding company income with respect to transactions in commodities	teia 12/31/04			−4	−10	−10	−10	−10	−11	−11	−11	−11	−12	−100
15. Modify treatment of aircraft leasing and shipping income (44)	(42)			−33	−172	−98	−75	−76	−88	−98	−108	−118	−129	−995
16. Modification of exceptions under subpart F for active financing income	(42)	Negligible Revenue Effect												
17. 10-year foreign tax credit carryforward; 1-year foreign tax credit carryback	(45)			−349	−271	−338	−500	−668	−779	−857	−942	−1,036	−1,191	−6,931
18. Modify FIRPTA rules for REITs	tyba DOE			−2	−7	−10	−12	−14	−15	−17	−19	−21	−23	−140
19. Exclusion of certain horse-racing and dog-racing gambling winnings from the income of nonresident alien individuals	wma DOE			−1	−3	−3	−3	−3	−3	−3	−3	−3	−3	−27
20. Reduce withholding tax applicable to dividends paid to Puerto Rico companies to 10%	Dpa DOE			−5	−7	−8	−9	−10	−10	−11	−12	−13	−14	−99
21. Repeal the 90% limitation on the use of foreign tax credits against the AMT	tyba 12/31/04			−265	−395	−376	−361	−348	−338	−329	−323	−319	−317	−3,371

22. Incentives to reinvest foreign earnings in the United States	(46)		2,788	−2,119	−1,267	−838	−553	−379	−300	−264	−192	−137	−3,261
23. Delay in effective date of final regulations governing exclusion of income from international operation of ships or aircraft	(47)		−24	−4	(5)	(5)	(5)	(5)	(5)	(5)	(5)	(5)	−28
24. Study of earnings stripping provisions	DOE					*No Revenue Effect*							
25. Interaction			3	192	248	253	410	429	450	473	497	523	3,478
Total of Tax Reform and Simplification for United States Businesses			**1,332**	**−3,108**	**−2,823**	**−3,415**	**−4,054**	**−5,689**	**−5,862**	**−6,096**	**−6,309**	**−6,612**	**−42,635**
V. Deduction of State and Local General Sales Taxes (sunset 12/31/05)	**tyba 12/31/03**		**−3,080**	**−1,915**									**−4,995**
VI. Fair and Equitable Tobacco Reform Provisions													
A. Revenue effects	DOE		1,098	1,089	964	964	964	964	964	964	964	1,205	10,140
B. Outlay effects (4)	DOE		−1,464	−964	−964	−964	−964	−964	−964	−964	−964	−964	−10,140
Total of Fair and Equitable Tobacco Reform Provisions			**−366**	**125**								**241**	
VII. Miscellaneous Provisions													
1. Qualified green building and sustainable design project bonds ($2 billion authority) (sunset 9/30/09)	bia 12/31/04		−3	−9	−15	−22	−27	−31	−31	−31	−31	−31	−231
2. Exclusion of gain or loss on sale or exchange of certain Brownfield sites from unrelated business taxable income (sunset 12/31/09)	PAa 12/31/04		1	1	1	−6	−18	−28	−38	−49	−34	−15	−185
3. Civil rights tax relief	josoa DOE		−5	−21	−29	−31	−34	−36	−38	−42	−44	−47	−327
4. 7-year recovery period for certain track facilities	ppisa DOE & before 2008		−13	−19	−26	−23	−14	−9	−6	−3	3	9	−101
5. Permit life insurance companies tax-free distributions from policyholder surplus accounts (sunset 12/31/06)	tyba 12/31/04		−78	−54	−51	−48	−48	−48	−49	−51	−52	−54	−533
6. Treat certain Alaska pipeline property as 7-year property	generally ppisa 12/31/04											−150	−150

APPENDIX:—Continued
ESTIMATED BUDGET EFFECTS OF TAX LEGISLATION ENACTED IN THE 108TH CONGRESS
Fiscal Years 2003–2014

[Millions of dollars]

Provision	Effective	2003	2004	2005	2006	2007	2008	2009	2010	2011	2012	2013	2014	2003–14
7. Extension of enhanced oil recovery credit to Alaska gas processing facilities	cpoii tyba 12/31/04						−32	−91	−101	−61	−23	1	11	−295
8. Method of accounting for naval shipbuilders	ca DOE			−26	−52	−99	−62	−42	−57	−35	−32	−38	−52	−495
9. Modify minimum cost requirement for transfer of excess defined benefit assets	tyea DOE	*Negligible Revenue Effect*												
10. Extension and expansion of credit for electricity produced from certain renewable resources—expand section 45 credit to include closed-loop biomass, open-loop biomass, geothermal solar, small irrigation, municipal solid waste, and refined coal to list of qualified energy resources	eposfqfa 10/22/04			−218	−279	−322	−366	−375	−261	−177	−135	−94	−49	−2,278
11. Allow the section 40 and section 45 credits to be taken against the AMT	tyea DOE			−10	−5	−4	−3	−2	−2	2	6	1	−3	−21
12. Inclusion of primary and secondary medical strategies for children and adults with sickle cell disease as medical assistance under the Medicaid program (48)	DOE	*No Revenue Effect*												
13. Temporary suspension of customs duty on certain ceiling fans (sunset 12/31/06) (4)	15da DOE			−19	−20	−5								−44

14. Temporary suspension of customs duty on certain steam generators (sunset 12/31/08) and certain reactor vessel heads and pressurizers used in nuclear facilities (sunset 12/31/08)(4)	15da DOE & DOE	....	−1	−1	−3	−3	−1	....	....	....	....	....	−9
Total of Miscellaneous Provisions	....	....	**−372**	**−459**	**−553**	**−596**	**−652**	**−573**	**−433**	**−360**	**−288**	**−381**	**−4,669**
VIII. Revenue Provisions													
A. Provisions to Reduce Tax Avoidance Through Individual and Corporate Expatriation													
1. Tax treatment of expatriated entities	tyea 3/4/03	....	96	50	59	63	67	77	90	100	109	119	830
2. Excise tax on stock compensation of insiders in expatriated corporations (rate tracks capital gains rate, applies to executives in affiliated groups)	generally 3/4/03	....	18	7	7	7	8	11	11	11	11	11	102
3. Reinsurance of United States risks in foreign jurisdictions	rra DOE	....	(29)	(29)	(29)	(29)	(29)	(29)	(29)	(29)	(29)	(29)	5
4. Revision of tax rules for individuals who expatriate	iwea 6/3/04	....	23	21	24	28	32	37	43	49	56	64	377
5. Reporting of taxable mergers and acquisitions	aa DOE	....	2	3	3	3	3	3	3	3	3	3	29
6. Studies	DOE	....					*No Revenue Effect*						....
B. Provisions Relating to Tax Shelters													
1. Provisions relating to reportable transactions and tax shelters	(49)	....	50	119	120	124	131	139	150	164	179	195	1,371
2. Modifications to the substantial understatement penalty for nonreportable transactions	tyba DOE	....	....	7	15	23	26	30	34	38	38	38	249
3. Modification of actions to enjoin certain conduct related to tax shelters and reportable transactions	da DOE	....					*Negligible Revenue Effect*						....
4. Impose a civil penalty (of up to $10,000) on failure to report interest in foreign financial accounts	voa DOE	....	....	(29)	(29)	(29)	(29)	(29)	(29)	(29)	(29)	(29)	3
5. Regulation of individuals practicing before the Department of Treasury	ata DOE	....					*No Revenue Effect*						....

APPENDIX:—Continued
ESTIMATED BUDGET EFFECTS OF TAX LEGISLATION ENACTED IN THE 108TH CONGRESS
Fiscal Years 2003–2014

[Millions of dollars]

Provision	Effective	2003	2004	2005	2006	2007	2008	2009	2010	2011	2012	2013	2014	2003–14
6. Treatment of stripped interest in bond and preferred stock funds	pada DOE			13	11	8	5	3	(29)	(29)	(29)	(29)	(29)	40
7. Minimum holding period for foreign tax credit on withholding tax on income other than dividends	apoamt 30da DOE			3	3	3	3	4	4	4	4	5	5	38
8. Disallowance of certain partnership loss transfers with partner level loss limits for transfer of interest in electing investment partnerships	ctada DOE			28	56	62	60	54	47	43	43	44	44	481
9. No reduction of basis under section 734 in stock held by partnership in corporate partner	Da DOE			6	12	19	23	27	28	30	33	34	36	249
10. Repeal of special rules for FASITs	after 12/31/04			(29)	(29)	(29)	(29)	(29)	(29)	(29)	(29)	(29)	(29)	5
11. Limitation on transfer or importation of built-in losses	ta DOE			51	99	147	164	180	198	218	240	264	290	1,851
12. Clarification of banking business for purposes of determining investment of earnings in United States property	DOE			40	34	34	36	38	40	42	44	46	50	404
13. Deny deduction for interest paid to the IRS on underpayments involving certain tax motivated transactions	tyba DOE				1	1	3	4	4	4	4	4	4	29
14. Clarification of rules for payment of estimated tax for certain deemed asset sales	toa DOE			55	28	7	3	3	3	4	4	5	5	117

15. Exclusion of like-kind exchange property from nonrecognition treatment on the sale or exchange of a principal residence	soea DOE	....	11	13	15	17	19	21	23	25	27	29	200
16. Prevent mismatching of deductions and income inclusions in transactions with related foreign persons	pao/a DOE	....	40	82	80	33	35	37	39	41	43	45	475
17. Deposits made to suspend the running of interest on potential underpayments	Dma DOE	....	150	−6	−6	−6	−6	−6	−7	−7	−7	−7	93
18. Authorize IRS to enter into installment agreements that provide for partial payment	iaeio/a DOE	....	52	10	5	(25)	(25)	(25)	(25)	(25)	(25)	(25)	67
19. Affirmation of consolidated return regulation authority	(50)						*Negligible Revenue Effect*						
20. Expanded disallowance of deduction for interest on convertible debt	diia 10/3/04	....	94	90	94	96	98	101	103	106	109	113	1,004
21. Reform the tax treatment for leasing transactions with tax-indifferent parties with additional coverage of Indian and intangible assets and assets subject to a fixed purchase price option with an exception for aircraft and vessels	(51)	....	589	934	1,416	1,955	2,474	2,923	3,352	3,805	4,293	4,819	26,560
C. Reduction of Fuel Tax Evasion													
1. Exemption from certain excise taxes for mobile machinery vehicles	(52)	....	76	95	95	95	95	95	95	95	95	95	931
2. Modified definition of off-highway vehicle	(52)						*Negligible Revenue Effect*						
3. Aviation jet fuel—move point of taxation of aviation fuel to the rack; provide that certain refueler trucks are treated as terminals	(53)	....	297	429	433	436	439	439	437	435	434	432	4,211
4. Dye fuel mechanically, security standards, and related penalties	(54)	....	....	42	46	47	47	47	47	47	47	47	417
5. Elimination of administrative review for taxable use of dyed fuel	Paa DOE						*Negligible Revenue Effect*						
6. Extension of penalty on untaxed chemically altered fuel mixtures	DOE						*Negligible Revenue Effect*						

APPENDIX:—Continued

ESTIMATED BUDGET EFFECTS OF TAX LEGISLATION ENACTED IN THE 108TH CONGRESS

Fiscal Years 2003–2014

[Millions of dollars]

Provision	Effective	2003	2004	2005	2006	2007	2008	2009	2010	2011	2012	2013	2014	2003–14
7. Termination of dyed diesel use by intercity buses	fsa 12/31/04	Negligible Revenue Effect												
8. Authority to inspect on-site records	DOE	Negligible Revenue Effect												
9. Assessable penalty for refusal of entry	1/1/05	Negligible Revenue Effect												
10. Registration of all pipeline or vessel operators required for exemption of bulk transfers; Secretary must publish list of registered persons (55)	3/1/05			56	125	127	128	129	129	130	129	129	129	1,211
11. Display of registration and penalty for failure to display	1/1/05 & pia 12/31/04	Revenue Effects Included in Line 10.												
12. Penalties for failure to register and failure to report	pia 12/31/04			1	2	2	2	2	2	2	2	2	2	20
13. Registration of persons within foreign trade zones	1/1/05	Revenue Effects Included in Line 10.												
14. Certain reports filed electronically	1/1/06	Revenue Effects Included in Line 10.												
15. Taxable fuel refunds for certain ultimate vendors	1/1/05	Negligible Revenue Effect												
16. Two-party exchanges	DOE	Negligible Revenue Effect												
17. Modifications to heavy vehicle use tax	tpba DOE			121	124	126	128	131	131	133	135	137	139	1,305
18. Dedication of revenue from certain penalties to the Highway Trust Fund	Pao/a DOE	No Revenue Effect												
19. Simplify the heavy truck tire tax (56)	(57)	Negligible Revenue Effect												
20. Taxation of transmix and diesel fuel blendstocks.	frsoua 12/31/04			74	107	108	108	108	108	108	108	107	106	1,043
21. Treasury study on fuel compliance	DOE	No Revenue Effect												

D. Other Revenue Provisions													
1. Permit private sector debt collection companies to collect tax debts	DOE	....		59	150	137	121	110	110	110	110	110	1,017
2. Modify charitable contribution rules for donations of patents and other intellectual property; provide for additional charitable deductions in future years based on income attributable to the contributed property	cma 6/3/04	....	307	318	330	342	356	369	384	399	414	434	3,653
3. Require increased reporting for noncash charitable contributions	cma 6/3/04	....	9	9	10	10	10	10	10	11	11	11	102
4. Provide that deduction for charitable contribution of vehicles generally equals the sales price	cma 12/31/04	....	30	251	253	256	258	261	263	266	269	272	2,379
5. Treatment of nonqualified deferred compensation plans	ada 12/31/04	....	158	135	44	21	20	18	144	189	172	151	1,051
6. Extension of amortization of intangibles to acquisitions of sports franchises	aoa DOE	....	52	88	71	37	22	21	19	22	24	26	382
7. Increase continuous levy for certain Federal payments	DOE	....	8	14	16	19	19	20	21	22	23	24	185
8. Modification of straddle rules	peo/a DOE	....	21	24	27	31	34	36	38	39	40	41	331
9. Addition of vaccines against Hepatitis A to the list of taxable vaccines (58)	(59)	....	1	2	2	2	2	2	2	2	1	1	16
10. Addition of vaccines against Influenza to the list of taxable vaccines (58)	(60)	....	26	29	31	32	32	32	32	33	33	33	314
11. Extension of IRS user fees through 9/30/14 (4)	ra DOE	....	25	33	35	38	39	41	43	45	47	50	396
12. Extension of Customs User Fees (4):													
a. Extend passenger and conveyance processing fee through 9/30/14	DOE	....	105	331	348	365	383	402	423	444	466	489	3,756
b. Extend merchandise processing fee through through 9/30/14	DOE	....	679	1,234	1,308	1,386	1,470	1,558	1,651	1,750	1,855	1,967	14,858
13. Prohibition on nonrecognition of gain through complete liquidation of holding company	doc/a DOE	....	13	15	17	19	21	23	25	27	29	31	220

APPENDIX:—Continued
ESTIMATED BUDGET EFFECTS OF TAX LEGISLATION ENACTED IN THE 108TH CONGRESS
Fiscal Years 2003–2014

[Millions of dollars]

Provision	Effective	2003	2004	2005	2006	2007	2008	2009	2010	2011	2012	2013	2014	2003–14
14. Effectively connected income to include economic equivalents of certain categories of foreign-source income	tyba DOE	....	....	5	7	8	9	10	10	10	10	11	11	91
15. Recapture of overall foreign losses on sale of controlled foreign corporation stock	DA DOE	....	....	3	7	8	9	9	9	10	10	10	10	85
16. Recognize cancellation of indebtedness income realized on satisfaction of debt with partnership interest	coio/a DOE	....	....	4	4	4	4	5	5	5	5	6	6	48
17. Deny installment sale treatment for all readily tradable debt	soo/a DOE	....	....	51	57	8	11	12	13	15	17	18	19	221
18. Modify treatment of transfers to creditors in divisive reorganizations	to/a DOE	....	....	8	9	10	10	10	11	11	12	12	12	105
19. Clarify definition of nonqualified preferred stock	ta 5/14/03	....	....	5	8	8	8	8	8	8	7	7	7	74
20. Modification of definition of controlled group of corporations	tyba DOE	....	....	3	5	4	3	2	2	2	1	1	1	24
21. Establish specific class lives for utility grading costs	ppisa DOE	....	....	13	31	53	72	85	96	106	115	118	118	806
22. Provide consistent amortization periods for intangibles	(61)	....	....	−152	362	500	521	447	402	345	285	214	161	3,085
23. Freeze of provision regarding suspension of interest where Secretary fails to contact taxpayer; remove listed and reportable avoidance transactions from interest and penalty suspension	tyba 12/31/03 & iaa 10/3/04	....	....	....	23	176	187	188	190	192	195	196	198	1,545

Provision	Effective												
24. Increase in withholding from supplemental wage payments in excess of $1 million	pma 12/31/04		111	43	5	(25)	(25)	(25)	4	7	8	8	186
25. Capital gain treatment on sale of stock acquired from exercise of statutory stock options to comply with conflict-of-interest requirements	sa DOE		1	1	1	1	1	1	1	1	1	1	10
26. Application of basis rules to nonresident aliens	doo/a DOE		14	16	18	21	23	25	27	30	32	35	241
27. Limit deduction for certain entertainment expenses (including company-provided aircraft) for covered employees (62)	eia DOE		172	201	209	217	225	234	244	255	264	272	2,292
28. Modify residence test in U.S. possessions	generally tyea DOE		3	8	12	16	25	35	41	49	58	63	310
29. Dispositions of transmission property to implement FERC restructuring policy (with reinvestment obligation (applies to sales or dispositions completed prior to 1/1/07))	ta DOE		−3,147	−1,823	172	939	955	964	970	845	507	15	395
30. Expansion of limitation on depreciation of certain passenger automobiles	ppisa DOE		137	136	99	−50	−98	−74	−39	−23	−13	−2	71
Total of Revenue Provisions			**611**	**4,135**	**6,987**	**8,257**	**8,845**	**9,482**	**10,255**	**10,838**	**11,158**	**11,388**	**81,966**
TOTAL OF PART SEVENTEEN: AMERICAN JOBS CREATION ACT OF 2004			**−5,719**	**−7,856**	**−4,226**	**2,570**	**6,519**	**2,401**	**1,841**	**1,975**	**1,498**	**1,201**	**213**
PART EIGHTEEN: REVENUE PROVISIONS OF RONALD W. REAGAN NATIONAL DEFENSE AUTHORIZATION ACT—FOR FISCAL YEAR 2005—EXCLUSION FROM GROSS INCOME OF TRAVEL BENEFITS UNDER OPERATION HERO MILES (P.L. 108–375, signed into law by the President on October 28, 2004)	**tbpa DOE**							***Negligible Revenue Effect***					

APPENDIX:—Continued
ESTIMATED BUDGET EFFECTS OF TAX LEGISLATION ENACTED IN THE 108TH CONGRESS
Fiscal Years 2003–2014

[Millions of dollars]

Provision	Effective	2003	2004	2005	2006	2007	2008	2009	2010	2011	2012	2013	2014	2003–14
PART NINETEEN: THE REVENUE PROVISIONS OF THE CONSOLIDATED APPROPRIATIONS ACT, 2005—APPLICATION OF THE ERISA ANTICUTBACK RULES TO CERTAIN MULTIEMPLOYER PLAN AMENDMENTS (P.L. 108–447, signed into law by the President on December 8, 2004)	DOE	*The Joint Committee on Taxation Did Not Estimate This Provision*												
PART TWENTY: CERTAIN ARRANGEMENTS MAINTAINED BY THE YMCA RETIREMENT FUND TREATED AS CHURCH PLANS (P.L. 108–476, signed into law by the President on December 21, 2004)	pyba 12/31/03	*Negligible Revenue Effect*												
PART TWENTY-ONE: MODIFY TAXATION OF ARROW COMPONENTS (P.L. 108–493, signed into law by the President on December 23, 2004)	asa 3/31/05			−1										−1

Note: Details may not add to totals due to rounding.

Source: Joint Committee on Taxation.

Legend for "Effective" column:

aa = acquisitions after
abiUSa = articles brought into the United States after
ada = amounts deferred after
aiiiTWWIIA = as if included in the Ticket to Work Incentives Improvement Act of 1999
aoa = acquisitions occurring after
apoamt = amounts paid or accrued more than
asa = articles sold after
asbmpoia = articles sold by the manufacturer, producer, or importer after
ata = actions taken after
ataro/a = amounts treated as received on or after
bi =bonds issued
bia = bonds issued after
bib = bonds issued before
ca = construction after
cma = contributions made after
cmd = contributions made during
coio/a = cancellations of indebtedness on or after
cpoii = costs paid or incurred in
ctada = contributions, transfers, and distributions after
da = day after
Da = distributions after
DA = dispositions after
di = distributions in
diia = debt instrument issued after
dma = distributions made after
Dma = deposits made after
DMa = disclosures made after
DMA = designations made after
dmo/a = disclosures made on or after
dmbo/a = designations made before, on, or after
doa = deaths occurring after
do/a = disclosures on or after
DOE = date of enactment
doo/a = distributions occurring on or after
Doo/a = deaths occurring on or after
Dpa = dividends paid after
dri = dividends received in
eia = expenses incurred after
ematma = elections made and terminations made after
epoia = expenditures paid or incurred after
epoid = expenditures paid or incurred during
eposfqfa = electricity produced or sold from qualifying facilities after
fpasoua = fuel produced, and sold or used, after
fpisa = facilities placed in service after
frsoua = fuel removed, sold or used after
fsa = fuel sold after
fsoua = fuel sold or used after
iaa = interest accrued after
iaeio/a = installment agreements entered into on or after
iwea = individuals who expatriate after
josoa = judgments or settlements occurring after
lf = losses for
lii = losses incurred in
oia = obligations issued after
pa = production after
Paa = penalties assessed after
PAa = property acquired after
pada = purchases and dispositions after
pao/a = payments accrued on or after
Pao/a = penalties assessed on or after
pca = productions commencing after
peo/a = positions established on or after
pfa = pleadings filed after
pi = production in
pia = penalties imposed after
pma = payments made after
ppisa = property placed in service after
pyba = plan years beginning after
ra = requests after
rma = requests made after
rra = risk reinsured after
sa = sales after
saptoea = stock acquired pursuant to options exercised after
so/a = sales on or after
soo/a = sales occurring on or after
soea = sales or exchanges after
sota = sales of timber after
ta = transactions after
tbpa = travel benefits provided after
teia = transactions entered into after
tma = transfers made after
toa = transactions occurring after
to/a = transactions on or after
tosa = transfers of stock after
tpba = taxable periods beginning after
trda = tax returns due after
tyba = taxable years beginning after
tyea = taxable years ending after
voa = violations occurring after
wma = wagers made after
wpoifibwa = wages paid or incurred for individuals beginning work after
15da = 15 days after
30da = 30 days after
90da = 90 days after

[1] Advance payment of 2003 child credit paid by rebate with safe harbor.

[2] Does not apply to any property with binding contract in place before May 6, 2003.

[3] Any dividend described in Internal Revenue Code section 404(k) would be taxed at ordinary rates. RIC and REIT shareholders receive tax relief to the extent that dividends paid by the RIC or REIT are qualified dividends received by the RIC or REIT. Taxed REIT income would receive the preferential tax rates when distributed as dividends. The provision excludes qualified dividends from investment income for the purpose of Internal Revenue Code Section 163(d). Certain anti-abuse rules, including the imposition of a 60-day holding period, apply. Certain foreign dividends would qualify for the preferential rates.

[4] Estimate provided by the Congressional Budget Office.

[5] Loss of less than $500,000.

[6] The provision applies to any period for performing an act which has not expired before the date of enactment.

[7] Generally effective for qualified individuals whose lives are lost in a space mission after December 31, 2002.

[8] Premium adjustments under Section 1839(i) of the Social Security Act for months beginning with January 2007.

[9] The estimate includes the indirect revenue effect that would exist if the Medicare subsidies to employers were taxable but the employers responded to the subsidies as if they were excludable.

[Footnotes for the Appendix are continued on the following page]

Footnotes for the Appendix continued:

[10] The indirect tax effects that begin in fiscal year 2004 are attributable to provisions in Title XI (enhancing generic competition, drug importation) which are effective upon the date of enactment. The provisions of Title I that affect employers (Part D program and related subsidies) are effective January 1, 2006.

[11] Although the tax exclusion will be effective for taxable years beginning after the date of enactment, the exclusion will have no effect until January 1, 2006, when the Medicare subsidies to employers will begin to be paid.

[12] The provision extending expenditure authority is effective on the date of enactment. The provision relating to the domestic flight segment tax for flight segments beginning after December 31, 2002, is effective as if included in the provisions of the Taxpayer Relief Act of 1997 to which it relates.

[13] The conference agreement also contains a provision relating to the antitrust status of graduate medical resident matching programs.

[14] Estimate does not include the effects on PBGC variable rate premiums which are the responsibility of the Congressional Budget Office.

[15] Provision includes interaction with item A.

[16] Provision provides penalty assessable by the Department of Labor for failure to provide notice.

[17] Negligible revenue effect.

[18] Estimate does not include the effects on PBGC which are the responsibility of the Congressional Budget Office.

[19] Provision applies to any employer that receives a notification under Section 4219(b)(1) of ERISA after October 31, 2003.

[20] For purposes of the child tax credit, effective for taxable years beginning after December 31, 2003; for purposes of earned income credit at taxpayer's election, effective for taxable years ending after the date of enactment and before January 1, 2006.

[21] This provision will have a negligible effect on penalty excise tax receipts. However it will have an indirect effect on income tax receipts through increases in employer-contributions for health insurance and corresponding decreases in cash wages. The table shows this indirect revenue effect, which was estimated by the Congressional Budget Office.

[22] The New York City Liberty Zone is defined as all business addresses located on or south of Canal Street, East Broadway (east of its intersection with Canal Street), or Grand Street (east of its intersection with East Broadway) in the Borough of Manhattan, New York, NY.

[23] Generally effective January 1, 2004, except for the bond provision which is effective for obligations issued after the date of enactment.

[24] The Economic Growth and Tax Relief Reconciliation Act of 2001 provides that the child tax credit and adoption tax credit are allowed for purposes of the alternative minimum tax for 2002 through 2010.

[25] Gain of less than $500,000.

[26] Effective as if included in section 201 of the Victims of Terrorism Tax Relief Act of 2001.

[27] Includes estimate for general transition and transition for binding contracts, if in effect on September 17, 2003, and for renewals of binding contracts if original contract was in effect on September 17, 2003.

[28] Effective as if included in the amendment made by section 101 of the Community Renewal Tax Relief Act of 2000.

[29] Gain of less than $1 million.

[30] Effective as if included in the amendment made by section 121(a) of the Community Renewal Tax Relief Act of 2000.

[31] Effective for debt incurred after date of enactment by SBICs licensed after date of enactment.

[32] The bill provides that the excise tax credit expires after December 31, 2010. If this bill is enacted, the Congressional Budget Office's subsequent baseline would not assume extension of the excise tax credit beyond its expiration because the requirement to assume extension of excise taxes dedicated to trust funds does not apply to excise tax credits paid from the General Fund. For purposes of this revenue estimate, therefore, it is assumed that the excise tax credit would expire as scheduled. This treatment generates changes in revenues after December 31, 2010.

[33] The provision would result in an indirect increase in farm program outlays of $171 million in the fiscal years 2011 through 2014.

[34] Tax credits would be provided for on-road and off-road uses of biodiesel.

[35] The provision would result in an indirect increase in farm program outlays of $64 million in the fiscal years 2005 through 2007.

[36] Estimate does not include a reduction in outlays from the Wildlife Trust Fund of $8 million for 2005 through 2014.

[37] Estimate does not include a reduction in outlays from the Aquatic Resources Trust Fund of $10 million for 2005 through 2014.

[38] Estimate does not include a reduction in outlays from the Aquatic Resources Trust Fund of $3 million for 2005 through 2014.

[39] Provision is effective as if included in the amendments made by section 101 of the Job Creation and Worker Assistance Act of 2002.

[40] Loss of less than $1 million.

[41] Base difference change effective in taxable years beginning after 2004, for taxes paid or incurred after 2004. Basket change in taxable years beginning after 2006. Pre-effective date excess credits carried forward to new basket that would apply under new system.

[42] Effective for taxable years of foreign corporations beginning after December 31, 2004, and for taxable years of U.S. shareholders with or within which such taxable years of such foreign corporations end.

[43] Effective for dividends with respect to taxable years of regulated investment companies beginning after December 31, 2004.

[44] Estimate accounts for interaction with reduction to 2 foreign tax credit baskets.

[45] Effective for excess foreign taxes that may be carried forward to any taxable year ending after the date of enactment. Carryback period effective for credits arising in taxable years beginning after the date of enactment.

[Footnotes for the Appendix are continued on the following page]

Footnotes for the Appendix continued:

[46] Effective for the first taxable year beginning on or after date of enactment, or for the last taxable year beginning before date of enactment, at the taxpayer's election.

[47] Effective for taxable years of a foreign corporation seeking qualified foreign corporation status beginning after September 24, 2004.

[48] Estimate does not include an increase in outlays of $126 million over the fiscal years 2005 through 2014.

[49] Effective dates for provisions relating to reportable transactions and tax shelters: the penalty for failure to disclose reportable transactions is effective for returns and statements the due date of which is after the date of enactment; the modification to the accuracy-related penalty for listed or reportable transactions is effective for taxable years ending after the date of enactment; the tax shelter exception to confidentiality privileges is effective for communications made on or after the date of enactment; the statute of limitations for unreported listed transactions applies to all taxable years for which the statute of limitations under section 6501 has not run as of the date of enactment; the disclosure of reportable transactions by material advisors is effective for transactions with respect to which material aid, assistance or advice is provided after the date of enactment; the investor list penalty is effective for returns the due date for which is after the date of enactment; the modification of penalty for failure to maintain investor lists is effective for requests made after the date of enactment; and the penalty on promoters of tax shelters is effective for activities after the date of enactment.

[50] Effective for all taxable years, whether beginning before, on, or after the date of enactment.

[51] Generally effective for leases entered into after March 12, 2004 with exception for pending transportation leases with FTA.

[52] Generally effective after the date of enactment, except for fuel taxes, effective for taxable years beginning after the date of enactment.

[53] Effective for aviation-grade kerosene removed, entered into the United States, or sold after December 31, 2004.

[54] Effective 180 days after the date on which the Secretary issues the regulations, which are required no later than 180 days after the date of enactment.

[55] Bulk transfers to unregistered parties would be taxed at the time of the transfer. The Secretary would be required to publish a list of certain registered persons by January 1, 2005.

[56] The revenue neutral tax rate on each 10 pounds of tire capacity above 3,500 pounds is 9.45 cents on tires in general and 4.725 cents for biasply tires.

[57] Effective for sales in calendar years beginning more than 30 days after the date of enactment.

[58] Estimated outlay effects provided by the Congressional Budget Office.

[59] Effective for vaccines sold and used beginning on the first day of the first month beginning more than four weeks after the date of enactment.

[60] Effective for vaccines sold and used on or after the later of the first day of the first month beginning more than four weeks after the date of enactment, or the date on which the Secretary of Health and Human Services lists the vaccine in the Vaccine Injury Compensation Trust Fund.

[61] Generally effective for start-up and organizational expenditures incurred after the date of enactment.

[62] Applies to individuals subject to section 16 of the Securities and Exchange Act of 1934 for private and public companies.